THE BISHOP

EMGEE

authorHOUSE®

AuthorHouse™ UK
1663 Liberty Drive
Bloomington, IN 47403 USA
www.authorhouse.co.uk
Phone: 0800 047 8203 (Domestic TFN)
+44 1908 723714 (International)

Published by AuthorHouse 09/19/2019

ISBN: 978-1-4520-7374-3 (sc)
ISBN: 978-1-7283-9343-8 (e)

Print information available on the last page.

This book is printed on acid-free paper.

DEDICATION

To those that have inspired me,
to those who have had faith in me,
and even to those
who have long since fallen by the wayside,
I thank you all

CHAPTER ONE

Madison was not amused.

The trip from the airport had taken twice as long as expected and now the taxi bringing her to her destination had stopped to drop her off quite some distance from the hotel's entrance.

She couldn't understand why…and checking her watch again, the spirited young American could not help but remark on the fact.

'In New York, cabs take you right to the door; why can't you do that?' she queried irritably.

'Well, love'; replied the wily old cabbie, indicating the hotel up ahead; 'I'd rather not get caught up in all that hullabaloo at the main gate there; you see, I've got to get back to the airport for another fare', he argued pragmatically.

'But, it's your job', the young American protested petulantly, irritated further by the man's questionable explanation.

…and besides, she thought to herself as she looked out of the taxi's window; what was the big deal, why was this guy being so difficult; it wasn't as if this was some kind of major political rally or international sporting occasion that the whole world was coming to witness…

…so, why all the fuss, she mused?

The cabbie just shrugged his shoulders.

'That'll be thirty five pounds, Miss', the cabbie announced with a patronising smirk, his chubby hand pointing purposely at the meter.

'Oh, whatever', Madison scowled indignantly, as she opened the car's door and swung her long legs out onto the pavement.

The young New-Yorker hopped out of the car, straightening her skirt in one, almost-choreographed movement…and as she took in her new surroundings for the very first time, she forced herself to take a couple of deep, calming breaths, before leaning back through the taxi's window and grudgingly handing over her fare.

She was still irritated…and unsatisfied…by the service that the cabbie had provided but as time was now of the essence, she didn't have the luxury to argue her case any further.

However, when she straightened up again and got her bearings, looking around left and right, the racket surrounding the event that she had been sent to cover suddenly hit her, and the penny quickly dropped as to what the cabbie had meant.

The approach road to the hotel drive-way where the event was taking place was completely jammed with cars, all hooting their horns and jostling for position.

Access to its private car-park had clearly been suspended due to the overflowing demand, all the kerb-side parking-spaces in the immediate vicinity had already been taken up…and still there was a long line of cars snaking off into the distance, filled with anxious drivers, all seeking out that most elusive of prizes, the Holy Grail of motoring; a space to park their car.

The traffic congestion in the area was complete and utter chaos.

Madison dumped her gum with a confident flick of her finger, and brushing back her sleek blond hair, she began striding confidently towards the hotel's front gate as if she was strolling down Fifth Avenue, her eyes still rather amazed by all the effervescence on the forecourt.

She reached the main entrance - managing to avoid the scrum that was taking place there between a couple of irate drivers - and waltzed directly through the glass-doors and up to the hotel's reception desk, where, with a typically patronising New York sneer, she produced her press-credentials from her designer hand-bag and asked concisely but insistently – and to no-one in particular - for directions to where *The Tournament* was being held.

Her confident, but somewhat arrogant manner instantly irritated the stiff, British protocol, but one of the hotel's younger employees, who had spied her stunning legs from afar, immediately took it upon himself to indicate a door to her, situated on the far side of the foyer.

'It's just over there, Miss', he declared timidly, gesturing discreetly.

'Thank-you', Madison replied with a taut smile, before turning on her heels and heading toward the door that the young man had indicated.

Beside the door in question, on which a small sign requested 'Quiet Please; Match in Progress', a short, middle-aged man dressed in a smart blue blazer with the chess association crest emblazoned on his breast-pocket and a plastic badge clipped to his lapel which read 'security' was sat at a folding table checking ID's.

It all looked very unprofessional and amateur to the sophisticated young New Yorker, but she flashed her press-card in his general direction all the same and was about to stroll on by when *the blazer* called her back, stopping her in her tracks.

'Excuse me, Miss', he enquired deliberately, biting his tongue in response to her rather supercilious attitude; '...would you like a programme and a media presentation folder for the tournament?'

Madison stopped and stared at him before cracking a stiff smile. She had no time to lose but in order to avoid any misunderstandings, she quickly back-tracked to the small table and gratefully accepted the information pack that *the blazer* was holding out to her.

'Thank you', she mumbled, before continuing on her way.

'...the match is already in progress...' *the blazer* called after her.

...and as she glanced back at him to acknowledge his warning, he raised a cautioning finger to his lips.

The confident American nodded her understanding and carried on walking.

Madison Chatfield was a journalist from Manhattan who believed that being punctual was part of her professional mandate and because she had been delayed in New York and then by the heavy traffic coming from the airport, she was in no mood for any hassle.

This was her first assignment on foreign soil and because of that she was quite unfamiliar with all the protocol, especially all the protocol surrounding the organisation of one of these strange events, but as she pulled open the door and walked through, the door closing silently behind her, she was more than a little taken aback by the frosty welcome she received from those assembled there; almost every head turning as one in her direction to admonish her with a chorus of 'shushing'.

Again, she was stopped in her tracks momentarily, but ignoring the inferred reprimand, the young journalist immediately turned to the first person she saw - *who was apparently keeping guard at the door for some reason* - and asked him rather loudly where she might sit - producing her press card once again as if it was some kind of *sesame* solution to any problem that these people might throw at her.

The man, also dressed in one of those striking blue blazers put a finger to his lips, and then pointed to the front of the room, whispering that he thought that there were a few spare seats left in the front rows.

Madison turned away and without so much as a nod of gratitude, she made her way towards the seats indicated, still oblivious to the amount of disruption that she was causing.

The young American oozed confidence to the point of arrogance and her eye-catching, blood-red suit served only to re-enforce the fact as she strode down the side-aisle, drawing the immediate attention of all those congregated there, like a red flag to a bull.

That…the clicking of her stiletto-heels…and the dazzling sheen reflecting off of her brilliant blonde hair, singled her out, among the multitude of drabbily-dressed spectators as she frayed an unerring passage towards one of the seats in the front row - and even though she still hadn't realised why everybody was looking at her, Madison returned every one of the disapproving stares that were flashed in her direction with a brash New York sneer of her own.

What is the big deal here? She thought to herself once again.

Her entrance had interrupted the almost religious silence in the room, and as she made her way along to a front-row centre seat, the disturbance she created was not too dissimilar to that of a movie-theatre, when people arrive late, after the film had already started.

Nevertheless, when she did finally sit down, Madison noticed - rather ironically - that the only two people, who were seemingly unaware of the rumpus she had caused, were the two people sat opposite each other, up on the make-shift stage at the front of the room.

Plunged in concentration, they seemed completely oblivious to the fracas - or at least that was how it appeared - treating the annoying interruption that this late-comer had created with all the disdain that one would, when confronted by someone who lacked the basic manners, respect and common courtesy known to be *de rigueur*, during the organisation of one of these, as they saw it, prestigious tournaments.

It was true; Madison really didn't understand what the game of chess was all about; she had never been interested in learning how to play...and growing up in Brooklyn, it had never really come up.

Nonetheless, she settled into her seat and looking around the room with bored detachment, she quickly deduced that the general consensus amongst those present was probably that she did not know the rules...nor did she understand the apparent efforts of brain-draining concentration and sophisticated tactical strategy that the two players up on the stage were clearly demonstrating.

However, in true British, stiff-upper-lip style, no-one was actually prepared to get up and tell her; they all just hid behind their disapproving stares, their wide-eyed looks of disgust and their whispered shushing sounds.

This was all just too much for Madison, all too British.

She took out her note-pad and readied herself to write down her observations, but looking around her again, she quickly realised that in this atmosphere of deathly silence she would probably find it nigh on impossible to find out what was going on without causing more mayhem... and so, having considered her options, she decided somewhat judiciously that for the present moment she would just have to sit tight, in blissful ignorance so to speak, concluding that it probably wasn't the right time to be asking anybody around her for any explanations.

The young journalist that she was, was frustrated by this social strait-jacket but Madison suddenly realised that while she couldn't be asking questions of the people around her, nothing could stop her from writing down her observations of the two strange characters sitting on the stage in front of her; it might not be of any use to her, when she came to write her article, but in the mean-time it would occupy her mind.

So, armed with the seed of an idea she set her mind to scribbling down a physical comparison of the two protagonists as they sat there, face to face, on this make-shift stage, separated only by a small square table, on which a strange collection of playing pieces in various random positions had been placed, the whole *tableau* framed by a heavy curtain of black velvet which did no more than exaggerate the pale features of the two players.

Both men were immobile, but whereas as the older of the two players was sat back confidently in the back of his chair, stroking his chin thoughtfully, the younger player was hunched forward over the table, cradling his head in the palms of his hands, in deep concentration, obviously staring defeat in the face but still searching for some kind of inspirational way-out of what seemed to be a lost cause.

Madison noted her observations conscientiously and when she looked up from her pad again, she was suddenly aware that not a single person in the entire room was moving; they were all frozen like statues, as if they daren't even risk breathing for fear of breaking the fragile, silk-like thread of concentration being exploited by the duelling titans.

You could have heard a pin drop in that room; it was that quiet...and even Madison herself could feel the tension.

A few more minutes passed by, and as the gripping drama continued to unfold before her very eyes the young journalist's thoughts turned to the catchy headline that she would have to come up with for her article, if it was to attract any kind of attention once published stateside.

She needed something original, something that would do justice to this epic encounter and capture the attention of the notoriously difficult readers of her newspaper's weekend supplement, she thought to herself sarcastically, but unfortunately, a little jaded after her long trip she was unable to come up with any spontaneous ideas.

Instead, bored by its lack of usual stimulus her creative mind started going off at a tangent…and rather than headline-grabbing blurbs, Madison began imagining surreal titles for the scene in front of her, likening it to one of those still-life 'tableaux' she had often seen hanging in museum exhibitions;

'Two Men sat at a Table' would probably sum it up, she mused to herself quietly.

The thought brought a lazy smile to her face, but the inertia on the stage and the frustration of not really understanding what was going on was beginning to eat away at the young journalist, over-extending her notoriously short patience threshold.

She was tempted yet again to ask her neighbour for an explanation as to the proceedings...but the tension in the air was so great, that it almost demanded that she wait a while longer before creating another disruption.

And so, as she sat there, none the wiser, completely lost as to what was going on, Madison's mind wandered again, back to the reasoning behind why she had been given this most incongruous of assignments for her debut in field-work.

She looked around at the rather bleak room, at the drab décor and the even more colourless populous, and it suddenly dawned on her why none of her more experienced colleagues had taken up the opportunity to come to England, to cover this strange sporting challenge.

It was a nightmare mission; a nightmare mission of magnanimous proportions; the graveyard shift that no-one wanted; that's why it had been thrust upon her.

There must have been any number of other more interesting assignments that Amanda could have allocated to her, to make her overseas debut, so why had her boss chosen to give her this particular one, Madison wondered, her mind quickly reliving that fateful day when Amanda had called her into her office to give her the '*good news*'.

Did her boss have it in for her, she wondered...was that it...?

...or was it maybe that somebody else in the office wanted her out of the way; she speculated, her thoughts gathering momentum.

Madison knew that she had ruffled a few feathers of late and that, as a consequence, she had had issues with a couple of her colleagues, but was that really a good enough reason to exile her here in this wilderness overlooked by the 21st century; she griped to herself.

Ever since that whole episode with Morgan - *an aspiring executive from the entertainment division whose insistent advances she had rebuffed on several occasions* - she had been ostracised by a number of those in the office keen not to get involved in her sexual harassment case after she had reported him to her superiors, but she knew in her own mind and in her heart of hearts that she had been right to stand her ground on that issue, by refusing to pay lip service to those beauty and fashion cronies upstairs who pull the strings and haunt the corridors of power.

Her conscience was her own but Madison also realised as she sat there daydreaming in this shabby room, that while her attitude and single minded crusade to succeed professionally was her driving force, it had almost certainly compromised her private life, driving away any possible pretenders and alienating her from the opposite sex.

Of course she regretted that enormously, but Madison knew that that was the price she had to pay – *and she was prepared to pay it* – in order to get on in the cut-throat industry which she had chosen as her profession. In fact, she was prepared to do just about anything to get ahead, to reach her goal…but she would never lower herself to acceding to the demands of a creep like Morgan.

Madison was strong willed and dedicated to her goals; she knew what she wanted and she went after it with unfailing resolve; she was the next shooting star – or at least she was in her own eyes - and she was determined not to crash and burn like so many others before her…but while she would do almost anything to enhance her reputation, she wasn't one of those women prepared to sleep their way up the corporate ladder - which had more than likely been her undoing over the last few months.

She knew however that despite her run-ins with Morgan, which had made her somewhat of a pariah around the office, her real goal, her real ambition was to get into the paper's fashion-department where she felt she would really be able to express herself and fulfil her potential…but she also knew that she had to start somewhere, and by making the most of this current mission, however much of a dead-duck it might seem to be, she knew that it would be a way of showing her peers and proving to all those that mattered - even her detractors - just how good she was and how determined she was to succeed.

She would show them what she was made of, she thought; all those stuck-up pseudo-socialites back in New York.

Madison had a career plan mapped out her in her mind; she wanted to move up as quickly as she could from her current junior role of stop-gap dogsbody...to writing feature articles or undercover exposés, and then make the big step up to an executive role, hopefully in the fashion department - and despite what anybody back in the office might think, she was determined to make this assignment a stepping stone to that future success.

Besides, this mission wasn't all bad news; when her time at *The Tournament* was over, she would have a few days to herself, time to relax and to do some shopping in London before flying back to New York.

At least this nightmare scenario had some perks, she concluded brightly.

♗

An accidental elbow in the ribs as the guy sitting next to her reached into his pocket brought Madison back to reality with a jolt...but still nothing whatsoever was happening up on the small stage.

She stifled a yawn brought on by the growing boredom, but then just when she was least expecting it, the whole room suddenly erupted.

Everybody was on their feet and rapturous applause could be heard all around.

Madison stood up too and without any explanation she was swept up in the rush for the door, carried along by the flow of the crowd's excited movement.

♗

Out in the foyer, where the wave of people had deposited her like a disowned pebble on the beach at low tide, Madison was still brushing herself down and trying to re-compose herself when one of the *old-brigade* organisers in his smartly-pressed blazer accosted her unexpectedly and began taking her to task over the kafuffle she had caused on her arrival.

Madison stood and listened graciously to the elderly gentleman biting her ear for a minute or so, but then, when he paused to take a breath, she held up her hand, stopping him in his tracks; she really had no time for officious oafs.

'Sir', she said, very calmly and very politely, having endured his remonstrations with undisguised boredom for long enough, 'If I had wanted to listen to a whining arse-hole, I would have passed wind - so quit crying, suck it up and let me through, grandpa'.

The old man's jaw dropped in disbelief and the look of sheer astonishment on his face showed the world that nobody had ever spoken to him like that in all his years; however, before he could riposte Madison dismissed him with theatrical contempt and proceeded to flash her press-credentials in the face of yet another of the '*badged*' organisers who was busy indicating directions to the after-game cocktail-party which was taking place in one of the adjacent rooms.

♝

In that room, throngs of people, obviously well-practiced in this strange world of tactical mathematics were already discussing - with quite some animation - the intricacies of the strategies used and the surprising result of the game that they had just witnessed, but for her part, the young American was still at a complete loss as to what was going on.

This had to change and to remedy the situation Madison decided that maybe a drink and a chat with a friendly barman might be just what she needed to provide her with both an explanation and some welcome relief from all the oppressive stares and mumbled under-the-breath comments that she had encountered thus far; it would also give her time to re-group, before she made another attempt at trying to understand just what she had gotten herself into.

With that in mind, she made her way to the bar through the crush of excited people and eventually - once the chattering crowd of enthusiasts which had congregated there, finally deigned to move away, she managed to get herself a drink.

The *wine spritzer* worked wonders on her parched throat and as she stood there sipping it, relaxing and contemplating the mayhem going on all around her, Madison suddenly realised that she was being spoken to.

Everybody seemed to have been avoiding her up to that point - because of the disturbance she had caused in the competition room - but to her great surprise, one of the contestants - the younger of the two - from the match she had just witnessed, had sought her out, and was bizarrely tapping her on the shoulder.

'G'day; owzagoin?' He drawled in his strange brogue.

Madison was rather taken aback by his question...and by his attire... and her expression did very little to hide her surprise. She hadn't noticed it earlier but the young man looked as if he'd just arrived from the Australian outback – a real cross between Crocodile Dundee and Steve Irwin…but despite his appearance he didn't seem to be the typical *okker*.

'Hi', she replied guardedly, still sipping on her drink.

The young man smiled at her sheepishly and offered to buy her another.

Madison didn't reply but raised her eyebrows inquisitively.

'Look, I just wanted to thank you for your help', the young man declared, before pausing and adding in a lower tone, '…even though technically, it wasn't the *done-thing*'.

The look on her face showed her confusion, but the young stranger quickly explained that, during the match he had been in real *strife*...but that thanks to her, his opponent had made an uncharacteristic mistake which had allowed him to draw the match - a match which he would have had to concede otherwise as a lost cause.

Madison smiled politely, if a little guiltily, and finished her drink.

'So, can I buy you another?' the young man offered again, indicating her empty glass.

She moved to decline his offer, but then immediately retracted her refusal, as her first inspirational, idea brainstormed her mind.

'Okay' the young journalist agreed, smiling at him disarmingly and turning on the feminine charm; 'but maybe you could return the favour for me', she suggested coyly.

The young man's features creased in turn; 'Whaddya mean?' he asked curiously.

'Well', Madison explained with growing confidence; 'as I have helped you out – as inadvertently as that might have been - I was wondering if maybe you could help me out in return by explaining to me exactly what the hell is going on here'.

'This is all new to me and I am a little bit…lost', she announced with a sweeping gesture of the hand, '…I need somebody to give me a brief summary as to what is actually happening here'.

'Sure thing, lady', the young man replied again in his Aussie twang, flattered that this sexy-looking American woman would ask him - of all people - to initiate her into the micro-cosmic world of tournament chess.

At that moment, the barman brought over her new drink and without a moment's hesitation the young man nodded in his direction to put it on his bill.

'Listen, Missy' - the young Aussie continued more boldly, 'I have some media commitments to take care of, right now, but if you're free later, maybe we could grab a drink and a bite to eat together, …*blow the froth off a few coldies* as they say back home…and I could explain it all to you in a little more detail; would you be right with that?' he asked cautiously.

Madison looked him up and down hesitantly, but then without further ado, she nodded her head in agreement. 'Why not?', she agreed, realising that a drink and a meal would be a welcome distraction...and a chance for her to get her foot in the door.

'It will have to be here in the hotel, though', the young man disclosed; '…if that's still alright with you? I don't like to disperse my energy during a tournament, so I'm staying right upstairs'.

'Fine', Madison agreed warily.

'I'll meet you in the lobby; let's say, at seven. Is that alright with you?' she questioned in return.

'That's sweet with me', the young man agreed. 'I'll see you then', he confirmed.

'Yeah, I'll be here', Madison drawled, still wondering if she was doing the right thing as she took a sip of her new drink.

The young man just about had time to finish off the beer that he was holding before he was hauled off by the local press, who had begun to crowd around them with their microphones at the ready, looking for a story and trying to get his impressions on the match - and more - especially his explanation as to its extraordinary outcome.

'The name's Gary, Gary Bridgewater', the young man shouted out to her over the scrum as he was dragged away.

'Hi, I'm Madison, Madison Chat...field', she yelled back, swallowing the last syllable of her name as the melee, with Gary at its core, exited the bar in the direction of another room which had been set up as the press-office.

Madison took a deep breath. It had been an inauspicious introduction into the world of tournament chess and having finished her second drink she decided that she had seen enough.

She placed her empty glass on the bar, thanked the barman for his service with a tight smile and left, as discreetly as possible, keen to avoid any further harassment or confrontation with the over-zealous organisers.

She made her way outside and as a little drizzle of rain began to fall she grabbed a taxi to her hotel, hoping that her luggage had been delivered there directly from the airport, just as she had requested.

It had been.

Relieved, Madison checked into her room and having unpacked her things, she immediately ran herself a hot, relaxing bath, reflecting as she lay there a few minutes later, immersed under a blanket of rose-scented bubbles on how a nice hot bath was, in her opinion, quite possibly the next best thing to paradise.

An hour or so later, the bath having revived and reinvigorated her travel-weary spirit, Madison wrapped herself in the towelling robe provided and settled herself down to study the press-folder and information pack for the Tournament - which she hadn't had time to look at earlier - hoping to pick up enough information so as to be able to at least comprehend and hold up her side of the conversation later on that evening when she met up again with this bizarre Gary character.

She scribbled down a few general questions about the game that she might slip into the conversation – and methodically worked her way through all the information she had been given, picking out a few of the more technical terms, that she would also ask Gary to explain, hoping that if this meeting with one of the players was successful, then it would give her a foot-hold and lead to her meeting some of the others.

Having done that, she then concentrated on how she would go about presenting her project to Amanda – deciding on an introduction, followed by a couple of explanatory interviews with some of the players maybe, a photograph or two, and possibly, the match results followed by a conclusion to tie up any loose ends.

A neat little journalistic package, she thought to herself - hopefully good enough, and concise enough to catch the chief-editor's eye, and yet possibly discreet and insignificant enough too, to get inserted onto one of the multitude of bland inside pages of the paper's week-end supplement.

Madison wasn't under any illusions; she knew that it would be tough, but somehow, she was beginning to sense, that this assignment was going to be her chance to break through, her first opportunity on the road to fulfilling her dream of breaking into television and ultimately becoming a major player on one of the major network's fashion rosters.

Her head spinning, she fell across the bed and dozed off for a while, her mind filled with images of the fashion shows in Paris and Milan – and of her…sitting proudly on one of those prestigious front-row seats, right next to the walkway; one of those seats reserved exclusively for the VIP's and the movers-and-shakers of the fashion industry – the 'crème de la crème', as they say in the biz.

Later that evening;

The post-competition clamour had all but ceased when Madison arrived back at the Tournament hotel and as agreed, Gary was there waiting in the lobby, when her taxi pulled up.

The young Aussie had clearly made an effort to spruce up his appearance for their meeting, hoping no doubt to make a good impression on her, but sadly, the garish green and gold aloha-shirt that he had chosen to match with a pair of dark leather trousers made him look even more absurd than the khaki shirt and shorts that he had been wearing earlier, and his unruly mop of blond hair, which he had clearly tried - and failed - to tame with a comb and some cold water did no more than crown what could only be considered as the most chaotic of sights, despite the welcoming grin on his cherub-like face.

Madison was not impressed. In fact, she was quite horrified by the sight of his gaudy attire as she walked through the door…but setting that aside and biting her tongue for once, she caught his eye and waved a polite hello in his direction, thinking to herself all the while, as she made her way over to him, that the poor guy was in desperate need of some serious make-over advice.

The young Aussie stepped forward to greet her in his customary relaxed manner and having exchanged the usual social protocols, he immediately took charge of operations, indicating the way into the restaurant with surprising confidence.

'I've just been checking out my Facebook page', he informed her, trying to break the ice.

'Do you know', he quipped spontaneously, '…that Facebook is the only place left on this planet where you can poke a girl and not get slapped in the face?'

Madison looked at him perplexed; she was not amused by his puerile attempt at humour...but just as she was about to comment on his tasteless witticism, a waiter came over and guided them to a table.

They took their seats and no sooner had she sat down Madison initiated the conversation by offering Gary another apology for the commotion she had caused earlier, during his match.

'I felt like I had the plague', she remarked; hoping that her comedic tone and feminine sensibility would ease his acceptance of her apology.

'No worries', the young Aussie replied positively, waving away her fears of retribution; '...but look, I have to tell you', he added, as the waiter handed them the menus; 'there is a lot of secret etiquette...and a whole load of un-written rules in our sport - that nobody actually teaches you or warns you about'.

'Of course, you weren't to know that, as a novice, so to speak – but to be honest, you did commit a cardinal sin this afternoon by breaking the code of silence', Gary insisted with false severity.

'I did' Madison jibed in a patronising tone, not really taking the bait.

'Yeah', Gary confirmed with a nod of the head.

Madison apologised again, though she was a little aggrieved at being considered a *novice* – even if it was the case; she felt it took something away from her desire to appear professional.

The waiter came over and took their orders and while their food was being prepared the journalist and the young pretender took turns exchanging background information about each other.

Firstly, Madison gave Gary a brief run-down of her mission, on why she was there and what she hoped to achieve...and then, having finished her explanation she pulled out a pad and a pen from her handbag...and readied herself to jot down whatever the young Aussie might say in reply.

This professional approach took Gary a little by surprise, but with his permission, Madison then began to interview him - for want of a better phrase - scribbling down a series of bullet-points about his life-story which she might possibly develop and expand upon later when creating her article.

Gary was a typical, laid-back Aussie but he fizzed with enthusiasm as he began to summarise his childhood and his background in Sydney. He was effusive too, about how he had gotten to participate in this, his first National Chess Master Tournament…and he took particular delight in informing his 'interviewer' of how proud he was to be the youngest competitor there.

He also revealed with a barely-disguised grin that his youthful exuberance and easy-going Aussie attitude had not gone down too well with the stuffy British Establishment…

Madison made a note, but she knew exactly what he meant on that score, from her own experience.

'…but I earned the right to compete in this tournament, fair and square, so there was nothing any of the grey-suits or blue blazers could do about it' he added contentedly with a shrug and a glint of mischief in his tone…

...and with that, Gary leaned back on his chair and smiled broadly with all the self-satisfaction that every Australian exhibit when they get one over on the *Poms.*

Madison noticed this and remarked that he was a typical Aussie.

'Nah', Gary countered, enjoying his role as the interviewee; 'that is not strictly true'.

'A typical Aussie enjoys his beer…enjoys *giving the ferret a run*…and enjoys the *Footy* and I'm not too keen on the *Footy*', he smiled cheekily after a brief pause.

'However', he quipped. 'I did once give up drink, cigarettes and sex simultaneously'.

Madison's brow creased quizzically waiting for the punch line.

'…It was the worst fifteen minutes of my life', Gary smiled naughtily, delivering the line with bravado.

Again, Madison was not amused by Gary's rather gauche and uncouth wit but she humoured him nevertheless with a stiff smile.

A pause followed as the food was served and Gary's enthusiasm suddenly cooled as he returned to the more serious side of the conversation explaining the fact that, although he was delighted to be participating in the tournament, his chances of progressing into the later stages were - unfortunately for him - relatively slim.

'And why is that?' Madison enquired curiously.

'Well', Gary revealed leaning forward again, 'I had hoped to make a big impression during this tournament…make a name for myself, but I have had to lower those expectations, since being drawn against *The Bishop*, in the first round.

'The Bishop…who is the Bishop?' Madison prodded, suddenly more intrigued, her journalistic instincts sensing a story; 'I noticed that even in the programme he is noted as such'.

'Aw lady, he is the man', Gary explained in his Aussie brogue; 'the guy is awesome, a real genius'.

Madison frowned, waiting for a more substantial clarification and as the waiter came back to check that all was well, Gary continued his explanation, revelling in the fact that he had this beautiful woman's full attention.

'The Bishop is the reigning champion here…and has been for as long as I can remember', he announced freely.

'After Karpov, Boris Spassky, Bobby Fischer and then more recently Garry Kasparov – *he* is widely recognised as the undisputed champion of his generation', Gary declared spontaneously, betraying an obvious admiration for the champion in his tone.

'In fact he would probably be the World Champion right now if only he would sign up for the title tournament…but for some reason, known only to himself, he refuses to do so', the young Aussie remarked, lowering his voice slightly.

'I don't think he likes the publicity or the media...you know, trying to invade his private space', Gary explained; 'Yeah, he shuns it all, and who can blame him, right?' he concluded quietly, looking for a sign of accord from across the table.

Madison nodded but didn't speak, not wanting to interrupt.

'Nah, *the Bishop* is a very private person', Gary continued, '…and so I suppose it's understandable…but if I was given the opportunity to become World Champion…I would jump at it...wouldn't think twice', the young Aussie insisted, revealing his deep-seated ambition.

Again the waiter approached but this time Madison waved him away.

'…in fact, that would be my dream, *down the track*', Gary mused triumphantly, '…to return to Oz claiming victory as I stepped off the plane as World Champion – just like Captain Cook did when he arrived to claim the land of my birth all those years ago'.

'Anyway', Gary concluded, coming back down to earth, 'that's why the tournament is being held here in Henley, so that *the Bishop* doesn't have to travel too far; that's how powerful he is in the sport', he confirmed, holding up the first two fingers on both his hands to punctuate the remark.

'And why the nickname...?' Madison interjected curiously, scribbling everything down - assiduously - and becoming more and more interested in this other character with every second that passed.

'Oh, he got *the Bishop* nickname, because he lives in a converted abbey', Gary asserted, before pouring them both a glass of water.

'...and apparently he lives there like a Monk, if you know what I mean', the young Aussie insisted with a smile.

Madison frowned but did not react.

'I reckon that his insecurity around women must have been born out of adolescent segregation during his school years', Gary surmised randomly.

'You obviously don't suffer from that', Madison commented with a wry smile.

Gary gave her a knowing wink but the young journalist - whose mind was working overtime - had clearly flared another story.

She sensed a tinge of cynicism in Gary's words, but there was no doubt that there was also a lot of respect in what he was saying about this Bishop character who he obviously admired and held in high professional regard.

'And so, as I was saying' Gary continued, getting back to his explanation.

'*The Bishop* usually annihilates the opposition in the qualifying rounds, and he was smashing me earlier...but thanks to your timely intervention' – he acknowledged, looking Madison straight in the eyes – 'I, Gary Bridgewater, from Sydney, Australia have lived to fight another day – having halved that game with the master'.

'...and that, for me, has already been an exploit'; he enthused, his morale soaring again.

Madison smiled again stiffly.

She really didn't know much about sport in general, and even less about this obscure game of chess, but she was still somewhat surprised to see such a joyous reaction over a drawn result.

'Surely, such enthusiasm should be reserved for a victory', she queried in her own mind.

She needed to know more – and so while Gary ordered in another round of drinks, she looked through her pad, and ran through the questions she had jotted down earlier in her room.

The main course was served, and as they ate, Gary quickly demonstrated his comprehensive - and concise - knowledge of the game of chess, at times showing Madison glimpses of an exceptional and deceptively high level of understanding as to the ins-and-outs...and the intricacies of the game, which she had to admit, contrasted totally with what she had expected from such a strangely attired and laid-back character.

Indeed she was most impressed by the clarity and the precision of the young Aussie's responses...to a point where she was even tempted to change her first impression of him…which was quite a rare occurrence for the New-York native.

Desserts were served and as they relaxed again after the rather intense question and answer session Gary agreed to explain to Madison once again, in greater detail, why his drawn match against *the Bishop* had been considered such a significant result.

'The game of chess', he explained, 'is all about tactics, concentration, and mental toughness; a bit like the game of cricket', he remarked, trying to make the comparison with another popular game from back home in Australia.

Madison didn't get the analogy and frowned once again, apologising for a second time for her lack of sporting knowledge…but rather than patronise or criticise her, Gary immediately sympathised with her, agreeing that actually both sports could be considered as interesting as watching paint dry for the uninitiated.

'It's just not my idea of sport', the young New-Yorker admitted candidly, appreciating his understanding.

'In the States, we have baseball, basketball, ice hockey and gridiron, which are all very physical games, where results are earned through the shedding of blood, sweat and tears - and forgive me for saying this', she announced a little facetiously, 'but what you do, doesn't seem much like sport to me'.

'I can understand that', Gary conceded honestly, '…being a lifelong Yankee fan myself'.

'You support the Yankees?' Madison remarked with a puzzled expression.

'Sure do...but that's another story', Gary joked, trying to re-focus on the discussion.

'Maybe we should disassociate physical sports like hockey and baseball from the cerebral gymnastics that we practice', he suggested intelligently; '...even though tactics, concentration and mental toughness are the basic ingredients for any sports...before technique, physical strength, endurance and contact are introduced'.

'Yeah, I suppose it's a fine line', Madison agreed, finishing her wine.

'Yes, exactly', Gary concurred.

The conversation continued for a while longer and despite her aversion for the topic - sport not really figuring very highly in her list of passions - Madison found herself slowly warming to her mission. It had been an eye-opening experience thus far and by the end of the evening, thanks to Gary's patient insight and detailed feedback, she had formed a pretty good picture, of what went on in the closed world of Championship Chess; a fact clearly evident in her excited scribbling as she hurriedly highlighted all the major subjects that they had covered during their conversation.

She also understood now why Gary's drawn match against this seemingly unbeatable *Bishop* character had been considered by many, as almost a victory - because of his opponent's apparently invincible reputation - and as the realisation of that particular detail began to sink in, the ambitious young journalist quickly came to the conclusion that she had stumbled upon a scoop here...or at least something that had the potential to be a scoop.

Nobody else could see it but as she looked around at her surroundings for any other novel ideas that she could use, Madison was convinced that there was probably more of a story to be had here than she had originally thought.

Her expression tightened again...and while Gary rattled on in the background, spurred on by her journalistic hunch, the young American instantly resolved to stay a few days longer than she had first planned, in order to find out more...

...more about the game, more about the Tournament - and although she found Gary charming in his own little way, and a rich source of information - more about this *Bishop* guy who she now saw as her primary target; an exclusive interview with him would definitely be the scoop she needed to show them back at the office, who she really was.

That would be her challenge, she told herself with a self-satisfied smile and as sweet as Gary was; she wouldn't be settling for - nor would she be satisfied with - the consolation prize.

At that point, Gary raised his hand and signalled to the waiter with a rather grand gesture that the bill should be put on his tab.

The hotel employee nodded back politely in acknowledgement and with that the young Aussie stood up and invited his guest to do likewise.

Madison put away her pad and as they made their way out of the restaurant, she turned to Gary and asked him about the possibility of getting an exclusive interview with *the Bishop*.

The latter cut her short immediately; '...an exclusive interview, you must be joking me', he said flatly; '*the Bishop* doesn't give interviews; I told you earlier; he guards his privacy, jealously; he avoids media attention whenever possible; the man is a notorious recluse and getting an interview with him would be nigh on impossible', the young Aussie concluded.

Madison frowned into the distance, a determined look in her eye.

'Is that so?' she stated cryptically; '...all the more reason to try, then', she confirmed challengingly.

Gary shrugged his shoulders.

'Do you think that there is any way that I could at least get to meet him?' Madison insisted, surreptitiously sowing the seeds of her plan.

'Well', Gary replied, seeing that his knock-back hadn't dampened her enthusiasm, 'the match continues tomorrow afternoon...so why don't you come along, and try your luck', he suggested in typical Aussie fashion, completely disregarding the usual protocol that would be in place around the event.

'I might just do that', Madison retorted confidently.

They were now standing in the middle of the hotel's reception-area and seeing his chance Gary chose that moment to invite Madison to the bar for a last drink; after all, the conversation had been of a serious tone most of the evening and it was time, he felt, that they lightened the mood a little.

Sadly though, this time, it was Madison's turn to cut him short as miming a yawn...and then claiming travel fatigue...she made it perfectly clear that she wasn't interested in 'that kind' of small-talk.

Instead, she began heading slowly towards the main door.

To say that he was disappointed by her reaction is an understatement but Gary could sense as he watched her go, that the young American journalist now had only one thing on her mind – and that was, finding a way to negotiate an exclusive interview with the enigma that was *the Bishop*...and so without rancour, he bit his tongue, accepted her refusal and followed her grudgingly to the hotel's main exit.

There, at the door, she thanked him for dinner, for his company. . .and for his patience, but before he could reply to her gratitude the expressionless doorman summoned her forward, having already opened the door to one of the waiting taxis.

'Taxi Miss', the man cried, poker faced.

Madison acknowledged the *uniform* with a brief hand signal and having bid Gary goodbye, she walked forward and stepped into the cab, thanking the young Aussie again through the taxi's window as it pulled away.

Outside the hotel's gates and back on the open-road, Madison sank back into the taxi's comfortable leather seat, peering out curiously into the gloomy night air outside. She reflected quietly on all that Gary had said over dinner, but then, in typical fashion, she decided that she was going to ignore the young Aussie's negative reaction to her suggestion.

The Bishop was going to be her scoop; she could feel it in her bones and as the taxi continued on its way she determined that she would do whatever it took to find a way of getting that exclusive interview with the elusive champion.

She continued to reflect on her strategy when she got back to her hotel…and as she lay there in her bed that night, listening to all the strange sounds, and pondering her first day in England, Madison was suddenly struck by the thought of just how lonely a hotel room could be; how they were just timeless places with no soul, no past and no future.

It was a depressing thought and it left her in a reflective mood but as she turned on her side, trying to find a comfortable position in which to sleep, it also galvanised the young journalist and spurred her on in her determination to pursue her dream of the perfect future...with even greater gusto.

CHAPTER TWO

The next day, when Madison got back to the tournament hotel, she immediately sought out her new friend Gary – who, with his usual free-wheeling, laid-back Aussie attitude quickly introduced her to several of the other participants who were all hanging out, in and around the bar and reception area of the hotel, waiting for their respective matches to be announced.

They were a pretty eclectic bunch of people and Madison - who had always prided herself on her observational ability - promptly began making mental notes on each of them, on those that Gary had actually introduced her to, and even on some of the others that he had not.

Every one of these strange individuals seemed to have his own way of preparing for the match ahead; some were relaxed, like her new friend Gary, others were pre-occupied or lost in concentration as they went over and over their game-plans in their minds...and a few others looked pale and nervous as they walked back and fore like worried students before an exam.

Madison took a seat in reception and taking out her pad she began writing down her observations - and making a few other notes for her article - commenting rather succinctly on how a number of the competitors seemed to be going through little rituals like boxers do, as reassurance and confidence builders before entering the arena.

The young journalist was pleased with the boxing analogy and underlined it with a flourish.

Then suddenly, just as she was putting her pad away, Gary appeared beside her...again...and invited her to join him in the bar, where, having organised the drinks and a table to sit at, the young Aussie - ever the jester and obviously still hoping to impress the young American - began pointing out one or two of the other contestants to her.

'Look', he said; 'over there', pointing to a guy who was sitting quietly in a corner booth keeping himself to himself.

Madison turned and glanced briefly at the guy that Gary was indicating.

'We call that guy *Trigger*', Gary divulged with an air of false sincerity.

‘Oh, you do, and why would you do that?’, Madison enquired, falling head over heels into Gary’s waiting jibe, her mind racing into overdrive as she tried to figure out the reason for the guy’s nickname before Gary could surprise her.

‘Does he carry a gun or is he just quick on the draw?’ she joked, picking up her glass.

‘Nah’, replied Gary glibly; ‘we call him *Trigger* coz he looks like a horse’.

The young Aussie then raised his glass and smiled at her contentedly, while Madison could do nothing but raise her eyes to the sky in disbelief - once again - at his puerile, male buffoonery.

The moment passed and while Madison continued to scan the bar, keeping her eyes peeled for her elusive prey, Gary took the opportunity to announce in his very own inimitable and unrefined way, that he had to go and *siphon the python* before getting ready for his match – adding that he would nevertheless be delighted to meet up with her again afterwards, if she was still around.

Madison didn’t have time to swallow the drink that she had in her mouth before Gary jumped up and disappeared towards the door.

Once again she found herself alone and so to fill in time while she waited Madison took out her pad once again and returned to scrutinising the other participants dotted around the room, jotting down random observations about each of them that she felt she might be able to incorporate into her article.

She recognised three of the scruffy journalists who had crowded around her the previous day, sat at a corner table, and while they were completely ignoring her despite her being the only woman in the room apart from the barmaid - she was struck by their attitude and the way that were respecting the players’ need for privacy in these tense moments before going into battle.

Back in the States, she mused; given their proximity and their accessibility, journalists of all sorts would be in the competitors’ faces until the very moment that they stepped onto the stage.

That restraint is so typically British, she thought to herself.

Madison continued scribbling and as she took another look around the room it suddenly struck her that there were no women among the contenders in the tournament; a fact which surprised her somewhat in this age of sexual equality...and she made a mental note to ask Gary about why that was.

On the other hand - the dearth of feminine participation aside - every other social group seemed to be represented in that bar. There was a group of geeky-types who reminded her of the Big Bang Theory (a TV series from back home), one who looked like a university professor, another in a sharp suit, a group of stereotypical students and even some people on the next table speaking a language that she didn't comprehend...but as she continued her observations it suddenly dawned on Madison that all of these people had one thing in common; a passion for the game of chess and a certain respect for their opponents; it was quite clearly a very serious business, for them all.

Madison put down her pen, took another sip from her drink and began to ponder the question again as to why there was no feminine interest in the game of chess.

It seemed somewhat of an anomaly but after another couple of minutes scrutinising the people in the bar, she concluded - rather arbitrarily - that tournament chess was probably one of the last bastions of male domination... and that maybe, because these chess-players were so wrapped up in their own self-contained, little world, they had no interest at all in sharing it with the opposite sex.

Then, she looked at it from a woman's point of view and realised exactly why there were no women around. The game of chess was...dull, boring, time-consuming and basically not much fun; that's why there were no women around, she concluded just as randomly.

After a while, Madison had profiled just about every person in the bar...but unfortunately for her, *the Bishop*, the one person that she had really hoped to profile wasn't one of them.

As was his habit – apparently - the man in question had arrived discreetly by a back-door only minutes before he was due to start his match - thereby avoiding the main crowd - and had been immediately ushered behind the scenes by the organisers, blocking any attempt that she or anybody else might make to try and intercept him.

She did catch a glimpse of him however, or at least she thought she caught a glimpse of him, from her seat in the bar as he was being ushered discreetly though a side door, recognising him, or at least the back of his head, from the photo in her portfolio - and unable to resist the temptation, her impetuous nature or her growing curiosity for the man, she got up straight away and tried to follow - but sadly, before she could confirm her suspicions the ever-vigilant blue-blazered organisers - who seemed to be acting like his personal body-guards - had spirited the man away through another door across the way.

Nevertheless, unperturbed, and unwavering in the pursuit of her goal, Madison immediately turned on her heels and with a determined look on her face she made her way directly into the competition room and plonked herself down in the centre-most front-row seat, deciding defiantly that this time, she would sit there and wait patiently for however long it took, for her chance to approach *the Master*.

The ambitious young journalist inside her was determined to do whatever it took to meet this guy, but this time she resolved to make a conscious effort to abide by the rules and respect all the regulations that Gary had now informed her of, which of course she had been completely ignorant of during the previous day's play, much to everybody's dismay.

One by one, the seats around her began to fill up and suddenly in a blast of respectful applause the two protagonists appeared from behind the heavy curtain, shook hands and took their places as before having been formally introduced by the MC much like at a boxing match.

Madison made a note of that as it worked in well with her previous boxing analogy.

The game got under way and as she sat there in all her splendour, being careful not to make any noise, but enthralled nevertheless by the growing tension of the situation and the adrenaline rush inside her, brought on by her chase for the scoop, Madison could not help but subconsciously try to attract *the Bishop's* attention, using the usual womanly wiles of regularly shifting in her seat, discreetly playing with her hair or crossing her legs and swinging her foot seductively.

Incredibly, it didn't work; *the Bishop* didn't seem to notice her, but on the other hand, Gary, who was completely destabilised by her antics, consequently lost all his concentration and soon found himself backed into a Zugzwang (*a position in which a chess player is obliged to move but cannot do so without disadvantage).*

Subsequently, the match was over in no time at all, and the smattering of applause that greeted the result - which was a lot less deafening than the day before – signalled plainly that the outcome was more conducive to the prevailing expectations.

Madison applauded with the rest of the crowd and as soon as the applause died down she quickly jumped up and rushed toward the small stage, hoping to use the opportunity to get some kind of comment from *the Master...*

It was a brave move but once again her plan was thwarted as the blue blazers quickly closed ranks around him.

She called out...but in spite of her efforts, the Bishop did not even meet her gaze.

Instead he just walked on by, completely ignoring her, brushing past her and the rest of the on-coming crowd without a second glance, as he made his way swiftly towards the fire-exit surrounded by his make-shift security cordon, before disappearing out of sight.

'Damn', she heard herself say out loud as she stamped her foot in frustration...but even though she was disappointed by his failure to stop and talk to her, Madison was nevertheless impressed by how clever this man was, when protecting himself and his privacy.

She had been foiled once again but even though she was a little disappointed at being snubbed, Madison now had proof that obtaining her scoop was going to be a sizeable challenge and in typical New-York style it only made her more determined not to give up the fight.

Moreover, his rebuttal had pricked her journalistic ego, and she knew that it would only serve to spur her on to continue her quest.

Indeed, to say that her curiosity had been roused by this brief encounter was now somewhat of an understatement, because with every passing moment the moody, enigmatic champion was slowly becoming an obsession in her eyes and one way or another she was convinced that somehow her future success, her future career, would be defined by her meeting with him at some point and getting her scoop.

Nonetheless, with *the Bishop* gone, Madison turned her attention back to consoling her new friend Gary after his crushing defeat, apologising to him yet again - this time for having distracted him.

However, even as she was doing so, Madison's mind was already racing ahead, trying to elaborate a strategy or engineer a way of getting the elusive champion to give her an exclusive interview.

Ideas and scenarios began crowding her brain...but before she could choose any of them, she was brought back to reality by Gary tugging on her arm.

'Hey; let's go to the bar and suck up some more of that amber liquid', he suggested flatly, leading the way.

'Yeah, why not', she agreed with a shrug of the shoulders; after all, accepting to join him for a drink in the bar was as good a way as any of trying to redeem herself, for precipitating the poor guy's competitive demise once again...

...but it would not be for long, she promised herself, as she turned and followed Gary's lead...because now, she had some much bigger fish to fry...

They made their way out of the function room and into the bar, Gary flanked by a number of his loyal supporters, all of whom were offering him their sympathy and their best wishes for next time...and as they approached the bar itself, Madison deliberately stood back from the crowd in order to study her new acquaintance more attentively.

She was starting to like the young Aussie and she smiled warmly at his boyish awkwardness as once again he took it upon himself to organise the drinks for her, himself and his immediate followers...

...but alas...now that she had found out about *the Bishop* - who was clearly going to become the new focus of her attentions, she had to admit, rather guiltily, that she was struggling to find a point of mutual empathy with the young pretender.

Nevertheless, once the drinks had been served, they found themselves a table and sat down, Madison ready and primed to comfort and console the day's valiant loser as he analysed the reasons for his defeat.

She braced herself for the post-mortem...and her part in it...but then against all expectations, Madison was somewhat surprised to discover that Gary wasn't too down-hearted at his loss; indeed he was quite philosophical about it...because after all, he had known that the odds would be stacked against him – especially after he had bruised the champion's ego and his reputation the day before.

All the same, he had lost...and despite his upbeat attitude Gary still needed to get the defeat out of his system...so, in typical Aussie fashion, over the next hour or so he did just that, sinking a succession of cold beers...or *tinnies* as he liked to call them...one after the other.

During that time, he and Madison discussed a number of issues, both current and personal...but just as they had started chatting about why there were no women on the chess circuit, their conversation was interrupted - without warning and somewhat annoyingly - by a rather tall middle-aged man, dressed in a tweed suit and carrying an empty glass.

Madison turned to look at the newcomer and recognised him immediately from the folder she had been given; however, if the bloodshot in his eyes was anything to go by, the man was already a few sheets to the wind and his unsteady manner made him look more like a stumbling John Cleese-type character from a Monty Python sketch than a potential chess-tournament winner.

'Hey Bruce, aren't you going to introduce me?' the man suddenly blurted out loudly, gesticulating wildly in Madison's direction and wavering ominously on his long, gangly legs.

The sound of the man's voice made the young Aussie cringe – visibly - but as he had just taken a large swallow of beer he didn't respond immediately - probably hoping that the man would go away without causing too much of a scene - but when the latter repeated his question, more theatrically and in a more peremptory tone, Gary simply had no other choice than to reply.

So; taking a deep breath and rolling his eyes in exasperation he raised a hand towards the towering stranger and announced in the most sardonic tone he could muster;

'Madison, this here is Rory Campbell-Brown...

...Rory, this is Madison, a journalist from New York who is over here to cover the tournament'.

'Enchanté', the new man purred, extending his hand in Madison's direction and taking the introduction as an invitation for him to sit down and join them.

Madison was shocked. She wasn't used to this rather presumptuous behaviour and she frowned in confusion as she looked across at Gary, no doubt hoping that he would explain to his uninvited *colleague* that they were in fact, in the middle of a private conversation and that they had no wish to be disturbed.

This was a blatant attempt at telepathic-transfer - *a talent known only to women who mistakenly assume that men can read their minds* – and unsurprisingly her efforts were in vain - as Gary clearly didn't pick up on the non-verbal message, which left the prickly New-Yorker with no other option or means of registering her disapproval of this man's highly inopportune imposition...than to deliberately decline his extended hand, while conveying her contempt and her indignation at his cutting short of their conversation through the steely look in her cobalt blue eyes.

It was a weird moment and prompted a rather awkward and uncomfortable silence at the table...but thankfully it only lasted for a moment or two; just long enough for Madison to make her point... and as Rory sat down opposite her, she quickly defused the situation by following up her passive-aggressive stance with a polite nod...and a smile; a forced smile it was for sure...but a smile nonetheless, as in spite of everything, she didn't want to antagonise the man unduly (*she might have to cross his path again during her stay*) and she definitely didn't want to attract any more attention from the other people in the bar. (*She had already created one scene in the hotel since her arrival*)

Meanwhile, Gary had taken another swig of beer from his glass...but before he could swallow it, Rory was already giving orders.

'Hey Bruce; get the beers in, would you...while me and the lady here get better acquainted', the facetious and rather overbearing shoe-horn suddenly insisted as he pulled his chair further forward.

This arrogant behaviour was clearly getting to Madison and it was quite noticeable that she recoiled in her chair somewhat as this invasive finagler got closer and closer; *she was, after all, from New York and had developed a certain wariness around men ever since her teenage years* - but what surprised her even more was the fact that Gary then did exactly what the new man asked, getting up and heading straight to the bar without demurring...only stopping momentarily to ask her - with a rather wobbly hand-gesture - whether or not she wanted her glass refilled too.

This sudden turn of events - and Gary's rather unexpected compliance – caught her a little off guard and in response to the young Aussie's shaky little hand-signal Madison could do nothing more than raise her glass – which was still half-full – and plaster an expression of complete bewilderment across her face; an expression which relayed both her confusion and her exasperation but did no more to convey what she actually meant to Gary than did her previous glare...and so, assuming that her raised glass meant 'yes, she wanted another drink', Gary simply nodded his head in reply before turning and squeezing himself between two rather large patrons as he made his way towards the bar, receiving an amicable slap on the back from one of them as he went past.

Almost immediately, taking advantage of Gary's absence, Rory relaxed into his chair and introduced himself again before launching into a tedious monologue about himself, about his career...and about his professional achievements, believing somewhat presumptuously that she (Madison) as a journalist, and an American journalist at that, would want to hear all about his exploits and the manner in which he had achieved them.

He was clearly trying to impress the journalist sat opposite him but alas, it didn't work.

Madison didn't like the idea of being cornered be a complete stranger... and forced almost to listen to his life-story. It made her feel uneasy, and again if it wasn't for the fact that she didn't want to create another scene in the hotel she would have told him to 'hit the bricks'...there and then, without a second's thought.

However, as she took another sip from her drink and remembered '*in extremis'* why she was there in the first place, Madison suddenly found herself swallowing her indignation and listening to Rory's story - for the first few minutes at least – offering a nod here and a non-committal response there - when she thought it was appropriate - in order to humour the man as he prattled on and on...and on about himself...

Now some of what Rory was saying was actually good background detail and Madison could possibly have used some of it in her article...but unfortunately, because of his obnoxious attitude and the unpleasant smell of his alcohol-laden breath that came wafting across her face in waves with every word he spoke – not to mention the way that he had hijacked her conversation with Gary and imposed himself at their table – she had taken an instant dislike to the man; a detail which sadly for him, trounced anything of interest that he might say...and that she might want to retain for her article.

Patience; patience had never been Madison's strong-point and eventually having indulged Rory above and beyond her usual limits she was already contemplating using the proverbial 'ladies-room' excuse to get away from him when out of the blue two pretty young women happened past the table, drawing his attention.

Both women were far too young for the aging roué...but that didn't stop Rory ogling them overtly, his eyes focussing shamelessly - and fixedly - on the fullness of their backsides.

This behaviour appalled Madison and for the first time in a long time she was lost for words...but as Rory caught her looking at him - out of the corner of his eye - she shot him yet another withering look, the expression on her face leaving him in no doubt as to how she felt about his lecherous conduct.

Now, this kind of reproach, especially from a woman, would have made most men uncomfortable and apologetic but Rory was in no way embarrassed or perturbed by Madison's disapproving and judgemental stare.

In fact, having realised that his attempts to impress her had fallen on deaf ears, he quickly brushed off the incident with a half-hearted shrug and immediately flipped the conversation from being about him...to being about her.

He leaned forward and brazenly looked directly into Madison's eyes.

'Do you know, Miss that your eyes are the colour of my Porsche?' he announced boldly, making absolutely no attempt to disguise the fact that his own eyes were once again roving, this time over the perfectly-formed curves of Madison's own upper-body.

She baulked understandably and quite theatrically at this cheesy comment; even in New York, she hadn't heard a weaker chat-up line.

Rory was clearly trying to unsettle her and make her feel vulnerable, but in typical New-York style Madison clenched her teeth and returned his impudent stare with interest, hoping that her eyes would once again convey both her contempt and her indifference to his advances without the need for her to provide a verbal framework.

She then flicked her hair disdainfully and allowed the stony look on her face to finish relaying the message.

The moment seemed to last forever, so in order to break the stalemate and not lose her self-control; Madison grabbed her handbag and began rummaging around in it.

She flicked through a couple of the bag's smaller compartments - making sure to take her time about it - and eventually pulled out her phone in order to check her messages...and to see if she had received any new e-mails; the intention clearly being that the diversion would somehow last long enough for Gary to come back and free her from the insulting presence of this sanctimonious jack-ass.

However, as she checked out the messages on her phone - which she had in fact already read – Madison suddenly felt as if Rory's eyes were crawling down the groove of her cleavage.

It was creepy, it was uncomfortable...and she was just about to set the annoying *schmuck* straight...with one of her famously stinging New York rebukes when in the nick of time Gary came back with the drinks, ultimately, saving her from the embarrassment of another scene.

And Gary was not alone.

In tow, right behind him, was another guy that he had clearly dragged away from the counter.

'Madison, this here is Cornelius', he announced with a lot more cordiality than he had used when introducing Rory; 'we call him Corny for short; he's Dutch...from Holland and he...'

'Let me guess...' Madison interjected as she made eye-contact with the new guy; 'he plays chess too'.

Gary smiled warmly and realising that the rest of his introduction was moot he put down the new drinks and started tidying up the other, empty glasses already on the table.

'Hallo; it's nice to meet you', Cornelius piped up in his clipped Dutch accent, the respect in his voice contrasting markedly with Rory's cavalier approach.

'It's nice to meet you too', Madison replied, dropping her passive-aggressive attitude and noticing – with a slight delay - that Cornelius held a striking resemblance to one of her favourite actors; Alexander Skarsgard. He had the same features and indeed the same hair (style and colour) but sadly that was where the similarities ended...as the accomplished Swedish actor - known for his brooding character roles - would never have been seen dead in the woolly jumper and corduroy trousers that Cornelius was sporting.

Predictably, Rory ignored the young Dutchman standing just behind him but as he took a sip of his new beer, he could be heard mumbling a few slurred words under his breath to the effect that Cornelius '...might play chess, but that he wasn't good enough to qualify for the current tournament'.

'Maybe not this year...' Gary interposed immediately on hearing Rory's disparaging whinge; '...but I guarantee he'll be here next year; won't you mate'.

'I'll drink to that', Madison declared, ignoring Rory's snide remark and raising her glass - which she chinked loudly against Gary's - pleased that she could smile again...out of encouragement for Cornelius of course... but also out of relief from the fact that she had been released from the oppressive one-on-one that Rory had been subjecting her to for the last fifteen minutes or so.

The sound of the heavy glasses crashing together, and the cheers that followed, rang loudly around the bar, attracting the attention of several other patrons, two of whom came straight over to the table in order to coax Cornelius back to where they had been stationed.

'Hey Corny...it's your round', one of them announced discreetly in a jaunty Irish accent, while putting his arm loosely around Cornelius's shoulder.

The latter smiled warmly. 'That's my cue', he said to all those at the table as he bid them a polite goodbye before following his friends back to the bar.

'Cute accent...' Madison commented as Gary sat back down.

'Yeah, it's the duck's nuts', Gary replied carelessly; '...he does alright with the girls too...because of it; the ladies love an exotic accent'; he affirmed, deliberately exaggerating his own Antipodean twang.

Madison looked at him and shook her head, rolling her eyes again, in false despair.

Do men never think about anything else? She thought to herself.

With Cornelius gone, the uneasy calm that Rory had brought to the table returned...and instinctively, not wanting the downbeat mood to fester, Madison immediately turned to Gary and commented on the fact that the three men sat at the next table were speaking a language that she did not recognise. (*She had picked up on it earlier while trying to avoid Rory's unsettling gaze.)*

'Talking about accents...' she said to Gary, trying to be as discreet as possible; 'do you know what language those guys next to us are speaking?'

Gary stared at the floor and listened carefully to the neighbours' conversation, hoping to impress Madison with his insider knowledge, but before he could reply, Rory held up his hand – as if he was back in school - and explained that the three men were Armenian…and that chess was the national sport in their country.

Madison raised her eyebrows in amazement. 'Really', she acknowledged.

'Don't mind him, he's just *flossing*', Gary interceded.

'*Flossing*?' Madison enquired curiously.

'Showing off', Gary explained.

Madison smiled stiffly; she had never imagined that the game of chess could be so popular...or indeed that it could have such a worldwide appeal, but since arriving at this tournament she had been surprised time and time again by the cultural variety of its devotees and the eclectic nature of its strangely insular world.

It was at that moment that one of the Armenians sensed her looking his way...and so as not to appear rude, Madison immediately raised her glass in his direction and spontaneously proposed a toast to Armenia.

Gary joined in without a moment's hesitation, Rory did not.

Nevertheless, the three Armenians acknowledged her toast and as things settled down again, Rory grabbed his beer and got up, excusing himself rather clumsily and letting Madison know that...'it had been a delight to meet her and that if she ever wanted to interview him…one on one…he was available at any time'.

'Maybe I could take you out for a drink sometime?' he offered; his invitation accompanied with a heavy wink of the eye.

'Sure', replied Madison curtly, 'I'll let you know when I'm thirsty'.

Rory smiled rigidly and walked away, seeking refuge at the bar…and as he did so, Madison noticed Gary growling irritably into his beer.

'Bloody Copperfield', he mumbled.

'Copperfield?' she enquired 'I thought you said his name was Campbell or something like that; I wasn't really paying attention'.

'His name is Campbell-Brown but where I come from, 'doing a Copperfield' means disappearing when it's your turn to buy a round'. Gary protested…

…before forgetting himself momentarily and adding, 'Yeah, the guy's as tight as a camel's arse in a sand-storm.'

Madison was going to say something but whatever it was, the thought suddenly escaped her.

'Listen, Maddy...'

'Madison', she corrected him.

'Listen Madison', Gary continued leaning forward, 'I'm not usually one to unload on other people but that kind of guy; well, I just don't like 'em, and the way he was checking you out earlier...well...'.

'It's okay, Gary', Madison reassured him confidently; 'I'm from New York. I'm used to it; it's no big deal, just forget about it'.

'Aahh; sorry Mad..., Madison, just don't take any notice of him; the guy's just a dog looking to bury his bone', the young Aussie insisted.

'Yeah...but who is that guy, anyway; why the deference?' Madison asked, still a little bewildered.

'The what...?' Gary asked, suddenly puzzled.

'The def....; why did you jump straight up and buy the guy a beer if you don't like him?' she persisted, re-phrasing her question.

'Oh that', said Gary, in a semi-whisper, recovering his composure.

'...Well, you see Madison, Rory there, sees himself as the rightful successor to *the Bishop*, and he has been toting himself around the corridors of every ranking event for some time as the pretender…the uncrowned king, so to speak'.

Madison frowned in silence.

‘Me...I’m new to this game’, Gary continued, ‘but that guy, that guy is part of the furniture and has been for years’.

‘So what; you look up to him, show him respect; is that it?’ Madison questioned trying to comprehend.

‘Him; nah; there’s only one person I look up to around here and that’s *the Bishop* himself; the rest of the guys here...are just wannabes’, the young Aussie confirmed, before taking another swallow of beer.

‘I see’, Madison acknowledged. ‘Well, I haven’t had to deal with that guy as yet, but from what I have already seen, he is not going to be one of my favourite people’.

That comment brought a smile back to both their faces, relaxing the mood again, and without further ado the conversation returned to what they had been discussing earlier, before they had been so rudely interrupted.

The rest of the evening flew by, during which Madison told Gary all about life in New York, and how, because of that, she felt like a fish out of water, here in this very English setting.

She also told him about her time at university – *enhancing the detail of her stories a little to make her anecdotes sound more interesting, as her time there hadn’t been that exciting* - and after a few more drinks, she even found herself telling Gary all about her hopes and aspirations for the future - both professional and personal - which the young Aussie lapped up enthusiastically between trips to the bar, assuming rather erroneously and somewhat presumptuously that her candour was some kind of indication that they had, in some way, on some level, made ‘a connection’.

(Little did he realise that Madison’s goal in revealing these personal anecdotes was simply to gain his trust so that he would do the same in return)

Nevertheless, Gary was clearly enjoying their chit-chat and in response to Madison’s rather surprising candidness, he did indeed open up to her, telling her all about himself and about his goals in life. He told her for example that he had never been to the United States, but that he had promised himself, that one day he would make it there, to New York City, in order to visit Yankee Stadium.

'Yankee Stadium', she repeated curiously, almost choking on her drink; 'the home of the New York Yankees baseball team'?

'Yeah; that's the one', Gary confirmed; 'as I said before, I'm a big fan... but I love music too…seventies and eighties music mostly'.

'...Seventies and eighties music'? Madison reiterated.

'Yeah; groups like *AC/DC*, *Men at Work* and *Midnight Oil*...and *Fox...; aaah, Fox*...with the inimitable *Noosha* on vocals', Gary revealed with a cheesy grin, suddenly buoyed by Madison's unexpected interest.

That dreamy look on his face told Madison that this '*Noosha*' woman must have been one of Gary's first crushes and for the next few minutes she listened attentively the young Aussie, nodding her head at appropriate moments as Gary, who was noticeably pleased to have found someone to talk to, told her all about the 'inimitable *Noosha*' and his other early musical influences.

Another subject they discussed was the cinema, both of them admitting to enjoying a good movie…and astonishingly they actually found some common ground there, although Gary harping on insistently about a couple of his favourite baseball movies – such as Bull Durham with Kevin Costner, Susan Sarandon and Tim Robbins or The Fan with Robert De Niro and Wesley Snipes - didn't do much for Madison's more sophisticated tastes.

All things said though - Madison was pleasantly surprised by the level of Gary's conversation up until then – but as the evening wore on and the effects of the alcohol began to kick in, his Aussie roots slowly became more apparent and he lapsed into a series of lame, bawdy jokes.

That signalled to Madison that it was time to leave.

It was getting late, so late in fact that they were the last ones in the bar...and when they finally made their way outside, Gary swaying noticeably, Madison was horrified to learn that there were no taxis available on the rank to take her back to her hotel.

That came as a startling surprise to her, as in Manhattan where she lived; taxis were always readily available 24/7.

'Wow, somebody needs to drag you guys into the 21st century', she commented dryly, looking at Gary's equally puzzled expression.

Then, it started to rain and as their eyes met in recognition of the English weather, Gary - clearly emboldened by the copious amounts of alcohol he had consumed over the course of the evening – made his move, throwing Madison an open invitation.

'You could always stay over...in my room', he suggested chivalrously with a barely-disguised grin.

Madison's eyes widened in disbelief; 'I don't think so', she replied with an amused look on her face and a hint of sarcasm in her tone…

…but even though she found Gary's invitation wildly inappropriate, she was nevertheless mildly charmed by the naiveté of the young Aussie's incongruous suggestion.

She smiled at him again, a little more stiffly…then refused him point blank once more.

'There is no way; it's just not going to happen', she insisted, looking askance at Gary's cheeky expression as she turned and made her way back to the reception area to demand that the concierge order her a taxi.

'I'm sorry madam; there are no taxis', the concierge announced politely in reply to her request. 'There has been an incident in London and the taxicab drivers have called a flash strike in protest'.

'What?', Madison exclaimed; 'you've got to be kidding me... what kind of place is this...some kind of parallel universe; you should have warned me', she insisted bizarrely.

The concierge looked at her, lost for words and shrugged his shoulders.

'Warned you madam...?' he repeated quizzically.

Gary, who was watching the discussion from afar, could see that the situation had the potential become 'volatile', and feeling more than a little responsible for having kept Madison talking so late, he decided to step in.

He moved forward and spying the concierge's name-badge, he quickly engaged the man (*Tony*) and asked him again if there was any way of organising transport for the lady, explaining that she needed to get back to her own hotel.

The concierge nodded politely, that he understood the situation but then explained once again, very diplomatically, that there was nothing he could do; one of their own had been attacked and the taxicab drivers had all stopped work in a gesture of solidarity.

'I would offer to have the courtesy bus take the lady back to her hotel...' he remarked,

'...but unfortunately it is gone midnight and the driver of that bus has clocked off too', *Tony* confirmed.

Madison was furious but still managed to contain herself.

'What time does that...that courtesy bus driver clock back in?' she enquired patiently.

'Seven o'clock, madam', replied the embarrassed employee succinctly.

'Then I shall just have to wait here in reception until he comes back', she argued logically, looking at her watch and hoping desperately that he would come up with an alternative solution.

The concierge smiled at her awkwardly. 'By all means, madam', he conceded politely.

'Oh, this is ridiculous', Madison suddenly fired off as her temper flared.

'Surely you can do something', she railed, slapping her hand down on the counter in frustration.

'I'm afraid not madam', the concierge repeated as the phone next to him rang and he excused himself with a gesture of the hand.

Madison was still fuming but luckily for the concierge, the alcohol she had consumed during the evening was slowly tempering that fire.

She was nevertheless still very angry and as she turned to follow Gary - who was already walking back into the empty foyer - she threw her hands in the air in despair.

'Can you believe this?' she questioned, as they each took a seat in the foyer's hard leather chairs.

Gary shrugged his shoulders...but caught up in the inertia of the moment, he didn't respond.

An hour went by, slowly...very slowly and having exhausted any small talk that they hadn't already covered in the bar they sat in silence for a while until tired, bored and a little cold, Gary quietly repeated his dubious offer for Madison to share his room.

'…no funny business', he promised; 'I'll sleep on the couch'.

Madison hesitated and consulted her watch again, glancing briefly out through the hotel's main doors to see that a sheet of monsoon-like rain was now flooding the forecourt.

She shook her head in frustration but eventually, having confirmed her terms, she took a deep breath and grudgingly agreed - even though it was against her better judgement - to accept Gary's offer of a warm bed and '*no funny business*'.

…and with that, they made their way upstairs, Madison deliberately ignoring the concierge as they waited for the lift on the far side of reception.

It was another awkward moment...but within minutes they were standing in front of Gary's room, both feeling a little apprehensive, and a little embarrassed by the circumstances that had led them to be there.

Nevertheless, doing his best to be the perfect host, Gary quickly inserted his key-card, pushed open the door and invited Madison inside; a gesture of chivalry that was once appreciated by women, but sadly, no more.

Instead, a look of drained consternation on her face, Madison immediately stepped to one side, telling Gary that it was his room...and as a consequence, he should lead the way...

'...and remember...no funny business', she added as she followed him in, glancing left and right along the corridor before she entered, to see if anybody was watching them.

Once inside the room which was surprisingly spacious, Gary took charge of the situation, deciding that, despite the late hour, the best thing for him to do - *in order to put Madison at ease and to reassure her that his intentions were good, if not completely honourable* – was to give her a cursory presentation of the room's amenities.

He reached for the switch, turned on the room's main lights and then leaving Madison by the door to compose herself, he wandered over to the bedroom door and pushed it open with a gentle shove.

'The bedroom is through here', he announced quietly; '...the sheets are clean and...the...the other light switches are here...there...and there..., he pointed out as he moved back into the middle of the room, doing his utmost to keep his cheeky Aussie manner in check.

In response Madison barely reacted.

She was still frustrated by the whole taxi-saga...and while Gary did his best to make her feel welcome, she just stood by the door, keeping a watchful eye on proceedings...making it perfectly clear to her host that she was primed and ready to make a quick exit from the room at the first sign that he was anything other than the easy-going, aspiring chess champion... and drinking aficionado...that she had gotten to know over the course of the evening.

She might be from New York, where she had seen and done it all, but her recent run-ins with Morgan at the office had made Madison even more wary of men than she had been previously and as a consequence, she had become extremely cautious in her dealings with them.

Gary picked up on her attitude almost immediately - *observation and the reading of body-language being two of his greatest assets when playing chess* - and despite the copious amounts of alcohol that he had consumed during the evening, he quickly realised that if he wanted his reluctant guest to stay over...and more...he would have to be a lot more persuasive.

And so, raising his voice slightly, in order to regain her attention and cut to the chase, he concluded his rather clumsy pitch for her trust by indicating the couch in front of him with a sweeping two-handed gesture.

'...and this is where I'm going to crash', he announced, '... as soon as you get yourself sorted in there'; a nod of the head in the direction of the bedroom accompanying the last word.

Madison smirked wearily in response and even stifled a yawn...but still she didn't move from her spot by the door.

'Look Mad...Madison', Gary said softly taking a few steps towards her, 'I've got a match in the morning and I need to get some shut-eye...so if you're going to stay...'

He didn't bother finishing the remark, but instead, in an effort to move things along, he grabbed an over-sized white t-shirt that was lying on the table and handed it to her.

'Ere you go; you can sleep in this', he suggested, catching her eye with a disarming smile.

'It'll be a lot more comfortable than that suit of yours', he assured her, gesturing towards her smart, blue business attire, '...and it's clean...never been used', he confirmed with another benign grin.

Madison accepted the cotton top, pouting unenthusiastically and sighing heavily as she did so.

'Thanks Gary, I suppose I owe you one', she mumbled through a tight-lipped smile.

The young Aussie nodded his head again and shrugged his shoulders.

'No worries', he replied simply, as he stepped back again, so as not to appear threatening to his guest.

A pregnant pause followed this exchange while Madison considered her options...and the incongruous nature of the situation...but then, without another word, she made her way into the bedroom, t-shirt in hand and closed the door behind her, making sure that it was shut really tight before she released the handle.

Once inside, she waited a few seconds...and then put her ear to the door for a few seconds more...before finally moving away.

Meanwhile, Gary who was a little disappointed by Madison's lack of '*community spirit*'...despite his promise of '*no funny business*'...watched the door close and shrugged his shoulders forlornly before pulling off his shirt and removing the cushions from the couch, ready for him to bunk down.

In the bedroom, Madison sat on the bed, listening carefully to what Gary was doing outside her door...

In fact, she listened for a good few minutes...her phone in hand (*in case she needed to phone for help*) and it was only when she felt certain that Gary was indeed preparing to settle down on the couch, that she slipped into the small *ensuite* bathroom, took off her top-clothes and pulled on the t-shirt that he had given her...before returning to the bedroom and sliding into the bed between the crisp white sheets.

It was then, and only then, that Madison realised that she had probably exceeded her usual quota of spritzers during the course of the evening because when her head hit the pillow the pressure of the spongy surface against her temple made it throb instantaneously.

It was well past one o'clock in the morning now and Madison had only just turned out the light and made herself comfortable after a really long and exhausting day when, all of a sudden, she heard a faint knock on the bedroom door.

The room was very silent and very still...and while she did feel a little uneasy, Madison didn't panic on hearing the door open as she didn't believe that Gary would want to harm her in any way.

'Mad...Mad...Maddy...I just wanted to say goodnight', Gary whispered in the dark, hoping very much that she would invite him to stay.

'Goodnight Gary...now get outta here', Madison replied in no uncertain terms.

'I...I...I don't suppose you'd like to get your gear off, would you...Mad?'

Gary whispered again to the back of her head, treading carefully so as not to alarm her.

This time Madison didn't reply but out of sight, under the covers, she formed a fist with her right hand ready to repel to any attempt that the young Aussie might make to force the issue.

'No, I didn't think so', Gary continued, answering the question himself, his voice dulled a little by the alcohol; '...but you can't blame a guy for trying', he mumbled to himself, as he crept back toward the door.

Madison relaxed again...and turning her head to watch Gary leave she smiled to herself and rolled her eyes, realising immediately that the young Aussie's feeble attempt at seduction had done nothing but confirm to her the sad, hopeless reputation of the stereo-typical British male - and by extension, the Aussie male - as far as their wooing techniques were concerned, in comparison to what she had always heard about the warm-blooded Latin-lovers of Europe.

There was however, a positive for her to take out of the situation. She had found out that these geeky chess-types were not all monks, after all. They were not all part of a celibate male conspiracy dedicated to world domination...and as she pulled the quilt back up to her chin, Madison found that knowledge somewhat reassuring and strangely comforting as her womanly wiles had always been a big part of her armoury.

Even so, she was not one to indulge in recreational sex...she found it all a little too messy and complicated...and while Gary was a nice guy, he just didn't do it for her...not in that way at least; besides, she was tired, her head was pounding and she was in no real mood for...romance.

Head down and disappointed, Gary already had his hand on the door-handle, and was about to go back to his make-shift bed on the sofa...when to his great surprise, Madison called him back.

His heart jumped at the thought that she might have changed her mind...that he might indeed 'get lucky' after all...and as he turned back around Madison switched on the light on the night-stand beside her and raised herself up onto her elbow.

Her tired smile encouraged him further...and when she smoothed out the quilt next to her, inviting him to sit down, Gary just couldn't believe what was happening.

However, as he sat down expectantly beside her, his hopes rising and his excitement flowing, Gary was immediately brought back down to earth, when - pulling the quilt all around herself and tucking it in at every corner - Madison looked him directly in the eye and with the sweetest of feminine smiles, said...

'I don't think I am going to be able to sleep now...so, as you're here... why don't you tell me more about this Bishop guy... just in case you overlooked something earlier'.

Gary was stunned; he was very patient for an Australian - because of the game he played - but given the situation and the circumstances he now found himself in, he was more than a little 'ticked off' by Madison's insistence that they re-visit the conversation that they had already had... rather than...

Nevertheless, still hoping that it might lead to something more, he politely acceded to his guest's wishes, running quickly once again, through everything he knew about his 'rapidly-becoming-annoying' adversary.

'Any other questions?' he asked finally having exhausted all his knowledge of the champion.

'No', Madison replied, stifling a yawn; 'I think we're done'.

'Anything else I can do for you?' Gary insisted hopefully.

'No, I think we're done', Madison confirmed more adamantly.

'Are you sure?' Gary repeated one more time.

Madison rolled her eyes wearily.

'Gary; I said I owed you one…I didn't say I'd give you one', she groaned, drawing a line in the sand that he dare not cross.

'Well then, I'll be on my way...' the young Aussie muttered with a shrug, his words clearly full of regret. 'I feel like a walnut...I mean I'm whacked', he corrected himself as he stood up, realising that Madison would probably not understand the Aussie slang.

'Yeah, me too; goodnight Gary and thanks again for all your insight', she whispered, as he turned to leave…

...and then guessing at his disappointment, Madison apologised once again as he reached the door...

'I'm sorry for any misunderstanding…and for insisting that you tell me your story again. I'm just a stubborn New-Yorker…and when I am working I try to avoid getting distracted', she explained, hoping that he would understand.

Madison knew in her own mind that she had to keep things professional; her focus had to be on her assignment and the scoop that she believed could potentially change her career path.

Gary nodded his head in acknowledgement...and realising that he had wasted his time hoping for anything else from his guest, he bade her goodnight and returned to the lounge area where his cold, uncomfortable-looking sofa-bed was waiting for him.

He took off his trousers and while he tried to get comfortable, wriggling this way and that, the young Aussie locked his hands behind his head and pondered on the day's events for quite some time, before finally drifting off into a fitful sleep.

Next morning however, Gary was in for a treat, as he carefully pushed the bedroom door open with the breakfast tray, not wanting to wake up his guest if she was still asleep.

The view that greeted him was the one he had dreamt of all night, or not quite.

Madison was lying across the bed on her stomach, facing away from him; the t-shirt he had given her barely covered her backside and the angle of her position allowed him a completely unobstructed view straight down the barrel of her beautiful tanned legs, illuminated conveniently for his delectation by an unwittingly collaborative bed-side lamp.

It was a sight for sore eyes...for sore Aussie eyes at least...and as her attention was focussed firmly on the lap-top in front of her, Madison was completely unaware of the spectacle she was offering her host.

Gary of course, had no such distraction...and standing in the relative obscurity of the morning's early light, he took full advantage of the situation, until eventually, coughing theatrically, he announced his arrival, with a cheery *g'day*.

This sound, the sound of his voice shattered the ambient silence in the room like a thunder-clap...and just as she had done earlier...Madison immediately tensed up, her whole body going into defence-mode, ready to fight off any potential threat.

'Clearly, this guy has no idea about privacy...or boundaries', she thought to herself as she snapped her laptop shut and scrambled to get herself together, pulling the bed's heavy quilt over her lower body for protection.

His guest's reaction made Gary feel a little awkward...as it was never his intention to scare her...but then realising that this was already the second time that he had appeared in her bedroom that night - without her consent so to speak - he decided that his best option...given the circumstances...was probably to stay by the door with his tray, until Madison gave him permission to venture further into the room; just so as to avoid any further '*misunderstandings*'.

This he did...and as he stood there shamelessly, reflecting on Madison's accelerated response to his unexpected presence...her hasty laptop closure... and her rapid dive for the covers...the young Aussie could not help but be reminded of the first time his mother had walked in on him, in his bedroom back in Sydney, and caught him surfing the internet.

The memory of that moment brought an instant smile to his face and while he waited patiently for Madison to collect herself, all Gary could think about was the similarity between the two situations.

In the meantime, having recomposed herself - *but still mortified by her host's repeat intrusion into her personal space* - Madison could do nothing but sit and glare at Gary, her eyes full of fury and scorn.

'What the fuck, Gary?' she blurted out indignantly, fixing him with an icy stare.

The reprimand was stern...and sincere...and yet despite its menacing tone, it seemed to whistle past Gary's ears without even making contact.

'Aaw, come on Mad...Madison', he replied in a slightly raspy voice, his wry smile making light of her rejection of him the night before; '...don't get all bent out of shape; I've brought you breakfast in bed', he added, trying to mitigate his way out of the situation.

Now, to say that Madison was livid with her host for his lack of respect (*for her privacy*) would be an understatement...but for some reason she just couldn't stay mad at Gary...and spying the tray - *realising his purpose if not his intention* - she decided that the best thing to do, given that she didn't really perceive him as a threat - *their previous conversation having already allayed any concerns or suspicions she might have had in that respect* - would be to bottle up her rage, bite her lip and acquiesce.

This she did, throwing her hands in the air...and having taken a deep breath to calm herself down she proceeded to greet her perky host with a more formal 'good-morning', before beckoning him forward with a cursory gesture of the hand.

Gary, who was still smiling to himself because of his childhood memories, acknowledged her signal with a slightly exaggerated nod of the head and while Madison busied herself again with the quilt - *making absolutely certain that the whole of her lower-body was properly covered and out of sight* - he stepped out of the semi-darkness and ambled nonchalantly into the room, whistling cheerfully.

That was when Madison got the shock of her life.

She hadn't noticed it before - *because Gary had been lurking in the shadows up until that point...and she herself had been preoccupied with making sure that her cocoon of protection was carefully secured* - but when she looked up again and saw him standing there, next to the bed, bathed in the light of the bed-side table, she just couldn't believe her eyes.

Her young host was stood there, bolt-upright, tray in hand, wearing nothing but his rather-tight *budgie smugglers* and a sleeveless vest.

Madison was flabbergasted. In fact she was more than flabbergasted. She was both flabbergasted...and appalled...because not only was Gary's attire completely inappropriate...it was also more than a little presumptuous... given the circumstances.

'Gary', she cried out in disgust as she turned and looked the other way; 'what the fuck do you think you are doing?'

Gary didn't respond immediately, caught up as he was in the inertia of the moment...but after a brief pause, a cheeky little grin did begin to spread across his lips as he raised the breakfast-tray a little higher.

Incredulous, Madison was just about to unleash a hail of New York lip on her impudent young host...but as she caught her breath and steadied herself, she suddenly realised that she couldn't be bothered; she was still feeling a little 'fatigued' from their 'drinking session' the night before... and having only had a few hours sleep, she wasn't ready for a long, drawn-out discussion on the rights and wrongs of Gary's tawdry and rather indecorous behaviour.

As a consequence, sighing wearily, she simply rolled her eyes and shook her head, choosing to ignore the issue, rather than get involved in another fatuous debate.

He was trying to disguise it, but this was in fact a desperate last-ditch attempt by the young Australian to seduce his American guest – as he was still secretly hoping that she would give him a ride. ***(Male psyche)***

Madison wasn't dupe, of course, but she preferred to think that 'it' (breakfast in bed) was a nice gentlemanly gesture, designed to save her from having to run the gauntlet of all those inquisitive looks in the Breakfast room downstairs. ***(Female psyche)***

Gary set the tray of food down on the bed and after an awkward moment of embarrassment and hesitation, Madison pushed a strand of blond hair away from her face, leaned forward and helped herself to a glass of fruit juice.

That broke the ice…and for the next twenty minutes or so, the two of them went about clearing the tray of all its contents, Madison, commenting somewhat ironically on the surprising quality of the English fare after what she had been led to believe about the British and cooking.

She was first to finish and having checked her mobile phone for the time...and for any new e-mail messages, Madison quickly disappeared into the bathroom to get dressed before emerging a few minutes later, asking Gary if it was okay for her to call down to the reception to make sure that there was a taxi waiting for her when she got downstairs.

'I have to get back to my hotel to change out of these clothes', she explained rationally as she headed for the desk, '…and I don't want a repeat of last night's performance'.

'Sure thing', Gary agreed, nodding his head a little despondently as Madison's hand reached for the phone…putting an end to any last hope he might have had of persuading her to stay and rumble.

The receptionist downstairs confirmed politely that there were indeed several taxis available outside the hotel…and reassured by the news - though sorely tempted to ask why that hadn't been the case the previous evening - Madison quickly thanked Gary for all his help and made for the door.

The young Aussie nodded his head again disconsolately and standing up just as she reached the door he stepped forward and handed her a small piece of hotel stationary with his telephone number on.

'If you're ever at a loose end when you get to London next week, give me a call', he mumbled, trying his best to hide his disappointment.

'Thanks Gary; I'll do that', Madison replied graciously as she accepted the wrinkled scrap of paper and hurried out of the room in the direction of the lifts, where luckily for her, one of the cabins was there waiting when she pressed the call button.

'Thank God', she murmured to herself, checking her appearance in the cabin's full-length mirror as she stepped inside.

She pressed the button for the ground floor, anxious to get away from the hotel as quickly as possible...or at least before anybody recognised the fact that she was wearing the same clothes as the night before...but the luck she had fleetingly enjoyed when entering the lift upstairs quickly deserted her when the doors opened on the ground floor and her gaze landed directly on the night-porter she had had to deal with the night before, who was still stood there, at his desk chatting to his shift-relief.

The latter sensed her eyes upon him...and tried to catch her eye in return...but Madison just screwed up her nose, raised her chin and walked on by, disdainfully ignoring his patronising stare as she hurried on towards the main doors and her waiting taxi.

It was 8.00 a.m. by the time Madison arrived back at her hotel in Maidenhead and in a desperate attempt not to waste any more time than necessary she asked the cabbie to leave the meter running and to wait for her, while she dashed up to her room to get changed.

Naturally, the cabbie was delighted to do just that...and as a result Madison was back at the tournament hotel within the hour, showered and changed, and just in time to see the first games of the tournament get under way.

The reception area of the hotel was abuzz with excitement; spectators and competitors alike, dotted all around in little groups making their final preparations...but not wanting to tarry in the vicinity for obvious reasons, Madison made her way directly into the competition room, where, trying to be a little more discreet than previously, she sat down in the first available seat towards the back of the room – hopeful that it would preclude her from attracting any more unwanted attention.

Once seated, Madison pulled out her pad as before...and as the MC at the front of the room announced the first match and its contenders to a rather sparse but polite round of applause, she readied herself to continue her research and her observations...scribbling down as many details as she could...trying to get a feel of the mood...and correlating as much information from her surroundings as was humanly possible without her ever being able to move from her chair or open her mouth.

It wasn't ideal and it certainly wasn't how things were done in New York but nevertheless Madison followed several matches that morning...and particularly the one that pitted the Armenian that she had acknowledged in the bar the previous day against the infamous Rory Campbell Brown... or as Gary liked to call him, *Copperfield.*

Of course she had no real bias as far as any of the results were concerned but secretly Madison hoped that *Copperfield* would lose...simply because of his obnoxious character and the way that he had treated Gary...but unfortunately true to his word, the man proved to be just as good as he himself said he was, and he won comfortably against the inexperienced young Armenian.

♗

There was a break for lunch after that match, and luckily for her - as she was nearer to the door than most - Madison managed to grab one of the small corner-tables in the bar - and order herself a drink - before the rest of the crowd came pouring in, filling up every inch of available space with noise and bulk.

Raucous laughter and excited conversations overpowered the initial silence and from her strategically-positioned vantage point in the corner of the room Madison was able to observe the spectacle with interest for a few minutes before her mobile-phone distracted her, to announce that she had received an e-mail.

She checked the message - which was from her boss Amanda asking for an update on events - but after a few moments of reflection Madison decided not to answer it...because of the noise...but also because she hadn't really completed her research and was not yet in a strong enough position to argue her vision of the article to her overly-demanding boss.

Instead, she pulled out her pad again and just as she had started to elaborate on some of the bullet-points that she had scribbled down earlier during the first few matches; first one, then another of a group of guys standing at the bar came over to her table and offered to replenish her glass.

Madison was flattered by their attempted chivalry but the bar was really crowded and the noise was hardly conducive to civil conversation so she declined their offers as politely as she could, explaining that she had overdone it the night before, and needed to remain alert and on-the-ball for the afternoon's session.

'I'm working here and I need to keep my focus', she confirmed pointing at her pad.

Both men smiled as if they had understood what she was saying... but still they tried to persuade her into joining them in another round of alcoholic socialising using all the usual lines.

Madison hated this kind of male badgering and despite their insistence which she quickly found rather irritating; she stood her ground and resolutely declined all offers from her bothersome admirers.

'Look...I'm sorry...I'm not trying to be difficult here guys but I have been sent here to do a job and that's what I intend to do', she announced bluntly as her patience began to run out.

'Whoa, okay lady', one of the patrons suddenly sneered at her; 'Yeah, we get the message', the second man confirmed as - disappointed by her lack of community spirit - they turned heel and made their way back to the bar chagrined and mumbling what could only have been a series of inaudible – as far as she was concerned - but undoubtedly uncomplimentary comments about her under their breath.

Is that all British men think about ...alcohol? Are they so repressed and uptight that they need the crutch of alcohol to systematically oil their social interaction? Madison wondered, before checking herself and biting her tongue as images of the previous evening she had spent drinking cocktails in that very same bar with Gary came rushing to forefront of her mind.

She frowned discreetly and returned to her writing, unfazed to any great extent by her rather ambiguous internal hypocrisy...but as she lifted her head up again a few moments later to make sure that a third guy from the group at the bar wasn't going to come over and try his luck, she wondered what the group of young English guys were thinking about her.

They probably think I'm a haughty, stuck-up, obnoxious American bitch', she mused to herself as she watched the group of young men now enmeshed in another boisterous discussion...but even that thought didn't really matter to her as she sat there ensconced in her papers because

Madison knew what her motivation was, what her goal was; she knew why she was there and nothing these guys or anybody else for that matter could say or do would ever sway her from that task.

Her focus was on her assignment…and nothing else.

The afternoon session reconvened an hour or so later and still trying to be as discreet and inconspicuous as possible Madison decided that she would follow *the Bishop's* second-round match from the back of the room... just as she had the morning session, taking up her seat as before, just next to the door.

Alas, unlike the morning session, the room was pretty jam-packed for the defending champion's match - *the majority of the crowd being middle-aged men dressed in navy-blue, grey or black* - and as a result Madison's attempt to melt into the crowd failed miserably; her rather-fetching salmon-pink ensemble standing out like a sore thumb among the sea of otherwise nondescript colour.

Nevertheless, keeping herself to herself as best she could and ignoring the casual stares from those around her, Madison spent the next couple of hours conscientiously studying her quarry, fishing for any angle, any detail that she might use in her forthcoming article.

Indeed, she watched *the Bishop* very closely, scrutinising his every move and noting with great perspicacity that while the man had very distinctive features, his face remained stiff and expressionless throughout the whole game; a fact which clearly made it very difficult for his opponents to read. His eyes too, she noticed, were steely-blue and impenetrable... which complemented his body-language perfectly, suggesting a confident, controlled and resolute character.

However, what impressed Madison most, was the champion's air of understated dominance and as she looked on, she couldn't help but marvel inwardly at the way he sat there, perfectly still, like a tiger ready to pounce; his impassive posture completely masking the fact that, at the same time, he was mentally stalking his opponent - on this occasion another Englishman – and wearing him down with just the intensity of his concentration.

This stand-off was repeated over and over – each time one or other made a move - but eventually, weakened by the sustained nature of this invisible, brain-crushing onslaught, the *Bishop's* opponent finally broke and left himself open to attack; an attack, which when it came was as sharp, as precise and as ruthless as any that the afore-mentioned feline might have contrived...and showed absolutely no mercy or compassion for the helpless victim who could do nothing under the circumstances but lean back in his chair and throw his arms in the air in a gesture of futility and exhaustion - both physical and mental.

The MC announced the result with his usual gusto...and in response, the audience rose as one...erupting with a wave of congratulatory cheers and applause, the force of which dynamited the prevailing silence and replaced it, in an instant, with a wall of sound.

This sound, this noise and the confusion that went with it - *as everybody got their breath back and gathered themselves and their belongings together* - went on for quite some time and using that disorder as the perfect cover... helped discreetly by a couple of blue-blazered officials...*the Bishop* managed to slip away from the podium and out the back door of the competition-room...before Madison – or anybody else for that matter- could get near him or realised what was going on.

Meanwhile, as he stepped off the podium, his poor, exhausted opponent could do nothing but shrug his shoulders and slap his hands together in frustration at yet another demoralising defeat.

Once again, *the Bishop* had outwitted her, Madison thought to herself ruefully as she turned and made her way out...but like a dog with a bone the young journalist was determined not to give up...and when she got back to her hotel that evening, tired and weary after a long day watching chess matches - each one more boring than the last - her persistence was finally rewarded with a surprise that not even she could have imagined.

Among the many phone messages that had been left for her at reception – *she had turned her phone off during the competition to respect the players concentration* – were several from her boss, two or three from her friends back home, and most surprisingly, a gold-embossed envelope inscribed simply with her name.

Madison flicked through the 'missed-call' slips rather dismissively... and then, with the duty-concierge looking on inquisitively, she turned her attention to the solitary envelope, looking at it from all angles.

She had no idea who it was from or what it might be...but then eying a crested paper-knife behind the concierge's desk, she asked the young man if she could borrow it.

'Unfortunately Miss, I cannot do that', the hotel-employee replied politely; 'there are Health & Safety rules that prevent me from...'

'You're kidding me, right...'? Madison interrupted.

The young concierge could only shrug...apologetically.

'You're telling me that you have rules against letting a client use your paper-knife', she persisted, a look of astonishment on her face.

'I'm sorry Miss...but yes...it's company policy...it's all to do with the fact that it could be used as a weapon...like airport security confiscates nail files', the embarrassed employee tried to explain.

It was no use; shaking her head in bewilderment Madison was no longer listening, her focus had already turned back to the envelope.

She was in no mood to be patronized after a long, hard day...and feeling a little galled by what she considered the concierge's pedantic dogmatism, she had slipped a nail under the flap of the envelope and torn it open with her fore-finger.

However, knowing that the concierge was still hovering, she didn't pull out the contents, she simply peeked inside...and on seeing what the envelope contained, her whole demeanour suddenly changed.

It took a few seconds for it to register but then her eyes widened, her heart skipped a beat...and a smug little grin began to dance...ever-so-slowly...across the shiny surface of her perfectly-formed lips.

It was an invitation; an invitation to lunch the next day...at noon, at the Crown Hotel in Amersham...and it was signed simply TB, which her feminine intuition told her without a shadow of a doubt, stood for Tobias Byron, aka *The Bishop*.

Madison was overcome with excitement, her previous fatigue suddenly disappearing as if by magic, but not wanting to give anything away, she simply smiled at the concierge, before turning heel and walking away, looking positively full of herself.

In truth, it took a supreme effort on her part not to punch the air in triumph as she walked away...but luckily for her, Madison managed to maintain her poise until she reached the lift and the doors had closed behind her.

Indeed, she managed to maintain her dignified posture all the way back to her room...and it was only when she was back behind closed doors that...unable to keep it to herself any longer...she allowed herself a long, long squeal of delight, as she clutched the prized invitation firmly to her chest.

The young journalist that she was, was elated; she just could not believe it; she couldn't believe that this was happening - especially after what Gary had told her about *the Bishop* – but she knew...in fact she was convinced...that this was going to be her moment of glory; as Andy Warhol once said, 'everybody is entitled to fifteen minutes of fame' and this was going to be hers.

Madison knew that with *the Bishop*, she had hit the jackpot; her gut instinct told her so...and as she kicked off her heels, she took out her phone and immediately '*Googled*' the whereabouts of...the Crown Hotel... in Amersham.

CHAPTER THREE

The next day, as she walked confidently into the Crown Hotel on Amersham's busy High Street, Madison tried hard to display her usual self-assurance. She certainly looked the part, full of energy and determination, but in reality, her stomach was in knots and her nerves were strained to their limits.

Nevertheless, with a quick glance left and right, she brushed back her hair and made her way directly into the small reception area.

It had been a long time since a man or indeed anyone had intrigued her as much as this *Bishop* character now did - as coming from New York, she thought that she had seen and done it all...and then some - but this guy was something else, this guy was something of an enigma…and having been more than a little captivated by his performances in the tournament she was really looking forward to the prospect of meeting him, one on one.

Madison had always been a stickler for time, believing that being punctual was a professional quality - or at least that being late was unprofessional - but as she stood there in the reception area of the hotel, looking around inquisitively at the beautifully quaint furnishings while checking her watch repeatedly, the young journalist suddenly realised that she was in fact way ahead of schedule for her mid-day appointment.

So, she took a couple of deep breaths to compose herself and then noticing a discreet sign on the far wall indicating the 'ladies-room', she decided to put the time she had on her hands to good use by popping into that most sacrosanct of sanctuaries - *used by women the world over in times of crises* - to check that both her make-up and her hair were still in perfect order.

'Confidence, attitude and strength', she whispered to herself as she looked in the mirror, repeating her own personal mantra…'confidence, attitude and strength'.

The vanity stop served its purpose to great effect and a few minutes later, Madison re-emerged into the hotel's reception area feeling a little more collected and slightly less anxious...even though the butterflies in her stomach were still making their presence felt.

She took a few more deep breaths, and having composed herself as best she could, she then made her way into the restaurant where a pretty young waitress - who just happened to cross her path on her way back to the kitchen - stopped and showed her to one of the unoccupied tables set back a little from the window.

Madison sat down...and as she made herself comfortable, two businessmen, sat at another table across the room smiled at her politely, acknowledging her presence.

This was nothing new to Madison; guys were always trying to hit on her back home...but not wanting to send them the wrong message by engaging with them, she simply ignored the men's smiles and looked the other away, her attention drawn instead to the clock on the wall as its hands approached...and then struck...twelve noon.

In an instant, the excitement and the anticipation that she had been feeling all morning, ratcheted up another notch...and at the very same moment, as if by magic, the restaurant's automated glass-door began to swing back on its hinges.

Time seemed to stand still for a moment...and then all of a sudden the man that she had been waiting for appeared in the doorway.

That's very precise, Madison thought to herself; perfect timing, and so in keeping with the type of person she imagined that *the Bishop* must be.

He didn't swagger, but walked into the room with confidence and poise, and as he approached the table where Madison was already seated, she immediately stood up again to greet him...and to thank him for the invitation...a quiver in her voice and a spasm in her stomach as their eyes met directly for the very first time.

It only lasted for a split-second, but as *the Bishop's* steely blue eyes locked onto her own, Madison froze momentarily; suddenly unsure as to how she should conduct herself.

This was a strange feeling for her, this feeling of indecision and it took the hitherto-bold New-Yorker somewhat by surprise. She had never been one to be overawed by this type of circumstance...by celebrity or by reputation...and yet for some reason, as she stood there in that restaurant, in the presence of this 'stranger' – for want of a better word - she felt, quite literally more intimidated than she had ever been before in her life.

The man had an undeniable presence about him; an aura or a demeanour that suggested he was protected by some kind of invisible force...or shield...ready to repel any kind of unwanted attention without argument or explanation...and while she had fixed him for only the briefest of moments, Madison immediately sensed his wariness if not his mistrust of the industry that she represented.

Nevertheless, he returned her greeting in a very refined university English, and extending a large muscular hand for her to shake, he casually pulled back his chair and sat down opposite her.

Madison took yet another a deep breath and did likewise, careful to suppress her nerves and her excitement, though still a little startled by her uncharacteristic lack of self-assurance.

Again, time seemed to stand still for a moment as they each settled into their seats...and while Madison did her best to weigh him up in that instant, she got the distinct impression that her host was doing exactly the same thing to her...and doing a far better job of it probably than she was doing with him.

Indeed, as she cleared her throat ready to make a more formal introduction of herself, her hands clasped tightly together in her lap for reassurance, Madison sensed his eyes upon her...reading her body language... and promptly sat up straighter in an effort to improve her posture.

She wanted to be the first to speak; she wanted to take charge of the conversation and she really wanted show her host that she wasn't intimidated by his presence – even though she was - but just as she was about to begin her presentation, the waitress came over with the menu-cards.

This took *the Bishop*'s quietly intense stare away from her for a moment and as he turned his head to listen to the pretty young waitress as she rolled off the list of chefs-specials, Madison cunningly took advantage of the circumstance to scrutinise her enigmatic host in greater detail, dextrously using the afore-mentioned menu-card as a rather creative if somewhat rudimentary prop.

Her first thought as she did so was that her host projected a quiet sort of maturity and confidence. He wasn't particularly tall - she knew that already - but his square chin and wavy black hair gave him a hint of Gallic charm.

His nose was rather cute for a man and as her natural dispositions kicked in, Madison noted instinctively just enough of that sadistic streak in the corner of his mouth that both arouses the female curiosity and masochistically frightens them into wanting to know more.

His overall facial expression was strong and business-like, and he was impeccably dressed...as usual...in an immaculately-cut three piece Italian suit which was the icing on the cake as far as the aspiring fashion-editor in her soul was concerned.

He was definitely the real deal, she thought to herself…and despite her initial apprehension, Madison suddenly felt an incredible energy from being in this man's presence.

In comparison, Madison had opted for a smart grey dress that morning... that she had picked out as being both demure and unthreatening, as her intention during this lunch was to focus all the conversation on her assignment…and not draw her host's attention away from that with any frivolous feminine fashion.

The waitress took their drinks-order and once the young lady had returned to her station, it was *the Bishop* who was the first to speak, breaking the tense silence with an inquisitive and somewhat searching question;

'So; what brings a beautiful young lady like you to these parts?' he enquired directly, speaking with measured precision...and hoping to catch his guest off guard with a little understated flattery.

Madison paused to take another breath and swallow hard, surprised by the question and its directness. She had been expecting – after all that she had heard and seen - to be confronted by an imposing wall of silence that she would have to break down brick by brick using all her journalistic skills and knowledge…and yet here he was, this giant of a man – as far as his reputation was concerned at least – asking her the simplest and most inane of questions.

She suddenly felt disarmed, but as she had done previously with Gary - trying hard to suppress the uncertainty in her voice - she quickly went through the whole routine again, briefly explaining that she was from New York, that she worked for one of the downtown papers there, and that she had been sent over to cover these *Chess Championships* in order to test her capacity to fulfil an assignment and to exploit it to the best of her ability.

'…and that is what I intend to do', she added in conclusion after a brief pause, her confidence level picking up again, having recovered from the initial shock.

The Bishop didn't react to her discourse straightaway but simply sat back in his chair with a look of dubitative intrigue on his face.

'Look, I realise that it is a tall order, but I am up for the challenge', Madison insisted with a little more self-belief.

'I see', her host commented flatly; '…and I have to say that I admire your forthright honesty', he added in the most cultured of English accents, leaning back again on his chair and using the time to reflect.

'I, myself have always felt that life is like a book full of chapters, and each of those chapters takes you on a different journey of discovery…of yourself. I wonder where this one will take you', he mused pensively.

Madison shrugged her shoulders; 'We'll just have to wait and see; only time will tell', she offered in reply with a taut smile.

'Just remember this, young lady', *the Bishop* put forward boldly; 'those who journey with their dreams discover life's richest bounty'.

Madison smiled again while absorbing his comment...but she remained silent.

'And just how do you intend going about completing this assignment of yours?' *the Bishop* then enquired, sitting forward again to pursue the conversation.

'Well', Madison mumbled, her confidence slowly ebbing away again as her host put her on the spot; '...if what I have heard is true...you sir, seem to represent this sport in all its glory, and with that in mind I was wondering if I might obtain an exclusive interview from you, to go along with my general brief and the information I will be collecting from the other participants, which I will then present to my editor with a résumé of the results from the tournament'.

♗

She wanted to...but Madison didn't dare mention the idea of a photo-shoot, remembering in-extremis his latent aversion to media exposure.

♗

'And why should I agree to do that?' *the Bishop* challenged bluntly, calming Madison's growing enthusiasm in an instant; 'I imagine that you have already done some back-ground work on me, and are aware that I do not particularly seek out this kind of publicity'.

'Yes', Madison replied calmly, 'I have been informed – and warned - that you do not particularly welcome journalistic intrusion, and that you prefer to avoid the media in general, but it's my job to at least try to persuade you otherwise'.

The Bishop sat back again and breathed deeply as if filling his lungs with inspiration.

'It is true', he agreed, 'that I do not solicit or welcome the attention of invasive journalists, or TV crews, but as you can see, I am not averse to meeting those that are just trying to do an honest job. I simply choose to avoid those prying, scandal-seeking paparazzi types', he confirmed, frowning at the thought.

Madison frowned too, relieved that she hadn't mentioned the photo-shoot idea. Coming from New York she was well aware of the concept of paparazzi and the intrusive nature of their activity but she still found it a little pompous on *the Bishop's* part to be so anti-media.

After all, she thought to herself; the guy plays chess - how hard can it be?

At that point, the waitress returned with their drinks...asking politely if they were ready to order.

This suspended proceedings temporarily and as she turned her attention to actually reading the menu laid out in front of her, Madison was somewhat surprised to see her host produce a monocle from his breast-pocket as he too, began to study the 'carte du jour'.

The moment passed without comment however, and having ordered a light lunch, they soon settled back down.

'Do you know young lady that a lot of people turn to stone...paralysed with fear when in my presence?' *the Bishop* announced casually as he poured her...and then himself, a glass of chilled water.

'I don't see why', Madison responded with false confidence, refusing to wilt under his intense masculine stare. 'You are very sure of yourself, but I don't see that as something to be afraid of...' she confirmed.

'Quite', *the Bishop* agreed, 'but vanity is a formidable armour', he argued rhetorically.

Madison smiled stiffly. For some reason, she had been expecting some kind of conflict or at least a refusal to co-operate from this man, but in fact he was being most personable...and having successfully negotiated the introductions...and the initial conversation...she was suddenly looking forward with even greater desire to unravelling the mystery of this man and finding out more about his larger-than-life personality.

However, while they did discuss a wide range of subjects thereafter, each one allowed *the Bishop* to skilfully side-step any further questions that she might want to include about her main goal for being there; the exclusive interview.

This left the journalist in her a little frustrated and while she didn't want to complain and ruin her chances of a possible scoop, Madison did feel that her host had operated a very clever role-reversal strategy on her, turning the meeting into a question and answer session on current affairs...with him asking most of the questions...rather than a preliminary discussion about her agenda.

Time went by, and having finished the meal they were just about to get up and leave, when Madison realised that she still hadn't gotten his name or indeed an answer to her pressing request for an interview.

'So, are we going to do this?' she asked hopefully, brushing herself down.

The Bishop paused again, 'I'm still not sure about that', he confessed obstinately.

Madison's shoulders dropped visibly.

'Listen Miss Chatfield'; *the Bishop* suggested sympathetically reading her body-language again, 'I would love to stay and discuss this with you further but I have a match in a couple of hours and I need to collect my thoughts and prepare myself for that…so…', he paused again as the waitress approached to start clearing the table;

'…what would you say to continuing this discussion over dinner tomorrow night? We can examine it further and I will make a final decision then'.

'Would that be okay with you?' he asked after another brief pause, prompting her to reply.

'Sure', Madison replied with false aplomb, shrugging her shoulders.

'Oh, and by the way…goodness knows how, but you know my name; what should I call you?' she asked boldly, regaining her poise.

The Bishop looked at her quizzically for a brief moment before breaking into a fleeting smile.

'The name is Tobias, Tobias Byron', he announced calmly; 'but my friends call me TB'.

Madison nodded in silence.

'I don't particularly like Tobias…so TB will be fine', he confirmed with gentrified civility.

This time, Madison smiled warmly, secretly delighted to have found out such a personal detail from this enigma of a man…and as they walked out of the restaurant she felt strangely honoured to have been authorised to call him by the name he reserved for his friends.

On her arrival a few hours earlier, she had assumed – again, after what she had heard - that trying to extract any information from the Bishop would be like pulling teeth...but on the contrary her host hadn't once hidden behind the mask of his persona; although she did wonder momentarily if by knowing his actual name, it didn't somehow take away some of the mystery of his character.

As they reached the reception area *the Bishop* reached into his jacket and gave her his card.

'Seven o'clock; tomorrow evening; I'll pick you up at your hotel', he confirmed rather brusquely.

They shook hands briefly, and although she was trying to show indifference and self-confidence, Madison's clammy palms immediately betrayed the inner tension that she had been feeling, but had managed to disguise up until that point.

However, this didn't go un-noticed by *the Bishop* and as she withdrew her hand self-consciously he took it upon himself to suggest that while she was in the area, she should try a couple of reflexology or Reiki sessions.

'They are wonderful for relieving tension, relaxing the mind and ironing out life's little stresses', he remarked with unshakeable self-belief.

Raising an eyebrow, Madison frowned at him momentarily but didn't respond.

'Oh, and if I might be so bold; grey is not your best colour', *the Bishop* added nonchalantly with a hint of lofty arrogance, as he turned and led the way out of the hotel and onto the pavement.

Taken aback, Madison gasped in response; that remark was a little more personal and left her feeling more than a little irritated after all the positive feelings she had garnered over lunch, but before she could react one way or the other to his rather unflattering critique, *the Bishop* was gone, cutting a purposeful stride down Amersham High Street as he went.

She watched him go and then scowled, shaking her head.

'Pffft…men…what do they know about colour', she thought to herself as she hailed a passing taxi to take her back to the tournament hotel.

Madison spent the rest of the day watching a succession of hopefuls have their dreams crushed by a ten ounce chess-piece and the astoundingly simple yet deceptively powerful expression *'checkmate...'*

This meant that she didn't get back to her hotel until very late that evening after a particularly protracted final session which had ended, annoyingly for her, in yet another stale-mate.

Nevertheless, as she entered her room, threw off her dress and made a bee-line for the bathroom in order to run herself a much-deserved bath - *exhausted as she was by the hours of mind-numbing, soul-destroying boredom she had had to sit through, especially as she had expounded quite a large part of her nervous energy reserves earlier in the day at lunch* – the ambitious young journalist didn't regret her fatigue one iota.

Instead, she was elated, elated that finally, after numerous failed attempts and several missed opportunities she - at long last - had her target in her sights.

Of course, she would still have to cover the tournament as a whole – she knew that was a given as it had been her original brief – but now that she had met him, one on one, Madison was convinced that there was only one person – as she had expected all along - who could carry the central focus of her article to its conclusion...and that person was none other than the enigmatic *Bishop* himself; he was the only one who stood out and had the charisma and the presence to carry it off.

All that remained for her to do now was to convince him that giving her an exclusive interview would be a good idea.

It wouldn't be easy; she knew that, she had read his background notes and had already been on the receiving end of his rather supercilious nature... but Madison loved a challenge and this man, she was sure, presented the greatest challenge she had had to face thus far in her fledgling journalistic career.

Besides, she surmised, as she checked her face in the mirror before the slowly rising steam obstructed her view, his dislike of the media aside, he was the obvious choice…with his intelligence, his controlled manner and his capacity to be direct and ruthless when required, the man was the embodiment the game he represented; a textbook case-study…

...and if his tournament exploits didn't get their attention, surely his roguish good looks and reclusive lifestyle, would more than make up for it in the eyes of the female readership of her paper's magazine, she mused to herself as she stepped into the bath and carefully lowered herself into the cauldron of liquid bliss.

She had been looking forward to that moment all day and as she stretched out her weary body, relishing the water's warm, velvety embrace as it slowly enveloped her tired limbs, Madison found herself chuckling indulgently to herself at her fretful attempts to cover every sector of her potential readership.

A heavy sigh - or was it a yawn – suddenly interrupted her anxious chortling and as she rested her head on the little pillow at the back of the bath, her mind finally relaxed.

Predictably, the day's highlight-reel began to flash in front of her eyes and of course the first thing that came into her head - as it had been uppermost in her mind most of the day - was her lunch with *the Bishop.*

Indeed, she hadn't stopped thinking about it all day; ever since she had watched him disappear down the high street; it had even distracted her from her journalistic duties during the afternoon session - going around and around in her head as she tried to analyse if there was any way that she could have extracted more information from his responses - but as she lay there now, relaxing and revelling in the miraculous revitalising qualities of nature's own body-repair solution Madison began to rationalise the situation more objectively.

It had to all intents and purposes been a relatively successful first meeting and most people would have been happy with that initial result, but the overzealous journalist inside of her, who was never quite satisfied, who always thought that there was more to a story than sometimes there actually was, had nevertheless been left feeling a little frustrated by its lack of real content.

Madison re-ran a couple of their exchanges through her mind, trying to analyse them more deeply in case there was any more to be gleaned from them...but then as she closed her eyes and took a couple of deep breaths in an effort to increase the oxygen flow to her brain, she suddenly realised that what she was doing was pointless. Her host had probably made a conscious decision to keep his distance from her during those exchanges… and was only going to let her know what he wanted her to know…which didn't really surprise her.

In fact, she had expected nothing less from a man whose mistrust of the media preceded him…and as she lay there, luxuriating in her own personal cocoon of scented delight Madison knew that she would have to work a lot harder if she was going to change *the Bishop's* mind and obtain the exclusive interview that she was now so desperately hoping for.

She began massaging the soap into her soft skin and in conclusion to her post-mortem analysis of their discussion Madison decided that, while she had been left unsatisfied by the content of their conversation, the experience overall had been a positive one; *the Bishop* or TB as she had been so flatteringly requested to call him, had been very polite and most deferential towards her by and large, he had answered her questions as graciously as anyone does when faced with an inquisitive journalist they are meeting for the very first time...and most importantly, she smiled to herself contentedly, he had spontaneously rewarded her efforts with a dinner invitation so that they might continue their chat…<u>and that</u>, she mused to herself proudly, was something she was very much looking forward to; spending some quality time alone with this enigma of a man, even if it was only across a table.

Yes, the whole experience had been perfect…or at least it would have been perfect, had *the Bishop* not blotted his copybook at the last minute with that rather indelicate comment on her choice of dress-colour, she suddenly rued, frowning to herself disappointedly...but as she closed her eyes and let her shoulders sink below the water-line, Madison happily dismissed the irritating comment - even if it had been rather perceptive and pertinent – as simply a moment of misplaced misogyny from a man bursting with an excess of testosterone.

That made her smile again, and slowly, as the water began to soothe away the day's aches and pains she calmly drifted off into a warm, peaceful paradise bursting with potential and opportunity.

Madison stepped out of the bath thirty minutes or so later...and wrapped up warmly in the fluffiest of white towels she sat down at the desk in her hotel room, pulled out her lap-top and diligently checked her e-mails, quickly answering the three she had received from her office - *careful not to reveal too much; anxious as she was to keep her scoop to herself until she had sealed the deal* - before swiftly turning her attention to those of a more personal nature, one of which was from her best friend Evie.

Evie was a typically stressed-out New Yorker who eked out a living as a legal secretary while she waited anxiously for a Mr Big-style sugar-daddy to come into her life and whisk her off to his luxury apartment on the Upper East Side. She and Madison had been friends and confidants for many years.

This tenuous and rather impersonal electronic exchange made the exiled New Yorker feel a little home-sick - especially as this was her first trip abroad - and so, in order to dispel those rather unwelcome, morale-sapping blues Madison decided that the best remedy for her would be to ring her best friend back in the States...which is exactly what she did.

'Hey girl; what are you up to?' Madison asked happily, delighted to hear her friend's voice again.

'Oh...I'm just about to have a three-way with Ben and Jerry', Evie replied jokingly, slamming the fridge-door closed.

Both girls laughed out loud and while Evie made her way into her tiny living room and slumped down onto her tired-looking sofa - having disposed of the usual social conventions - Madison immediately launched into the story of her trip so far; how she had met Gary, how they had had dinner together, how he had invited her to stay in his room and how... despite the ambivalence of the context...she had spent the next couple of hours, making him repeat everything he had already told her about the game of chess while they sat tantalisingly close to each other on the bed.

Evie listened intently to what her friend had to say, realising intuitively as she tucked into her tub of ice-cream and folded her legs comfortably underneath her, that she probably just needed someone to talk to, but as soon as Madison paused to take a breath, she didn't miss the opportunity to chip in.

'Isn't it strange?' she remarked facetiously, 'just like Susan Sarandon's character said in the film Bull Durham; a guy will listen to anything if he thinks it's foreplay'.

Madison chuckled out loud again as she gravitated from the desk to the bed, comforted by the sound of her friend's voice...but before Evie could drag her into that most dangerous of minefields she quickly set her straight - with a little mock fury in her voice – insisting that nothing of *that* sort had gone on.

All the same, as Madison settled herself on the side of the bed and reflected momentarily on her friend's rather banal yet strangely insightful comment, it suddenly struck her that Gary had referenced the very same movie during their dinner conversation.

What a coincidence that is, she thought to herself, as she paused to ponder the rather unusual happenstance.

She relived the moment briefly in her mind…and as Gary's rascally face stared back at her, in her mind's eye, the sparkle in his mischievous eyes revealing the obvious nature of his libidinous desires, Madison was suddenly overcome with a feeling of loneliness and isolation as she sat there in her soulless hotel room.

It unsettled her for a moment but putting it down to the fact that this was her first visit abroad, that she was probably a little home-sick…and that the sound of Evie's voice had probably accentuated her sudden lack of morale, she brushed it off in customary fashion.

However, the feeling had clearly undermined her usually unshakeable self-belief and it prompted her into telling Evie about how fragile and susceptible she had felt during her meeting with TB earlier, even though - at the time - she had disguised her vulnerable state very well.

'TB?' Evie questioned, a little perplexed.

'Yeah; TB. He's the Mr Big around here', Madison explained, very matter of fact.

'People over here call him *the Bishop;* it's some kinda nickname they have for him, but to his friends, he's TB', she asserted casually.

'…and you two are…friends?' Evie enquired intrusively, her tone suggesting that she wanted to know more.

Madison ignored her friend's more prurient curiosity and quickly began relating what had happened over lunch.

However, in true New York style Evie was impatient to get to the point.

'Yeah, yeah, but what's he really like?' she interrupted hastily from across the pond, hoping for some spicy girl-talk.

'Oh, you mean physically', Madison teased, enjoying playing with her friend's obsession to find Mr Right, her own moment of doubt summarily dismissed and replaced with a renewed positivity and optimism.

'Well', she replied, deliberately drawing out her answer; '…movie-star good looks, eloquent, cultured; everything a woman looks for really', she revealed nonchalantly, a mischievous smile spreading across her face.

'Everything...?' Evie enquired with more urgency.

'Well, he is confident…and in control…and his conversation is as precise and efficient as a Swiss-watch', Madison insisted, delighting in her friend's desperation.

'And……….' Evie shrieked into the phone.

'…and…he has great poise', Madison responded to her friend's cajoling, realising as she said it, that while *the Bishop* really did have great poise, that poise could quite easily be mistaken for arrogance.

A brief pause followed that reflection, but just as Madison was about to tell Evie about TB's dinner invitation, a desperate shriek of frustration came hurtling down the line, breaking the silence.

'Well, if you're not going to tell me anymore about this guy; I've got some news of my own', Evie announced loudly, interrupting Madison's introspection and bringing her back to reality.

'I've met a new guy too', Evie declared eagerly.

'You remember that workshop I was looking into…which specialised in the art of seduction and striptease...for women who feel the need to boost their self-confidence…you know, the one run by that Big Mamma

Gina woman at her studio in Manhattan?', Evie stated emphatically, her voice getting a little more excited.

Madison frowned, and then remembered her friend mentioning it a few weeks before; 'Ahaa…' she replied courteously, though the details were rather sketchy in her mind.

'Well…I joined up'. Evie shrieked, ignoring her friend's noticeable lack of enthusiasm.

'You did…and how did it go?' Madison asked, trying to sound a little more interested.

'Well, guess what?' Evie screeched again, this time more stridently.

'I went for a latte after that first session with some of the other girls on the course, and at the coffee-shop, I met this guy Rick; he works on Wall Street'.

'Wow; that's a quick return on your money', Madison remarked, her comment more than a little tinged with sarcasm.

'So, did you make-out with him', she enquired naughtily, knowing her friend's usual M.O. (*modus operandi*).

'Nah, just some friendly flirting this time', Evie revealed in rebuttal; 'he's still got to earn the rest', she confirmed coquettishly.

'What was the chemistry like?' Madison insisted curiously, her mind still analysing her own meeting with *the Bishop*.

'I just told you; I don't know; I haven't been in the lab yet', Evie chuckled before scooping out another spoonful of cold comfort and licking the spoon.

'Well; good luck with that; keep me posted', Madison replied, smiling to herself and bringing the call to a close, happy to have spoken to her friend but too tired to prolong it any further.

'Will do', Evie agreed, and with that, they both hung up.

♗

Madison placed her phone on the bedside table and made her way back into the bathroom to get ready for bed.

However, an hour or so later, restless and unable to find her sleep - *despite her rather intense and exhausting day* - she started to reflect upon the enormity of the task ahead of her...and began to wonder whether or not she was really up for the challenge.

The Bishop had been so sanguine during lunch, so full of his own self-belief...and meeting him, one on one, had been somewhat of an ordeal - *an intimidating experience in fact, even for someone with her natural confidence and character* - and at times she had felt like a lamb going to slaughter...

...so as she lay there in her bed, ensconced in her quilt, Madison could not help but ponder if this was really such a good idea after all?

♗

Of course she had tried not to show any weakness during their exchanges over lunch but she knew that her usual self-belief had deserted her fleetingly on a couple of occasions when this seemingly powerful...and yet disarmingly charming individual had confronted her...

...and as she lay there, analysing the situation while idly contemplating the bland opacity of the ceiling in the room's half-light, she suddenly found herself questioning whether or not she was pushing the envelope a bit too far in pursuing an exclusive interview with a man who was such a force of nature...despite all her previous bravado to the contrary.

A few more minutes went past, but then as her confidence steadily returned Madison slowly began to appreciate that despite his reputation and her uncharacteristic uncertainty, *the Bishop*, had actually been very up-front and honest with her during their conversation - almost to a fault in some cases...even though his parting words - which lacked the subtlety and consideration that he had shown up until that point – were very harsh and still rankled with her as a woman; *despite her knowing that his comment on the colour of her dress was very pertinent as she had purposely dressed down for the occasion, so as to avoid distracting him from the reason for their meeting.*

Her thoughts then began to wander further afield and as she tried to break down her approach going forward Madison quickly recognized that the next major obstacle she would have to negotiate would be to get her elusive...and very secretive...new case-study to open up and reveal anything about himself...as during their lunch-time conversation he had managed, with an exceptional degree of aplomb, to side-step any personal questions from her, thereby shielding his private life from any prying examination with great proficiency.

Madison couldn't quite get a handle on this guy but the more she thought about him, the more she was intrigued by the fact that a man could fascinate her so – and despite her latent trepidation about the size of the task ahead of her she was desperate to know more.

She began wondering how she could possibly gather up enough information about him for a credible scoop and then, in a last moment of clarity before it closed down for the night, her brain unexpectedly gave her the answer to her question by reminding her that he had invited her to dinner…thereby offering her the perfect opportunity to further her research.

That thought put a smile on her face and within no time she had relaxed and drifted off to sleep, her head filled with the speculation of what she might find out during this impending new *tête-à-tête.*

♝

Next day, Madison spent the whole morning in the tournament hotel's reception area, interviewing a steady stream of the other competitors who, having gotten accustomed to her presence in their midst were slowly lowering their defences and pocketing their wariness.

Most of them were foreigners in England, just like her, and as she listened to their life-stories and their explanations as to how they now found themselves participating in this prestigious tournament - which incidentally provided her with a wealth of insight and background information for her article - Madison found herself being strangely more interested than she ever thought possible by the game of chess.

These people, like Gary who she had already met of course, were such an eclectic mix, coming from far and wide, from every culture and every race, but what really astounded her, as one person succeeded the next in the seat opposite her, was the similarity of all their stories despite their diverse origins.

Their backgrounds covered the whole spectrum of humanity, from exiled refugees to obscure heirs apparent…and yet they all seemed to share a common goal…they all seemed to have the same dream…that of becoming the next chess-champion of the world; a fact which she, as an American, still found rather perplexing and relatively narrow as a life-goal in comparison to her own lofty ambitions of running a fashion magazine… but that was their dream and who was she to question that.

However, what was even more surprising as far as Madison was concerned - *as she ran through her checklist of questions for the umpteenth time* - was the unanimous consensus of opinion that each of them put forward about the hierarchy of their rather insular and close-knit community; i.e., that *the Bishop* was the undisputed master...and that Rory was, well…a pretentious nobody.

'Have you not noticed how he pompously imitates the regal mannerisms of yesteryear when answering a question?' one of the young Indian contestants remarked.

Madison didn't follow up on that comment directly but having met Rory, she simply smiled politely at her interviewee's inquisitive expression and let her silence do the talking for her.

The young Indian got up and left…and while the next person made his way over to join her, Madison sat back in her seat feeling pretty pleased with herself…pleased with her morning's work, pleased that a number of his peers had confirmed her first impressions of Rory - or *Copperfield*, as she preferred to call him, thanks to Gary – in that he really was a pompous, obnoxious wannabe…and pleased too, that her journalistic hunch to pursue *the Bishop* as the focus of her article was also turning out to be the right one; it was now just a question of making it all work for her.

That thought brought the image *the Bishop's* face clearly to the forefront of her mind's eye and bizarrely, as she waited for her last interviewee to settle into the seat opposite, it prompted her subconsciously to check the time on her mobile phone.

Wow; its twelve thirty already…where did the morning go, she wondered to herself as she turned to double-check the time on the clock on the wall behind the reception desk?

The Bishop's next match is set to begin at one o'clock and I certainly don't want to be late for that, she reminded herself, putting her mobile-phone back into her handbag.

The last interviewee, a shy Norwegian was very reserved and not very talkative which suited Madison perfectly in the circumstance…and twenty minutes or so later, having thanked him for his humble contribution and packed away her new state-of-the-art digital voice recorder, together with the rest of her journalistic paraphernalia, Madison was soon making her way into the main competition room, ready to take up her usual seat for the afternoon's session.

It had been a very interesting morning; she had gathered lots of useful information from the other competitors which she might or might not use in her article, but this was what she had really been looking forward to… this and spending some quality time, later that evening at dinner...one-on-one...with the man she hoped would provide her with her break-out scoop.

She settled into her seat, and as she did so, the anticipation which had built up over the course of the morning suddenly manifested itself in Madison's stomach, reminding her that she hadn't eaten anything since breakfast…but before she could do anything about it, the lights in the room were dimmed, the MC was standing there on the podium and the introductions were being made to a rousing set of applause.

Later however, once the match had been concluded and *the Bishop* had swept aside yet another unfortunate opponent with another typically masterful and ruthlessly efficient display of mental agility - Madison did retire to a table in the hotel coffee shop in order to grab something to eat and review the notes that she had made earlier.

It had been another eventful day and as she sat there enjoying a light snack from the counter, paper from her files scattered randomly around her on the table, her mind drifted off at regular intervals with thoughts of what might happen later that evening - when she was scheduled to come face to face once again with the enigma that was...TB.

Naturally, she was still a little apprehensive about having dinner with the man who seemed to be so revered and respected in this rather uniquely insular community - especially after the mixed messages he had sent out during their lunch date the day before - but she also knew in her gut that this was the guy who was going to be her meal-ticket to a better career… and while some might think that that was a little selfish and egotistical of her, to be so single-minded, she couldn't wait to get started.

An hour or so went by...and having satisfied her hunger and finished putting her paperwork into some kind of order, Madison was feeling much better about herself.

She checked her mobile-phone once again...for the time and for any messages - of which surprisingly there were none - and was just about to pack up the rest of her things when all of a sudden; out of the corner of her eye, she spied *Copperfield* walking into the eatery.

Of course, she knew that that wasn't his real name, but for some reason she just couldn't get Gary's nickname for him out of her head; it just seemed so appropriate.

'Well, well, well; if it isn't the journalist with attitude', the abrasive Scot commented loudly from across the way, completely ignoring the other patrons sitting nearby.

'Young lady, I think we got off on the wrong foot the other evening, so I would like to apologise', he offered with exaggerated gallantry as he walked over and sidled up creepily beside her.

Madison cringed as he approached and wary of his intentions she glanced at him poker-faced, to let him know that she wasn't interested in talking to him.

This stopped him in his tracks but then, just as she was about to relent and accept his apology, unable to quit while he was ahead, the obnoxious nuisance allowed his mouth to open again.

'Maybe we could still have some fun together', he announced boldly - almost licking the words into her ear, his insufferable grin, his whisky-laden breath and his lecherous stare blatantly betraying the libidinous plans...that he was having rather a difficult time in hiding.

Madison's face convulsed instantly at the thought of this man touching her and as she twisted around to face him directly, her whole body shuddered with repulsion in reaction to her understandable disgust.

'Believe me, I'm already laughing…on the inside', she quipped sarcastically and very emphatically, much to the delight of another couple sitting in the next booth…

Of course, it was never going to happen; Copperfield was a non-entity as far as Madison was concerned – indeed, he was not even in the equation, and his leering look, on top of what she had already gleaned from her previous meeting with him, not to mention what the other competitors had told her about him earlier in the day, did little to alter her feelings of antipathy towards the guy.

…and with that Madison swept a stray lock of hair behind her ear, picked up one of her notebooks and began busily flicking through its pages once again in the hope that her unwanted admirer would get the message and leave her alone.

'Whatever…' Rory huffed as he turned away, snorting in disbelief at her complete and utter rejection of his advance; 'I've no time for hormonal women'.

The couple in the next booth both smiled warmly in concurrence as Madison shook her head again in disgust…but as she watched him walk away, she felt a little sympathy for poor *Copperfield* who in reality was more to be pitied than he was to be scorned; destined as he was to always be second-best at what he did, as long as the invincible and incomparable *Bishop* reigned supreme over the game that was his life.

CHAPTER FOUR

That evening, Madison decided to power-dress in order to boost her confidence; not that she really needed it…but *the Bishop's* criticism of the grey dress she had worn the day before still rankled with her and she was determined not to re-live the embarrassment for a second time; even though in retrospect, she was no longer convinced that his comment had been a deliberate attempt to offend her feminine sensibilities.

Nevertheless, this time she picked out her favourite navy-blue suit; the one in which she felt most at ease. The skirt was rather short, but as it show-cased her legs magnificently she came to the conclusion that it struck a good balance between her desire to appear professional...and her innate inclination to appear feminine...at the same time.

She would also wear her three-quarter length coat over her suit, just in case the weather turned cold later in the evening.

The digital display on her mobile-phone hit 7PM and with perfect British timing, a call came from the concierge's desk downstairs to inform her that her taxi had arrived...and that it was waiting for her outside.

Madison thanked the man for his call and having checked herself out one last time in the full-length mirror; she slipped on her coat and made her way downstairs, where, guided by the ever-deferential and smiling young valet she was ushered over to the cab where *the Bishop* was waiting.

The latter nodded to acknowledge her...and as she stepped into the cab they exchanged a brief but polite salutary greeting, before Madison settled herself in and the taxi slowly pulled away from the kerb.

Surprisingly, Madison didn't feel overawed by the situation as she sat there expectantly, but because of his reputation and of course her need to make a good impression - in order to succeed in her enterprise - she decided not to initiate the conversation after the opening greeting, hoping naturally that *the Bishop* would take that lead.

However, this was not to be, and rather than engage her - even in the most banal of social interactions - *the Bishop* just sat there in silence looking all debonair and vain, his hands placed comfortably in his lap and his eyes looking straight ahead, following the car's progress as it cut a swath through the cool night air.

Several minutes passed by and the silence in the car grew steadily more intense, but unwilling to compromise her position or say anything out of turn Madison stuck to her guns and indulged her host in his rather unsettling and somewhat annoying control trip, finding herself reduced to staring at her own reflection in the side-window and wondering quietly where he was taking her and what she had gotten herself into.

It took another twenty minutes or so, but eventually the cab pulled up outside the Villa d'Este, a chic little Italian restaurant, slightly off the beaten track in the village of Marlow...and as they came to a halt, having held her tongue for the duration of the ride, Madison could not help but ask in her brash New York twang, why he always reserved tables in restaurants that were so far away from where they were staying.

'Discretion' was *the Bishop's* only reply as he leaned forward and handed over the fare to the cab-driver.

Madison shook her head and rolled her eyes cynically as she opened the door and stepped out...thanking the cabbie simultaneously for his service.

The Bishop followed her out...and without further consultation they walked directly into the restaurant, where in a complete reversal of their previous meeting, *the Bishop's* very first gesture, as she took off her coat, was to compliment Madison on her appearance.

'A great improvement...' he remarked, in a warm but slightly monotone voice.

This unexpected word of approval took Madison by surprise somewhat, but before she could react with any great satisfaction to his comment, *the Bishop* immediately flattened her again, by adding...with a furtive glance at her hem-line...

'...but probably a little OTT for the prudish mentality of rural-England'.

Stunned, Madison smiled at him through gritted teeth...but as she handed her coat to the waiting employee she was still somewhat pleased to have prised a compliment out of her host...because even though it had been followed by a derogatory counter-remark; it was nevertheless, a first.

The busy restaurant manager sensed the tension and immediately showed them to a table, where, with typical English protocol he pulled out Madison's chair for her...in the most gentlemanly fashion... and invited her to take a seat with a guiding gesture of his other hand.

Madison thanked him appropriately, but as she made herself comfortable, pulling the chair forward, she immediately felt the weight of her host's stare upon her once again, scrutinising her with what she perceived as misogynist disparagement.

This was the last straw for the young journalist; she had had enough of his games and his unprovoked criticism but just as she was about to explode and let rip her volatile New York tongue, *the Bishop* cleverly anticipated her reaction and immediately tempered his previous remark by adding very honestly, as he took his seat, that he found it most appealing to see a woman looking so confident and comfortable with what she was wearing.

'I admire that in a woman', he disclosed frankly.

'Personally', he said, continuing his thought, 'I hate to see women flinching in low-cut, cleavage-revealing dresses…or fidgeting…or pulling down constantly on the hem of a short skirt, in obvious embarrassment. It shows a complete lack of confidence in their choice of clothing', he declared assertively.

Madison looked at him incredulously but didn't respond.

'If a woman is not comfortable with what she has chosen to wear, then she should not be wearing it; do you not agree, Miss Chatfield?' *the Bishop* suggested with indisputable logic.

'I guess so'; the young American concurred, never having really thought about it.

'…by the way...' *the Bishop* queried, rather haughtily, ignoring his guest's relatively non-committal response; '...Chatfield…that's not a very American-sounding name?'

'No, it's not'; Madison agreed impassively. '...my grandfather was English', she pointed out by way of explanation.

The Bishop nodded with understanding and then returned to the initial conversation.

'Surely these women know damned well, that plunging necklines and short skirts are going to draw male attention...so why do they do it, if they do not welcome that attention?', he continued pedantically.

'Right?' he advocated after a brief pause, hoping for a reaction.

'Right', Madison agreed nonchalantly as she reached into her handbag for her note-pad.

'...and what is worse', *the Bishop* continued, pursuing his thoughts and not really allowing his guest time to settle, '...are those women who dress up sexily – but then ruin the whole effect by throwing a scarf around their shoulders, to hide their cleavage...or tie a jacket or even a jumper around their waists to hide their hips'.

'What's the point in that?' he questioned, leaning back comfortably.

Madison didn't reply, assuming that his question was rhetorical.

'...seriously, what is the point', *the Bishop* repeated, waiting this time for her to reply.

'Well...I suppose it's a confidence thing', Madison ventured carefully, shrugging her shoulders.

'My point exactly', *the Bishop* affirmed; 'women should not bow down to fashion or peer-pressure; if they're not happy with it, then they shouldn't wear it. It's as simple as that', he concluded, pleased to have made his point.

Madison smirked, noticing that he was analysing her; gauging her reactions...and as she searched her note-pad for the questions she had written down...and wanted to ask during the evening...it suddenly dawned on her - as they were handed the menus by a suave-looking Italian waiter - that *the Bishop* was a great observer of human social behaviour, and that no doubt he had a marked preference for the fairer sex.

The look on his face as their eyes met briefly over the menus confirmed her suspicions and while she was flattered by that...and by the fact that he had started the conversation on a topic that she would feel more comfortable with – i.e. fashion; even though his observations were a little sexist - the young journalist inside of her wanted desperately to steer the discussion towards the real reason she was there – i.e. her article.

However, it would not be that easy as *the Bishop* or TB as she had now been beseeched to call him...immediately countered her imminent attempt to divert him onto that path...*inferring with a rather dismissive wave of the hand that they would get to that part later*...by asking about her background.

'Tell me more about the USA...and about New York', *the Bishop* suddenly urged as he sat forward again with intent. 'I have never been there but I am somewhat fascinated by your country and its culture', he revealed.

'Is that right?' Madison replied; humouring him, and not wanting to lose sight of the prize that was being dangled in front of her eyes.

She was a little frustrated by her host's delaying tactics but Madison had never been one to capitulate when confronted with an uncooperative respondent...and so, in order to indulge her host, she plastered her most obliging smile across her face and proceeded with great aplomb to review a number of general topics, all to do with the American way of life.

It was a nervous start but Madison soon relaxed and was beginning to enjoy the chat about life in New York - even if certain details were making her a little home-sick - when suddenly, *the Bishop* stopped her dead in her tracks with a question right out of left field;

'Tell me this Miss Chatfield', he asked bluntly, his diction very precise and perfectly clear; 'why is your country based on so much hypocrisy and contradiction?'

Once again Madison was stunned...and her face congealed, almost instantly in an expression of puzzled confusion. His question had caught her off-guard and for the first time in a long time, in a very long time, she was left speechless.

An awkward silence followed, but then rather strangely *the Bishop* repeated his question... quite matter of fact.

'I hope you don't mind me asking this...' he maintained calmly, '...but in your capacity as an American journalist, could you please tell me, why it is that your country is based on so much hypocrisy and contradiction?'

Again, he was met with a frozen smile and a stunned silence from across the table as Madison tried valiantly to rally, while struggling at the same time to conceal her dismay at his searching question.

‘Okay Miss Chatfield’, *the Bishop* remarked without relenting...despite noticing her discomfort; ‘could you please explain to me how…and why… the gun lobby, the religious activists and the anti-abortion groups manage to hold a great country like the United States of America to ransom? I mean, America pretends to lead the world – and in many respects, it does’, he continued; ‘but in the political arena I just cannot understand why it affords so much grace and favour to these groups and activists who hold such vintage ideas...tell me why that is…please. I just want to understand, I just want to hear it from the mouth of an American citizen’, he asked again, deliberately antagonising her, his slightly raised tone drawing the attention...and a couple of furtive glances...from the neighbouring tables.

Aghast, Madison was still dumbstruck and could only grimace in embarrassment as she fiddled with her pen trying to collect her thoughts…

...so without pausing for reflection, *the Bishop* pursued his brutal interrogation.

‘Let me put it another way’, he added hastily.

‘Why do those who front 21st century politics in America allow themselves to be influenced by these minority groups who want a return to the Middle Ages with their archaic beliefs and their antiquated ideals; ideals which have so clearly been superseded by the recent progresses in technology and advances in knowledge awareness; what is their hold on the political community of your country...why do they hold so much sway?’, he insisted forcefully, though his manner was still composed and unruffled.

Madison sat there dumbfounded and looking a bit glum, caught up as she was in the inertia of the moment. ‘Where was all this coming from’? She wondered.

‘Oh, don’t get me wrong, young lady; *the Bishop* continued pontificating.

‘I agree that abortion for example, should be controlled to avoid abuse, but returning to a blanket ban as some people in America would have it, would only set things back to a time where women risked dying – them and their babies – in botched back-street DIY clinics; why can’t the people in these misguided pressure groups see that?’ He pressed.

This time, Madison wanted to respond but wisely she bit her lip.

‘We all know that unwanted pregnancies will always occur – people will always have sex – so why not face the problem head on, discuss it, and plan a solution – rather than close our eyes and hope that it will go away by hiding behind an unenforceable law. A blanket ban is just ridiculous, and the mere fact that the leaders of your country are bending to the outdated demands of these people leaves me perplexed', *the Bishop* railed passionately, his voice rising an octave or two, which again prompted a couple of casual stares from the patrons sitting at quite close quarters in the cosy little restaurant.

Madison was getting a little uncomfortable. In fact, she was getting more than a little uncomfortable but she managed nevertheless to remain dignified and keep a lid on it, thoughts of her scoop and what it would mean to her career tempering her reaction.

'If anything, Pro-life and Anti-abortionists should become more socially responsible', *the Bishop* declared dogmatically.

'Why – as they would advocate - bring unwanted children into the world – no matter how they were conceived', he reasoned, looking at Madison and waiting for her response, a quiet but intense stare in his eyes.

The latter glanced around vaguely in the direction of the waiter...doing her best not to reveal her inner turmoil and hoping desperately to deflect her host's attention away from her; it didn't work.

'Surely these people can understand that there is an argument for rape victims, under-age pregnancies, socially or mentally challenged women and those with foetuses that have malformations to be given the choice as to whether they want to proceed with a pregnancy; after all, you had the Eugenics Movement in place in America until the 1960's which sterilised handicapped people to prevent them from re-producing; surely that set a precedent', *the Bishop* argued; '…so, I ask again; what hold do these people have over your political community?'

Madison took a sip of water, and looked around again for the waiter as *the Bishop* continued his rant, the simmering cauldron of her volatile temperament threatening to boil over at any time.

'Is it that the majority of Americans who live in the conservative Mid-West and constitute the bulk of the votes cast during the elections, are in fact not living in the 21st century but are still entrenched in ideas of a bygone age?'

'Is that the reason?' *the Bishop* queried after a pause.

Madison, occupying her hands with the glass of water, shot him a disdainful glance but despite her increasing resentment...and her desire to offer an explanation...to defend her country from this stinging attack, she was still unable to find a suitable parry.

The Bishop's barrage of questions, all perfectly reasonable and all flawlessly logical left her without a defence and quite literally the young New-Yorker - despite her journalistic training – just didn't know how to answer. She was not a political journalist and felt that *the Bishop* was deliberately exposing and exploiting that particular deficiency in her armoury.

'…and pray tell me', *the Bishop* continued, playing the devil's advocate and revelling in his dominant role; '…could you please explain to me as an American what the complex ties are between the Office of the President, the Justice Department, and the Church concerning the hypocritical façade of morality which the US maintains for the outside world'.

'After all, legal and illegal gambling is rife throughout America, prostitution is widespread and paedophilia is completely out of hand – especially in the Church'.

He paused before adding ….

'In fact, several high-profile cases have recently revealed that the Church is a hot-bed for child abuse the world over'.

For information;

The Archdiocese of Los Angeles was recently forced to pay out $660 million to over 500 victims of sexual abuse by priests.

'So how does all that balance out with the Mid-western bible-punchers', *the Bishop* preened, rattling the young American's cage and continuing his relentless antagonism.

Madison felt trapped. She had no answers to this onslaught of heavy rhetoric and she was rapidly losing patience with her host...but finally, just as she was about to throw in the towel, she was saved by the waiter who suddenly appeared at the table with a reassuring smile.

'Are you ready to order?' he asked politely, in a soft, calming voice, bringing a moment of sanity back into Madison's world.

'Yes, of course', they both replied, turning their attention back to the menus and taking turns to pick out their meals.

The young waiter made a note of their order...and Madison enjoyed the moment's respite filled with talk about food and wine…but as soon as he walked away again leaving her to her fate, she knew that she would have to steel herself once again for the next wave of *the Bishop's* laser-guided questions.

She did try to pre-empt his next onslaught by asking if he was a regular at the restaurant, but with a wave of his hand which could have meant yes or no, *the Bishop* dismissed her frivolous question and returned to his anti-American tirade, trying to draw a reaction from her by commenting on the paradox between the Puritanical hypocrisy of the political body in the United States – and the fact that the majority of the worst web-sites on the world-wide internet system, concerning those most delicate subjects, were produced or originated in the very heart of that very same country.

'In fact, if what I have heard is true…there is a whole valley in California which is given over to producing this material', he confirmed.

Mortified, because of the rather intimate setting, Madison began to smoulder.

The Bishop was really pushing her buttons and testing her beyond her usual limits.

'Boy, that's heavy stuff…but I guess that's just the way it is'; she managed to comment with a controlled smile.

'I have to tell you, Miss Chatfield', *the Bishop* declared; 'I despise the public front of sanctimonious shock and moral outrage that Americans display when confronted by any form of exploitation of a sexual nature, at whatever level – while behind the scenes, the wheels of the US economy are oiled by the multi-million dollar turnover and profits grossed from the very production of millions of those questionable videos sold world-wide'.

Madison looked across the table at him, questioning his remark with raised eyebrows.

'Take for example, the hypocrisy of the *Nipple-gate* episode at the 2004 Superbowl with Janet Jackson and Justin Timberlake', he pursued; '...where, because a few inches of breast-flesh were revealed during the half-time performance, the American censors made a pathetic attempt in the following weeks, at hypocritical Puritanical protectionism, by insisting that subsequent live events were taped and screened with a two minute delay in order to avoid the potential for any further revealing or embarrassing situations'.

'There must be a problem somewhere; it all lacks coherence; the whole country is just one big hypocritical contradiction', he surmised... 'on the one hand they are producing the majority of the world's X-rated material... which is available to anybody and everybody the world over at the click of a button... while at the same time censoring TV stations for broadcasting a glimpse of breast-flesh, the nipple itself having been carefully covered up beforehand by a discreet shield', he stated self-righteously.

For information;

A recent study by Mr Benjamin Edelman of the Harvard Business School even suggested that the States considered stalwarts of conservative and religious values consume more internet pornography than the States which would normally spring to mind – 'some of the people who are most outraged are turning out to be biggest consumers of the very things they claimed to be outraged by', he claimed (if that is not hypocrisy)

In the same way, the sexually repressed teenage children of these same hypocritical, puritanical parents use the prom-dance and the spring break period to affirm their independence and cut the umbilical cord of parental control. In fact, the prom-dance, which was originally a teenager's first brush with adulthood has now become stereotypically synonymous with sexual promiscuity and echoes with shouts of 'let's get laid', while its big brother, the spring break is now no more than an excuse for alcohol-fuelled, drunken debauchery and even more shouts of 'let's get laid' but this time... as many times as possible.

'I don't think so', Madison replied firmly, a hint of her usual confidence suddenly returning.

'Listen, young lady, *the Bishop* stated smugly; '…you Americans revere JFK as an icon and yet while he promised that his administration would display a new morality, it is well-documented that he had several extra-marital affairs…notably with Judith Campbell Exner and Marilyn Munroe to name but two'.

'How hypocritical is that; can you see what I'm driving at here?' he asked in the next breath.

Madison sat there wide-eyed as the waiter came with the wine.

'Look…what do you want me to say?' she countered finally, once the latter had filled their glasses and gone off again to his other duties.

'I don't have the answers to all your questions', she admitted, shrugging her shoulders and folding her arms in front of her defensively.

This was new territory for the young New-Yorker. She had never before been on the receiving end of such a barrage of unquestionable reasoning where she literally had no defence, but something else was bothering her too; she was hating the way that *the Bishop* was talking down to her, almost paternally…especially when there were not that many years between them.

Sure, there was an age gap, but it wasn't that big.

The waiter returned again with their meals offering Madison another short respite but as he left, *the Bishop* leaned forward across the table once again to focus her attention and suck her back into the conversation.

'I could go on', he whispered, 'but if the great American public really wants to naively believe that these values are still alive today, in 2014; then we must leave them in their little bubble and respect that'.

He then sat back again and as Madison breathed a sigh of relief, hoping that the lesson was finally over and that he was at last going to allow her to concentrate on eating the wonderful meal that had now been placed in front of her, *the Bishop* paused for a moment before nonchalantly driving home his point with another slice of scathing sarcasm.

'It would be very honourable', he announced blithely, 'if that were the case, if these values that Americans hold so dear were still respected...but unfortunately', he continued, 'the reality of the 21st century tells us, and shows us in black and white every day - or is that in digital multi-colour - that those beliefs, anchored in a long-forgotten past, no longer apply'.

'The politicians might still be trying to pull the wool over our eyes and make us believe that that is the case; big-brother, media moguls and censors might also still be trying to avoid showing their citizens the real world – but come on America – wake up and smell the coffee'.

'Not so long ago, you were going to throw out your President, Bill Clinton and lapidate him for sexual misconduct…the only problem was, that there wasn't one politician who felt honest enough to throw the first stone'.

Madison stopped eating and looked up, her reaction tantamount to being of the same opinion.

'I applaud Bill Clinton', *the Bishop* went on, '…not for abusing his position, that was and still is…unforgivable, as he himself has since admitted'.

'No, I applaud him for sticking it out, and facing down his critics, calling their bluff and daring any of his political enemies to stand up and accuse him, face to face, to cast the first stone if you will, knowing full-well that their own reputations would then be put on the line, churned up and exposed to the light of day for the vultures to pick over as his had been, were they to make that stand'.

'What is it that the Bible says; Judge not, lest ye be judged', he quoted.

'…and as I said earlier, none of them was prepared to do that, which basically speaks for itself'.

Madison nodded silently, a look of consternation on her face.

'Let me tell you this, young lady'; *the Bishop* pursued again without stopping to take a breath.

'This incoherence and the double standards that are so glaringly obvious to outsiders…are what leaves your country wide open to constant attack by all those controversial political activists who delight in exposing and exploiting the *Achilles heel weaknesses* of the American system.

People like Michael Moore have created polemic situations – just to embarrass the incumbent administration, to fuel their own ego and to swell their own bank balances…and they will continue to do so until a future Administration calls a halt to this hypocrisy and makes some major changes.

That said; of course I understand that everybody has a right to their own opinion…even Michael Moore, but the media exposure that he now commands through his films - *which are often no more than conjecture, rumour and unsubstantiated allegations and are sadly based more on conspiracy theories than on fact, while lacking in unbiased credibility* - allows him and people like him, who have access to the media, the opportunity to express themselves, and their ideas, to a worldwide audience - which only serves to magnify the embarrassment of the incumbent political community while chipping away at its credibility…and that situation will continue until the loopholes and the incoherencies are addressed.

Here in England, successive governments have ruined what was Great Britain; most notably New Labour under Tony Blair and Gordon Brown who has since gone down in history as the worst Prime Minister we've ever had – but despite that, it seems to me that we don't live under such a regime of total, universal hypocrisy as appears to be the case state-side… though I must admit...and it would be wrong of me to deny it...that there is an element of that here too', he admitted in conclusion.

Again Madison didn't reply, preferring instead to let her mind simply drift off into a safe haven where she suddenly remembered a quote from Abraham Lincoln that she had learned at school; 'it is better to remain silent and be thought a fool, than to speak out and remove all doubt'.

The Bishop drew breath at that point and tasted his meal appreciatively before continuing.

'It seems to me', he pursued, 'that, in the make-up of the human psyche, nature has built in a need for power…originally tied to dominance and survival probably…but nowadays, this power, and political power in particular, has morphed into an uncontrollable monster, systematically corrupting anybody who comes into contact with it.

Unfortunately, this power has become a necessary evil in the running of our everyday lives…and regrettably it doesn't discriminate; it's a universal scourge which happens the world over; even the most decent, law-abiding men and women who have gone into politics with the most honourable intentions have found that the demands of being a part of the political process has gradually and inevitably forced them into degrees of dishonesty and corruption.

I suppose that it is all a question of managing IT as best we can', he mused philosophically.

IT, of course…being power…and its by-product 'greed'…which was hi-lighted not so long ago here in the UK during the expenses scandal, where many of those in the political community were discredited after having been found to be abusing the system for their own ends.

Madison looked up rather circumspect, scratching her head and running her hand idly through her sleek blond hair.

'You wouldn't know this, I'm sure, but a league-table which ranks countries according to the honesty of their politicians and public officials recently placed the UK at No.20...below countries like Qatar. How humiliating is that for our wonderful leaders?' *the Bishop* remarked rhetorically.

'Yes...the thirst for power and greed are human traits that are never going to go away', he reflected...'and so, dare I say it...as we strive towards the utopia of a perfect world, we will inevitably have the need for watchdogs like Michael Moore - like him or not - to pull back on the reins of this monster, from time to time, in order to remind the politicians of why they are there…who put them there and most importantly, their obligations while they are there, for the good of the people who elected them and not just to fill their pockets and feather their retirement funds.

It's just a shame that moral integrity and economics don't mix…' he lamented...' because it has been proved time and again the world over... that politicians are always ready - and willing - to compromise their beliefs, if it means keeping their seat on the gravy train'.

Madison was trying to appear sympathetic to all his arguments...and interested in what he was saying, but the truth was that she was beginning to feel intellectually brow-beaten by *the Bishop's* constant verbal battering... and at this point she just wanted to escape to the relative security of the ladies-room, in order to recompose herself and relieve the overwhelming pressure on her brain...but once he had paused again to savour another delicious morsel, *the Bishop* returned to his narrative...and it was a narrative; it was no longer a conversation; Madison, having given up all thoughts of a riposte to his protracted arguments, preferring instead to concentrate on her food.

'If only we could take a leaf out of the book of the ancient Japanese samurai culture', *the Bishop* bemoaned, seemingly out of nowhere.

'They believed that with power came responsibility; they followed a strict code of honour and loyalty, which was respectful and protective of their ancestors and their elders; they upheld and defended their heritage and traditions – and all that it represented'.

'These are basic human qualities and ideals which still exist but which are no longer held in any esteem; ideals that the politicians and the youth of today in the western world – would do well to heed, in order to improve their own understanding of life'.

'The samurai was a simple, some would say naïve, way of life; live your life in the respect of others – it's as easy and naively utopic as that'.

'What's wrong with that ideology?' *the Bishop* questioned.

Exasperated, Madison simply ignored him, wishing simply that the ground would open and swallow her up.

'These days – most politicians blow with the wind, as long as they get the votes they need to keep them in power. They are not interested in ideology or the needs of their constituents. They are only interested in keeping their seats on the gravy-train so that they can maintain the lifestyles to which they have become accustomed...while they merrily fill their ever deepening pockets with whatever they can get their hands on'.

'Everybody knows that; they are the same the world over' he chanted, repeating his doctrine from earlier.

'So I say; forget the hypocrisy America – update the constitution and open your eyes to the real world. You have to admit that something exists before you can address it; Man's faith should be in his own humanity; his spirituality based on his own past and his children's future'.

The Bishop took hold of his glass at this point and sat back in his chair, pausing to allow Madison to assimilate all that he had said.

She did so, and though she hadn't given any reply to his thrusting arguments trying to maintain her composure while she polished off her delicious Italian meal, she was nevertheless quite annoyed at his barrage of criticism of her country…and a little frustrated at not having been able to find a parry to counter his many attacks.

And so, reverting to her natural sarcasm, knowing that she would probably be priming the grenade for yet another onslaught, she told him, rather tongue in cheek that the USA didn't need the samurai code to protect them, they had the CIA.

Sure enough, TB took the bait and threw his hands in the air in despair.

'The CIA', he exclaimed in horror.

'Let me tell you, young lady...'

She interrupted him; 'please stop calling me that. My name is Madison or Miss Chatfield'.

This time, it was *the Bishop* who was stopped in his tracks.

'Very well then, Miss Chatfield', he insisted.

'...and while this is all very interesting, I would much rather you talked to me...and not at me', she added, with commendable spirit.

The Bishop paused for moment and his expression tightened but he quickly regained his composure.

'As I was saying', he continued, with a little more diplomacy; '...it is true that in the USA you have the CIA, and it is one of the most powerful agencies on the planet – because of the financial backing and governmental subsidies that it receives – but it is also one of the most dangerous organisations ever to come into existence'.

'The whole agency is riddled with paranoid suspicion, corruption, incompetence, short-sightedness, naiveté and misguidance'.

'That agency, of which you are apparently so proud…lies, cheats, deceives, betrays and kills; all in the name of the USA'.

Madison recoiled. She had pushed a button and realising the fact, she smiled to herself facetiously with a sense of contented self-satisfaction.

'And another thing', *the Bishop* added, venting his absurdly knowledgeable cerebral mass.

'The CIA was created to protect the USA from attack…and the only time that the USA was attacked...on 9/11...and should have been able to rely on their intelligence and count on the protection of these dedicated counter-terrorism agencies, they messed it up through the incompetence and the systematic failure of all those concerned; and then of course, to compound their error and cover their tracks they proceeded to invent the false WMD stories in order to support President Bush's knee-jerk decision to invade Iraq'.

'Do you need more proof?' He asked plaintively.

Madison's eyes flashed with annoyance and her pout relayed her answer.

'I'm sorry to tell you this…but every time the CIA has gotten involved in whatever conflict, wherever in the world, it has got it wrong and millions have suffered – so how much should the American people really trust them?', *the Bishop* concluded.

For information;

To illustrate the Bishop's position here is a non-exhaustive list in the public domain of some of the work carried out by the CIA

(Also known as the Department of Dirty Tricks)

taken from a documentary made by Sky Television in the UK

- *The CIA started out employing known Nazis after 2nd World War – offering them exemption from prosecution for intelligence information on Soviet Union*
- *The CIA has used drug schemes to try to warp and control minds*
- *The CIA manoeuvred to overthrow the democratically elected leader of Iran to install the puppet Shah.*
- *The CIA supported Mbutu in Congo - a known dictator and tyrant*
- *The CIA tried to pass spy-planes off as UFO's*

- *The CIA financed and organised the botched invasion of Cuba at the Bay of Pigs*
- *The CIA meddled in Indonesia with black/covert operations leading to the massacre/slaughter of over 500,000 communists*
- *The CIA participated in narcotics trafficking in Laos during the Vietnam war – The American army ended up full of drug addicts*
- *The CIA sponsored the assassination of Che Guevara*
- *The CIA organised the Phoenix programme which systematically and summarily assassinated 20,000 Vietcong leaders*
- *The CIA helped overthrow President Allende in Chile and installed Pinochet in his place*
- *The CIA meddled in Cambodia leading to the arrival of Pol-Pot and the Khmer Rouge – 2 million were subsequently assassinated*
- *The CIA supported the Angolan civil war*
- *The CIA was embarrassed by the hostage situation in the US embassy in Iran when they organised the disastrous rescue attempt which failed pitifully killing 8 personnel*
- *The CIA meddled in Nicaragua, selling arms to Iran (Khomeini) to finance the Contras*
- *In Afghanistan, the CIA financed the Mujahiddin against the Russians…and finally…*
- *It is said that the CIA made up to 600 assassination attempts on Fidel Castro; all of which failed.*

At that point, Madison grabbed her notebook and her handbag; she had had enough and she wasn't going to take any more; she felt disabused and her bruised and battered mind needed a rest.

This man was too overpowering, and despite her desperate desire to use his story for her scoop, she was ready to leave.

'…and one last thing', *the Bishop* added, driving home his unquestionable and indomitable personality.

'I hate the lack of respect that the White-House media-spin-doctors have now introduced to the office of President; they are completely undermining the dignity and prestige of the position'.

Madison's expression didn't change, but then she clicked.

'First, there was that silly video of Bill Clinton walking around an abandoned White House at Christmas, washing the presidential limousines by hand etc. – and then we were treated to George Bush chatting with his dogs in the Oval Office…and finally we had to suffer his dog Barney presenting his Christmas videos from the White House, one of which even featured our very own Tony Blair'.

'Now, this might be funny to some lame press-officer but politics is a serious matter and the office of President should not be ridiculed like that. Not in my opinion anyway', *the Bishop* declared rather self-righteously.

Madison took a deep breath and reconsidered her position, finally having to admit that *the Bishop* was right in what he was saying…and that he clearly understood the realities of American life - probably more and better than she did herself.

She also had to recognise that behind all his ranting against her country, the man was actually a moralist, a defender of society committed to traditional values and somebody who despite his antagonising commentaries, clearly respected the executive office of the President of her homeland.

This prompted her to give him a second chance…and putting her bag back down she tried to defend her country's political system as best she could, arguing that the politicians always tried to be politically correct, and that those videos shot in the White House were simply a light-hearted way of connecting with the ordinary folk.

The Bishop smiled or at least half-smiled at her attempt at conciliation but then, enjoying the exchange he swiftly countered her comment with another sweeping statement.

'Political correctness Miss Chatfield is just a collective hypocrisy which prevents us from giving things their real name...much like spin or the artfully manipulative, double-edged discourse used by smooth-tongued diplomats', he proclaimed triumphantly; 'it's just sugar-coating'.

That stopped Madison in her tracks once again but luckily for her she was saved from the ignominy of further scrutiny by the arrival of their next food course, and while it was being served both she and *the Bishop* withdrew into their own private worlds.

However, the respite was short-lived and as soon as the waiter had left again *the Bishop* was back on her case.

'Another example of hypocrisy…or contradiction at least…is the fact that the President of the United States ends each and every speech he makes with, God Bless America', he remarked casually.

'Oh…and why is that?' Madison snapped, with a scowl on her face, her patience reaching its limit.

'Well', he explained; 'the *God concept* in religion is all about peace; how can a person like your previous President for example, so intent on war and destruction invoke God every time he spoke; surely there is another paradox there?' he reasoned calmly.

Madison was in a real predicament. She was having difficulty trying to deflect *the Bishop's* thunder and as there was no parry to that last statement, or at least none she could think of in that instant, she decided to change the subject once again…after all, she was supposed to be interviewing him about chess and as yet they hadn't even mentioned the word.

'Look, I get it'; she conceded, trying to bring that particular subject to a close; 'you don't like Americans'.

'Oh no, that's not true', *the Bishop* countered ruefully, brushing back his mop of black hair.

'Let's just say that Americans in general, lack subtlety, and while that arrogant, blustering, get-up-and-go attitude of refusing to take a backward step has allowed them to create the society in which they now live, it is unfortunate...but nonetheless true...that because of it, many people around the world dislike them for it.

'Personally, I have nothing against Americans. I just abhor hypocrisy in all its forms and as I said earlier, politicians worldwide are guilty of it. It is just that the USA are such an easy target as they pretend to be morally outraged by what goes on in the rest of the world when they are often the worst offenders in their own back-yard'.

'You should not go around the world handing out lessons when you are morally corrupt yourself', he concluded very matter of fact.

Madison nodded and shrugged again before trying to steer him away from politics and back to chess – but frustratingly *the Bishop* side-stepped her question once again, preferring instead to ask her more about her job as a journalist in New York.

It wasn't what she wanted, it wasn't the direction she wanted the conversation to go in, but at least she felt on more familiar territory talking about what she knew...because despite her attempts at ignoring his criticisms she was getting rather uncomfortable discussing her country's political short-comings.

Besides, she was not a political journalist and was now certain – if she had ever been in doubt - that her host's knowledge of the subject far outweighed her own in that particular area.

So, she relented and while they ate she began telling him more about herself, about the office she worked in and about the jealousies that went on there, the words suddenly rolling off her tongue with ease.

'I am hoping that this assignment will be my launching pad...that my boss will finally draw a line under the past, see who I really am and give me another chance to show her what I can do', Madison disclosed, suddenly revealing much more than she had intended to compensate for her lack of *talk-time.*

It all sounded very shallow and superficial after the heavy political bludgeoning that her host had just subjected her to, but finding herself back in her comfort zone Madison finally began to relax again.

Unfortunately, she relaxed a little too much and her revelation that she wanted to meet Mr Right someday, to buy a big house with a white-picket fence and settle down with a couple of children left her wide open to another blast; another devastating theory.

'Those are all projected desires and unrealistic hopes', *the Bishop* commented with cold indifference as he sipped another mouthful of wine, having taken a moment to analyse her soliloquy from every angle.

'You Americans are all too pre-occupied with superficiality', he pursued.

'I don't know if it's because you're lacking in history, but as I was saying earlier about your politicians being pre-occupied with what the rest of the world thought about your morality, American women, and particularly New Yorkers, seem to be obsessed with becoming the ideal stereo-typical woman'.

'Why not be an individual; why not be yourself?' He suggested challengingly; 'you don't have to conform to the social template'.

Madison threw him a look of withering disdain and launched her hands in the air in despair.

'Look, I get it, you really don't like the USA, do you?' she blurted out, tired of *the Bishop's* constant tirade of criticism…even though she knew in her heart that everything he had said rang true.

A pregnant pause then followed as he reflected on her comment and went over all that he had been saying in his mind…and then realising that he had indeed been preaching over and above, *the Bishop* slowly came back down to earth and took a few deep breaths himself before continuing.

A young couple were being seated at a table across from them and *the Bishop* could not help but notice the young woman's alluring figure and enhanced attributes.

Madison saw him looking and followed his gaze, curiously.

'You like...' she commented impudently.

The Bishop looked at her and smiled.

'I do appreciate the beauty of nature...but what is it with you women, especially you American women, that you have to mess with that nature?' he remarked, ever the master of conversational transition.

'...why the obsession with implants and cosmetic surgery?' he insisted.

Madison found his question rather personal, and somewhat extrapolated from their previous topic, but seeing where his question had originated she decided to answer it in order to humour him - eager as she was…still…to please him in her quest for the inside story, despite the tongue-whipping she had just taken - especially as she knew that she would rather talk about anything else at that point than go back to discussing politics, where she felt she was on shaky ground.

'Again, it's a confidence thing; women feel more feminine with a shapely figure', she explained rationally, '...and, as for the cosmetic stuff... well that's just us being vain and not wanting to grow old', she added boldly, defending the sisterhood.

'Well, I don't believe that we should mess with nature…under any circumstances;' *the Bishop* retorted firmly, crinkling up his nose. 'All this

Nip and Tuck surgery; it's so unnatural, he confirmed with a strange wave of the hand.

He then mentioned having seen some examples of breast implants, which because of their size had in fact had the opposite effect on him.

'Real passion-killers', he joked bizarrely, riding rough-shod over any delicate feminine sensibilities that Madison might have about discussing such issues.

The young journalist raised her eyebrows in disbelief of what she was hearing.

'Did anybody in the female media, which drives this obsession, ever think to stop and ask men if that was what they were looking for in a woman...because if they did, they would probably have gotten a surprise', he reasoned out loud.

'Out-sized breasts are such a turn-off, just like pantyhose' he stated, very matter-of-fact.

'Yuk', he mimed to himself; 'There is no bigger turn-off for a man than pantyhose...and might I say that wearing them shows a distinct lack of imagination on the woman's part...and...a certain loss of her desire to seduce; wouldn't you agree, Miss Chatfield?'.

Madison gulped, as once again he put her on the spot.

'Well...', she said, composing herself, putting on her fashion journalist's hat and trying to defend the woman's point of view, even though she felt the conversation was going off at a quite bizarre tangent.

'...they are practical...and comfortable...but I do see your point about them not being too sexy', she agreed hesitantly.

The Bishop smiled at her vanilla reasoning...but as the conversation progressed over the next half-hour, Madison found out that her host was also against *piercing* any other part of the body other than the traditional ear-lobe, and that even tattoos or...tramp-stamps as he called them were a *no-no* as far as he was concerned.

In fact, she discovered that he was quite a traditionalist for the most part and didn't agree with any visual mutilation of the human body whatsoever.

'Nature should not be messed with', he maintained, time and time again.

However, after much discussion and a lot of hypothetical conjecture

Madison did finally manage to convince him that a reasonably sized, discreetly placed, tattoo could be decorative.

It was a small victory, a minor concession after what had been an interminable rear-guard action but it was another concession nonetheless.

Desserts were served and as Madison tucked into her tiramisu *the Bishop* treated her to another history lesson, explaining how tattoos had originated in the Maori culture as a way of covering up or disguising the marks left on the skin by eczema...and revealing that it was only recently that it had evolved and turned into a social statement, symbolising anything from the spectrum of the human psyche – be it spiritual, love, loyalty, protection, power or bravery.

'...and...' he added subtly, '...it is also another way for a woman to draw attention to herself...like a logo on a t-shirt', which, he suggested, was there solely to draw attention to her breasts.

Madison blushed slightly and shrugged her shoulders for the umpteenth time, bowing to his reason.

'...and then of course, there's your obsession with colouring your hair', *the Bishop* added, developing his thought; 'that's another way of drawing male attention, like birds with their plumage...colour attracts the eye'.

'Did you know that four out of five women dye their hair; why is that?' he suddenly questioned rhetorically.

'Why are women never satisfied with what Nature has given them? You paint your faces; redden your lips and your fingernails, you stick false eye-lashes on your eyes'.

'I have to admit, as a red-blooded man, that I have never, not once, checked out a woman's eyelashes'; he stated ironically, a hint of mockery in his tone.

'What you women will do, to draw attention to yourselves just amazes me'.

'You're forever inventing new hairstyles and adding shiny, noisy ornaments such as earrings and necklaces, bracelets and belt buckles all to draw the male eye'.

'Then there are the high heels you wear to accentuate your posture... and the perfume'.

'You're all obsessed with your appearance in your perennial quest to seduce a man'

'It's all so shallow and superficial; nothing about you is real'.

'Whatever happened to natural attraction – and what's wrong with growing old with dignity and grace?'

'It must be difficult to find the right balance between the angel and the painted-lady with all the different facets of the female personality and psyche', he commented critically.

Madison looked at him, open mouthed.

He was preaching again and she was beginning to see why this man was a bachelor – his opinion of women was highly questionable and most unflattering.

An ironic paradox...or the reasoning behind the Bishop's point of view

The illusory nature or the cynical trickery of today's modern women

Women spend their whole lives screaming; look at me; look at me; look at me; look at me.

This is because attraction is a biological imperative for the female of the species and has been hard-wired into their psyche over a million years of evolution. It is an innate part of their DNA to find a partner and as a consequence, women spend millions of pounds every year improving the physical aspects of their bodies just so that they can fulfil their natural role of attracting male attention.

It is unfortunate however, that despite all the progress that has been made, the resulting effect of all this pecunious outlay quite often serves no other purpose than to make them look more false and more un-natural.

Indeed, everything about women these days - in the seduction game at least - is false and un-natural.

It begins with their hair, which is more often than not coloured or altered with hi-lights (only one woman in five has her natural hair-colour).

Then, if it is not as thick and as lustrous as the 'because you're worth it' slogan-writers say it should be, they add extra extensions just to make sure.

After that, they shave / exfoliate their skin, moisturise it, wax it or cover it with a layer of powder to hide any blemishes before applying a layer of fake tan and adding the obligatory perfume.

The next step is to paint their nails (often false) and apply longer eye-lashes before they coquettishly add a little mascara for extra effect.

Then, by reddening their lips with the latest lipstick they hope to make them look plumper and more inviting than they actually are.

Once the painting and decorating is completed, it is time to get dressed and this begins with a pair of control pants / Spanx, worn both to sculpt the body and to keep a wayward booty in check – this underwear is then matched with a padded or uplifting bra which women hope will showcase their best assets while simultaneously keeping them in place.

...and finally, having completed the transformation process, from natural beauty to superficial vamp they put on a set of clothes which are as revealing or as daring as their moral-code will allow, and top that off with some high-heeled shoes (which make them look taller than they actually are) together with some shiny, noisy jewellery, all of which is geared to attract attention and get them noticed.

Now; it may all be superficial and false, but women do all this to make men look at them and desire them more, and despite what they might say or how they might react when approached, they secretly crave compliments on their 'toilette' (appearance) having gone to all the trouble.

However, the paradox is that in these days of rampant feminism, a man has to respect so many boundaries when approaching a woman that he is more likely to get slapped with a sexual harassment suit than a puckered smile if he dares to get too close.

Also – it has to be said that – as nature has proved time and time again over millions of years, and the feminist mantra has consistently confirmed in its male-bashing diatribe for the last forty; no matter how much attention has been given to the hair and make-up, the only part of the female body that most men are really interested in seeing is, the 'gateway to heaven'...and yet paradoxically that particular part of the female anatomy is more often than not, its least aesthetically pleasing feature – having a less than attractive appearance.

Of course, women are well aware of the fact that - driven by their natural instincts - this is the centre of a man's interest in them, and having resorted to the scalpel, collagen and botox in every other area of their bodies, desperate as they are to conform to the un-natural and unhealthy standards laid down by the fashion industry movers and shakers; they are now beginning to falsify this particular area of interest too, through cosmetic rejuvenation,(labioplasty and / or vaginoplasty) thereby completing the transformation and falsification of every inch of their once unblemished, naturally-designed bodies.

Conclusion; Women spend all their time trying to create the illusion that they are someone other than who they really are; why can't they just be themselves?

It would be so much simpler and less stressful for all concerned.

At that point, Madison snapped and barked back at him.

'Don't you think that men have some rather annoying faults and habits too?' she countered.

'I'm sure they do', *the Bishop* replied flatly, delighted to have finally drawn the young American out of her reserve.

'Well, let me tell you', Madison continued, trying to evacuate the pent up frustration that had built up during his one-man onslaught while she indulged him.

'As you seem to know so much about it, you should come to New York and see for yourself', she challenged.

'I might just do that', *the Bishop* stated with a wry smile.

They had talked all evening, but hardly ever about chess and so despite their final clash over how Americans order their coffee – *Madison had asked for a double decaf non-fat latte* – and her growing aversion to this overbearing, self-opinionated maverick of a man, the young journalist managed to recompose herself enough to ask if they might continue their discussions over lunch the next day – as she really did need to find out more about his occupational hazard and the reason for her being there in the first place – the game of chess.

The Bishop hesitated for a moment...and then, taking a deep breath, he politely refused her invitation – explaining that he had a match to prepare.

'Let's say I call you when I am ready to resume this discussion', he added calmly.

Madison was more than a little disappointed by his refusal but decided almost instantaneously that it was maybe a blessing in disguise – as it would give her more time to re-group after the verbal mauling he had just given her.

They got up to leave, and as he held her coat for her – *the Bishop* leaned in and whispered in Madison's ear; 'You should really lose that strut...and the high toting attitude; that's what I was talking about earlier; it's all a façade – a smokescreen that you hide behind'.

Disarmed, Madison felt awkward and insulted.

'...it shows a real lack of self-confidence', *the Bishop* insisted. 'I'm telling you, young lady; forget the superficial image, and be yourself; you'll feel much better about life', he concluded as they stepped outside.

Out on the pavement, Madison turned to face him with a look of resolute determination on her face, ready to take him down a peg or two for his presumptuous comments...but even though she was seething inside, she had to bite her tongue again for the sake of her article.

A prolonged moment of silence was the only sign of her rage as they waited for a taxi to pull up to the kerb, and rather than compromise her position - and the chance of another meeting with the enigmatic champion with an outburst that she might regret - Madison simply pasted a false smile on her face as she signalled a cab which had stopped a few metres further on.

'If you don't mind; I'll take this one...' she announced firmly, turning her host.

'Be my guest', *the Bishop* replied without contestation...and with that Madison mumbled a prickly goodbye, before throwing her head back, pivoting on her heel and making her way over to the waiting taxi, leaving *the Bishop* no other option than to call another forward.

Back at her hotel, Madison felt emotionally drained. She didn't know what to think of this guy.

All evening, he had deliberately antagonised her in order to undermine her confidence, making her feel inadequate and foolish.

She felt morally bruised, humbled and frustrated by what had happened at dinner but then, as she lay in her second bath of the day, trying to relax and process the day's events in her mind, she suddenly realised why.

'Of course'; she cried out, thumping the wall with her hand. She didn't see it at the time but the guy had simply used the most tried and trusted rule of all military tacticians; attack being the best form of defence.

He had outsmarted her by taking immediate control of the conversation in order to put her in her place, before she could unleash her feisty American character on him and show her cutting journalistic prowess. That had been very clever of him, Madison had to admit; the man was obviously an expert in strategy and tactics.

'Oh, the wisdom of hindsight', she bemoaned as she rested her neck comfortably on the back of the bath-tub for support...

...but pleased to have at least resolved the enigma of her evening's work Madison quietly slipped under the water and enjoyed the revitalising suds as they worked their magic on her stressed-out body...

...and later, as she stood in front of the mirror in her blue-silk pyjamas brushing out her long blond hair, she conceded that while *the Bishop* had won the first round of their particular contest she was determined to match him in his audacious mind games *quid pro quo.*

She felt better about herself for having resolved the riddle, and as she got into bed that evening Madison began analysing her encounter with *the Bishop* in greater detail.

Sure, the man was obnoxious and confrontational, and while she wanted to disparage him for that...and for the personal comments he had made about her...the more she thought about it the more she had to admit that there was very little satirical subterfuge in what he said; everything was just very factual, straight-forward reasoning, backed up with unquestionable logic.

Unfortunately, as a journalist, she found that realisation irksome and unhelpful...as truth, logic and honesty are hard to spin into sensationalism for a Sunday magazine article – even if they can be controversial at times - but while *the Bishop* was clearly very dogmatic and unequivocal in his arguments he was no less pragmatic and down to earth in his analysis...and that was something that surprised her to some extent considering his latent arrogance.

Of course, she couldn't agree with his overtly contemptuous and misogynous comments about women, but that aside, the rest his ideas were infallibly reasoned and she knew that no journalistic argument or cross examination from her would have had the slightest chance of success against his vastly superior intellectual acumen...much as that pained her to admit.

The sound of a door slamming in the hallway outside her room and the strident laugh of a boozy young woman suddenly brought Madison back from the edge of slumber-land.

This commotion frustrated the young American and as she tossed and turned in annoyance at being disturbed, her mind continued to explore the different components of her encounter with *the Bishop* earlier that evening.

She found herself revisiting the more harrowing moments of the discussion - where *the Bishop* had really put her passive-aggressive mask to the test - and as she began to analyse it, Madison found it somewhat frustrating that rather than repel or deter her, his pontificating comments had actually made him even more fascinating in her eyes...in a *Fatal Attraction* kind of way.

In fact, *the Bishop* had been nothing like the distant mathematician or theoretical visionary that she might have expected from someone who spent his time elaborating complex tactical strategies. On the contrary, he had been intriguing...and absorbing...and despite his sanctimonious, judgemental nature Madison suddenly realised that - without even trying - he had surreptitiously overwhelmed…and subjugated her even…with his intelligence, even though, at the time, her American pride had prevented her from recognising it or admitting it.

There was however no denying that there was a moody and uncommunicative side to *the Bishop's* character too - which she felt was probably down to an excess of testosterone – but despite that and despite his critical preaching which really dragged on at times, she had been unexpectedly captivated by his contrasting mix of prudish, ultra-conservatism and progressive modernity...and while she couldn't necessarily explain that on any intellectual level, she did feel a subliminal connection, a strange empathy with the guy...which was quite ironic really, after she had previously classified all British males as hopeless in the seduction stakes.

Another scream from next door, jolted Madison back into full consciousness, and then another...and another as the couple in the next room got hot and heavy.

It was a little unsettling for someone who just wanted to get to sleep on this side of the wall but rather than create a fuss or ruin the mood for her amorous neighbours - who were clearly intent on putting another dent in the headboard - Madison decided to get up and make a start on the framework of her article. Her mind was full of ideas anyway, especially after her encounter with *the Bishop* earlier, so having popped into the bathroom to freshen herself up, she smoothed out the quilt where she had been lying, turned on the radio to drown out the rhythmic banging noise coming from next door and spread out all the different components for her article on the bed before her.

Then, sitting cross-legged in the middle of it all, her laptop handily placed on her right side, she set about creating a broad outline for her expose which she would then be able to send on to the office as a rough copy.

This took some time but as she was doing it, Madison couldn't help but feel that somehow this trip was going to make a lasting impression on her life...and this one thought kept her mind focussed on what she was doing, forcing her to be extra careful and pay greater attention than she normally would when deciding who and what she was going to write about in an article.

She began by piecing together the characters of those players she had met since her arrival, using the photographs - from the original file - that were now scattered all over the bed in front of her; Gary...those that he had introduced her to...those that she had interviewed such as the Armenians and Rory or *Copperfield* as she liked to call him now...and then of course, the man himself, *the Bishop*, Tobias Byron who was quite naturally given centre-stage in her temporary collage.

It took her a little over two hours to marry up each person's photograph with the comments she had made in her little pad, to which she added a few other quotes extracted from each of their interviews...but finally, her eyes too tired to focus any longer, she had to call it a day.

Madison wasn't used to working late into the night but circumstances and the nagging fixation that this assignment was going to be her sesame into the world of mainstream journalism had spurred her on...and as she put her pen down, having decided on the provisional layout for her article, she felt one of those deeply satisfying yawns travel up through her body and out through her carefully moisturised lips, rewarding her for a job well done but reminding her also that it was time for her to go back to bed.

She leaned over to turn off the radio, listening carefully for signs of continued activity in the room next door, and reassured that her neighbours had finally concluded their amorous interlude, she closed down her laptop and quietly gathered together all her different papers, which she then transferred - in an untidy pile - onto the desk on the far side of her room.

It was almost 3.00 a.m. and stretching her arms high above her head while arching her back wearily Madison shuffled herself quietly back into bed, turning out the light for the second time that evening…and as she drifted off into a well-deserved slumber, her body filled with wonderful fatigue, she was quite surprised at just how much she was looking forward to *the Bishop's* call...and to round two of their discussion...despite the intellectual hammering that he had rained upon her earlier that evening... because she knew that her article would be all the richer for it...and as things stood, that was all that mattered.

CHAPTER FIVE

The next day, dressed in her softest green cashmere dress, Madison spent her whole morning waiting around the hotel, alternating from her room to the reception-area and back again – all in anticipation of *the Bishop's* call.

However...it never came, and by noon she was getting bored and frustrated, so rather than hang around aimlessly waiting for a call that might never come, Madison decided to act on some of the advice that *the Bishop* had given her...the first time they had met.

She went up to the concierge - on one of her many visits to the lobby to check for undelivered messages and calls - and while she was there, she took the opportunity to ask the young man behind the counter if he knew the number of a person who offered reflexology or Reiki sessions.

Now she wasn't quite sure what Reiki was. . .or indeed what it entailed but the concierge did. . .and without missing a beat he immediately got on the phone to book up a couple of sessions for her, for later in the week; the details of which he handed to her on a sheet of hotel stationary.

Madison thanked him discreetly...as if he had just booked her an escort and felt her cheeks flush unexpectedly as she turned and made her way back to her room grabbing a couple of magazines from the news-stand as she went.

The afternoon dragged on, and at 7pm, as *the Bishop* still hadn't called, Madison decided to ring the hotel where the Tournament was being held, in order to find out if there was anything going on that she should know about, to ask for the day's results and hopefully find out the whereabouts of the elusive champion.

The call was brief but she managed to find out that *the Bishop* had once again disposed of his challenger in record time...and that, as the tournament was taking a break after several very hectic days, he wasn't expected back in the hotel until the day after next.

Fantastic, Madison thought to herself as she thanked the *blue-blazer* for his help; he's bound to ring now, she reasoned, as she made her way back to her room for the umpteenth time. . .

...but alas, several hours later he still hadn't called...and left to her own devices Madison was reduced to spending the evening on her own, working on her article.

The following morning, *the Bishop* still hadn't called and after a token breakfast of dry toast and coffee Madison found herself once again wandering aimlessly around the hotel, looking more than a little downhearted.

She was feeling a little stressed too...because of everything that was going on, and noticing that the concierge was free she walked over to him again to ask if there was any way that he could ring the person he had booked for her Reiki / reflexology session and find out if it was possible to bring the appointment forward a day.

The young concierge recognised her from the day before and nodded politely.

'I can try Miss, but I can't promise anything', he declared with a smile as he picked up the phone with one hand and flicked through a list of telephone numbers with the other.

Madison returned his smile with a half-smile of her own to show her appreciation of his efforts and while the young man dealt with her request, she discreetly turned her head to look around the lobby, just in case *the Bishop* suddenly appeared out of nowhere unexpectedly.

'4 pm, Miss…; we can move the appointment to 4 pm. today', the concierge announced respectfully, trying to regain Madison's attention without startling her.

'No sooner...?' she grumbled ungratefully; 'its 10.30 now; I was thinking more like 11.30 or 12', she added, looking at the time on her phone.

The concierge, still holding the phone, tried again, insisting heavily that his client was one of his best customers...but despite his valiant efforts he could not convince his interlocutor on the other end of the line to bring the appointment any further forward...and in the end Madison had to choose between the later time of 4 p.m. or stick with the original appointment, booked in for the next day.

She thought about it for a moment and then shrugging her shoulders a little disconsolately, she settled for the 4 pm. slot.

The concierge nodded again and having confirmed the appointment, he politely said goodbye to his contact and put down the phone before informing Madison that she would receive a call in her room, from the front desk when the therapist arrived.

Madison thanked him again for his help, but as she walked away, she was still feeling fed up and a little annoyed that *the Bishop* hadn't called her, even though he had not given her any specific time-line for the call.

She thought about maybe going into London for a few hours, to do some shopping or to meet up with Gary – but then as she wandered back to the lift she immediately dismissed that idea, as she was determined to be there...if and when *the Bishop* did call...despite her growing disappointment.

After all, as far as she was concerned; *He* was now her meal-ticket and she had no intention of giving that up without a fight.

Back in her room Madison slouched across her bed and started to flick through the magazines that she had picked up the day before in the foyer of the hotel...and within no time at all she had fallen asleep again...out of sheer boredom.

The afternoon slipped by…until around about five minutes to four, when all of a sudden the phone on the bed-side table sprang into life, waking her from her slumber.

It was the concierge, who as promised was ringing to announce that her therapist had arrived and that she was on her way up to the room.

Madison thanked him fuzzily and rubbing her eyes, she rushed into the bathroom to splash some water on her face before the therapist arrived two minutes later…and indeed she was still brushing her hair in front of the mirror when a loud knock on the door forced her to curtail her pampering.

'Who is it?' she asked in typical New York fashion, to gain those extra couple of seconds in which to check out her appearance – *nobody in New York opens a door without first verifying who is on the other side; not even in a hotel.*

'My name is Alessia', came the reply in a strong Italian accent; 'I'm here for your therapy session, Miss Chatfield', the young woman confirmed from behind the closed door.

Madison opened the door cautiously and was a little surprised to see a stunning young woman standing on the other side, her arms filled with her own portable table and all the equipment she needed to do her job.

'Come on in', she blurted out after a moment's hesitation; trying not to look too awkward or embarrassed.

The young therapist nodded and stepped forward.

'I'm sorry...this is my first experience of alternative therapies and I'm not quite sure how it is supposed go down', Madison explained, gesturing for the young woman to carry on in.

'Oh, I see', the pretty brunette remarked; '...don't worry, there is nothing dangerous in here', she confirmed motioning casually to her bags.

Madison smiled stiffly; 'of course not...it's just that I have never done anything like this before'.

'I understand', the young therapist sympathised, looking at her client with a caring smile...and with that she pulled out a leaflet from one of the side-pockets of her bag and handed it over.

'These are all the treatments we do', she announced as she put her bags down on the floor; 'just have a look through it...and tell me what you would like me to do', she added, her Latin accent just about filtering through her English idioms.

Madison accepted the leaflet graciously and while the young therapist busied herself setting up her table, she sat down at the desk to study its contents.

Most of what she saw was unfamiliar to her, to say the least, but as she went through the list - out loud - the young therapist was only too happy to give her a brief explanation about each of the treatments on offer, be it Reiki, reflexology or acupuncture and the benefits that each of them could contribute to a person's overall well-being.

'Look...Alicia...' Madison declared moodily, trying not to take her frustration out on the young therapist; 'I have no idea which of these therapies I should go with; what would you suggest for a first-timer like me?' she enquired looking for some professional guidance.

'Well, Miss Chatfield, why don't you go for the de-stress massage and maybe the reflexology to start with...those are the two most popular ones... and if you like, we can try something else next time', the young therapist suggested, picking up on Madison's irritability.

Madison nodded; 'fine, let's go with that', she agreed...'oh, and by the way, my name is Madison', she offered in a lighter tone, remembering that she hadn't properly introduced herself.

'...and my name is Alessia', the young therapist retorted, taking the opportunity to correct Madison's earlier slip of the tongue.

'Okay; so what happens next?' Madison asked as she stood up, suddenly eager to get started with the treatments after her initial reticence.

'Well; if you could just slip into the bathroom and strip down to your underwear, that would be great', the young therapist announced quite matter of fact; '...then...if you just want to wrap a towel around yourself for your own comfort and tie your hair back...', she added after a pause as she donned her monogrammed tunic and went about preparing her lotions and oils.

Madison did just that and a few minutes later, she was laid out on the table, face-down, ready for her first-ever massage. She still found the situation a little weird, being in a hotel room - dressed only in her underwear – in the company of a woman she didn't know, but once Alessia's expert hands got to work on her tensed-up muscles and knotted nerves she soon got over her initial embarrassment.

Fifteen minutes or so later, the intoxicating bouquet of aromatherapy oils filled the air in the room with wonderfully evocative scents ...and as Madison relaxed...and her body enjoyed the pampering, her mind slowly disconnected from all the frustration that had built up over the past couple of days.

Alessia's hands were working miracles in every nook and cranny of her body and the resulting quietude was filling the young journalist with renewed confidence and optimism...not to mention a physical well-being the likes of which she hadn't felt since she was a child.

The session lasted almost two hours - between the massage and the reflexology - but when Alessia finally signalled that her work was done, Madison still didn't want it to stop.

In fact, she took quite a while to react to Alessia's prompting when the latter tapped her on her shoulder...but then, having sat up groggily and wrapped the towel back around her glistening body, Madison was full of praise for what the young therapist had done.

'Thank-you Alessia', she whispered almost, as she jumped off the table, 'I really didn't know what to expect from all this...but you have seriously re-booted my morale over the last couple of hours'.

Alessia smiled warmly; 'that's not the first time I've been told I have magic hands', she commented as she reached out a steadying hand to help Madison find her balance again after her two hours of indulgent pampering.

Madison returned the smile and went off to the bathroom...to get herself together again...while the young therapist simply removed her tunic and went about her business, packing away her table, ready for her next appointment.

She reappeared from the bathroom a few minutes later, a glass of cold water in hand. . .and still feeling on top of the world Madison asked Alessia if she could add another session to the one she had already booked for the day after next.

'Of course', Alessia replied, taking out her diary.

Madison sat down at the desk, still a little unsteady on her feet.

'I have an early slot next Monday at 10am or...' Alessia announced flicking through her very busy schedule looking for times and dates that would be convenient to her new client.

'That would be good for me', Madison agreed without really thinking it through, her brain still in a fuzzy haze.

'Fine', replied Alessia making a note. '...so that's 2pm on Friday and 10am Monday', the young therapist repeated to make sure that everything was clear.

'Yes', Madison concurred vaguely, her thoughts still trying to catch up.

'Oh...and what about payment? She asked, slowly regaining her lucidity.

'Don't worry about that...' Alessia confirmed in her cute Italian accent as she picked up her equipment; 'it's all taken care of downstairs...we bill the hotel and the hotel bill's you; it's a standing agreement'.

Madison nodded her understanding...and with that, the young therapist turned on her heels and went on her way with a smile.

Madison watched her go...and once the door had clicked behind her and she was on her own once again, she could do nothing but collapse back onto her bed, pull her robe around herself more snugly and enjoy the last sensations of residual warmth proffered on her body by her first taste of holistic pampering.

'Damn, that girl was good', she mumbled to herself as she finally got up the energy to make her way back to the bathroom and turn on the taps for her bath; '...nobody has ever made me feel like that before...ever'.

An hour or so later, relaxed after her massage and refreshed after her bath, Madison wandered back downstairs; she hadn't eaten all day and the rumblings in her stomach were gently reminding her of the fact.

However, the hotel restaurant wasn't quite ready to receive guests – a fact which would normally have exasperated the impatient young New Yorker - but today, rather than complain, Madison just looked around the vicinity for somewhere she could sit while she waited for the doors to open.

She looked to the right and then to the left but unfortunately, there were no seats nearby - which she did find a little frustrating - but still managing to maintain her calm Madison simply retraced her steps back to the reception area and quietly took a seat in one of the easy chairs situated opposite the main desk - picking up a local newspaper which had been left there earlier, as a distraction.

She made herself comfortable and had just started flicking through the pages of the tired tabloid she had picked up...when her attention was suddenly drawn to the concierge's desk...where the young employee that she had pestered regularly over the last two days - about the fact that she was expecting an urgent call - was waving to her discreetly and pointing to the phone he was holding in his other hand.

Madison's heart missed a beat and a thousand thoughts flashed through her mind; ...was her patience finally going to be rewarded?

She stood up and casually strolled over to the desk, using those precious seconds to calm her nerves and clear her voice.

It could have been her office calling; it could have been the tournament hotel with news of another change to the schedule; it could even have been Evie calling out of the blue to surprise her, but Madison knew; her feminine intuition told her that it would be 'him'.

'I was trying to reach you in your room, Miss Chatfield...but...', the young concierge informed her, swallowing the rest of his phrase, as he handed her the receiver.

Madison didn't really hear what the young man was saying but she smiled at him stiffly nevertheless and mouthed a succinct thank you in his direction as she took hold of the phone.

'Madison Chatfield speaking', she announced professionally, her grip on the hand-set much tighter than it needed to be.

There was a pause...during which her heart skipped another beat but then, just as she was about to hand the receiver back to the concierge *the Bishop's* deep voice came on the line filling the void.

He presented himself calmly and then, with a certain authority in his tone - probably due to his typically-English accent - he asked her if she would be free to join him again for lunch the next day.

This time it was Madison who paused as she closed her eyes in thanks while resisting...with some difficulty... the overwhelming urge to punch the air...as a shiver of anticipated triumph ran enthusiastically down her spine.

The moment passed...and as the concierge moved away to respect her confidentiality Madison sneakily flicked through the pages of the newspaper she was still holding, to simulate her consulting her agenda.

She deliberately made him wait for her reply, clicking her tongue for his benefit on the other end of the phone as she did so, and only after she had cleared her throat one more time, did she gladly accept his invitation.

The Bishop acknowledged her response with a curt reply of his own but before Madison could ask any secondary questions - displaying his usual guile - he quickly rattled off the address of a quiet little country pub-come-restaurant that he knew...where he assured her they would be able to have lunch and continue their discussions without being disturbed.

This caught Madison a little short; she would have liked to confirm that they would at least be talking chess this time and not deviating from that into the realms of whatever else he might want to discuss, but unfortunately she never got the chance...as once he had confirmed the time of their appointment - 1pm - *the Bishop* promptly hung up.

'Is everything alright, Miss?' the concierge enquired politely, returning to his post.

'Yes...thank you', Madison replied as she handed the phone back to the concierge with an appreciative nod; 'everything is just fine'.

And with that, she turned and walked away, smiling to herself contentedly as she headed for the restaurant; her stomach doing somersaults in her mid-section - thanks to the emotion and the hunger pangs - but her outer demeanour, confident and calm, revealing absolutely no sign of that inner turmoil.

Chequers Inn: the next day...

It was a perfect afternoon with bright sunlight and not a hint of wind in the air when Madison's taxi pulled into the car-park of the quiet little pub in the picturesque village of Wooburn.

The Bishop was already in-situ, waiting for her calmly at a table in the garden which had been strategically placed under a huge oak tree that was very charitably offering its shade to some of the pub's lucky patrons.

He spied her from afar...and as their eyes met, a strange frisson ran down the length of Madison's spine. She felt her stomach clench too with a familiar mix of excitement and dread...and as she got out of the cab her legs suddenly turned to lead.

Another annoying flutter in her stomach then caused her to swallow hard as she turned to make her way over to him...but despite this metaphysical irritation her step was surprisingly assured.

'Confidence, attitude and strength', she whispered to herself, repeating her own personal mantra; '...confidence, attitude and strength'.

The Bishop stood up with gentlemanly propriety and as she greeted him in her usual deferential manner smiling warmly and professionally, he immediately indicated a chair opposite him for her to sit on, which she gladly accepted.

'Might I say, you look very attractive today Miss Chatfield', he commented, gesturing towards her attire as they sat down.

She was wearing a zesty-lemon coloured print dress and contrasting black short bolero jacket, her hair loose but held in place by a colour-coordinated matching slide.

Madison was taken aback by the unexpected compliment but she thanked him all the same, wary nevertheless that he might yet add a...*but...* to the end of his comment...but he didn't.

She herself was not usually one for handing out compliments or platitudes but remembering *the Bishop's* utter distrust of the media in general and journalists in particular she attempted to return the compliment with one of her own, remarking politely on the cut of his Italian-silk suit.

The Bishop cracked a smile for the first time and handed her a glass of red Fetzer wine to taste.

'I hope you like red wine', he commented optimistically, arching his right eyebrow inquisitively.

'I do', Madison replied with the same enthusiasm as she made herself comfortable, 'but I really need to talk chess today', she reminded him, having been rather underwhelmed by his less than forthcoming responses last time around.

'Oh yes, of course', *the Bishop* acknowledged; 'your article'.

'Very well then', he acquiesced compliantly; 'where would you like to start?'

'Let's start at the beginning', Madison suggested trying to be objective and professional, still somewhat amazed that this pleasant, obliging individual was the same obnoxious character that she had dined with the other evening...and with that she reached into her bag, pulled out her note-book and laid it on the table beside her.

The Bishop smiled again. 'Pen and paper at the ready, you look like one of those eager young hacks who loiter outside the doors of a locker room after a major sporting triumph in the hope of getting an exclusive quote from the game's MVP', he commented teasingly.

Madison smirked stiffly at the reference; 'they are just the tools of the trade without which I cannot do my job...' she retorted as politely as possible, being careful not to compromise her scoop.

'...just like the pieces on your chess-board', she added resolutely, clicking her pen deliberately.

'Good analogy', *the Bishop* consented as he raised his glass and took another mouthful of wine.

'Now then...what would you like to know about me Miss Chatfield?' he asked as he sat back confidently and scrutinised her face.

Madison took a deep breath. She was slowly becoming infatuated by this rather eccentric figure of a man and was desperate to ask him more about his personal life - which she, and she was sure her readers, would be more interested in - but given the circumstances, and reminded of her university professor's motto 'that we only ever see two sides of a person; what we want to see and what they are prepared to show us', she decided that she should hedge her bets and begin her preparations to scale the mountainous task ahead by laying down some neutral groundwork first.

The Bishop's career had already been well documented in the portfolio that she had been given earlier – so rather than go through all that again, especially as she didn't know how much time he was going to allow her before he abruptly called a halt to proceedings, which he was capable of doing at any time, she decided to set the ball rolling, by asking him how he prepared for a match, hoping secretly to work in some more personal questions later, once the conversation had moved on.

She flipped a couple of pages in her notebook to compose herself and still amazed at how much his conciliatory attitude contrasted with the acerbic verve of their previous meeting, she turned to the list of questions that she had prepared earlier.

Then, with the customary clearing of her throat she began her interview.

'So, what do you do?' she enquired eagerly, trying not to appear as if she was prying too much; 'how do you work up your concentration before a match?'

'Do you have any special relaxation techniques; do you do yoga, for example...or introspective meditation?' she asked boldly, her pen poised at the ready.

The Bishop nodded approvingly and raised his eyebrows, impressed by the precise nature of her question.

'No', he replied indolently; 'none of that...I follow the *Kahuna Training Method*'.

'The...*what*...method?' Madison blurted out in bewilderment, the expression on her face confirming her confusion.

The Bishop smiled at her over his glass and spelt out the word for her; 'Ka – hu – na'.

'It is a method where...rather than concentrating all one's energy on one's own mind...and interiorising everything, you do the complete opposite...by increasing and fine tuning your senses, thereby amplifying your awareness and your sensitivity to all that surrounds you'.

'The Kahuna Method unlocks your powers of observation and concentration...and as an added bonus...it also works to relax you and energise your body by helping the flow of KI-energy', he explained calmly.

Kahuna Training Method; - a journey

The Kahuna training method is an ancient Hawaiian method – mostly non-verbal – which requires the student to listen, observe and apply himself.

Dignity and respect are cornerstones of the Kahuna training method.

The Kahuna training method uses motion, posture, positioning and leverage to help KI energy flow naturally through the body through the practice of 'ka'alele au'.

Like a wave washing over you – it increases the flow of KI energy - helping it to flow through the body more freely – thus relaxing it and tuning senses.

This, in turn – amplifies the student's awareness and sensitivity – and this constant expansion of awareness of oneself and others leads to more tolerance and compassion for them

Also, it allows for a better understanding of time and space – which has now branched into a Hawaiian form of 'feng shui', used for positioning and balances in space and environment.

It's a mind, body and spirit experience. Mind over body develops awareness.

We come from *the Source* and in the process of rediscovering this source, we find our self.

External beauty comes from a relaxed and balanced internal state of well-being.

'I see', Madison remarked, nodding her head slightly, though in reality she had no idea what he was talking about.

'So, you read minds', she announced carefully, trying to appear worldly.

'I open my awareness in order to soak up the energy that surrounds me', *the Bishop* explained more emphatically.

'And how long does that take?' Madison asked consulting her notes.

'Between two and three hours', *the Bishop* replied again, graciously.

'Okay, and aside from that; do you use...or study tactical manuals, Madison pursued bravely reading her question literally as it was written on the page.

'From time to time', *the Bishop* acquiesced, 'but just as reference books really', he added qualifying his statement.

'...and if I might be so bold...why do you bother to continue playing?' Madison asked out of the blue, trying to throw in a question from left field; '…you are unbeaten in years; what drives you to still compete?', she insisted carefully.

The Bishop sat back and reflected for a moment; then, setting his glass down on the table, he answered her politely, his face a mask of imperturbable calm.

'My thinking is this;' he explained; '...without comparison, everything loses its meaning'.

Madison nodded and smiled appreciatively at his response...and after a moment's reflection she diligently wrote the words down underlining them twice. That's a line I can use, she thought to herself as she paused to take a sip from her glass.

At this point *the Bishop* noticed one of the barmen from the pub walking past and called him over with a polite 'excuse me'.

The young man, recognising who it was that was calling him, stopped in his tracks and immediately made his way over to the table, despite the fact that his hands were already full of empty glasses collected from a neighbouring table.

The Bishop greeted him cordially and while the two men began discussing what was on the lunch menu, Madison took the opportunity to study her subject, realising as she did so, that there was thankfully a lot more to him than the boorish recluse she had first thought; the last comment that he had made having confirmed to her that he was just as committed to the game of chess as she was to journalism.

'How does fresh salmon and salad sound to you, Miss Chatfield?' *the Bishop* suddenly asked out of nowhere, the sound of his voice swiftly re-focussing her attention on the present.

'Salmon...that's fine with me', Madison agreed courteously, pretending to write in her notebook assiduously when in fact she was doodling a caricature of her host.

'Two salmon specials', *the Bishop* confirmed to the young barman who, having glanced at Madison for her confirmation, nodded his head politely before taking his leave and strolling back inside.

'The food here is very good...so I thought that we could just keep this lunch on a more informal plane', *the Bishop* disclosed calmly, gesturing loosely towards the table with his hands.

'Sure', Madison agreed. 'You obviously know the place so I will bow to your greater judgement', she added, her tone sounding more patronising than she intended.

'So, tell me Mr Byron', she asked craftily moving on swiftly so as not to dwell on her unfortunate tone; 'do you have a special diet...or anything like that to help with concentration and memory retention for example?

They do say that salmon is good for you...for example', she insisted, trying to work her way into her host's world, on a more personal level.

The Bishop shook his head, shifting his gaze slightly.

'No, nothing like that...' he replied again rather abruptly. 'I am careful with what I eat but I don't deprive myself...if I feel the desire', he confirmed, the tone of his voice suggesting innuendo but by no means blatantly flaunting it.

This question and answer session continued all through lunch until Madison had more or less exhausted the list of questions she had prepared... and only when their plates had been taken away again, did she try to slip in a few more personal questions in an effort to squeeze out as much information as possible for her article, not knowing whether *the Bishop* would answer or not, or at what point he would unbendingly bring the discussion to a close.

She stayed on safe ground most of the time but she did manage to ask him about what he did in his spare time, throwing in – as a justification - that he had learned quite a lot about her at dinner the other evening.

That made him smile.

'You really are very resourceful Miss Chatfield', he commented without batting an eyelid, acknowledging her journalistic ruse.

Madison returned his stare, enjoying the mental gymnastics and the verbal exchange.

'Tell me about your house', she continued with growing confidence, her enthusiasm and her fascination reflecting more and more in her tone.

'Well', *the Bishop* answered forthrightly without breaking eye-contact, 'I live alone...but that is not to say that I am lonely; I find the solace... inspirational', he added after a brief but evocative pause.

Madison paused too at this point; with all the negative comments that he had made previously about women, it suddenly dawned on her that maybe he was gay...and that that was why he had such a low opinion of women.

She knew that she might regret it...but she had to ask; her readers would want to know.

'I don't wish to pry...and you are quite entitled not to answer this question if you don't want to...as it is rather personal and none of my business really', she advanced, treading carefully – 'but...are there any special women in your life?'

The Bishop took a deep breath and fearing the worst Madison braced herself, ready to be engulfed in a verbal backlash of epic proportions, but this time, much to her relief, there was no such tyrannical reaction.

'Well', he confirmed simply, rubbing his chin. 'Let me see now; I think that it is safe to say that I am no Lothario...but as your compatriot actress Julia Roberts once quoted from the female perspective;

Women in my life come and go
I'm glad they come
I'm glad I come
And then ….. they go'

Madison swallowed deeply, the pink hue of embarrassment blooming on her cheeks.

'So; nobody special then', she prodded, continuing her sensitive research, a bourgeoning smile on her lips.

It was a strange moment but after a deliciously long silence, during which *the Bishop* delighted in Madison's mild discomfort, he eventually countered her remark and her unintentionally patronising tone, by producing another gem from the vast wealth of his seemingly unquantifiable social knowledge.

'I don't know if you are aware of the fact, young….. Miss Chatfield', he corrected himself, 'but polygamy is tolerated in 84% of the world's cultures;

...so tell me this', he added languorously as he took another sip of wine; 'what are the advantages of monogamy; do you think that the ecclesiastics held the absolute truth when they invented it in the 17th century?'

Madison looked up from her notebook but *the Bishop* didn't leave her any time to respond, before continuing his lecture.

'Did you know, for example, that pagan tribes had been celebrating fertility and sexuality for centuries before the Puritans came along with their *guilt concept*...with their ideas that sex was wrong, that sex was evil?', he questioned, his tone suddenly taking on a harsher edge.

Again, Madison had no time to reply, her blank stare and her raised shoulders being the only indication of her response.

'Maybe you didn't know', *the Bishop* declared, answering his own question; '...but surely, you realise young lady – *he couldn't help it this time* - that in today's society where old, traditional concepts are constantly being challenged it is not surprising that those established yet misguided ideas on sexuality have now lost their impact', he affirmed decisively.

Madison grimaced and continued scribbling, trying hard not to show her unease.

'So the answer to your question Miss Chatfield...very concisely...would be no...' *the Bishop* continued, pursuing his thought; '...nobody special...I prefer a modern lifestyle, unfettered by the shackles of social commitment'.

'I see'; Madison concurred, clearing her throat and swallowing dryly to cover her embarrassment, he mind categorising him instantly as yet another commitment-phobe.

♝

She would dearly have loved to know more about his philosophy on life but at that point Madison decided to avoid any more questions of a personal nature; she wasn't in the mood for another one of his speeches.

Unfortunately though, *the Bishop* was not one to leave a stone unturned and once he was on a roll...there was no stopping him.

'Too much is often made of our sexuality', he suddenly announced with almost regal conviction, interrupting Madison's moment of reflection.

'As Freud once said...sometimes a cigar is just a cigar', he mused smugly.

'Life is not about the number of breaths you take, but about how many moments in that life take your breath away', he then quoted, leaning back in his chair and taking a moment to ponder his own perspective.

'Whose quote is that?' Madison asked earnestly; trying to recover her professional composure like a seasoned journalist.

'That? Oh I don't know where I first heard that phrase', *the Bishop* admitted rather nonchalantly, 'but it's rather pertinent don't you think?' he offered magnanimously.

Madison just smiled stiffly, her attention suddenly distracted by a couple of school-children playing on a climbing frame in the garden across the way.

'Women...and men for that matter...do not always enjoy all aspects of their sexuality', *the Bishop* suddenly stated very matter of fact.

'Do you enjoy new experiences, Miss Chatfield?' he asked casually, leaning forward again and looking her straight in the eye.

'Yes, I suppose I do experiment new ideas from time to time', she agreed without qualifying her statement further.

'True pleasure is worth waiting for' *the Bishop* remarked cryptically looking off into the distance; '...it confirms depth of sincerity...', he appended as his mind clearly drifted before returning to the present, '... but enough of all this aimless reflection...tell me more about dating in New York', he insisted in a more upbeat tone, catching Madison completely off guard.

'You want to know about dating... in New York', she asked...surprised by the suddenly frivolous nature of his question.

'Is that such a shock to you, Miss Chatfield?' *the Bishop* remarked probingly.

'Well, to be honest with you; it kinda is...' Madison confirmed; 'You don't strike me as someone who would be interested in that kind of thing...and I'm pretty sure that you wouldn't like it anyhow', she added dismissively, putting her pen down and sitting back.

'Try me', *the Bishop* countered, not one to be brushed off that easily.

It was going off subject a little, digressing slightly, but having endured so much of the *Bishop's* pontificating and patronising behaviour over the last couple of meetings; Madison suddenly decided very daringly that this would be a good time for her to get some pay-back…and so, for the next twenty minutes or so, she deliberately set out to shock her host by explaining all the ins-and-outs of the current dating game; New York style.

She told him all about speed-dating, about check lists, about questionnaires and about the new trend for 2 to 5 minute parking-lot inquisitions – which had *the Bishop* cringing in disbelief, much to her hidden amusement - but then not wanting to scare him off completely, she tempered her mischievous discourse by explaining that there was also another tendency in New York which was a throwback to centuries past, where several rendezvous' were organised and chaperoned or supervised by a girl-friend – where the intended couple could get to know each other better before they were finally allowed to go it alone.

The Bishop smiled enigmatically at that last comment, his expression midway between mild amusement and incredulity…but before he could begin to analyse what had been said, Madison delighted in preceding him, adding balance her argument by informing him that she herself would prefer a more direct approach – hoping possibly, in her sub-conscious that that thought might take root in his psyche.

'I hear that here in England, relationships are struck up a lot quicker, once the initial connection has been made', she remarked impishly, looking over the rim of her glass; '…but then I have also heard, rather paradoxically as it turns out, that this is just where the British seem to fall down; they lack any kind of technique in making that...connection', she concluded contentedly while swilling the last drops of wine around in the bottom of her glass.

The Bishop sat back again, having listened carefully to Madison's rather colourful depiction of stateside social protocol and a little amused by what she had said, he took a moment to reflect on it before finishing his glass and giving her his considered response.

'I'll tell you why the situation has come to this – and why you Americans have had to resort to all these pre-arranged, organised, surreal dating processes', he began to explain.

'It is because men no longer dare to approach women; the seduction process has been hi-jacked by feminism. These days, men are afraid of being hit with a lawsuit or a claim for sexual harassment if they come within a metre of a woman – be that claim real, alleged or bogus...', he suggested.

'...and to prove my point'; he added gruffly, 'just look at the increase in the number of single people...and the boom in singles clubs'.

'...and dare I say', he added again before Madison could intervene, '... the increase in the male homo-sexual community'.

'How sad is that...' he commented rhetorically though rather tongue-in-cheek, '...that to avoid sexual harassment charges and spurious lawsuits from money-grabbing women, men are now preferring to group together with their own kind'.

Madison huffed mockingly and looked right past him, over his shoulder, not daring to look him in the eye.

'Of course it's not the main reason...but it is a contributing factor... and furthermore, the fact that domestic violence is also on the increase confirms the suggestion that there is an on-going break down in communications between the sexes', *the Bishop* persisted directly, getting into his pontificating stride.

'...and... if you will allow me to be so bold, Miss Chatfield', he added, leaning in closer to avoid being heard by the people at the next table; 'you only need to look at the infinite number of 'female-friendly' toys that are now available for their exclusive use to see that men are no longer up to the demands of this generation of liberated women'.

Madison recoiled in horror at this last comment hiding her embarrassment behind a disapproving smile – *even though she knew that it was true; all her girl-friends had a little 'helper' stashed away in their bed-side table drawers* – and once again she was lost for words. This man seemed to have a depth of knowledge on...*any*...given subject and it made her feel quite inept.

'Paradoxically', *the Bishop* continued; 'your world, Miss Chatfield, the world of fashion...which is where you ultimately want to be, isn't it?', he prompted, '...that hasn't evolved in the same way; there is no coherence there'.

Madison rolled her eyes and took a deep breath, readying herself for another onslaught.

'Quite rightly, the feminists reject objectification...', *the Bishop* proclaimed firmly, '...but while women are busy protecting themselves with legislation to prevent men bothering them, they are nevertheless continuing to gall them and bait them by dressing provocatively, wearing revealing clothes and inviting suggestive behaviour in the way they act'.

'Women are constantly dangling and flaunting their sexuality in front of men, almost taking a sadistic pleasure in frustrating and taunting them...tantalising them...but these days when men react to this natural stimulus, which is in-bred in their psyche by the way', he confirmed pertinently, 'those women immediately retreat behind those same sexual harassment laws'.

'Now, I understand that women are only obeying their biological impulse to attract attention...but men are not made of stone, Miss Chatfield', he argued with growing passion; 'so tell me this...', he pursued, railroading straight over any delicate feminine sensitivities she might have about discussing such issues; '...at what point does flirting become sexual harassment; where do you draw the line?'

Madison shifted in her seat. This was getting a little scary. The tone of his voice...and the content of his argument was making her feel a little uncomfortable...again.

'Oh, of course, I am not condoning rape', *the Bishop* insisted unequivocally, 'but I am trying to offer a reasonable explanation to the increasing number of incidents we have seen splashed over the front pages in the past decade'.

'Plunging necklines, short skirts and low-riding jeans, that reveal the panty-line at best and the outline of the thong whale-bone at worst, are like red flags to the morally inept and uneducated animals of today's western society...and as a man, I can understand the adrenaline rush that other men might feel – born out of the accumulated frustration of seeing the goods paraded constantly in front of them, in the shop window so to speak, and being told not to touch'.

Madison looked across at him, questioning his remark and was just about to counter again, to defend the sisterhood when her mobile phone began to ring.

She looked at the caller ID...and seeing it as an opportunity to curtail *the Bishop's* latest rant, she informed him that it was her boss Amanda, calling from New York for an update and that exceptionally, she would have to take it.

The Bishop nodded his understanding and without further ado, Madison got up and walked away from the table, looking for some privacy to take the call.

The delicate subject of rape was never re-visited and an hour or so later, once they had finished lunch and enjoyed a second cup of coffee, *the Bishop* graciously offered to drive Madison back to her hotel.

'That would be very kind of you', she agreed, putting away her notebook; 'I was just about to call myself a cab'.

'It's not a problem', *the Bishop* conceded...and with that, having paid the bill and thanked the young barman for his service, he led the way back to the car park, unaware that Madison had tarried at the table to check that she hadn't forgotten anything.

Moments later however, having brushed herself down and checked her mobile phone for any more messages Madison followed him out into the car-park - which had filled up quite considerably during the time that they had been sitting there - her mind wandering and wondering what kind of car he might have.

Another piece of information I could use as part of his profile, she thought to herself as she scanned the different models, her article and its contents as ever uppermost in her mind.

The Bishop had sauntered on ahead and as she manoeuvred her way around a couple exchanging hugs at the gate and caught sight of him again through the cluster of parked cars now separating them, Madison suddenly noticed that there was something strangely seductive about him, about the way he walked, about his presence and the confidence he exuded.

He must have sensed her looking at him and he turned around in an instant to see where she was.

Madison raised her right hand to apologise for the lost ground and when she saw him turn again and approach a gleaming silver-grey Aston Martin, parked on its own, away from the immediate crowd, stationed very precisely within the confines of the painted white lines which marked out each car's individual parking-space; she knew intuitively that that would be his ride.

'About time', he chided playfully as she approached.

'I cannot believe that you drive the same car as James Bond', she remarked casually as she finally caught up with him, a reassured smile curling slowly along her perfectly-defined lips.

The Bishop shook his head in mirth and opened the passenger door for her with a gentlemanly flourish.

Madison pursed her lips in another wry smile and without further ado she got into the car, thanking him with a flirtatious toss of her thick blonde hair.

Unruffled by her gesture, *the Bishop* quickly closed the car-door behind her and walked around to the driver's side before sliding in behind the wheel, Madison's eyes following him every step of the way.

What a fascinatingly strange man, she thought to herself...inappropriate and quite insensitive at times and yet immensely intelligent and extremely well-mannered at others.

Madison was feeling quite good about herself - for a number of reasons - as she sank down into the car's luxurious leather seat; the conversation they had just had over lunch, had been much more entertaining and insightful than their previous meeting; she could feel the potential of her article slowly emerging with what she had gathered today on top of what she already had back in her hotel room...and although she would never dare to admit it, she could even feel - in *the Bishop's* gentlemanly manner - that there was something there to suggest that he quite liked her too, or at least that he didn't dislike her – which in her journalistic mind she thought she might be able to use to her advantage at a later date; *after all, he had offered her a lift back to her hotel which he was under no obligation to do.*

The car's engine roared into life and as they drove off down the narrow country lanes in the direction of her hotel Madison quietly relived the key moments of their lunchtime encounter...realising as she did so that while she had seen another side of him, she had only just scratched the surface of the enigma that was TB.

That evening, Madison enjoyed another long, leisurely soak in the bath and having revelled in its luxuriant warmth for over an hour she finally got out just as the water was getting cold.

She wrapped herself casually in the towelling robe provided by the hotel and hugging herself contentedly she walked back nonchalantly into the bedroom.

It had been the most rewarding day of her trip so far and as she settled down in front of her lap-top, ready to write up her notes on the day's events - while they were still fresh in her mind, just in case she overlooked a detail which might have its importance / significance in the final analysis - she was filled with the enthusiasm and the optimism of someone who knew exactly what the future held in store for them.

Glancing to her left, at the pile of dossiers she had now accumulated on the various players, she reached over and took hold of *the Bishop's* file which of course was first to hand.

She flicked through it briefly before setting it down on the desk next to her, just in case she needed to consult it again, and then, pulling out her note-pad she began to tap away at her computer, making sure that she didn't miss anything out by crossing out her remarks one by one as she transferred them from the note-book to the lap-top.

This took some time and as she worked Madison could not help but glance across at *the Bishop's* file from time to time where the rather flattering photograph of the man himself - pinned conspicuously on the front-cover next to his profile - seemed to be staring right back at her.

She tried to ignore it at first, but the more she thought about him - through what she was writing - and the more her attention was drawn to his photograph with its enigmatic smile, the more she felt her infatuation with *the Bishop* growing.

'Stop trying to distract me', she scowled at the photograph, after her latest glance...and with that, with false anger, she turned the file face-down.

It took her longer than she thought it would to complete, but eventually, after several hours, during which she found herself reliving one or other of their exchanges almost word for word in her mind…on several occasions… Madison was finally satisfied, after much shilly-shallying that she had summarised and indexed every detail of what had been discussed earlier over lunch on her computer.

She closed the main file with a sigh of satisfaction...and having taken a moment to stretch out her stiffened limbs and release a mighty yawn, she subsequently fired off a couple of e-mails to keep her bosses happy before deciding to spend the rest of the evening relaxing in front of the TV.

She closed down the computer and moments later - as she slid into bed, still dressed in her comfy robe - Madison grabbed the TV remote from the bed-side table hoping to find something on one of the channels that might interest her.

She began zapping through the different channels but unfortunately there were no decent films on the movie channels…or at least nothing to her liking…and apart from the usual slew of soap-opera re-runs, the only other choice left to her was a stand-up comedy show, which alas she couldn't be bothered to watch...because of the accents...and the British humour, so rather than persist in trying to find something worthwhile, she simply turned off the TV, turned out the lights and slowly drifted off to sleep, safe in the knowledge that, professionally at least, her endeavours were finally meeting with some success.

CHAPTER SIX

The Tournament came to an end a couple of days later in typical fashion with *the Bishop* emerging victorious once again over a resigned and somewhat disgruntled Rory Campbell-Brown – aka *Copperfield*.

It was a fairly low-key ending - without any real pomp or ceremony - to what had been a rather intriguing competition…and while nothing 'official' had been arranged for her by the organising committee - Madison did try once or twice - as everything began to wind down - to get another interview...or at least some magnanimous closing comments...from the enigmatic champion that was TB, before he disappeared into the shadows again like the invisible man that had become his trademark...but sadly, it wasn't to be.

She had been hoping to wrap up her mission with a flourish and another spectacular quote from the master, but in the end Madison wasn't too surprised...or downhearted by his vanishing trick as it fitted in rather well – if not perfectly - with the whole concept of mystery with which he surrounded himself; a premise that she was hoping to convey and exploit to excess in her article...

...and besides, with what she had read about him, with what Gary and the others had told her about him, and with what she had managed to extract from him herself with all her charm and journalistic creativity during their meetings, she considered – as she enjoyed another relaxing visit from Alessia - that she now had enough material in her possession for a decent article...and one that - she was certain - would prove to her bosses back in the Big Apple that despite what they might think of her, she hadn't wasted her time in England.

In fact, she was more than pleased with the results of her assignment - even though, as a journalist she was always striving for more – and as she checked out of her hotel the next morning, Madison was intent on rewarding herself for what she considered *'a job well done'* with a couple of exciting, fashion-packed days in London before she had to fly back out.

Yes, the mission itself had gone very well but this was the part of her trip that she had really been looking forward to. Madison was a fashion aficionado who had spent hours during her teenage years reading all about London's iconic boutiques...and this was going to be her first chance to experience them first hand.

It was also going to be an opportunity for her to get more acquainted with the world-renowned quirkiness of the British fashion scene, and maybe pick up a few new ideas...because despite her current lot...as a poorly-considered junior-staffer, her goal down-the-line was - and always had been - to carve out a career for herself in the world of fashion...and to one day hold a position of great responsibility at the very pinnacle of that esteemed profession.

London was wonderful, just as she had expected; the boutiques in Oxford Street, Regent Street, Bond Street, Carnaby Street and the King's Road all lived-up to their long-standing and hard-earned reputations as leaders in the fashion trade...and while she was there, Madison spent as much quality time as possible visiting each and every one of them, cramming as much shopping and research into her days as was humanly possible.

Time went flying by, and while the shops and the city were a major distraction for her, Madison's mind would not let her escape her recent past...which inevitably led to her thinking about *the Bishop...*

...because of her article of course...but also because of the intriguing discussions she had had with him. In fact, her infatuation with the man was such, that on day three of her London adventure she even found herself poring over some fancy lingerie in one of the city's more renowned department stores and wondering if one day he might like to see her wearing it.

She knew of course, that in reality she would never dare...or indeed have the recklessness...to buy any of the items on offer; it just wasn't her thing...but as she continued to browse through the different types and styles - 'for research purposes only' she told herself - one of the store's employees, who just happened to be lurking nearby saw her looking at the new collections and casually walked over to where she was standing.

Madison sensed her presence from afar...and before the young woman could make eye-contact with her, she quickly put the 'lacy-ensemble' that she had picked up back on the display counter and walked away; scoffing to herself humorously and shaking her head incredulously at her surreal thoughts as she ambled back out of the store through the huge glass-doors.

Outside, Madison had just set foot onto the crowded London pavement when, as if by some strange telepathic coincidence, her mobile phone began playing its tune in her pocket.

It rang once; it rang twice...and for a moment she was tempted not to answer it as she was really enjoying her *alone-time*...but even so...ever the professional, she decided to check the caller ID just in case, on the off chance that it was her boss calling with an urgent memo...or heaven forbid, Evie with another one of her vital new updates on her search for Mr Right.

She pulled the phone out of her pocket and looked at the screen...but as the caller's number had not registered she found herself in a bit of a catch twenty-two situation; either she took the call and found out who it was... and all that that entailed...or she let it go to voice-mail...

...but if she let it go to voice-mail and the caller had withheld the number, then she would not be able to call back and would never be able to find out who it was that had called.

Naturally, her curiosity would not allow that to happen, so without further ado, she pressed the little green button and took the call.

'Hello, Madison Chatfield speaking', she announced warily as she raised the phone to her ear, looking for a place to stand, away from the bustling crowd.

'Hello Madison Chatfield speaking', came the reply in a deep, monotone voice that she recognised instantly as that of *the Bishop*. 'How would you like to join me for dinner this evening?' he asked impassively.

Madison was stunned for a moment...understandably...but as she stood there, in the middle of Oxford Street looking up at the cloudless sky she was also very flattered that he had called.

She covered the phone's microphone with her other hand, taking another moment to compose herself - so as not to appear too eager - and then having cleared her throat noisily she responded to his invitation with a succinct affirmation.

'Sure; why not?', she consented flatly, though her heart was beating so loud in her chest that she was certain anybody passing by must have heard it.

'...8 PM at Cliveden House in Taplow; is that okay with you?' *the Bishop* enquired, his voice as steady and as controlled as always.

'...8 PM it is', Madison agreed courteously.

'Wonderful; I will text you the address', *the Bishop* confirmed with economic courtesy before hanging up...bluntly.

For information;

Cliveden House in Taplow is a grand stately-home, steeped in history and was once the scene of a much-publicised political scandal back in the 1960's.

Bemused, Madison hung up too...and as she put away her phone and looked around for a taxi to get her back to her hotel, she suddenly felt her whole being flood with a new sense of adventure.

Of course, she didn't know what to expect from this new encounter with *the Bishop* or indeed why he had decided to call and invite her out, but after all that had gone on before, she wanted it to be a success, no matter what, so that her stay in England could end on a positive note.

And so, after a brief stop at her hotel...to make some arrangements... and to check her wardrobe for something suitable to wear Madison spent the rest of the day preparing herself to look her best.

This started with a visit to the waxing and tanning salon a few doors down from her hotel where she endured that most painful of feminine beauty treatments; the arm and leg wax.

That was followed by a trip to the Spa where she treated herself to another of those relaxing massage rubs, this time with essential oils which she was hoping would evacuate the stress that had slowly and somewhat inexplicably begun to build in her mind since she had received his call...

...and then finally, she moved on to the hair-salon, where a creative young stylist managed to magically transform her usual straight up-and-down style into a more sophisticated, trendy look - with just the addition of a wave and a soft curl - while a couple of beautiful young Thai women performed simultaneous miracles on her hands and feet, polishing both sets of nails to perfection.

In all, it took over four hours to complete...but nothing boosts a woman's confidence like a four-hour pampering session and as Madison stood in front of the mirror in her hotel room later that afternoon, taking one final look at the finished result, she could not help but feel sexy for the first time in a while, guessing that her sub-conscious was just as thrilled about this rendezvous as she was.

And so it was, that on the stroke of 7 PM., perfumed, oiled and dressed to kill as they say, in an amazing new Versace dress, Madison walked out of her room and made her way down to the hotel reception in the lift.

She was really looking forward to the evening ahead and was excited by the prospect of crossing swords again with *the 'notorious' Bishop*. In fact, she couldn't wait to see what he was like in a more relaxed setting now that the tournament was over...and she wouldn't have to be badgering him for ideas to put in her article...

...unless of course, he revealed something new that she could use...she mused to herself mischievously, as the lift doors opened.

That thought reminded her of who she was – an insatiable journalist ready to pounce on the slightest weakness or indiscretion - and the roguish smile on her face confirmed the fact as she exited the lift and strolled casually through the reception area and out of the hotel's main doors...

to some rather admiring glances from both the concierge and a couple of male guests who were there to check in.

The valet who was stood outside saw her coming from afar and as their eyes met, he immediately turned and waved a taxi forward for her.

Everything seemed perfect at that moment...but just as the valet was opening the taxi-door for her to step inside, Madison suddenly turned on her heels without warning and went back into the hotel, mouthing a series of expletives to herself, her actions leaving the valet completely in the lurch and totally bemused.

It was quite unlike her to do such a thing, but out of nowhere Madison had been overcome by a sudden wave of nervous tension as the reality of what she was about to do unexpectedly dawned on her...and the ensuing emotion which she had felt right to her core had left her feeling a little nauseous in the moment – probably because she hadn't eaten much all day.

She needed to compose herself again before setting out...and clutching her abdomen discreetly she quickly made her way to the ladies-room, next to the bar, thankful and relieved that nobody else was in there.

The ladies sanctuary was tastefully decorated, as all these places tend to be, and its calming hues quickly soothed Madison's rattled nerves as she checked her face and her make-up in the mirror for signs of imperfection.

She was not one to be nervous on any occasion and this episode was quite out of character for her, but within a few minutes the discomfort in her stomach had passed and she was ready to go again.

She made her way back outside and spying her once again, the valet immediately called another cab forward – indicating to her with a polite double-handed gesture - that there was a taxi ready and waiting if she still needed it.

Madison smiled at him awkwardly, stepped forward and thanked him for his indulgence.

The young valet nodded; they shared a little quip about her moment of over-excitement and without further ado, she got into the waiting cab, careful not to snag her dress on the door as she did so.

'Cliveden House, please', she announced distractedly as she tried to sit down without creasing her skirt.

'Sorry Miss; what was that?' the cabbie retorted, looking in his rear-view mirror with a frown.

'Cliveden House, Taplow', Madison repeated with more inflection in her voice, while checking the address on the e-mail that *the Bishop* had sent to her phone.

'Do you know where it is?' she asked anxiously, waiting for the cabbie's confirmation.

'I do, Miss', the man replied, sighing with audible irritation as he tapped the destination into his GPS (*global positioning system*) before engaging the car's first gear.

'Okay then', Madison declared with delight as she made herself comfortable, reassured that everything was once again going to plan after her unexpected false start.

They set off and as they began making their way through the sparsely populated streets of London's west-end, navigating carefully between the buses and a multitude of other cabs, Madison suddenly felt like a nervous debutante making her way to her first Prom.

In fact, it felt somewhat surreal, sitting there in all her finery while she was chauffeured to her destination, and her unease clearly showed in the way she kept fidgeting and repeatedly brushing down her dress, a gesture which strangely mirrored the actual events of her own senior Prom night ten years or so earlier.

It was a weird moment of *déjà-vu*, but prompted by the subliminal comparison in her mind, Madison suddenly found herself thinking back to that fateful night of angst-riven embarrassment all those years ago, with all its frivolous pomp...and its questionable teenage traditions...and as she looked out of the taxi's rain-stained window she instantly saw herself again, swathed uncomfortably in the garish-pink Prom-dress that her mother had insisted she wear that night.

How she had hated that dress; it had been so wrong for her; wrong shape, wrong colour, wrong length...and worst of all, it did nothing to complement either her hair or her shoes; the whole thing had been a disaster, she thought to herself as she turned her head to look out of the opposite window trying to switch her focus.

It did the trick for a moment but as the streets began to whizz by outside, the memory of that dress came racing back to the forefront of her consciousness and like a bitter pill she could almost taste the embarrassment that she had felt that evening rising up again in the back of her throat.

It was somewhat disconcerting, especially as her delicate stomach had already upset her plans once that evening...but before she could dwell any further on her nightmare of teenage humiliation, Madison was suddenly thrown off balance by the taxi swerving violently to the left and then the right again, as it narrowly missed an oncoming motorist who was obviously in too much of a hurry for his own good.

'Hey', she cried out as she struggled to right herself again with the help of one of those conveniently-placed restraints.

'Sorry about that Miss', the cabbie announced apologetically, glancing briefly in the rear-view mirror.

Madison grimaced and grabbed her stomach.

'Are you alright, Miss?, the cabbie enquired in a concerned tone, thinking about his cab and how long it had taken him to clean up from the last person who had been sick in the back.

'I'm fine', Madison replied as she steadied herself once again, raising a hand to reassure him.

'...are you sure?' the cabbie asked again, looking for further confirmation.

'Yeah, I'm fine', Madison repeated, while deliberately avoiding eye-contact and holding on tight to the restraining strap as a safety precaution, '...must be something I ate earlier', she quipped sarcastically, trying to play down her discomfort.

The cabbie smiled stiffly into his mirror, reassured that he wouldn't need to get the bucket out again...but before he could come up with another clever remark to lighten the mood, a crackling call came through on the two-way radio in front of him, asking if he was available for another fare.

'No; sorry dispatch, I can't pick up on Regent Street', he replied curtly into the hand-held receiver, 'I'm on my way to Taplow...'

'Okay, let me know when you've dropped off', the young voice on the other end retorted hastily, his words breaking up slightly as the communication came to a rather abrupt end.

'...Will do', the cabbie concurred with indifference, as he applied the brakes for yet another set of traffic lights.

'Kids', he mumbled to himself without any explanation, as he leaned forward simultaneously to replace the hand-set in its cradle.

The avoidance manoeuvre had jarred Madison out of her musings...but as the taxi pulled away from yet another set of red-lights...and the mood in the cab settled back down to its normal uneasy silence, the film of her disastrous prom-night immediately started up again, right where it had left off - as if it had somehow been put on hold - and played all the way through to its annoying conclusion with a mischievous and taunting persistence.

It was a crying shame, but sadly that whole evening had been a complete debacle for Madison...and as she sat there suspended in time, reminiscing rather reluctantly about the events of that night, her date...the dress...and the fight that had broken out between several of the alcohol-sodden young bucks on a neighbouring table half-way through the festivities, her mood clearly shifted towards the glum, drawing yet another quizzical look from the cabbie up-front via his rear-view mirror, though this time no words were exchanged.

Yes, for Madison, prom-night had been a total nightmare...and yet paradoxically, it had also been a blessing in disguise, she suddenly remembered...because it was the very next day - as a consequence of that fiasco and of her mother's insistence that she should wear that horror of a dress – that she had decided, unilaterally and without any consultation whatsoever, to make a career for herself in fashion.

That had been her 'eureka moment' and the memory of her mother's disapproving face - as she told her about her plans over breakfast that morning – suddenly brought a smile, albeit a wry smile, back to Madison's hitherto poker-faced demeanour.

Of course, she still felt a little disheartened by the fact that she hadn't yet managed to break into the fashion business *per se*...but she was within touching distance now...she knew that, working for the Supplement, and despite all the obstacles that had since been put in her way, she was still confident that one day her time would come; it was just unfortunate, that like most things in life, that particular opportunity was taking its time to present itself...

That thought, that reminder that she hadn't as yet progressed in her lofty ambitions - despite her best attempts - suddenly dampened her mood again...and as she pondered the reality of her aspirations - and the lack of progress she had made thus far - the nerve-jangling anxieties that had haunted her during that disastrous prom-night all those years ago suddenly resurfaced, prompting Madison to take out her compact mirror and check her make-up one more time.

Meanwhile, the taxi continued on its way and as they joined the main thoroughfare out of London, picking up speed as they left the city behind, Madison hit the reset button in her mind and turned her attention back to the evening ahead.

She began wondering what *the Bishop* had in store for her...and having settled down again to enjoy the ride, she started to work her way – very methodically - through the mental check-list she had composed for herself, of all the little quirks that he had mentioned during their previous conversations - on what he liked or disliked in the way women dressed - in order to be sure that she wouldn't be giving him any ammunition or excuse to criticise her during the evening.

He had told her that he didn't think grey was her colour; her dress this evening was her favourite shade of royal-blue; *check*.

He had told her that he didn't like short hemlines; the flared skirt of her designer dress ended quite demurely just above her knee; *check*

He had told her that he didn't like thrusting cleavages; the Sabrina neckline of her dress with its tailored bodice...and its clever design...shaped that area of her body beautifully while covering it up completely; *check*

...and he had told her...

Oh no; that was one concession that she wasn't prepared to make... she thought to herself...

...he had told her that he didn't like women who wore pantyhose...

...but that, she had decided, was non-negotiable; there was just no way.

It was inappropriate and way too personal...and besides, as this evening's encounter was not technically a date, just two people meeting for dinner, there was no real reason for her to have complied with that particular foible – even though she had unconsciously picked out the sheerest pair of hose in her collection without really thinking about it.

Of course, this was all completely against her feminist ideals - to be complying with *the Bishop's* rather sexist demands - and normally she would never have allowed herself to be dictated to in this way - but for some reason, a reason that she couldn't actually explain in the moment – it was clear that Madison was really hoping to make a good impression on her host over dinner...

...maybe even change his opinion of her...

...and if to do so, meant her having to play by his rules for once... then for one night only...she was prepared to do just that and suspend her feminist principles as a consequence; though only temporarily.

Obviously, Madison knew that this invitation to dinner wasn't a date as such, but it was the first time that she and *the Bishop* were going to meet post-competition...and because their previous meetings had all been somewhat strained because of the circumstances and their respective roles, this time she wanted him to see another side of her, not the journalist or the *culturally-less-aware* American, but the woman, the real her.

That was her goal at least, but for that reason - because she wouldn't have her professional mask to hide behind - she felt a little vulnerable and it was showing ever so slightly in her countenance.

They were now on the M4, making good progress towards her destination; the traffic was heavy but fluid and they still had plenty of time in front of them...but then without any fore-warning the whole shebang suddenly came to a grinding halt.

'Sorry Miss...rush-hour', the cabbie explained wearily, muttering to himself that this was why he didn't really want to take this fare in the first place; the M4 was always blocked at this time of the day because of Heathrow Airport...and he knew it.

Madison looked around inquisitively but not one to be discouraged by such a minor hitch - she was after all from New York - she simply nodded her understanding before checking the time again on her phone which was handily placed in a little pocket sewn onto the outside of her handbag.

'I do need to be there by eight; are we going to be okay?' She asked judiciously, craning her neck to listen to the cabbie's mumbled reply, her eyes flashing briefly with annoyance.

'I should think so...but there's just no telling...' the cabbie retorted flatly, gesturing towards the sea of red brake-lights stretching out ahead of them.

Outside, in the fading light, it was suddenly pandemonium; cars edging forward either side of them with scant regard for the highway-code as irritable drivers jostled for position, their lights flashing on and off arbitrarily, as they each made their own stilted commute back to the suburbs.

Whatever happened to all that stiff upper lip British reserve, Madison wondered out loud as she observed the chaos...while up front the cabbie busied himself with the two-way radio trying to inform his office of the situation.

It was a surreal moment, especially considering the circumstances but thankfully, only a short time later, the blockage cleared - as if by magic - and they were on their way again.

'Must'ave been one of those phantom hold-ups', the cabbie announced by way of explanation as they slowly picked up speed again.

'Yeah', Madison agreed with a nod, not really understanding what he meant, but just pleased that they were moving again.

The taxi quickly regained momentum and within no time at all the rural scenery outside was once again skipping past the window at an ever increasing pace.

They had lost a little time - because of the hold-up - but as she looked out at the darkening sky, Madison was confident that they were still ahead of her carefully-calculated schedule, if only just.

Nevertheless, as she sat back in her seat, she couldn't resist another quick glance at her phone, just to be sure...and that was when she had her first shock of the evening.

It was already 7.40 PM.; the hold-up had eaten into her planning much more than she had imagined and as she stared blankly at the screen, thinking for all the world that it must be a mistake or a technical glitch, her eyeballs bulged in disbelief.

Suddenly, she was on red alert and even though she still had twenty minutes in front of her, the young journalist inside her instantly began to wonder if she should call *the Bishop* or send him a text to inform him of the possibility that she could be delayed.

'How much longer should it take to get there?' she suddenly blurted out, as the pressure and the weight of expectation began to build in her mind.

'Another ten...fifteen minutes Miss', the cabbie replied gruffly as he checked the cab's own digital-clock display.

That's cutting it fine, Madison thought to herself, bringing up *the Bishop's* number on her phone's LCD screen. (*She had put it in her contacts when he had texted her the address*)

She thought about it for a moment, wondering what she should say... or how she should phrase it, but then in a moment of surprising lucidity or one of foolish over-confidence that only time would expose, she decided against making the call, choosing instead to pin her hopes on her driver getting her there in time.

It was a gamble and one she might live to regret, but Madison was determined not to show *the Bishop* any sign of weakness during the evening...not even in her punctuality…and as she put the phone away she prayed that her audacity would be rewarded – or at least that it wouldn't backfire on her in any way.

She sat back again in her seat, tense but excited...and while they continued to hurtle ever closer to their destination a succession of scenarios played out in her mind as to how the evening ahead might unfold.

Of course, the possibilities were endless...but despite her creative thinking, none of her imaginary scenarios seemed feasible or practical in reality (*probably because - despite their previous encounters - it was impossible for Madison to factor in the unpredictability of the man she was about to spend it with)* and yet, it was that unknown element, that unknown quantity that made things all the more exciting for her...and indeed, as she sat there rocking gently from side to side as the taxi slowed and moved more cautiously over the increasingly uneven roads, it was that part of the evening that she was looking forward to most.

Her thoughts continued to wander and as she was pondering one particular scenario - *which had made her screw up her nose and grimace slightly, as it featured another of His tedious intellectual rants* - Madison suddenly felt the cabbie's eyes checking her out again in his rear view mirror.

The searching look in his eyes made her feel a little uncomfortable, but distracted by her own musings - and unsure as to whether he was still worried about her wellbeing or whether he was being deliberately leery - she simply ignored his heavy gaze, preferring instead to remain in her own private world of imagination, potential and possibility.

And so it was, that after a trip of nearly fifty five angst-filled minutes, the cab finally turned into the majestic driveway of the grand estate of Cliveden and rolled up to the courtyard of the house where *the Bishop* was waiting patiently on the steps to welcome her.

The taxi came to a halt and *the Bishop* - dressed impeccably as usual - immediately stepped forward, gesturing politely to Madison in the back seat as he approached the cab-driver's window and paid her fare...adding a rather large tip for the grateful driver who thanked him sincerely for his generosity.

That should have been the end of the transaction but discreetly handing the cabbie his business-card *the Bishop* then asked him to collect the lady again from his address three hours later.

The cabbie took the card, winked knowingly at his generous benefactor and then put it in his breast pocket; an improvised military salute sealing the deal.

Meanwhile, having checked her appearance one last time Madison stepped out of the car shaking with trepidation...and anticipation, though she really need not have worried because she looked absolutely stunning.

Her dress was subtle but sexy, her hair was perfect and her make-up, having been touched and retouched any number of times during the trip was faultless.

She stood by the car waiting to greet her host for the first time since their memorable lunch at Chequers, and in that moment she felt more nervous than she had ever done in her life-time – despite having had her fair share of gallant...and less gallant...escapades back in New York.

Just then, *the Bishop* turned to face her and as his eyes met hers, Madison could see - without him having to say a word - that she had succeeded in her mission; she had dressed to impress...and if his reaction was anything to go by, all those hours spent primping and preening in the beauty salon had been well worth it.

Little did she know however, as she stood there waiting for him to lead her inside...that in that moment she bore an uncanny resemblance to a girl *the Bishop* had once known - a long time before - and it was <u>that</u> memory that had made his eyes linger on her for longer than they possibly should have.

The taxi pulled away and then, like the regular client that he obviously was, *the Bishop* quickly guided Madison inside the imposing mansion and on towards the terracotta-walled restaurant where for the duration of the meal, he was the perfect gentleman, effortlessly charming and scrupulously polite. They were simply two people enjoying each other's company, exchanging the usual run of the mill chit-chat about life and current events that anyone else would take pleasure in, while indulging themselves in the culinary delights of one of the country's finest *cuisines.*

Nevertheless, the whole experience was a little strange for Madison – especially after their previous encounters - and she was more than a little wary at first, expecting *the Bishop* to explode at any moment into another of his Anglo-American stand-offs, but it never happened; there was no confrontation, no incendiary comments and no speeches.

In fact, even though it wasn't a '*date*' as such, it had that feeling to it... and because of the easy, relaxed atmosphere Madison was able to play to her own strengths and show *the Bishop* how well-informed and articulate she really was about those areas in life that she was passionate about.

This freedom filled her with confidence during the meal...and buoyed by the stress-free mood she couldn't help - as the coffee was served and the dinner drew to a close – but revert to type by asking a more personal question of her host, having waited for a suitable opening to do so, all evening.

Of course, she knew that she was probably playing with fire by doing so, but as a journalist she also knew that it would be remiss of her not to try. . .and so, swallowing a large gulp of vintage Dutch-courage, she quietly mentioned to him that she had seen him at work - which had been mightily impressive, she added as an aside - but that to complete her profile of him she would really have liked to visit his home to get an idea of the man behind the maestro.

'Besides; coming from New York I have never heard of anybody living in an abbey before', she declared with self-deprecating caution, hoping to press home her argument, while dabbing her lips delicately with a napkin.

The Bishop, cup in hand, raised a solitary eyebrow and paused deliberately.

'You...want to see where I live' he commented calmly and deliberately, his eyes thoughtful and intense.

'Yeah; I think it would complete the picture', Madison responded again, her attention suddenly drawn to the spectacular row of chandeliers hanging above their heads.

The Bishop put down his cup, sat back in his chair and steepled his fingers in front of him.

Suddenly a charged silence descended over the table and for a moment the ambient noise...of the restaurant...and all the babbling conversations taking place around them...seemed to merge into one cacophonous wall of sound, isolating the two of them temporarily from the rest of the world.

It was Madison's turn to pick up her cup and as she leaned back in her chair, steeling herself for *the Bishop's* inevitable rebuke...and possible tongue-lashing, her mind immediately began work on the wording of her professional '*I didn't mean to pry but...as a journalist, I had to ask*' apology.

Clearly, she had stepped over the line with her request for access to his most private world...but nevertheless, Madison thought that it had been worth a shot...and as she observed her host, his eyes half-closed as he considered his response, she suddenly realised that her fascination with him had evolved and grown over the last few weeks from one of mild infatuation into one of...secret admiration.

Time seemed to stand still for a moment and feeling a little uncomfortable with what she had just realised - and not wanting to sour the mood with her uncensored curiosity - Madison was just about to retract her request when the *Bishop* suddenly looked directly at her, fixing her straight in the eyes and started to nod his head approvingly; barely discernible at first and then more visibly.

'Very well...why not?' he agreed quietly with guarded pleasure as his mind secretly congratulated itself for correctly predicting...or at least anticipating...the next stage of the evening's distraction.

Madison was stunned. She had never imagined in her wildest dreams that he would actually agree to her request...and her shock was all too evident in the way she immediately cleared the catch in her throat again to confirm his words.

'Are you serious?' she questioned cautiously, her expression taking on a note of surprise.

'I never say anything that I do not mean Miss Chatfield', *the Bishop* replied formally with a hint of mischief in his eye, before calling for the bill.

This response set Madison's pulse racing and although she couldn't or shouldn't have allowed her imagination to interpret isolated facts beyond their meaning, she couldn't help but secretly wonder - as she held her cup to her mouth, without actually taking a drink from it – if there wasn't an ulterior motive to her host's unexpected indulgence, especially as his eyes had been playing games with hers all evening.

She scrutinised his demeanour once again while his attention was focussed on the waiter...and as strange as it might seem...the more she thought about it the more Madison found herself feeling attracted to this enigma of a man...though she was completely at a loss to explain the alchemical shift as it had never really been her intention.

The Bishop paid the bill and a few minutes later, as they waited in the Mansion's magnificent, Italian-inspired Great Hall for the liveried valet to bring the car around to the front of the building, Madison was suddenly engulfed by a bewildering array of emotions, her brain overflowing with a multitude of unanswered questions.

Was this going to be a watershed moment in her life...was *the Bishop* going to make a move on her in the privacy of his own home...or was he really inviting her back to his place just to show her around...in order to satisfy her unrelenting journalistic curiosity...?

...but if he did....if he did make a move on her, should she consent... Madison wondered to herself, her mind working its way quickly through the pitfalls and the consequences of such an event; ...she was certainly tempted...but would it be unprofessional of her to do so in the current circumstances, she mused hypothetically?

The question went around and around in her head...and even as she stepped into the Aston...and the valet closed the door behind her; she had still not resolved her prospective dilemma.

They drove to the abbey via a series of twisting back-roads in almost complete silence and thirty minutes or so later, after a succession of ever-narrowing tight bends they finally came upon the hidden entrance to *the Bishop's* home, tucked away neatly in a quiet little hamlet on the outskirts of Oxford.

The Bishop pulled the car into the driveway and as he did so, the sound of its tyres crunching noisily on the white gravel stones beneath them, announced their impending arrival.

That sound made Madison perk up again and as the car rolled forward to its usual station in front of the old-fashioned, detached garage-block to the left of the house, she quickly cleared her throat again to mask her excitement at having finally arrived.

This renewed interest drew *the Bishop's* attention momentarily and as their eyes met, the fuzzy feeling in Madison's stomach - that had been dogging her all evening - suddenly returned, ramped up by the anticipation and the uncertainty of just what might happen next.

The sensation was more than a little irritating, but desperate as she was for her first glimpse of the amazing home she had only ever heard of in passing conversation, Madison simply held her breath and consciously ignored the discomfort while she leaned forward in her seat to do just that.

It was quite dark outside and although there were a couple of courtesy lights on, dotted randomly around the perimeter of the courtyard, they were relatively diffuse and did not provide much in the way of illumination.

The lights in the abbey's ground-floor windows didn't offer much help either, but by squinting through the shadows, Madison was at long last able to get her first peek at the master's home.

Wow, that's impressive, she thought to herself; solid and impregnable – just like its owner.

She couldn't wait to see inside...and racing ahead of the game, her mind was already wondering if the abbey's interior design was just as representative of its owner's character; ...cold, angular and conventional...

or whether it was, on the contrary, in any way similar to the mental picture that she had often conjured up in her head...a hundred times or more... while writing up *the Bishop's* profile.

Time and reality were momentarily suspended while she contemplated these imaginings...but then, just as she was coming to her senses again... Madison was suddenly blinded by the powerful glare of the motion-sensitive security lights which automatically lit up the immediate area in reaction to the car creeping closer to the garage.

It made her jump back in shock, the expression on her face worth a thousand words.

'Sorry about that; I should have warned you...' *the Bishop* remarked very matter of fact as he brought the car to a halt in front of the first of three garage doors.

'That's okay'; Madison retorted with false indulgence - articulating the first thing that popped into her head, so as not to allow her annoyance to show through in her voice.

The Bishop smiled impassively...and while he turned back to switch off the car's ignition, Madison quickly recomposed herself, opened the car door and stepped outside.

The night air was crisp and cool, after the snug warmth of the air-conditioned Aston Martin and pausing to take a couple of deep breaths - to fill her lungs with fresh air after the rather somniferous journey - Madison could not help but throw an accusing glare back over her shoulder at the annoyingly indiscreet security lights, whose modern design seemed so incompatible and out of place in comparison with the rest of the surroundings.

Then, having registered her withering disdain for the unrelenting inanimate objects, she quickly made her way around the car and on towards the cobble-stoned path that lead to the abbey's front door.

The Bishop saw her going on without him - without so much as a backward glance - and worried that she might fall and hurt herself, he called out to warn her about the dangerous gravel underfoot, knowing from previous experience how treacherous it could be, especially for a woman in heels.

However, Madison didn't seem to hear his call - or if she did, she chose to ignore it - and it was only when she almost lost her balance on the craggy, uneven surface, that she carefully adjusted her step so as not to fall flat on her face.

It was a close call, but avoiding the fall seemed to galvanise the young American and as she steadied herself again, her natural New York strut suddenly re-emerged to help her gloss over the momentary loss of poise.

She paused briefly to check that her heel hadn't been scratched and then, with no more than a mumbled expletive, she threw her head back and continued on her way without breaking stride again until she reached the quaint little path that separated the courtyard from the house.

Once there, she took a moment to compose herself and get her breath back, checking her heel once more for damage...but as she raised her eyes and saw *the Bishop's* extraordinary residence standing before her in all its glory for the very first time, it literally took her breath away again…and despite her attempts to maintain both her poise and her blasé New York attitude, her inner surprise was clearly evident in her widened stance and her open-palmed gesture.

'Wow; it's magnificent...truly magnificent', she remarked enthusiastically, suddenly finding her voice.

Her enthusiasm was indeed genuine...Madison had studied architecture during her creative classes at University and had learned to appreciate its finer points thanks to the amazing talent of her lecturer, Mr Walters, on whom she had had a crush for the best part of two semesters...but alas, *the Bishop* didn't hear her complimentary comment; he was still out of ear-shot; double-checking the car-doors and fiddling with his keys...

...and even if he had heard...and had reacted to her exclamation, Madison probably wouldn't have heard him anyhow...because as she stood there in transfixed fascination, a thousand thoughts running through her head, the only sound she could hear at that particular moment in time was that of her own thumping heart.

The abbey's dour grey exterior was indeed very impressive... but while its appearance was one of medieval splendour, it was not too ostentatious... and although the stonework was worn and uneven in places, it only added to its character in Madison's eyes...and as she stood there in the night air, contemplating the abbey's quiet grace and its amazing neo-classical style she could not help but be enchanted...even if she was a little disappointed that there were no gargoyles adorning the walls; something that had always fascinated her, even as a child.

It's not quite the magical castle of every girl's dreams...she thought to herself facetiously; but on the other hand, it's probably as close as you are ever going to get, the little voice in her head informed her in quiet reprimand.

Then, out of the corner of her eye Madison's attention was suddenly drawn to the Moon's reflection in one of the abbey's upstairs windows...and as she turned to check it out, her creative mind – which had unexpectedly clicked into gear given the circumstances - was immediately captivated by the mesmerising maze of ivy branches that crept every which way over the abbey's upper facade.

The anarchic foliage seemed to cover the walls completely in places; its interwoven, intertwined branches forming a natural if somewhat ephemeral cladding (protection) for its imposing host...from both the weather...and the prying eyes of those that weren't necessarily welcome in its surrounds.

This feature of the abbey's appearance really appealed to Madison's artistic instincts and as she stood there wide-eyed, looking in amazement at this uniquely individual dwelling, she was tempted to reach into her handbag for her phone, to take a photo of it for her files.

She even began the motion, but then remembering at the last minute how susceptible - if not completely paranoid - the *Bishop* was about preserving his privacy...and anything to do with his personal life; she grudgingly yet sensibly resisted the urge.

At that moment, without any warning, the powerful security lamps above the garage doors - which had been providing the only real light up until then – suddenly switched themselves off again, instantly distracting Madison from her musings and creating a rather dark, eerie silence in the compound around her.

It was both scary and electrifying all at once but as the night wrapped itself around her, rather than feel intimidated by the sudden murkiness Madison found the hush in the courtyard almost magical - as if the world had suddenly decided to hold its breath, as if time had suddenly been suspended.

She blinked a couple of times, her eyes taking a second or two to adjust to the semi-darkness, and just as she was beginning to wonder what was keeping her host from joining her - her desire to see inside the house making her more than a little impatient – Madison suddenly sensed him behind her. She didn't need to turn around, she knew exactly where he was; she could feel his presence, such was the intensity of *the Bishop's* aura.

Overhead, the moon suddenly broke through the night clouds and as if the planets were somehow surreptitiously conspiring to create the perfect mood for them, their path was suddenly lit by a shaft of filtered moonlight.

'Shall we...?' *the Bishop* announced quietly as he came level with her, extending his arm politely, indicating that Madison should go first.

'It's what we're here for', the young American replied a little brashly, catching his eye as she stepped forward.

The Bishop smiled affably with great restraint and without further ado, he quickly fell in behind his guest, the waft of her perfume tickling his senses enjoyably as he followed on at a safe and respectable distance.

The path to the abbey's front door wasn't that long but as she advanced, a flirtatious smile playing discreetly on her lips, Madison's sense of anticipation that something amazing was about to happen seemed to grow exponentially.

A hundred scenarios rushed through her head but as she got closer to the door, those teasing thoughts only added tension to the adrenaline that was already coursing through her body and the butterflies in her stomach which had almost settled - for the first time since she had left her hotel earlier in the evening – were forced to take flight once again.

However, she managed to keep her inner turmoil to herself and as *the Bishop* caught up with her, she deliberately flashed him a smile, thereby masking her discomfort with some true New York grit.

'Welcome to my humble abode,' *the Bishop* announced dryly, as he took out his keys.

Madison didn't reply, but quaking with excitement and champing at the bit to get inside, she simply bowed her head and took a step back to allow him easier access.

The Bishop could sense her eagerness despite her outward show of restraint and in a move clearly designed to build up the tension further and prolong his guest's anxious wait, he purposely took his time in unlocking the door.

It seemed to take him forever – especially as far as Madison was concerned - but eventually he managed it and with a hefty shove of his left hand, the gateway to his private domain was finally thrown open to her willing and long-awaited inspection.

The sense of anticipation in the air was almost palpable and as *the Bishop* stood aside, and gestured for her to step forward - having first reached inside and flicked on the lights - Madison felt another wave of excitement ripple through her body.

Their eyes met fleetingly - drawing out the ripple for another millisecond or so - but before *the Bishop* could repeat his invitation Madison quickly recomposed herself and stepped forward.

She didn't know what lay ahead, she didn't know what to expect and she certainly had no idea what *the Bishop* had in mind - if anything other than what they had agreed - but as she stepped over the threshold of His home for the very first time, an expectant smile on her lips and a mischievous twinkle in her eye – what she did know was that whatever happened in the next couple of hours or so, she was up for the challenge.

Inside, the abbey oozed masculinity...and as she ambled into the entrance-hall - which was surprisingly spacious and not at all what she had imagined - Madison's senses were immediately assaulted by the strong mix of testosterone and polished leather. It was a heady combination and as she wandered further, into the centre of the marble-covered floor she felt momentarily overwhelmed.

The sensation stopped her in her tracks, forcing her to close her eyes for a brief moment to regain her composure but then without a second thought she quickly cleared the catch in her throat and glanced back over her left shoulder to check that *the Bishop* had indeed followed her inside.

She tried to catch his eye...but alas he was still busy securing the door... and so while she waited for him to join her - feeling a little awkward, stood there alone in the middle of the entrance-hall, her curiosity radar on full alert - she began to turn on herself slowly to take in as much of the decor as she possibly could.

It was the first time that she had ever been inside an abbey or any building as old as this one was...and as her 21st century New York consciousness tried to come to terms with these strange new surroundings, the first thing that caught her eye was the magnificent chandelier that dominated the vaulted ceiling above her head.

It was spectacular and almost took her breath away...but as she wheeled around further lowering her gaze incrementally over the rather sparsely decorated walls, she was even more impressed by the two matching doors that opposed each other across the entrance-hall.

Each of them was beautifully carved out of solid wood, and the heavy wrought-iron hinges which held them in place seemed to stand out proudly against the polished wooden grain of their surround. The locks in the doors were of the same sturdy constitution and as she leaned forward slightly, to get a better look Madison could even see the keys - keys the size of which she had only ever seen in movies - protruding enticingly from the cast-iron key-holes.

Both they and the doors themselves were obviously part of the original decor and as she stood there, a little frustrated in her over-eager desire to see more, Madison couldn't wait to see what treasures were hidden behind them.

Another shiver of anticipation ran down her spine but even though she was tempted to walk over and take a peek, she knew that she would have to bide her time and wait patiently for those particular secrets to be revealed to her...

...after all, she thought to herself; now that I have finally worked my way into *His* home, I don't want to get kicked out before I have had a good look around.

♗

Behind her, *the Bishop* suddenly flicked another switch...and much to Madison's surprise a corridor of light appeared in the far wall...extending away from her beyond a set of stylish glass-panelled doors which she had inexplicably failed to pick up on during her initial panoramic scan.

These doors obviously led through into the main part of the house and as she took another quick look around to see if there was anything else she had missed, Madison was suddenly struck by how immaculately tidy everything was; there was no clutter, no mess, no disorder to be seen...anywhere...and as if to complete this rather sanitised setting, she also noticed how all the doors were firmly shut too; an instant reminder, if she needed one, of the *Bishop's* almost obsessive, controlling – if not OCD - personality.

♗

The extra brightness from the light in the corridor had by extension illuminated a small display cabinet, set into the wall right next to the double-doors and seeing it as an opportunity to resume the conversation Madison immediately gravitated over towards it, unable to resist her journalistic need to pry any longer.

The Bishop, who was still stood in the doorway, watched her veer off towards the glass case and following in her wake, having locked the door, he immediately began his explanation of its contents, with his usual detached calm, before she could question him about it.

'...Ever since the media saddled me with the nickname, I have literally received hundreds of those pieces', he informed her, gesturing towards the display case full of chess pieces - all of them bishops;

'...in ivory, in jade, alabaster, ceramic, granite, marble, glass, ebony, aluminium, silver; ...you name it; I've got a bishop made from it', he remarked pleasantly, monitoring his guest's reaction.

'So I see', Madison replied quietly, drumming her fingers lightly on the display cabinet's glass pane while she filed away some of the different materials that he had mentioned in her head...for future reference.

'You know, someone once suggested to me that that collection looked like a load of old sex toys...' *the Bishop* suddenly commented out of the blue, trying to lighten the mood.

'Do you play with toys Miss Chatfield?' He enquired mischievously, catching Madison off-guard and deliberately exploiting the ambivalence of the mood.

'...Toys?' Madison queried with a cursory glance in *the Bishop's* direction.

'Toys are for childr...oh, you mean those toys...' she clicked before completing her sentence.

'No...I'm pretty conservative when it comes to that kinda thing', she riposted with surprising self-assurance…trying to rise above her host's obvious attempt to destabilise her…while masking her sense of outrage at his inappropriate and uncharacteristically familiar enquiry.

'That's strange for a New Yorker', *the Bishop* commented, continuing his teasing remarks as he unlocked the double-doors.

'...for a New Yorker; ...what is that supposed to mean?' Madison demanded in as measured and as diplomatic a tone as she could manage under the circumstances so as not to compromise the situation, yet almost reprimanding him for the remark.

'...for a New Yorker', *the Bishop* replied with clipped precision, hunching his shoulders and repeating her words insistently as he opened one of the glass-doors.

'Well, I read recently that those that live there - in New York that is - tend to have a reputation for being a little...wild, when it comes to that sort of thing', he persisted, the corners of his mouth creasing briefly into an ironic smile as he raised his arm and gestured politely towards the corridor.

'You really shouldn't believe everything you read', Madison declared confidently...'and I should know...I write it', she added as she slipped through the doorway and into the brightly-lit corridor, an engaging smile on her face and a renewed spring in her step, pleased with herself that she hadn't risen to *the Bishop's* rather obvious and deliberate provocation – at least not to any great degree anyway.

'I'll remember that...' *the Bishop* confirmed resolutely as he followed her through.

'Second door on the left', *the Bishop* announced as he tracked his guest down the corridor, placing a soft hand in the small of her back as he guided her adroitly into the abbey's small reception room.

Madison registered his touch but didn't respond, stepping confidently into the room as if she had been there a thousand times before.

'Wow, this is amazing', she remarked with genuine wonder as she walked in and span around twice looking at the mahogany wall-units and the array of shiny teak cabinets.

'Thank you', *the Bishop* retorted quietly, smiling politely at his guest as he invited her to sit down on one of the beautiful antique-green Chesterfields before she got giddy.

'Errm, right here?' she questioned, disappointed that *the Bishop* was not going to follow the usual social protocol and offer her the grand tour of the property that she had been expecting.

'Yes, right there will be fine', *the Bishop* confirmed courteously with a suave smile.

Madison frowned discreetly but then reminding herself to be patient... and telling herself that 'all good things come to those who wait', she quietly made her way over to one of the leather chairs, and sat herself down on the edge of its cushioned seat, making it plain by her body language that this was only to be a temporary halt.

'Would you like something to drink Miss Chatfield?' *the Bishop* then asked with his usual cool detachment.

'Well, I don't want any more alcohol but I would like a glass of water... with ice and lemon', Madison conceded politely, doing her level best to keep the tone as courteous as possible as she choked back her frustration and suddenly realised that her throat was far drier than she thought thanks to the car's air-conditioning system and the nervous tension that was building within her core.

The Bishop nodded his understanding and quietly walked over to the drinks cabinet, checking his watch discreetly as he went; inwardly savouring the chess-like game of cat-and-mouse that he was playing with his guest.

Meanwhile, perched carefully on her seat, Madison heaved a quiet sigh of dissatisfaction as she began looking around at the room's extraordinary decor.

The experience thus far had been fascinating, and spurred on by the quality and the refinement of the furnishings that now surrounded her – the sight of which had instantly renewed her desire to see more - Madison immediately began work on a new plan, a new way of manoeuvring her host into accommodating her request for greater access.

Her thoughts began to wander as she searched for a new approach but before she could decide on a new strategy, her attention was quickly brought back to the present by the sound of ice-cubes clinking noisily into crystal glasses.

The noise broke the ambient silence that had settled over the room and as she looked across to where *the Bishop* was standing, Madison could not help but notice how broodingly sexy the man was. He was busy fixing the drinks and had his back turned to her, so she could only see his black mane above the collar of his Italian suit but *the Bishop* had such strong shoulders and such a commanding presence, that for a moment, she felt all of a quiver.

His whole demeanour oozed subtle strength and a deep-seated masculinity, and as the wine from earlier in the evening started to take effect, relaxing her mood, lowering her protective barriers and shuffling the deck of her priorities, Madison's thoughts digressed momentarily from her original mission and she began imagining that beneath the unruffled surface that he presented to the world *the Bishop* was like an untapped volcano ready to erupt.

The image distracted her briefly but unlike all the men she knew who were incapable of doing both simultaneously, her brain was still working correctly, her self-control was still intact and within a split second she had regained her composure.

The Bishop walked back over with the drinks and having made sure that she was comfortable he took a seat across from her.

For a moment, there was an awkward silence, Madison sipping her water slowly and waiting patiently for her host to take his usual lead.

She was dying to be told that the tour that she had been expecting was next on the agenda but much to her dismay, as *the Bishop* sat back in his chair and stared silently off into the distance, his mind plunged into sudden retrospection, he showed no sign that he was about to indulge her in that way.

That left the journalist inside her feeling immensely frustrated after the evening of revelations which had brought her to this point, but while she was in no mood to hear him deliver another of his rambling soliloquies - however compelling it might be – Madison knew that she would probably have to endure it and bide her time a while longer before bringing up the idea of a guided tour once again.

In the meantime, she looked around the room hoping to find a conversation-starter...and admiring the decor which was both tasteful and expensive, she suddenly commented on how impressive it all looked.

That jump-started the conversation which was a little cagey at first - as if the two of them were still sizing each other up - but eventually the mood relaxed again and after a little more light conversation, having avoided the elephant in the room for as long as she possibly could Madison finally built up the chutzpah to ask for the guided-tour which she had thus far been denied.

'...in order to get a better idea of who you are' – she explained, trying to hide her inquisitive nature under a blanket of professional interest.

'Who says I want you to know who I really am?' *the Bishop* countered a little churlishly, taking her to task, in a move designed to brush off her persistence and escape further scrutiny.

'Well...the people who read....' she began before he interrupted her again, cutting her off mid-sentence.

'You know Miss Chatfield', *the Bishop* remarked in measured, even tones, as he settled further into his seat, 'it is a popular misconception that people in the public eye somehow lead more exciting lives than everybody else, but the truth is...it's just not the case; it's an illusion'.

Madison knew that he was deliberately yanking on her chain.

'...but that is why you invited me back here, isn't it?' she commented with emphasis, a hint of her frustration managing to escape her control.

The Bishop stared off into the distance pensively and left the question hanging.

'I'm sorry but old habits die hard'; she announced, having taken a moment to regain her composure, 'I've always had a problem with boundaries', she blurted out. 'It goes with the job...but you did invite me here, so being a crazy American I just assumed….' Madison surmised tilting her head appeasingly in an effort to press home her case.

'I too, must apologise...for my lack of enthusiasm'; *the Bishop* suddenly responded, rising from his chair; 'it's just that...how can I say this without offending you?...I'm pathologically distrustful of anybody who tries to get too close to me', he declared solemnly, a dead-pan look on his face.

'I understand that...but I just want an over-view of Tobias Byron the man and not Tobias Byron the chess-master', Madison insisted, waving away his concerns, trying to be resourceful and refusing to take her eyes off the prize.

She felt exhilarated by the exchange and as she traced the rim around her glass with her fore-finger, a mischievous smile flickered across her face.

'Never assume anything', *the Bishop* affirmed resolutely as he walked over to drinks cabinet to put down his glass; '...but that said, Miss Chatfield...', he continued as he walked back towards her, '...I do appreciate your candour...and in recognition of that and of your unswerving determination, I will, on this one occasion make an exception and show you around my home'.

'Thank-you', Madison trilled with a twinkle in her eye, doing her best not to reveal her conflicting emotions or the metaphysical turmoil percolating through her body.

The Bishop nodded politely, his eyes crinkling indulgently at the edges.

'Shall we then ...?' he remarked, with a chivalrous arm motion towards the door.

'Sure', Madison replied with alacrity, putting down her glass and springing to her feet; her sense of triumph etched clearly on her face as she straightened her dress and headed for the door, stopping only - as an after-thought - to wait for her host to catch up.

The Bishop took a deep breath and stepping forward, led the way out of the room with Madison following close on his heels. He was still feeling a little uncomfortable, a little reluctant that she had manoeuvred him into agreeing to her request, but having given his word and relented for once - against his better judgement - he decided to follow through on his promise.

They crossed the corridor in silence - but for the sound of Madison's clicking heels - and almost immediately stopped in front of another heavy wooden door carved into the abbey's imposing stone-work.

There *the Bishop* paused for a moment, as if he was still fighting with his natural instincts of self-preservation, but then grabbing hold of the door's solid-looking handle, he twisted it tightly to the left and with one strong shove, he pushed it open, before instinctively leaning inside for the light-switch and standing back again to allow Madison to precede him.

'After you, Miss Chatfield', he announced politely with another gallant hand-gesture.

'Thank you Mr Byron; you are such a gentleman', Madison replied with a wry smile before taking her first step inside.

'Wow, this is amazing', Madison remarked out loud, as she stood just inside the door, '...and it's not hard to see where the inspiration came from' she added, gesturing towards the room's minimalist decor of white walls and chequered black and white floor...which contrasted completely with the traditional furnishings of the room that they had just vacated.

The Bishop, who had followed her inside, grimaced discreetly but he didn't react to her pejorative comment as he saw it, preferring instead to register his irritation with a simple clearing of the throat.

Madison sensed his disquiet and realising too late, the impertinence of her observation - *and the tenuous nature of her position* - she immediately tried to defuse the situation - and the potential for an unnecessary misunderstanding - with a rousing if somewhat blatantly-obvious over-reaction.

'Yep, this really is spectacular', she declared, as she walked forward a couple of paces before turning to face her host, hoping that her super-sized compliment would somehow smooth over her previous slip of the tongue.

The Bishop was by no means bluffed by her awkward attempt at verbal camouflage but the beautifully-designed, acoustically-perfect conservatory was indeed spectacular; in fact it was his pride and joy...and suddenly basking in her belated recognition and appreciation of his home, he accepted her compliment with good grace.

♗

Madison took a deep breath to recover her composure and glancing sideways in order to avoid her host's rather piercing stare, she pretended that one of the framed prints that lined the walls on either side of the door had caught her eye.

'Who's the artist?' she enquired inquisitively as *the Bishop* ambled further into the room behind her and looked on impassively as she slowly gravitated over towards the line of art-work...to inspect it in greater detail.

The Bishop smiled stiffly, somewhat surprised by his guest's question.

'Erm, well...those prints are mostly from Jack Vettriano's collection', he replied after a brief pause, his raised eyebrow and his stunned tone clearly revealing his surprise that Madison would in any way be interested.

'He's a contemporary Scottish artist', *the Bishop* added indulgently, '...and that particular print, the one right in front of you, is called *Man of Mystery*', he confirmed contentedly, pleasantly buoyed by his guest's prolonged pause in front of the said print.

'How fitting', Madison blurted out impulsively, her mouth unable to censor her words before they were spoken.

The Bishop just smiled benevolently and shrugged his shoulders.

'So, what goes on in here?' Madison then enquired, trying to take charge of the conversation and lull her host into revealing more about himself.

'Well...mostly I use this room to relax...to read...and of course...to play the piano', *the Bishop* responded, gesturing firstly towards the large angular sofa and comfortable chairs situated in the bespoke glass extension…and then to the white baby-grand situated on the far side of the room.

'Wow, you really are a man of many talents'; Madison acquiesced, suddenly feeling a little inadequate as she stopped unintentionally in front of a print entitled *Private Dancer* and gazed upon another entitled *Game On*, both of which evoked a simmering sexual tension not unlike what she was secretly experiencing within.

'Thank you for the compliment', *the Bishop* replied as he wandered over and sat at the piano, scrutinising his guest's aesthetic with rapt interest as she moved from one framed-print to the next, her hands linked loosely behind her back or brushing her cheek thoughtfully.

'This art-work really is stunning', Madison affirmed; '...I've never seen anything quite like it'.

'It is...isn't it...?' *the Bishop* agreed...as he opened up the keyboard and started to play his own rendition of Beethoven's *Fur Elize...*,

'...although *music is the only sensual pleasure without a vice*', he announced cryptically, quoting Samuel Jackson before the swell of the melody drowned out his voice.

Madison didn't quite understand what he meant by that; it seemed a little out of context in terms of what had been said up to that point but not wanting to get into another interminable discussion about it, she just smiled politely and drifted over to join him by the piano, where she stood and listened in subjugated fascination for the next couple of minutes until her host concluded his musical interpretation, which she inevitably rewarded with a brief but very loud applause.

'That was amazing...truly amazing', she exclaimed with a little too much enthusiasm, deliberately stroking her host's ego.

The Bishop looked up, clearly revelling in her flattery and applause, and as their eyes locked - carried along by her appreciation of his talent...and by her unexpected interest in the art-work that graced his walls - he slowly got up from the piano-stool and invited her to continue the tour around the rest of his home.

'I thought you would never ask', Madison responded promptly with a smile, gesturing for him to lead the way.

They walked quietly out of the conservatory, and by-passing the beautifully-crafted wrought-iron spiral staircase *the Bishop* showed his guest into the kitchen...where once again, she was taken very much by surprise.

In her own mind, for some reason, Madison expected it to be small and cluttered, dominated by an old coal-fired range with lots of copper-bottomed pots and pans hanging from the ceiling - just like she had seen in so many British movies over the years - but in fact the kitchen was fashionably appointed with reclaimed oak floorboards, opaque glass splash-backs and stainless steel work-surfaces.

'Wow; I really wasn't expecting such a contemporary design', she declared in a complimentary tone as she wandered around the granite-topped breakfast-bar; '...you know, because of the age of the building...' she added with a swirling hand-gesture, trying to qualify her statement.

'Really...what were you expecting?' *the Bishop* enquired simply as he leaned back casually against the door-frame; 'something out of a Jane Austen novel...?

'Yeah, something like that', Madison replied a little distractedly, not realising the patronising profundity of her host's comment.

'Well, to be honest...' *the Bishop* explained placidly as he wandered further in, '... it probably did look something like that before...but we had a fire a year or so ago and the whole place had to be gutted and redesigned'.

'Oh, I see', Madison concurred as she watched her host walk over and open another wooden door.

'This is the wine-cellar' he announced with indifference, '...and through here...' he explained while walking through a heavy stone archway,'... is the dining-room'.

Madison paused for a moment, not wanting to be rushed...and only once she had taken in as much as she could of the kitchen, did she follow *the Bishop* through.

This room, the dining- room was absolutely stunning and Madison immediately froze on seeing its splendour; from the oak-panelled walls, to the vaulted ceilings and the huge bay-window, she was simply blown away by its eclectic mix of old and new.

'Wow', she whispered to herself, secretly frustrated that she didn't have her phone with her to capture what she was seeing...before she realised that *the Bishop* probably wouldn't allow her to take pictures anyhow.

'...and that's about it...that concludes the tour', *the Bishop* announced rather brusquely, with a relieved shrug of the shoulders, '... apart from the usual service rooms etc...' he added as an after-thought, hoping that his guest had seen enough.

Madison nodded, took one last look around and followed her host back out into the corridor.

She knew of course, that she hadn't seen everything; that *the Bishop* had only shown her what he thought she would be interested in, or more precisely, what he was prepared to reveal to her...and as they made their way back to the reception room where it had all started, she couldn't help but ask about the upper floors.

'Can I see upstairs?' she enquired candidly, tilting her head slightly and playing on her host's uncharacteristically indulgent mood.

'I hardly think your readers would be interested in anything up there', *the Bishop* retorted dismissively; checking his watch discreetly and realising that the taxi he had surreptitiously arranged wasn't due for another ten minutes or so.

'Aaw, come on, you'd be surprised what my readers want to know', Madison insisted, flashing her most ingratiating smile.

The Bishop frowned then smiled back stoically, rueing the fact that he still had ten minutes to fill.

'Very well then', he declared reluctantly, indicating the spiral staircase; 'Ladies first...'

Madison flicked her hair confidently, and resisting the temptation to punch the air in triumph, she made her way swiftly over to the staircase, before her host could change his mind.

The light in the stairwell leading upstairs was a little more subtle than it was in the rest of the house, and all of a sudden, as Madison stepped carefully onto the bottom stair and began her ascent - *without a second's thought for the social convention that would deem it unwise for a woman to find herself alone, especially at night, in the house of a man she hardly knew* - the air around them thickened with intrigue.

Of course, she was well aware of the potential danger - she had seen it a thousand times in the movies - but as she made her way upstairs, climbing slowly and steadily, one careful step after the next because of the height of her heels, it only added to the excitement and the anticipation that was pulling her inexorably onwards and upward.

Meanwhile, behind her, at the foot of the staircase, she could feel *the Bishop's* penetrating stare, watching her every move through the stairway's open ironwork.

She glanced back over her shoulder to see where he was, and without meaning for it to happen, their eyes met, forcing them both to look away uneasily. It was only a fleeting glance but that was enough to send Madison's heart racing and make the adrenaline in her veins - which was already flowing pretty freely because of the situation - begin to boil.

The mere fact that he was allowing her upstairs, into the very heart of his jealously guarded, personal domain - into what would be considered by many to be forbidden territory - had rekindled the stirrings she had experienced earlier and the promise, albeit abstract, of potentially concluding the evening with a flourish of passion...just as her host had done earlier at the piano, did little to assuage her enthusiasm.

She reached the top of the stairs and as she took a moment to recompose herself, glancing curiously up at the small brass chandelier that lit up both the stairwell and the immediate corridor, the *Bishop* promptly joined her, ready to continue the tour.

He immediately took charge once again, leading the way down the corridor and showing her into several of the abbey's guest-rooms which - *while they were perfectly clean and tidy* - clearly hadn't seen any guests in a while; he showed her into the communal bathroom, and into another couple of rooms tucked away in a corner which she could only describe as 'works in process', and then finally, knowing that there would be no way of avoiding it - and realising that he was too short on time to argue – he even allowed her a peek into the privacy of the master-bedroom.

'Wow; now this is the real deal', Madison proclaimed loudly, as she pushed past her host, opening the bedroom's heavy wooden door on its hinges to its fullest extent.

The decor in this room - as opposed to the other rooms he had shown her - was a lot more ostentatious. The original beams and joists that interlocked in the walls and ceiling were very much in evidence as a design feature; the red velvet curtains that hung proudly on the wall were both rich and heavy, the dressers either side of the windows were clearly antiques and taking centre-stage against the wall on her right as she walked into the room was the strangest looking bed that Madison had ever seen.

'That's a Mongolian rocking bed', *the Bishop* announced somewhat smugly, noticing his guest's puzzled frown on seeing the wooden artefact...

'...fabled to have once belonged to the notorious Genghis Khan, ruler of all and founder of the Mongolian Empire', he added knowledgeably from his position by the door.

'Really', Madison stated simply, as she twirled and scanned the rest of the room underwhelmed by weird bed's alleged history.

'Yes, really', *the Bishop* insisted, stepping forward and giving the base of the bed a nudge with his foot so that it swung gently on its frame.

Madison shrugged incredulously, though her mind was suddenly racing.

'May I?' she questioned with a fleeting smile, ignoring *the Bishop's* probing stare and pointing towards what she assumed to be the en-suite bathroom.

'Be my guest', *the Bishop* agreed, checking his watch once again, as soon as his guest's back was turned.

'Thanks', Madison acknowledged once more as she walked around the rather-imposing wooden bed and made her way towards two frosted-glass doors on the far side of the room.

'Are you sure that you're okay with me doing this?' she asked again, glancing back over her shoulder with a slightly patronising and ambiguous smile, as the tension in her lower abdomen ratcheted up another notch.

The Bishop - looking brooding and mysterious as he leaned back stiffly against the door-jamb - didn't answer her facetious question but simply raised a hand to wave her on.

Madison continued...and reaching the frosted-doors, she paused only briefly to regain her composure, before sliding them open, to reveal the most beautifully designed bathroom she had ever seen.

♗

When she had walked into the bedroom, she had been amazed; ...now, Madison was impressed. The sight of the bathroom with all its gleaming chrome and mirrors instantly took her breath away and as she stepped inside the pristine - and immaculately tidy - grooming-studio, her senses were immediately overwhelmed by the musky scent of masculinity that came rushing towards her.

She closed her eyes for a moment and inhaled deeply, before retreating again quickly, not wanting to linger for too long in this, his most personal of personal spaces.

She turned around one hundred and eighty degrees, and with the smell of his masculinity now embedded in her brain, her eyes were suddenly drawn, almost by instinct back to the bed; her journalistic curiosity taking an uncharacteristic back-seat for once to her natural drive as her secret desire and her sense of destiny mushroomed out of all proportion.

The bed looked strangely conspicuous and yet so inviting...and as she walked around it, she felt her cheeks blush and the butterflies in her stomach tingle at the thought of what it would be like to spend a night in that bed with this strange, enigmatic man.

'Nice bathroom', she murmured as she re-joined her host by the door.

The Bishop nodded politely; 'it's new; as you can imagine, there was no bathroom in the original plans', he explained simply.

'Yeah, I kinda guessed that...' Madison acknowledged, catching his eye.

'So, what's next?' she enquired boldly, looking deeper into his eyes and trying desperately to maintain her professional focus.

The Bishop had loosened up more than she had expected and he had probably shown her more of his home than he had ever intended.

However, while this was all very interesting, the expectation - as far as Madison was concerned, coming from New York - was that dinner was a precursor to physical intimacy…and after inhaling his intoxicating essence for the last half-hour or more, she was aching for him to cross the line first and make a move on her, even though she knew that to allow such behaviour would break every self-imposed rule she had ever made about remaining professional at all times.

There was just something about the way he looked at her that made her whole body quiver inside and she was in no mood to resist.

The Bishop paused briefly, cleared his throat, and then raised a hand to indicate the way out.

Madison was disappointed, and as she moved to exit the bedroom, wondering what else he was going to show her, she could not help but turn and look back, her eyes drawn back inexorably to the unusual-looking rocking bed.

'How do you keep it all so clean?' she asked as they walked back down the corridor, changing the subject on purpose to stultify her emotions.

'Pochemuchka', *the Bishop* exclaimed with sudden dismay.

'Sorry; I didn't quite catch that', Madison retorted, slightly bewildered.

'Pochemuchka', *the Bishop* repeated dispassionately; 'its Russian...it means 'a person who asks a lot of questions''.

Madison rolled her eyes discreetly and forced a half-smile.

'I relish my solitude…but I do have a lady that comes in three times a week', *the Bishop* then replied after a brief pause; 'she takes care of everything for me'.

'...A lady?' Madison repeated.

'Yes, a lady', *the Bishop* confirmed.

'And she cleans the house?' Madison insisted.

'Yes, she cleans the house', *the Bishop* repeated diplomatically.

'Is that all she does?' Madison continued, the insinuation in her voice revealing her growing frustration.

The Bishop smiled stiffly but did not react.

'...so how do you alleviate the boredom of this solitary existence?' Madison continued with a coquettish sideways glace, clearly struggling to keep her libido in check.

The Bishop sensed her expectation but true to character he did nothing to assuage her desires, preferring instead to remain placidly silent and ignore her innuendo as he led the way back downstairs.

Frustrated, Madison followed him down, making sure not to lose her footing on the stairs shiny steel steps and just as they reached the bottom, she noticed another large door on the ground floor that she had not yet seen behind.

'What's in that room?' she asked inquisitively.

'I'm sorry, young la...Miss Chatfield, but that room is off-limits', *the Bishop* intimated without further explanation.

'Oh, I'm sorry, I didn't mean to pry'; Madison retorted contritely, with another winsome smile; *despite having scrupulously and systematically inspected all the other rooms she had been shown into, in the minutest detail.*

The Bishop frowned jadedly and at that moment, just as Madison turned her head back to face him, the headlights of a car swept into the courtyard, filling the abbey's hallway with a momentary wash of extra light.

Then, chimes sounded in one of the rooms upstairs, echoing through the stair-well.

'Aaah, your carriage awaits'; *the Bishop* announced suddenly, his remark blind-siding his guest completely.

'I'm leaving?' Madison asked, somewhat aghast, looking around sharply and meeting his gaze again.

'Of course', *the Bishop* confirmed succinctly...with his usual controlled calm.

'I'm leaving now', Madison repeated insistently, a look of exasperation and disappointment on her face.

'...Are you serious?' she added with dramatic intensity.

'Yes, you are leaving now', *the Bishop* repeated noting the confusion in her eyes.

'It's getting late, but thank you very much for your company'; he confirmed quietly. 'It's been a most enjoyable evening and I hope that you have now seen enough to complete your article'.

'Yes, I suppose I have...but...' Madison mumbled grudgingly.

She was stunned; she didn't know what she had been expecting but it certainly wasn't being shown the door like this.

The Bishop ignored her obvious disillusion and gathering her belongings from the reception room he quickly guided her towards the door, his hand placed gently at her waist, a gesture which – although not deliberate or intentional – sent frustrating tingles of excitement racing through Madison's body once again.

They reached the front door which he opened in gentlemanly fashion... and just as she was about to turn around and show her disappointment more petulantly, with a mouthful of New York reality, *the Bishop* leaned in unexpectedly to place a consoling - almost apologetic - goodbye kiss on her cheek.

The gesture took Madison by surprise and as she turned her head, their lips met inadvertently in a gentle kiss; the frisson making her tingle all over once again.

'An old English tradition', *the Bishop* joked, pulling back sharply, his mind quick to react to the potentially embarrassing situation.

Stunned again, but for a different reason this time, Madison didn't react; she simply stepped back and walked out, strutting into the cool night air with a toss of her blond hair and a veiled snarl of frustration on her lips.

The Bishop followed her out, and catching her up as she made her way towards the waiting taxi, he politely opened the cab door for her and closed it again behind her, once she was safely seated inside.

'Have a safe flight home, Miss Chatfield', he announced through the closed window with one of his inscrutable smiles.

Madison returned the smile with a pout, but didn't speak.

Then without further ado - and masking his relief behind his serious demeanour - the *Bishop* calmly made his way around to the driver's window to discuss payment for the trip back to London.

The transaction was concluded after another brief exchange and seconds later, with a courteous wave of his right hand in the direction of his generous benefactor, the cabbie selected a gear with his left and released the car's brakes.

This prompted the taxi's idling engine to instantly pick up the revs... and as it pulled away slowly - its tyres crunching noisily on the fore-court's white-gravel carpet; *the sound of which echoed crisply in the cooling night air reminding its passenger of how excited and full of expectation she had been upon hearing those same noises on her arrival only a short while earlier -* Madison sat back impassively on the back seat and thumped the door beside her in melodramatic fashion, deciding stubbornly not to wave or even glance back at her enigmatic host.

CHAPTER SEVEN

(Part One)

The taxi began working its way back to London through the labyrinth of narrow lanes deserted overnight by the local population and as she settled down for the hour-long ride, Madison couldn't help but glance back briefly once or twice with a look of 'what might have been' in her eyes.

How she would have liked to have stayed a while longer at the abbey... and how she would have really liked *the Bishop* to have caressed *her* as delicately and as dextrously as he had caressed the keys on his piano, she thought to herself mischievously.

The thought brought an instant hue of colour to her tense cheeks but as she sat back quietly, projecting an outer calm while her insides churned annoyingly with confusion, Madison was primarily filled with feelings of disillusion. She felt thwarted, mystified and bitterly disappointed by the rather abrupt anti-climax to what had started out as quite an exciting evening.

Indeed, *the Bishop's* incivility had dealt a crushing blow to her usually unshakeable ego...and she didn't know quite what to make of it. She wasn't used to being shown the door like that and her pride - both personal and professional – had been badly bruised.

That hurt was bad enough for her to contend with, but what perplexed her even more was the baffling array of mixed messages that *the Bishop* had been sending out all through the evening.

She thought that she could read men; she thought that she knew what they wanted...which was usually always the same thing...so, what had gone wrong?

Had she said something or done something to annoy him? She wondered cautiously.

Had she misread the situation?

What was it about *the Bishop* that meant he didn't respond like any other man she had ever met...she pondered...because as far as she was concerned, there had been more than a hint of chemistry between them all evening.

She had felt it build from the moment he had greeted her at the restaurant, right through to the moment he had thrown open his bedroom-door for her...

...and having felt that tension and made all that effort to be on her best behaviour so as not to ruin the moment, she was now at a loss to understand or explain why this enigma of a man had never made any serious attempt to put the moves on her.

Her trusty intuition had let her down for once...and as she sat there on the back seat of the cab, her body tingling with a combination of adrenaline and rage, Madison couldn't help but rant to herself.

Whoever would have thought that in England...'Would you like to come back to my place for a night-cap actually meant just that...a night-cap?' she mused ironically as she gazed aimlessly out through the car's windscreen at the seemingly never-ending hedge-rows, illuminated one after the other in recurring fashion by the car's powerful headlights as they went rushing towards them.

The taxi veered to the right to take another twisting bend and as she was swayed by the motion Madison suddenly caught sight of the cabbie's reflection in the rear-view mirror.

At first, she thought nothing of it, but then it suddenly dawned on her that she had seen him before. It took a moment for her to place him...but then the penny dropped. It was the same driver as before...he was wearing a cap now which altered his appearance slightly, but it was definitely the same driver.

She hadn't picked up on it earlier because of the fading light and the fact that she was completely wrapped up in her emotions when she had first gotten into the car - but seeing him now she instantly realised that *the Bishop* had never had any intention of inviting her stay overnight.

That realisation was galling and made her want to scream at what she considered social misrepresentation...but it did little to alleviate her frustration.

However, rather than create a scene which might possibly end up with her being left at the side of the road in the middle of nowhere…in the middle of the night…Madison pulled out her phone and began flicking irately through the messages that had arrived over the past couple of hours as she had turned it off before meeting *the Bishop* at the restaurant.

The first two messages were from her boss Amanda which she scanned through with indifference; then there was one from Evie which made her roll her eyes in disbelief. . .and then finally there were a couple more from an ex-boyfriend...which she immediately deleted without even bothering to open.

Frustrated, she simply shrugged her shoulders and put her phone back into her handbag; she was in no mood to respond.

A few minutes later, the taxi emerged from the last of the countryside's sleepy little villages and made its way onto the M40 where, with an audible sigh of relief from the driver up-front, it quickly began to pick up speed for the run into London.

Meanwhile, on the back seat, collecting her thoughts again carefully, Madison began reliving the evening's events one more time, wondering to herself if there was anything she could have done differently to bring her truncated evening to a more satisfying end.

In her mind's eye, she saw herself in the restaurant chatting away quite happily, she saw herself in *the Bishop's* car where she was certain there was a definite buzz of anticipation when their eyes had met...and she saw herself walking around the abbey, enjoying its eclectic mix of old and new...but nothing stood out; nothing to tell her where she might have gone wrong.

Then, as her thoughts jumped around randomly and the image of *the Bishop's* magnificent bedroom appeared temptingly before her eyes, Madison shivered naughtily at the thought of her and the man himself ensconced comfortably under the covers of his unusual swinging bed, locked in a passionate embrace.

The fleeting image instantly turned into a full-blown cameo - the details of which were of a rare clarity - and as the taxi continued to eat up the miles Madison's fertile New York mind had no trouble in embroidering...and elaborating on those details.

The mere thought of his swinging bed was undeniably erotic in itself...and by the time her cameo had reached its inevitable crescendo, the hormones in her body were hurtling around her system like a washing machine on a fast spin cycle.

It felt wonderful and weird at the same time; the images in her mind had inflamed her senses once again, and as she sat there in silence, enjoying the erotic slide-show in her head, another naughty ripple shivered down Madison's spine.

Her body shuddered for a split second as the heightened emotion slowly subsided and as the taxi reached the outskirts of London, surprising its passenger with the swiftness of its return journey, Madison found herself blushing once again at her reflection in the back-door window.

It was a strange almost surreal moment, but as they made their way into the heart of the capital, the harsh street-lights that lined the city's pavements quickly brought back her focus, and by the time they pulled up outside her hotel Madison had all but regained her customary composure.

It was still quite early, barely eleven o'clock, and knowing that she wouldn't be able to sleep after the disappointment of her evening - and because of the pent up frustration still circulating around her body – Madison decided that when she got back to her room she would call Gary.

The young Aussie was always good for a laugh and with his selflessness and his witty - albeit puerile – anecdotes, he was the one person – *notwithstanding the fact that he was the only person she knew in London* – she knew who would be able to take her mind off her frustration, contrasting starkly with what she had just experienced from *the Bishop* whose staid, exasperating personality had left her feeling somewhat disgruntled and dissatisfied.

'A little light relief would do me good right now', she thought to herself as she checked her hair in the mirror.

'...besides, I have made all this effort; somebody might as well take advantage of it', she mused as she took out her cell-phone once again and punched in Gary's number from the scrap of paper he had given her.

Gary arrived at the hotel thirty minutes later, trying desperately to disguise his self-satisfied grin, convinced as he was - given the hour - that this was a booty-call...and that finally, this time, he was going to get his chance with Madison.

He quickly made his way upstairs on the nod of the concierge and having found Madison's room half-way down the corridor on the third floor, he stopped in front of it for a moment to compose himself before knocking.

He still couldn't believe that this was actually happening and as he stood there awkwardly in front of her door, he had to take a couple of deep breaths and clear his throat twice, before knocking.

'This is sweet', he mumbled to himself, remembering *in extremis* to remove his cherished green and gold beanie as he heard the lock of the door click.

'Hi; it's me', he announced guardedly drawing back his shoulders and looking both nervous and eager at the same time as Madison's face appeared on the other side of the door.

She smiled, 'I know it's you Gary; I called you, remember'.

The young Aussie nodded silently, not wanting to do or say anything that might ruin his chances.

'I just need to slip into something more...comfortable', Madison signalled in rather clichéd fashion as she left Gary to close the door...and headed into the bathroom.

Gary concurred without comment, gesturing discreetly for her to go ahead...and then, once he had closed the door, he simply walked over to the bed and sat down quietly still wondering to himself if this was really happening.

Madison reappeared five minutes later, dressed in a pair of brown leather trousers and a comfy cashmere sweater so as not to appear overtly flirtatious or coquettish.

'I'm all yours, Gary', she declared playfully, forgetting herself momentarily and cruelly raising the young Aussie's hopes.

'I mean...I'm ready, I'm good to go', she corrected herself, instantly extinguishing those same hopes almost as quickly as they had been ignited.

Gary looked at her and immediately realised that this was not a *booty-call* after all.

'So, what are we doing here exactly?' he asked diplomatically, trying not to communicate his disappointment.

‘Well, you said that if ever I was in London and I wanted to go for a drink, then I should call you...so I called you...’, Madison explained bluntly as she headed for the door.

‘...For a drink?’ Gary confirmed looking a little downcast.

‘Yes...for a drink’, Madison reiterated as she turned to face him, her mind suddenly catching up with the young Aussie’s more fanciful ideas.

‘Okay then...no dramas’, Gary agreed, as he got up from the bed, his beaming smile from earlier having morphed slowly into a solemn look of acceptance.

Madison gazed at him from the door, understanding his disappointment and his frustration at not getting what he had come for... which coincidentally, seemed to mirror her own experience from earlier in the evening.

Being from New York, Madison knew all about the booty-call concept; about receiving a call late at night to go and join somebody in a hotel room... and she was well aware of how the current situation could be interpreted...

...but just as she had had to do earlier, Gary would have to do the same... and ‘suck it up’, over a nice cold beer...she thought to herself bombastically.

Gary joined her at the door, just as Madison finished her mental analysis of the situation...and without another word - although they did exchange a complicit glance – she quietly led the way out.

Downstairs, they quickly grabbed a cab...and having swallowed his pride on the ride down in the lift, Gary promptly offered to take Madison to his favourite bar where they could meet up with a group of his friends who were part of his regular crowd.

That wasn’t exactly what Madison had in mind - and initially she screwed her nose up at Gary’s impromptu suggestion - but then, seeing the crumpled look on his face...and secretly empathising with the fact she had already burst his balloon once that evening, she was suddenly struck by a case of guilty conscience and decided somewhat uncharacteristically to relent, agreeing to accompany him to the bar on the condition that she would leave whenever she saw fit.

Gary concurred again, whole-heartedly, and having informed the cabbie of their destination, he simply sat back in his seat, grinning like the cat that got the proverbial cream, while Madison - remembering the time-difference between New York and London – quietly took out her phone again and checked it once more for messages.

Fifteen minutes or so later, the taxi pulled up outside Gary's favourite haunt; a very colourful establishment named the Pickled Parrot situated right in the heart of Fulham.

Madison got out first while Gary paid the fare and as she stood there on the pavement, in the cooling night air, looking curiously at the brightly-painted property, the pouting New-Yorker immediately wondered what she had let herself in for.

The music from inside the bar was blaring out into the street and as Gary joined her, and ushered her inside, a guiding hand in the small of her back, the expression on Madison's face spoke reams about her hesitant disposition, after the contrasting opulence of Cliveden House and the Abbey, both of which she had left only a few hours earlier.

The bar was very, very busy and as they made their way through the crowd, looking hopefully left and right for a table to sit at, several of the boozy patrons recognised Gary and slapped him on the back with a welcoming word or a bawdy comment.

The young Aussie acknowledged each of them with a smile or a short greeting and as one of them pointed out a table that had just become available, he quickly guided Madison over to it and pulled out a chair for her, trying his best to treat her with as much gentlemanly propriety as he could in the rather cramped circumstances.

His friends were all over in the far corner of the bar playing darts, but having made fortuitous eye-contact with one of them as he was ushering Madison inside, Gary immediately confirmed his presence to the others with a booming 'Hey fellas', and a flamboyant wave of the hand...which each of them acknowledged in their own way, before returning to their game.

Gary then sat down next to Madison and a few minutes later - once the game they had been playing was over - his friends began sauntering over to join them, curious to meet his new acquaintance.

♗

The first person to come over was a rather stout, rotund figure grasping a mug of beer to his chest.

'Madison; this is Kev', Gary announced over the sound of the music; 'we call him the bed-swerver...'

Madison frowned, turned to look at Gary and then smiled, waiting for a more complete explanation; but despite her obvious bewilderment, none was forth-coming.

'That is Carl, the chubby-chaser...' Gary continued, pointing to the person following on behind Kev, seemingly oblivious to Madison's confusion...

'...this here; is Dave, my flatmate...' he then declared reaching over to slap palms with a geeky looking mature-student-type who just seemed to appear beside them at the table...

'...and over there, at the board, you have Katie and her brother George', Gary concluded cheerfully with a flourish.

'Fellas, this here is Madison; she is from New York', he then proclaimed proudly, pausing for the full dramatic effect...and the expected appreciation of his friends.

All at once, a chorus of hellos rang around the company to welcome Madison into their midst...but before she could respond to their greeting, the band - which had been taking a breather after a particularly raucous number - launched into yet another rip-roaring Irish classic drowning out any possibility of a verbal exchange.

Madison did try, but - realising that there was simply no way she could compete with the decibels that the band was producing - she could only shrug her shoulders and raise her hands in the air apologetically in recognition of their salute.

The introductions over, Carl immediately pulled up a chair and sat down; Kev remained standing just behind him, and because he was due to play next, Dave quickly disappeared again back to the dart-board area.

'So, what do you think of the place?' Gary asked succinctly turning to face Madison once again.

'Nice...if a little loud', she replied, putting a finger to each ear.

'Yeah; it used to be run by some Jamaican guy...hence the name...the Pickled Parrot...' Gary explained, '...and when the new owners bought it and transformed it into a typical Irish pub...they couldn't decide on a new name, so they just kept the old one'.

'Oh, I see', Madison responded, feigning interest.

'Yeah, I love it here...it reminds me of home', Gary added, trying to prolong the conversation; '...it's not the actual music itself I like, so much as the camaraderie and the sense of community that the music spreads throughout the pub; that's what I like...', he confirmed tenaciously.

Madison simply nodded...and prompted by his words, she glanced over to where the band was regaling the punters with a compilation of Celtic music - *not too dissimilar from that played by the Pogues* - although there was no way she could actually see them through the mass of human bodies that separated them.

Gary followed her gaze and when he noticed her scanning the bar and looking at the TV behind the counter - which was replaying some grey-hound races from earlier in the day - he immediately seized on the opportunity to reel off another of his childhood memories.

'That reminds me of home too', he announced with a hint of nostalgia in his voice, his eyes suddenly fixed on the TV too.

'Yeah, I used to go down to the races at Wentworth Park in Sydney with my dad', he explained briefly, realising all of a sudden that Madison probably wasn't interested.

'Did you?' she remarked, nodding politely at his rather obscure and unfamiliar references.

There was a lull in the conversation at that point as a fire-crack of applause sprang up in the crowd to welcome the band's next offering, but as that noise subsided, Gary tried to jump-start the stunted mood once again.

'Anyhow boys; my throat's as dry as a dingo's donger', he announced suddenly, lapsing into his native dialect for his friends benefit...and temporarily forgetting his erstwhile charm offensive on Madison.

'It's my shout, boys, so what'll it be? He confirmed, jumping to his feet and looking at his friends for some encouragement.

'I'll just have a glass of Chardonnay; if that's okay', Madison stated quietly as she readjusted her sitting position and her posture.

'Sure, no worries', Gary responded considerately; 'Carl...Kev; same again?' he enquired as he moved nimbly around the table and headed for the bar.

'Yeah; cheers *Gaz*', they both replied with raised glasses as Gary disappeared through the crowd, leaving Madison alone and feeling a little uncomfortable in the company of two hitherto complete strangers.

Carl saw an opening and immediately pulled his chair closer...

'It's nice to meet an American woman', he announced candidly trying to relax the mood and engage Madison in a conversation.

'Thank you', Madison responded politely though she was clearly on her guard.

Carl tried to follow up with another socially-acceptable...'Where did you say that you were you from?'...but before he could finish his question, Kev, who was now standing next to him, interrupted him.

'Yeah, that's true', the bigger guy interjected, '... it is nice to see an American woman...and you're definitely a *looker* if I do say so myself', he commented brashly.

'...however...' he added after a brief pause.

Madison cleared her throat, ready to unleash a suitable response to what she expected to be another insulting jibe.

'... there is one thing I've always wanted to know about America...', he blurted out tactlessly, with scant regard for social etiquette or for Madison's feminine sensibilities; 'I mean; what is it with you people over there, that men are called guys, and women call each other guys too?', he observed with reasoned logic.

'Is it a unisex society or something like that?' he queried, slurring his words a little.

The atmosphere around the table suddenly fell silent despite the noise from the band in the background.

Madison shook her head and then very diplomatically, reigning in her passive-aggressive nature, she began explaining to Kev and to the rest of the table as Gary arrived back with the drinks, how...

'...in the States we have what we call Positive Discrimination laws which state that you cannot discriminate against somebody for reasons of faith, colour or gender'; she declared with her own cool, calm logic.

'...so, you all call each other guys; in that way no-one feels discriminated against', Kev confirmed obnoxiously labouring the point with annoying exactitude.

'...guys are guys, women are guys; you are all guys, right?' he insisted... deliberately driving home his point and putting Madison on the spot.

'Yeah, even actresses are called actors over there'; George added, out of nowhere as he joined the table with Dave and Katie.

'That's crap;' Kev cut in, 'and I'll tell you why', he insisted taking over the conversation.

'...because at 'the Emmys'...and even at 'the Oscars'...they still hand out awards to the best lead actress...and the best supporting actress...so clearly the idea that women are 'actors', he stated emphatically, emphasising the 'ors'... 'is bullshit...' he asserted, his words suddenly drowned out by the music.

Madison took a deep breath and felt the hair stand up on the back of her neck; she had already had her fill of Yankee-bashing from *the Bishop* and after her evening's disappointment she was ready to explode...

However; rather than cause a scene and embarrass Gary in front of his friends, she decided with commendable restraint, given her frame of mind - to let it go this time, and allow this Kev character some leniency because of his inebriated state.

'Don't listen to Kev', Gary said, nudging her with his arm and defusing the situation somewhat; '...he's a lawyer and a nice guy really but he can be a sanctimonious bastard sometimes, usually when he has had a drink; although I have to say...', he added, defending his mate, '...that maybe he's not entirely wrong'.

Madison turned and looked at Gary rather circumspect as he continued.

'I mean; surely the fact that you are not allowed to differentiate between the sexes is political correctness gone mad...don't you think? I mean... when you cannot even call a woman, a woman, for fear of highlighting her feminine traits...that's going too far...isn't it?' Gary suggested with his own logical analysis.

'You mean you can't call a woman a woman over there?' asked Carl quizzically, a little lost.

'Nah mate', Kev confirmed as he swilled down the rest of his pint; 'she could have you up in court for sexual harassment for that. That's what they do over there. If you look at a woman; I'm sorry, I mean a '*guy*', the wrong way over there; they can take you to court. It's the ultimate victory for the feminists, that nobody can call them women...in case it's misconstrued as something pejorative and meaning less than equal...' he chimed triumphantly.

'Where we come from, we don't really adhere to the gender surrender philosophy of new-age man' George explained rather facetiously, leaning in towards Madison to make himself heard; '...all that metro-sexual nonsense...', he added, shaking his head disapprovingly.

'...and don't forget the 'we are pregnant' concept', Kev remarked, raising his arms and two fingers on each hand to punctuate his comment, before going off to take his turn at the dart-board.

'...WE are pregnant', he bawled out over the music. '...how pathetic is that?'

The brutality of Kev's criticism – which was clearly over the top - left everybody at the table feeling a little perplexed...but before anybody could do or say anything, Kev was back, having forgotten his beer-glass.

He emptied the dregs from the glass and then fixed Madison once again.

'...Don't your guys...the male ones I mean, have any balls?' he suddenly insisted with an instantly recognizable hand-gesture; '...or have they all been so emasculated by today's feminine society that they daren't even explain the reality of life to their female guys', he questioned, continuing his unflattering and argumentative tirade.

Madison felt a little disabused by Kev's unprovoked antagonism but wisely, she didn't respond, not wanting to give the guy the satisfaction of dignifying his remark with a reply; although, her eyes did narrow considerably as her exasperation started to show.

'Okay fellas; that's enough...give her a break Kev...and stop your whinging', Gary suddenly advocated, raising his tone.

'This is all very inconsiderate...and in poor taste. We came in here...' he motioned towards Madison and himself, '...for a quiet drink; not to criticise and discuss American culture'.

'I apologise for my friends,' he whispered into Madison's ear, with a wink in his eye and a cheeky grin on his face - hoping desperately to keep his options open.

It was an awkward moment...but as luck would have it the music started up again at that point, drowning out any further exchanges and reducing Kev to an unapologetic shrug before he turned and walked away with another dismissive hand-gesture.

Madison meanwhile, sat there poker-faced and seething.

Dave and Katie got up at that point and went over to join Kev - to take their turns at the dartboard - and as they did so, a couple more girls arrived to join in with the game.

'I don't know what it is, but I've always got tight pants when she's around', Dave suddenly remarked to Kev as he pulled his darts from the board and glanced in the direction of the more curvaceous of the two new girls.

Katie, who was standing right next to Dave, overheard his comment and immediately gave him a sharp dig in the ribs for his trouble, coupling it with a disapproving stare, as she stood up in defence of the sisterhood against these disrespectful and discourteous males.

Carl then walked past them on his way to the toilets…and spying the same young lady, he whispered into Dave's ear; 'blue-balls?'

Dave nodded his head apologetically, and they both grinned - Carl winking naughtily at Katie's scowl - as he disappeared through the door leading to the men's' toilets.

The band finished their set a few minutes later and across the bar - once the rapturous applause for the band's performance had died down - several members of a rugby team on a stag-night picked up where the band had left off, repeating the chorus of their last song over and over and over;

'**...**in heaven there is no beer,
...that's why we drink it here,
...and when we're gone from here,
...our friends will be drinking all the beer; Hey!

(Repeat)
...in heaven there is no beer...'...etc.

They were drumming their hands on the tables and singing along karaoke-style, but before they got too carried away, the barman quietly dimmed the lights - ever so slightly - and put on a selection a seventies music, which got as loud a cheer as the band had received previously.

The atmosphere in the bar changed almost instantly, from one of raucous conviviality to one with a more muted tone...and within no time at all everybody's mood had softened again as the nostalgic melodies of the past began to work their well-worn magic.

However, ten minutes or so later, just as things had begun to settle down, a medley of classic Roxy Music songs suddenly had the crowd back on its feet again, singing along unreservedly with the group's lead-singer Bryan Ferry, as he belted out his mega-hits in his own, distinctive and inimitable style.

People sat at the adjoining tables immediately joined in, as did Gary and Carl...and as the strobe lighting in the bar's ceiling kicked in - transforming the mood further - others began dancing with their hands in the air while those who could not move between the tightly-packed tables simply bopped and boogied where they stood, clutching their glasses of happy-juice carefully to their upper bodies in a massive communion of ecstatic delight; even Madison - who was still secretly fuming with Kev - found herself getting caught up with the adrenaline rush, her foot tapping under the table and her body swaying discreetly in time to the music.

Everybody seemed to be having a whale of a time and then suddenly when one particular song, '*This is Tomorrow*' came blasting over the sound-system a strange phenomenon seemed to take place.

The song began as any other, but half-way through it, after an amazing saxophone solo the barman / DJ deliberately interrupted the tune and held it...

For a moment, the whole crowd seemed to freeze and hold its collective breath, as if suspended in time, waiting for the lyric to start up again...

The silence was deafening...but then, having held up the beat for a good three seconds, the barman / DJ counted it back in, two...three... thereby allowing everybody to exhale again as Ferry pounded out the next line; '*truckin' by the railroad station, I'm on the road again...*'.

It was a surreal moment, the purest instant of collective silence and mass discipline that Madison had ever witnessed...and as she sat there, surrounded by the eclectic mix that made up the British population, she could only marvel at the power of music...and how easily it could connect and unite people, even tempting the traditionally repressed Brits out of their legendary reserve.

The bar calmed down again after that amazing crescendo of energy and having exhausted themselves singing and dancing, most of Gary's friends came back to the table for a moment's respite; though stalwarts Kev and Dave preferred to stay at the oche to continue playing darts.

The chatting and joking resumed in earnest and as the alcohol began to play its part in bringing down the barriers that divided them - Madison slowly began to mellow and enjoy the light-hearted, tongue in cheek banter of Gary's friends, joining in when she felt she could, and charming all those in earshot with her New York wit, when she was allowed the ego-massage of centre stage.

The guys even took it upon themselves to flatter her on the odd occasion...complimenting her on both her steely nature...and her sense of humour - and while Madison knew instinctively that they were only doing this to make up for the earlier attacks that their friend Kev had inflicted on her and her metro-sexual countrymen - she accepted the compliments with good grace.

The mood around the table morphed into one of relaxed camaraderie and as Katie disappeared to the ladies-room Madison decided to use her absence – as the only other female - to wind-up the guys, to antagonise them and get some pay-back for her earlier verbal drubbing.

'Tell me guys', she asked candidly … 'and please don't take this the wrong way...but I've heard it said around New York that people over here in England...people involved in a certain lifestyle...', she put up air-quotes at this point, '...engage in what qualifies as...reprehensible activities (*more air-quotes*) after-hours in pubs like this;...is that true?', she enquired bluntly, deliberately teasing the guys who were all instantly rocked back in their seats by her unexpected and controversial disclosure.

'Well...is it true...?' Madison asked again in a loud whisper, as she looked around the table at each of the stunned male faces...revelling in her moment of sweet revenge.

Still nobody spoke but unable to hide their innate curiosity for anything remotely related to '*the naughty or the freaky*' – as they called it – the guys were suddenly all ears again, hoping to learn more of what Madison apparently knew...and they did not.

Gary leaned forward and looked directly at Carl, hoping that - being English - he might know something about these strange goings-on.

'Well Carl, you're from this neck of the woods...what are you hiding from us?' he asked quietly, his tone playfully menacing.

Carl's jaw dropped in shock and unable to speak he could only shake his head, shift uncomfortably in his seat and look sheepishly to his left at George for some kind of moral support or assistance...

...but George couldn't offer anything either and he just shrugged his shoulders and pasted a vacant 'don't look at me' expression on his face trying desperately to escape any further scrutiny.

So; all heads then turned back to Gary, but he simply imitated George's apologetic shrug, picked up his beer and sat back casually, waiting patiently for somebody else to step up to the plate for once in order to break the enduring silence.

The stalemate lasted a good twenty seconds...but then, unable to contain her impudent joy any longer, Madison threw her head back and burst out laughing.

'I'm sorry guys'; she spluttered with a facetious grin, her mocking tone scarcely masking her hidden delight, 'I'm just messing with you'.

'I just wanted to see your reactions...and I have to say...' she added with a click of her fingers; '...that I have never in my life seen a group of guys turn so instantaneously into a pack of hungry, salivating wolves'.

Carl looked at George and both smiled awkwardly to hide their embarrassed male blushes but as Madison turned to Gary to get his reaction - savouring her triumph with more than a hint of self-satisfaction in her eyes - cries of 'skull, skull, skull' suddenly rang out across the bar, saving him from her forensic stare.

Everybody immediately turned to watch...and assuming that she would not be familiar with what was going on; Gary quickly took it upon himself to explain to Madison that 'skull' was an Australian term for knocking back a drink in one.

On the other side of the bar, Dave who had apparently just lost the last game of darts - was standing in the middle of a circle of people, beer dripping copiously down his chin as he tried to engulf his pint in one continued action.

The packed gallery was cheering noisily, waiting for him to give up...

or worse...throw up...but having done this before on numerous occasions (*each time he lost in fact)* Dave easily managed to consume the pint of Irish nectar and put the empty glass upside-down on his head (*thereby signalling the successful completion of his task*) without too much trouble...although the shirt he was wearing was a mess, having mopped up the overflowing spillage.

It was getting pretty late at that stage...so once everybody had finished ribbing Dave and his party-trick, Katie and George got up and announced that they were going to *bail-out*, which they did almost immediately to a chorus of friendly jeers.

This signalled the beginning of the end for the group of friends, as after their departure, the evening quickly wound down...and one by one the others began to drift away as the bar started to clear out.

Gary and Madison said their goodbyes too, and as they walked back to the taxi rank a little worse for wear - Gary draping his arm loosely around her shoulders in a protective embrace – Madison suddenly realised that, just as he had done in the hotel that night, Gary had taken care of her; he had warned off his friends when they had started attacking her and he had been both considerate and funny during the evening, which had cheered her up no end after her earlier disappointment with *the Bishop* at the Abbey.

Thirty minutes or so later, having had to wait around a while for a taxi, Madison and Gary were back in the warmth of her hotel room.

They were cold and hungry…and once she had sorted herself out, checked her phone and popped to the bathroom, Madison suggested to Gary that she should ring down to reception to ask the night-porter if he could maybe organise some hot coffee for them...and a sandwich.

'It's a bit late for that, don't you think?' Gary observed wistfully, discreetly eyeing the bed.

'No it's not; it's the least I can do for messing up your evening', Madison countered, her lips slowly curling upward into a genuine smile as she reached for the phone.

'Okay then, a *sanger* it is', Gary agreed with that genial air of self-deprecation that defined him, his mind - awash with alternative ideas - not picking up on Madison's attempted sarcasm, as he leaned casually against the desk, still hoping to end the evening on a high.

She picked up the phone and twenty minutes or so later – even though it was nearly three o'clock in the morning - one of the hotel's immaculately groomed employees duly arrived at the door with a plateful of freshly-made egg-sandwiches and a pot of steaming hot coffee which, when he was invited in, he dutifully set down with the utmost professionalism and discretion on the desk beside Gary.

Both Madison and Gary thanked the young man for his service and while she signed the docket - adding a reasonably generous tip to the charge to avoid any awkward explanations - Gary played host and began serving up the coffee.

It was another surreal moment - *them acting almost like an old, married couple* - and as soon as the young man was gone - and she had carefully locked the door behind him New York-style - Madison seemed to subliminally reinforce that age-old cliché - and underline the apparent and yet unspoken complicity that now seemed to exist between her and Gary - as she quickly made herself comfortable on the bed and began sharing out the sandwiches, just as Gary himself was making his way over with the cups of coffee which he carefully set down on the bedside table, before jumping onto the bed beside her, grabbing a sandwich as he did so.

♗

A charged silence descended on the room at that point and as they both tucked in - strangely enjoying the somewhat-incongruous late-night snack - they each got lost in their own head-space;

...Madison sat upright against the head of the bed, trying not to smile as she relived her evening and weighed up her options, wondering casually what it would be like to spend the night with Gary...

...and Gary - laying untidily across the bed at her feet – searching unwittingly for any excuse he could, to distract her from those very-same secret musings in order to get himself to first base.

A few minutes went by without either of them speaking, but then just as Gary polished off his second sandwich, the calm that had settled over the room was brutally ripped apart when the latter noticed Madison reaching awkwardly for one of the cups he had put down on the bed-side table just behind her elbow.

'Holy Dooley' he cried out with a note of genuine concern in his voice 'You need to be careful; that coffee is steaming...'

Surprised by his alarmed tone, Madison immediately checked her movement and recoiled slightly, her lips parting in a half-smile.

'Holy Dooley...? ', she teased with a snigger, repeating Gary's vanilla expletive; '... are you serious?'

'What; ...would you prefer something a little more colourful?' Gary protested quietly, defending his choice of phrase.

Madison paused in reflection. 'My my; are you always this thoughtful and considerate?' she asked nonchalantly, the veiled ambivalence in her voice not lost on the young Aussie.

'I try', Gary conceded with a renewed smile as he waited patiently to see what would happen next...

Nothing did, but the jocular interlude had relaxed the mood a touch more and while Madison was busy plumping up a pillow to put behind her back for more support, Gary decided to take the initiative.

'Another sanger...?' he proposed politely, offering Madison the plate.

'Nah, I'm done', Madison declined with a small gesture of the hand as she reached again for her coffee.

'Smooth', Gary murmured as he helped himself to another bite, his thoughts still very much focussed on trying to work out his chances of 'doing the naughty' with his attractive but as yet unresponsive snack-buddy.

Madison leaned back on the pillow, making herself comfortable again and while Gary finished off the last of the late-night snack, she quietly cleared her throat and began debating in her own mind what she wanted to happen next.

She was feeling a little fatigued and a little intoxicated from the alcohol she had consumed during the evening, both at the restaurant and at the bar, but as she took her first sip of coffee - being careful not to burn her mouth after Gary's prescient warning - she made a brave attempt to sort out her jumbled thoughts...and process the conflicting emotions which were running amok in her brain.

The Bishop snubbing her earlier in the evening had left her feeling rejected, disgruntled and somewhat unappreciated. The man had been rude and obnoxious...in her eyes, and despite the tension and the frustration that had built up during the evening - a frustration she could still feel in her restless limbs - she quickly came to the conclusion that, the exasperating, abbey-dwelling recluse had blown his chance...and that he no longer deserved to enjoy the indulgences that she had been prepared to lavish on him...

Gary got up at this point, distracting Madison from her deliberation and as her eyes followed him around the room, in silence, it suddenly dawned on her - for the very first time - that Gary was quite a hunk...not her type by any stretch of the imagination...but quite a hunk nevertheless...

That realisation surprised her somewhat and as he stopped right beside her to pick up his cup from the bed-side table, his shirt half-pulled out of his jeans and his hair in its usual unruffled state, she could not help but inhale the sweet mixture of manly sweat and beer that emanated from his person.

The whiff went directly into her brain, subconsciously tickling her senses and as Gary returned to his seat at the foot of her bed, his cup clasped tightly between his strong, masculine hands, Madison could not help but scrutinise the young Aussie's profile for a few brief moments before discreetly averting her eyes again, and focussing wistfully on the patterned bed-spread beside her, so as not to draw his attention.

The moment passed without comment and having folded her legs into a more comfortable position beneath her and taken yet another sip of coffee, Madison returned to her reflection.

The Bishop - despite all his qualities - had indeed disappointed her...and her frustration as she sat there mulling over the images of her last moments at the Abbey - which were subconsciously feeding her disenchantment - was real, very real.

How could he just blow me off like that, she kept thinking to herself as her mind replayed the scene over and over...

…and then - as if to drive home her disillusion - as she shifted her position once again, *the Bishop's* face suddenly appeared in front of her eyes, teasing her with his maddeningly impossible movie-star looks, his wonderfully chiselled jaw and his intense if somewhat disquieting smile.

It was almost as if he was taunting her...and the recollection of what she had missed out on earlier in the evening - through no fault of her own that she was aware of - immediately twisted her face into a disgruntled frown; a frown which was only alleviated a minute or so later when her focus turned back to Gary who was still sat there patiently biding his time at the foot of her bed.

Of course, there was no comparison between the two; *the Bishop* in her head was a selfish egotist who had taunted her all evening and left her feeling embarrassed and discontented, while Gary here - though he didn't have *the Bishop's* personality or good looks - had selflessly changed his plans and stepped up to the plate when she had called – even if his motives were not particularly gallant – and he had done so without question and without rancour.

He had also taken her under his wing to some extent while introducing her to his friends – something she was certain *the Bishop* would never have done – and had both defended and protected her with real altruism on a couple of occasions already.

The bizarre juxtaposition of emotions was making Madison's head spin but these last thoughts brought a little smile to her lips and as she wrapped up her increasingly fuzzy rationale, she decided that it was time to relieve the ambient tension and shore up her self-esteem...and that Gary because of his proven generosity of spirit would be - just for the evening - her chosen instrument of release.

Now this probably wasn't the most moral reasoning as to why she should succumb to Gary's obvious expectations as he sat there waiting patiently, but Madison was no longer thinking straight; her hormonal radar was going haywire and with her inhibitions reduced if not negated completely by the alcohol she had consumed during the evening, she felt that this was as good a reason as any to give in to Gary's wishes; especially as she hadn't seen any *action* in a while.

♝

Gary of course was blissfully unaware of Madison's ethical turmoil but even as the level of coffee in his cup decreased and his window of opportunity slowly disappeared it was clear in his body language that he still had every intention of somehow burrowing in beside Madison before the night was through.

♝

At this point, Madison shifted her position once again - being careful not to spill what was left in her cup...and having finished her coffee with one last swallow she put the cup down on the bedside-table and decided it was time to make her move.

'Enough talking; get over here...' she suddenly announced, her nostrils flaring as she patted the mattress next to her.

Gary looked around and hesitated momentarily, not sure that he had heard correctly...but before he could ask her to repeat what she had said, Madison pounced on him, like a tigress, forcing him onto his back in one swift movement.

'You are okay with this...right?' she asked with a facetious grin and a sarcastic chuckle as she straddled him assertively, pinning him to the bed.

'Hey; fortune favours the brave is what I say', Gary replied, still disbelieving that this was actually happening as he blindly placed his cup on the floor beside him and reached up to grab his assailant by the hips.

Madison's eyes flashed with a hint of unquenched desire and without another word she began ripping open Gary's shirt, subconsciously taking out her pent up frustration on her unsuspecting but willing victim.

Time stood still for a moment but having exposed Gary's rather impressive and deceptively muscular torso Madison quickly got up off the bed, kicking off her shoes as she did so.

She strode over to the wall and within seconds - having hastily turned the light-switch down to a lower setting - she had slipped out of her outer clothes, pulled back the covers and gotten into the bed.

Gary was still a little bewildered by this sudden change in Madison's behaviour but realising that this was no time for him to be asking questions, he quickly followed her lead, getting up and throwing off his own clothes with alacrity as he raced to join her under the covers - a self-satisfied smirk spreading rapidly across his face - before she changed her mind.

They both stared at each other for a moment from opposite sides of the king-sized bed – which was a little awkward - but then taking the lead, Gary reached out a hand and any remaining hesitation was quickly overcome.

He moved closer and kissed her tentatively...on the cheek…Madison reciprocating graciously with a gentle peck to his upper-lip.

The next kiss was a lot more passionate...and full of promise...but unfortunately, after all the time that they had spent working up to this moment, the resulting clinch was an unmitigated disaster; done and dusted within ten minutes...or so, and in the most unimaginative belly to belly, missionary position.

Gary tried to make it last longer - desperate as he was to make a good impression on Madison - but despite her ego-stroking encouragements, the whole experience was a catastrophe, a fiasco; there were no sparks between them, no chemistry and ultimately no real tension release either...and as she looked on in frustration as Gary rolled over and discreetly tucked his little soldier back into the barracks, Madison immediately began to regret what she had done.

She rolled over onto her side of the bed too, hoping that she would wake up in the morning to find out that this was all just a dream, but the frustration and the embarrassment she was feeling made her whole body restless...and despite the late hour, the alcohol and the intimate interlude, she just could not switch off her brain.

She tossed and turned for quite some time but eventually, unable to find that elusive sleep-cycle Madison just lay there on her back, in the late-night calm, reviewing everything that had happened to her since her arrival in England, trying to file it all into some kind of logical order.

So much had happened since she had landed at Heathrow only a week or so earlier - but in spite of the fact that Gary was asleep on the pillow beside her, the images that were uppermost in her mind were those of *the Bishop*, his home and his enticingly intriguing swinging bed.

Next morning, as they shared the copious breakfast for one - which for obvious reasons of convenience and discretion Madison had had delivered to the room – both parties avoided talking about their less than memorable coupling of the night before...

Indeed, Madison couldn't help but grimace at the thought of what she had done.

...and instead, as they tucked into the delicious French pastries and hot, steaming coffee, Gary - hoping to avoid any awkward silences - deliberately monopolised the conversation, commenting whimsically on his crazy friends' nicknames from the night before…and then telling Madison all about how much he was missing his home in Sydney.

Madison herself was not really in a very sociable or forgiving mood, but with a forced smile on her face, she listened nevertheless to Gary's infectious, almost endearing monologue about his home, his family and his country...and eventually, between sips of revitalising coffee and mouthfuls of tasty, freshly-baked pastry she slowly began to warm up and sympathise with his situation as she too was missing her home of New York and couldn't wait to get back there.

'What is it that you miss most?' she suddenly asked out of the blue, her journalistic instinct to find out more detail unexpectedly springing into life.

'Well', Gary pondered as he swallowed half a croissant; 'In the G.O.D.'s, I used to enjoy sitting at the café Rossini on Circular Quay between eight and nine in the morning...

‘Circular Quay…?’ Madison interrupted; ‘Isn’t that the place where the ferries arrive in Sydney?’

‘Yeah, that’s right’, Gary confirmed. ‘I always found it rather fascinating to sit there with a freshly served latte and watch the ferries as they deposited wave after wave of suits and corporate uniforms onto the busy wharves of Sydney harbour’.

‘It reminded me of the boats of yesteryear which used to arrive at those same docking points in the harbour, laden with droves of frightened cattle...or sheep’

‘... and just like those poor, startled beasts of the day - once they were on dry land again and had found their feet - all those people would then disperse in much the same way...in all different directions...’

‘...though I have to say...the suits of today were usually glancing nervously at their watches and mobile phones as they made their way into the town and not just looking for some fresh grazing...’

Madison cracked a smile. ‘That sounds very interesting, almost cathartic’, she confided as she ripped open another croissant and took a sip of orange juice, realising somewhat belatedly that there was actually more to Gary - behind the self-deprecating mask that he chose to show to the world – than she had first thought...despite his short-comings in the bedroom.

‘Yeah, I used to really enjoy that’, Gary admitted pensively.

CHAPTER EIGHT

(Part Two)

After breakfast, Madison decided that she was going to do some last-minute shopping…and to show Gary that she harboured no ill-feelings towards him, she invited him to join her, secretly hoping that like most men, he wouldn't be interested in doing so...

...but surprisingly, that wasn't the case.

Madison had underestimated the degree to which Gary had been smitten by her, and despite his slightly dishevelled appearance, he agreed to join her, feeling somewhat compelled to do so in his own mind, as if their brief coupling had somehow imposed a certain obligation on him.

However, playing the faithful companion would prove to be the wrong move for Gary, because a while later, as Madison wandered through the aisles of yet another bustling department store still looking for more gifts and souvenirs for her friends back home, it was all he could do, to shuffle along aimlessly behind her, looking totally bored and nonplussed, like any other man accompanying a woman on a shopping trip.

He tried to show a little interest in what she was doing but after a few hours, he was clearly losing the will to live - metaphorically speaking - and so, in an effort to revive his flagging morale, he came up with an excuse to bail out; informing Madison that shopping wasn't really his *bowl of rice* and that anyhow, he needed to get home to take care of the three S's and change his gear as he was going 'go-karting' later that afternoon.

Madison didn't hear him at first; she was too busy admiring the beautiful, crystal glassware that she had just happened upon; but after he repeated his pretext a little louder - and with a little more gusto - she did stop what she was doing to throw him a cursory glance.

'If you need to go Gary...then go', she announced impassively, fixing him momentarily before turning her attention back to the glass ornament she was holding in her hand, her brain clearly otherwise engaged converting the price of the object in her hand into US dollars.

'I'm not holding you prisoner here', she continued with a wry smile, putting the first ornament down and picking up a second, just as an elderly couple stopped opposite them to look at the pottery displayed on an adjoining shelf.

She didn't dare say it but Madison was somewhat relieved to hear that Gary had other things to do, as he was clearly slowing her down in her quest.

Gary was disappointed by her apparent indifference and the ease with which Madison was more or less dismissing him, but at the same time, knowing that she was flying out the next day, he felt a little awkward and uneasy at leaving her in this way - without any kind of closure on their brief encounter the night before.

He personally, would have preferred a more harmonious farewell, with a few words of mutual encouragement from either side for a happy and prosperous life, but unfortunately the proximity of the elderly couple - who seemed to be deliberately hovering there while they discussed the merits of a two-handled soup-bowl - rendered any private discussion impossible, and so he was left with no real option other than to simply wave goodbye, turn tail and begin his rather delayed walk of shame.

'I'll see you around then...' he mumbled miserably to the back of Madison's head as she continued to rummage through yet another rack of souvenirs; apparently oblivious to his words which were instantly gobbled up by the hustle and bustle of the store.

It was quite a poignant moment and as he turned away, scratching his head in disappointment, Gary felt almost ashamed, as if he was somehow abandoning her, like so many men do after the fact.

Madison sensed his hesitation and as she glanced over her shoulder to watch him go, she immediately felt the guilt-charged stares of the elderly couple standing opposite her burning into her cheek.

It made her feel a little uncomfortable but unperturbed by their unspoken disapproval of her ways, she promptly stared right back at them... and with interest, swallowing back – *in extremis* - the urge to tell then to keep their noses out of her business.

However, after a brief pause, suddenly regretting her rather flippant, passive-aggressive attitude...and guilted-almost into a reaction by the demeanour of the old British couple, Madison unexpectedly had second thoughts.

She put down the picture-frame she was holding, and whirling around in an anti-clockwise direction to avoid any direct eye-contact with the elderly couple she calmly puffed out her chest and began striding after Gary, trying urgently to catch up with him before he got swallowed up by the milling crowd.

'Hey Gary, wait up, I've changed my mind; ...I've had enough of this too', she announced with an impudent smile, putting a restraining hand on his shoulder to slow him down and catch his eye.

Gary stopped in his tracks, apologising immediately to a group of people whose passage he had blocked.

'So; what do you say...would you mind if I tagged along...to see where you live?' Madison enquired with another inscrutable smile, her mind racing, thinking about her article and any background info she might be able to gather on Gary, just as she had done with *the Bishop.*

Gary shrugged his shoulders in silence.

'Sticky beak syndrome is it?' he replied glibly, subtly manifesting his mood.

'Sticky beak syndrome...?' Madison retorted, her brow creasing quizzically.

'It means...never mind...' Gary remarked after a brief pause, his mood lifting visibly '...but I do have to warn you...' he continued in a more apologetic tone, '...that it probably won't be very pretty...'

'Pretty...'? Madison frowned.

'Yeah; neither I nor my flat-mate Dave is the tidiest of people'. Gary explained, almost in jest.

Madison's face screwed up instantly at the thought of two young men living together in 'unsupervised squalor', but not one to be easily deterred, she paid for her shopping and without further ado, the two '*amigos*' headed for the exit.

Outside, Gary suggested that they take the Tube as Central London was completely grid-locked with traffic – *another first for Madison who only ever travelled by taxi in New York* - and only twenty or so minutes later, there they were, standing in front of the tiny two-bedroom flat that Gary shared with his mate Dave.

♗

Gary took out his keys but before he opened the door he pressed the doorbell a couple of times, to warn Dave that he was coming - just in case.

The sound of the doorbell was rather shrill but vaguely familiar.

'Where have I heard that sound before?' Madison piped up curiously, while brushing aside a stray wisp of hair that had been blown across her face by the wind.

'Oh, that's Dave's idea', Gary explained, 'he rigged it up a couple of weeks ago... he's a bit of a whizz with the old electronics', he confirmed, pressing the button again.

'Do you recognise it?' Gary asked, curious to find out the extent of Madison's musical knowledge.

'I think I might have heard it before but I can't quite place it', she admitted, humouring him politely though in reality she had no idea.

'It's a slightly modified version of the sax riff from '*Who can it be now*' by Men at Work...they're an Aussie band', Gary explained with a cheesy smile as he pushed the door open and stepped inside.

'That's original', Madison agreed, as she took a deep breath and followed Gary inside, measuring her steps carefully as she balanced unsteadily on her designer heels.

'Yeah, I'm thinking of putting it on my phone too...as my ring-tone', Gary remarked, his voice trailing off as he led the way through the tiny hallway and into the main living-area.

♗

Dave, Gary's flat-mate wasn't at home but the acrid smell of stale alcohol and cold pizza, which had been trapped in the flat all day, immediately rushed towards them, prompting Madison to screw up her nose and take a step back.

'Dave must have had some friends over last night', Gary explained apologetically; as he rushed over to crack open a couple of windows leaving Madison by the door looking both aloof and aghast at the same time.

'...So; what do you think of Casa Mio?' he enquired breezily, arms outstretched biblically, as he turned again to face Madison who was still stood quietly in the doorway, trying to focus her thoughts, while her eyes - unaccustomed to such untidiness - scanned almost reluctantly around the room, noting the discoloured cream doors and the hideous seventies wallpaper.

'Well, it's certainly not the Plaza', she replied dispassionately trying to conjure up a believable response as she glanced around at the discarded beer bottles and soft-drink cans that littered the room, '...but I suppose it does have a certain...*lived-in* appeal', she added with sarcastic restraint, after a brief pause.

'...and this...this is the lair', Gary continued with a sweeping gesture – *seemingly oblivious to the mess as he walked across to a door on the other side of the room, narrowly avoiding a half-eaten pizza that had been carelessly dropped on the floor and left* - feeling it incumbent upon him – as *the Bishop* had - to show his guest around.

♗

Unsurprisingly, Madison was not impressed. Indeed, she felt a little awkward - and with her enthusiasm to see more, clearly on the wane - she held her ground for a moment, biting her lip in thought, while she surveyed the room again and decided whether it was worth continuing.

The mess aside, the small living-room was dominated by a huge flat-screen TV, a couple of tired-looking leather sofas placed in a v-formation in front of it and a strange triangular-shaped coffee-table, which she guessed was made of glass but couldn't be sure as it was almost completely obscured by beer-cans, gaming magazines and dirty plates.

'Hello...' Gary suddenly insisted in a stronger tone, interrupting

Madison's visual inventory of his home with a wave and another gesture towards the door to his room which he had just pushed open.

'You wanted to see where I live; this is where I live', he announced cheerfully.

Again, Madison hesitated, taking the time to clear her throat, before speaking.

'Look Gary, I don't wish to offend you in any way but I think I've seen enough', she suddenly blurted out, her mind regretting increasingly her behaviour the previous evening.

Gary's face fell and his shoulders dropped...but then feeling compelled to follow through on her request - as it was indeed she who had asked to see where he lived - Madison grudgingly relented in her stance and stepped forward into the centre of the room, squeezing herself carefully between the two worn-out old sofas.

However, that was as far as she got before she stopped in her tracks once again, taken aback as she was by the sight of what had suddenly caught her eye as she glanced away to her right.

'What the hell is all that?' she cried out in disgust, waving an outstretched arm in the direction of a small dining-table in the corner of the room which was piled high with more dirty plates and other kitchen utensils, together with an accumulation of take-away packaging from a variety of fast-food outlets.

Gary grimaced painfully, on seeing her reaction.

'It doesn't usually look as bad as that', he explained with his usual laid-back attitude, trying hard to save his credibility while shrugging his shoulders apologetically to convey his growing embarrassment.

Madison cringed visibly as their eyes met across the room...and while she took a moment to reconsider her position, unable to feign any kind of socially-acceptable indifference, she lowered her gaze cautiously to the floor to check where she was standing – just in case.

Gary saw her hesitate, and thinking on his feet, he quickly repeated his summons...beckoning Madison forward once again.

'Come on Mad..., nearly there', he teased, trying cleverly to brush aside her obvious displeasure...and divert her attention away from the sorry state of his humble abode.

His comment immediately re-focussed Madison's concentration.

'I've told you before Gary; its Madison...not Mad...not Maddy...just Madison', she responded with a hint of petulance, not realising that she had taken the bait.

'Yeah; sorry about that', Gary confessed, acknowledging her reprimand with a sly smile and another gesture towards his door.

Another brief pause followed, but then as the penny dropped in Madison's outraged mind, she could not help but roll her eyes and shake her head in disbelief at Gary's smart ruse.

'You did that on purpose, didn't you?' she suddenly affirmed through tight lips, secretly disappointed that she had been outwitted by Gary's juvenile ploy.

Gary's face morphed into one of caricatured shock but just as he was about to protest his innocence, and deny any ulterior motive or premeditated wrongdoing on his part with one of his myriad of *okker* expressions, Madison simply shrugged her shoulders in a gesture of resigned compliance, and stepped, or rather tip-toed back around the sofa, deciding ultimately in her own mind to indulge her host in his courteous efforts, but only until she could think of an excuse to get the hell out of there, which she hoped would be sooner rather than later.

Her path around the sofa led her past the tiny adjoining kitchen, and despite Gary's hurrying insistence, Madison took advantage of the fact that the door was slightly ajar to stop to take a peek inside. It was only the briefest of peeks but it was long enough for her to see the leaking-tap and the stained sink stacked with yet more unwashed crockery.

The sight made her screw up her nose once again...and she frowned noticeably as she turned away, ironically regretting her over-active curiosity, but as she joined Gary at his door - having decided judiciously to avoid the bathroom which stood adjacent to the kitchen with its faded ceramic door-plaque, she did her best to disguise her consternation and appear unruffled.

'There you go', Gary announced tongue-in-cheek, pushing his bedroom-door back on its hinges, seemingly oblivious to Madison's moral discomfort; '...my own personal Kirribilli'.

‘Your own...Kirri...billi?’ Madison questioned, looking the young Aussie directly in the eye.

‘Yeah, Kirribilli’, Gary repeated, ‘it’s the official residence of the PM in Sydney’.

Madison looked at him again, her patronising eyes still agog from what she had already seen...and as she held her breath and shuffled across the threshold of Gary’s personal domain, she was already dreading what she was about to discover on the other side of the door.

‘Okay then...’ she mumbled to herself as she stepped inside; ‘...let’s get this over with’.

The room was in semi-darkness, mainly because the curtains hadn’t been opened properly; a fact which made Madison a little jittery, but when Gary followed her inside, made his way over to the window and pulled the curtains back - as they should be - allowing a swathe of natural light to flood into the room, she was both reassured and pleasantly surprised - contrary to her apocalyptic expectations - to see that his room was a lot more ordered than the rest of the apartment.

It was quite small and unassuming, and its sparseness didn’t really reflect Gary’s fulsome personality, but considering what she had witnessed elsewhere in the flat, Madison found Gary’s room remarkably tidy.

The un-made bed did draw an over-the-shoulder look of scorn from the hyper-critical New Yorker, but what really caught her eye were the full-sized film posters that dominated two of the walls.

The first one, ‘The Natural’; one of Robert Redford’s most successful films (it won four academy awards) faced his bed on the left-hand wall while the second, ‘Field of Dreams’ - one of Kevin Costner’s biggest box-office triumphs - hung modestly on the right hand wall above the bed.

Madison immediately interpreted this as being part of the young Aussie’s stunted male maturity, but the posters spiked her curiosity and as she turned to ask him for a more detailed explanation a sudden draught, from out of nowhere, caused the bedroom door behind her to close slightly, revealing a third, smaller poster which had been attached to the back of it; this one from the Vin Diesel film ‘Fast and Furious’.

Gary, who was still trying to make a good impression, was busy tidying a small desk in the corner of the room - which clearly doubled up as his grooming point - and as he stooped to pick up a stray pen which had fallen from the desk onto the floor, he noticed Madison looking at the posters - and more poignantly, the judgmental look on her face.

Again, he grimaced, but before she could speak, he quickly jumped in to explain.

'I know, it's probably not the done-thing at my age... but these posters are my inspiration', he revealed with almost philosophical vindication; 'they tell me that if you dream, anything is possible', the young Aussie added pensively as he ran a finger protectively over a strip of Sellotape holding down one of the corners that was beginning to peel away.

That was the first serious thing she had ever heard Gary say...and for once Madison was lost for words, as she stopped to reflect and mentally compare his motivational tools with those of *the Bishop* who probably had a whole library of books at his disposal in order to accomplish the same end-result.

A heavy silence followed Gary's modest admission - which Madison was tempted to break with an uncharitable analogy between the 'Fast and Furious' poster and his performance the previous evening - but wisely she refrained from doing so, in order to spare his blushes...deciding not to emasculate him any further after what she felt had been a rather humbling revelation.

It wasn't like her to pass up the opportunity to run her mouth but this time she did, even surprising herself with her restraint, though she did allow herself a secret snigger as she turned and followed Gary out of the room.

What's in there, she asked curiously, jerking her chin in the direction of a second door as they exited the room.

'Oh, that's Dave's room; you really don't want to go in there', Gary warned, shaking his head dissuasively…and for once Madison didn't need to know any more.

Back in the living-room not wanting to sit on the sofa for fear of catching something, Madison stationed herself over by the window and the fresh air supply while Gary disappeared back into his room, only to reappear a few minutes later with his hair brushed, and wearing a red sleeveless jersey.

The aspiring fashion-commentator that she was had to bite her lip about his strange choice of clothing, but rather than criticise his incongruous style she commented instead on the way the jersey showed off his strong biceps and ripped beefy shoulders.

She hadn't noticed it to any degree the night before, but the truth was that she probably hadn't had the time; she sniggered to herself again, naughtily.

'Yeah, it's a replica jersey', Gary declared; 'back home, my brother Joey is a squad member for the Sydney Swans'.

'Huh; the Sydney Swans?' Madison queried, a little bemused.

'..It's a *footie* club', Gary explained enthusiastically, monitoring her reaction.

'Oh, right', Madison nodded, assuming an air of practiced aloofness though she had absolutely no idea what he meant, given her complete ignorance of sports.

'Look; me and a couple of the boys are meeting to go karting', Gary then blurted out, a hint of impatience in his voice.

'You wouldn't want to tag along for that too, would you?' He offered politely, not thinking for a moment that Madison would be interested.

The latter looked him in the eye, challengingly.

'Well, I don't know; I've never heard of that either, so it's gonna be a little out of my comfort zone…but hey, I'm always looking for a new challenge, so why not?', she replied defiantly, a tiny smile twitching at the corners of her mouth.

'Okay then Missie, on your head be it', Gary remarked acquiescently offering her a high-five to which she didn't respond.

'You're on', Madison replied quickly and confidently, suddenly caught up in Gary's contagious enthusiasm.

They set out once again for the Tube station and no sooner had they left, still disturbed by what she had seen - and unable to keep her thoughts to herself - Madison couldn't resist turning to Gary and chiding him gently – in a slightly mocking tone - about the state of his apartment.

'You really need to get that place cleaned up', she remarked with a reproving glance, '...and you should also think about investing in some new sofas...and maybe...get the *super* to have a look at that leaking tap', she added before realising too late that she was preaching.

Gary wasn't really listening…and in response to her suggestions, he just blew out his cheeks apathetically and nodded in agreement, his preoccupied mind already racing ahead to what his mates were going to say when they saw him arrive at the track with Madison and her designer shopping-bags in tow.

However, as they crossed the road at the end of the street, looking both ways so as not to get run over, he did allow himself a passing smile in response to her somewhat incongruous use of the word 'super' rather than 'landlord' or even 'concierge' which any British resident would have tended to use.

Needless to say, this gentle ridicule didn't go entirely un-noticed by Madison, but as they turned into the underground station concourse almost immediately thereafter - along with fifty or so other harassed commuters - she decided not to question it, preferring instead to turn her attention to her shopping-bags, in reaction to a warning poster on the wall that informed all passengers using the Underground system that thieves and pickpockets were in operation in the area.

The Kings Cross Circuit was only a couple of stops down the line but as they emerged from the underground-exit and made their way towards the small courtesy coach which was waiting to take them - and a number of other racing enthusiasts - directly to the track, Madison suddenly began to reconsider her decision.

She had never done anything like this before and unsure that she could actually go through with it, she intentionally held back for a moment - pretexting a stone in her shoe - in order to give herself a moment to think up a valid reason, as to why she couldn't possibly get on-board the waiting vehicle.

She stepped aside from the flow of people, not wanting to hold up those coming behind her, and finding a convenient wall to lean on, she calmly put down her bags and removed her shoe; a gesture which instantly drew a number of curious glances from other commuters who were exiting the Underground behind her; among them, an elderly couple who smiled at her sympathetically as they shuffled past and a young mother, desperately trying to keep her brood together, who glanced at her briefly as she too hurried past, chasing her youngest, who having escaped his mother's clutches, was clearly making a break for freedom after the uncomfortably restrictive environment of the crowded underground system.

Others rushed past too, but as she stood there, shoe in hand - waving it blatantly in the air in order to dislodge the imaginary grit – Madison suddenly began to rue the impetuous nature of her character.

Why had she agreed to do this, she wondered...secretly castigating herself for that overly zealous part of her persona which had so often gotten her into trouble in the past.

...and karting...of all things, she muttered to herself as the child - who had run-ahead earlier – suddenly came running back past her, grinning cheekily, with his exhausted mother in hot pursuit.

That brought a smile to Madison's face but even as she watched the worn out young mother corral the little boy, grab his arm and drag him back to join his siblings, her over-active mind was already hard at work, searching for the perfect solution to her own dilemma; an excuse that would allow her to both save face and avoid her getting dragged along to participate in an activity in which she had absolutely no interest.

Her brain clicked into over-drive, sorting quickly through her loaded memory-banks...and almost immediately it came up with a number of excuses, any one of which could have been her saving grace.

However as she contemplated the scene around her - Gary, the coach and the view across the Thames – Madison suddenly decided, rather atypically, that none of the excuses she had come up with was particularly fitting or appropriate for the situation in which she currently found herself...and so, not wanting to appear churlish in Gary's eyes, she chose quite simply to disregard them all as unsuitable.

Meanwhile Gary - who had continued on his way and hadn't noticed that Madison had stopped - suddenly realised that she was no longer by his side and turning to see where she was, he immediately back-tracked, ready to offer his arm or his hand - for balance purposes – should she need it.

It was another honourable gesture on his part and even though she didn't actually need his help – being the independent woman that she was - Madison rewarded the young Aussie's kind concern with a warm appreciative smile as she bent her knee adroitly and carefully slipped her shoe back onto her foot.

Gary returned that enigmatic smile, enjoying the exchange...but as he did so, the coach driver - who had been standing patiently by his vehicle's open-door ready to greet those getting on-board – began bellowing out a rallying cry to all his would-be passengers, ruining the moment.

'Two minutes, ladies and gentlemen; we leave in two minutes', he shouted, his dry tone prompting an immediate response from Gary who quickly glanced around and raised an apologetic hand in acknowledgement of the fact that maybe they were the ones holding up the coach's imminent departure.

'Are you right?' he asked earnestly, turning back to Madison once again.

'Crisis averted', the latter replied with a fixed grin as she re-gathered her bags.

'Do you need a hand carrying all that stuff?' Gary enquired, gesturing towards the bags full of shopping.

'No, I do not', Madison quipped brusquely, her tone this time revealing just the slightest hint of her frustration at her inability to come up with a credible excuse not to be doing this.

'Okay...smooth', Gary mumbled tactfully, as he turned away and headed for the coach, expecting Madison to be following right behind.

Unfortunately though, she didn't.

Instead...gripping her bags tightly and smirking impudently at another couple who just happened to be making their way into the underground at that moment, Madison stubbornly held her ground, clearly exasperated now by her inability to come up with an argument, convincing enough to exempt her from what she now considered was going to be a complete and utter waste of her precious time.

'Are you coming, Miss?' the coach-driver suddenly called out again, his words not really registering in her brain, but just penetrating her ears enough to snap her out of her self-critical trance.

Madison still didn't move, determined to register her lack of enthusiasm...but when Gary looked back again in reaction to the driver's enquiry, she knew that she had no other option than to step forward and follow his lead, even though it made her feel like a fish caught on a hook being inexorably reeled in towards a fate that she did not deserve.

That feeling; the feeling of helplessness really irked her but as she meandered slowly towards the coach's open-door - making an uneasy peace with her situation despite her reluctance – Madison's prayers were suddenly answered out of the blue, when, in the most perfectly timed moment of happenstance, just as she prepared to climb on board, her phone began to ring.

She looked at Gary and he looked back at her, his face tightening slightly.

'I'll have to take this; it might be important', she announced defensively, trying hard not to smile at her good fortune as she reached into her handbag to fish out her phone.

The driver heard the phone too and with a glance at his watch, a flick of the chin and an accepting hand-gesture; he signalled that Madison should stand aside if she was going to take the call, so that those behind her could board the coach unhindered.

Of course, Madison had absolutely no problem with that and grateful for the last-minute reprieve she readily took a backward step to allow those behind her to brush past and take up their seats.

Gary stepped down too, feigning indifference but groaning inwardly as he grudgingly joined the driver on the pavement...and while Madison sauntered off - clutching her phone with covert delight - he and the driver found themselves striking up a rather awkward and disjointed conversation – mainly about sport - when the latter thought he recognised the crest on Gary's jersey.

Madison didn't wander far, just far enough to get herself some privacy, and once she felt that that was the case, she calmly cleared the catch in her throat and took the call, keeping a careful eye on Gary and the driver who returned the courtesy with undisguised curiosity as they stood there sharing their manly small-talk.

The call wasn't important. It was just Evie, checking up on the time of her flight back to New York - and of course wanting the usual chat - but just as she was confirming her flight-details, Madison was suddenly struck by an unexpected flash of inspiration which made her eyes twinkle with cunning.

'Hon, I have to go...I have a driver here, waiting for me' she announced brusquely, deliberately curtailing the conversation, before Evie could get too involved.

'Oh, okay, time-out; I get it; call me when you...' Evie responded swiftly, trying to sign off rapidly before the line went dead.

She wasn't quick enough…because using the pretext of subtlely smoothing a couple of rebellious hairs back into place Madison was already putting her devious new plan into action. She had noticed that Gary and the driver were momentarily occupied with a random passer-by who was walking her dog, and taking advantage of their distraction she had sneakily turned away from their gaze, in order to end the call without them seeing what she was doing.

However, while she did indeed end the call to Evie, Madison didn't remove the phone from her ear, and turning back towards where the two men were waiting, a look of obvious disappointment plastered theatrically on her face, she then pretended to extend the call - striking up an imaginary conversation with herself - hoping to use that as an excuse when she got back to the coach, to renege on her incommodious commitment to go 'karting'.

The call seemed never-ending and all of a sudden, getting a little fidgety, the driver quietly turned to Gary and informed him that his 'girlfriend' would need to hurry herself if she was going to get on the coach, as he had a schedule to keep.

Gary frowned, nodding his head in silence, and once the driver moved away to take up his place behind the wheel, he immediately raised both hands in the air and began waving in Madison's direction, trying in vain to catch her attention in order to hurry her up.

Of course Madison saw those signals, if only out of the corner of her eye, but engrossed in her imaginary conversation she deliberately ignored them, hoping beyond hope that one way or another the coach-driver would lose patience with her and decide to leave without her…without them.

Unfortunately though, that didn't happen, and it was only when Gary began walking towards her - with a certain amount of purpose - that she raised a hand in acknowledgement of his gesticulations, conveying her assent that it was time for her to wrap up her performance.

However, while Gary turned around again to make sure that the coach did not in fact leave without them, Madison deliberately dragged 'the conversation' out for another minute or so - as if she had all the time in the world – so that it wouldn't look too suspect when she did eventually 'hang up'.

She paused briefly; then exaggerating her sad-face a little further, and slightly encumbered by her rather voluminous shopping bags - which she had loaded onto the one arm in order to take the call - Madison calmly made her way back to where Gary was standing, phone in hand, to announce the bad news that her boss urgently needed some files e-mailed to her in her office in New York.

'I'm sorry; I need to get back to my hotel', she explained shamelessly, holding the sad expression for longer than was necessary.

'Go on; you're bailing on me?' Gary exclaimed, gobsmacked by Madison's shock announcement.

'Yeah, I'm sorry', she retorted with false regret. 'I have to do this...'

Gary's face fell once again as did his shoulders, but making a brave attempt to disguise his chagrin he immediately recomposed himself and offered to accompany her back to the hotel; a gesture which made Madison feel a little uncomfortable.

In fact, it made her feel more than a little uncomfortable, it made her feel rather guilty that he was actually considering cancelling on his friends in order to return to her hotel with her...and so...taken aback once again by the young Aussie's unselfish and easy-going nature, she decided somewhat unusually to put her obnoxious New York attitude aside for once, to back-pedal on her charade and to go along with Gary's jaunt, uttering a track-covering, 'what the hell; her boss could wait', as she turned and headed rapidly for the coach's open door before she changed her mind again.

Gary followed her onto the coach, looking a little bemused as to her sudden change of heart but there was no time for any explanation as they quickly found themselves two seats, one on either side of the central aisle, about half-way down the coach, and the driver, not wanting to be held up any longer, immediately closed the doors, looked in his mirror and pulled away.

♗

Strangely, the slight delay – caused by Madison's 'phoney' phone-call - had inadvertently ramped up the expectant mood inside the coach…and that air of excitement – which seemed to be prevalent amongst most of its passengers – soon gained its late-arrivals.

All around them animated conversations filled the air and within no time both Gary and Madison began to feel the thrill of excitement infusing their mood.

In fact, the anticipation amongst those in the coach was almost palpable and as it made its way along the Thames embankment, the overall mood of those inside was one of thrill-seeking adventure.

♗

The journey from the tube station to the race-track only took ten minutes or so and as they stepped off the bus in Indian file - a little later than Gary had pre-arranged because of the slight delay - Dave, Kev and George were already there waiting.

Kev, wearing his habitual frown, was the first to spot them, and with his usual sarcasm he immediately commented on the contrast between

Gary's garish red football jersey and Madison's casual - but nevertheless stylish - powder-blue cashmere roll-neck jumper and designer-jeans.

'Sorry, we're late fellas', Gary murmured as they approached.

'No worries', George and Dave cried out in unison, their minds clearly more concerned with what they were about to take part in.

Kev meanwhile, just greeted them with a nod and a grunt.

'So, what's the sub-text here?' Dave asked curiously, looking at Madison and then back at Gary.

'Yeah, what's going on?' George followed up inquisitively.

'Well guys', Madison announced boldly, stepping forward and taking charge.

'Gary here, wants to race; I, on the other hand, am here to kick all your butts', she declared confidently – albeit a little tongue-in-cheek - revealing her competitive spirit and a hint of her natural arrogance despite her complete and utter neophyte-status.

'Yeah, right', Kev scoffed scornfully with a supercilious smile, taking Madison's facetious challenge and her pretentious attempt at bravado far too seriously, as he turned and led the way inside.

'That guy's a jerk', Madison muttered under her breath, making subtle eye-contact with Gary; '...I was just trying to lighten the mood'.

'Yeah, we know, but 'figjam' doesn't get American humour', Dave interjected, doing his best to smooth over the lingering animosity between Madison and Kev, held over from their encounter at the Irish bar the night before...',

'...and he certainly doesn't reckon on getting beat by a girl...' George chipped in as the roar of engines and the screeching of tyres came thundering out of an opened door behind them, drowning out the end of his sentence.

'Figjam?' Madison queried with a sideways glance.

'I'll let you explain that one', Dave remarked, looking at Gary.

'It's just another nick-name we have for Kev', Gary explained succinctly without elaborating any further.

Madison frowned but accepted that it probably wasn't the time to ask for more clarification.

Again, the raucous noise of revved-up engines exploded out of the opened door behind them, acting like a siren-call to all petrol-heads… and as their testosterone levels suddenly spiked on hearing the inexplicably seductive sounds, Dave and George quickly turned and followed Kev inside, itching to get started.

Gary and Madison, shrugging their shoulders, were left to bring up the rear, and as they stepped into the cacophonous cauldron and headed for the reception area, Madison was immediately struck by the pervasive smell of warm oil and petrol which instantly filled her nostrils.

She screwed up her nose instinctively but her face tightened even more dramatically on seeing the track for real…and the portraits of a number of what she could only presume to be former World Champions adorning the walls surrounding it.

It looked a daunting prospect for anybody, never-mind a novice like her and as the next race started and the noise of the karts reduced any normal conversation to an inaudible shouting match, she began to re-assess once again whether she could or should actually go through with it.

After all, this was really way out of her comfort-zone, and she had no intention of risking life and limb for bravado's sake...but then Kev's comment and his begrudging sexist attitude towards her, started to replay over and over in her brain and with that in mind, having calculated the risk as best she could, Madison determined that she would go for it and that whatever else happened during the race, by hook or by crook, she would beat Kev to the finish line.

That settled, taking her courage in both hands, Madison joined Gary and the others in the busy the pit-area where they were all kitted out in their obligatory matching coveralls and colourful size-appropriate helmets ready to go racing.

They then had to stand in line and wait for another two races to conclude before their names were called out over the loud-speaker...but it wasn't that long before the track marshals were calling them and five other people forward to take up their positions in the karts on the starting-grid.

Madison swallowed nervously and quaking with both fear and excitement she carefully stepped into her kart (No.20).

It was a wobbly moment and seeing her obvious novice-attitude one of the track-marshals immediately came over to offer her a helping hand… and to check her safety harness.

'I got this', she remarked, rejecting out of hand the guy's invasion into her personal space...but the marshal insisted that the rules were the rules and that it was his job to make sure that her harness was correctly attached.

Madison relented and raised both her hands in the air to allow the marshal to do his job, glancing simultaneously over at Dave who gave her a reassuring thumbs-up…but as the marshal tried to give her the safety instructions which all drivers were obliged to listen to, the noise from the other karts gunning their engines - *and noticeably Kev's, who had made sure that he was already ahead of her by jumping into the kart placed directly in front of hers* - drowned out whatever he was trying to say.

Nevertheless having checked that her harness was firmly secured, the marshal moved on to the next kart where Dave was already strapped in and ready to go.

Madison was a picture of concentration as she sat there waiting for the start...and as her excitement grew, her body tightened in anticipation, her hands gripped the wheel, her eyes fixed firmly on the track ahead of her and her lips became a thin line of resolute determination.

Her foot, trembling with emotion, hovered over the accelerator pedal and as she waited for the 'off', she realised that she had never before felt more nervous and more excited all at the same time.

The track-marshal checked with the rest of his team that all the drivers had been secured and checked...and then ten seconds later, having taken up his position at the side of the track, he raised and then dropped the chequered flag signalling the start of the race.

Madison hit the accelerator pedal hard but in the cauldron of noise that exploded around her, she immediately found herself wedged between Dave and another driver as they went around the first corner.

The noise from the karts' powerful engines was deafening, but somehow Madison managed to maintain her position as the driver on her right span 180 degrees...and Dave - who had drawn level with her on her left-hand side - held back chivalrously when he could so easily have forced his way through.

It was a nervous start but Madison quickly got the hang of the pedals... to the point where she was soon bullying her way through the field - her competitive nature coming to the fore - as George too, allowed her to go past unchallenged.

Madison found it exhilarating...to be part of such a hands-on celebration of speed...and while she hated the dumb-blond stereotype, she had learned early-on in life that there were times when it worked to her advantage; <u>this</u> was one of those times and as she whizzed past yet another competitor she couldn't help but holler her delight into her helmet, at the top of her voice.

The race was going well; the pace was fast...and furious...and Madison was really enjoying the thrill of overtaking her fellow competitors, forgetting all about her earlier reluctance to participate in the challenge.

Hyped-up on adrenaline, she was flying...and having started ninth on the grid, she was suddenly running sixth, right behind Kev. . .and she was even closing in on him...while, at the back of the field, Gary, Dave and George were battling it out in their own personal dogfight.

♗

Another lap went by before Madison could catch up to her new nemesis Kev...but sadly, as she tried to follow him past yet another driver - with the blood rushing to her brain...making her a little light-headed – her concentration wavered momentarily and she clipped the rear of the other driver's kart sending <u>her</u> off course...and <u>him</u> spinning into the protective barriers which lined the track as part of the safety measures.

♗

Only three laps remained after that, before the chequered flag was lowered once again...and having made that mistake Madison suddenly found herself trailing Kev by quite some distance.

Nevertheless, she was determined to push on...and as fate would have it; on the next lap, which was the penultimate lap, 'cock-sure' Kev - pushing too hard – made a mistake of his own...and somehow - *probably because she was so desperate to get one over on him* - Madison managed to catch up again...just as Kev was battling it out with another driver to take over third spot.

Lady-luck was clearly on her side, Madison thought to herself...but having pulled out all the stops to catch back up to Kev, she decided to play the waiting game for the next lap or so, doing little more than follow the two karts in front of her around the circuit at a safe distance... biding her time...but ready to pounce...if ever the opportunity to over-take one of them presented itself.

Meanwhile, out in front of her, the duel between Kev and the other driver started to escalate out of control as they jostled for position...bumping each other and bouncing off of each other, time and time again - *like a couple of those crazy sand-buggies from the Mad Max films* – as they made their way at a furious pace around and around the circuit.

Both were really on the limit and neither was prepared to concede as they focussed firmly on their race within the race...on who would finish in front of who...as the chequered flag was waved.

It looked more than a little scary from where she was sitting but Madison had no intention of getting involved in the testosterone-fuelled dog-fight...though she knew in her own mind...that if either of the guys in front of her made a mistake – *and especially if it was Kev* - she would have absolutely no problem in taking advantage of the situation.

And then it happened; serendipity seemed to take over...because...as they went around the next bend, like two rutting stags, the guys' karts, came together with a crunching thunderclap of noise sending them both spinning out of control and into the protective barriers.

The crash bore all the hallmarks of deliberate foul-play...from one or other of the protagonists...but Madison had no time to waste on analysing who was at fault; this was her chance to capitalise and in the midst of the chaos and the confusion created by the two stranded karts, she managed to pick her way past with an audacity and technique worthy of a professional driver.

It turned out to be the pivotal moment of the race...as subsequently neither Kev nor his rival had time to get back up to speed...to mount a realistic challenge against Madison before the chequered flag was waved again and the race was ended.

And so it was that Madison finished third - which was quite an exploit for somebody who had never set foot in a kart before - and while she hadn't won, which did rankle with her a little, she had nevertheless finished way ahead of Kev...and that...given the context, was all that really mattered to her.

For information;

Kev finished fifth, Dave finished sixth, Gary finished in seventh place and George brought up the rear in ninth.

Madison enjoyed a self-congratulatory lap of honour around the circuit...and then having parked the kart according to the marshal's instructions; she quickly unfastened the safety harnesses and stepped out of her idling machine.

Her legs were a little unsteady and her heart-rate was out of control... and as she took off her helmet and brushed back her hair, Madison had to take a couple of deep breaths - to regain her composure - before she walked off the track with a casual strut...and a look of intense pleasure written all over her face.

She was buzzing...and the smug, self-satisfied smirk - *having struck a blow for the sisterhood* – said it all.

'Wow; what a rush that was', she screamed to herself over the deafening roar of the engines being fired up behind her for the next race.

Dave, Gary and George quickly joined her, the former and the latter chanting enthusiastic shouts of 'awesome' and 'that was the duck's nuts' as she greeted them, hands akimbo.

'Beginner's Luck; hey boys', a disgruntled looking Kev mumbled with a sneer, as he too joined the group, looking at Dave and George for their support, his ego bruised and his pride dented.

'Nah mate; you got stonkered by a girl', Dave shouted out glibly, milking the moment and revelling disloyally in Kev's obvious dismay.

The others all joined in too...to commiserate with Kev...and to throw in a little gentle ribbing of their own for good measure, but the focus quickly turned back to Madison as George turned to her and complimented her, on her performance.

'Wow; that was some race for a first-timer', he enthused, offering her a high-five; 'I'm impressed'.

'Yeah, you said it mate', Gary agreed congratulating Madison too with a friendly thumbs-up; 'the girl drives like Jehu'.

'Hey; if that was beginner's luck; who wants a second run', Madison suddenly proposed as she ran her fingers through her hair again, keen to repeat her exploit.

It seemed like a logical thing to do...and to say, given the situation, and the propensity for young men – normally - to enjoy this kind of thing... but surprisingly there was very little enthusiasm among the guys to repeat the experience - which Madison found a little odd.

Nevertheless, with a little persuasion, and encouraged by Gary... and George who was the first to get on-board with the idea...Madison eventually goaded them all into agreeing to a second race, Kev in particular suddenly relishing the thought of revenge.

However, a few minutes later, as they stood in line for the next race, the air around them heavy with the noise of the engines and the smell of hot petrol, the driver that Madison had clipped earlier came over to complain about how she had cut him up, out on the track during the race.

Still pumped with adrenaline, and not realising the depth of the guy's grievance, Madison whipped around in a flash and smirked as she looked at the guy.

'Yeah, sorry about that', she riposted, one hand raised, punching the air victoriously, and sounding more than a little insincere.

The guy was obviously a pretty sore loser and not content with Madison's trite apology, he was getting rather heated...looking for more of an explanation from her...but once again, before things got out of hand; Gary stepped in and quickly sorted him out with his quiet confidence and his unshakeable Aussie cool.

'Mate, what's your beef?' He asked in a controlled, meaningful tone. 'You want to fight with a girl?'

The irate driver was fuming, almost frothing at the mouth with anger and ignoring Gary's question, he continued proffering obscenities at Madison, forcing Gary to step further forward...and to up the tone.

'Listen mate, you'd better knock it on the head now unless you want some Aussie dentistry', he insisted more forcefully...and with a considerable amount of front.

'Yeah; take it down a notch, buddy', George chipped in, closing ranks.

The guy eye-balled Gary...saw that he had back-up in the shape of Dave, George and possibly Kev...and decided to back off, grinding his teeth, wagging his finger and mumbling menacingly at Madison as he hobbled away.

Then suddenly, Gary wheeled away too...coughing and spluttering noisily.

'Okay fellas', he asked through grimaced features, '...who's opened their lunch?'

'Say what?' Madison enquired getting a little exasperated by the crazy antipodean vernacular.

'Oh, that would be me', Kev revealed with a smirk as he walked away too, abandoning his malodorous cloud and lengthening his stride deliberately in order to distance himself as quickly as possible from the immediate vicinity.

'Eew', Madison cried out in disgust, as she recoiled, waving her hand in front of her nose and screwing up her face in revulsion as the pungent smell spread, polluting the space around them and leaving them all gasping for clean air.

Everybody vacated the area and as they regrouped a little further along, Madison turned to Gary and pointed an accusing finger at Kev.

'That guy's toxic', she fumed indignantly. 'In the US we use the word toxic to mean bad-news, but in this case I literally mean he's toxic'.

The second race was far less spectacular.

Madison didn't have her lucky 'Number 20' kart and this time it was Gary who won with Madison, playing it safe, only coming in seventh.

However, as they stood in line again, ready to give their helmets back at the desk, surrounded by more bruised egos and disappointment than actual race winners, Madison turned to the guys and admitted that the whole experience had been more than exhilarating.

'In fact, while it was completely outside my comfort zone, it was… without doubt…the most fun I have ever had with my clothes on', she remarked enthusiastically...which raised a great Aussie cheer from the guys that went up to the rafters and rebounded back down in a rapturous echo, much to the amusement of a couple of passers-by who had been in the race with them…and who were just leaving.

That brought the excursion to an end...and as the group of friends walked out of the Karting centre, in Indian file and onto the Euston Road, chatting amongst themselves and reliving their particular highlights of the day, all thoughts suddenly turned to deciding what they were going to do next, and where they were going to eat.

The sun had already set and the cold wind that seems to haunt the streets of London - no matter the time of day - had inevitably picked up.

'This spanner weather sure tightens up your nuts'; Gary joked as they made their way to the Tube station.

Madison scowled again at his puerile humour but the rest of them simply agreed with him.

The group of friends reached Kings Cross station still squabbling over where to eat...but as they got to the Tube-station's main entrance, Madison checked the time on her mobile phone and informed them all that it was time for her to go.

'I still have a few things to sort out before my flight', she announced casually.

'No worries', George replied amicably, nodding his understanding and thrusting his hands in his pockets.

'Yeah; that's cool', Dave chipped in, '...but you're quite welcome to stay and eat...' he hastened to add, looking around for Kev who had already gone on ahead.

Madison's face creased into a half-smile. 'Thanks...but no', she persisted resolutely. 'I really have to go'.

Gary then stepped forward and motioned towards the shopping bags that he had been helping her to carry.

'Do you need a hand getting all this stuff back to the hotel?' he asked with a sparkle in his eye...playing out his role as unofficial chaperon... but also hoping - no doubt - to join her back at the hotel with a view to cementing his brief liaison with her in some way...

Madison recognized the tone of his voice and saw the look in his eyes. It was a nice gesture and she really did appreciate it...but this time she had to decline Gary's offer.

'Rain-check', she proposed, wrinkling her nose and crushing the young Aussie's burgeoning optimism in an instant, as she thanked him for everything he had done for her, not only there in London, but also during the tournament...*her theory on the seduction techniques of English men...and by extension Australian men...having already been proved two-fold the previous evening.*

'No sweat', Gary replied bravely as he handed over the bags.

Madison took them off his hands...and then, with a kiss on the cheek... and a wave to the rest of the group, she jumped into a nearby taxi - making sure that she had all her purchases – and was gone.

It had been an intense couple of days...and that evening, as she lay on the bed in her hotel room, with her laptop, writing the conclusion to her article, after a long, luxurious bath, Madison took a moment to reflect on the highs and the lows of her first stay in England.

The whole experience had been somewhat of a culture shock – a contrast between her and her American sophistication – *the Bishop* and his standoffish Englishness – and Gary; Gary with his unflappable, laid-back Aussie cool; all of which had opened her eyes to a world of diversity that she would never have known had she stayed in New York.

This realisation brought a smile to her face and as she rolled over onto her back...and lay there, ensconced in her white, fluffy robe with her hands clasped loosely behind her head, Madison could not help but close her eyes and re-live a few of the more amusing and intriguing encounters of her stay;

A number of situations - and the faces connected with them - suddenly appeared in front of her mind's eye;

- Gary in the hotel bar...in the 'pub'...and at the race-track...
- Rory when he had cornered her in the bar... (Eeew)
- The face of Gary's friend 'Corny' who really did look like Alexander Skarsgard...
- A few of the other contestants she had interviewed...
- Alessia, the Italian masseuse...
- Gary's friend Kev and his thunderstruck face after he had lost out in the race...

  ...and of course, last but not least...,
- *The Bishop* - who naturally took pride of place in her mental review, despite his unpardonable late-night dismissal of her...

This muddle of images - filled with a whole host of emotions - used up the last of Madison's usually-unfailing energy reserves...and after one last look at her phone - *to check for any last-minute messages* – exhausted by the mental and physical rigours of her day, she finally crawled under the covers, turned out the light and drifted off into a night of well-deserved slumber.

The next day; Madison flew home; back to the Big Apple, back to reality and back to the people she knew.

CHAPTER NINE

On the weekend after she got back, Madison arranged to meet up with her best friend Evie in Central Park; something they did from time to time, whenever they hadn't seen each other in a while...or when either one of them felt the need for some 'girl-time'...usually because of a man...

That particular day, was a perfect early-summer's day with bright sunlight and not a cloud in the sky and as she made her way to hers and Evie's usual meeting-spot...right in front of the Met Museum...Madison couldn't help but marvel at how her city - the city of New York – welcomed... and embraced...people from all over the globe.

This really is the melting-pot of the world, she thought to herself as she looked around, seeing people from all nationalities, all cultures and all walks of life just going about their lives and 'doing their thing' without a care in the world.

I wonder why we can't all just live in peace like this, she mused to herself, her thoughts suddenly harping back to the images of war and desolation that she had seen on the morning news.

A few minutes later, having reached 'their spot'...but still wrapped up in her thoughts about peace and humanity...Madison was suddenly shocked out of her musings by the ear-piercing sound of a shrieking chid.

It was a deafening scream and alerted by the noise, everybody in the vicinity immediately turned around to see where the cry had come from... and as Madison turned around too, she saw a small plastic ball come rolling towards her; a little girl...who could not have been more than four years old...following it in hot pursuit.

Madison stopped the ball with her foot and having steadied herself for a moment, to regain her balance, she pushed it back gently in the direction of the little girl who quickly picked it up with both hands and ran back to her mother a few yards away without so much as a word.

Madison smiled discreetly to herself, somewhat amused by the little girl's behaviour and as she turned around again thoughts and happy memories of her own childhood suddenly replaced those of war and carnage that had been squatting her mind all morning.

It was then that Evie arrived, tapping her gently on the shoulder and snapping her out of her nostalgic reflection.

'Hey girl...long time, no see', Evie chirped, her face breaking out into a beaming smile.

Startled out of her musing, Madison pivoted around in an instant, flashing a smile of her own.

'Hey you', she replied, happy to see her friend; '...I'm back'.

'I can see that', Evie exclaimed, throwing open her arms and grabbing her friend by the waist in order to give her a huge, 'welcome-back' hug; a gesture which – for some strange reason - incited another couple of young women who just happened to be passing by at the time, to turn to each other and give each other a kiss.

The re-connection made, the two friends composed themselves once again...and having decided which direction they were going to take...this time it was a clockwise direction...they set off on their usual walk.

Evie was bubbling with expectation. Naturally, she was pleased to see Madison again...as it had been a while since they had last caught up... in person...but more importantly she was desperate to hear all about her friend's trip to England...because in the meantime...her own life in New York had been decidedly lacking in any kind of pizzazz.

This was no surprise to Madison of course; she knew all about Evie's inquisitive nature...and so...as they set off on their walk along the foot-path, right next to the jogging track, she quickly indulged her friend's unbounded...and somewhat pervasive...curiosity by launching into a full... and very detailed description of London... its fashion houses...and its architecture.

'That's all very nice hon...', Evie commented as they ambled along, enjoying the sunshine.

'I know you're into fashion and all that...but...but what about the story...' she enquired after yet another description of a tiny niche-boutique that Madison had found near Oxford Street.

'Oh that', Madison remarked somewhat distractedly as she reached back to tighten the elastic-band holding her long blond hair in a tight pony-tail.

'Well...that; that was something else', she replied teasingly, with a wry smile and a hint of intrigue in her voice.

Evie's eyes suddenly sparkled. 'I'm listening'.

Madison scoffed deliberately and then went on to tell her friend all about the Tournament, about how it was held out in the 'middle-of-nowhere', about some of the people involved...and even about Gary.

'Any chemistry there...?' Evie prodded, always avid for a snippet of spicy detail.

'No; nothing like that...' Madison lied impassively – *deciding not to mention her moment of weakness with the young Aussie* - '...but he was a nice guy and gave me a lot of inside information about the Tournament...and what goes on etc'.

Evie shrugged with disappointment as without warning a group of jogging fanatics raced past them, leaving a trail a sweaty odour in their wake.

'Eew', she remarked as she wafted the air in front of her face with both hands.

'There was another guy though...' Madison suddenly continued, her lips curling upward in a genuine - but slightly chagrined - smile.

'Tell me more', Evie responded eagerly, as a couple of stragglers from the jogging-group struggled past her, wheezing from the effort.

'What's he like...and don't skimp on the detail?' she insisted as a couple of elderly people came towards them from the opposite direction, holding hands and smiling.

'Well', Madison explained, having nodded politely to the elderly couple; 'It's the guy I ended up writing the whole article around'.

Evie's eyes suddenly widened. 'Aha...?'

'Yeah; he is the most intriguing man I have ever met', Madison revealed; 'the guy's brilliant...'

'...but...I'm sensing a 'but'...' Evie interjected, her head swivelling around inquisitively.

Madison paused.

'Yeah, because he's...so. . .obnoxious...and arrogant...and...and while he might have the most perfectly chiselled features and gorgeous blue eyes I've ever seen', she added in order to satisfy her friend's unbridled curiosity; '... he is just another one of those infuriating guys that you know you should really stay clear of...'

'...but somehow always manages to draw you in', Evie interrupted, finishing her friend's sentence.

'Exactly', Madison confirmed; 'he's a nightmare'.

'Really; tell me more' Evie insisted again, desperate for more detail, for more juicy gossip.

'Well', Madison continued. 'It's strange really, but the guy has...an inexplicable aura around him...like a force-field of confidence. . .'

She paused again while Evie waited expectantly...

'This is a guy...who could psycho-analyse me and paraphrase Shakespeare all at the same time', she added with a scowl and a hint of irritation in her voice.

'. . .but he was suave and sophisticated too, even though he could be unpredictable and a little uncommunicative at times', she pursued.

Evie was caught up listening to her friend...when all of a sudden...out of nowhere...two more young guys dressed in Lycra ran past them...almost knocking her over.

'Hey', she blurted out, in annoyance.

'Nice butt', one of the guys called out as he ran by...only to receive a disapproving nudge in the ribs from the more respectful guy running with him.

'Pervert', Evie called out again in reply, admonishing the guy's sexist comment, but secretly enjoying the 'flattering' remark all the same - *if it could be called 'flattering' in this age of political-correctness* - even though it was actually Madison's 'butt' that had caught the guy's eye and not her own.

The guy looked back over his shoulder with a cheeky grin on his face... and then without further ado, he quickened his pace and disappeared off into the distance.

'So...what's the situation with this guy?' Evie asked, turning back to Madison and trying to reboot the conversation after the interruption.

'Well, I don't really know', Madison admitted. 'There is no doubt that he is moody...and frustrating at times; in fact he can be a real a-hole...but for some reason...and I really can't put my finger on it, I feel a connection with the guy'.

'I know it's irrational...but I think I'm infatuated by the guy...despite his misogynous nature and his tendency for patronising comments; he is just so compelling; I'm spellbound', she confessed.

'Wow, I see', Evie concurred, glancing back momentarily at another hunky guy who had just crossed their path.

Madison stopped in her tracks and looked off into the distance, caught up in the sudden inertia of the moment.

'You know Evie, this guy has so much natural talent...and he is so accomplished in what he does...that he is revered...revered...given almost regal status...by his peers...'

She raised her hand in a kind of regal wave to back-up her point.

'...even if it is only in the tiny, insular world of chess'.

'And…talking of talent', Evie smiled, with that knowing look in her eyes; '...don't keep me in suspense here...'

Madison smiled at her friend, knowing exactly what she wanted to hear.

She paused again...deliberately; 'All I can say is...that his kisses are spectacular'; she lied again, knowing that in reality she had only ever experienced that one fleeting...and unscripted...goodbye-kiss with *the Bishop* at the door of the abbey.

'I'm impressed', Evie admitted, '...but I thought we'd decided on a moratorium on men…after that last episode?'

'Hey, don't patronise me', Madison retorted in mock anger as she checked the time on her phone...though there was a hint of petulance in her tone; 'besides...isn't it a girl's prerogative to change her mind'.

'I'm not so sure', Evie replied.

'Me neither', Madison agreed, revealing the confusion in her brain. 'I am a thinking person...some would say a calculating bitch...and not one prone to irrationality. . .and yet here I am getting obsessed with a guy that I hardly know', she disclosed.

Evie nodded her understanding, but gauging her friend's mood she refrained from commenting.

'We are totally incompatible...in so many ways...but I just can't seem to get this guy out of my head', Madison continued, her voice suddenly softening with a romantic edge as she remembered back to that delicious preamble at the abbey before *the Bishop* had sent her home.

'Hey', Evie shouted out, giving her friend an elbow to the ribs to bring her back to reality; 'we decided a while back that no such prince existed, right. . .'

'. . .apart from the artist formerly known as', she clarified, giving Madison the eye.

'We decided that love is no more than a spider's web, spun by men to trap women...to lure them into their grasp for their own self-satisfaction', she scoffed, quoting her own personal feminist mantra.

'Oh, don't be so cynical...and pessimistic', Madison retorted, holding her ground. 'It might be a cliché, but this guy is different: men have been trying to bribe their way into my pants for as long as I can remember, but not him'.

'. . .Besides', Evie warned, cutting in and completely ignoring Madison's case for the defence, 'transatlantic romances never last; trust me, it will only lead to tears'.

Madison looked away, disappointed by the scorn that Evie was pouring on her experience in England...though in her heart of hearts she knew that her friend was only trying to protect her.

And yet, she thought to herself again; why should she refuse to live out a potential romance with someone, under the pretence that one day it would end...even if it was - as things currently stood - only in her own head?

Besides, she pondered further...just like Carly Norris (*the main character in one of her favourite films, 'Sliver'*) she was just an ordinary girl looking for some action to relieve the boredom...and what's more, she mused further still, Sharon Stone who played the role of that adventurous young woman in the film...has since gone on to become a Hollywood legend; a living example of what every woman should strive to become; confident... successful and wealthy; a 21st century woman in complete control of her career and her life; so hey, why shouldn't she do that?

After all, what was the harm; Madison thought to herself? Meeting *the Bishop* had revived her slumbering libido; he had made her want to rediscover the full richness of her senses again - *something she had not felt since 'the incident' a few months back* – and even if he had refused to close the deal that night at the Abbey – just thinking about him now made her feel that much more alive, and that could only be a good thing.

The sound of music coming from a group of hipsters - sat in a circle on the grass to their left, singing songs and holding coloured balloons – suddenly interrupted Madison's reflection...and as she and Evie walked along a little further, each in their own heads, two more couples walked past them going the other way.

They crossed without acknowledgement...but then one of the women did a double-take, and recognising Evie almost after the fact, she turned around and called out her name.

'Evie...?'

Evie turned around and acknowledged the woman - and the other people with her – offering them all a casual wave...

However, she didn't stop or try to engage with any of them…and instead just carried on walking, looking straight ahead.

'Who's that?' Madison asked nonchalantly, giving her friend a quick sideways glance.

'That...is my colleague Rita...and the guy she's with; that's Mike'. Evie explained, feeling compelled to respond; 'I don't know who the other two are...'

'Wait a minute; Mike...is that the same Mike that you used to...?'

Madison didn't have time to finish her question.

'Yep; the very same...and now he's married to Racy Rita', Evie snapped ruefully, gesturing towards the disappearing foursome.

Madison frowned and put her arm around her friend's shoulder, giving it a sympathetic squeeze. Mike had been a big part of Evie's life a few years earlier...and at one point she even thought that he might be 'the one'; sadly...it wasn't to be.

♗

Another pause for reflection followed that rather awkward moment and as the two women resumed their walk Madison's thoughts immediately wandered back to *the Bishop.*

Was this really just an infatuation or could there something more to it? She wondered.

She felt weird; she had never been in this position before.

She had told Evie all about *the Bishop* - as she always did with the men she dated - but for the first time in her life she had stopped short of mentioning the real juicy details...the abbey...the swinging-bed...or even the fact that he drove the same car as James Bond...

Why was that; was there an explanation for it? She puzzled.

She knew that Evie would devour that kind of information...and that kind of detail...but for some reason she hadn't wanted to share it with her.

Why was that; why had she wanted to keep those particular details to herself, Madison asked herself.

After all; it didn't really matter now; she would probably never see the guy again...so why not reveal all...?

♗

Evie was getting tired and seeing a bench free off to the side, she led the way over to it and sat down.

She was clearly torn up by what she had just seen...and by the memories that had inevitably resurfaced in her mind – and as she sat there brushing down her jeans she couldn't help but comment again on Madison's new obsession.

'Listen hon; I know that it has been a while since you've had a serious relationship...but why do you always attract...and fall for...the creepy type?' she remarked; a little perplexed.

'This guy's not creepy' Madison scolded as she sat down next to her friend; 'stop saying that...; he's a one-off, that's for sure, but he's not creepy'.

'Remember that last guy; what was his name? David', Evie commented disapprovingly.

Madison stared straight ahead and reminisced for a moment; flashbacks of her short time together with David suddenly filling her mind.

She had had a hot steamy affair with the property developer a year or so earlier but the way things had ended had left a permanent scar on her heart... and since then, her social life had hit the skids.

'Yeah, I remember David', she declared; 'but I'm telling you, TB is not like that'.

'TB?' Evie queried, raising her eye-brows.

'His name is Tobias but his friends call him TB; it's all to do with what he does and who he is…but I told you that already', Madison explained.

Evie remained unconvinced…though naturally she understood that sexual attraction could be possible without love and commitment after a prolonged period of celibacy.

However, still looking through her own narrow prism, she then asked her friend what the chances were of 'TB' committing to a relationship, and a transatlantic one at that.

'Commitment, forget commitment', Madison retorted, taking Evie by surprise, 'sometimes it can just be a case of enjoying the moment'.

Stunned into silence, Evie just shrugged her shoulders and with that, they got up again and pursued their walk, each of them lost in their own thoughts.

Of course Madison understood her friend wanting to protect her, she knew all about the 'incident' and the lawsuit…but Evie didn't know the Bishop; she hadn't met him and was thus, in all honesty, unable to comment objectively on him, wrapped up, as she was, in her sadly cynical, New York mentality.

'By the way', Madison prompted, trying to lighten the mood with some positive energy; 'What's the news on Rick; you know, that guy you met in the coffee-shop?'

Evie shook her head dismissively.

'Pump and dump?' Madison guessed out loud.

'Eeew; that sounds so gross...but yeah; pump and dump', Evie repeated disconsolately, her emotions rising to the surface once again.

Madison reached out again with a consoling hand...and as she looked up at the sky with its fluffy white clouds, the two women wandered off for another lap of the track so that the healing process could begin.

CHAPTER TEN

A few weeks later, sat in her cubicle on the 20th floor of her newspaper's high-rise, Madison was slowly getting back into the drudgery of her daily routine when...out of the blue...she received a call from her boss, Amanda, asking if she would...'pop up and see her after lunch'.

Amanda Brooke;

known around the building as 'the Nanny' because of her striking resemblance to the actress Fran Drescher...was the paper's Features Editor and one of those single-minded, straight-talking New Yorkers, so focussed on climbing the corporate ladder that she had no time for nurturing friendships...or even working relationships...with her fellow employees. Nevertheless, her reputation around the office...and amongst her peers in the wider New York media-elite...was unparalleled and demanded immediate respect from anybody who met her...even if her assertive tendencies, her fierce loyalty to her employer's board of directors and her lack of empathy towards anybody she considered her subordinate meant that Madison, like most of her colleagues, found her cold and unapproachable.

The call came not only out of the blue...but as quite a surprise to Madison as she and Amanda had often clashed and rarely saw eye to eye.

The two women had one of those fractious working relationships that many women experience when working together...and while it wasn't a personal vendetta as such, nor a mutual dislike of each other, the animosity between them just seemed to stem from 'the insecurities that any woman of her boss's age feels in the presence of a younger, more attractive version of herself'; at least that was how Madison would explain it.

And so, on the rare occasions when they did meet up for a department briefing or the odd one-on-one discussion Amanda never missed an opportunity to let Madison know who was boss, often trotting out one or other of her legendary back-handed compliments or trademark put-downs to put her in her place.

However, Madison had never been fazed by her boss's little 'woman-on-woman' jealousies...and mocking gibes...and over time, she had gotten used to it, accepting that those gibes were all part and parcel of their rather-volatile professional relationship.

That said; this friction between the two women was not only down to Amanda's rather focused approach...or her sometimes dubiously-brusque manner; it was also because Madison herself was very outspoken and very headstrong...and while these character traits might well have been considered useful...and even laudable by some...in the competitive world of journalism, they had inevitably led to her crossing swords with Amanda on numerous occasions; over her job description...over her career prospects... and even over the silliest, most insignificant and ridiculous of office-based protocols.

Now, most people would have shied away from this kind of confrontation with their boss but not Madison. She always fought her corner and while she rarely won the debate...Amanda's opinion ultimately holding sway…as a general rule...a measure of compromise was usually found and agreed upon.

...and yet...ever since 'the incident' and the sexual-harassment suit that had followed - *which had brought more than its fair share of scrutiny and unwanted attention to the newspaper...and had led to their most explosive and acrimonious quarrel yet* - the two women had barely spoken, helped largely by the fact that they worked on different floors...but also due...in no small part...to the paper's executive – *of which Amanda was an integral if somewhat peripheral part* – seemingly making a conscious and deliberate... albeit unofficial...decision to ostracize their junior employee by excluding her from any meaningful or significant journalistic involvement in the paper's activities as 'punishment' for her legal claim against them...

…and indeed…in the immediate aftermath of the case…despite working in the same department Amanda had clearly stone-walled Madison on a number of occasions and even avoided bumping into her around the office; in fact, since her return from England they had yet to cross each other's paths.

As a result, come one o'clock when she showed up at Amanda's office, Madison was ready for yet another confrontation.

She knocked on the door…quite firmly, but then seeing…through the glass-panel…that her boss was on the phone, Madison decided to hang back and wait to be invited in, hoping thus to avoid any unnecessary awkwardness that her 'bursting-in' might create.

Amanda heard the knock, looked up absentmindedly and without breaking off from her phone-conversation, motioned for Madison to 'come in and sit down'.

Feigning nonchalance, Madison did just that, sauntering in as she had done on so many previous occasions; her confident demeanour belying her apprehension as she made her way over to the beautifully-crafted, leather chair that was placed so deliberately opposite her boss's rather impressive desk.

Madison sat down on the edge of that chair and with her arms crossed in front of her, she waited on tenterhooks for her boss to finish her call, readying herself for what she could only assume was to be yet another lecture or dressing down.

An uneasy silence prevailed in the room but then Amanda suddenly got up from her chair…and while still on the phone…she walked over to a pile of magazines that were stacked on a cupboard off to the right and began flicking through them.

Sat there feeling like a lemon, Madison followed her boss with her eyes and…*while Amanda was turning her back, clearly looking for a reference in one of the magazines*…inspired by her trip to London…she could not help but put her 'fashionista' hat on…and mentally critique her boss's sartorial style.

Amanda was dressed as usual in one of her perfectly-tailored trouser-suits with a contrasting silk blouse and a pair of matching Jimmy Choo heels. She looked immaculate...every bit the ruthless executive stereotype...and while Madison was loath to admit it...her boss was still very attractive... for her age; she was trim and fit and clearly 'high maintenance' but while Madison could see the appeal of the business-suit with its sharp-lines and elongating allure...not to mention the aura of authority that it projected... she felt that her boss's style lacked variety, which in her opinion was the essence of every woman's wardrobe.

♗

Just then, Amanda found what she was looking for...and having sorted the problem posed by her caller in her usual brusque manner she concluded the conversation with one final exchange and sat back down behind her desk, smiling stiffly.

The underlying tension between the two women was almost palpable.

Amanda sat forward and steepled her fingers in front of her face, her thumbs resting gently on her chin...and then after a brief pause, and with practised detachment, she announced;

'Madison; I wanted to see you to congratulate you on the quality of your article. I found it original, articulate, enthralling and written with a flourish and a panache that exceeded all my expectations'.

♗

The article; 'A fascinating insight into the little known world of chess' had appeared a few weeks earlier in the paper's 'Weekend Supplement'.

♗

Madison's taut facial expression suddenly altered. In fact she was stunned; shocked to receive such praise from her boss who rarely gave out compliments or indeed expressed any kind of appreciation for the work she oversaw...and all she could reply as she relaxed in her chair and brushed aside a few loose strands of shiny blond hair...was; 'Thank you'.

Amanda smiled stiffly, and then held up the supplement, open at the page of Madison's article.

'This guy...' she said, pointing at the photo of *the Bishop* taken from the tournament press-folder; 'this guy not only fits the cliché; tall, dark and handsome...but he's also got that hint of danger about him that gets us women so worked-up; don't you agree?' she commented, her tone suggesting more than just a passing interest in the broodingly-handsome, English champion.

Madison looked at the article but didn't react, other than to throw her boss her best passive-aggressive smirk and to inform her somewhat flippantly, that in reality he wasn't that tall.

'Listen hon', Amanda continued, waving away Madison's churlish comment; '...your article was so interesting and so surprisingly well put together that even I̲ am intrigued...and curious to know more about this Bishop guy; so, what more can you tell me about him?', she enquired.

Again, Madison declined to comment, wary of her boss's intentions... and rather than say something she might regret she just shrugged her shoulders finding her boss's behaviour strangely out of character.

'...Oh, come on Madison, don't be so defensive', Amanda insisted, a distinct note of irritation in her voice. 'If we can get this guy...this enigma of a guy fronting a story; I think that we could increase circulation substantially over the next cycle...and we might even get our female readers talking about the game of Chess for a couple of months...wouldn't that be something?' Amanda pursued, trying to use the sisterhood as a means of convincing Madison to open up.

'I mean the possibilities are endless...so what do you say?' she added as she sat back confidently in her chair.

Oh; so now you're playing the sisterhood card, Madison was tempted to blurt out...thinking back to her boss's lack of compassion or support after 'the incident'...

...but she resisted...just...

...and mindful of her position, she took a deep breath while she pondered Amanda's question.

Madison was actually in a bit of a quandary at that moment…for a couple of reasons; the main one being because she didn't really know much more about TB than what she had already written in her article…other than those details that she wanted to keep private…but also, having detected more than professional curiosity in her boss's tone, she had to question Amanda's motivations in all this.

'There's not much more to say', she finished by admitting, sensing that they had reached an impasse…and not wanting her boss to gain any advantage from exploiting what she herself had worked so very hard to achieve.

'I see', Amanda concurred with a throwaway hand gesture, though the look in her eyes screamed that she didn't believe a word of it.

'So, is that it; are we done here?' Madison questioned as she got up to leave.

Amanda pushed back on her chair and reached into the top drawer of her desk, pulling out a thick green folder which she laid carefully on her desk.

'I have another assignment for you', she announced casually, stopping Madison in her tracks.

She had almost reached the door but Madison turned around and stood there with a mix of curiosity, contempt and cool insolence plastered on her face.

She was more than a little wary of Amanda and it was clear that she was on her guard…because of her rather precarious situation within the company…but nevertheless she was interested to hear what her boss had to say.

'I have been discussing this with senior management and through my contacts in the business, I have managed to set up an exhibition match in Boston', Amanda announced calmly, holding the file under the palm of her hand.

'An exhibition match...?' Madison repeated, her eyes suddenly showing some enthusiasm as she took a few steps forward.

Amanda rolled her eyes. 'Yes...an exhibition match', she reaffirmed. 'Now, I don't expect you to organise it all', she stated rather dismissively, 'I'll deal with that...but I do want you to invite this guy over to participate in it. You will cover the show as our representative, show him around maybe, and then do a follow-up article for us; what do you think?' she concluded looking expectantly at her junior colleague.

Madison frowned in false reticence, and then paused...looking at her boss, rather circumspect.

'Could you run that by me again?' she asked, secretly delighted to be offered a second assignment...and the opportunity to get her boss to repeat herself, which she did so very rarely.

Amanda growled into her throat and her nostrils flared but she repeated the offer once again.

Madison listened carefully, nodded her understanding and then queried the location. 'Why Boston...?' she asked.

'It was decided upstairs...that it would be better to organise this kind of event in a smaller venue like Boston...to gauge the public reaction...and the interest it might create...before possibly bringing the idea to New York... where, let's face it...', she explained, pausing for effect; '...it would probably be swamped by the sheer mass of cultural activity going on here'.

Madison nodded again, seeing the logic...and despite pretending to give it some thought, she quickly agreed to take on this new challenge... even though she had no idea if she could pull it off.

'Very well; let's talk...'

Amanda's phone interrupted her; she checked the caller ID and put it the caller on hold.

'Let's talk details tomorrow...' she said continuing her charm offensive, '...but in the meantime I want you to get started on that invitation', she confirmed before dismissing her junior employee with another wave of her arm.

Madison nodded again; she still had her doubts about her boss's motivation but as she walked out of her office and down the corridor towards the lifts, barely avoiding a couple of harassed executives rushing in the other direction, she couldn't help but smile to herself.

However, as she reached the lifts, Madison suddenly realised that in spite of the plaudits that she had just received from her boss; she hadn't really been very thorough in her research when finding out about the organising structures of the game in England...because when she thought about the organisers of the event...or the game's representatives...the only things that came to mind were images of grumpy old men in blue blazers... shushing her and looking down their noses at her; she had no real contact details for those in charge.

Nevertheless, she was determined not to let that put her off; failure would not be an option if she was to achieve her goal, she thought to herself.

'Ping'.

The sound of the lift door opening snapped her mind back to the present…and back at her desk a few minutes later Madison immediately set to work Google-searching anything and everything to do with British chess organisations, her only thoughts being; if she could succeed in this new project, as she hoped she would, it might just give her the necessary leverage to ask Amanda for a transfer to her dream job on the fashion team...and that...that was all the motivation she needed.

The next day, Madison met up with Amanda again and together they went through the details of her new assignment point by point; the dates, the venue, the times, the hotel that had been reserved and all the contact numbers she would need during the forthcoming event.

The meeting was very professional, concise and to the point, providing Madison with all the information she would need to carry out her assignment...but then just as she was about to pack up her things and leave there was a faint knock on the door and a young man walked in.

'Oh yes; one last thing Madison', Amanda informed her. 'This is Todd Klingenschmidt from Marketing. He will be your 'contact' here at the paper during this assignment; my eyes and ears so to speak, in case any issues arise', she confirmed rather ominously.

Madison looked the new guy up and down without comment. Todd Klingenschmidt was just another of those stereotypical city-boys who seemed to wear a permanent sneer on his face, but he nodded politely in Madison's direction and she acknowledged him in turn, with a tight smile.

Amanda motioned for Todd to sit down and then quickly ran through what she and Madison had already discussed to bring him up to speed.

Ten minutes later, Madison got up...and having carried out the usual social protocols she left the office with a hard-copy of the assignment tucked neatly under her arm…noting as she walked that there was a noticeable spring in her step that hadn't been there in a while.

♗

The next day when she arrived at her office, Amanda was greeted at the lift by her assistant Gayle who quickly informed her…with quite some urgency…that Mr Hines wanted to see her in his office. *(Bruce Hines was the paper's Chief Executive Officer)*

Amanda smirked at the news...as if she was expecting it…and without a hint of concern or unease she carried on down the corridor, walking calmly into her office with her assistant Gayle, following cautiously behind.

She sat down at her desk and barely had time to breathe before Gayle started running through a whole host of other 'less-important' messages… that were nevertheless awaiting a reply, and despite her dislike for this kind of early-morning ambush…a fact that was well-known around the office…she proceeded to reply to all of Gayle's questions and requests for information with her usual no-nonsense, self-confidence.

Gayle made a note of all these instructions and as she turned to leave, she took a moment to remind her boss that she also had a couple of important appointments in her diary later on in the day.

'I'm well aware of my diary, Gayle…' Amanda replied in muted irritation, picking up the phone at the same time; '…but thank you'.

♗

And so it was that twenty minutes or so later, having dealt with a number of 'important' calls, Amanda got up from her chair, picked out a number of files from the pile sitting on her desk and made her way up to the paper's executive suites situated on the top-floor of the building, the expression on her face a mix of consideration and malice.

She reached Bruce's office; just as Svetlana Joric, the paper's HR Rep was leaving and the two women exchanged a brief smile before Amanda swept into the office with her usual assured stride.

Inside, she was met by the strained expressions of three of the paper's most senior representatives; Bruce, who was sat behind his desk, Conrad Elliott (the paper's CFO; Chief Finance Officer) who was leaning up against the desk and Milton Harvey, the paper's lawyer who was sat on one of the leather couches.

Amanda greeted each of them in turn...with a great deal of familiarity... and then walked directly over to the drinks cabinet to pour herself a small glass of water before sitting herself down on the other couch…without being invited…and making herself comfortable, clearly at ease in the company of these powerful men...despite her rank in the paper's hierarchy.

'Amanda, I have just been informed (by Todd Klingenschmidt) that you have given that...that young woman a new mission', Bruce remarked, bristling with frustration.

'I have...' Amanda replied casually.

'But that isn't what we agreed', Bruce continued, unable to hide his irritation; 'you were supposed to find a way of getting rid of her'.

Amanda paused, took a sip of water and considered her response with great calm as all three men focussed their stares on her.

'Well Bruce', she explained; 'I could hardly sack her for helping to increase our market share the other week; could I?'

...and with that she placed three files on the table in front of her...

'Take a look at the figures gentlemen; the numbers don't lie...; I mean... her article was even trending on social networks at one point', she added, sitting back a little more comfortably and folding her arms in contentment.

'That's immaterial', Conrad interjected, looking a little perplexed.

'Exactly; that was not your remit', Bruce blustered, his exasperation starting to show; 'I want her gone', he insisted.

'That <u>is</u> what we agreed...' Milton confirmed brushing off an imaginary speck of dust from his trouser-leg.

'Well gentlemen…' Amanda reasoned; '…maybe this time she won't do such a good job and we can use that as leverage to ease her out'.

Bruce frowned, exhaled noisily and bit his lip.

‘Look Amanda, we’ve discussed this...and it was agreed...’ Conrad remonstrated, as he moved towards her, hands outstretched.

‘I’m well aware of what was agreed Conrad...’ Amanda retorted, putting down her glass and getting up in almost the same movement; ‘...but I’m not going to put my reputation on the line...or have my name associated with an accusation for wrongful dismissal just to satisfy your corporate ego’.

‘Besides, I thought we were trying to avoid any more negative publicity for a while’, she added pertinently and very matter-of-fact whilst glancing at each of the men in turn.

A brief silence descended on the room as all three men looked at each other feeling the other’s discomfort.

‘So...are we done here...?’ Amanda asked, her eyes scouring the room again.

Bruce threw his hands in the air but as nobody had anything else to say, Amanda simply turned on her heel and walked out, leaving the three men to continue their bureaucratic scheming amongst themselves.

♝

It took a while…but a month or so later - after an intense campaign of persuasion by Madison and the event’s organisers - the contractual differences with the English Chess Association had all been ironed out and an invitation had been sent out for *the Bishop* to appear in the exhibition match in Boston which – as previously agreed - Madison would be duly assigned to cover.

All that was left to do was for the ECA to convince *the Bishop* himself that he should actually consider doing it.

However, that process was far from straight-forward…and the ECA committee members had had to go on a real charm offensive themselves during those few weeks, meeting up with *the Bishop* on several occasions to discuss the deal with him...mindful of his reticence and knowing full well that he would always have the last word...but also hopeful of persuading him that the exhibition-match would be an ideal opportunity for them to show-case their champion and expose the game of chess to a wider audience...through the inevitable media coverage...while pushing its development as a spectator sport to a whole new level.

(Of course the fee that was on offer from the sponsor was also a great incentive for the ECA to encourage *the Bishop's* participation but they knew that that would not be the deciding factor in his decision)

It turned out to be a difficult and drawn-out negotiation but eventually, *the Bishop* was convinced by the committee's arguments...and despite his initial reluctance to get involved - due to his profound aversion to the media and to the inevitable circus that surrounds such events - he finally consented to putting the needs of the game first, and agreed to attend.

Boston...a few weeks later;

It was a sunny afternoon in Boston when flight BA213 from London finally touched down at Logan International Airport...and as arranged, in her official capacity of chaperon - *for want of a better title* - Madison was there to meet it, ready to smooth *the Bishop's* passage through the rest of the airport's procedures after what she knew would have been a very arduous US Customs process.

Unsurprisingly, she was a little nervous about meeting him again, after the way that things had ended that night at the abbey...but as she stood there, behind the barriers with her friend Evie, waiting for him to emerge from the restricted area behind the heavy metal-doors, Madison was resolved to making the most of this new opportunity to prove herself.

It wasn't in the budget but Madison had invited Evie along all the same; not only for the company...and the moral support...on the trip up from New York but also to cheer her friend up after a string of romantic disappointments... and of course...more pertinently to meet the Bishop who she (Madison) had clearly fixated on since her trip to England.

It might be a little awkward at first; she knew that...after what had happened at the abbey, but Madison was determined to use this event to impress her bosses...to show them what she was made of...to show them what she was capable of...and in doing so, she hoped...not only to confirm the potential that she had already shown glimpses of during her assignment in England...but also to soften their position - if not their attitude - towards her; a state-of-affairs that had poisoned her life every day since '*the incident*' all those months ago.

She truly believed that this was going to be her chance to shine; her chance for redemption as such – *even though she had done nothing wrong* - and she couldn't wait to get started, to show off her organisational skills... and to set in motion all the things that she had put into place in order to make *the Bishop's* stay...and the event itself...a huge success.

Time was moving really slowly...as it always seems to when you are waiting, but an hour or so into their penance the board above the girls' heads - which had been regularly updating itself and adding to their impatience - suddenly updated itself again, this time to announce that his flight, the flight that they had been waiting for, had landed.

'This is it', Madison cried out, turning to her friend and grabbing her in an unexpected bear hug...before realising her lack of composure and taking up a more professional pose.

Evie breathed a sigh of relief and winked cheekily at the guy standing next to her while Madison recomposed herself and swept her hair back over her shoulders in readiness to welcome her charge to the United States.

The girls looked at each other one more time and as they did so, the nervous tension that had been building between them all day suddenly cranked up another notch, making them quiver almost as they waited impatiently for the man himself to appear from behind the cold, impersonal steel-doors of the US border control.

That tension only added to the nervousness that Madison was already feeling...because she knew that the responsibility and the success…or failure…of this venture had been placed squarely on her shoulders.

She also knew that there were those back in the office - whose feathers she had ruffled previously - who were just waiting to see her fall flat on her face, and who would be only too pleased to rub her nose in it, were that to happen.

However, rising above all that negativity, Madison was nevertheless very excited too...and looking forward to meeting up...once again...with the enigmatic chess-master.

Moments later, people began to shuffle through from the restricted area behind the security doors...and the mood of expectation in the waiting crowd immediately began to swell - almost to a crescendo - as the first passengers came forward and faces began to beam with the delight of recognition and the relief that loved-ones, friends or family had arrived or returned home safely.

The trickle of people became a stream and the stream became a constant flow of humanity as hundreds of passengers began making their way out into the airport's main arrivals hall.

It took quite a while for everybody to filter through...but eventually the tide slowed to a drip and just as quickly as it had blossomed, the spontaneous excitement dissipated once again.

Only then, when both girls were beginning to think that he had missed the plane...or maybe that he was being kept behind by the Border Control officers for some unforeseen security reason...did the doors open one more time and the man that they had been waiting for so patiently, appeared before their very eyes, sauntering casually down the row of barriers as if on a Sunday afternoon stroll.

He was wearing that same arrogant expression that had had such a devastating effect on Madison the first time that they had met in that hotel restaurant in Amersham but to her great surprise...and disappointment... he walked right past her and Evie without any kind of acknowledgment or recognition.

She called out; 'Mr Byron...', and as he turned his head in response, their eyes met, locking momentarily as he changed direction and walked calmly back towards them.

They greeted each other politely...her with a wry smile and him with a subtle nod of the head...but despite their outward reserve, there was no denying the unmistakeable chemistry that fused between them, even though - because of the situation - neither was prepared to admit it.

Madison then introduced her friend Evie and as they made their way out through the small crowd of waiting relatives still clustered around the exit, TB reached into the carrier-bag he was carrying and handed Madison a gift as a thank you for all the hard work that she had obviously accomplished in organising the event.

Surprised, she thanked him for the gesture and continued guiding him towards the waiting photographers, who she had organised to be waiting in a quiet corner of the building...leaving Evie to follow a few steps behind.

There, playing her role to perfection, Madison introduced *the Bishop* to the 'paps' with a brief summary of who he was and why he was in Boston. . .and having fulfilled her remit she then stepped aside so that the photographers could snap the British champion from every angle.

She hated ambushing him like this – especially knowing his abhorrence of such things - but Madison needed maximum exposure for the event and she knew that this was the best way of getting it; the reward, she hoped would be worth...or at least would justify...the expected fallout.

However, she needn't have been so concerned.

The Bishop stood proudly in front of all the flashing lenses...and for the next ten minutes he complied admirably with all that was asked of him while....unable to resist the temptation...Madison faded into the background and sneaked a quick peek at what he had bought for her.

Surprise, surprise, she thought to herself; it was a book; 'The Mistresses of Cliveden; three centuries of scandal, power and intrigue in an English stately home', by Natalie Livingstone.

Madison looked at the cover and recognised the name of the stately home where they had had dinner that time...but then biting her lip she also remembered that that was the same evening that he had invited her back to the abbey and humiliated her by sending her home...or at least back to her hotel...disappointed and unfulfilled.

What was this? She wondered. Some kind of coded message that she should read more....she wouldn't put it past him...or was he rubbing her nose in it; asserting his control over her in some way by reminding her of that evening...or...could it be a more subtle reminder of what had been a wonderful evening...right up until...

Or...maybe he was feeling guilty...

...No, that wasn't it, Madison reasoned, tutting to herself and shaking her head dismissively.

Having spent time with the man, she knew that he would never admit to any infallibility of that order.

She thrust her hand back into the package and pulled out a second item; it was a bottle of perfume...Fendi perfume...that he had clearly picked up in the duty-free store at Heathrow before flying out. No doubt, a last minute attempt to be civil, she grumbled to herself as she stuffed both items back into the shiny carrier-bag

♗

The photo-shoot over, they were ushered towards a waiting car by airport security and as they did so, Madison felt obliged to apologise to *the Bishop* for having sprung the photographers on him, knowing full well that he detested the media...and especially having his photograph taken... but then surprising her once again, showing perfect self-control, he simply nodded his head in an understanding fashion, and motioned her and her friend into the car, without further comment.

His luggage loaded in the trunk, the car headed off and a couple of minutes later, once they were comfortably ensconced in the relative calm of the rented limousine, with Evie sitting quietly opposite, keeping herself to herself, Madison duly took out her note-pad and began to run through the itinerary of *the Bishop's* stay, informing him first that she had booked him into the Fairmont Copley Plaza hotel for the duration of his stay - *one of the most luxurious hotels in Boston* - and that any expenses he might occasion during his time there - within reason – would be covered by an expense account.

She also informed him that she and Evie would be staying at the hotel too, so that she could be on hand - as his chaperon - if there was anything else that he might need; avoiding his gaze as she said it but hoping clearly that he would pick up on her lame attempt at subtlety.

He fixed her with a stare which she held for a moment before ultimately averting her eyes, and shifting uncomfortably in her seat, using her trusty note-pad as a distraction.

The Bishop sat back in his seat and in that instant he realised that the brash facade and abrasive posturing Madison had displayed in England had all been a facade, thereby confirming his first impression of her.

The rest of the itinerary was pretty straight-forward and Madison concluded her professional spiel by saying that if there was anything else he would like to do while he was there...as far as cultural activities were concerned...then he should let her know and she would be only too pleased to organise it for him.

'Thank-you Miss Chatfield; you are too kind', was his only response as the limo turned off the highway and approached the entrance to the hotel.

The limo came to a halt and as they clambered out acknowledging *the Bishop's* gentlemanly, 'ladies first' gesture, Evie threw a bewildered glance in her friend's direction and couldn't help mouthing the words 'who is this guy?', to her as discreetly as possible as she recomposed herself quietly on the pavement.

The hotel's porters greeted them with the usual welcoming manner and while they (*the porters*) took charge of removing *the Bishop*'s suitcases from the rear of the car, Madison confirmed arrangements with the limo-driver for the rest of the day, agreeing with him that if there were any change of plans, she would call him on his mobile number.

The trio then checked in at the hotel's beautifully appointed reception and within no time they were in the lift and on their way up to their rooms; everything was going like clockwork.

When the lift stopped, Madison stepped out first, followed closely by *the Bishop*...while Evie, who was feeling a little awkward, hung back a little waiting to be invited to join them.

'Come on hon; keep up', Madison blurted out, getting a little carried away by her role.

They arrived at *the Bishop's* room and having opened the door for him, Madison invited him to take the lead, as she handed him his key-card.

It was a little over-the-top, Madison knew that; she knew that she was treating her 'guest' with as much deference as she would royalty, but she was so desperate to make a good impression that she was even prepared to swallow her pride...to a certain extent...if it meant her succeeding in her mission at the end of the day.

The Bishop went inside...and then curious to see for themselves, Madison and Evie followed in behind, almost falling over each other, as they marvelled at the room's wonderful layout and plush furnishings.

Their 'guest' was already checking out the wardrobes...and having given the room his approval, he went over to the window, where looking out and down at the swimming-pool area, he noticed a line of tanned. . .or not so tanned. . .topless sun-worshippers basting in the hot sun.

'Don't you just abhor those white lines?' he remarked somewhat bizarrely.

This rather unusual comment took both women by surprise and not knowing what to say...or how to react in the moment...they just looked at each other, shrugged their shoulders and nodded at him politely, mumbling an unconvincing 'yeah, I suppose so' under their breaths, before Madison quickly changed the subject, announcing that she was certain that he would like some time to himself to unwind before meeting up again. . .and that, if it was alright by him, they would reconvene again, at six, down in the hotel bar before going to dinner.

The Bishop simply nodded in agreement and with that, the girls left him to get unpacked and went back to their own room...which they had booked into earlier...to do the same.

Madison went straight into the bathroom to take a shower, to get rid of the sweat and the nervous tension that had built up during the day. *(She would have preferred a bath but with the two of them in the room there just wasn't going to be enough time.)*

Meanwhile Evie relaxed on the bed and began flicking through one of the magazines that featured Madison's article. *(The latter had brought a few copies along for publicity purposes and potentially to give one to the Bishop)*

'Who's this guy in the corner?' she asked casually, pointing to a thumbnail photo of Rory.

'Oh, that guy's a creep', Madison replied, coming out of the bathroom half-dressed to look at the photo before going straight back in.

'He looks like the snowman out of 'Frozen'; what was his name...?' Evie questioned.

'Olaf', Madison shouted out.

'Right...Olaf', Evie concurred; 'he looks like that guy'.

Then turning back the page and seeing *the Bishop's* photo Evie took out her phone and 'googled' him.

'Geez, this guy is a mystery', she announced.

'What...?' Madison questioned, appearing again in the bathroom doorway.

'I just 'googled' your bishop guy...and well...'

'I know', Madison concurred, giving her friend a quick sideways glance.

'There are just a couple of write-ups about him from chess tournaments; his Wikipedia page is barely three lines long...and there is not even a photo; he's practically a ghost', Evie complained, suddenly exasperated.

'I know', Madison concurred again before disappearing back into the bathroom.

'Maybe there's more on his Facebook page?' Evie suggested, raising her voice.

Madison popped her head around the bathroom door.

'Really; do you think he is the kind of guy that has a Facebook page?' she queried.

Evie shrugged.

'He doesn't; I've checked', Madison confirmed, before disappearing once again.

Stepping out of the shower a few minutes later, Madison stood in front of the mirror, checking herself out while towelling her long blond hair.

'So what is it about this guy that you like', Evie pursued; '...the obvious physical attraction aside, I mean?'

'You can't fool me', she added; 'I saw those stolen glances in the car'.

'I really don't know', Madison answered, re-entering the room, swathed in a couple of those over-sized hotel towels; 'I suppose it's just the force of his personality'.

'Yeah right...no, I can see that...' Evie reasoned; 'he's clearly not the kind of guy who just wants to hit it and quit it'.

'Just the kind of guy you're looking for', she added after a brief pause.

'How do you know what I'm looking for?' Madison countered.

She was uncomfortable discussing the Bishop because while she felt an almost gravitational pull towards him, she really didn't know where she stood with him.

'But, enough about him' Madison said changing the subject; 'what are you looking for hon?'

Evie rolled onto her back and her eyes seemed to glaze over.

'Me...?; I want a hot, sweaty body on top of me, pinning me down, heaving; I want hot passionate lips pressed firmly against my own; I want... hands...and caresses...and...'

'Okay, okay, I get where you're going...' Madison interrupted, hardening her tone.

'By the way'; Evie enquired innocuously; 'I forgot to ask you, what was in that bag...at the airport?'

'Oh that', Madison replied nonchalantly.

'Perfume; what do you think?' she asked holding out the gift.

Evie took the bottle from Madison's grasp and having examined its shape, she sprayed a little of the scent on her wrist.

The smell was intense at first but once it had had time to breathe, the aroma was quite pleasant.

However, Evie didn't like it. 'It's not for me', she declared giving the bottle back.

Madison smiled; 'Well, I quite like it', she announced brightly, turning back around and spraying a cloud into the air which she walked through with intent before walking back around the bed.

'He also bought me this', Madison explained, handing Evie the book.

Evie took hold of the tome and read the title.

'A book about mistresses', she mumbled; 'hmmm...am I missing something in the sub-text here...?' she enquired.

Madison shook her head and disappeared once again into the bathroom, images of the evening she had spent at that extraordinary residence suddenly flooding her mind.

Evie put aside the book and the magazine, turned on the TV and began zapping through the channels looking for something interesting to watch.

There <u>was</u> nothing interesting as far as she was concerned so rather than blur her mind with rubbish she got up and began laying out the clothes she was going to wear for dinner.

'What do you think?' She called out to Madison; 'sexy or demure?'

'What?' Madison questioned, coming out of the bathroom still swathed in Terry towels.

'Sexy or demure', Evie repeated holding first one dress then another up against her body.

'...Demure, definitely demure', Madison advised, not wanting her friend to upstage her in any way in front of her guest.

'You do know, that this guy of yours is a little weird, don't you?' Evie remarked, reflecting on *the Bishop's* strange demeanour as she checked herself out in the mirror.

Madison didn't reply as she was now back in the bathroom, towelling her hair.

'I think it's just as well that I've tagged along', Evie continued.

'Oh, he's really not that bad', Madison countered, appearing yet again in the doorway.

'He's not? You could have fooled me' Evie retorted continuing her theme.

'Listen Evie', Madison reasoned, sitting down on the bed beside her friend; 'all I'm asking you to do, is not to judge him too harshly before you get to know him; okay'.

'Okay hon ...but all I'm saying is that my overwhelming first impression of this guy is that he is a jerk', Evie concluded unmoved as she riffled through her suitcase looking for suitable underwear to go under her dress of choice.

'No, he's not', Madison argued, taking *the Bishop's* defence and contradicting her friend again, a hint of irritation creeping into her tone.

'He might be unconventional, he might be unorthodox, but he's no jerk; you'll see', she confirmed as she strolled back into the bathroom to finish doing her hair.

Evie shrugged her shoulders; 'yeah, we'll see…' she mumbled to herself as she too started to get undressed.

♗

Later, downstairs in the bar, while they were waiting for Evie to join them, *the Bishop* took the opportunity to ask Madison if she had liked her present.

'Yes I did; thank-you...for the book...and the perfume; it's not what I usually wear but...'

'I know it's not what you usually wear...' *the Bishop* interrupted; '...but it's what I think suits you best'.

Madison stood there aghast and recoiled visibly, lost for words.

'The scent is strong with a subtle hint of grace and elegance', *the Bishop* intoned with authority, accompanying his description with an airy hand-gesture.

Madison was stunned and more than a little taken aback that this man who she barely knew had actually put so much thought into his choice of perfume...and not just picked up the first thing on the shelf like most men would have done...

'Well...thank-you...again' is all she could come up with in reply as Evie suddenly appeared in the bar's doorway, wearing a beautiful, moss-green polka-dot dress.

♗

Madison raised her hand to catch her attention and Evie immediately joined them at their table...where, ever the gentleman...*the Bishop* immediately sat back and complimented her...very politely...on her choice of attire.

‘Thank you, thank you very much kind sir’; Evie replied coyly, trying to sound sophisticated or as sophisticated as possible, while at the same time feeling a little uncomfortable at *the Bishop's* close scrutiny of her outfit; ‘I just love polka-dots’.

Evie's obsession with polka-dots had begun years earlier, after she had seen the film Pretty Woman and been blown away by Julia Roberts's beauty in that stunning chocolate-brown and white polka-dot dress.

In contrast, Madison looked very formal in her rather staid business-suit as she felt she needed to maintain her professional persona throughout her mission; at least in TB's presence.

The barman came over to take their order; the drinks were served and for the next twenty minutes or so the three of them sat there exchanging small-talk and soaking up the relaxed mood.

The barman came over again a while later to ask if they wanted another round...and Evie was keen...but thinking about getting an early night, Madison immediately held up her hand and suggested that they decide instead on what they were going to do for dinner as their schedule the following day was going to be very taxing.

She had already pre-booked a table at the hotel's cosmopolitan restaurant as a contingency, and she voiced that option...but having pondered the idea for a moment *the Bishop* suddenly proposed an alternative;

‘I'm sure that the hotel restaurant is...wonderful...but why don't we go for a walk around Faneuil Hall and the historic centre of Boston instead... to get some fresh air...before looking for a place, a little less formal, to sit down and eat?’ he submitted.

Madison knew all too well about *the Bishop's* interest in American culture so it was no surprise to her that he would want to do that...but nevertheless she was more than a little taken-aback by the fact that he was prepared to embrace the rest of the city's citizens sharing his cultural experience with him; him being such a hermit and all.

Ten minutes later;

The trio walked around Boston city centre taking in the sights...and then strolled through Chinatown stopping from time to time to look at menus or admire an interesting view, before finally opting to go for a meal at a small restaurant called Radius recommended by the guide-book, which served delicious French cuisine; Madison having made a note in her brief...and remembering Cliveden...that her guest particularly appreciated refined cuisine.

It was indeed a pleasant experience and during the meal, the conversation was light and non-confrontational until somehow they got onto the subject of Hollywood...probably through Evie admitting that she wasn't used to all this five star treatment...which suddenly changed the mood.

'It's like being in Hollywood', Evie announced breezily, the two glasses of wine she had consumed having loosened her tongue.

The Bishop swallowed what he was eating and then slowly turned to face her, morphing for the first time since his arrival into his alpha-male role.

'Hollywood is a state of mind, but it is superficial and shallow', he commented.

'I don't know about you, but personally, I don't buy into the Hollywood concept', he continued; 'the Disney dream ending where they ride off into the sunset, get married, have lots of children, and all live happily ever after etc.

Evie looked at Madison. 'What did I say?' she asked perplexed.

'Let it go', Madison whispered.

The Bishop then took hold of his glass and unperturbed by the girls whispering he continued his thoughts out loud.

'Most stories of young-love in those films end on a 'happily ever after' theme, which is all very well...and I don't object to this - but the reality of life tells us differently, surely?'

He looked at the girls waiting for a reaction but sensing a sermon coming on, Madison preferred to focus her efforts on getting the waiter's attention.

The Bishop leaned forward, fixing Evie directly.

'Tell me, young lady…'

Madison interrupted; 'Her name is Evie.'

The Bishop glanced at Madison but she didn't see his stare as she was too busy waving the waiter forward.

'So, tell me…Evie', he questioned; 'why is it, do you think, that American films always have to have a moral ending where good defeats evil, when reality and life in general often proves to be the contrary?'

Evie looked at Madison for advice on how she should answer her guest's rather intimidating argument but as none was forthcoming, she let rip on her own.

'Okay wise-guy', she replied; 'that is solid gold…bull…crap. Hollywood is all about entertainment and escapism; you're not meant to believe it'.

She paused and then continued. 'It's abstract idealism; we all know that it's not real but for the two hours that we sit and watch a movie, we are transported into another dimension where reality is suspended; that's all it is', she explained.

'But don't you see that as rather shallow?' *The Bishop* insisted in reply, secretly impressed by Evie's succinct explanation.

'No, I do not', Evie retorted holding her ground. 'I see it as harmless cultural Prozac'.

There was a lull in the conversation after that, as the waiter came over and Madison asked him to push the service along, anxious to avoid another one of *the Bishop's* self-indulgent speeches…but then, not to be outmanoeuvred, the man himself shot another question at Evie.

'Answer me this, then Evie', he persisted rather annoyingly; 'if Hollywood is just a distraction not to be confused with reality, then why is the city of Los Angeles amongst others, so hell-bent on destroying its female population with all that cosmetic surgery; boob-jobs, botoxed-lips, liposuction and even vaginal rejuvenation…in order to conform with what Hollywood portrays?', he trumpeted self-righteously.

Evie pouted disdainfully with veiled animosity, but unable to offer another reasoned parry she could do nothing but concede.

'Good point; touché', she acknowledged, finishing her wine.

'You see Evie', *the Bishop* insisted again like a dog with a bone; 'the mainstream media as epitomised by Hollywood, forces young girls to try and meet unattainable, idealistic criteria in their formative years; all to conform with the '...because I'm worth it...' generation'.

'Their own vanity has become the centre of these young girls' universe; it is so wrong', he persisted yet again.

'You sure are one happy person', Evie complained, gesticulating airily with obvious irritation.

'Happiness...as a goal...is a myth too', *the Bishop* announced smugly. 'People are just brain-washed – by society, religion or the TV advertising executives - into thinking that they want more than they already have'.

'Wow, you really are the life and soul of the party', Evie grumbled with just the slightest hint of anger in her voice; 'you should get a life'.

'What was it that Socrates once said?' Madison interjected out of nowhere; 'Happiness is just un-repented pleasure'.

The Bishop bowed his head in admiration, impressed that Madison could actually quote the fabled Greek philosopher and in recognition of that fact he suddenly sat back in his seat, relinquishing his mental hold on Evie at the same time.

Pleased with herself, Madison decided to change the subject...and lighten the mood...by explaining to their guest how she and Evie had met. . .and become the best of friends.

'We lived in the same apartment complex and had done for years, but we had never met until one day we both went to see a show being performed by Chris Rock', Madison revealed.

'Chris Rock is a comedian from Brooklyn', Evie interrupted to explain, '...and talking about Chris Rock', she continued, 'you remind me of a sketch he once did, about being conservative about some things and liberal about others ....'

The waiter re-appeared at that moment with the next course and Evie lost her train of thought, so after a brief pause, Madison took up her story again, where she had left off, on how she and Evie had met after the show trying to get into the same cab.

'Yeah, that was some episode and ever since, we've been the best of friends', Evie added, 'though I have to admit that Madison was always on the fast track and she moved out of our building pretty soon after...she got herself a place in the city...but I still live out in the suburbs', she concluded.

'Ah, suburbia', TB commented with irony; 'a place where they tear down trees and name streets after them'.

'You're such a wise-guy', Evie riposted, flicking her chestnut-coloured hair disdainfully, her frustration growing by the minute.

'So, how do you like living in the city', *the Bishop* asked, ignoring Evie's comment and turning his attention back to Madison.

'Well', she replied honestly, trying to drop a broad hint; 'in New York as in most big cities there is an undercurrent of loneliness, desperation and sadness but apart from that, I wouldn't want to live anywhere else'.

The Bishop nodded his head in understanding.

The conversation pretty much ebbed and flowed from there on after, drifting along tediously towards the end of the meal as Madison and TB concentrated mainly on the schedule for the forthcoming event…until it was time to leave.

Meanwhile, feeling a little ignored, Evie pulled out her phone and started texting which Madison didn't pick up on at first until eventually she leaned in and whispered playfully in Evie's ear; 'You do know that more than three texts in an evening is considered stalking'.

Her friend's face creased into a half-smile but she didn't say a word.

Little did Madison know, but Evie...and through her, her friends...had been posting and re-posting her article on Facebook and tweeting and re-tweeting it on Twitter ever since it had appeared in order to get it noticed.

Later, back in their room, as they got ready for bed, Madison and Evie dissected the evening in great detail, picking over the bones of everything that had happened.

Madison lay across her bed...dressed in a pair of blue-silk pyjamas while Evie who was wearing an old American-football shirt and pair of cute boy-shorts was still fussing over her nightly skin-care routine.

'Well, there's no risk of boring small talk with that guy', Evie suggested sarcastically as she slapped on her rejuvenating cream.

Madison rolled onto her back casting her mind back through the day's events...but not wanting to get into another discussion about *the Bishop*, who was already occupying more space in her thoughts than she cared to admit, she ignored her friend's comment and remarked instead on her American football shirt (NY Jets No16; Vinnie Testaverde), revealing that she knew somebody else that wore replica shirts and that perhaps she should introduce them.

'If he's anything like as exciting as that Bishop guy, you can forget it', Evie complained petulantly; 'my God, only a masochist could love such a narcissist', she insisted.

'No; don't worry, the guy I'm thinking of is the complete opposite'; Madison reassured her, ignoring her friend's disparaging comment and picturing Gary in her mind's eye.

'They are like chalk and cheese; couldn't be more different', she confirmed.

'...but TB's not that bad, is he?', she enquired after a reflective pause, knowing that she could count on Evie to be direct and straightforward even in awkward circumstances.

'Well, what can I say; where do I start?' Evie responded, as she slumped onto the bed next to her friend.

'He has a rather annoying personality; he is cheerfully-challenged, haughty and contemptuous, and his persistent cynicism is depressing...but that aside, I suppose he is okay', Evie conceded in conclusion, sensing her friend's burgeoning attraction to the object of her critique.

'Touchdown', Madison exclaimed emphatically, punching her fist in the air, trying to derive a measure of solace from her friend's rather tacit and sarcastic approval.

'But seriously', she added, as she got into bed; 'he's not that bad; he just hides behind his intellect to avoid expressing any emotion'.

'Aha', Evie concurred...and with that, Madison reached up and put out the light, ending the day on a reassuringly positive note.

Next morning;

After breakfast and with perfect timing, the limo was ready and waiting outside to take them to the venue for a small press-conference and presentation of the event which was due to take place the following day.

Everything went smoothly...but...after the presentation had concluded *the Bishop* pulled Madison aside and asked her discreetly to have a word with the organisers. He feared that, while she was doing a good job, the one-off game against a local university professor lacked any serious challenge to his talent…and in order to add a little extra interest to the event's appeal, he wanted her to organise twenty five blind games on top of the exhibition match.

Madison was shocked when he explained how this worked…but when she presented the idea to the organisers they were absolutely delighted to add another feature to the event and immediately set about arranging it.

Then, delighted to be able to inform Todd of this extra component to the challenge, Madison accompanied *the Bishop* back to his hotel...where – as was his custom - he isolated himself in his room for the rest of the day to work on his concentration.

He (*the Bishop*) wasn't interested in dining out that evening, so having checked that room-service had his order...and having written up her notes and called Todd back in New York to inform him about how things were progressing, Madison and Evie decided to go out for dinner just the two of them.

It had been a long day for both of them, but as the two girls were getting ready later, titivating themselves side by side in the bathroom Madison in her underwear and Evie wearing only her bra - *displaying her exhibitionist tendencies* - the following conversation took place.

'I'm all hot and horny' Evie announced, rocking her head from side-to-side and shimmying her hips as if practicing her dance moves.

Mildly amused by her comment Madison gave her friend a sideways glance.

'Hey; don't knock it', Evie continued; 'the hip roll is a powerful seduction tool if used right...and tonight I might just get laid through using it; it's about time my dug-out got filled with some new talent'.

'Eew...' Madison replied; '...chance would be a fine thing...but if you are going to go there you might want to trim the field first ...and tidy up the mound', she chided with mock outrage, continuing the baseball-themed chit-chat.

'You're one to talk; look at your underwear; it is so wholesome', Evie retorted, her mouth curling into a grin.

'Wholesome; what does that even mean?' Madison replied aghast.

'It means...oh, never mind...we need to get a move on...' Evie stammered.

'Pochemoosh...' Madison mumbled trying to imitate *the Bishop's* erudite indignation.

'What does <u>that</u> mean?' Evie quizzed.

'It means...oh, never mind', Madison answered flatly as she disappeared back into the bedroom where she slipped delicately into a pretty cotton print-dress.

A few minutes later Evie emerged from the bathroom too, looking stunning in a black crochet dress.

'It hides a multitude of sins...but the heat is on', Evie explained, rolling her eyes naughtily; 'I need to get laid'. She was clearly in a mischievous mood.

Madison shook her head but having decided where they would eat, the two friends set off, receiving a number of admiring glances as they walked down the hall towards the elevators.

They walked to a small restaurant not far from the hotel and having been seated and offered a free cocktail by the charming French waiter they spent the rest of the evening discussing the usual mundane absurdities that all girlfriends talk about when they get together…although both avoided talking about *the Bishop* for very different reasons.

That said; despite her apparent disillusion with the male genre, Evie seemed to enjoy her evening enormously, flirting outrageously with both the waiter and the restaurant manager, while Madison on the other hand could not stop her thoughts from wandering back to her charge.

The following day; the day of the match, was another beautiful Boston day and despite Madison's nervous anxiety beforehand, *the Bishop* had no problem winning both the exhibition match and the twenty five blind-challenges without even breaking into a sweat, showing flashes of incisive brilliance at times, as he slowly won over the initial scepticism of the watching crowd who began to cheer a little more with every winning move that he made.

It took him just under two hours to complete his triumph, and after the final game, once the last challenger to his supremacy had been bamboozled into submission, *the Bishop* stood up and graciously acknowledged the acclaim of the crowd, his confident demeanour showing through magnificently as he milked the prolonged applause...

...and for once, he didn't find the attention distracting or intrusive; indeed he found it most flattering.

Throngs of people came up to congratulate him on his extraordinary feat and amongst them one person – delighted to have witnessed his prowess - gave him two invitations to a film premiere that was taking place that evening.

The Bishop accepted the tickets courteously and immediately handed them to Madison, informing her quietly that he had no interest in 'those kinds of events'.

She looked at him a little surprised but didn't question him and took them off him gladly, certain that she would be able to find somebody who did.

The Bishop then went about fulfilling all the other media duties that were suddenly thrust upon him after his brilliant display...but as soon as it was feasibly possible, he pulled Madison aside once again and announced... in his usual abrupt manner...that he would not be attending be the ensuing cocktail party that had been organised in his honour;

'I know people back in England who organise that kind of shindig...' he explained bluntly...

'I'm sorry...' Madison interjected; '...shindig?' she repeated a look of mild amusement spreading rapidly across her face at his use of such a word.

'Merriment...joviality', *the Bishop* clarified using a throwaway hand-gesture to emphasise his point.

'Oh I see...a shindig', Madison repeated again, stifling a snigger.

'Yes...a shindig', *the Bishop* reiterated, ignoring her attempt to tease him; '...and they just use such events as an excuse to pour as much champagne as they can into people before sitting back and waiting for the inevitable to happen...which usually means someone making a fool of themselves. That just isn't my cup of tea', *the Bishop* added with a hint of disdain.

Madison nodded her understanding...and as another group of spectators came over to them, praising *the Bishop* and showering him in congratulations, she quietly stepped away, took out her mobile phone and began arranging for them to slip away.

Having done that...and seeing that *the Bishop* was still surrounded by several of his adoring fans…which made her smile quietly to herself, knowing how much he was probably loathing all the attention...Madison went to find Evie who...looking stunning in her blue-silk polka-dot shift-dress...was stationed discreetly in an alcove chatting to a couple of smart 'executive-types'.

Now Evie was clearly enjoying her chat with the two guys...and so, not wanting to interrupt, Madison simply stood in her friend's eye-line, trying as best she could to get her attention with the use of a couple of discreet hand gestures.

It didn't work; Evie was far too engrossed in her conversation, so realising that she was pushed for time, Madison had no choice but to sidle right up to her...and smiling generously at the two men...who both returned her smile...she leaned in towards her friend and quietly whispered in her ear that she and *the Bishop* were leaving, if she wanted to tag along.

Evie listened with one ear and then frowned in disappointment.

'Thanks hon, but I think I'm good', she announced, glancing back at the two guys; 'besides...I don't think I could sit through another one of your Bishop's tedious lectures.

'He is not my Bishop', Madison protested in a loud whisper, glancing sideways to check the whereabouts of the man in question.

Evie smiled facetiously.

'Well maybe not...' she remarked calmly, looking around in turn for *the Bishop's* location; '...but heads up girl; the guy likes you...'

Madison was stunned by that comment...and while she took a moment to process the implications of what it could mean...*spying the complimentary-tickets in her friend's hand*...Evie quickly reached out and grabbed them, before turning on her heel and walking away in the opposite direction with careless abandon, waving the invitations above her head and assuring Madison that she was 'bound to find someone at the cocktail party who would like to accompany her to the glitzy event later that evening'.

Still rooted to the spot by the thoughts rushing around her brain... and her friend's rather brazen audacity, Madison could do nothing... for a second or two...but shake her head in bewilderment...and as Evie disappeared into the crowd she (Madison) had to take another few ticks to regain her professional composure, before wheeling away herself and going to look for one...or other of the event's sponsors in order to inform him of *the Bishop's* decision to leave.

The crowd in the hall was still quite plentiful but after a few minutes searching Madison came across two of the sponsors...together with their wives...in a corner discussing the event's success.

She approached the small coterie with restored poise...and once the usual courtesies had been dispensed with...together with a couple of mutual compliments on how well everything had been coordinated (from the men)...and how amazingly talented *the Bishop* was (from the women)... Madison quietly informed the group of the change in plans.

Naturally both men were a little disappointed by the news; their wives too...and one even asked if there was any way that their 'VIP-guest' could be persuaded to reconsider...to stay a while longer and perhaps even to make an appearance at the cocktail...but Madison just shook her head; 'No I don't think so', she replied apologetically; 'he is very tired and just wants to go back to his hotel'.

'Very well', the elder of the two men agreed with a nod of the head... and with that Madison excused herself and made her way back through the crowd towards the back-entrance of the building...where she had arranged for the limo to be waiting...signalling to *the Bishop* as she went by, that he should follow her as soon as he was good and ready, which he did almost immediately.

Outside;

He caught up with her just outside the building...and with his usual courtesy, *the Bishop* quickly opened the limo-door and invited Madison to get inside, before following in her footsteps and pulling the door closed behind him.

Madison made herself comfortable on the bench-seat and for the first time since she had walked out of Amanda's office all those months before she relaxed and let forth an almighty sigh of relief. After all her hard work, the 'chess-challenge' had been an undeniable success and the pressure of her responsibilities had at last been lifted from her shoulders.

Now, she thought to herself, as she looked askance at her fellow passenger, it was time to find out more about this strange, enigmatic man who had...for some inexplicable reason...become such an object of fascination in her eyes.

The limo pulled away and as it joined the flow of early-evening traffic Madison caught *the Bishop's* eye...and she smiled at him politely. It was a genuine, open smile; a smile that said thank-you for a 'job well-done' and much to her surprise *the Bishop* returned the sentiment with a smile of his own; a tight, uneasy smile…but a smile nonetheless.

♗

Neither of them spoke during the ride back but as *the Bishop* was sat across from her...albeit at an angle...it gave Madison the perfect opportunity to study her charge and to make a more precise mental note of his rather distinctive features...just in case she needed them for future reference.

'TB' as his friends called him, had an almost-regal bearing about him and while she had not always found him...amenable...she had to admit that every time they had met he had carried himself with a kind of masculine grace and elegance that clearly set him apart from all the other men she knew.

He was very confident and very self-aware too...without being overly arrogant...although he could be a little wearing and obnoxious at times... but, she thought to herself, the contrast between him and that other guy... Copperfield...for example...could not be more glaringly obvious...and as he sat there full of life and relevance only a metre or so away from her it slowly became clear to Madison, that she was more than a little taken with him.

She then noticed that he was slowly opening and closing his right hand...repeatedly...but not wanting to break the ambient silence with another potentially-irritating enquiry she didn't mention it, assuming simply that it was probably some kind of cramp that had set into his fingers after playing chess for hours on end.

Then, all of a sudden, *the Bishop* sensed her gazing at him...but before he could engage her, Madison quickly diverted her attention back out the window...at the road ahead...only to be brought back into the moment seconds later by the ping of a message arriving on her phone.

She reached into her pocket, pulled out her phone and glanced at the screen. On it was a selfie from Evie...of her...and some random guy holding the premiere-film invitations...and the sight of her friend...and her mischievous grin...immediately made Madison scoff unexpectedly and chortle out loud.

This drew *the Bishop's* attention once again and for the very first time since they had met in England, he noticed and appreciated her bewitching natural smile.

♗

It was then that...out of nowhere...probably driven by the adrenaline running through her veins...and the fact that she hadn't eaten all day... Madison suddenly leaned forward and instructed the limo driver to drop them off at Grill 23...rather than the hotel...where she thought that she and *the Bishop* might enjoy a real American food experience, away from the madding crowd; just as he liked it.

They were almost back at the hotel but the driver instantly acknowledged the change of itinerary...and as *the Bishop* raised an eyebrow in surprise...he quickly indicated to turn right, off the main highway, in order to follow the new heading.

♗

At the restaurant;

At the restaurant, Madison ordered chicken piccata with roasted pine-nuts and a side-order of salad for them both. It looked and smelled absolutely delicious...and as she hadn't eaten all day she wasted no time in tucking in.

As a consequence, they ate in relative silence, any verbal exchanges kept to a bare minimum, which suited both parties to begin with.

However, in between mouthfuls, unable to reign in her curiosity indefinitely, Madison did take a time-out to ask her distinguished guest why it was that he was so reluctant to join in with things...with social events etc, making reference to the cocktail party and to his refusal to accept the film-premiere invitations.

Looking slightly irritated, *the Bishop* sat back in his seat, inhaled deeply through his nostrils, took another drink of wine and then looked at her intensely over the lip of his glass.

'Hey, I'm just doing my job', Madison blurted out, trying to justify her question and pre-empt his impending ire as she wiped her mouth carefully.

'Don't say that', he responded wearily;

'That's just the typical excuse used in any conflict...notably by those perpetrating genocide..."that they were just doing their job"; it's a stock-standard, generic response...but it can never justify or excuse such actions', he affirmed, his assertive tone allowing him to cleverly side-step the question she had actually asked.

Taken aback again, Madison felt his put-down was a little over-the-top - and frankly uncalled for - but quickly changing tack, she decided to indulge her guest after his stressful afternoon and throw him a compliment on his talent...and on the way he had won all his challenge matches.

This time *the Bishop* smiled graciously and raised his glass, thanking her for her kind words.

Then, drawing a comparison between himself and Madison, he returned the compliment, provoking a sudden rush of heat to the usually-blasé New Yorker's stomach, which took her by surprise.

'I can see that you are highly motivated Miss Chatfield...and I have to applaud you for your drive and determination in the pursuit of your goals', he remarked with sincerity...and a hint of admiration.

'...and your organisation of today's event was a perfect example of that', he added, discreetly monitoring her reaction.

'Thank-you; that's very kind of you', Madison replied, wiping her mouth again carefully, to hide her self-satisfied smile.

The Bishop acknowledged her thanks with a barely-discernible nod of the head...but as she basked in this rather surreal moment of mutual appreciation...even though the organisation of the day's event had not been down to her entirely...Madison still couldn't help feeling confused about how she felt towards this enigma of a man. She knew that she was beginning to enjoy his company but she didn't quite understand why being in his presence had such a visceral effect on her.

'We are both talented individuals', *the Bishop* continued in a surprisingly measured tone, 'and talented people are always looking for challenges'.

'The maths is simple', he pursued, leaning forward; '....by meeting those challenges and striving to fulfil our potential, we evolve intellectually and spiritually as individuals'.

'You and I Miss Chatfield...are intellectual equals...and while we might not have much in common we both know what a wonderful feeling it is... to know what you want, to go after it and to get it; to believe you deserve it. You and I both have that', *the Bishop* reasoned purposefully.

Hearing those words sent another shiver down Madison's spine and her eyes lit up with genuine gratitude. She smiled again graciously and without realising it, she reached up to her face and ran her fingers through her beautifully-coiffed blond hair.

'Well, they do say that 'opposites attract', she interjected, trying to introduce a degree of levity into the conversation.

'Yes indeed, opposites do attract...like magnets', *the Bishop* agreed...

'...but then 'the flip side of attraction is repulsion', he thought to himself, remembering Freud's quote.

'Dessert?' the young waiter suddenly announced...shattering the moment...and bringing the discussion to a temporary halt.

The Bishop shook his head politely; Madison followed suit and while the young waiter went about his business...clearing the plates and tidying the table...she spent the whole time studying her arcane table-companion looking for a flicker of complicity in his eyes and wondering if they were somehow secretly engaging in some kind of emotional foreplay over dinner.

She then held out her glass for a refill, and as the waiter had just moved away, *the Bishop* duly obliged, filling her glass and returning her thoughtful stare with interest.

Madison smiled again, evasively, and looking at her glass she ran a finger lazily around its lip.

'That is very chivalrous of you', she announced as she took a sip of wine...savouring the dry tangy flavour.

'No, no it isn't, not at all', *the Bishop* replied brusquely, pausing for a moment to fill his own glass.

'Why isn't it?' Madison asked, knowing that she was letting herself in for another of his insufferable speeches or patronising diatribes.

'Why?' *the Bishop* responded, picking up his glass; '...because sadly, Miss Chatfield, the art of chivalry and indeed the art of seduction itself died many years ago with the rise of feminism'.

Madison looked puzzled...I had to ask, didn't I? She thought to herself.

'Why...cause and effect?' *the Bishop* continued without being prompted; '...because the rise of feminism led to women taking charge of their sexuality and their fecundity...via 'the contraceptive pill'.

'This led to sex being more freely available...because women were being more promiscuous...and as a consequence, men no longer have to put any effort into seducing women; they no longer have to work for it...'

'...ergo, the end of chivalry', he explained candidly.

Madison grimaced; annoyed with herself that she had opened her mouth again without thinking first.

'...and...not forgetting of course...that the radical feminists now feel that it is beneath them to have a man open the door for them or offer them a seat on a crowded train...', *the Bishop* added in conclusion while discreetly flexing his hand...out of view.

'Well...; it was about time women got some power...in this modern world...' Madison commented in reply, her brow furrowing slightly; '...even if it is only over their own bodies'.

'Except...of course...here in the USA', *the Bishop* then interjected out of left field.

'I'm sorry; what was that?' Madison spluttered, shifting uncomfortably in her seat.

The Bishop sat back again and took another sip of wine.

'All I am saying...is that it is so sad to see a country like the USA... which because of its size should be setting the example to humanity...have so little courage in the political arena; I mean the political cowardice of

American politics is an absolute disgrace', he continued, getting a little more animated.

'Look at the Republicans', he added, throwing his hands in the air, 'they are political dinosaurs; the way they are clinging onto their guns and their religion...while at the same time depriving women of their right to choose on abortion. It just shows how far behind they have fallen in the modern world'.

Madison frowned again, in silence.

'They decry anything to do with sex...' *the Bishop* started to rant; '...and then do the complete opposite in their everyday lives; watching pornography, having extra-marital affairs...and hiring hookers etc. etc.'

'But do you know what the worst thing is Miss Chatfield...?' he growled with insistence.

Madison shrugged impassively.

'...they do all that...and then on Sunday, they go to church, praise the Lord and then leave their families on the church steps to go and meet up with their mistresses. That's what really infuriates me', he moaned. 'How many Republican politicians have been caught with their pants down, having affairs or sending inappropriate selfies to young women while still going to church every Sunday?'

'Hey, you cannot pass judgement on people like that; not all republicans are like that', she countered, trying to defend her countrymen.

'Oh, no judgement', *the Bishop* pursued; '...but for me you cannot play the church-going family man in front of the cameras, when you are sexually and morally incontinent the moment that those cameras are switched off; its hypocritical and if there is one thing I abhor more than anything else it is hyp...'

'Hypocrisy', Madison interrupted. 'I know you've told me before...like a million times...but tell me, where is all this anti-American bile suddenly coming from? I get what you're saying; I really do...but I find this relentless cynicism about everything very...wearing', she said, wondering how her trying to pay him a simple compliment had somehow turned into them discussing sleazy politicians sending 'dick-pics'

The Bishop was still shaking his head in dismay at her comment when out of the blue, two women at the next table suddenly burst out laughing drawing his attention...and prompting Madison to glance across too.

The conversation about their most recent dating disasters was clearly hilarious and the two women were so wrapped up in their conversation that they didn't notice that they were being watched.

However, Madison thought she recognised one of the women as Dianna Agron...an American actress who had played the role of Quinn Fabray in the TV series Glee...and the irony was not lost on her...after what she and *the Bishop* had just been discussing...that the character Dianna Agron had played in Glee, had been Captain of the Celibacy Club and had 'somehow' managed to get herself pregnant.

In the moment, Madison thought about mentioning it to *the Bishop* and even began to speak...but then she quickly revised her decision, not wanting to give him any more reason to criticise her fellow countrymen... notwithstanding the fact that he probably wouldn't get the 'Glee' reference anyway.

♝

The next thing she knew her phone was ringing...

Madison quickly reached into her pocket again and checked the called-ID. This time it was Todd, probably ringing on behalf of Amanda to find out how the event had been received.

'I have to take this', she informed him, almost in a whisper; 'it's my office'.

The Bishop frowned again but he didn't comment; he didn't have to, the disapproving look on his face said it all.

Nevertheless Madison took the call and having briefed Todd as succinctly as possible with the promise that she would call him back as soon as it was more convenient, she hung up.

♝

During the call;

The Bishop leaned back again in his chair...and for the duration of the call he studied Madison, imagining what she would look like naked...and how much he would like to take her to bed...but then, as she hung up, he quickly dismissed the idea out of hand.

Madison put her phone away and as soon as she had done so, *the Bishop* immediately reprimanded her for taking a call on her mobile while in his company.

'It might be the accepted convention these days, and I didn't say anything in the car earlier, nor did I embarrass your friend the other evening...but I find it the height of bad-manners to answer a phone and carry on a conversation while sat at a table...in company', he opined indignantly.

Madison rolled her eyes, getting tired of her guest's constant judgmentalism and couldn't help but riposte.

'Get over yourself', she snapped back at him defiantly; 'No disrespect... but this is the 21st century, not Victorian England'.

'You need to lighten up', she added before taking a large swallow of wine.

The Bishop didn't respond but quietly enjoyed seeing the real Madison revealing itself at last because...despite his initial doubts about her, he found her intriguing and beguiling...though he would never tell her that of course.

An awkward pause followed but happily it didn't last long and they were soon back on track discussing the history of Boston...and notably that most iconic of events, the Boston Tea Party, Madison enjoying yet another history lesson.

They finished the meal not long thereafter and as she was settling the bill with her company card, *the Bishop* suggested that they walk back to the hotel rather than call for the limo to pick them up.

'I need some fresh air to clear my head before going back to the room', he announced in a more conciliatory tone.

Madison looked at him curiously, a little taken aback by this sudden show of spontaneity...especially as no-one in America walks anywhere... but after what Evie had said earlier, she wondered if this was in fact *the Bishop's* roundabout way of letting her know that he had taken a liking to her too, that he enjoyed her company...and that he wanted to prolong it a while longer...

...but then, in the same instant the devil on her other shoulder immediately contradicted that thought, suggesting that, despite his congratulatory comments in the restaurant...she just couldn't see the inscrutable Englishman actually admitting to something like that.

Confusion reigned in her brain…but nevertheless, as the waiter pulled her chair back for her, Madison agreed to *the Bishop's* suggestion and moments later they were making their way out of the restaurant and onto Berkeley Street.

It was only a short walk back…but as it had been quite a long day, both parties were more than a little thankful to get back to the comfort... and relative anonymity...of the hotel.

Dinner had been pleasant...if a little strained at times...but the walk back to the hotel had been just long enough to blow away the transient annoyance of their most recent disagreement and as they walked through the main entrance, greeted by a number of polite smiling faces, both Madison and *the Bishop* were more than satisfied with their day's accomplishments.

Predictably, Madison's phone pinged...again...; it was Todd...again, and while she moved away tactfully to take the call, *the Bishop* ambled over to the front desk to check with the concierge if there had been any messages for him.

The smiling young woman behind the counter immediately checked *the Bishop's* room-number and to his great surprise she informed him politely that there had been so many messages of support and congratulations for him, that the duty manager had had them all delivered to his room... together with a complimentary bottle of champagne.

The Bishop looked at her and then at Madison...who had just crept up behind him...and for the first time since they had met, all those months ago, he had been rendered speechless.

The look on his face...of shock and incredulity...was priceless...but it only lasted a second before he regained his composure enough to thank the young receptionist for her competence...and tell her to thank the duty-manager too...on his behalf...for his kind gesture.

He then paused for another moment or two, to reflect on this unexpected turn of events, after which...still a little bemused...he turned and followed Madison over to the lift where she was waiting quietly with her own thoughts, wondering what might happen next, once they got upstairs.

They both stepped into the cabin...standing quietly side by side...until out of nowhere...throwing subtlety to the wind while playing discreetly with her earlobe...Madison suddenly broke the silence by asking...in a very considered tone...if he would be needing any help with drinking the champagne – thereby testing the water...and the possibility that he might invite her to his room to continue the evening.

This was strangely out of character for her; Madison wasn't one for casual encounters...or one-night-stands...that one mistake with Gary aside...but much like that evening at the Abbey and probably because she was still hyped up on the success of the day, the adrenaline in her veins...and the hormones in her brain...were creating a chemical reaction within her that was somehow short-circuiting her higher reasoning and driving her somewhat-irrational fascination for this man.

The Bishop, who was still wrapped up in what the concierge had just told him...was a little startled by her remark but in reply to her questioning look, he simply raised an eyebrow and fixed her with one of his penetrating stares, wondering if this was just an idle remark...blurted out to temper the awkwardness of the moment...or whether there was indeed something more behind Madison's rather tenuous suggestion.

He sensed an invitation in Madison's eyes...

...and could easily have prolonged the exchange to discover if there was any truth to his suspicions...with some well-chosen innuendo of his own...

...but after a brief pause, he chose to believe that the remark was just a throwaway line, uttered impulsively to fill in the silence...and so responded quietly with his usual inscrutable hubris;

'I think we should leave that until another day; don't you Miss Chatfield?'

Madison nodded in agreement and shrugged her shoulders;

'Sure; it has been a long day', she acknowledged, even if the ambiguity of his remark left her a little bemused...

...though it was more than just bemusement, she suddenly felt dispossessed by his rather dismissive tone...and the renewed silence in the cabin...filled with rejection and embarrassment...left her feeling more than a little uncomfortable...

...until the lift suddenly stopped on her floor, that is...and her hopes were raised again when...having invited her to step out...*the Bishop* followed in her wake.

Nothing was said but Madison quietly led the way...and as she walked along the corridor with her 'escort' in tow...trying to act like it was no big deal...she suddenly felt her pulse start to race.

They approached her door and as they did so, Madison glanced around discreetly.

Her heart started to pound like crazy; she experienced that butterfly frisson in her stomach that she hadn't felt in a long while...and all manner of weird and random thoughts started running through her head.

What if Evie came back early?

What would Amanda say...

...and...more importantly...

What would Amanda do...if she found out?

...and if they were going to do this; surely his room would be the better option?

As they reached her door *the Bishop* suddenly slowed his pace to create a little separation and add a little decorum to the proceedings.

'Anticipation is a wonderful thing', he remarked cryptically.

'Anticipation?' Madison questioned, endeavouring to make sure that they were on the same page.

'The champagne...' he confirmed.

Of course...the champagne', Madison repeated.

'...but thank you once again for all that you have done today', *the Bishop* added. 'I really did enjoy it'.

'Likewise', Madison replied casually as she opened her door, not wanting to acknowledge the stirrings in her stomach as she waited for him to make the next move.

The Bishop smiled awkwardly but stood his ground...and in that one moment the corridor was so still that Madison could hear nothing but the sound of her own shallow breaths.

She was on tenterhooks and paused again...deliberately...

...holding the door ajar, and allowing *the Bishop* ample time to either make a move...or to excuse himself politely and walk away.

The moment was almost surreal...time seemed to stand still...but in that instant *the Bishop* paused too, for just a fraction of a second.

It was almost imperceptible in his demeanour...but in her heightened state Madison sensed the hesitation more than she noticed it...and with that, the expectation of the preamble down the corridor suddenly disappeared.

'Well; goodnight Miss Chatfield; have a good night's sleep', *the Bishop* suddenly announced;

'...you've certainly earned it', he added, repeating his earlier tribute...

...and with that, he turned to leave, cleverly avoiding any further eye-contact.

Madison could not believe what was happening...and as she stood there in silence and utter disbelief, a multitude questions jostled for answers in her head.

She was desperate for some kind of explanation...as to why he had accompanied her to her door...if he had no intention of joining her in her room...but knowing *the Bishop's* rather complex character she decided that that was not the moment to pursue an immediate clarification...

...and as a consequence of that uncharacteristic passivity the evening came to a crashing halt at that point with just a furtive glance back at him as he disappeared down the corridor, almost in slow-motion.

The Bishop reached the lift moments later and resisting the temptation to turn around, he carefully pushed the call-button. He then took a deep-breath to collect himself and a few seconds later, the lift-doors opened.

He stepped inside...and as the doors closed again behind him...like the curtains bringing a stage show to an end...he disappeared out of sight with Madison putting on her bravest face and bidding him one final goodnight with a cursory wave of the hand from her doorway.

She then closed the door behind her...and as she walked into her empty room, her mind awash with a thousand wasted scenarios...none of which had her standing there alone...Madison dropped her bag on the desk and clenched her fists, to stop herself from screaming out aloud in frustration.

Meanwhile...inside the lift;

The Bishop pressed the button for his floor...and then reaching into his breast pocket he pulled out a tiny piece of paper. He unfolded it slowly, looked at it contemplatively for a few moments and then folded it again carefully before returning it safely to its place next to his heart...

The note read;

I will be forever grateful
for the way you saw all my faults
and loved me regardless

affectionately yours

J x

Back in her room;

Madison took off her jacket and threw it angrily onto the bed. She then kicked off her shoes and stormed directly into the bathroom, unable to hide the look of disappointment written all over her face.

She leaned on the wash-basin with both hands and looking in the mirror, she tried to clear her head, control her breathing, and make sense out of what had just happened.

'Well; that was an anti-climax' she scolded herself; she had put herself out there only to be rejected and humiliated yet again without a second thought.

The realisation that he (the Bishop) had snubbed her once again made Madison feel more than a little embarrassed and she hated herself for letting her guard down like she had.

She closed her eyes and as she hung her head in despair, her shoulders dropped. She was crestfallen by the presumed rejection but not one to dwell upon the negative she quickly snapped out of it…and as she loosened her hair and reached for her brush a couple of nagging thoughts suddenly crept into the back of her consciousness.

'Maybe he has a problem with intimacy...' she thought to herself...

...or maybe he is just a closet romantic caught in a time-warp, a throw-back to the days of long-since abandoned Victorian values', she mused, caricaturing *the Bishop* to make herself feel better.

Nevertheless, Madison was confused. She knew that he wasn't gay; he had told her as much previously, so why couldn't they connect on a more intimate level, she wondered, refusing to believe that a man of *the Bishop's* undeniable intelligence would not have been able read the perfectly clear, universally accepted signals that she had been sending out all evening.

...or there again...she thought more objectively; could it be that he simply had more self control...and more respect for the professional nature of their relationship; that he didn't want to mix business with pleasure...?

Oh well, she thought, as she completed her night-time routine; she'd put it out there and he didn't bite; it was his loss, she concluded…

…and with that she turned out the bathroom light and shuffled off to bed.

The next day, they all enjoyed a leisurely breakfast together in the hotel's Huntington restaurant and while Evie spent a good half-hour rambling on profusely about her evening at the film premiere, getting her own back on *the Bishop* who had a tendency to monopolise the conversation, she could see that her friend was a little distracted...lost in her own thoughts.

Something was clearly amiss, Evie thought to herself...but not wanting to create a scene...if one was to develop...in front of the hotel's other guests; she let it slide and kept it to herself for the time being.

Now of course, Evie had no idea about the reason behind her friend's subdued state...having gotten back rather late the previous evening...but assuming that it had something to do with *the Bishop*, as they came out of the breakfast room and Madison veered off once again to take yet another call, she quickly seized on the opportunity to grab *the Bishop* by the elbow and usher him to one side so that she might give him a piece of her mind.

'Okay wise guy', she scowled at him; 'you might be well-read and you are certainly the most opinionated guy that I have ever met...but I think you need to work on your people-skills'.

For only the second time that he could remember, *the Bishop* was again lost for words. This seemingly random and unprovoked attack had caught him off guard and as he tried to get his head around it…and unravel its meaning…the relaxed mood that he had been enjoying up until then… over breakfast…was suddenly replaced with an altogether more hawkish, more quizzical demeanour; his body tensed, his lips tightened and his eyes narrowed into a confused frown.

'You bought my friend a book...a book' Evie insisted unflinchingly; '... that's a rookie mistake here in New York'.

Still baffled, *the Bishop* raised an eyebrow and continued to look at Evie in utter disbelief.

'...Not if the person receiving it likes to read', he suddenly countered, quickly regaining his usual poise.

Evie held her ground, remaining steadfast for a few moments;

…being from New York, she was used to dealing with strong, confident men.

'Fine', she conceded eventually...getting a little flustered and rolling her eyes...

'...all I'm saying is that... you need to know...that here in America we make bi...g gestures', she insisted again enunciating the words very slowly and clearly; 'we don't buy people we...appreciate...books. We put more effort in; we try to be more creative.'

'Point taken Miss Finch', *the Bishop* acknowledged calmly, brushing down his sleeve.

'Huh...', Evie nodded...and having made her point, she turned on her heel, tossed her head defiantly and walked away, trying her best to hide the smuggest of grins.

Later that day, they all flew back to New York as *the Bishop* would be catching his connecting flight back to London from there, early the next morning.

Having decided to go the extra mile when planning the event, Madison had thought that her distinguished guest might appreciate the chance to see the Big Apple...'up close and personal' so to speak...if only for a day, before flying back to England...although after the previous evening's debacle she was probably starting to regret it...

The flight from Boston to New York…which took just over an hour and twenty minutes…was pretty uneventful…although the ambient calm inside the cabin was disrupted a couple of times by a nervous passenger sat a few rows behind them, when the plane bobbed and weaved in some unexpected turbulence …but other than that the trip went without a hitch.

Of course, Madison and Evie sat together during the flight…and when they weren't texting on their mobile phones they spent the whole time discussing the fashions in a couple of magazines they had found on board; an activity which they both revelled in and one which undoubtedly helped to heal Madison's bruised ego…and boost her morale…after the disappointment she had suffered the previous evening.

Meanwhile…across the aisle...where he was sat quietly on his own, *the Bishop* spent his time during the flight, with his eyes closed and his mind plunged deep in thoughtful reflection.

Back in New York…

For his last night 'stateside' Madison had booked *the Bishop* into the world-renowned Hotel Pierre on 5th Avenue …and when the cab pulled up outside this most iconic of addresses she could see in his rather-understated demeanour that she had made the right call.

'Chequered floors', *the Bishop* mumbled to himself, as he exited the cab to be greeted by two smiling doormen…in pristine liveries...

'...Nice touch', he added with muted appreciation as he stood back to admire the magnificence of the hotel's 1930's architecture.

Madison, who had followed *the Bishop* out of the cab, turned to Evie looking for a reaction to this latest remark...but coming around from the other side of the vehicle the latter just rolled her eyes and shrugged her shoulders as two very-courteous young valets suddenly appeared, seemingly out of nowhere, to deal with their luggage.

With a shrug of her own and a flippant wave of the hand, Madison dismissed the matter and immediately took charge of operations, explaining to the two young valets which cases were to go inside and which were to be set aside for her and Evie to take home with them.

Then, having tipped the two young employees quite handsomely, she joined Evie and *the Bishop* in the porch-way and they all went inside.

Madison led the way over to the reception desk and while she dealt with the formalities of *the Bishop's* registration, the man himself hung back and took the opportunity to further admire the hotel's spectacular décor...

...and Evie slipped away discreetly to find the ladies-room.

The paperwork was quickly taken care of...and once *the Bishop* had signed in and gone off to his room to get settled in...Madison fulfilled one of her last official duties by returning to the reception desk to make sure that the bill for his stay would be sent to her newspaper's accounts-office...

The receptionist confirmed the arrangement and while she was there, at the desk, Madison also asked, rather brazenly, if the hotel could put a room at her disposal for a couple of hours later on in the day...where she and her friend (Evie) might get changed...as *the Bishop* (their guest) had suggested in the cab that they have one last dinner together before he flew out...to celebrate the success of their collaboration and to thank her once again for all her hard work.

The receptionist immediately called her manager and for a small extra charge...to cover the cost of house-keeping...it was agreed that a room would be made available.

Madison thanked the young woman...and having double-checked the arrangements with Evie, the two friends sauntered back outside where they retrieved their luggage and jumped into separate cabs, as both needed to go home to get a change of clothes.

Later that afternoon;

By 4:30 PM, the girls had returned to the hotel with their change of clothes and were already getting themselves organised in the room that had been made available to them.

Evie was in the shower...and Madison was laying out her clothes on the bed when, all of a sudden, out of the blue, there was an unexpected knock on the door.

Madison stopped what she was doing and with her usual relaxed attitude she walked over to the door and answered it, to find a young man standing there, dressed in the hotel's livery holding a package, wrapped beautifully in paper carrying the hotel's logo.

'Miss Chatfield?' he asked politely. 'Aha', Madison responded nonchalantly.

'Package for you', the young man announced.

'Thank-you...' Madison replied calmly.

She took the package and having tipped the young man his due; she laid it on the desk and opened it carefully, recognising immediately the pink and black brand colours on the box inside.

'Whatever could this be?' she wondered.

Then, opening the box, she breathed in sharply and immediately slammed it closed again before Evie could sidle up behind her and take a sneaky peek for herself.

The box contained a beautiful set of lingerie from 'Agent Provocateur' and a small card inscribed simply with two little words 'Thank You'.

Madison was gob-smacked.

Yet again, *the Bishop* had taken her by surprise, but as she took another look inside the box she couldn't help wondering if this was just him messing with her head again or if there really was some kind of subliminal message hidden therein.

Evie, who was still in the bathroom half-way through putting on her make-up, had heard voices.

'Who was that?' she enquired casually, as she checked out her mascara.

'Oh that...' Madison replied by the bye, appearing in the bathroom doorway;

'That was only the most expensive set of lingerie that I have ever seen', she announced impulsively, producing the elegant wine-coloured unmentionables from the chic designer packaging.

Evie looked at her friend's reflection in the mirror and huffed dismissively;

'Men; they are so...predictable; do they never think about anything else?' she crowed, a hint of despondency in her voice. 'They are just a load of old perverts...'

'Remember...?' she insisted; keen to remind her friend of her most recent misadventure.

'Of course I remember...' Madison countered, looking at her friend ponderously before returning to the bedroom; '...the memory of that day is burned into my brain like it was yesterday...but still...I don't agree'.

'They are selfish...and unreliable', Evie insisted again, puckering her lips before putting away her gloss.

'Hey; what's gotten into you all of a sudden?' Madison shouted out as she continued sorting through her clothes.

'They might be a little awkward at expressing themselves, and yes, there are those who are only after one thing, but I'm telling you that there are a few diamonds among them'.

'In your dreams hon', Evie retorted from the bathroom; 'in your dreams'.

Madison appeared again in the door frame.

'Well, if you ask me; I think that men are so used to being criticised and shunned by women these days...that they don't realise how desperate we are to experience genuine kindness...and when a woman does actually pay them any attention they get confused…and gauche, and don't know how to react', she suggested, her mind suddenly flashing back to the previous evening.

Evie turned to look at her friend.

'You've been listening to too many of that guy's sermons', she remarked.

Madison shook her head and smiled.

'That said...' Evie continued, as she joined Madison in the bedroom having donned one of the hotel's robes; 'I was only saying the other day that your underwear drawer needed updating and...hey presto...'.

She motioned towards the package; 'you see…great minds', she added as she dug out her brush from her handbag and disappeared back into the bathroom.

Madison shook her head and returned to sorting her clothes.

She had brought a selection of dresses back with her...and having tried each one up against her body...and checked it out in the full-length mirror placed intentionally on the wall for that very reason...she decided to go with a classic, blue Roland Mouret for their last dinner together, applying the same dogged determination to her charm offensive as she did to everything else in her life; following her own personal maxim of always trying to impress while remaining as discreet as possible about her intentions.

A little while later;

Despite her facade in front of Evie, Madison was still very confused by the mixed signals that *the Bishop* was giving her...

- what with the snub at the abbey...

- and then the awkward moment at her door the previous evening in Boston...
- and now the delivery this afternoon of the rather alluring if somewhat clichéd gift-set, *which everybody knows is loaded with meaning...*

...and as a consequence, once she was prepped and ready, she decided to make her way down to the hotel's lobby a little earlier than was scheduled... hoping to catch *the Bishop* on his own...so that she could confront him about it...and find out exactly where she stood...before Evie...who always took longer than her to get ready...joined up with them.

She informed Evie of her intentions and having prepared her belongings for the concierge to collect later in the evening...leaving them all neatly grouped on the bed...she made sure that Evie knew to do the same and then headed out.

♗

Madison had arranged with reception for the concierge to collect their belongings from the room...which she would then pick up from the concierge's desk the next day

♗

In the lift, on the way down to reception, Madison quickly worked out what she was going to say...

- *about Boston...*
- *about his gift...*
- *and especially about that evening at the abbey which probably rankled with her more than the other two put together...*

But then as she watched the numbers on the LCD display steadily decrease she wondered if Evie was right after all; that *the Bishop* was indeed just like any other man with a one-track mind who just enjoyed objectifying women...

She huffed out loud.

...But he wasn't...was he; she reasoned; last night in Boston had had proved that already...

So...

- *Maybe he was self-sabotaging...?*
- *Maybe he was deliberately doing things to creep her out in order to ward her off, to keep her at a safe distance and stop her from wanting to get closer.*

After all, she always had the impression that he was testing her...

...or was it all a double bluff? She just didn't know.

All these questions were running around her head in a whirlpool of confusion...and she was desperate for answers, but when the lift doors opened and she exited the cabin into the hotel's busy reception-area, she did so with style and confidence, shoulders back and chin up.

True to form, *the Bishop* was already there, standing by the book-stand, looking as smooth and as suave as ever; a fact which never failed to impress Madison...*she liked the way he dressed and the way he always seemed so totally in control*...and as she approached she could see in his demeanour that she had made an impression too.

Their eyes met in a fusion of unspoken attraction but before Madison could engage him, before she could ask any questions, *the Bishop* jumped in first...

'Did you like the gift...?' he asked in a warm but monotone voice.

Madison's first instinct was to throw him a look of defiance and disbelief at his audacity but the simplicity of the question disarmed her somehow...tempering her reaction.

'I did; thank-you', she confided in response, trying to remain very dignified while blushing ever so slightly; '...but I...'

'Are you wearing it this evening?' *the Bishop* enquired again discreetly, with his usual irrepressible charm.

Madison leaned back aghast.

'Bah; I'm, I'm sorry Mister Byron...sir, but that kind of information is highly classified', she retorted modestly, brushing a few imaginary strands of shiny blond hair away from her face, while at the same time thinking to herself how inappropriate both the present and the questions were...

...unless of course there really was an ulterior motivation to his actions…

In fact, Madison wasn't wearing his present as she felt that it would be not only unprofessional of her to do so; it would also be a little weird; after all, she was working and the gift was a little too personal coming from someone who she had never even kissed...not properly at least.

Still, the air crackled with sexual tension and Madison could feel beads of perspiration slowly forming on her forehead.

So much for my perfect make-up, she thought to herself as she looked away, hoping for some kind of distraction...and luckily for her, she was indeed spared any further blushes when at that very moment Evie just happened to arrive, wearing the most daring of red dresses, the neckline of which plunged so low that it would put most to shame, though it did show-case her natural assets to perfection.

She was obviously very proud of her figure and after her confidence-boosting evening out in Boston at the premiere, she had clearly jumped at the chance to show it off again.

Madison and Evie exchanged compliments...and not wanting to feel excluded *the Bishop* joined in too, adding his moderate endorsement to the mutual admiration of the moment.

'I'm going for sexy...but stylish', Evie announced, wiggling her hips and shoulders in an improvised shimmy...while adding a spicy 'If you catch my drift' to her Marilyn Monroe-inspired pout.

Madison looked at her friend rather circumspect...but deciding not to prolong the moment any longer than was necessary...she quickly turned and led the way out, rolling her eyes and shaking her head with incredulity.

Evie and *the Bishop* looked at each other too...waiting to see who would move first...but before they followed in Madison's footsteps Evie quickly leaned in and whispered in *the Bishop's* ear;

'I'd be careful if I were you; that kind of attention can go to a girl's head'.

The Bishop smiled at her impertinence and countered simply with; '... the chase is all part of the thrill'...

...and with that he held out a hand and gestured for Evie to precede him.

Evie smiled back at him and just as she turned to follow in Madison's wake she sensed a guy standing at the reception desk off to her right. She barely registered the guy's face, but she was well aware of him blatantly checking her out.

'Hey, stop looking at my ass', she scolded loudly...*which of course drew the attention of everybody in the surrounding area*...before winking at the guy and continuing on her way with a little extra swing in her hips...and an undeniably self-satisfied smile on her lips.

The unlikely trio jumped into a cab and made the short trip to the restaurant, *the Bishop* politely declining Evie's suggestion *en-route* that they should stop for a drink at Serena's Wine Bar beforehand... explaining that his flight was early the next morning and that he wanted to get an early night.

Evie was naturally disappointed and shrugged her shoulders theatrically at his knock-back but...for once...she took his dismissal of her idea with good grace, not wanting their 'goodbye-dinner' to turn sour before it had even begun; even though she couldn't understand why anybody...in New York for the first time...would want to get to bed early.

Meanwhile, sat impassively between them, Madison swallowed deeply, before clearing her throat noisily. Was that another surreptitious hint as to his intentions? She wondered; was tonight the night?

They walked into the 'Cafe Boulud'...a wonderful little restaurant situated not far from the Carlyle Hotel...and were immediately shown to a table, where...as they sat down...Madison showed her local knowledge by mentioning the fact that Marilyn Monroe used to drive to the Carlyle Hotel, all the way from her Connecticut farm-house, just to enjoy a clandestine tryst there, with her lover, JFK.

The comment instantly opened the door for *the Bishop* and as the waiter arrived to announce the chef's specialities, he immediately quoted JFK's private motto, while looking directly into Madison's admiring eyes;

'Life is too short and painful; so never refuse pleasure when it is offered'.

Madison froze momentarily, both in confusion and embarrassed delight...marvelling once again at *the Bishop's* vast eclectic knowledge while at the same time trying to decide if there was any hidden subliminal meaning to his remark.

She thought about it for a millisecond and then regaining her composure as the waiter moved away, she found a clever response of her own.

'That explains Jackie O's pet name for her husband...' she joked, pausing momentarily to gauge *the Bishop's* reaction.

'What was it...?' Evie questioned indifferently, without taking her eyes off the menu.

'...Bunny', Madison revealed with a tight grin.

'That could have been Clinton's motto too', Evie retorted, with a snort...and they all smiled at the dubious parallel she had drawn.

However...moments later, once the girls had enjoyed their chuckle, *the Bishop* once again jumped to ex-president Bill Clinton's defence, just as he had done, during his first dinner with Madison back in England.

'I have to say that I disagree with the general consensus', he said, 'that Bill Clinton's presidency should be reduced to a caricature of that one episode'.

The girls looked at each other with arched eyebrows, knowing that once again they had hit a nerve.

'Oh god; I feel another lecture coming on', Evie whispered quietly... but loud enough for him to hear.

'That said...' *the Bishop* continued, ignoring Evie's facetious comment...

and Madison's look of dismay; 'I think that it was right of him to come clean about the problems he had had during his time as President. It set the record straight...allowed him closure...'

'...and his declaration about those events now stands as a warning to all those who are called to serve, of the pitfalls awaiting them, if they stray from their official line'.

The girls looked at each other again, rolling their eyes in unison.

'He did the right thing...for his own sake, for that of his family...and for the posterity of his time as President, so I say, Bravo, Mr President', *the Bishop* asserted in conclusion, raising his glass.

Madison joined in and chinked glasses with him...to humour him more than anything else…but Evie did not; though she did manage to force a smile.

'Well ladies, you may well mock, but I believe that if you have to judge him', *the Bishop* started again, directing his gaze at Evie; '...then judge him on his results as President...and not on his actions as a man who gave in to temptation – during a time when he was stressed out and under extreme pressure'.

'After all, just because he holds the office of President; that doesn't make him Superman; he's just a regular human being made of flesh and bone like the rest of us'; he insisted padding out his argument.

The girls had already switched off from his moralising tirade but to wrap up, *the Bishop* tried one last time to explain to them that what he was expressing was not based on a political affirmation but on a humanitarian one.

Madison nodded. 'Sure, but let's not get into it again', she commented, hoping to curtail the discussion.

The Bishop agreed...grudgingly...but sadly his tendency to lecture had spoiled the mood and having once again felt the force of his tongue, Evie retracted into her shell.

She had not appreciated his outburst and as a consequence she ignored him most of the time thereafter, preferring instead to sit back and spend her time checking out the talent on the neighbouring tables...or fiddling with her phone, which naturally provoked more than a few irate looks and non-verbal exchanges between her table companions.

She did try to rally a couple of times, notably when *the Bishop* criticised a popular reality-TV icon, but on the whole it was left to Madison to keep the discussion going with a stream of nostalgic memories of her first time in New York...and a couple of more-risqué anecdotes from the office which, while they lacked the intensity of *the Bishop*'s lectures, did manage to lighten the mood again….slightly.

The conversation tailed off eventually and by ten o'clock they were all but done.

However, as they got up to leave Madison somehow managed to persuade *the Bishop* to join them for one last drink in one of Manhattan's trendy, up-market night-clubs.

Of course, he wasn't really keen initially...having already explained about his early flight...but eventually Madison talked him around and he caved.

'Just one...' she insisted '...to celebrate the success of my mission and to toast your first...'

'...and probably last...' Evie interjected...

'...time in New York'.

The deal was sealed and they headed out.

In the club;

In the club, *the Bishop* was as always, the perfect gentleman, and while she still didn't like him very much, Evie had to admit...as she sat there quietly with her raspberry mojito, enjoying the leering glances coming at her from all angles...that...with his undoubted intelligence...*the Bishop* could probably charm the pants off of any woman he wanted if he put his mind to it.

He just seemed to have a presence about him which meant that when he entered a room, he did it with such confidence that every man's head turned and every woman's heart skipped a beat…and much to her dismay, she had to recognise that there was simply no denying that.

A while later, tempted by the music, the girls got up to dance, and holding out a hand, Madison invited *the Bishop* to join them.

Unsurprisingly, he refused...very politely, but all the same...remaining completely impervious this time to her cajoling persuasion.

Disappointed but not disheartened, Madison immediately turned on her heels and made her way to the dance-floor...expecting Evie to follow on behind...which she did.

However, before she left the table, Evie quickly turned around...and using her finger to signal for him to come closer...she leaned down and whispered into *the Bishop's* ear, trying to be as discreet as possible.

'Maddy really enjoys flirting...and showing off...' she said in a low voice; 'but it's all smokescreen and mirrors;

...in reality she is very shy when it comes to men', Evie disclosed trying once again to intercede on her friend's behalf.

The Bishop looked at her...again...perplexed.

'Yeah, she hides the reality of her fragile, true-self behind the strong image she tries to project...but it's all a charade', Evie added in a hushed tone.

'I will say this for her though' she continued having checked that Madison had not come back to listen; 'she does love to dance; it whets her appetite...

...and you do know Mr Intelligence that dancing is the vertical expression of a horizontal desire...don't you?' she murmured coquettishly as she slowly stood up straight.

The Bishop's impassive demeanour didn't change but as Evie backed away and turned to leave, he did look beyond her, at Madison's disappearing silhouette.

'All I'm saying...' Evie concluded; '...is that sometimes, just sometimes, she doesn't want your opinion, she just wants your validation...'

...and with that, without waiting for him to respond, she turned and boogied off in the direction of the dance-floor where Madison was already being surrounded by a swarm of potential suitors.

Now Evie was not the most discreet or tactful of people...but while the clarity of her message could not be clearer, *the Bishop* still declined the invitation to join them on the dance-floor; preferring instead to remain seated where he was and to reflect calmly on what she had just said.

He ordered another round of drinks and while he sat there quietly... mindful of his reputation...he deliberately ignored all the admiring glances he received from those passing by...and the wealth of eye-candy that abounded on the surrounding tables.

Instead, in his usual discreet manner, he just sat there quietly - looking a little awkward it had to be said - keeping his eyes and his attention fixed solely on Madison and Evie as they tore up the dance-floor, dancing and gyrating rhythmically to the incessant beat of the music which seemed to drown out all other activities.

'You girls are certainly attracting a lot of attention out there', he commented when they finally came back to the table.

'Well', Madison quipped, brushing her hair back and picking up her glass; 'like anybody else; I want to be respected for my brain…but a girl still needs to know she is attractive and sexy', she jibed as a subtle dig in retaliation for his emotional passivity.

The girls sat down and as the new round-of-drinks was served, all the animosity from earlier in the evening suddenly dissipated. *The Bishop* congratulated them both again on their dancing and then trying to be more open-minded he took them both by surprise yet again;

'I haven't seen anybody *Merengué* like that since that Colombian singer...what's her name...Shakira...did as much in that video' he informed them out of nowhere.

Evie burst out laughing. 'Are you serious; you've actually heard of Shakira...?' she questioned, looking at Madison who was equally stunned.

The Bishop grimaced but accepted the ribbing with good grace, as he took another sip of his drink, not wanting to pick a fight with Evie over something so trivial.

Merengué – this is a hip-shaking dance from the Dominican Republic which has Cuban influences and is known as 'dirty dancing' in the 'hypocritically puritanical' USA.

The girls each took a sip from their glasses, Evie still cackling with delight at the fact that *the Bishop* actually knew of Shakira...but also in reaction to the less than subtle expression of a man across the dance-floor who quite clearly had the 'hots' for her… and moments later, having cooled down and regained their breath, they disappeared back to the dance-floor; Madison complaining to Evie as they went that she didn't know what else to do to provoke a reaction from *the Bishop*; the man just seemed immune to her feminine charms.

Evie threw her hands in the air with a 'don't beat yourself up about it gesture', then added rather patronisingly that; 'subtle wordplay is lost on men' - but as she brought her arms back down, lost in the beat of the music and the swing of her hips she accidentally knocked against one of the waitresses who just happened to be passing by with a full pitcher of Margheritas on her tray.

It was unintentional of course, but the ice-cold drink went all down the front of Evie's dress, taking her breath away and bringing her evening to a maddening and unexpectedly premature end.

Evie was naturally mortified by what she had done...and as she stood there apologising to the waitress for her clumsiness, everybody in the immediate vicinity suddenly stopped what they were doing to look at her.

Horrified, Evie apologised again...this time offering to pay for the spilled-drink...but then concerned about the damage to her favourite dress, she immediately rushed back to the table... her hands folded strategically over her chest.

Once there, she quickly grabbed her purse...and clutching it tightly against her upper-torso...while gesturing animatedly to her rather uncomfortable state of affairs...she hastily explained to *the Bishop* that she was leaving.

Of course, *the Bishop* was more than a little surprised, not having witnessed the incident...but before he could respond to her distress Evie had already turned to leave throwing him nothing more than a cursory wave goodbye.

As she turned away, she bumped straight into Madison who was just arriving back at the table with a bunch of napkins that she had grabbed from the bar.

'I got these for you...are you okay?' Madison enquired sympathetically.

'Yeah hon. I'll be fine', Evie replied, taking a couple of the napkins and giving her cleavage a brief wipe.

'Wait here; I'll get 'you know who' and we can all get outta here together', Madison proposed, still trying to manage the evening.

'No, no; don't do that hon; don't spoil your evening for me...' Evie countered, handing back the napkins.

'...besides...' she added, leaning in and whispering in her friend's ear. 'I think you should stay and grab your chance'.

Madison screwed up her face; 'I think that ship has sailed'.

'Nonsense; just be spontaneous for once…and don't over-think it', Evie suggested with a knowing smirk and a discreet jerk of the head.

Madison smiled affably at her friend's suggestion but feeling in some way responsible for what had happened...even though she was completely blameless...she immediately dismissed Evie's idea, offering instead to accompany her out to the taxi-rank.

'No hon; I'll be fine', Evie declared reassuringly as she leaned in again and kissed Madison goodbye on the cheek. '...Now go...' she insisted, winking discreetly and nudging her friend back in the direction of the table before making her way out.

Madison shrugged her shoulders and smiled again fleetingly, calling after her friend to text her nevertheless when she got home so that she knew she was safe.

She then returned to the table and sat back down opposite *the Bishop*... and all those people around them who had stopped to look went back to what they were doing.

However, the incident had literally poured cold water on the evening and the mood at their table had gone completely flat too.

As a consequence, Madison and *the Bishop* finished their drinks... pretty much in silence...and twenty minutes or so later they too were back in a cab, on their way back to his hotel.

Madison was still hopeful...as this was his last night...that *the Bishop* might invite her in, but once again, true to form, he didn't. Instead, he left her sat in the cab, completely frustrated yet again despite all her best efforts to force his hand in the seduction stakes.

He was certainly a special breed but for some reason...which she couldn't quite figure out yet...he seemed emotionally unavailable, despite his bachelor status and his oft-clever innuendo.

The evening...and *the Bishop's* first visit stateside...ended there...on the pavement outside the hotel...with just brief exchange of tight smiles, an earnest goodbye from him, a polite wave of the hand from her...and the slamming of the cab door...much to the cab-driver's annoyance.

The next day *the Bishop* flew back to London without seeing Madison again...though as her final professional courtesy she did call his hotel early the next morning to wish him a good flight...explaining that she had a busy schedule and couldn't make it to the airport.

However, that was a lie - because across town, up in her apartment, on the 43rd floor of her tower block, Madison was still in her PJ's.

Pleased with what she had achieved...as far as her mission was concerned, she was nonetheless disappointed that she had not succeeded in her personal goal of bridging the yawning emotional gap between herself and the frustratingly-enigmatic Englishman...and as she ended the call and looked out of her window, at the quirkily-geometric Manhattan skyline that epitomised New York, she couldn't help but roll her head back on her shoulders and scream in frustration at the top of her voice, motioning at the same time to throw her phone across the room.

Madison Chatfield was on an emotional rollercoaster and she didn't like it.

The de-brief, a few days later...

On the Tuesday morning, a call came down from her boss's office, informing Madison that Amanda wanted to see her at 2PM sharp.

So at 1.45 PM, full of confidence, Madison stopped what she was doing and made her way upstairs.

Her mind was full of positivity but then as she waited her turn for the lift...behind two male executives who hadn't noticed she was there...she couldn't help but be saddened by their conversation...

'Sum up marriage in three words' she heard the younger of the two men say.

'I only need two'; the slightly more mature executive answered, 'misery and heartbreak'.

Madison was a little taken aback and wanted to hear more but the lift arrived at that moment and the two men slowly ambled inside.

'Misery...and. . .heartache', the younger man repeated with a frown as the older guy pressed the button for the ground floor. 'Hey, but that IS three words; misery...and. . .heartache', he remarked as he noticed Madison waiting...and beckoned her forward, holding the lift-door open for her.

'No, I'm good; I'm going 'up', she motioned pointing her finger skyward, pretending not to have heard what had been said.

The two men nodded and smiled...as the doors then slid together with a dull 'thunk'.

Minutes later, still filled with a sense of achievement, Madison entered Amanda's office, a triumphant look plastered all over her face.

However Todd Klingenschmidt was already there looking positively smug and self-satisfied...which immediately dampened her enthusiasm.

Amanda, for her part, was ...as always...tied up on the phone and all Madison heard as she crossed the room was; 'Listen up hon; could you just e-mail me the rest of that story because right now I'm bored and life is too short...'

...and with that she just hung up the phone and tossed it on the desk, before looking up and pretending to be surprised.

‘Ah yes; Madison, take a seat’, she intoned as she made herself comfortable again in her big leather chair.

Madison sat down, crossing her legs confidently and brushing an imaginary crease out of her skirt.

‘Right…’ Amanda began, leaning forward and getting straight to the point; ‘Todd here tells me that you didn’t quite ‘get it done up in Boston’.

Todd turned and looked at Madison, grinning disloyally and pursing his lips like he had just sucked on a particularly sharp lemon.

‘He what…?’ Madison spluttered, taken aback by the accusation.

‘He doesn’t think that you did a good job…that you completed your mission…satisfactorily’, Amanda clarified reading from the report that Todd had sent her on her tablet.

Lost for words initially, Madison was about to interrupt…to demand what Todd had found lacking in her work…but before she could, Amanda continued with her summary.

‘…however, I have been in touch with the sponsors up in Boston and they couldn’t be more pleased with the way you handled things’, Amanda announced more impartially.

Madison didn’t respond but she did give herself an imaginary high-five…and Todd a sarcastic stare.

‘Still…’ Amanda continued, glancing at Todd; ‘I myself, am not wholly convinced with your performance Madison, and I will tell you why…’

She sat further forward, put her elbows on the desk and clasped her hands beneath her chin.

‘You didn’t commission a photographer…’ she stated quietly.

Madison was stunned and this time she couldn’t hold her tongue. ‘But I…I had the Press there…and the local…’ she tried to explain.

‘Bup, bup, bup; don’t interrupt me…’ Amanda snapped back at her junior employee swatting away her explanation, like an irritating fly.

‘When you are given a mission like this, you need to hire a photographer…to get some exclusive close-ups…and maybe a few more insightful clichés of the event…but you didn’t…and sadly that is going to cost us money…’ Amanda explained, her brow furrowing slightly.

Madison grimaced and crossed her arms in front of her defensively.

'...and when I say us', Amanda continued, 'I mean me; I mean that I am going to have to go to the media now and pay for the rights to publish any clichés that I might find suitable...out of my budget'.

Madison apologised acknowledging that she had slipped up on that one detail...and at that point Todd leaned forward and handed Amanda a piece of A4 full of figures.

Amanda looked at the print-out, frowned briefly and put it to one side.

'Now the 'photographer-thing' might have slipped your mind...or not...'

'...But I...' Madison began to interrupt again.

Amanda raised a hand.

'...the 'photographer-thing' might have slipped your mind...or not...', Amanda repeated, '...but you must realise Madison that it is a false economy to save the photographer's fee – whose work you then have copyright over – when you have to pay...

'...Over the odds', Todd interjected, a half-smirk on his face.

'...Yes, over the odds...' Amanda concurred, '...and sometimes twice, thrice or even ten-times over cost-price...for the same photos when you get them from an independent pap or media outlet'.

Madison nodded her understanding while mentally kicking herself for giving Todd...and by extension, the top bosses...a metaphorical stick to beat her with.

Then, all of a sudden, right in the middle of their discussion, Amanda's phone began to beep.

'Okay; that's all for now', she announced, picking up her phone and looking at her 'diary-prompt'; 'we'll just have to wait and see if your copy is worth the extra investment', she advised, signalling that the meeting had come to a rather abrupt end.

Madison got up to leave and as she turned to walk out, feeling belittled and more than a little frustrated, Amanda immediately called her back.

'Madison', she said as her phone burst into life once again; 'e-mail me the finished copy of your brief before Friday's deadline and we'll take it from there'.

Madison nodded and walked out... kicking herself again for not having hired a photographer...and seething at Todd who seemed to be doing his level-best to undermine her work and her job at the paper.

CHAPTER ELEVEN

After the high of being involved in organising the exhibition match…and being the centre of attention in a way, as *the Bishop's* personal assistant, life was suddenly pretty flat and mundane for Madison in the weeks that followed, and understandably it took her a while to get back into the routine again...of simply writing generic copy for the humdrum articles that were assigned to her.

Indeed, the ambitious young journalist that she was found it more than a little soul-destroying…and there were times when she really hated her job...but as the days wore on she was nevertheless pleased that she had it, as it had allowed her to get away from her mother's constant criticism and repeated derogatory comments on how much of a disappointment she had been to her.

Even so, as she sat at her desk one morning, contemplating her future, Madison knew that it was all part of the game...part of the waiting game... and just like in a game, just like in a game of chess for example, she knew that she would have to bide her time and wait for the right opportunity to present itself...

...and she was convinced...that when that day came, she would be there, like a coiled serpent ready to strike.

It was at that moment, just when she was imagining her day of triumph, that Madison was suddenly startled from her daydreams by the sound of footsteps, as off to her right, a young, elfin-faced intern had stopped by her cubicle carrying a couple of internal memos for her to sign.

The poor girl was obviously new to the job and as she stood there, nervously chewing her bottom lip, she flinched visibly in anticipation of Madison's fiery rebuff, having been warned by other staff-members to watch out for 'the blond at the corner desk'.

Her reputation for asserting herself...and not taking any 'bullshit' had clearly begun to precede her around the office, Madison thought to herself...and out of sheer boredom and downright frustration she could quite easily have unleashed that volatile temper on the poor girl...

...but this time it never happened; instead, she simply looked up and smiled at the new intern who – having gotten her signature for the internal records - quickly turned around and scampered back to whence she came.

Madison guessed that Amanda or someone else 'upstairs' had left instructions with the HR department to inform these juniors to be wary of her...because of the 'trouble' she had caused...

...and indeed, at one time she might well have gnashed her teeth at this kind of annoying interruption...

...but she was more intelligent than that...and she refused to play the bosses game; she refused to assume the role of loose cannon that they were trying to impose on her as they pursued their agenda of black-balling her... to punish her for breaking rank and standing up to them.

And as she sat there at her desk, still revelling in her previous analogy about her current situation and the game of chess, Madison's thoughts suddenly turned to *the Bishop*.

She thought about his eloquence...and about his immense capacity for self-control...and in that single moment she realised just how his influence had begun to subliminally affect her; she was more patient, more considerate and less aggressive now...and in her opinion, she definitely had him to thank for that.

Leaning back in her chair, Madison looked around the floor at the rest of her colleagues, each one in their own little world, and as she did so the memories of her time in London, in Boston...and even right-here in New York with *the Bishop*...with TB - ambled slowly across the pages of her mind.

It was a comforting moment but as the images slowly began to fade again she could not help but expel a deep sigh, filled with longing...and an overwhelming sense of unfinished business.

His absence seemed to be inducing a permanent lethargy in her; as if part of her essential core was now missing from her life...but the reality was that he was in England and she was in New York...so reluctantly she brushed those thoughts aside and carried on with her work.

That was how it was for the next couple of weeks but then for no apparent reason the mood in the office…and around the water-cooler…suddenly changed after her article about the exhibition match in Boston was published…in a beautifully-presented two-page spread…albeit towards the end of the weekend magazine.

Madison came into work on the Monday morning, not having been informed that her article was going to feature over the weekend, to find a copy of the magazine opened at the page of her article displayed on her desk.

She was stunned…she hadn't even seen Amanda since the 'de-brief' and as she slumped into her chair, she couldn't believe her eyes when she saw that the editor... in his infinite wisdom... had even included a few photos of the event in his layout and notably one of her – *the one from her photo ID* - next to her name.

It was her breakthrough moment.

Madison punched the air and immediately made her way up to Amanda's office...on the off chance that she could get to see her and thank her for whatever she had done (investing in the photos etc).

The ever-present Gayle waved her through…and acknowledging the latter's smile with one of her own Madison quietly knocked her boss's door before opening it slowly and gingerly poking her head around.

'Amanda; I just wanted to thank-you for your help with the article', she whispered almost, not wanting to disturb her boss any more than she had to.

Amanda clenched her teeth and smiled rigidly as her employee invaded her space without an invite.

'Oh, are those the other photos you procured?' Madison asked curiously as she advanced, noticing a photograph sticking out of a folder marked 'Bishop' on Amanda's desk.

'They are...as it happens', Amanda replied.

'Is it okay if I take a look', Madison asked again, gesturing towards the folder.

'Be my guest', Amanda agreed as her phone pinged once again.

Madison picked up the folder and began flicking through the photos... most of which were of *the Bishop*...recognising those marked with a red-cross that had been retained for her article.

'He has a very distinctive, a very distinguished look about him, doesn't he?' Amanda remarked, as she held out her hand for the folder, her demeanour and the look in her eyes barely able to disguise the fact that she too was not averse to the masculine charm the enigmatic English champion.

'Yeah, he does', Madison whispered, almost to herself, as she handed back the folder.

'Look Madison…', Amanda said, skilfully bringing the conversation back to the article as she put the folder away; '…Management are still on your back because of the lawsuit...and you will just have to deal with that until the dust settles...but I think you did a great job. I think that you showed initiative and promise, and you confirmed with this article that the article you did in England wasn't a fluke...'

'Thanks Amanda', Madison replied.

'And now...' Amanda advocated, motioning her younger colleague towards the door with a double hand-gesture; 'I have work to do...'

'Of course', Madison acknowledged, '...but thanks again', she repeated.

'Shoo...' Amanda urged, bringing the moment of unexpected complicity to a close.

From that day forth Madison's reputation within the industry began to build. The reviews she received from her peers became more encouraging; the support she received from readers seemed to be growing exponentially…and even around the office the praise seemed to be more forthcoming, although at times...she still found herself questioning the degree of its sincerity.

Indeed, even her 'enemies' up in the boardroom seemed to be thawing towards her, as without asking for it, she received a small bonus in her pay-packet at the end of the month which she also made a point of thanking Amanda for...as she would have had to sanction it and sign-off on it.

All of a sudden Madison was on top of the world and the next time she met up with Evie for coffee, they talked about it for hours, about the success of her article, about her new-found popularity around the office – *although reluctant respect was probably a more fitting description* - and of course, about *the Bishop* and his influence in all this.

Evie was very supportive...as ever...but once Madison had stopped gushing, she tried to rationalise everything that was happening…and analyse each of the afore-mentioned criteria, in an effort to keep her friend's feet firmly on the ground.

'Listen', Evie said; 'you are doing a good job 'Mad'; the success of your articles proves that; your boss is slowly recognising the fact, albeit grudgingly, and no doubt her army of sycophants will soon fall into line too.

'As for that English guy; TB was it?' she confirmed. 'You have several things in common with him;

- you're intelligent – he is too
- you read books; I assume he reads books too…'

Madison nodded...then interrupted; 'yeah, but sometimes, no matter how many books you read – there are some things you never understand'.

'...but...' Evie interjected; '...here's the thing; he is in England...and you are here in New York. So what's the big deal; I don't get it; why the fascination?' she queried having already stated the obvious.

Madison stared out of the window, looking off into space.

'I don't know why; I can't explain it and that's the frustrating thing about it', she lamented.

'When I was younger, I was a bit of a handful and got myself into god knows how many scrapes. I was a nightmare…and consequently I learned every which way of how to get myself in and out of trouble with men – but dealing with this guy, this *Bishop* guy, is just a whole new ball-game', she conceded.

Evie smiled with understanding.

'I thought I knew every angle...every little thing about what makes men tick...but I've got this guy under my skin and I just can't find the key to unlocking his protective shield; he is so...inscrutable', Madison admitted, continuing her self-analysis.

'Aah, the frustration; it's just eating away at me', she groaned almost missing her mouth with her cup in distraction.

'Maybe we should go out on the town some time to get your mind off of that guy; you never know, we might get lucky', Evie suggested trying to move away from Madison's rapidly-becoming obsessive infatuation.

'Yeah, we should do that', Madison agreed, her eyes finally letting go of the mental images of TB and returning to her friend's enquiring expression.

Evie immediately began suggesting venues and after a few rejections from her more up-market friend they settled on a little bar in the Village that both had heard good reports about, deciding to meet there at 7PM on the following Saturday.

The two friends then paid for their coffees, embraced warmly and went their separate ways...

...but as she began her walk home through the gleaming landscape of glass skyscrapers, world-renowned hotels and swish penthouse apartment-buildings, Madison couldn't stop her thoughts from drifting back to *the Bishop*...almost of their own accord. Her brain seemed determined to explain the enigma that was Him...and then, as she turned into Lexington Avenue and the wind caught her hair, it suddenly struck her...

Approval; that was it; for some reason she had been looking to gain his approval, his respect; that was what she was trying to do all this time; that is what had fuelled her fascination...her obsession.

Madison was overjoyed, delighted that she had finally figured it out... and she was still giving herself an imaginary high-five when...without warning...a homeless guy pushing a shopping trolley filled with junk...

suddenly appeared out of nowhere, right in front of her…forcing her to take evasive action…or at least to deviate from her path.

'Hey', she cried out, almost stumbling on her heels; 'you wanna be more careful with that thing'.

The guy barely acknowledged her…but he did shrug his shoulders and throw her a disparaging glance before he went on his way, mumbling to himself and spewing a relentless torrent of uncensored profanities to no-one in particular.

'Pffft…New York', Madison uttered to herself, as she brushed herself down…even though the guy hadn't actually come into contact with her…

…and with that she continued on her way.

Now the homeless guy's untimely eruption into her path had interrupted Madison's reflective process but as she arrived back at her apartment, she was nevertheless pleased that she had managed to figure things out in her head.

For whatever reason it hadn't worked out between her and *the Bishop*… and whether she had been successful in gaining his approval would always be up for debate… but at least she now had some clarity in her own mind and hopefully that would be enough to allow her to put him behind her… and move on with her life.

Frank's Bar; the following Saturday

As agreed earlier in the week, Madison and Evie met up on the following Saturday and headed off to enjoy an evening of 'restrained indulgence'.

It was a cold New York evening and expecting just a quiet drink and some girlie chat Madison had dressed accordingly...and rather casually...in her trusty leather trousers, a chunky, cable-knit sweater and her comfortable Prada boots, while Evie…who always dressed to impress on a night-out…

was clearly on the prowl in her tight, colour-blocked woollen dress and heels.

However, when they entered the bar Madison was somewhat surprised...and a little disappointed...to find a group of Evie's friends were already there waiting for them.

She had been hoping for a nice quiet evening with her friend...and had no interest in a girls' night out...but Evie being Evie, with her gregarious, sharing nature was...as always...up for a good time and she insisted they go over and say 'Hi'.

♗

'Madison; these are my gospel girls', Evie announced, interrupting one of the women who was regaling the company with a story of how she had gone out the night before and met up with a load of 'cute guys'.

Madison acknowledged the group as one...and baring her teeth...she managed to force a reluctant smile.

Evie then introduced her as 'the girl who wrote the articles' and almost immediately a chorus of congratulatory remarks rang out around the table.

Naturally, this led to an invitation for them to sit down...and as Evie disappeared to the 'ladies room', Madison found herself once again marooned at a table, in a bar, in the company of people she had never met.

The women - *each of whom had their mobile phone placed in front of them on the table for easy-access...if they weren't actually texting* - were all discussing the drama being played out in the latest reality TV show...and in the next hour or so Madison found herself rolling her eyes at Evie on numerous occasions to express her frustration at the frivolous content of the conversation.

She felt spectacularly awkward and while she didn't want to think about *the Bishop*, and what he might say about such triviality she couldn't help but compare one with the other.

After all, she had spent a lot of time in recent months listening to *the Bishop* pontificate on the mysteries of life, on international politics and myriad other topics of real interest and she just couldn't understand why these women would find the banalities of cable TV so interesting.

Indeed, a tug of war going on in Madison's head and as she contemplated the scene, she began to wonder if she should stay...or if she should go.

However, she stuck it out and tried to enjoy it, putting up with the ambient frivolity for a little while longer…but when the conversation turned to discussing the newest shade of lip-gloss being promoted by some internet cutie or other...despite her best efforts...Madison just couldn't take it any longer.

She could feel the indignation rising up inside her like a volcano and while she had managed to keep a lid on her temper for the last few weeks this...this shallow bunkum was just too much for her.

'What the fuck; what is wrong with you people; who the fuck do you think you are?' she suddenly blurted out angrily, a flash of annoyance sweeping across her face.

The women stopped chatting and all eyes turned to Madison who instantly calmed her breathing and quickly regained her self-control.

'I'm sorry; I just don't need to listen to this crap; I'm outta here', she announced, before getting up suddenly and heading for the door, ignoring Evie and leaving all the other women looking blank, confused and a little bemused.

Outside the bar, Madison came across a group of people chatting, laughing and joking but she was in no mood for levity - and just carried on walking… trudging slowly along the road feeling miserable and frustrated.

Her morale was clearly at rock bottom and despite her recent understanding of the situation, *the Bishop* was still driving her crazy...or at least the thought of him was...and try she might to get him out of her head, she just couldn't...

…and the worst part of it was that her obsession with him was starting to have a detrimental effect on her social life.

But, what more could she do to declare an interest, she wondered to herself, casually dismissing her recent, self-determined ruling that she was going to put the whole thing behind her; she had already laid her cards out on the table…a couple of times…but on both occasions there was no sign of him making a move; the guy seemed immune to her womanly wiles.

She knew, as a woman, that like all men, *the Bishop* intentionally avoided discussing certain subjects but why wouldn't he let her in...if only on a physical level? She reflected.

There was clearly an attraction there...or at least she felt that there was...

And it was not that she didn't meet his intellectual standards; she was pretty sure that she could give as much as she got in that department... so what was it that was preventing him from opening up to her, she wondered...or is this really what infatuation feels like?, she speculated.

For the first time in her life Madison didn't know what to do and it was driving her insane.

As she walked along, pondering her thoughts, the cold, dank evening air was slowly turning her lips blue so when a taxi-cab slowed down next to her, Madison raised her hand to signal him to stop.

The cab pulled up alongside her and as she opened the door she looked up at the night sky.

What will be, will be, she mumbled to herself, as if to wash away her negative thoughts and restore her confidence…

I believe in karma and karma has a way of balancing the scales, she then thought to herself…

...and with that she got into the cab and made her way home, her self-belief revived but her maddening dilemma still unresolved.

However, the solution to her problem did materialize a month or so later.

Madison was going about her work as usual when one morning, out of the blue; the mail-guy dropped a letter onto her desk along with the usual handful of junk mail. She was very busy and barely registered the fact at first…because she received a handful of circulars and other paraphernalia on her desk most mornings…but the strange yellow envelope immediately caught her eye and when she picked it out of the pile and started toying with it, she quickly spotted the English stamp on its top right-hand corner.

Turning it over, she then saw the ECA's crest – which she remembered from those garish blue blazers – which stood out prominently on the letter's reverse-side.

Curious and secretly excited, Madison looked around her to see if anybody was watching her.

A few people were talking on the phone; others were rushing around with sheets of paper in their hands but as nobody seemed to be paying any attention to her, she took out her letter-knife and opened the envelope, with as much nonchalance as she could muster, just in case.

As expected, the letter was from the board of the ECA, announcing that they were organising a ceremony for *the Bishop* where he was going to be honoured for his services to the sport…and presented with his official title of British Champion…

...and…as she had done such a wonderful job in covering the tournament in England and the subsequent event in Boston – which had led to a marked increase in the sport's overall profile since, in both the USA and in the UK - the ECA wanted to reward her for her contribution by inviting her to attend.

Madison's spirit leapt and her eyes brightened instantly at the news... but she had to read the letter over again just to make sure that she had her facts straight before she would allow the wave of joyful emotion to engulf her.

Having done that, her heart-rate suddenly rose out of control and she felt a little hot under the collar. In fact she was stunned, but after a few minutes…once that initial surprise and excitement had abated…Madison quickly recomposed herself, closed down her computer and made her way up to Amanda's office…to show her boss the invitation and to ask her for her permission to attend.

Unfortunately though, her boss, Amanda - who had watched her junior colleague blossom considerably since her escapade in England - was still under strict instruction to keep her in line…because of the sexual harassment suit she had brought against the company…and as a consequence of those orders...she was forced to refuse Madison the time off to go to England despite the latter's impassioned plea.

Madison was naturally devastated and...quietly fuming...she stormed back out of her boss's office without even waiting to be dismissed.

The next few days were a constant torment for Madison to the point where she even re-considered her position with the paper but having allowed her time to calm down, Amanda called her back into her office, primarily to reprimand her for storming out on her. . .but also to inform her that after a lot of 'soul-searching' she had re-considered her request...and had decided that she would allow her the time off to go on the trip after all.

In the intervening period – she (Amanda) had met with her hierarchy and agreed the arrangement in principle.

That said; in order to demonstrate her authority...and show those upstairs that she was not rolling-over completely as far as Madison was concerned...Amanda also informed her that rather than the eight days she had requested, she would only be allowed to take four.

That news made Madison grimace with frustration and dismay but she was nevertheless delighted. . .and two weeks later, she arrived back in London, where, to her great surprise, it was Gary who was there waiting for her at Heathrow, acting as the ECA's official representative.

Smiling broadly from ear to ear, he explained with an apologetic shrug that he had been asked to step in, as none of the old-guard had forgotten the first impression she had made on them on her previous visit...and as a consequence they had all refused the 'honour' of coming to meet her.

'Ya scared 'em all off Mad'; he joked in his wonderfully direct Aussie brogue.

Madison, although a little disappointed after the sympathetic of the invitation, just replied with a shrug and an impudent little smile.

Now, it had been almost six months since her last visit...but once they were over that initial moment of surprise and awkwardness, Madison and Gary greeted each other as if it were yesterday, Gary pulling her in close for a hug.

In fact his hug was a little too close for comfort, as far as Madison was concerned...

...but then realising that the young Aussie had clearly taken a shine to her, despite their doomed tryst, she understood his actions...and while she was not un-appreciative of his efforts and his show of affection, she knew that things had changed, that life had moved on and that her main focus now was on *the Bishop*.

She pulled away respectfully. . .and before she could say or do anything else, Gary immediately took hold of her suitcase and led the way out of the terminal, where they were lucky enough to grab one of the waiting taxis.

They quickly settled themselves in for the ride into London and five minutes or so later, just as the taxi hit the roundabout filtering traffic from the airport onto the motorway, the Simpson's theme tune suddenly sprang to life in Gary's pocket, filling the cab with sound and ringing loudly in Madison's ears.

It was his mobile phone ring-tone.

The two of them looked at each other for a moment; then Gary excused himself, pulled out the phone...and having checked the screen... he quickly explained that he had to take the call as it was from his friend Murray in Australia.

Madison nodded in agreement, shifted away from him...across the seat...as far as she possibly could and looked out the window while Gary then engaged in the following conversation;

G – 'How's life, mate?'
M – 'No worries!! - I got myself a new Sheila'.

G – 'A new 'Sheila'?'
M – 'Yeah mate; a bush-fire blond'. (Red-head)

M – 'You should see her in the raw' (naked)
G – 'You little ripper!!' (Words of praise fail me)

G – 'What's the chick's name?'
M – 'Dawn!'

G – 'Dawn? Are you kidding me? I know her, you drongo (idiot); she's the local bike!!' (Hooker)

M – 'Are you serious?'
G – 'Of course I am, you droob'. (Idiot)

M – 'But, she's like a wild-cat in the sack; she goes like the clappers!!'
G – 'Listen Murray, I know all about her reputation, and so does everybody else'.

G – 'Mate, I hope you've remembered your gumboots'. (Condoms)
M – 'Nah, I don't use them – they never seem to fit; I prefer to get off at Redfern'. (Withdraw)

G – 'Ah mate, if I cracked a fat, (got an erection) and she was the only Sheila around, I'd still rather flog the log (masturbate) than spear her bearded clam'. (Have sex with her)

G – 'So, when are you coming over?'
M – 'Dunno mate, coz Roz is crook, (ill) she went out yesterday and got pafo (pissed and fell over); that's why I was calling'.

G – 'Aww mate; sorry to hear that; so when are you coming then?'

M – 'Dunno, but soon mate, promise ya'.

G – 'Okay, see you then mate and look after Roz…'

M – 'Right; will do Gaz; cheers then…'

G – 'Bye Muz; see you guys soon'.

M – 'Yeah…looking forward to it'.

Gary then turned to Madison to finish his explanation.

'That was Murray; he and his sister Roz are planning to come over to England for a visit. You'd like Murray; he tells some ripper yarns'!

'Good jokes', he then reiterated, reverting back to his Anglo-tongue.

Madison smiled with the hint of a smirk but she didn't comment.

'I have to admit though', Gary shared, as he opened his wallet and took out a few snapshot photos, which he handed to Madison, '...talking to Murray makes me a little home-sick for Oz'.

'That's Murray, there', he confirmed, pointing to the first and second pictures of a rugged, thick-set Aussie bloke who apparently only ever wore a wide Australian bush hat.

Once again the Crocodile Dundee character immediately sprang to the forefront of Madison's mind, but given that Gary was sharing a private moment with her, she decided to bite her tongue.

The third photo was of his brother Joey, kitted out in his Sydney Swans jersey, the replica of which Gary had worn to the karting-track that time.

Madison recognised it much to Gary's delight...even though her thoughts flashed instantly back to Evie and her fetish for wearing out-sized replica jerseys as pyjamas.

Thirty minutes or so later, they arrived at the hotel in west London... and taking his responsibilities as ECA representative very seriously, Gary quickly went about making sure that Madison was settled in comfortably in her room...even handing her a copy of the presentation details in case she hadn't brought her own...before he left without any bother, telling her on his way out that if she needed anything...anything at all...she had his number and all she had to do was call; otherwise, he would see her at the presentation the day after next.

Madison thanked him politely for all his help and once he had left, she began to relax, unpack her cases and look forward - with great expectation - to enjoying another wonderful stay in the English capital.

That evening, Madison dined alone in the hotel restaurant and… almost as if she had been expecting it…when she walked out of the dining room, on her way back upstairs, she heard the concierge call out her name.

'Miss Chatfield…' the hotel employee articulated politely in his posh British accent;

'…this was just delivered for you', he declared, holding out a small, embossed envelope.

Madison approached the desk with a casual glide and accepted the envelope with a warm, friendly smile.

'Thank-you', she remarked…her voice barely audible as she turned the envelope over and slid her thumb under the flap.

'You're welcome Miss', the concierge replied, before turning to answer the call of another guest, who had just arrived at the desk asking about theatre tickets.

The moment was a little surreal and all of a sudden Madison's mouth felt really dry as if she knew that her destiny or indeed her whole life might just depend on what she was about to discover.

She waited another second or two before opening the envelope and then taking a deep breath…which she held in anticipation… she slowly freed the contents of the envelope from its paper prison.

Inside Madison found a matching notelet which she immediately flipped open with her thumb…barely taking the time to register the text that was written…before her eyes were drawn almost instinctively to the bottom of the page…and to the signature…or at least to the stylishly written initials…that were penned there.

Almost instantly, her heart leapt in her chest…and a split-second later a broad beaming smile began spreading, right across her face as she recognised those initials; 'T.B.'

'Yesss…' she whispered to herself, but just loud enough for the concierge to hear.

'Good news…Miss?' he queried kindly, noticing his guest's sudden change of mood.

Madison looked around and nodded politely. Then, moving a little further away from the concierge's desk…and his ear-shot…she took another deep breath and began reading the note all way through, from top to bottom.

It was of course the message she had been waiting for…praying for, ever since *the Bishop* had left New York after his Boston visit…*it was another invitation to the abbey*…and having read the note…twice, Madison quietly back-tracked to the concierge's desk to thank him again for his diligence before she sauntered back up to her room, where she waited almost an hour - *so as not to appear too eager* - before calling the number on the bottom of the note to confirm her acceptance of His invitation and to find out what time exactly he would be expecting her to arrive.

After that, she decided to go straight to bed, bringing to a close what had been a very long, exhausting…but ultimately successful start to her trip.

However, as she lay there in her bed, unable to sleep Madison just couldn't get the note and its contents out of her head;

- Why didn't he just call? She wondered.
- He could have just called.
- That's what most guys would have done
- After all; he had her number. Right?

...but that was just it, wasn't it? She suddenly realised; *the Bishop* wasn't like most other guys; he didn't do the obvious thing...

…and as she turned over, pulling the pillow tightly underneath her chin she quietly understood that <u>that</u> too was another reason why she found him so fascinating.

The next morning, she ordered room service...and as she sat at the little table, nibbling on a muffin and a banana…and drinking cup after cup of strong black coffee, Madison couldn't help but relive everything that had transpired on her previous visit to the abbey.

It had been exciting…and informative…and frustrating…and humiliating…and as she sat there thinking about all those things and about her first visit back to the abbey today, she suddenly felt a little light-headed.

I need to stop drinking so much coffee, she said to herself as she got up and made her way into the bathroom…but then as she stopped and looked at herself in the mirror Madison suddenly realised that she would probably never be able to go back to the abbey ever again…or indeed look *the Bishop* in the eye…without her brain instantly dragging images of that mortifying evening out from the archives of her mind.

Later that day... after a trouble-free ride of just under an hour through the verdant glory of the English countryside, Madison's taxi pulled into the abbey's driveway and came to a halt right next to *the Bishop's* sparkling Aston Martin.

Her head filled instantly with memories of the excited anticipation that she had felt on her first visit to this rather unconventional domain… and she smiled to herself inwardly…but then as she gazed out at the upper floor of the building … those wonderful memories of elation and expectation were quickly replaced by those of vexation and frustration from the disappointment that had followed.

Her brow furrowed slightly at the recollection…and as she pondered her reception by the master of the house, the butterflies that had began to flutter once again in her stomach immediately tempered her inner joy at being back.

Meanwhile, on hearing the sound of tyres crushing the gravel on the driveway, *the Bishop* put down the book he was reading and gazed briefly out the window of his study to see the taxi coming to a halt.

He checked his appearance vainly in the hallway mirror and then opening the front door, he strolled out to meet his guest, arriving just as she was about to open the car door.

He did the honours in gentlemanly fashion...and as she got out, he could not help but cast a discreet but approving eye over her elegant deportment.

Madison looked delightful and her face melted into a rich smile as she caught his attention and they greeted each other more formally.

'I thought that kind of chivalry had been lost forever', she commented thanking him for his gallantry, while reminding him of their conversation in that little restaurant in Boston.

'Courtesy and manners cost nothing', *the Bishop* replied, nodding in acceptance of her compliment and motioning for her to make her way towards the house while he took care of her fare.

Madison did just that, taking a few steps and then stopping for a moment to breathe in some fresh air before slowly continuing along the quaint, cobble-stoned path.

The Bishop paid off the cab…and quickly caught up with his guest to lead the way with his usual genteel courtesy.

However, much to Madison's surprise, instead of guiding her into the house, her host directed her politely around to the back garden, via a side-gate and a leaf-strewn alleyway that ran along the side of the main building.

Then, carrying on without further explanation, he led her along a stepping-stone path…through a flourishing rose garden…and on past a little thatched cabin which was set slightly back from the edge of the garden and hidden discreetly among the flora.

Madison stopped for a moment, to try and take it all in…to marvel at the array of different flower-beds that framed the garden, each of which was filled with a blaze of coloured flowers…but as soon as she did so, *the Bishop* waved her on, indicating that they were almost there.

He continued walking and…like the children behind the Pied-Piper… Madison followed his lead in silent contemplation, past an open-fronted gazebo…which looked more like a shelter…and all the way to the far end of the grassy lawn…and through a strange-looking latticed archway which led surprisingly to yet another part of the property.

Here though, it was like walking into another world; the garden took on a more unruly aspect as it extended off into the distance, as far as the eye could see, into what could only be a series of orchards, Madison surmised, if the fruity smell in the air was anything to go by.

For once, she was lost for words and as she looked around, Madison's first impression of the garden was that it reminded her of one of those magical Victorian walled gardens…often mentioned in 19th century literature…which always seemed to be brimming with trees packed full of ripe luscious fruit.

Enchanted, she turned to her host for confirmation of her assumption… that the more unruly area of the garden was an orchard;

'So…you grow your own fruit', she commented inanely, stating the obvious, but really just looking to make conversation.

'I do', *the Bishop* confirmed politely…and while Madison continued to process the fruit-laden assault on her senses, he duly showed her to a secluded little grove in the far corner of the orchard where he invited her to take a seat on a charmingly-ornate little bench in the shade of a strange-looking juniper tree.

Madison jumped at his offer as the intoxicating smells of slowly maturing fruit were making her a little light-headed; coming from New York, she had never experienced anything like it and she was starting to feel a little disorientated.

In fact, as she sat down, she felt like she had stepped into a parallel universe, like Alice through the looking glass; the latticed archway symbolising the portal between the two worlds.

The Bishop then produced a pitcher of iced-water, seemingly out of nowhere, and as Madison made herself comfortable, he offered her a glass of the refreshing liquid which she accepted gladly…resisting her natural instinct to ask for something stronger.

He poured a glass for himself too, and then placed the pitcher on a small wrought-iron table next to her before taking a seat himself on the other end of the bench.

It was a wonderful sunny day and both Madison and *the Bishop* sat there in silence for quite some time thereafter, drinking the chilled water and enjoying the tranquillity of the surroundings…until finally *the Bishop* decided to jump-start the conversation by complimenting her on her dress and its pretty olive-green print.

Madison thanked him for the comment and brushed her thigh lightly, smoothing out an unwelcome crease.

'It's idyllic here', she remarked, regaining her composure.

'It is indeed', *the Bishop* concurred.

♗

The social foreplay dispensed with, the conversation turned once again to women and relationships…and for the next couple of hours, Madison sat mesmerised, as she listened to *the Bishop's* cultured English accent, enjoyed his quirky turn of phrase…and marvelled at his clear, concise diction.

There was something so seductive and compelling about his words, and when he wasn't on one of his tiresome crusades she felt that she could listen to the calm authority in his voice for hours, which she did, more or less for the rest of the afternoon contributing only a meagre opposition.

He asked about Evie…and about her job…and about herself…and whether she had met anybody interesting of late…and with barely concealed self-interest, all Madison could reply to that question was;

'...without a doubt, Mr Byron…you are the most interesting and fascinating person that I am ever likely to meet'.

The Bishop smiled at the compliment.

It was the first time she could remember him doing so and boosted by the connection that she felt she had made, Madison returned the question enquiring about his recent past.

However, *the Bishop* was not dupe and recognising her ploy he immediately sidestepped the question by commenting on how women always tended to use their manipulative charms for their own ends…

'…just look at Samson and Delilah', he stated emphatically.

Madison frowned…but unmoved by his efforts to destabilise her…she responded immediately by remarking on his wariness of women…and the fact that he often made references to names from the past – which she saw as him showing off his culture - in order to avoid the embarrassment of answering a personal question.

The Bishop took a moment to reflect on her comment and then replied again simply…still avoiding the question…that he respected and admired people who had the courage and the moral fibre to stand up and be counted in the face of adversity; especially those women in history who had made their mark despite their fair nature and the submissive character of their existence.

'Cleopatra is another of those I admire', he confessed. 'Now she was fascinating'.

'Did you know young la......Miss Chatfield?' he corrected himself; '…that Cleopatra enjoyed her domination over men so much that one of her favourite pastimes was performing fellatio on them', he revealed, as if trying deliberately to unsettle her.

'Ppfffhhh…'

Madison almost choked on her water, shocked by the impertinence of *the Bishop's* remark and for the next few seconds… as he glanced mischievously over at her, delighting in her stunned expression…she was unable to respond.

Once again, he had caught her off guard with just a single phrase…but while she couldn't help but marvel at his wealth of knowledge…historical and otherwise…Madison still couldn't understand his continued attempts to shock her with the more salacious titbits of it.

After all, there was no need for it…and yet she was beginning to see a pattern developing…as every time she felt them getting closer, every time she felt that she was connecting with him, he would push her away again by making another scandalous comment in order to stop that connection from crystallising.

'Yes', he continued smugly, enjoying her embarrassment; '…indeed, she was notorious for her liking of it', he insisted, finishing off the last few drops of water in his glass.

Madison's mouth hung open slightly and her eyes widened further in shock as the memories of her own dreams of getting close enough to *the Bishop* himself to do something similar, made her blush.

'I like a responsive woman', *the Bishop* commented ambiguously.

What did he mean by that?, she pondered, as a subliminal image of the two of them in an intimate embrace flashed through her mind and ignited a rush of excitement in the pit of her stomach.

Then she remembered his words on that infamous Boston night;

'...True pleasure is worth waiting for'.

It had been a beautiful afternoon...with the sun in and out of the clouds...but as the temperature began to cool *the Bishop* proposed that they move indoors and maybe grab a bite to eat.

'Yes...please', Madison replied; the immediacy and the slightly over-enthusiastic tone of her response instantly betraying the façade of nonchalant indifference that she had been trying to project up to that point.

The Bishop smiled, but in true English style, he didn't pick her up on her eagerness.

'Ladies first...or shall I lead the way?' he asked.

'By all means; go first', Madison agreed with a simple hand-gesture.

'Very well', *the Bishop* concurred, responding in turn with a calm, benevolent smile.

They walked back slowly through the garden...stopping momentarily at the thatched shelter so that *the Bishop* could recover a newspaper that he had left there previously...and then carried on to the house...Madison taking great care as she followed on behind...not to snap or scuff the heels of her new designer shoes, as she negotiated the flag-stoned path that led the way there.

The Bishop reached the house first and waited politely by the back door for a moment or two, until Madison caught up. Then, with a quick flick of the wrist...and quite a hefty push...he slowly opened the sturdy-looking portal before standing back...with his usual gallantry...and inviting her to step inside.

Inside the abbey;

The Bishop led the way into the kitchen and while Madison excused herself to go and freshen up, he served them both a light snack from the fridge...*which had clearly been prepared in advance*...together with a glass of fresh orange juice, which he somehow managed to spill…and was still wiping up when Madison reappeared.

'Butterfingers…', she remarked casually, as she sauntered back into the kitchen, making light of her host's unusual lack of dexterity…but secretly enjoying the hangdog expression on his face.

'Indeed; …sorry about that' *the Bishop* replied, his face suddenly contorted with embarrassment, as he binned the sodden paper-towel and motioned…once again…for her to sit down…which she did willingly.

The informality of the setting was somewhat strange…given the circumstances of their previous encounters…*in posh hotels and restaurants*… but as they sat there eating…at the breakfast bar…in the intimacy of *the Bishop's* beautifully-appointed kitchen...and continued the conversation that had begun all those hours earlier in the garden…Madison could not help but spend most of the time wondering what her host's intentions were…and why he had bothered to invite her back to his home;

Was it an apology for last time...? She wondered…or for what had happened in Boston...?

…or was it just another thank you for the work she had done stateside…?

She didn't know and she couldn't decide…but as she sat there enjoying the experience Madison was convinced that *the Bishop…this man who had so obsessed and fascinated her since the very first time she had laid eyes on him…*would surely not have gone to all this trouble simply to chew her ear.

Another hour passed…and as the daylight dwindled outside…and the clock on the kitchen-wall struck seven, *the Bishop's* mood seemed to change…as if obeying some kind of self-imposed curfew.

He glanced up at the clock and without even finishing his last thought, he instantly cut the conversation short…looked directly into Madison's eyes and asked her politely, if she wanted him to call her a cab.

'Not necessarily', she replied confidently, '…not just yet anyway… unless of course you have other business to attend to', she added boldly.

The Bishop raised an eyebrow, smiling benignly - and while he still wouldn't admit to it, the look in his eyes told the intuitive and worldly young American that she wasn't the only one sensing the elephant in the room.

Madison didn't want to believe that he had only invited her over because he enjoyed their verbal exchanges; she really felt a connection with the Bishop and she needed to know if he did too.

I can't go on like this, she thought to herself...drifting along on the current of circumstance. I have to know one way or another if there is anything in this. I have to find out, I have to make a move, she concluded, suddenly remembering her host's comment earlier in the day that he liked responsive women, women with character.

Madison stood up in the middle of the kitchen and moved towards her host…offering to help him clear up, but hoping more than anything that he would make some kind of move on her.

The Bishop stood up too, sensing her intention…and for the first time in a very long time, a glint of desire flared in his eyes.

There had been an undoubted spark…of attraction…of sexual chemistry…between the two of them…ever since the first time they had met, and seeing that look in his eyes now, Madison instantly felt her inner regions tremble in anticipation.

'Is that look what I think it is?' She asked with a hint of devilment in her voice.

‘Well’, *the Bishop* replied, his voice taking on a more sensuous tone; ‘there is no shame in the exultation of the spirit…mind body and soul… and as you have decided to stay a while longer…’ he pursued, deliberately toying with her, ‘I thought I might play some more piano for you; I find music is a wonderful auditory aphrodisiac…’.

Madison smirked and swallowed nervously, her heart suddenly pounding with uncertainty.

I don’t need any ‘auditory aphrodisiac’; she thought to herself; I just need…

…and with that…feeling suddenly compelled to show her colours… she took her courage in both hands, put a finger to *the Bishop’s* lips…to shut him up…and then kissed him.

♗

The kiss was gentle at first but as *the Bishop* began to respond, succumbing to the sensuality of the moment, it quickly became very passionate…and all the tension and suppressed feelings that had built up in the months leading up to this moment were suddenly released as he wrapped his arms gently around her waist.

The heady sensations shot right up into Madison’s head, making her scalp tingle…and as *the Bishop’s* grip on her tightened, she deliberately lingered there…prolonging the moment for as long as she could…her eyes half-closed as she melted with the pleasure beginning to course through her body.

Finally though, *the Bishop* did release her…and having unwittingly ruffled his hair, Madison quickly brushed it back into place in a wordless apology…before pulling back and looking away, slightly flushed around the cheeks and rigid with the fear of delayed rejection.

Time seemed to stand still for a moment, but then, rather than rebuke her, *the Bishop* simply took her face in both his hands and returned the kiss, making her heart beat faster and harder until she felt as if it was going to burst out of her chest.

It was the most passionate of kisses and one that simply took Madison’s breath away.

This was a pivotal moment in their 'relationship'...and a moment so unspeakably sensuous that *the Bishop* just couldn't deny the feelings running through him any longer.

For a long time, he had not wanted to let anyone in…not wanted to let anyone get close to him…*which is why he had subjected Madison to all manner of tests since they had first met all those months ago*…but despite all his attempts to dissuade her or to sabotage any potential relationship that might develop between them, here they were…standing in his kitchen, in this most natural of human contexts.

Clearly, it had been a while since he had found himself in such a serendipitous situation…but as he stood there in the privacy of his own home…looking directly into Madison's eyes…*the Bishop* could no longer see any reason why he shouldn't let his guard down for once and enjoy the moment for what it was…or for what it might be.

And so…without another word…he simply took Madison by the hand and led her quietly out of the kitchen towards the spiral staircase in the hallway; Madison following willingly, but with her legs like jelly just barely able to carry her weight.

Upstairs, *the Bishop* pushed open the door to his bedroom and with a sweeping gesture of the hand, he invited Madison inside.

She hesitated momentarily…gazing at him with that challenging look in her eyes that all women have when seduction is in the air, but then as she stepped forward across the threshold of his private lair and penetrated his masculine domain…albeit for the second time, a sneaky grin began to curl in the corners of her mouth, relieving the tension slightly, as her eyes came to rest on his unusual swinging bed.

There it was, she thought to herself; the bed of her dreams, and as she moved closer to it and touched the timber structure of this amazing piece of antiquity with its almost magical, magnetic attraction, Madison knew intuitively that what was about to happen was going to be a life-changing experience for her.

The Bishop followed her inside, closing the door quietly behind him… and while Madison revelled once again in the moment, brushing the bed's wooden framework lightly with her fingers, he dimmed the lights, lit a candle on the dresser in the corner and then discreetly lay flat a framed photo which…up until that moment…had held pride of place on his bedside table.

Of course, with her curious nature and the innate capacity for jealousy…that every woman suffers from when it comes to a potential rival…Madison immediately picked up on what he had done – *and secretly scolded herself for her lack of observation, having no recollection of seeing the photo on her previous visit* - but realising that this was not the moment to be conducting a cross-examination, she decided…reluctantly…against asking any probing questions.

The flame from the candle in the corner…suddenly rose…then flickered…as it settled into a steady burn…creating an almost-mystical atmosphere…and as *the Bishop* turned to face her; the hesitation that he had hinted at downstairs suddenly disappeared and gave way to a much more confident Lothario.

As she stood there, Madison's heart thumped in anticipation and as *the Bishop* moved closer, she couldn't help but admire his wonderfully chiselled features in the half-light of the candle's shadowy glow.

She was going to say something…to compliment him on his perfect cheek-bones or his stylishly tousled hair…but then as another tremor of emotion rolled maddeningly through the depths of her being she quickly realised that words…or indeed flirting of any sort…would be altogether superfluous at this point.

Their eyes locked…and for a moment, they just stared at each other, each of them recognising that something of significance was about to happen between them.

The Bishop took another step forward, backing Madison up against the bed's wooden frame and as she reached behind to steady herself…unable to react otherwise…she could do nothing but watch in silence as he reached out and began to undo the buttons on the bodice of her dress…slowly and methodically, one after the other.

The drama of the moment was truly intense; the sexual rush that she was feeling inside was incredible…and Madison could feel her heartbeat quicken again…in anticipation…as the last of her buttons gave way…and the top of her dress fell open on either side revealing her lacy wine-coloured bra to *the Bishop's* intense, masterful gaze.

The tension in the room was at its zenith…but then without warning and to Madison's great surprise…and disappointment… *the Bishop* suddenly stopped what he was doing…and took a step back, his face full of unintended perplexity.

She was wearing the present he had given to her in New York.

'You like?' she asked quietly, an inquisitive smile playing slowly across her face.

'I do…' *the Bishop* replied almost in a whisper; 'very much so…'

Madison was delighted; she had built this moment up in her head to such a degree that she just could not stop herself…and acting almost on impulse in reaction to his approval, she took a step forward…away from the bed-frame…and slowly shook her hair loose before running her fingers through it like so many grains of soft sand.

Her confidence was clearly growing and as the anticipation in the room built and built until she could resist it no longer she slowly reached up and pushed the dress off of her shoulders…first the right, then the left…as she waited expectantly for *the Bishop* to make his next move.

The sudden silence was thick with possibility…but rather than rush the moment, *the Bishop* just stood there for a second or two…in quiet contemplation of the sight before him…the expression on his face slowly relaxing into one of discerning…and respectful…appreciation.

Madison meanwhile, felt a little awkward…standing there somewhat exposed …but as the suspense began to reach its peak she felt another shiver of emotion slowly ripple down her spine.

The passion inside her was beginning to spread exponentially and as *the Bishop's* gaze lowered slightly and fastened firmly onto her hips, she felt those stirrings of desire starting to ignite her core.

Her pulse began to race and caught up in her own excitement, Madison felt her stomach churn with expectation.

Finally, she thought to herself…after all these months of uncertainty and doubt…after all the missed chances and wasted opportunities she was…at long last…on the cusp of reaching her goal of seducing this elusive, enigmatic Englishman; they had been dancing around each other for so long…but now, the time had come.

The candle in the corner suddenly crackled and flared, drawing Madison's attention momentarily but then spurred on by her heightened expectation…and her unalienable impatience…Madison's natural instinct took over and she took the initiative once again.

She looked *the Bishop* straight in the eye…and then noting that her initial nervousness had dissipated, she reached for the waistband of her dress, hooked her fingers into the soft pliable material…and with a coquettish swivel of the hips…her head tilted slightly to one side…she slowly eased the dress over her thighs in one fluid movement and let it go, allowing the delicate green fabric to glide effortlessly down her legs…and pool quietly on the floor around her feet.

She paused for a moment and then, channelling the sexual energy that was now flowing freely through her veins, she slowly lifted her left foot off the ground and kicked the dress away with her right.

'Ta…dahhh…' she whispered quietly, as she stood there confidently, arms outstretched.

The candle's soft, romantic lighting cast flattering shadows on Madison's newly-exposed curves…and this time, having taken another moment to appreciate the tableau before him, *the Bishop* did step forward to embrace her, brushing his fingers gently against her cheek.

He took hold of her upper-arms and kissed her again…softly at first... and then more passionately...causing a long, protracted moan of relief and pent-up tension to vibrate deep in Madison's throat.

She could almost taste the urgency in his kisses…feel her senses suddenly awash with the strong, intoxicating spice of his powerful masculinity…and reassured that they were finally on the same page, she slowly succumbed to *the Bishop's* commanding embrace.

Madison had often envisioned what it would be like to be in this position but she had never dreamed it would be so exhilarating.

His arms went around behind her…and with one dextrous movement of his fingers, the clasp on her bra sprang open and the lacy garment that she had been wearing up to that point begin to slide unerringly down her arms and onto the floor.

Madison was still a little nervous...after all that had happened between them on previous occasions…but this time without another word, *the Bishop* then took her by the hand and led her over to the warm comfort of his bed, pulling back the heavy quilt and helping her to get under the covers…*because of the unusual swinging movement…*before stripping off himself and quickly joining her between the crisp white-cotton sheets.

She was acutely aware of everything that was going on at that point, every little gesture, every little detail and as she lay there, preparing to enjoy her victory, Madison's keen photographic memory was capturing every delicious moment and secretly storing it all away for future reference.

A full night of love-making lay ahead of them, a night bursting with intensity and all-consuming passion, but as the night was still young, both Madison and *the Bishop* spent quite some time…*once they had gotten over the initial awkwardness of those first few moments that everyone experiences when they jump into bed with a new partner for the very first time* …kissing each other…passionately…and caressing each other…feverishly…until they had finally put each other at ease and established that oh-so important mutual trust - *so vital to an intimate relationship* - that allows two people to relax and enjoy each other's body thereafter with unrestrained delight.

Typically, *the Bishop* was a master of seduction and as the strange bed swayed quietly beneath them on its sturdy iron couplings, his expert hands quickly took charge, moving slowly but inexorably towards those parts of Madison's body that filled her spirit with fire…every touch of his fingers, every touch of his very dexterous fingers…eliciting sensations in her body the likes of which she had never experienced before.

It was immensely pleasurable and as she lay there quietly, in a moment of respite…Madison couldn't believe how wonderful she felt. There was simply nothing in her past that could compare with how she was feeling in that moment, that could have prepared her for such a heightened state of excitement…because she simply had never met anyone quite like this man, like *the Bishop*; someone who literally took her breath away…and as her mind swirled with myriad emotions and flashing images of all those moments they had spent together…but which had remained unfulfilled… she suddenly realised that she was only just managing to keep it all together.

Her body was alive and every muscle was tensed in readiness; her hips yearned for that time-honoured release but only after what seemed like an eternity, did *the Bishop* finally breach the entrance to her temple, pushing into her very slowly…just a centimetre at a time…provoking what could only be described as a series of wonderfully garbled sounds from her mouth…that meant nothing…but spoke volumes as Madison felt her body stretching around that of her lover.

It was a very sexy, very intense moment and when their pelvic bones did finally meet uniting them at last, a fiery explosion erupted almost immediately deep in Madison's core releasing a seething volcano of desire that had been smouldering there for months.

Madison was finding it difficult to breathe…because of the intensity of the emotions she was feeling…but nevertheless…caught up in the moment…she wrapped her legs around *the Bishop's* back and then found his lips again…kissing him passionately once or twice…before she was forced to break away again…to catch her breath…as the pleasure from their combined heat started to ripple up and down her spine in one continuous motion.

The bed began to rock …and as it did so, Madison tensed up a little more, suppressing her moans as best she could, while *the Bishop* began to thrust into her…starting slow and steady…but then picking up the tempo…and synchronising his movements with the rhythmic swinging of the bed.

Those thrusts from his strong masculine pelvis became harder…and deeper…and in next to no time Madison was meeting each of them with a thrust of her own, until without realising it, she found herself involuntarily letting slip a series of 'oh my god, oh my god' gasps as each stroke hit home deep in her core.

She was now helpless to resist…and as *the Bishop* continued his thrusting motion, the swinging ceiling above Madison's head and the warm amber light coming from the candle in the corner only added to the disorientation of her senses. She tried to remain lucid, she tried to remain 'in the moment' but *the Bishop* was overpowering her with such force… that before long her body was drenched in sweat and tiny beads of physical exertion...witness to the effort that she was generating...were beginning to pool in her navel like the droplets of rain that congregate in a flower's core.

Madison was in heaven…enjoying the 'human-experience' like never before…but then all of a sudden, taking her by surprise yet again, *the Bishop* rolled over and pulled her down on top of him, tight against his chest.

His hands immediately grabbed her butt-cheeks…and as he pulled her against him with quite some force, more cries and even more moans escaped her quivering lips as her body reacted instantly to the fire sweeping through her inner regions.

Completely overwhelmed, Madison struggled to breathe. Never before had she known such immense pleasure…or been so thoroughly possessed… and while the fire within roared higher and higher, sending a constant stream of unbridled delight into her pheromone-soaked brain...to the point of making her vision blur with multi-coloured lights...a whole host of unfamiliar emotions began to sweep over her in a torrid surging tide.

The wonderful sensations were driving her crazy...and then without warning, *the Bishop's* breathing suddenly became louder and harsher too, intermingling with her own animal-like groans...*which were increasing exponentially*...as he guided them both towards a towering climax.

Madison knew that she was close...but nevertheless she wanted to delay the inevitable...and hoping for a moment's respite...she put her hands against *the Bishop's* chest and...gasping for air...managed to push herself up into a straddle position, arching her back instinctively.

She took a couple of deeps breaths and as she did so, the sweat-soaked sheet that had been covering them both up to that point, fell theatrically from her shoulders to settle gently around her waist.

The Bishop took a moment to catch his breath too; in fact he took several moments...and then fixing Madison's expression once again, he looked for the tell-tale signs; *her breathing had definitely become more laboured and her face, neck and chest were clearly flushed from all the exertion;*

She was close and he knew it...

Madison knew it too; her stomach muscles were slowly tightening and she felt the tell-tale spasms deep inside her which told her instinctively that she was on the cusp of a mind-blowing orgasm.

Consequently, *the Bishop* took hold of her thighs in both hands and continued his thrusting...until, after a long moment of steady rhythmic pumping the circular grinding motion of his hips against her delicate soft tissues finally sent Madison over the edge...and unable to hold it off any longer, she let herself go, drowning in the powerful waves of carnal delight.

Her eyes rolled back in her head...and with her tousled blond hair covering most of her face, her body convulsed as she exploded with maddened pleasure, her hips writhing uncontrollably, lost in the sea of lust that had overwhelmed her entire body; indeed, her orgasm had hit her like a falling anvil and Madison felt as if her whole body had been shattered into a thousand pieces.

It was amazing; in fact it was more than amazing and Madison rode the emotion for as long as she could…until eventually, struggling for breath, she collapsed forward back onto *the Bishop's* chest, before slipping off him and laying by his side panting as if she had just run the marathon, the perspiration gleaming on her skin and her brain…for the next minute or so…an intellectual desert.

In truth, it was several minutes before Madison's orgasm subsided completely and while she waited for the emotion to quiet, she snuggled into the crook of *the Bishop's* arm basking in both the physical and the intellectual satisfaction that she felt, from having manoeuvred this strange enigmatic man into bed.

This is heaven, she thought to herself as her wits and her equilibrium slowly returned…but then a few moments later…much to her surprise… *the Bishop* raised himself up onto his elbow and announced that he was primed and ready for round two.

'Oh please, you gotta be kidding me, right?' she joked, breathless and exhausted.

But *the Bishop* wasn't kidding; he had resisted the siren's lure for longer than he cared to remember and after months of self-imposed celibacy he had a lot of catching-up to do.

He quickly got back into position…being careful to shift their combined body-weight back into the middle of the bed…and before Madison could really argue the fact, he was dominating her again, just as he had done before.

'Please', she whispered; 'I can't do that again, not so soon'.

'Oh yes you can', *the Bishop* asserted, brushing aside her flimsy rebuttal.

Madison really didn't think that there was any more passion…or desire left in her worn out body…but refusing to be beaten (*competitive nature*) she tacitly agreed to round two and much to her amazement *the Bishop* managed to prove her wrong once again as she climaxed twice more…in quick succession…sending blood pounding into her brain and driving all coherent thoughts from her head.

'My God', she whispered, as she lay there breathless and bereft of all energy; 'you sir, are insatiable'.

The Bishop leaned down and kissed her again, pushing his breath deep into her lungs...and then after another series of short, rapid thrusts...he climaxed too before collapsing heavily on top of her pinning her to the mattress.

Madison was crushed under his weight but as she stroked his sweat-sodden hair, she could feel his heart pounding in his chest through her skin as his body continued to twitch uncontrollably for a couple of minutes on top of hers.

Exhausted, *the Bishop* finally rolled off to the side, and lay there on his back for some time catching his breath, the sudden separation sending a cold shiver right through Madison as the sheen of perspiration covering her drained body instantly cooled; in fact, they both lay there, mentally paralysed and breathing heavily for several minutes.

Never before had Madison ever felt so gloriously sated, her body throbbed, her muscles hot and languid from the succession of prolonged orgasms, but even as she was revelling in the dreamy aftermath of the afterglow *the Bishop* was already gearing up for the next round.

The rest of the night was a blur, dedicated to Venus and all her sisters… and by the end of it, Madison was as limp as a rag-doll; her floppy arms and her floppy legs, a sure sign that her body had given all it had to give.

The next morning, as dawn broke, Madison awoke with a warm glow emanating from her core…even though every muscle in her body was aching from all the impossible positions *that the Bishop* had forced her into during the night.

She blinked owlishly as the light of day hit her eyes and although she was exhausted after a very short night's sleep, she felt invigorated; her adrenaline levels still clearly on a high.

Even so, she didn't move for the first couple of minutes, preferring instead to use the time to scan all around the room…yet again…but eventually she had to get up as she needed to answer nature's call.

Beside her, *the Bishop* was still completely out of it, so doing her best not to rock the bed and disturb him, she slowly climbed out and… grabbing the sheet to cover herself…she quietly tip-toed into the bathroom to use the 'Lucy' and run herself a bath, a hot, revitalising bath, as they had both worked up quite a sweat during the night's frenzied activity.

She tried to be as quiet as possible in the bathroom, but the sound of the running water soon roused her sleeping partner and Madison could hear him moving around in the bedroom.

A little embarrassed, she went to the door to apologise for waking him... but as the water in the bath was too hot for her to get into immediately; *the Bishop* cleverly lured her back into bed, the time that it cooled.

Madison couldn't believe it; she had reached sexual saturation while the Bishop was ready to go again; who is this man, she wondered to herself.

Now, normally Madison wouldn't have been able to do this…feeling that she had already squeezed every ounce of energy out of her body in order to keep up with *the Bishop's* gymnastics during the night…but amazingly, but with a little gentle persuasion and a few well-placed kisses, she could not help but give in to his demands one more time.

However, unlike the previous evening, this time it was more of a snuggle and a cuddle…than any full-on action…and once he had satisfied his desire to hold her in his arms one more time, *the Bishop* respectfully left Madison in peace to go and take her bath, while he…as the master of the house…gallantly got up and went downstairs to sort out breakfast.

Madison finished her bath and…having first sneaked a peek at the photo on his bedside table that he had tried to hide…she joined him down in the kitchen twenty minutes or so later...wearing his favourite Italian-silk robe…which she had found hanging on a hook in the bathroom…and her hair wrapped tightly in a towel.

The Bishop frowned in dismay at the sight of her in his preferred morning attire but he didn't pick her up on it…as she probably looked better in it than he did…and as she sat down opposite him at the breakfast bar, he instantly forgave her as he quietly announced what was on offer.

Madison smiled lazily. She was ravenous from the endless coupling of the night before and her first thought was coffee...and then more coffee… before she decided that she should probably eat something too, as the previous evening's meal had been rather light on calories and her nocturnal exertions had most definitely used up any reserves of energy that that meal might have provided her body with.

The Bishop offered her some fruit juice…and then some toast with marmalade…which she accepted gladly…and while she set about eating that, still re-living the events of the night before in her mind, he wandered out to the front porch to pick up the morning paper which was always delivered to his door around about 7 a.m.

'What time do we need to get going?' Madison asked suddenly as she stood in the kitchen doorway, toast in hand, her voice breaking the silence and startling *the Bishop* as he was about to turn around and make his way back along the corridor.

'The presentation is at two, so we should be leaving here at about midday', he declared irritably, not appreciating being caught unawares.

'Okay; that's fine by me, but I will have to swing by my hotel to get changed', Madison advised. 'I wasn't expecting to stay overnight so I don't have a change of clothes', she added, gesturing to her current attire as she disappeared back into the kitchen.

The Bishop looked at the door to the kitchen and then thinking better of it, he decided to go into the conservatory to read his paper, hoping to find a moment of peace and quiet there while Madison finished her breakfast.

Unfortunately though, he had no sooner set foot in the glass covered dome, when Madison appeared behind him, holding a fresh plate of buttered toast.

'Would you like a piece, hon?' she asked brightly.

The Bishop turned and threw her an icy look. He was rather set in his ways and not altogether at ease with having a stranger in his house…despite the fact that they had just spent the night together…but more importantly he was a stickler for tidiness in his solitary existence and the thought of her trailing crumbs all through his house filled him with abhorrence.

Firstly, he retorted rather brusquely; 'don't call me hon or honey; I hate those terms of endearment, and secondly, NO, I do not want anything else to eat; thank you very much'.

Madison was stunned a little by his rebuff and had to catch her breath for a second or two before she could apologise for her over-enthusiasm.

'I'm sorry; I didn't mean to…'

'It's fine', *the Bishop* interrupted, 'just be careful with that…' he added, pausing deliberately for effect and motioning towards the plate of toast.

He was clearly perturbed by his guest's lack of house-etiquette…but to calm his disquiet and take his mind off of her rather presumptuous attitude…he quietly put the newspaper to one side and sat down at the piano…

This was one of the ways he used to master his emotions and focus his thoughts.

Meanwhile, still by the door…and still chewing on a crust of toast, Madison watched him in quiet admiration for a moment or two...before sauntering languidly over and joining him on the piano-stool, shifting him over a little with a gentle nudge of her hips.

This audacity surprised *the Bishop* somewhat, and while he ruminated on the situation…and how he could avoid letting this intense young American get too close to him, Madison immediately tried to defuse any growing animosity between them by asking him politely if he would play that tune again; the one he had played to her the first time that she had been there.

The Bishop looked at her…smiled at her benignly…and then did just that, launching immediately into the tune that she had requested…just like a performing dog.

Madison was more than a little pleased with herself; she had managed to lower *the Bishop's* usually steadfast and unyielding defences with just a dash of feminine charm…and while she sat there beside him, mesmerised once again by his undeniable talent, listening attentively to the sound and tempo of the music, she proceeded to calmly ignore his subsequent grimacing…and looks of disapproval, to enjoy yet another piece of freshly-buttered toast.

It only lasted a couple of minutes but Madison was charmed once again by the haunting melody of the tune…and when *the Bishop* had finished playing, she immediately put her plate down on the top of the piano in order to applaud him, unaware that she was committing another house-etiquette faux-pas in doing so.

The Bishop thanked her politely and then making little tsking noises with his tongue he quickly removed the plate from the piano's shiny, varnished surface and placed it on top of his newspaper.

Madison looked at him with raised eyebrows but with her spirits buoyed…and assuming that their night of passion had somehow given her license…or perhaps entitlement even…to know more about him, she proceeded to ask her new lover…rather tentatively…about the photo on his bed-side table, her journalistic instincts – *or perhaps even more simply her natural feminine impulses* – suddenly coming to the fore.

The Bishop looked at her again and true to his reputation; he blanked her, as like all men, he intentionally avoided discussing certain issues.

A pregnant pause followed…but after a few moments, the journalist in her would not be denied, and Madison asked again more insistently.

'C'mon...who is she...you can at least tell me her name ...?'

The Bishop grimaced, coughed nervously and took a deep breath.

'That...is a private matter and I would rather not discuss it', he stated trying to shut her down.

Madison could only smile as she licked her buttery fingers; 'I see...but...'

At that point, *the Bishop* raised his hand to stop her talking...and stood up.

He had no desire to get into an embarrassing argument with Madison, so instead of answering her question he decided to try to throw her off the scent her by offering her a compromise instead.

'Look, I understand that you would want to know more about me but there are some things in life that are private...and should remain so', he commented.

'Yeah, everyone has secrets; right', Madison agreed.

'Indeed', *the Bishop* concurred, '...but if you are really that curious about me...'

He stopped talking and simply motioned for her to join him.

Madison got up from the piano and followed her host back down the corridor to his study, pleased with herself that she had managed to negotiate this very rare chance to find out more about him.

However, she thought to herself as she caught up to him; while she admired his attempts at distraction...offering her a visit of his personal sanctuary as a diversion...it didn't mean that she would forget about the photo; her journalistic curiosity...and ultimately her female nature...would just never allow that to happen.

The Bishop took a key from inside a miniature ornamental chess-board that sat on the antique dresser in the hallway and unlocking the door, he pushed it open and invited Madison to step inside.

She did so, walking slowly into the room to find herself in a deceptively large study, covered with thick shag-pile carpets and furnished with a beautiful ensemble of sturdy leather sofas.

The red-velvet walls were lined with book-shelves finished in expensive mahogany and above her head the vaulted ceilings were spectacular.

A rich Persian rug emblazoned with *the Bishop's* very own initials held centre-stage and above that hung a photo of the 1st Duke of Wellington.

The Bishop followed Madison's gaze; 'the world's greatest ever strategist', he remarked calmly.

'…And a notorious ladies man', Madison added with a somewhat patronising tone.

On the far wall of the room, between two beautiful stained-glass windows, Madison noticed a couple of paintings by Edward Hopper and to her right above his desk, there were a couple black and white photos... of gangsters from the 1930's...taken by New York photographer Arthur Fettig (aka Weegee).

Madison knew her New York history and commented on them.

'Oh, so you <u>do</u> like Americans', she remarked sarcastically, remembering all their previous conversations.

'Did last night not teach you anything?' *the Bishop* replied, thawing slightly and enjoying the verbal jousting.

Madison blushed slightly…and feeling a little intimidated all of a sudden…by the testosterone-rich environment of the room, she carefully made sure that the robe she was wearing was wrapped as tightly as possible around her body and that the belt at her waist was tied securely.

The Bishop didn't say anything but as he watched her reaction he was more than a little impressed by the fact that Madison knew her New York history.

Then, through a small archway, in a recessed alcove or snug as some people would call them...Madison noticed a signed photograph of Bob Newhart hung on a wall above a snooker table.

'That's a little strange', she commented as she approached. 'This photo seems somewhat out of place'.

'Precisely', *the Bishop* acknowledged, as he walked up behind her… 'and that's what gives me the psychological edge when I'm playing…my opponent's mind is distracted by that very thought'.

Madison shrugged her shoulders…but this time she didn't comment on his reasoning; she had no interest in the technicalities of psychology and instead, her attention was drawn to another series of framed photographs of people she didn't recognise.

With her buttery fingers Madison had smeared the glass on the photo of Bob Newhart…and so before he moved on the Bishop whipped out his kerchief to wipe it off.

In doing so, the note he kept in his pocket came flying out too and fell on the floor.

Madison saw the note but the Bishop didn't offer any explanation; he just bent down and put it back in his pocket, before turning to the photo and wiping off her fingerprints.

'Who are all these people?' she enquired, scrutinising the faces.

'Those are people who I admire from the game of snooker', *the Bishop* explained pointing to the respective photographs; 'Ronnie O'Sullivan, Jimmy White and Alex Higgins'.

'So, you obviously like this game', Madison remarked after a pause, indicating the table.

'Yes I do', *the Bishop* admitted without restraint. 'It's a bit like chess but it takes concentration, mental toughness, precision and tactical awareness to a whole new level by adding an extra ingredient; flamboyance'.

'I see', Madison acknowledged.

'…..and that there, is George Best, another flamboyant genius', *the Bishop* pointed out on the opposing wall.

Madison nodded her head, not recognising the name but silently acknowledging that the last guy had a very sexy grin.

She then moved back into the main part of the room...and on a shelf full of books clearly dedicated to her host's favourite subject, psychology, a thin volume squeezed between two rather heavy tomes suddenly caught her eye.

Madison pulled it out, intrigued by its title.

'Payback is a Bitch', she read out aloud. 'I haven't read this, but it sounds like something I might like. What's it about?' She asked curiously.

'Oh that', *the Bishop* mumbled, grabbing it out of her hands and replacing carefully on the shelf.

'I don't think you would really like that', he commented cryptically.

'That book is a study into the psychology of evil, where a nefarious devil-like character called Daniel Vatspoynter infiltrates a happy family and spreads his gangrenous poison within their midst – infusing his hateful evil into their unsuspecting hearts and corrupting their previously unpolluted minds with as many despicable sins as possible – avarice, covetousness etc.'

'Eew; you're right'. Madison protested as a cold shiver ran down her spine. 'I definitely wouldn't want to read about anything like that. It sounds disgusting, sordid and immoral', she declared.

'It is, believe me, but don't worry', *the Bishop* reassured her; '....to cut a long story short – what goes around, comes around...the bad-guy gets his come-uppance....and the family dances on his grave condemning him to eternal damnation, singing 'payback is a bitch'.

'Hence the title', Madison concluded.

'Hence the title'; *the Bishop* confirmed, finishing his brief synopsis... and with that, as he was still a little uncomfortable about her being in his private space, he guided her back out, while explaining that the hero of the novel, Marcus had been modelled on the fabled character Dunstan; a blacksmith who supposedly un-shackled the devil and made him promise in exchange, to never again enter any house with a horse-shoe over the door.

'That's why people still hang them over the front door of their houses even today; for Good luck', he revealed.

'Did you know that?' he asked, guiding his guest out of his shrine of inspiration and back to the neutrality of the conservatory.

Madison shrugged; 'No, I did not know that', she replied.

'Anyhow', *the Bishop* commented; 'enough of all this; we need to get ourselves ready; the presentation is at two.

Back upstairs;

While *the Bishop* disappeared into the bathroom to take a shower, Madison busied herself getting dressed. She was still trying to get her head around the situation; around everything that had happened since she had arrived at the abbey the previous afternoon.

Everything about *the Bishop*...and indeed everything about the abbey... intrigued her now and this morning's revelations were no exception.

Who could have guessed what was behind that door, she thought to herself as she straightened-out her dress; the library, the snooker table, the portraits...the...

And then, thinking about the portraits she suddenly remembered the piece of paper that had fallen out of *the Bishop's* pocket when he had wanted to wipe the glass clean.

I wonder what that was, she thought to herself; another secret, another piece of intrigue; something else he didn't want to share; he didn't say anything at the time, gave her no explanation so it must have some personal significance, she concluded.

And then, while checking her appearance in the full-length mirror attached to the wall, she unwittingly spied the shirt that *the Bishop* had been wearing earlier, draped over the chair by his dresser.

She thought about it for a moment and then listening for a change in the water falling in the shower...that might indicate that *the Bishop* was about to reappear...she tip-toed across the room, reached down into the shirt's pocket and found the little piece of paper.

She took it out quietly...and hesitated for a moment, knowing that she probably shouldn't be doing this...but she just couldn't help herself.

However, before she could open the note and read it, Madison heard the shower-water stop running and the shower-door open.

Quickly, she stuffed the incriminating note into her bra and pushing the chair aside, she pretended to be looking for something on the floor.

'What are you doing?' *the Bishop* asked appearing behind her in a towel.

'Oh', she replied calmly, pretending to scour the area. 'I think I lost part of my earring last-night…'

'You did? Then, if I were you…I would look in the bed rather than over there by the dresser…' he suggested as he grabbed a pair of nail-clippers from the bedside drawer and returned to the bathroom.

Madison nodded. 'Yeah, that would be more…'

She didn't need to finish as *the Bishop* had already gone, but feeling guilty…and with her heart thumping uncontrollably in her chest, she decided…against all her journalistic…and feminine…instincts to put the note back without reading it.

Later;

They left on time, if not just before, at 11.50 a.m. to be precise, and as he eased the car into gear the *Bishop* enquired casually if she had found her earring.

'As a matter of fact…no, I didn't…' Madison replied, '…but it was loose anyway, so I could have lost it anywhere', she added with a throwaway gesture, trying to cover her tracks.

The Bishop simply nodded his head…and without another word he pulled out of the drive and headed into London, parking the car upon their arrival in the underground car park of the hotel in which Madison was staying.

He kissed her again tenderly...and before she got out of the car, Madison asked him playfully if he was sure that he didn't have a girlfriend, because he did that really well.

The Bishop smirked but didn't reply. Instead, he got out of the car and like a perfect gentleman; he came around to open her door, giving her his hand to assist her exit from the car.

They took the lift up to the hotel and while *the Bishop* stopped at the lobby and made his way out to the taxi rank…having agreed with her that he would go on ahead, to the presentation…Madison carried on up to her room where she could get changed and freshen up.

Energised by her intimate interlude with *the Bishop*, Madison rushed inside getting undressed as she went, going straight into the shower before quickly fixing her hair…which she hadn't been able to do properly at the abbey…and getting back into her professional persona by changing into her usual, everyday business-suit.

It was all a bit manic, because she didn't want to be late for *the Bishop's* big day but then as she was applying her lipstick in a last-minute attempt to look more presentable, it suddenly struck her.

In the reflection of the mirror, she noticed the underwear that she had just discarded, laying haphazardly on the bed where she had thrown it… and as the penny dropped she found herself frozen in mid-stroke, standing perfectly still for a few seconds, her eyes fixed firmly on the aforementioned item.

She didn't usually wear sexy underwear; she never had, but all of a sudden she realised that wearing those particular undies last night had given her the extra confidence she needed to make a move on *the Bishop*… and she began to wonder if by buying them for her, he had not only taught her a lesson in self-confidence but also shown greater insight and read her better than anyone had ever done before.

Could he really be that observant or was it just a coincidence, she speculated as she made her way by taxi to the presentation which was being held at the ECA's central London offices.

No way; it must have been a coincidence, she decided, no man could ever know a woman that well; not in such a short space of time at least; there was just no way, she convinced herself as the cab dropped her off; simply no way.

The presentation…*at which the Bishop was presented with a beautifully-crafted, crystal-glass decanter in the shape of a bishop chess-piece…*went very well and despite their night of passion, both Madison and *the Bishop* remained very discreet during the ceremony.

That same discretion also applied to the ensuing after-party…held in a bar across the road...where, determined to avoid any un-necessary scandalous whispering Madison chose to sit with Gary and some other chess aficionados...who - *caught-up in the mood of role-models and sporting-idols which was the order of the day* - were discussing the pros and cons of Gary's hero - Kerry Packer; an Australian businessman and sports innovator who had revolutionised the game of cricket back in the seventies.

Gary was waxing lyrical about all that Kerry Packer had done for cricket and for Australia, playing to the audience in typical fashion…when all of a sudden the man they all loved to hate, Rory Campbell-Brown poked his head around the door of the bar, his snooty gaze flicking around the tables, left and right as he searched for a 'sympathetic' face.

He saw where Gary and Madison were sitting and his eyebrows instantly knotted in frustrated anger. His cheeks flushed with a rush of blood…and ignoring the greetings of several other players and officials, he walked into the bar and made his way directly over to their table.

Madison sighed as she saw him coming; she hadn't really gotten to know him but in stark contrast to *the Bishop*, her opinion of this guy was that he was rude and crude.

Gary looked up too and seeing Rory approach, he grimaced in frustration at the thought that once again the annoying larrikin was going to interrupt his conversation…and sure enough, he did just that, sitting down in a spare seat without even being invited.

A couple of the people who were sat there quickly got up and moved away…and then, with contemptuous disregard for his Australian contemporary…and complete indifference as to whether she was interested in talking to him or not, he began questioning Madison with insistence - his pungent breath thick with alcohol - as to why she had never consulted him about his thoughts on the game; '…After all, you seem to have consulted every other player at that Tournament back in March', he rasped indignantly.

Barely able to suppress her disdain Madison feigned contemplation… patronisingly…but then as Rory waited expectantly for her reply, she simply shrugged her shoulders and informed him - trying to be as polite as possible - that by the time it had come to his turn, she had gathered ample content for her article and no longer felt the need for his input.

This rather dismissive but succinct comment left Rory - or Copperfield as she liked to call him – more than a little aggrieved as it detracted greatly from the self-importance that he tried to attach to himself, but nevertheless, determined to incrust himself once again and regain a semblance of self-respect from this brazen American journalist, he reigned in his indignation and continued his cringing 'charm offensive' on her, rolling out his usual, worn-out string of lame, scarcely-veiled flirtations.

Madison sat back and took a deep breath, revolted by most of what he had to say, as every word that came out of the guy's mouth was dripping with double-entendre and crude sexual innuendo, but while she gave as good as she got most of the time in the ensuing exchanges, she did have to look to Gary to intervene on several occasions in order to stop his fellow player from harassing her, not wanting to make a scene or commit another social faux-pas herself as they were celebrating *the Bishop's* presentation.

Gary's response however was somewhat less subtle or considered.

'Stop badgering her; you Dalek', he riposted, sending Rory packing after one particularly crude comment.

Humbled slightly by that rebuke, Rory did back off a little after that… and while he continued to chew Madison's ear as to the stories he could have told her about his life on the circuit, Gary returned to sipping his beer quietly and contemplating two young women in water-tight dresses who were sat decoratively at a nearby table, his mind wandering into the stereotypical fantasy of what it would be like to be in bed with the two of them…at the same time, in a three-way.

The storyline was just getting interesting in Gary's imagination when all of a sudden Madison stepped in front of him obscuring his line of vision and breaking the visual connection with his dream-girls.

'I can't listen to any more of this trite nonsense', she declared impatiently, staring into Gary's eyes. 'I'm going to the ladies-room to get away from this creep'.

Gary nodded his head in understanding, but still distracted a little by the remnants of his imaginary cameo, he could not help but watch as Madison turned and walked off, focussing all his attention on her swaying hips...and affording them as much appreciation as the next man.

However, as he enjoyed the view, an annoying little buzzing noise brought his attention back into focus; it was Rory, trying to talk to him.

'Did you know Bruce that women never really listen to you; they are not interested in what you have to say; they are just waiting for their turn to speak - and when they don't get that chance they don't like it', he growled, slurring his speech slightly.

'Hey, Missy; would you like to get a room later?' he called after Madison, trying to demean her with his misogynous comment as she disappeared through the door.

That was the final straw for Gary; Rory had been winding him up for long enough.

He put his hand onto the Scot's left arm and began to tighten it, suggesting that Rory should apologise to Madison for that last comment.

'Who are you...her body-guard', the older man rasped with his usual mean-spirited temper, trying to pull his arm away.

'Nah mate; I'm just looking out for her, that's all; keeping her away from wolves like you', Gary replied, the tone in his voice suggesting an underlying strength that wasn't to be messed with.

Rory huffed, looked at the young Aussie and then looked away shaking his head as the former released his arm; he paused for a moment but then recognising he was in the wrong, he wisely took Gary's comment as a cue that he should probably vacate the area.

He got up and went over to the bar where, having brushed down his jacket and recomposed himself, he started gloating all over again about his winning performances and his career high-lights to one of the two young women that Gary had been eying up previously who was herself at the bar waiting to get served.

The second young woman immediately joined her friend at the bar, hoping probably that Rory was going to get the next round in, which he did surprisingly; though probably only in a moment of weakness because of the guilt he was feeling over what he had said to Madison...and the fact that the eyes of the chess association members, sitting across from him at the bar, were now focussing their attention very firmly on him.

'Here's to winning', he announced with false chivalry as he held up his glass, inviting the girls to do the same.

The two girls looked at each other and smiled as they chinked glasses with the wavering Scot, but then as Rory turned to leave, they cleverly surrounded him, doing their utmost to engage him in a little more conversation, trying tenaciously to persuade him to stay, not wanting to lose their benefactor so quickly.

'Hey, some guy over there just said that we look like sisters; what do you think?' one of the girls chirped in, pulling back on Rory's sleeve.

He stopped and looked at the first girl, then at the second, then back at the first.

'Nah, they were just taking the piss'; he replied, and with that he pushed past them and walked off to chat with one of the other ECA members who had congregated with *the Bishop* on the far side of the bar, leaving the two girls with their mouths agape and downright flabbergasted.

A few minutes later, Madison re-joined Gary at the table and two minutes after that Rory returned too; this time with an apology and a round of drinks for them all 'on the house'.

Madison was unmoved by his apology and after yet another off-colour remark about her legs, she felt that she had reached the end of her tether… and could no longer restrain her natural response.

She took hold of the pint of beer that was sitting in front of her annoying tormentor and threw it in his face, soaking his shirt, his tie and his lucky tweed jacket, as it dripped to the floor.

Then she sat back and glared at him, daring him to make a scene; *she was clearly annoyed with him but in reality she felt that Copperfield was probably more to be pitied than to be scorned.*

The initial shock of the cold liquid hitting his face took Rory's breath away but once he got over that, a series of unrepeatable expletives followed as he jumped up and began brushing himself down as best he could.

'Well, I have to say that I have never been so insulted before in all my life', he spluttered as he finished brushing his trousers.

'No? Then you should get out more', Madison retorted shaking her head with understandable incredulity.

'Rory mate; you're such a girl', Gary chipped in, adding to Rory's obvious ridicule…and with that, without another word, the tall Scot turned and left, grinding his teeth together discontentedly.

In the mean-time, having shared a glass of champagne with the senior members of the ECA, *the Bishop* had also left discreetly…as was his habit… thereby adhering to his own strict self-imposed social convention.

She was very disappointed that he hadn't even stopped to inform her… or to say goodbye, but there again, knowing how he protected his personal life, Madison wasn't too surprised that *the Bishop* had quietly slipped away; after all, they weren't officially a couple as such…and even if that was the case, she knew that there was no way he would allow anybody to be privy to that information…at least not until he was good and ready.

So, she got up too…and having thanked the organizers for their invitation, embraced Gary warmly for his company and shaken the hands of a few others who were there, Madison made her way back to her hotel.

She was feeling a little disgruntled after the highs of the night before, as despite understanding the situation, she knew in her mind that she would nevertheless have preferred *the Bishop* to have made some kind of gesture towards her…to show that he was thinking about her as much as she was thinking about him.

He should have done something, she was still complaining to herself as the taxi dropped her off at her hotel…but then as she trudged back to her room and threw herself onto the bed despondently, sighing deeply, she was suddenly overcome with joy and a little guilt when she saw the bouquet of flowers that had been delivered in her absence…and the card attached to it, signed TB.

She immediately rang him to thank him but the call went straight to voice-mail, and though she tried several more times between then and the moment her flight left the next day, she never did get through to him…. and he never returned any of her calls.

The next day;

During the long flight home, Madison was restless and fidgety as she relived the night she had spent with *the Bishop* over and over in her mind. She was frustrated that she hadn't managed to say goodbye to him properly, and as she sat there in her seat ruminating she felt somewhat abandoned… and in need of a friend…or at least someone to share her frustration with… so…who else could she call…or at least text, but her best friend Evie…even though she hadn't connected with her properly since walking out on her and her friends almost two months previously;

Just on the way home from England. Let's catch up. M,

…she tapped out as the flight attendant hovered, waiting to offer her some refreshment.

The plane was quiet thereafter…apart from the low, constant drone of the engines…and as a band of fluffy white clouds raced past the window next to her, Madison settled down to take a nap.

She woke up a little while later to find the guy sitting next to her sound asleep too, sprawled as best he could in the tight confines of his under-sized seat. The situation made Madison feel a little uncomfortable and so to let him know that he was crowding her, she nudged the guy's elbow a couple of times, gently but firmly.

Eventually, he took the hint, mumbled an apology and moved his arm a little…but it was so cramped in coach that it made little difference.

Unable to settle again Madison decided to send another couple of texts and write down a few bullet points about the presentation; just in case

Amanda asked...although not surprisingly her mind kept flashing back repeatedly to the abbey.

Not long after that, the captain's voice came on the intercom to announce their impending arrival at JFK…and minutes later the flight attendants were coming down the aisles to check that all the tray-tables had been put-away, that all the seats were in the upright position and that everybody's seat-belt was secured ready for landing.

CHAPTER TWELVE

Back in New York;

Madison opened the door to see Evie standing there with a couple of bottles of wine.

'Right, I'm not taking no for an answer, I want to know everything, and I mean everything', she said as she brushed past.

Madison followed her friend into the living room and stood watching as she opened the first of the bottles, poured two glasses and handed one to her.

Then she dropped into a nearby chair, took a mouth full of wine and smiled up at her.

'Okay; go! Shed the light girl; shed the light', Evie prompted.

'Hey, you need to stop hanging out so much with those gospel girls', Madison commented breezily.

'So…?' Evie goaded impatiently, her bright eyes flashing with excitement

'Well, hon; sorry to disappoint you but there's not much to say. The presentation went well…' Madison began, brushing her hair out of her eyes.

'Oh who cares about the presentation; what about…you know…' Evie interrupted keenly

'Well; he was his usual self…'

'Obnoxious?' Evie announced.

'…Self-assured and confident', Madison countered, taking a sip from her glass and shifting nervously in her chair.

'Annoying…?' Evie riposted; 'cold, aloof, pompous…impolite'.

'…Fascinating, inscrutable and absurdly conservative', Madison proposed instead. 'The guy is just so intense…and deep'.

She would never admit it, even to Evie, but when she was in his company, Madison felt herself in a state of permanent wonderment.

'…But was there any spark', Evie pushed.

'No, nothing like that', Madison replied almost choking on her reply, wanting to keep anything to do with her and *the Bishop* on a more personal level…to herself.

'You know me; I'm looking for a relationship that has depth and meaning, that will stand the test of time...and I'm not sure that that guy is', she replied drily, biting the inside of her cheek, knowing that she was not telling the whole truth; '…but at the same time; I…I can't explain it… but I'm totally hooked on the guy', she added throwing a hand in the air.

Evie frowned, disappointment etched on her face.

'Well hon, the first thing I would say is...that you can't force attraction; love chooses its own path'.

Madison rolled her eyes.

'Well; how about this', Evie offered airily; 'I know it's a cliché…but maybe he thinks he's too old for you?

Taken aback, Madison riposted instantly; 'Don't be so facetious, E', she protested as the twelve-year age gap rushed through her mind…

'…besides…', she added as if to defend her position; 'I've had endless hours to think about it and I've come to the conclusion that compatibility is more a function of intellectual equivalence than actual physical years'.

'Wow', Evie commented, a sceptical look on her face; 'the guy really is getting into your head'.

The two women spent the next two hours catching up…and having finished most of the wine Evie got up to leave…hugging her friend tightly and kissing her on the cheek.

'Just remember; the only thing that matters is being with someone who makes you feel that you matter and if that guy can't see that…well'.

Madison nodded indifferently and waved her goodbye.

Next morning;

Madison woke up the next morning in much better spirits than she had been the night before.

She made herself some coffee, and in between reading the newspaper and eating her usual bowl of cereal she pondered what had been said, deciding to play the long game…

Back in the office over the next few weeks, Madison began to hear a few sneaky comments here and there about how she had changed, how she was more patient, less impulsive, more approachable and less prickly.

This of course set the rumour mill in motion and thanks to the office whispers; it soon spread around the whole building, like wild-fire, that she was *in love.*

Even Amanda was intrigued…and when she called her into her office one day to thank her for the back-ground work she had recently completed on several of her other assignments, she (Amanda) could not help but comment on the fact that she (Madison) had mellowed of late…and had seemingly left behind some of the brash New York, 'in your face' attitude.

'Listen hon; I'm only saying this because it's the talk of the office', Amanda stated; '…so would you like to corroborate or deny the rumours washing around this place?' she asked with her usual air of haughty superiority, never one to beat around the bush.

Surprised by her boss's comments Madison just shrugged her shoulders; her ears had been burning too, but she hadn't really thought about why she had suddenly become flavour of the month with the gossip-mongers.

Yes, her trip to London had been most enjoyable on many levels but as far as she knew, nobody knew the details of what had happened there; she certainly hadn't told anybody, so there was no reason for everybody to be getting pointlessly excited.

It must just be her turn to be singled out by the coffee-machine crowd, she decided using her usual logic, her eyes narrowing in thoughtful reflection as she sat down opposite her imposing boss…

…but then as she made herself comfortable, it suddenly struck her; it was true, something he had said, something he had done must have rung a bell in her sub-conscious because all of a sudden she was enjoying her femininity again, flirting and playing with her sexuality.

The Bishop had done that; he had given her that confidence; the confidence to show her softer side again. He had stripped away all the false hypocrisy of the person she was trying to be and brought out the real 'her' – someone who was actually a stronger, more confident and more dynamic person than the pretentious bitch she had been pretending to be.

He had shown her that you didn't have to conform, to succeed – you just had to be yourself. It was a great lesson.

♗

Amanda was still waiting for verbal reply to her question but Madison quickly disappointed her by calmly dismissing the rumours for what they were, office gossip designed to occupy the shallow minds of those with too much time on their hands….

…and anyway, she thought to herself; even if there had been a grain of truth in the scandalous hearsay doing the rounds, she certainly had no intention of revealing it to her boss and having her private life held up for discussion on the office gossip grapevine.

Her boss smiled at her dispassionately; being the mature woman that she was, Amanda wasn't fooled in the slightest by Madison's muted denial but on this occasion she decided not to insist any further.

'Listen hon; that's fine by me; what you do in your own time is up to you; I was just asking', she assured her, taking out a file from her top drawer.

'Besides, it's no big deal, and anyhow that's not why I called you in here', she declared, softening her usual harsh tone.

Madison relaxed, relieved that she wasn't about to be grilled by her boss whose notorious reputation swept all before it when it came to interviewing and interrogation techniques.

♗

The mood relaxed momentarily after that, but then as Madison caught her breath and cleared her throat Amanda immediately tightened it again by getting up, walking over to the door of her office and closing it firmly.

Though she would never admit it…as she and Madison had never really seen eye to eye…Amanda had been quietly impressed by her junior's transformation of late - as had several other members of her hierarchy who had commented on the fact - and despite the latter's denials to the contrary, she knew as her boss, having interacted with her on a regular basis, that Madison had matured as a person.

She also knew, as a professional, that Madison's work had been second to none recently and deserved some kind of reward, despite of the memo that had been sent down from the boardroom regarding promotion and advancement possibilities for this particular employee.

This had left Amanda in a rather unenviable position.

She was caught between wanting to fulfil her professional role of department head on the one hand…by rewarding a deserving employee who was showing immense potential, even though she didn't particularly like her, and who might quickly pose a threat to her if she continued to progress at her current rate…and respecting the company's covert - albeit twisted and unfair - internal policy on the other.

However a few days earlier a situation had developed and fallen into her lap which was going to allow her to kill two birds with one stone; a situation which, if she exploited it correctly would allow her to off-load Madison to another department under the guise of rewarding her for her work, while at the same time maintaining her position and respecting the memo sent down from above.

Amanda regained her chair and sitting back confidently against the plush leather seat; she took a deep breath and began her announcement.

'Right, here's the deal', she announced, concealing her usual contempt for her younger colleague.

'It's pretty simple really; Gretchen, our Fashion editor has asked for a new assistant to share her workload…and…after careful consideration, taking into account your aptitude and your organisational skills, I have put your name forward for the position', Amanda proclaimed calmly... looking directly at her junior.

Madison's eyes sprang open in shock and a look of complete astonishment spread rapidly over her face.

She wasn't sure that she had heard right......but before she could speak, to ask Amanda to repeat what she had just said, her boss continued.

'Look, I know it's only a glorified PA role and you are vastly over-qualified to take on such a role, but you have always wanted to get into the fashion department and this could be your chance; it might be the only one you get', Amanda insisted facetiously after a brief pause, hinting at Madison's situation in relation to the on-going saga of in-house politics.

Madison instantly sat up straighter and listened carefully to what Amanda was saying - *analysing every word that she spoke as she elaborated on the details of her offer* - a little wary of the fact that her boss was letting sentiment encroach on her decision-making for once, however false and hypocritical that behaviour appeared to be.

Here was a person who usually had no compunction whatsoever about trampling someone else's feelings...and indeed often delighted in her reputation as a cold-hearted bitch, so why would she be offering her a helping hand, she wondered.

Madison sat there stunned but stoical as Amanda concluded her description of the job-offer, and while her outward demeanour was one of a person nonchalantly unimpressed by what she was hearing, her mind was secretly ablaze with a thousand ideas, revelling in the fact that she had even been considered for this new role - regardless of its junior rank - because she had known for quite some time that the board-members had issued clear instructions to her department-head that she should not be offered any assistance in her attempts to climb the ladder after the embarrassment and prejudice she had brought on the company's reputation.

However, she could not help but feel a little suspicious.

Amanda picked up on this and sensing her employee's hesitation, she intervened again in the latter's thought process, by suggesting that she was well aware that this new role would only be a side-ways move for her - at best - but that, because it was 'only' a junior role and a side-ways move... and not a promotion as such - she would find it easier to persuade those upstairs to sanction it - the look in her eye revealing that she understood why Madison was less than enthusiastic in her response.

Madison's expression took on a note of surprise as her boss's final words hung in the air.

She and Amanda had never gotten on very well and yet here she was trying to shoe-horn her into the department of her dreams, albeit as a dogsbody.

Why would she be doing this? She wondered. What was her agenda?

Almost a minute passed by, but after a final moment of reflection Madison decided that, despite the fact that it meant that she would be starting at the bottom again, it was too good an opportunity for her to turn down as far as her long-term career-plan was concerned; the fashion department was where she wanted to be and with her work-ethic, perspicacity and determination, she knew that, given the chance, she would soon to make her mark there.

'That's settled then', Amanda confirmed breezily. 'I'm just on my way upstairs now, so I will let you know the outcome of our discussions as soon as I get it', she confirmed in conclusion.

Madison nodded in agreement and stood up, trying desperately hard not to show any emotion; she then thanked her boss politely and prepared to leave.

Amanda nodded her head too in reply; 'Don't thank me, you did the work, you deserve the chance', she announced huskily, smiling duplicitously.

'Trust me', she added reassuringly with a glint in her eye as she gathered her paperwork together for her meeting.

Madison didn't trust anybody, especially her boss who had sided against her during the afore-mentioned inquiry but nevertheless, because of the news; she was starting to have a little difficulty keeping the lid on her excitement, and couldn't wait to get out of the office in order to express her emotion.

'Okay then; we're done here', she agreed as Amanda finally dismissed her.

Madison walked out and once she had closed the door and was out of ear-shot of her boss's office, the neuron connections in her brain lit up like

Krakatoa and she squealed at full volume, the grin on her face widening from ear to ear as she made her way back to her desk, convinced as she was, that if she was going to be given her chance, she would grab it with both hands, she would prove all those that doubted her wrong, and through sheer hard work, determination and focus, she would succeed in her goal of reaching a senior role in the fashion department.

She was in a state of complete elation as she sat back down at her desk but while she sat there congratulating herself - because she knew that it was her who had done all the work - she also knew that meeting up with *the Bishop* and writing those articles on him had played a major part in her being offered this chance.

She knew that she owed him…and those articles…a lot and as she tried to get back to work, her thoughts suddenly filled with images of him and the time she had spent with him, in London, in Boston and most importantly at the Abbey.

A call from the editor's department brought her back down to earth at that point…but it was an hour or so later, while she was still trying to get her head around the simple task of writing out a bullet-point report, that Amanda called her on the phone to confirm that her move had been approved and that she would be assigning an intern to her for the rest of the week to help her with the transition and to take over the assignments that she hadn't quite finished.

Madison calmly conveyed her appreciation once again, put down the phone and pounded her desk with her fist.

'Yes', she cried to nobody in particular; 'I'm outta here'.

She couldn't believe it was happening and to settle her nerves Madison decided to go for a walk around the office to stretch her legs. She would have loved to tell somebody her good news, share it with somebody, anybody but she couldn't. She didn't really have any friends as such in the office, everybody was so bitchy; especially the women…so instead, she waited another half hour or so and then, feeling a little more composed, she took out her phone and rang Evie who as usual was delighted to hear from her.

They exchanged social niceties and then without telling her why… wanting to keep it a surprise…Madison suggested they meet up for a drink after work as they hadn't seen each other for a few weeks.

Evie was a little surprised by this and asked if anything was wrong but Madison just repeated that they hadn't seen each other in a while and she just wanted to catch up.

In fact, Madison didn't tell her because she wanted to see the look on her friend's face when she did tell her.

They arranged to meet up at 6.30 p.m. and then hung up.

Later;

The two friends met up in their usual bar in the middle of downtown Manhattan which was about half-distance for them both to travel from their respective jobs.

Madison broke her news and to celebrate they immediately ordered a bottle of champagne.

Then as they caught up with the rest of the news, Madison finally let it slip that she and *the Bishop* had actually 'connected' after all, before going into greater detail which, because of its raunchy content, drew a series of gasps and exclamations from her friend.

'I knew it. I knew that there was something that you weren't telling me when I came over that night', Evie shrieked.

'I'm sorry; it was just…all so spontaneous and unexpected', Madison enthused.

'Aha', Evie replied, a little circumspect remembering *the Bishop* from his last visit; 'I heard that spontaneous and unexpected actually meant premeditated in that kind of situation', she joked concealing her dislike for her friend's new lover.

Madison blushed.

'So, let me get this straight', Evie resumed; 'you have found yourself a guy who has a certain flair for playing board-games…and has a flawless technique for giving you orgasms'.

'Oh my God, I wish I could find one of those', Evie griped mockingly.

'Multiple orgasms', Madison corrected her in a low tone, 'and might I say that on behalf of the sisterhood; I wish that a few more men would acquire that particular skill', she insisted in a whisper.

'I've always felt that long and thick did the trick', Evie sniggered, and with that the girls both enjoyed a chuckle at the expense of men in general - but then Madison's expression changed and she became a little more serious.

'Yeah, that part of it was wonderful, but it's more than that', she stated furtively.

'TB made me feel all those things that I had never felt before….and he made me feel alive', she lamented, 'more so than any of my previous relationships which have all left me feeling so woefully unsatisfied', Madison concluded.

'Wow; you are really hooked', Evie exclaimed, pouring another round of celebratory drinks.

'Yeah, it was intoxicating; he was intoxicating…pretty much like this', Madison confirmed, raising her glass.

'So, when are you going to see him again?' she asked; 'Have you made any plans?'

'No, not yet', Madison replied evasively retreating into her own mind.

'Do you think you love this guy', Evie insisted; 'coz that was the impression I got last time we met'

'No', Madison retorted without reflection; '…at least I had never envisaged falling in love with him up to this point. Oh, I don't know; you know what men are like when it comes to commitment…

…Besides, I don't want to think in those terms yet; my hopes have been dashed too many times already in the past'.

Evie sighed and took a sip of champagne. 'Listen hon, you can't blame yourself for letting somebody into your heart', she reasoned, tempering her usual suspicious neurosis concerning all things masculine.

'Love is always a risk that you have to take', she continued, 'but be careful sweetie; we don't want you opening up a healing wound again', she warned, making allusion to Madison's most recent relationship with a certain David.

'Oh, God no', Madison agreed as the barman came over to offer them a cocktail of their choice paid for by one of the bar's other patrons.

The girls checked out the guy with a quick glance to their right…but it had been a long day and it was getting late so they politely refused his offer…via the barman…and decided to leave a few minutes later, Madison's celebratory mood over her new position having been pushed to one side by thoughts of her new emotional state of mind.

The friends separated outside the bar and as Evie walked off and hailed a cab Madison decided to walk for a few blocks in order to clear her mind, resolving eventually to take a more philosophical approach to her life.

If *the Bishop* wanted to pursue a relationship with her, he knew how to get in touch with her, but in the mean-time, she could not let thoughts of him cloud her judgement; her new job would have to become her first priority because she could not afford to fail in that department; there was just too much at risk.

She decided not to dwell on it and as the weeks went by and he didn't call…proving her right…Madison realised that she had made the right choice.

During this time, while, Madison's position in the fashion department began to take shape and slowly crystallise in New York, back in England on the European chess-circuit, Gary's reputation as an awkward opponent to play against began to grow too.

His ranking improved enormously and all of a sudden he found himself making his way quite easily through the early rounds in the smaller tournaments, becoming one of the toughest opponents on the circuit and even beating Rory a couple of times, though the pompous Scot did crush him too, in return, on several other occasions.

Of course, while the lesser mortals fought it out in a series of tournaments all over Europe, as the undisputed champion *the Bishop* didn't need to play in these minor events as he had no need for ranking points.

That said, ever the consummate professional and always watchful of who might one day be in a position to dethrone him, he did follow most of the events through the winter, via the internet, and was often quite impressed by the young Aussie's physically relaxed yet mentally focussed attitude.

Indeed, he made a note to mention it next time he met with the ECA.

Six months went by, until one day Amanda rang Gretchen in her office and asked her to send Madison up to see her.

It was a strange request and Madison was a little surprised when Gretchen told her about it as Amanda had hardly crossed her path since the day she had offered her, her transfer…but nevertheless she made her way up to Amanda's office a while later having confirmed her arrival beforehand with Gayle.

As she did, Amanda invited her to sit down…and then prefacing her disclosure with a little small-talk, which was unusual, she enquired casually as to how she (Madison) was getting on in her new role.

Madison paused deliberately then enthused at how inspiring it was to be working with somebody like Gretchen who was so full of ideas.

'That's good', Amanda retorted, grimacing slightly at the barely disguised criticism as she flicked through the file she was holding.

'Anyhow', she proceeded, putting down the file in front of her and getting down to business; 'the reason that I have called you in here…asked you to come in', she announced correcting her tone, 'is that…after the success of the Boston chess challenge last year, the newspaper's top-brass want to repeat the experience, but this time in New York'.

'…Another exhibition match?' Madison asked dubiously.

It had worked once, and with a fair amount of success in Boston…but to repeat it, and in New York of all places, well, she just wasn't sure.

'Yes, another exhibition match'; Amanda retorted, growing a little impatient; '…some new guy on senior management wants it to happen and it's their call'.

Madison sensed that Amanda was hardly enamoured by this new project but she kept the rest of her thoughts to herself and waited to hear why her old boss…who was still technically her current boss once removed…had called her in, as this new project had nothing to do with her and her new role in the fashion department.

'So, as I was saying', Amanda continued.

'The people upstairs want to do this…and they want to know who you would recommend to cover it, as you made such a good job of covering the event last time around'.

'They are asking me?' Madison gasped in complete surprise.

'Yes…' Amanda replied a little patronisingly; 'I know it might sound a little ridiculous, but yes, they are asking you for your input', she confirmed, her contempt for her junior employee surfacing momentarily.

Madison sat back in her chair, taking a deep breath; both relieved and disappointed at the same time.

She was relieved that her bosses hadn't designated her as their automatic choice to organise the event again, because Gretchen had just recently given her the monumental task of researching the background of the current trends…and the tendencies and influences of the new collections due out shortly…and it was a huge work-load,

…but there again, she was nevertheless a little disappointed that this match was going to be organised without her being involved…because, despite the fact that *the Bishop* had never been in touch with her since their one memorable evening together, all those months ago, the game of chess had oddly enough opened doors for her and given her the chance to be where she was today.

Furthermore, she had gotten to know some of the game's strange characters…and somehow, for some reason, she felt that she owed them and the game something in return.

Madison pouted for a second dragging out Amanda's obvious discomfort at having to delegate this responsibility.

'I'll think it over and let you know', she announced, as she got to her feet, '….but I really need to get back to my desk now, if there's nothing else', she affirmed with assurance.

'Very well', Amanda agreed, stifling a snarl; 'you've got until the end of the week to come up with a name'.

Madison thought about it long and hard over the next couple of days, making short-list after short-list of names, before striking them out one by one, as the hours and days went by, usually for the most outlandish and dismissive reasons.

Who could she propose, who <u>should</u> she propose? Who in the office deserved her chance?, she found herself wondering.

Obviously none of those who had blanked her after her misadventure with that creepy executive, Morgan; not that they would ask or expect her to put them forward for such an assignment.

Or should she…?

Maybe it was time to forgive and forget, Madison thought to herself.

Maybe she should be the bigger person and let bygones be bygones.

It might turn out to be the big break that they were waiting for, just like it had been for her.

They might even do a better job than she had done and end up… marrying *the Bishop*.

That thought stopped her in her tracks. She couldn't have that.

She had resolved to put her dalliance with the chess-master in the past, but like many good resolutions, it did not seem so attractive when it came time to actually putting it into practise.

What about one of the younger new interns? She pondered; somebody too young to catch his eye.

'No; that wouldn't work either', she thought, dismissing the idea almost immediately.

Her reputation would be riding on this recommendation and if the person she chose made a mess of it, it would reflect back badly onto her, and the top brass, not to mention Amanda, would have a field day hanging her out to dry.

Nah, she decided finally. This is a shark's world. Screw them all.

On the Friday afternoon, having imagined every possible scenario Madison finally returned to Amanda's office and gave her, her appraisal of the situation, informing her politely that after mature reflection she had come to the conclusion that there was only one suitable candidate for the assignment that was on offer.

Amanda stopped what she was doing and leaned back in her chair, expectantly.

'Okay then, let's hear it; who is it?' she asked brusquely, raising an eyebrow and encouraging her young colleague to get on with it.

Madison took a deep breath.

'It's me', she announced with a sparkle in her eyes and a previously-unheard confidence in her voice.

'You?' replied her boss, the degree of surprise in her voice forcing her to lean forward.

'Yes...; me' Madison confirmed, brimming with self-assurance.

Amanda paused; then sat back in her chair to consider her options, the expression of surprise on her face slowly replaced by a mischievous smile as she warmed to the idea.

Madison noticed this change in her demeanour but she remained on her guard as the memory of her boss's betrayal and the months of being cold-shouldered by her were still fresh in her mind.

'Listen Madison; believe me; that was not my intention when I asked you to consider somebody for this role; I wanted to see if you were capable of delegating someone, putting your faith, your trust in someone', her boss explained…

'…apparently, it is not that easy for you'.

This time it was the expression on Madison's face that suddenly betrayed what she was thinking; perhaps it <u>had been</u> a miscalculation on her part to propose herself.

'However', Amanda continued, interrupting Madison's moment of self-doubt; '…it is a good idea and does show initiative and the ability to take responsibility'.

Madison's expression brightened again.

'…but only do it if you are sure', Amanda insisted; 'there is no pressure from me on this one. I could quite easily designate somebody else'.

'No, it's okay. I'll do it', Madison confirmed, '…as long as Gretchen is okay with it'.

'It is only for a couple of days and as I did get to know a few of the people involved last time around, it seems to me that it's only right that I do it', she concluded.

'Fair enough', Amanda agreed, getting up. 'I'll have a word with Gretchen and once you have sorted out the details with the guys down in publicity and accounts, I will look forward to seeing what you come up with.'

Madison smiled to herself, pleased to have successfully negotiated the discussion with her usually ruthless and uncompromising boss.

♗

The phone rang at that moment breaking the silence but rather than answer it, Amanda simply ignored it, picked up a bundle of other files from her desk and walked toward the door, obviously on her way to yet another meeting.

Madison looked at the phone and wondered who it could be; how could her boss not answer?

'Voice-mail will get that', Amanda announced as she reached the door and stopped in her tracks, turning around to see Madison's contemplative demeanour.

'Oh, and by the way, I quite fancy meeting that Bishop guy myself after all you wrote about him last time around….so when you do get the schedule sorted, make sure that I get a copy of it', she proclaimed… revealing her feminine side for the first time that Madison could ever remember.

'…that way I can have Gayle put it in my agenda; you never know, I might be able to fit him in somewhere', she declared ambiguously whipping her head around as she walked away, though the innuendo was completely lost on her younger colleague who was too stunned to speak as she prepared to follow her boss out.

♗

Indeed Madison couldn't move for a moment after that, as she stood there, engulfed in a feeling of complete disbelief, watching her boss disappear slowly down the corridor.

She knew that Amanda usually avoided anything that created a wrinkle in her tight schedule, but all of a sudden, out of the blue, for some un-known reason she was preparing to make an exception for TB.

That realisation made Madison suspicious but the mere thought of her boss getting together with *the Bishop* made her physically shudder, and she knew it would probably weigh heavily in her decision as to whether or not she would get involved with him again herself…and to what extent.

♗

And so it was that after a few meetings with all the departments involved, Madison assumed the responsibility of overseeing this new event which she knew would probably go a long way to shaping the rest of her career.

It was all a bit of a rush but within weeks she had the whole thing arranged and just needed confirmation from the English Chess Association before she could finalise the dates and get the stamp of approval from her bosses.

She had written to the ECA at the beginning of the process with a formal invitation, and hoping that it might reignite their friendship - she had also sent a copy of the letter to *the Bishop* himself together with a hand-written note suggesting that perhaps he could persuade the ECA to allow Gary to be part of the trip.

She hadn't explained her reasons for doing this, as it would probably complicate things with TB, but she did feel that she owed the young Aussie, and knowing that it had always been his dream to see New York, she saw this invitation as a way of making that dream come true and thanking him for looking after her when she had needed it in England.

♗

Meanwhile, back in England, *the Bishop* was well aware that for the game of chess to survive and thrive on the international stage… there were three things it would need to increase its popularity and take e it to the next level;

1) A charismatic world champion who would appeal to a greater and younger audience
2) More media involvement; press, TV and internet etc…and
3) Greater sponsorship

…so when the ECA called him in to discuss the letter that they had received, it wasn't long before they all agreed that it would be in the game's best interest to accept the invitation to repeat the 'challenge experience' in New York.

However, having given his undertaking that he would indeed participate in this new venture, *the Bishop* immediately tempered the rest of the committee's enthusiasm by mentioning the fact that while he felt a responsibility to the game and its future, he was nevertheless torn between that responsibility and his desire to keep his private life…private.

'Gentlemen', he began, looking around the table, 'I am a product of the previous generation and while I do not consider myself to be over-the-hill in any shape or form, I do suggest that if we are going to use this trip to lay the foundations for the future of the game, it would probably be an astute move by this committee to include somebody on the trip who would encapsulate that new dynamic'.

'I agree entirely', said the president of the committee as a series of mutterings broke out around the table on hearing *the Bishop's* suggestion.

They began considering candidates…and of course Rory Campbell-Brown's name was thrown into the hat.

He seemed to be the obvious first choice, as he was apparently already destined to be *the Bishop's* natural successor when the latter did eventually stand down…but the mention of his name instantly provoked discordance from several quarters.

Indeed, several of the committee members raised strong objections to him being put forward, citing his obnoxious elitist manner…and his tendency to spend too much time in the bar as their reasons, but on the other hand he did have one or two old-school supporters who did speak out and defend him and his loyalty to the game.

The discussion rumbled on for quite some time but by the end of it, the consensus seemed to be that raising Rory's profile and presenting him as the future of the game would probably have an adverse effect on people - especially the younger generation who were going to be their target market - and possibly toll the end of any international interest in the game.

The Bishop could see that there was still some disagreement on the matter, so taking it upon himself, he looked at the president sat across from him at the table and gesturing discreetly with a brief hand signal, he announced that he wanted to say a little more.

The president raised both his hands out in front of him asking for quiet and once the discussion had died down, he gave *the Bishop* his consent to take the floor as it were.

The latter stood up, adding dramatic effect to what he was about to say.

'Listen everybody', he began, 'Rory Campbell-Brown has worked very hard to get himself where he is today and we should all respect his accomplishments; indeed he has been a worthy adversary for me on many occasions, so we should not be dismissive or underestimate his undeniable talent and achievements'.

'However, I have to say that in my considered opinion and for all the other reasons you have just mentioned, I don't see the man as the future of the game'.

'The game of chess is crying out for an injection of youth and a personality who could attract a younger audience – a charismatic character, somebody different, somebody like…Gary Bridgewater for example', he concluded taking most people by surprise.

The Bishop couldn't really relate to the talented young Aussie but it was not that he didn't like the rising young talent; he just felt that they had very little in common - and while that fact could be a problem during any transitional period, if that ever came about, he knew in his heart that he shouldn't let it stand in the way of his intuition and his experience as a veteran of the tour, both of which were telling him that the young Aussie was exactly the breath of fresh air that the sport needed.

…and with that, he sat back down, glancing around him to see that the majority of the committee members were in agreement with his reasoning - even though there were still a couple of dissenting voices from the old guard.

The president then spoke up and having given his opinion supporting *the Bishop's* suggestion, he put it to the vote.

Each of the members present was asked for their judgement on the matter and once everybody had had their say, a vote was cast and it was decided, rather heartlessly, that Rory would be passed over for the trip to New York in favour of Gary, who, due to his age and his recent run of results, seemed to embody the new breed, the new generation of players that the game needed to look to…in order to survive and flourish.

However, Rory was livid when he was informed of the decision the next day and immediately rang the ECA president to ask if he could appeal against the committee's resolution.

His request was refused on a technicality, but instead of creating a stink as everybody might have expected from him, Rory decided to accept the decision graciously and show the committee how wrong they all were about him, by putting all his efforts into winning the next tournament and building up his ranking points so that he could challenge for his ultimate goal, which was that of the world crown.

Meanwhile, Gary's reaction when he heard the news was more predictable and spontaneous.

'You're joking me mate; that's sweet', replied the young Aussie when he was told, his mind immediately extrapolating the possibility that this would be another chance for him to impress Madison.

CHAPTER THIRTEEN

This time, Madison's budget for the event was somewhat greater than what she had been given to play with in Boston and so, in order to impress her guests... and to make sure that everything ran smoothly...she decided to book them into another of New York's more exclusive hotels for the duration of their stay; the Hotel Gansevoort on 9th Avenue.

More specifically, she reserved two luxury rooms at the hotel...one for the Bishop and one for Gary ...the cost of which would be taken care of in the budget...and then organised two further rooms for herself and Evie to stay in, for which she would be picking up the tab personally.

This was to thank Evie for being her BFF...and also to thank her for agreeing to support her once again during the event...despite her obvious dislike of the Bishop...but more importantly - as far as Madison herself was concerned – it gave her the perfect excuse to stay at the hotel too...to be on hand if there were any problems ...or any issues to be resolved...

...and...in the event that the Bishop might want to spend some quality time alone with her, she could be on hand and amenable for that too!

Arrival;

The flight bringing *the Bishop* and Gary from London wasn't due to land at JFK until late afternoon, so before she made her way to the airport, not wanting to be caught out by any last-minute hitches, Madison arranged to meet up with Evie at the hotel at around 11:30, where they could drop-off their overnight bags...and she could make sure, one last time, that all her plans were in place.

At 11:10, Madison was already in the hotel lobby...waiting patiently for her friend to arrive.

At 11:20, knowing only too well that Evie had punctuality issues, she started to pace back and forth in the lobby…getting slowly more irritable and anxious with every minute that ticked by.

At 11:25 and every couple of minutes thereafter, Madison found herself checking her phone again…and again…expecting at any moment to receive a call…or a text from her friend to say that she (Evie) was running late.

'I really don't need this extra stress', she whispered to herself as she scrolled one more time through her phone messages.

At 11:38; She pulled up the 'contacts' list on her phone and was just about to scroll down to Evie's number when in that instant the hotel's main door opened and Evie herself walked in, all excited, wearing the most stunning Tropicana print dress…*which in passing made the rather-staid business-suit that Madison was wearing look quite plain.*

'I know; I know, I'm late…again, I'm sorry but I had to put on the dog' (New York-speak for get dressed up), Evie explained.

Madison breathed a sigh of relief. She was both annoyed and relieved, but rather than express either she just stood there, shaking her head and rolling her eyes.

♗

The two friends exchanged hugs and their usual familiarities, and then promptly made their way over to the reception desk where…assuming her professional role…Madison immediately checked over every detail of her reservation with the receptionist who...with equal professional competence...confirmed that everything was indeed, in order;

'Two rooms on the 8th floor overlooking the Hudson to be charged to your company account and two further rooms situated on the 6th floor… also with a view of the Hudson …to be charged separately to…Miss Madison Chatfield', the young receptionist recapped.

'Yes, that's me', Madison responded, handing over her card.

'Thank-you', the young employee replied politely, accepting the card for payment.

♗

‘Two rooms?’ Evie questioned, as Madison collected her card and they moved away from the counter; ‘I assumed that we would be sharing…like in Boston’.

‘My treat…’ Madison quipped with a fleeting smile as she finished putting away her card.

This was disappointing news for Evie as she had hoped to be sharing a room with her ‘bestie’ like they had in Boston…but with her curiosity-radar now on high-alert she was just about to pursue her line of questioning when out of nowhere the hotel’s commercial director came walking over towards them, introducing himself with a warm friendly smile.

‘Good morning ladies; welcome to the Gansevoort’, he said, extending a polite hand.

‘Morning,’ Madison replied, smiling back at him with inscrutable poise.

She introduced herself…and then introduced Evie…and a brief discussion ensued…about the hotel and its facilities…which concluded with the hotel executive asking them, very politely, if they would care for a complimentary coffee…in the lobby.

‘That would be a great idea; thank you’, the two women replied, showing their gratitude to the man for his kind gesture…and satisfied at that point that she could do no more to further her logistical planning, Madison finally relaxed.

The hotel executive nodded respectfully...and while the two friends wandered off to find themselves a couple of plush lobby-chairs where they might continue their conversation…and enjoy the hotel’s surroundings… he immediately turned to the receptionist and asked her to arrange the complimentary coffees for them.

‘So, are you going to let me in on the why?’ Evie asked as she settled into one of the stylish lobby-chairs, her eyes flickering mischievously.

‘Do I need to…?’ Madison riposted, trying to hide the smile spreading across her face.

‘No…I guess not’, Evie replied with a snigger; ‘…but hey…thanks all the same for the…‘goody’, she added, raising her arms to their surroundings, before sitting back to enjoy the complimentary coffee which seemed to appear out of nowhere on the table in front of them, thanks to the hotel's wonderfully efficient personnel.

It was a moment of calm, before the storm that was inevitably going to descend on them...what with the pressure, the stress and the weight of expectation that Madison was going to be faced with over the next couple of days...but brushing all that aside, Madison immediately took the opportunity of them sitting there together, just the two of them, to inform Evie that not only had she invited her along for her support, but also as a kind of chaperon for Gary as she herself was hoping to be spending some alone-time with TB.

Evie smiled naughtily over the lip of her coffee-cup; 'Aha, now I see what you're up to', she remarked.

Looking slightly amused, Madison, just shrugged...

'You do realise that what you are doing is a 'set-up'', Evie added '... but then again', she continued, as she glanced around at her surroundings; 'maybe this is just the kind of pick-me-up that I needed'. *(After yet another... in a succession of romantic disappointments)*

Madison just nodded in response and took another sip of coffee.

'So...anyway' Evie then enquired after a brief pause, her mind returning to the conversation; 'what's the situation then...between you and this TB guy; are you two playing at...friends with benefits?'

'Oh, I really don't know what we are; if indeed we are anything... after all this time', Madison replied, rolling her eyes; '...but I'm keeping my options open just in case'.

'I see', Evie concurred, crossing her legs and brushing down the skirt of her dress.

The two friends then finished their coffees...and while Madison went back to her office to go over the final schedule and make sure nothing had been changed or forgotten, Evie decided to hang around the hotel and use her time more productively by checking out its spa facilities.

Later that day; JFK airport…

The flight from London arrived with only a slight delay…and as *the Bishop* and Gary came through the automatic security-doors thirty minutes or so later, *the Bishop* sauntering some way behind his more eager companion, Madison was there…as arranged… to meet them.

Greetings were exchanged on all sides but it was all very low-key as neither man wanted to let the other know the level of their previous involvement with her.

Indeed, the only acknowledgement Madison got from *the Bishop* was the briefest of stares as she turned and led the way out to the exit where the town-car that she had booked was waiting.

They all climbed into the car and within no time they were making their way back into Manhattan via the Long-island expressway, exchanging only a few polite comments about the flight and the traffic along the way.

Evie hadn't joined her friend on the trip to airport…as her presence wasn't officially sanctioned by Madison's employers (insurance reasons)…and because Madison feared that Amanda would find out somehow… either from Todd… or some other source…and hold the fact that she had flouted the rules against her in some way or another, she wasn't prepared to take the risk.

Barely an hour later, the two men were checking into the hotel with all the smooth efficiency that Madison had planned for. The formalities had been taken care of with minimal fuss…and within no time they were making their way up to their rooms with Madison…once again…leading the way.

The elevator doors opened on the 8th floor and stepping out first Madison quickly took charge again, preceding them down the corridor and indicating Gary's room to him on the left…with a polite hand gesture… before stopping a little further on, in front of a second room, where *the Bishop* would be staying.

The latter thanked her respectfully for her diligence…in a controlled and focussed manner

…and then without another word, he slipped the key-card into the lock, coolly pushed the door open and walked inside.

Madison stood there for a moment, still smiling politely, but then having checked left and right…just catching the back of Gary's head as he disappeared into his room…she took a deep breath and then…just as the door in front of her was about to close…she followed *the Bishop* into the room, hoping…optimistically…for some kind of sign that the enigmatic Englishman remembered the night that they had spent together. *(Oh, she wasn't expecting him to sweep her off her feet and embrace her with passion or anything like that, but just a little sign of recognition would not have gone amiss.)*

It never happened, despite her obvious loitering…and so, masking her disappointment behind her professionalism, Madison simply reminded her esteemed guest that she had made dinner reservations for them all at 8 p.m.…and informed him that she would be '…down in the hotel bar from 7 p.m. onwards if he wanted to join her…them…for a drink beforehand'.

She then told him her room number…just in case he needed to call her…for whatever reason… and confirmed to him, rather tongue in cheek, that she would be doing everything in her power to make sure that his second stay in New York was more memorable than the first.

The Bishop thanked her again…though he showed no visible reaction to her veiled invitation…and once he had checked out the room and its amenities Madison left him alone to settle in.

She then stopped off briefly at Gary's room, to confirm the dinner reservations with him too…and while she was there she also took the opportunity to apologise to him once again for that 'other time' in London.

The young Aussie accepted her apology graciously and did the same in return, remembering that his performance on that particular occasion had not been the most memorable either.

'So, we're cool…right…and we never speak of it again?' Madison confirmed.

'Sure thing, Mad., we're cool' Gary concurred, yawning and stretching his powerful arms above his shoulders; '…we were just two friends sharing a moment'.

'Okay, just so that we are clear', Madison insisted; 'I just don't want there to be any awkwardness between us'.

'Hakuna matata, Mad; hakuna ma…tata' Gary responded as he lobbed his suitcase onto the bed.

'Oh, and this evening…' Madison added, almost as an afterthought; '…my friend Evie will be joining us for dinner…so I would appreciate that you didn't mention our little 'encounter' to her either…or indeed to *the Bishop* for that matter'.

Gary looked a little puzzled…but he quickly reassured her…again… that he wouldn't say anything;

'Don't worry Mad; it's all good…my lips are sealed; it's our little secret', he declared in his usual laid-back style…before leaning forward expectantly, hoping for a cheeky little kiss.

Taken aback, Madison baulked in disbelief at his presumptuous manner…especially after what they has just discussed…and recoiling deliberately, she raised her right hand and pushed him away with a finger against his lips…the look of incredulity on her face making it perfectly clear that she had no intention of repeating her 'mistake'.

Gary was confused…and bemused, wondering if he had read the signs wrong…but before he had time to voice that confusion, Madison quickly interrupted his reflection with another brief reminder for him to be downstairs by seven…and without waiting for him to respond to that, she promptly turned to leave, abandoning the young Aussie to his puzzled thoughts and his re-evaluation as to why she had invited him to New York in the first place.

Later; 6.45 p.m.

As the organiser of the event Madison made sure that she was the first one ready.

She knew from past experience that the men would be on time…or at least *the Bishop* would…so having checked herself out from behind one last time in the mirror she made her way out of her room, and walked next door to Evie's room.

♗

'E…Are you ready?' she called out, a little impatiently as she knocked on the door, knowing her friend's tendency to keep here waiting.

'Hey girl, you can't rush perfection', Evie replied, coming to the door still dressed in her robe.

Madison frowned, a little circumspect. 'I'm sorry E; I…I can't wait for you', she exclaimed.

'That's okay; go on ahead M; I'll catch you up…five minutes…ten… max', Evie asserted, holding her robe closed with her free hand.

'Okay, but hurry up', Madison retorted; 'We'll be in the bar'.

'I'll meet you in there', Evie replied a little flustered as she closed the door.

♗

Madison rolled her eyes, took a deep breath and made her way down to the hotel's reception-area so as to be there, ready and waiting when her guests emerged from the lift.

And…just as she had predicted, the two men arrived only a few minutes later, *the Bishop* groomed to perfection as always, his shirt and tie matching perfectly with his immaculately cut Italian silk suit, and Gary, dressed as only Gary knew how…though he had made an effort…in a seersucker shirt and cargo pants.

She greeted them both again briefly and before Evie joined them, she quickly explained to them, that her friend would be joining them for the evening…if that was alright with them; 'she has been helping out with a few things connected to the event so it's a chance for me to thank her', Madison lied.

The two men nodded politely without comment

Then, turning to Gary…and trying rather deliberately to under-play her friend's somewhat ebullient character…she explained to him that Evie;

'...might be a little shy to begin with...and a little rusty around men; if he could just be a little indulgent with her'.

'Of course', Gary agreed, nodding his head with understanding... while standing next to him *the Bishop* looked directly at Madison and raised his eyebrows in curious reflection; *he had already met the rather feisty Evie last time around and in his opinion she was no shrinking violet.*

Madison ignored *the Bishop's* look of bemusement...but as she turned to lead them to the bar she could not help but smile to herself as he leaned forward and complimented her discreetly on her vintage black and white print dress...just as she had hoped.

'It's Prada', she gloated proudly, as she continued walking.

Not to be left out Gary instantly took *the Bishop's* lead, concurring with him that Madison looked pretty awesome...but then, having been informed of her friend's rather skittish disposition around men, he could not help but crack a joke, in his own inimitable style, as they entered the bar;

'...And don't worry Mad; if that little lady friend of yours is rusty, I've got just the right tool to give her a tune up', he bragged.

Madison groaned audibly on hearing the comment and looked at *the Bishop* for support in condemning Gary's contentiously sexist remark... but the latter just shrugged his shoulders; 'Don't look at me, you invited him', he protested quietly.

In the Bar;

'Okay guys; take a seat over there and I'll be with you in a minute', Madison announced, excusing herself.

The two men nodded again and continued on into the bar to find themselves a table, while Madison headed back into the lobby to wait for Evie...again.

She took out her mobile-phone, pulled up her contact-list and tapped on Evie's name, smiling politely at a couple of guests who just happened to be passing.

The connection was made after twenty seconds of panicked anxiety.

'Evie, where are you?' Madison asked, a little discomfited by her friend's tardiness.

'I told you', Evie replied; 'you can't rush perfection'...and with that the lift doors opened and she made her second appearance of the day...in all her glory...still clutching her phone to her ear.

Meanwhile, in the bar, Gary and *the Bishop* had found themselves a table.

'Mate, how good is this then?' the young Aussie commented, overjoyed at just being there.

Remaining stony-faced, *the Bishop* didn't answer, but the hint of a smirk did germ fleetingly at the corner of his mouth.

Now, most people would have lost the plot faced with such an awkward situation but not Gary, he felt right at home. Nothing seemed to faze him, even sitting across from the Bishop; though of course, he did have the advantage over most people, having already faced the master across the chessboard.

A silent pause followed as Gary looked around and *the Bishop* checked his watch.

Then, just a few moments later, Madison and Evie appeared at the door.

Gary instantly stood up, caught Madison's eye with a silent wave of the hand, and motioned them over.

Of course, the two men had already seen Madison's outfit and had complimented her on it in the customary manner...but when they set eyes on Evie's dress, it was something else.

She looked stunning; her chestnut coloured hair looked sleek and polished...and the neckline of her emerald-green halter-neck dress plunged impressively into her deeply tanned cleavage.

Both men watched appreciatively as the two women made their way to the table.

'Crikey, I like what I see there', Gary exclaimed unashamedly.

Again *the Bishop* didn't comment but he did get up from his seat and gesture for the two women to sit down, which they did…together…forcing him to change sides and take up the seat next to Gary.

The usual exchange of social protocols then followed…and remembering Madison's request to make her friend welcome Gary immediately complimented Evie on her dress.

'Why thank-you kind sir', Evie replied a little melodramatically; 'You know, the sisterhood put it out there that we dress up for other women… as some kind of rivalry thing…but the truth is, we don't; we do it for you guys and I have to say…we really appreciate it when you notice'.

Moments later, a bottle of champagne was brought to the table… to celebrate their arrival…and once the glasses had been filled Madison immediately took it upon herself to propose a toast, welcoming the two men to New York and forecasting the success of the exhibition-match.

'…To success!' she announced as all four glasses met over the centre of the table in a clinking of crystal.

'To success', the others reaffirmed in unison.

The conversation thereafter was light and friendly for the next half-hour or so, everybody enjoying the surroundings and 'shooting the breeze' New York style, until once again Gary broke the mood of sophistication with another of his *fair-dinkum* comments.

'This is like a Barbie back home', he observed, much to the company's displeasure; 'you girls on the one side and us blokes on the other'.

All three of his table-companions looked at each waiting to see who would pick up on Gary's comment but although they were all left a little confused by his rather incongruous remark, nobody felt the need to humour him by asking him to explain.

A while later, before they all headed out to the restaurant, Madison and Evie left the two men chatting amiably at the table and disappeared to the ladies-room, to powder their noses.

Gary waited until the two women were almost to the door and then brazenly elbowed *the Bishop*...gently...in the ribs before asking him what his first impressions were...of Evie.

The Bishop picked up his glass and glanced briefly in the direction of the two women as they made their way out – *Evie, hanging back a little behind Madison, revelling ostentatiously in the hungry masculine stares of several of the bar's patrons who were following her every step* - but he didn't dignify Gary's question with a response, knowing full well where the young Aussie was going.

Thwarted momentarily, Gary picked up his glass too and a few seconds later - ignoring *the Bishop's* blatant attempt at political-correctness - he voiced his opinion on their new acquaintance with great candour whether his rather staid companion was interested or not.

'I'm not gonna lie', he smirked; 'I felt a little 'tickle in the pickle' when I saw her come into the bar. I mean I wouldn't kick her out of bed; would you?' he asked rhetorically, knowing that *the Bishop* probably wouldn't answer.

'Yes mate, I would dearly love to give that girl an Australian kiss', he announced, swilling down the last few drops of champagne.

'An Australian kiss; what in God's name is an Australian kiss?' *the Bishop* asked curiously, being coerced out of his silence...and yet fearing the worst.

'An Australian kiss is the same as a French kiss...but 'down under'; Gary chuckled to himself smugly, making a rather questionable gesture with his hand.

The Bishop frowned at his companion's rather puerile and vulgar humour and began drumming his fingers on the table as his impatience started to show.

Fortunately, the girls came back pretty soon thereafter and without further ado the four of them quickly moved on to a little restaurant called

Meet situated a couple of blocks away from the hotel on Washington Street, where Madison had reserved a table.

The restaurant served typical Mediterranean cuisine and as Madison had calculated, Gary spent the whole meal trying to put the bite on Evie, in his usual roguish manner, attempting to impress her with a series of questionable if not seriously bad jokes.

At one point, he put his hands in front of his face and started waving them around wildly.

'What's this?' he asked.

All around the table blank stares looked back at him.

'…the Australian salute', he sniggered. 'You guys get it? We're forever swatting flies'.

Madison shook her head but nobody was really amused.

However, unperturbed by their lack of enthusiasm; Gary turned to Evie to tell her another bawdy joke.

'A man goes into bar flashing a state of the art watch.
He sits down and starts to explain the watch's sophisticated
workings to a girl who was sitting on the stool next to
him, telling her that his watch talked to him.
'Oh yes', she replied, intrigued '…and what's it saying now then?'
'Well', he said unfazed…'it's telling me that you
are not wearing any underwear'.
The girl looked at him amused and giggled coyly;
'It must be broken then', she countered, 'because I am wearing underwear'.
And at that point, the guy put his watch up to his ear and calmly says;
'Damned this thing must be an hour fast'!!

Evie was not impressed; in fact, she was shocked.

'Hey', she said, 'this is New York and we are more sophisticated than that; you are not in the minor leagues here', she pouted.

Gary threw up his arms in defeat at their lack of a sense of humour but immediately seized on the baseball reference.

'You know, you're right' he said apologetically. 'This is a whole new ball-game, being in the city of baseball; I'm a real fan, you know. I've been into baseball all my life', he continued trying to erase his faux-pas.

'As a pitcher or a catcher' (*homosexual innuendo*), Evie asked him cheekily.

Gary didn't answer.

There was a lull in the conversation after that and all of a sudden, out of the blue *the Bishop*'s posture stiffened, he wiped his mouth with a napkin and began to stand.

'If you ladies would excuse me for a moment, I need to use the men's-room. I'll be back shortly'.

(*This was most unexpected and took Madison by surprise as the Bishop had impeccable manners and would not normally leave a table mid-meal*).

'Yeah; I could use the little boys' room too...' Gary declared, looking for an excuse to get away from the table in order to re-group.

He threw down his napkin and followed in *the Bishop* footsteps.

In the men's room *the Bishop* immediately isolated himself in one of the cubicles while Gary strolled over and stood at one of the urinals.

'You and Maddy seem to be getting along', Gary commented out loud.

The Bishop didn't answer, not wanting to discuss his personal life, especially not in the men's room.

A minute or so later *the Bishop* joined Gary at the wash-basins.

'So, what do you think of Evie', he asked (*forgetting that Gary had already told him in the bar*)

'As I said before; I think she's got some grunt' Gary commented, surprised that *the Bishop* would ask him.

The Bishop smirked briefly and without another word he turned on the faucet, just as Gary had finished washing his hands.

'Okay mate; back to the sizzlers' the young Aussie said as he headed for the door.

The Bishop shook his head and looked deeper into the wash-basin mirror. Then, as the door closed behind Gary and he reached to turn the tap off, he suddenly began to shiver uncontrollably, as if his body was going into spasm. It only lasted ten seconds or so and he didn't seem unduly fazed by it, but another guest who had just entered did stop to ask if he was okay.

He reassured the guy that he was fine and having washed his hands again, *the Bishop* returned to the table as if it had never happened.

At the table; while the men were away

'What's wrong with Chewbacca?' Evie asked with an insolent smirk.

'Chewbacca; really?' Madison retorted, looking at her friend with disapproval in her eyes.

'Well, he does look like a bear with a sore head tonight', Evie remarked.

'He's not…he's just…intense', Madison pointed out, taking *the Bishop's* defence.

'Aha', Evie muttered.

'Look E; I've told you before; the guy's a riddle wrapped up in an enigma' Madison explained.

'I know…I'm teasing. Just be patient M; sooner or later everybody tells their secrets to someone'.

'Whatever', Madison replied trying to cut the conversation short.

And with that, Evie started looking around the restaurant, at the décor…and across the way at the other diners where she thought she recognised film producer Judd Apatow and his wife Leslie Mann sat with another couple.

'Isn't that…?' she started to say…

…but before she could finish her sentence, Gary rejoined the table, stopping her short.

'…Maybe not', Evie quietly mumbled to herself, dismissing her observation out of hand, as *the Bishop* followed a few moments later.

The next course was served, but once the waiters had moved away again, rather than continue talking to Gary after his rather questionable joke, Evie turned her attention to *the Bishop* who was now sitting there quietly keeping himself to himself;

'Did you know that Madison received a prize recently for that article she wrote about you guys...and the world of chess?' she remarked assertively, trying to consolidate or even enhance her friend's reputation with him.

The Bishop raised an eyebrow and nodded discreetly but feeling rejected and a little put out by the fact that Evie was ignoring him in order to talk with *the Bishop*, Gary reverted to type and quickly came out with another example of his annoyingly boorish, Antipodean humour;

'Prizes; he said; '...are like haemorrhoids; sooner or later every arsehole gets one'.

Madison recoiled again in shock at this crude comment which she felt was quite unbecoming and unworthy of Gary who she now considered a friend.

'Gary!' she reprimanded; 'That's out of line'.

Meanwhile Evie who was just as outraged, gave the young Australian such a filthy look that he almost had to go back to the men's room to wash it off.

The vulgar comment had lowered the tone and put a damper on proceedings but while Madison and *the Bishop* returned to their food, Evie got up and stormed out, disgusted, grabbing her coat from the attendant as she went; she clearly wasn't used to...and didn't appreciate...Gary's rather crude, tongue-in-cheek Aussie humour.

'Go; get her tiger', *the Bishop* whispered unpredictably into Gary's ear, encouraging him to follow their distressed dinner-companion out...

'...And don't forget to apologise to her...you idiot', Madison added for good measure.

The Bishop was a bit of an anarchist, who found the potential for mayhem rather exhilarating - which was quite a paradox for him really, considering the anally-controlled lifestyle that he led.

Confused, Gary felt a little out of his comfort zone. Coming from Australia he had no experience of dealing with this kind of sophisticated... and highly-strung female temperament; *the women he knew were far more robust creatures, used to his roguish behaviour and his earthy humour...* but nevertheless he took *the Bishop's* cue...and following Evie outside he managed to catch up with her a few doors down at the local K-mart where he could see through the window, she was already waiting in line to buy a packet of Kleenex.

He paused outside for a moment, still unsure as to how he was going to play it...but when another customer came wandering out, loaded down with a couple of six-packs, he took advantage of the open door to go inside and wait patiently by the counter, while Evie finished up with the cashier.

The store wasn't very big and Gary felt a little awkward, standing there on his own, seemingly without purpose...*a fact which didn't escape the store's other patrons, many of whom threw him a wary glance or a suspicious look...*but then, when an elderly couple slowly filed past him, forcing him to vacate the space he was occupying, Gary suddenly spied a shifty-looking individual at the far end of the store who was clearly helping himself to some free alcohol.

'Woah; take a hike there, mate', he blurted out, having spotted the guy.

Heads turned and a number of customers...*probably used to the scenario being New York natives...*slowly moved away, keeping their eyes firmly on the potential threat.

However, the guy in question was totally unfazed by all the attention and simply raised his hands in the air and shrugged his shoulders as he ambled up to Gary to confront him;

'Who are you; Roy Rogers?' he taunted the young Aussie threateningly.

In that moment, the mood in the store shifted considerably; tension filled the air...but while other customers backed away, finding refuge behind shelves in other aisles...unimpressed by the ruffian's ominous manner, Gary - who was to be fair, a couple of sizes bigger than his aggressor - stood his ground, flexing his considerable frame.

'Aah mate', he quipped, standing tall and lapsing once again into his native slang; 'you're all foam and no beer'.

The tough-guy stood there looking puzzled for a moment…but then a split-second later, he lunged at Gary, trying to land a haymaker of a punch on the young Australian's jaw.

Gary, fortunately for him, had surprisingly good reflexes and seeing the fist coming from a long way off; he swerved to one side dodging the blow with ease…and then moving to his right, as quick as a flash, he downed his assailant with the most gut-wrenching kick to the groin.

The guy fell to his knees for a second…and then keeled over onto the floor, grimacing and writhing in pain.

He reached for his groin with both hands and as he did so, a bottle of branded bourbon slipped slowly out of his jacket and rolled onto the floor beside him.

Alerted by the commotion, the shop-keeper and his assistant were immediately on the scene, ready to assess the situation and take the appropriate action - and as Gary was the only one still standing, they took a firm grip on him in order to prevent him from doing any further damage to his adversary, although a simple glance at the crumpled heap at their feet would have quickly shown that no further fighting would be taking place, at least not between these two opponents.

Several witnesses then began shouting out their versions of what had happened and it quickly became clear for all to see that Gary was the innocent party and that he had merely acted in self-defence.

It was a moment of surreal drama, but once he had been vindicated and cleared of all wrong-doing by the other customers' statements, the shop-keeper and his assistant quickly released their hold on Gary's arms and patted him on the back in thanks.

However, during the confusion…while the explanations and shouted comments were being exchanged between the shop-keeper and the witnesses…the would-be thief had slowly gotten to his feet and…taking advantage of the disorder…was about to strike again.

He lunged forward again, screaming and shouting, still trying to land a blow on his cool-headed adversary, but despite his ire and his obnoxious demeanour the guy's half-hearted attempt at revenge was immediately thwarted by a posse of people…customers and staff alike… who quickly overpowered him and pinned him back against the shelves before immobilising him down on the ground. He continued to struggle… and threaten all those who were holding him down…while trying to break free…but then, two more burly staff-members appeared…seemingly out of nowhere…and after a brief struggle they picked the guy up and marched him unceremoniously towards the back of the shop, notifying Gary, the shop-keeper and the rest of the stunned customers that they would take care of the problem from there-on in.

Evie…*having watched in bewilderment as the scene had unfolded in front of her*…paid the cashier for her tissues, and with a cursory glance in Gary's direction, she walked out of the store inviting him to follow her.

There, out on the pavement, Gary immediately began to apologise for the rumpus in the store…and for his inappropriate behaviour at the restaurant…but before he could finish doing so, three young women approached them out of nowhere, giggling.

They all ignored Evie and crowded around Gary taking him completely by surprise; then one of them shouted out a count of three and all three of them simultaneously lifted up their tops, brazenly exposing their charms to the young Aussie's stunned gaze, while the one in the middle asked him rather bluntly who in his opinion had the best looking pair.

Gary was stunned, but as he was trying to comprehend what was going on, the three young women simply turned and walked away again without even waiting for his reply, no doubt pleased to have fulfilled a dare that they had made up between themselves.

Meanwhile, as she watched the three young women disappear, a disapproving scowl on her face, Evie suddenly realised that her show of petulant outrage at Gary's silly jokes earlier in the evening had been a little misplaced not to say hypocritical when this kind of thing was happening on the streets of New York.

'Okay, okay', she stated loudly, jealously trying to protect her new-found hero and pushing him back in the direction of the restaurant; '… the show is over'.

Gary looked at her a little confused, his puzzled expression still quite evident on his youthful face.

'Hey', she repeated; 'reel your eyes back in there mister; this is New York', she added vociferously; 'that kind of thing happens here all the time, get over it'.

His brain was still scrambled but when he finally came to terms with what had just happened, Gary's first thought was that he had found his personal paradise in coming to New York.

'If that's the case', he said with a cheeky grin; '...this is where I want to spend the rest of my life'.

'Everybody says that about New York', Evie confirmed, softening her stance, smiling and taking Gary by the arm - and as they strolled back to the restaurant, the thought of living in New York percolating deeply into the young Aussie's mind, a reveller across the street echoed what Gary was thinking as he wandered off in the opposite direction singing the chorus line of the classic song 'New York, New York'.

Back at the restaurant, Evie spent the next ten minutes telling Madison and *the Bishop* all about what had just happened, in all its melodramatic detail while Gary - who usually made a conscious effort to avoid speaking in Aussie verve when in company but couldn't help himself on this occasion because of the adrenaline pumping through his veins - interrupted her repeatedly to insert a detail, whenever she accidentally omitted one.

Evie found that a little annoying…and threw him a patronising look every time he corrected or interrupted her…but as she was clearly impressed by his heroic actions she eventually decided to sit back and let Gary have his moment in the spotlight.

Gary acknowledged her gesture with a brief nod of the head and immediately took up where Evie had left off; however, a few minutes into his story…seeing that Madison was starting to yawn…he decided to make his version of events as brief as possible, summing up the episode very simply in his own words by announcing that he had seen a guy trying to get some 5-finger discount and he had intervened;

'There was nothing to it, really', he announced humbly. 'The guy was spitting chips because I'd seen him trying to steal a bottle of bourbon, so I gave him a Woolloomooloo uppercut'.

'He kicked him in the groin', Evie translated.

'You were taking a risk there, Gary', Madison chipped in; '…this is New York; that guy could have been armed'.

'Yeah, that's true…and if there had been one around, I would have called for a cop…but these days pizzas arrive quicker than the police', Evie complained.

The Bishop - who had ordered a cognac in the meantime - had been strangely quiet during all this hero talk, but as he sniffed the aroma of his preferred amber nectar and peered through the glass of his snifter he suddenly began whispering to himself.

'As my name-sake Lord Byron once said; 'Sometimes, it is easier to die for the woman you love, than to actually live with her'', he announced in a rather poignant tone, before swirling his glass and swallowing half its content in one gulp.

Madison looked at Evie and then at Gary wondering if she had missed something, but it was obvious from their reactions that neither was any the wiser.

(The Bishop's comment was in stark contrast…and slightly out of context… with what they had been talking about - and nobody had really understood its meaning or its significance, but none of them was prepared to question him about it either.)

She glanced back at *the Bishop* sensing that he was a little subdued and not his usual self, but before she could enquire further, the waiter came along holding a small silver tray on which the bill sat menacingly.

'Toby here, will sort that out', Gary announced in his tactless Aussie vernacular, still pumped up with adrenaline.

In that moment, a sudden hush descended over the table and all that Madison and Evie could do was look at each other and swallow deeply as they braced themselves in anticipation of the come-back that was surely about to follow.

It didn't happen.

Instead *the Bishop* remained stoically dignified, realising that Gary was probably still hyper after his brush with the New York crime scene, and while Madison took the check and placed her card on the tray, he simply folded his napkin carefully and prepared to leave.

They all got up following his lead and as if no New York outing would be complete without it, the evening was concluded with a visit to a nearby club where, as they walked in, a Marc Bolan tribute band was performing their rendition of a vintage T-Rex song; New York City.

The atmosphere in the club was decidedly raucous but as the party of four waited patiently to be seated the band enjoyed a decent round of applause for their efforts before... *after a brief pause to re-tune their instruments*...they launched into a medley of 'seventies-songs' which, although a little surreal, seemed to fit in perfectly with the club's rather psychedelic décor created by its hi-tech lighting system.

'Sh...oot; this is awesome', Gary blurted out as he looked around, remembering at the last second to keep his language in check.

In fact, Gary was in heaven because it just so happened that he loved seventies music and on hearing the intro to one of the biggest hits from that era, he immediately sparked into life, draping his arms around Madison and Evie and announcing excitedly; 'Let's crank it up a gear, girls'.

Gary being Gary, he didn't wait for them to respond...and while a hostess arrived to lead the rest of them to a table, he started making his way through a sea of people and directly onto the dance-floor, where...

hyped up on adrenaline…he began playing along with the band on his very own air guitar.

In the meantime, Madison, Evie and *the Bishop* were shown to a table…and within no time an efficient young waitress had taken their order and returned with their drinks.

The mood around the table was quite convivial and while they all sipped politely on their different potions…enjoying the décor and the retro-vibes that were reverberating around the club…the two women could not help but cringe with embarrassment and mortification as they gazed at Gary out there on the dance-floor making a complete and utter fool of himself.

(And to be fair, his awkward attempts at dancing were indeed beyond parody.)

It was almost thirty minutes later, when…the band having finished their set…Gary finally re-joined them at the table, his shirt stuck to his back and sweat seeping out of every pore of his body…

…and as he called for a refreshing, life-restoring beer or a 'swifty' as Gary called it, they all agreed that there was no getting away from it; he really was one crazy guy.

'I have done some crazy stuff in my time', Evie commented, looking at Gary, '…but I've never done anything like that'.

Madison looked across and raised a knowing eyebrow.

'…though I did once try to ride one of those mechanical bulls…' Evie continued turning back to the table; '…during Spring-Break…and ended up flashing my underwear to the whole crowd…before I was dumped… very unceremoniously…onto the floor'.

'The story of my life really', she sighed. 'So yeah; that was the wildest thing I have ever done', she concluded, looking directly at Madison for corroboration.

The latter didn't comment but secretly smiled to herself as she raised her glass to her lips; she had known Evie for a long time and as far as she knew, that episode with the mechanical bull didn't even rate in the top twenty of her friend's lifetime misdemeanours.

However, Evie was a friend…and a loyal friend at that…and there was no way that she was going to rat her out or embarrass her in front of the two men.

'What about you, Chewy; what did you get up to back in the day?' Evie asked trying to bring *the Bishop* into the conversation.

Madison shook her head but had to stifle a snigger.

'Nothing so gregarious; I can assure you', *the Bishop* replied with his usual poise, unaware that the two women were smiling at his expense.

Gary meanwhile was still psyched up and as he looked around, a couple of pretty apple-bottomed, young women caught his eye.

'I want to get wild and have some fun', he said, placing his hand on Evie's thigh and squeezing it gently.

'Come on, let's dance', he insisted; 'this is my first time in New York; let's get hot and crazy'.

Evie's response was a look of quiet indignation.

'First of all Gary', she replied, removing his hand from her thigh and brushing down her dress; 'I have a strict 'look but don't touch' policy".

'Aaw, come on Bronco Bill; saddle-up', Gary insisted.

Again Evie resisted but then as other people began to drift away from the tables and onto the dance-floor, she finally gave in.

'You know I wouldn't normally do this…' she said looking at her friend and waiting for her response; 'but sadly that's the best offer I've had all week'.

Madison just shrugged and took another sip of her drink.

This was to be a defining moment.

Gary then took hold of Evie's hand and as he guided her through the different groups of people standing, chatting and flirting, he glanced back over his shoulder and grinned widely at *the Bishop*, as if to thank him for his encouragement earlier in the evening.

The DJ had taken over from the band and to launch his set he was playing 'Get up and Dance with me' by 'Walk the Moon'

They reached the dance-floor and as the music began to throb in their ears, Gary immediately gestured for Evie to dance in front of him while he clapped and gesticulated by her side in a 'Travolta-like' fashion, much to the amusement and enjoyment of the packed gallery surrounding them.

Evie hesitated for a moment but she really enjoyed being the centre of attention for once, and within no time she was twirling and shaking her booty like a 'good-un'.

Meanwhile, Madison looked on longingly from afar; she would have loved to get up and dance too, but she knew from prior experience that *the Bishop* would refuse to join her.

This left her feeling a little disconcerted, especially as *the Bishop* was not saying much in the way of conversation…and while she was forced to sit there kicking her heels and nursing her drink, having chosen to stay and keep him company…almost as part of her professional duties, the beat of the music seemed to taunt her and frustrate her as it resonated around the room and vibrated through the floor into the soles of her feet.

She was itching to get up on the dance-floor and was tempted to ask him again, but as she glanced sideways at him, the blank expression on *the Bishop's* face quickly warned her off and she grudgingly resigned herself to the fact that he would probably never indulge her in her passion for dancing.

Just then, the dance-floor really started to fill up with people grooving to the beat - and once the initial tension had subsided, Evie and Gary truly began enjoying themselves amongst the growing throngs of sweat-soaked bodies seething all around them, their minds entranced by the strobing lights above them which flashed relentlessly with dazzling subliminal promise, until eventually, after a run of several consecutive frenzied dance routines, the music finally slowed down and they were forced to stop to take a breather.

At this point, the club was pulsing with men on the prowl, and seeing two rather ungainly characters approaching her rapidly from a distance, Evie decided that it would probably be safer for her to close the distance between her and Gary, just in case the two men created a scene around her.

She took a couple of steps forward into the protective haven of Gary's arms and as they embraced loosely for the slow dance, and the two men went bouldering on by without even acknowledging their existence, her rather full cleavage brushed ever so slightly against the young Aussie's chest.

Although a little bemused by Evie unintended gesture, Gary mistakenly took it as a come-on and because of the adrenaline still pumping through his veins, he suddenly became a little over–zealous at the thought that he might be making a connection.

Nevertheless, he continued to hold Evie loosely and respectfully, trying not to draw her in too closely, but as they danced, and the music lulled them in closer, his hands slowly wandered down her spine and came to rest - inevitably - on the soft curves of her hips.

Evie immediately pulled away, arching her back and threw him a warning glance.

'That's naughty', she remarked saucily...but as she didn't push him away, Gary took that as a green light and wrapped his arms more tightly around her waist pulling her closer.

They danced that way for a moment or two...and then leaning forward and craning his neck a little awkwardly, Gary suddenly planted a sloppy kiss on Evie's mouth, his slobbering lips coming down hard on hers, crushing them almost...and showing his obvious inexperience in these matters.

The kiss was gauche and juvenile; Gary's overenthusiastic exuberance lacking any sophistication or technique, but as Evie pulled away to get her breath back, she knew that if ever a girl could read a man's mind, she could read Gary's, right at that moment...

However, instead of slapping his face and walking away in disgust, as the music continued and the mood softened further, she stayed close, but not too close, enjoying the attention and the power that her femininity was affording her.

Twenty minutes or so later, it was time to go.

Madison came over to them on the dance-floor and having watched them slow-dancing together for a couple of minutes - with their hands clamped tightly on the upper part of each other's buttocks…*which forced their hips together in a wild premise to the evening's end*…she told them to 'get a room', before announcing with some explanatory hand-signals that she and *the Bishop* were leaving.

She then turned and quickly made her way back towards the table, only to see that during her brief absence *the Bishop* had struck up a conversation with one of the waitresses who had been taking care of them during the evening.

Slightly exasperated, Madison stormed up to the table glowering at *the Bishop*…who had not had much to say to her all evening…and ready to tear a strip off the young employee for simply talking to him and being polite, *which she was only doing, in all probability, to increase her tip*…but instead, taking a deep breath, she managed to keep her composure and just threw her rival the secret glare; the glare that women all over the world recognise as a signal that says 'hands-off, he's mine'.

Then, digging into her purse as the waitress stepped back warily; she pulled out a handful of dead presidents (one hundred dollar bills) and handed them to the young woman with a duplicitous smile.

'For our tab; oh, and keep the change hon', she announced rather flippantly as she busied herself closing her purse.

The Bishop looked at her a little puzzled and got up from the table just as Evie and Gary arrived back from the dance-floor.

They were dripping with sweat but before they could catch their breath or quench their thirsts, Madison grabbed the receipt from the girl's tray - for her expenses account - and began making her way unerringly to the exit.

Evie immediately looked at *the Bishop* assuming that he had said or done something to upset her friend - and then at Gary - but as nobody was forthcoming with an explanation, she just grabbed her purse and followed in Madison's footsteps with Gary and then *the Bishop* bringing up the rear.

Evie caught up with Madison at the door and pulling her to one side, she questioned her discreetly as to why she was acting so erratically.

‘I’m just tired, I guess’, Madison shrugged, not wanting to reveal her true feelings while the men were in earshot – and with that she raised her arm assertively to hail a cab.

Back at the hotel, they all decided on a night-cap in the bar to finish the evening, though this was mainly on Evie’s insistence, because she had been denied a last drink in the club and her throat was parched after all that dancing.

This time they sat down at one of the tables nearer to the bar and as they relaxed in the plush armchairs, the barman served up two cognacs for the men and two rather sweet raspberry liqueurs to the women.

Tongues finally loosened and the discussion once again turned to relationships…and inevitably to sex…but after a rather steamy comment from Gary about a friend of his back home, Evie blurted out that they should change the subject.

‘I’m getting horny’, she chirped with an element of sexual mischief in her smile as she looked over at Gary.

She too was now high on adrenaline and hormones and they were obviously starting to dictate her behaviour.

The night-cap took her over the top and finally Evie could resist no longer.

She got up and holding her hand out limply in Gary’s direction, she mumbled those immortal words of courtship; her eyes glinting with barely-disguised excitement; ‘take me to bed, stud’.

Uncharacteristically though, Gary didn’t react immediately. He just sat there with his mouth open, looking a little confused.

‘Hey’, Evie insisted a little louder, slurring her words slightly and cocking her head to the side; ‘this is a booty call…’

‘It is?’ Gary exclaimed, recovering his enthusiasm and looking over at Madison for her approval.

‘…besides, these two will be a lot more comfortable if we’re not hovering over them’, Evie added.

The latter just shrugged her shoulders. ‘It’s your call…….stud’, she commented repeating Evie’s appreciation of him.

‘Yabba, dabba, dooo’, Gary hollered as he rushed to Evie’s side.

'Gary; have you got a raincoat?' *the Bishop* suddenly called after his young colleague.

'What's that?' Gary questioned, looking puzzled.

'Have you got your English riding jackets?' *the Bishop* insisted.

'Oh, you mean my love-gloves. Yeah mate, I'm good, but thanks for offering', Gary confirmed.

Madison looked at *the Bishop* a little shocked…but he just smiled back at her benignly.

'Safety-first', he explained.

As the happy couple walked away, Gary turned and winked again at *the Bishop* while his hand slipped down a little lower over the curve of Evie's peachy-backside.

Without looking, Evie slapped his hand away.

'Hey, hold your horses there…' she chided with a giggle as they disappeared towards the lifts.

The Bishop turned to Madison.

'What were you saying earlier about …shy and rusty?' he commented, a heavy note of sarcasm in his voice.

Madison shrugged her shoulders again.

'Maybe she's also a little more spontaneous too, when acting on a biological impulse', she concluded as she polished off her drink, hoping that he might pick up on her barely-disguised meaning.

It was to no avail.

'You don't like Evie, do you? Madison asked, feeling protective of her friend, as the incongruous couple disappeared towards the lifts.

'On the contrary' *the Bishop* countered, raising his glass; 'I find her delightfully…crazy'.

Upstairs, revived by Evie's invitation and boosted by the adrenaline rush, Gary felt a strong urge to take charge of the situation, and as soon as they were alone...and the door was closed behind them, he pulled Evie close and kissed her, hard on the lips once again.

Evie could almost taste the young Aussie's urgency in that moment but the kiss itself was no more than a frantic melding of lips and skin without any real technique or romantic deftness.

Evie could also feel Gary's enthusiasm against her thigh and as he leaned in for another rather awkward smacker, she could feel herself being slowly backed her up against the wall.

'Whoa; back up your truck there fella', she protested...putting a hand out to slow things down for a moment...but still, the young Aussie's crude assault had fired-up her passion...and though she wasn't sure if they had ripped their clothes off or not, within seconds they were both naked and stumbling awkwardly over to her bed.

Meanwhile downstairs in the bar, Madison and *the Bishop* had begun discussing the more mundane matters of the schedule and the arrangements she had made for the next couple of days; the interview she had arranged, the exhibition match and the photo-shoots, but try as she might, despite several obvious allusions from her, touching her hair and shifting in her seat, *the Bishop* never once hinted at copying their more liberated companions' example.

In fact, as he sat there opposite her, swilling the last few drops of his cognac, *the Bishop* was rather uncomfortable with the whole situation, because in his own mind, he had calculated that the evening they had spent together at the Abbey was only ever going be a one-off situation; a chance for his body to exult and indulge itself for a few hours in some risk-free, non-committal passion.

Madison had been leaving the next day to go back to New York – and logically, as far as he was concerned, they would never have had to meet again if circumstances hadn't dictated otherwise, but now here they sat.

They concluded their discussions with Madison making one last desperate...but ultimately futile...attempt to communicate her repressed passion to the object of her desires, announcing to him - as subtlely as she could possibly put it - that it was time for bed…but he didn't pick up on her prompt…or if he did, he preferred to ignore it.

Her hopes dashed and her ego bruised, Madison got up, confirmed their meeting time for breakfast and then turned to leave.

The Bishop got up too and ever the gentleman, he walked her to the lifts in the lobby; a gesture which briefly ignited a flame of hope in her soul, but sadly that was where they were to part company.

He did kiss her on the cheek and brush a stray hair back behind her ear as they waited for the lift to arrive - *which caught her a little off-guard* - but then he took a step back, as the lift doors closed between them, leaving Madison both breathless and confused as she began the ascent to her room…all on her own.

She was disappointed and that disappointment was compounded way past the point of frustration when she wandered past the door to Evie's room.

She would have liked to discuss her situation with Evie, as she usually did, but if the muffled sounds coming from underneath the door were anything to go by, her friend was clearly otherwise-engaged with Gary.

Madison crept closer and carefully put her ear up against the door. She was tempted to knock; she even clenched her hand into a fist and raised it ready to strike, as she waited patiently for an appropriate lull in activity in which to announce her presence…but that moment never seemed to arrive.

She waited and waited, but all she could hear from behind the door were the constant and unmistakable sounds of flesh pounding flesh - and Evie's voice seemingly overtaken by unbridled desire.

There was no question that these were the sounds of passion…and the cadenced rhythm of the bed's sprung-mattress which also echoed loud and clear in Madison's ears, served only to confirm what she already knew, that her friend and Gary were dancing again, only this time to the horizontal tango.

Curious and intrigued, she listened for a while longer, enjoying the moment vicariously, but then hearing footsteps coming along the corridor and not wanting to be found eaves-dropping, she quickly slipped into her room, next door before anybody appeared and saw her acting suspiciously.

That said, even the solid walls between the rooms could not block out the most recognisable whimpering and moaning sounds which continued almost unabated from Evie's room next door. Gary was riding her friend with the gusto of a young stallion and seemingly doing a far better job of it than he had when they had spent the night together, Madison surmised.

It was a strange thought to have, but as she stood in front of the mirror getting herself undressed, Madison was suddenly reminded of the 'Fast & Furious' poster on Gary's wall back in London and as she went through her nightly cleansing and moisturising routine, she couldn't help but chuckle naughtily to herself at the memory.

She got into bed and not long after, the noises from the room next door fell silent.

Madison sighed with relief at this; it had been a long day, and she was exhausted, but feeling a little disconsolate she pulled the second pillow down alongside her...punching it a few times in frustration; she had been looking forward to a night full of passion herself, but to her great regret *the Bishop* had not invited her to join him as, ever the professional, he had refused to compromise his concentration and the energy levels that he needed for his commitments the next day.

The following morning, after a pretty restless night's sleep, Madison was already walking towards the lift when Evie suddenly appeared out of her room and came wandering up behind her, a dreamy look in her eye and a look of absolute bliss on her face.

'Morning M', she said as she caught up to her friend.

'Morning E', Madison replied as she pressed the 'down' button.

A brief pause the followed...and without looking at each other...the following exchange took place;

M – 'I came up to see you last night...'

Evie – 'You did...?'

M – 'Aha...'

Evie - (rubbing her neck, much to her friend's amusement) 'I didn't hear you knock'

M – 'I didn't…I didn't want to…disturb you…'

Evie – 'Oh, I get it. What exactly did you hear?' She asked with a hint of devilment in her voice.

M - 'Oh, nothing much', Madison replied telling a little white lie; '…just enough to know that someone was definitely having a really good time in there', she added.

Evie shrugged her shoulders; 'Hey girl, I've told you before; you can't rush perfection'.

M – 'I thought that was…; never mind…'

At that moment, the lift doors opened and…Evie motioning for Madison to go in first…they shuffled inside, joining two other guests who were already in the cabin.

In the breakfast room;

In the breakfast room, they met up with Gary who was already sat at one of the tables…looking somewhat drawn and pale…and as she prepared to sit down, Madison casually informed them that *the Bishop* had preferred to have his breakfast delivered to his room.

'That man knows how to live', Gary commented as he threw back half a litre of orange juice, noticing that on the table across from them an odd looking man was wearing the 'do not disturb' from his room around his neck.

Madison could see that Gary was the worse for wear and that…by contrast...Evie was bursting to talk, but it wasn't the right time or place to be discussing what she knew would be a delicate subject, so with a flash of her eyes and a discreet shake of her head she communicated her thoughts to Evie who understood them immediately, and acknowledged the fact with a tight smile of her own.

The two friends usually shared everything but Evie quickly realised that for once it would probably be better not to talk about what had happened between her and Gary until later in the day when she and Madison were alone.

Besides, she knew that her friend had a full schedule in front of her and didn't need the distraction…or the details…of her sex-life clogging up her thoughts, no matter how desperate she was to brag about it.

And so, for the rest of breakfast, they ate in relative silence, speaking only to ask for more coffee and to make brief complimentary comments on the beautifully arranged buffet, the superb all-round quality of the food… and the amazing selection of breads, pastries and hot dishes on display at the counter.

All three of them enjoyed their fill and having washed it down with the usual procession of morning coffees, Madison called up to *the Bishop's* room to inform him that they would be leaving within the next half-hour, her rather clipped tone bringing a look of astonishment from Evie and a raised eyebrow from Gary.

Even so, thirty minutes later, everybody was ready and waiting in the hotel lobby.

Madison called them all together and while they waited for the valet to call their car forward, she took a moment to summarise the day's itinerary for them.

'First of all', she announced in a confident tone; 'the guys are going to be interviewed at the television studios at 10 a.m., then I have organised a quick sight-seeing tour of New York…for those interested', she insisted, looking at *the Bishop* and knowing almost certainly that he wouldn't be…'and that will conclude with a visit to the venue where the exhibition match will be taking place tomorrow…so that we can all, and by all I mean me, familiarise ourselves with the layout etc.'

She paused at that point to take a breath and all three of the others simply nodded or shrugged affirmatively.

'After that, it's back here for a quick change and then we have reservations at One Little West Street for dinner, she concluded.

'I hope everybody likes American Tapas', she asked rhetorically as she led the way out to the car.

Again, Evie and Gary looked at each other a little incredulously before following her lead in amiable silence; while *the Bishop*, who clearly hated being dictated to, deliberately hung back a little as if pretending not to be associated with them, the expression on his face one of pained coercion.

They all got into the car and moments later it pulled out into the morning traffic to a chorus of frustrated horns, from people who should have known better…as New York, like any other major city is regularly grid-locked in the morning by the sheer volume of commuter traffic.

However, it was only a temporary setback and within no time at all they were pulling up at the television studios where Madison had cunningly managed to call in a favour.

(A few months earlier it just so happened that Madison had worked on an article with one of the producers of a little known culture show that aired on a cable network targeting the New York metropolitan area…and she had persuaded that producer to give her some air-time to promote the exhibition match in exchange for her getting a personal introduction to the Bishop… though, of course, she hadn't told him that.

She was under no illusion that the interviews would have any impact on the success…or not…of the event that she was organising but in her eyes Madison saw it as another feather in her cap that she could mention when it came to making her report to Amanda.)

It was just before 9.30 a.m. when the car pulled up outside the TV studios and deposited its passengers at the front door.

Madison got out first and the others followed on behind, in single file…with *the Bishop*, looking a little over-dressed in his Italian suit…and Gary a little understated – as usual - in his mismatched, casual-garb.

The programme's producer (who had worked with Madison previously) met them at the door with her team of professionals; introductions were made…and while Madison dealt with the technicalities, *the Bishop* and Gary were led away to the make-up room to be groomed for their first ever television appearance.

The interview was to be all about the Bishop promoting the exhibition match of course, but Madison had suggested that Gary be a part of it too, in order to cover a wider demographic; especially as he was 'potentially' the future of the game.

She was so well organised in her preparation for the up-coming event that it only took Madison a couple of minutes to get the AD (assistant director) and his script up to speed with all the relevant, factual information concerning *the Bishop* and Gary, and once they were satisfied that they had everything they needed and had gone away to distribute the sheets that she herself had provided, Madison and Evie were shown to a kind of 'green-room', situated away from the hustle and bustle of all the studio activity where they could sit and talk in peace until they were called upon once more.

'So…you and Gary seem to hit it off last night', Madison commented discreetly stating the obvious.

'Yeah, I suppose we did'. Evie replied blushing ever so slightly.

'…but hey, what can I say?' she continued; 'you know; it just happened spontaneously after he had gotten my attention with his dazzling moves on the dance-floor'.

She paused for a moment and then looked at her friend trying desperately to stifle a chuckle.

However, she couldn't hold it in and all of a sudden her face began to crumble as she exploded in embarrassed laughter, her infectious joy making her friend smile too.

'…and…' Madison asked more insistently, without being specific about the question.

'Well, the first thing I have to say is that he's different, so unlike the typical smug, conceited American males that we are used to meeting around here …and grateful…soooo grateful', she added, doing her best to stifle yet another snigger.

Madison shook her head and looked off into the distance hearing approaching footsteps.

'There was no instant phwoar chemistry', Evie continued, reflecting on the previous night's events, 'but the way he took on that guy at the store, well that did something to me…' she admitted.

'Mind you', she complained, remembering their first embrace; 'he's a sloppy kisser'.

'Eew', Madison lied as if she didn't know; 'that's too much information'.

'So…never mind me, what about you and Mr Grumpy?' Evie suddenly enquired turning the tables.

'Nothing to report', Madison shrugged disconsolately as voices and footsteps brought them back to their current situation.

Evie sensed her friend's disappointment and despite the fact that there were people milling around not far from them, she wrapped her arm around her shoulders and jokingly offered to share Gary with her; a thought that was so gross that they both burst out in uncontrolled laughter yet again.

At that moment the producer of the show, suddenly emerged from a side-door with *the Bishop*, Gary and several other studio employees in tow…and with a cheeky wink and a discreet hand-gesture, she made it clear that the two women should join their group as they made their way over to the studio where the interviews were going to be taking place.

Madison and Evie got up as one…and followed on as the small group of people continued on their way, along a series of identical-looking corridors until they finally ended up at the heavy padded door of the studio, where tossing her hair flamboyantly - for *the Bishop's* benefit no doubt - the producer pulled it open and invited them all inside.

The mood suddenly changed and as all the little helpers went scuttling about their work in order to create the magic, Madison, Evie, Gary and *the Bishop* were all introduced to the show's presenter by the floor-manager.

Jeff Johnson was a typical American news anchor with white teeth and a cheesy smile who instantly clicked into character, taking charge and indicating the chairs on set where the men should sit, while Madison and Evie were ushered off into the wings by yet another studio employee, time of course being of the essence.

It was the first time that both Madison and Evie had ever been in a TV studio and as they stood there at the side of the set, amongst an array of monitors, with cables trailing all around their feet and technicians of all sorts running here, there and everywhere, both were in awe of the fact.

However, while Madison managed to maintain her composure Evie could not help but let her emotions get the better of her; her excitement bubbling over like cheap bubbly.

Meanwhile, on the set, the interview was soon in full swing and with his confident manner and enigmatic style *the Bishop* soon had the presenter eating out of his hands as he slipped modestly into the role of spokesperson for the game of chess, answering each of the latter's questions on its merits with his usual tact, finesse and cerebral mischief-making while shamelessly promoting the exhibition match that he was there to plug.

(Gary said very little other than to acknowledge the presenter's introductory greeting but for the young Aussie it was enough for him just to be there.)

It was a very polished performance and as Madison and Evie looked on with appreciation, the producer came over to them with a thumbs-up, her features beaming with satisfaction, as she thanked Madison for giving her the opportunity to meet *the Bishop*.

'He's amazing, isn't he?' she gushed.

Madison smiled at her and nodded her head.

'Yeah, that he is', she agreed pensively; 'that he is'.

After the interview, as they all stood in the studio's reception area Madison announced that the next thing on their schedule was a tour of New York.

'I thought you in particular might enjoy this Gary', she said looking at the young Aussie; '...as it's your first time here, but I'm sure it will be fun for everybody', she insisted, knowing full well that *the Bishop* would probably not be interested.

Indeed, that was what she was hoping for...her intention being to send Gary and Evie off sight-seeing so that she could spend some quality time alone with *the Bishop*...and as expected, her devious plan seemed to be working when Gary showed his appreciation with a whoop and an enthusiastic but mystifying shout of; 'Lock it in Eddie', which made no sense to anybody but himself.

Evie looked at him waiting for an explanation...and then at Madison but words seemed to fail her, so shrugging her shoulders after a brief pause she simply let it slide; 'that's fine by me, I love New York', she declared consensually.

However, as Madison had hoped, *the Bishop* then informed them that, having already seen what New York had to offer on his previous visit, he would prefer to go back to the hotel to rest up and be with his thoughts.

'Would you like me to join you...; is there anything you need?' Madison questioned pertinently, trying to mask the easily detectable innuendo in her voice.

'No, no thank you', *the Bishop* replied dishearteningly; 'just a taxi back to the hotel will be fine'.

Madison was disappointed...again...and was tempted to stamp her feet in frustration, but rather than make a fuss over his rebuttal of her offer, she kept her cool and marched over to the studio's reception desk, where within minutes...with the help of the young woman sat behind there, she had organised a cab for him.

The cab arrived a few minutes later, and once *the Bishop* was safely on his way back to the hotel, Madison, Evie and Gary jumped back into the town-car and went off in search of Manhattan's hidden secrets.

CHAPTER FOURTEEN

Later that evening, while Madison and Evie were still up in their rooms getting themselves ready for dinner, the two men made their way down to the bar where they had all arranged to meet up again.

As was generally the case, *the Bishop* got there first, but when Gary arrived to join him a few minutes later, strutting like a peacock as he passed a table full of women near the door, the young Aussie was more than a little surprised to find his hero sat in the corner, huddled almost dejectedly over his glass, deep in thought, looking like the weight of the whole world was on his shoulders.

Gary found this more than a little bizarre, because for him personally, it had been a great day and things could never have been better; what with the visit to the TV studio and the guided tour of New York, not to mention him hooking up with Evie the night before...

No, no doubt about it; he was having the time of his life since they arrived in New York.

'Could I get a beer, mate?' Gary called out to the barman as he made his way nonchalantly over to the table where *the Bishop* was sitting.

He was going to sit down without asking...but sensing that the mood was a little tense he quickly reigned in his cocky bravado, opting for discretion over valour, and instead of expressing his usual, self-satisfied, swaggering 'joie de vivre', the young Aussie simply asked *the Bishop*, with renewed respect - after the champion's stunning performance at the TV studios earlier in the day - if it was okay for him to take a seat.

The Bishop seemed strangely distracted...and at first he didn't react, lost as he was in his thoughts...but Gary repeated his question and at the second time of asking the master nodded his assent...although his muted response was barely recognisable as a reply.

Gary took a seat...feeling a little uncomfortable in the great man's presence when he was in this kind of mood…but once the barman had brought him his beer, his confidence returned and he instantly began looking around for a topic of conversation.

He would have dearly loved to discuss chess with his idol but Gary knew that he had to abide by the unwritten rule of the game…which stated that players should never discuss tactics or technique with other players, rivals or adversaries…and so rather than break with that age-old tradition, the young Aussie sat back, took a gulp of amber liquid and gently initiated the conversation by thanking *the Bishop* for his encouragement the previous evening.

The master looked up, his eyes thoughtful and intense, but he didn't speak.

Gary waited, took another swallow and then trying to lighten the mood again, he cunningly complimented *the Bishop* on his knowledge of the finer points of the female psyche, confirming that the latter's alleged reputation as a lady-killer had obviously not been usurped; not that the young Aussie knew anything about it really but he was quickly learning all about the power of flattery after spending time in the master's company.

A pinched smile finally cracked on *the Bishop's* sallow face and he chinked his glass mannishly against Gary's before finishing off his drink and calling for another round.

The young Aussie took this as a compliment of his own and pleased with himself for having restored a more balanced mood to the proceedings, he polished off his drink too with a loud exhalation of contentment.

He was going to ask *the Bishop* why he was so 'bummed out', but then, as his mind clicked into gear, he suddenly remembered a conversation that he had overheard earlier, while in the car with the girls, where he had gotten wind that things were not quite right between him (TB) and Madison.

He thought about it for a moment and as he knocked back another brew, bolstered by his initial success in engaging *the Bishop* and believing that one good turn deserved another - i.e., *the Bishop*'s advice for him to follow Evie - he decided to try to provoke another reaction out of the master by commenting on Madison.

'You want to be careful with that Madison', he said unselfishly; 'she attracts the boys like flies in the Australian outback'.

The Bishop remained impassive for a moment but then lifting his head slowly he smiled again tightly at his young colleague, instantly changing the mood.

The mention of her name suddenly improved his mood…considerably… and over the next couple of minutes Gary could literally see *the Bishop* gradually coming alive again, preparing himself to offer his young student yet another life-lesson in female psychology.

♗

'Take last night…' he suddenly announced '…when Evie walked out of the restaurant. It was a test…she did that to see if you would follow'.

'She did', Gary exclaimed, a puzzled look on his brow.

'Of course', *the Bishop* explained, his tone strengthening; '…and you did, which confirmed to her that you were interested in her'.

'Her behaviour - whether it be consciously or sub-consciously - was calculated to give you a chance to show your interest and take it a step further', *the Bishop* began lecturing.

'You think so', Gary pondered as he swallowed more beer.

'Listen Gary', *the Bishop* affirmed; 'it's quite a simple dynamic. If you make a move and the person you are interested in follows – then that is a clear indication, a clear sign of attraction…' he concluded.

Gary nodded… impressed and intrigued by *the Bishop's* effortless capacity to unravel the mysteries of the female psyche…and to explain the different facets of the mating game…so taking advantage of being in the presence of a genius as he saw it, he dared to ask the master for a few more pointers on seduction technique, explaining that while he liked Evie…*She 'banged like a dunny door in a gale' was how he put it…*the whole 'thing' was all over a little too…quickly.

The Bishop leaned back in his chair at this point and gazed at Gary contemplatively; men were not usually so forthright about these matters and he was loathe to get involved, but seeing that Gary's request appeared quite genuine, he decided to give his young colleague the benefit of his experience.

'I have no idea about your 'technique'', he said, putting up air-quotes, 'but from what you are saying, you probably need to relax', he advised; 'take your time and be more attentive…less impetuous', he lectured again.

The Bishop was warming to his young companion; he was a little awkward at times but his honesty was refreshing…if a little too direct on occasions.

Indeed it was somewhat embarrassing, the way that Gary had struck up the conversation, but as relationships with women was another one of those subjects that the Bishop had learned to master over the years, he knew that he was on solid ground and would be able to offer some strong advice to his young colleague, especially as one-on-one was and always would be, his favourite dynamic.

In reality, the Bishop was just pleased to have found a level on which he and Gary could connect other than chess.

Gary took a moment and then agreed with *the Bishop's* summing up; 'yeah, that would be right, I suppose; when I'm on a good wicket, I tend to get carried away', he tittered, slipping back into his Aussie verve.

'Gary, you are a great prospect in this game', *the Bishop* confirmed; 'you have a great future ahead of you and I understand your youthful enthusiasm but when it comes to women I think that you probably need a lesson in subtlety, tact and manners', *the Bishop* suggested on a more serious note.

'Yeah, that would be right too, I suppose', Gary agreed, nodding his head and shrugging his shoulders almost apologetically.

The Bishop leaned forward again to focus Gary's attention and keep the contents of what he was about to say just between the two of them.

'Women love to relinquish power; they like nothing better than to fall into the strong arms of a man and take on the submissive role'.

'However, you have to remember Gary, that in spite of the roles we play, the game of seduction is an exchange of contracts…and within the rules of that exchange…foreplay plays a major role; and I cannot stress it enough how important that particular component is to the construction of a lasting relationship'.

This time it was Gary's turn to sit back…but that did not deter *the Bishop* from completing his explanation.

'As you well know; we men reach a sufficient level of excitement for sex within two minutes of encountering the right stimuli.

Gary nodded silently, getting a little embarrassed.

'...well, unfortunately or fortunately, depending on how you view it, women need about twenty minutes to reach that same level of excitement; hence the need for foreplay', he explained.

Gary was stunned. He had never seen relations between men and women studied as if it were a science before...and once again *the Bishop* had blown him away with his superior knowledge.

'So what do I do?' asked Gary struck with renewed admiration, his eyes wide as saucers.

The Bishop grimaced as if pondering the solution, then replied; 'You must realise young man, that in these post-feminist times, women have become more demanding; they are enjoying their sexuality a lot more and men need to adapt to this new set of rules', he declared.

Gary leaned forward again, determined not to miss a single word of advice that oozed so confidently out of the mouth of the master...but unfortunately just as *the Bishop* was about to dispense the most important component of his counsel, the young Aussie's focus was distracted by a picture in his mind's eye of Luke Skywalker from the Star Wars films listening to the wise words of Yoda...and he missed what was said.

'Sorry mate; you lost me there. What was that last bit', he interrupted.

The Bishop frowned and took a deep breath before repeating himself.

'...all I'm saying is that women expect a lot more from their partners these days and as their demands have increased, they have invented a host of new ideas to entice men to become more adventurous'.

'True', Gary agreed again.

'...for example, many women have taken to 'tidying up the shop front' so to speak', *the Bishop* explained, 'and that in turn has led to previously taboo practices like oral-sex becoming more popular and acceptable', he reasoned.

Gary smiled foolishly at this comment like many people do when discussing the intimate details of human behaviour, but *the Bishop* was not put off and ignoring his colleague's smirk he continued his argument.

'...however, men must realise that women are not just making a conscious effort to improve the aesthetics and present themselves at their best – down there – for their own benefit; they are in fact tending to that area these days with all the care and attention that they dedicate to the rest of their feminine hygiene, because it is the expectation nowadays that oral-sex is a normal part of any intimate relationship', *the Bishop* disclosed.

'Yeah, that's true'. Gary agreed. 'I had noticed that they have been chopping down the old map of Tasmania of late'.

'So..., if you enjoy that kind of thing too, you might like to try that as a way of slowing things down', *the Bishop* concluded wrapping up the lesson.

'...and by the same token, by simply prolonging the foreplay, you would also be extending the duration of your endeavours', he added as an aside, picking up his glass and polishing it off again.

'Remember Gary; a woman can say more in a sigh than a man can say in a sermon' *the Bishop* whispered, quoting Arnold Haultain.

'Thanks mate, you're a legend', Gary replied, showing his gratitude.

'One last thing', *the Bishop* suggested as he spied the girls arriving in the distance. 'If a woman makes the first move, then she's already warmed up; just dive straight in; last night for instance was a prime example'.

'Champ, you're on fire', Gary ovationed, just as the girls joined them interrupting the lesson.

Meanwhile; upstairs, just before Gary had left to go down to the bar;

Madison was still fixing her appearance when Evie came a-knocking;

'I need to 'snap a yam' she announced directly, '...and I can't do it with Gary there'.

'Be my guest', Madison replied motioning towards the bathroom.

Evie quickly disappeared into the bathroom...and re-emerged just a few minutes later...with her phone already...or still...placed firmly against her ear.

All Madison heard was...'I know; I ate the whole enchilada' and the promise that she (Evie) would tell the person on the other end of the call all about it when they met up next.

'Ready?' she asked impatiently, barely able to contain her excitement.

'Wow, I haven't seen you this excited since...since last night', Madison remarked.

Evie shrugged with feigned indifference.

'By the way; that dress needs a belt', she suggested, pointing at Madison's outfit.

'Do you think?' Madison questioned, looking at herself in the mirror. 'I don't think I have one that goes with it'.

'Here take this one', Evie suggested…and with that she took off the belt she was wearing and handed it to her friend.

Madison put the belt on and took one more look in the mirror.

The belt made all the difference to her silhouette and defined her figure even more-perfectly than before.

'Wow; that's perfect; thanks E', she acknowledged as she turned and followed her friend out, still amazed that she was ready before her for once.

'What are you guys talking about?' Evie asked curiously.

'Oh, just enjoying the simple pleasure of male-bonding', *the Bishop* announced, with a hint of sarcasm as he smoothed down his tie nonchalantly.

'Well, the car is waiting', Madison announced, to the men's appreciative smiles and with that, they all made their way out to the forecourt, the men taking the opportunity to once again compliment the ladies on their stunning outfits.

Madison was dressed in a fuchsia-coloured cashmere dress with a scooped-neck …now belted at the waist thanks to Evie…which showed off her figure to perfection…while standing next to her, Evie was wearing a more risqué, zebra-patterned print-dress that hugged her in all the right places…much to Gary's obvious delight.

After a short ride, the car dropped them off at the American Tapas restaurant…and they had just been seated at their table and been handed the menus…when a herd of beefy manhood came rumbling through the restaurant's main door and made its way to the bar area accompanied by the raucous sound of a chorus of 'Hell Yeahs'!

Everybody in the restaurant tried to ignore them but the cabal of city-boys were being rather loud and unruly, and though he was desperately trying to hold his tongue, *the Bishop* could not help but comment on their behaviour, drawing a parallel between them and the sexist wolf-pack culture that seemed to him so prevalent in American College football teams and even to a lesser degree in the professional ranks of the game.

'Don't you find it strange that whenever groups of American men get together they seem to revert back to loud, uncouth, chest-beating numskulls?' he observed in muted irritation.

'Yeah well, in life, everything's a hustle', Evie commented. '…at least it is in New York… and anyway, those guys are just letting off steam', she argued, defending her countrymen and smiling politely at Gary.

Feeling a little awkward, the waiter stepped away for a moment, leaving them to decide on what they would like to eat and while they were discussing the merits of the menu, one of the guys from the rowdy group at the bar suddenly broke off from the pack and headed towards the men's room, informing his friends rather graphically of his intentions – which of course brought the inevitable volley of questionable comments from them in return.

He began making his way between the tables to the back of the restaurant…where a stairway led down to the rest-rooms…and as he did so, passing by their table, he suddenly recognised Madison.

'Well, well, well; who do we have here then?' he exclaimed theatrically stopping abruptly next to their booth.

Both Madison and Evie turned to acknowledge him with a polite nod of the head and a tight smile, but *the Bishop* who was so obviously full of disdain for the culture that the young man represented, simply threw him an indifferent glance without speaking.

Gary however did speak; turning to face the stranger directly and extending a hand to him, he presented himself as Gary Bridgewater, enjoying his new-found celebrity.

'And who might you be, mate?' he asked confidently in his charmingly informal manner, assuming erroneously that the stranger had recognised him from his television appearance.

'David, David Kirk', the stranger announced curtly, a hint of aggression in his tone; 'Madison's ex'.

The girls looked at each other uncomfortably and the mood at the table tensed dramatically...but rather than being impressed or intimidated by the stranger's demeanour Gary quickly defused the New-Yorker's brash arrogance with his own brand of self-confidence.

He cocked a curious eyebrow in the stranger's direction and then repeated the guy's name with a measure of jocular irony.

'Kirk, you say; K.I.R.K. as in Capt. James T of the Star-ship Enterprise', he announced pertinently to the surprise of all those within earshot.

Evie stifled a chuckle, just about, while Madison covered her mouth with her napkin to hide her joy as the stranger's face turned crimson with embarrassment.

He stared at Gary menacingly for a couple of seconds but then seeing the young Aussie's rather imposing physique and not wanting to humiliate himself any further, he turned around and started back to the bar, completely forgetting that he had been on his way to the men's room.

'Life is just like a pen; you can cross some things out but you can never erase them', *the Bishop* quipped with a mischievous twinkle in his eye, looking over at Madison whose mouth curled up at the edges in recognition of his comment.

Then she turned and looked at Evie and together they burst out laughing as her ex, the guy that had broken her heart, all those months ago, retreated back to his friends - unsteadily - with his tail between his legs.

Gary just shrugged his shoulders feeling a little crest-fallen all the same.

'I thought he was a fan', he explained, as the waiter came back to take their order.

The two women looked at each other again, relieved at the way Gary had defused what could have been a rather embarrassing episode, but then once they were certain that David was out of sight again - and in an effort to put the whole incident behind them and move on - they turned their attention back to the menu, their eyes feasting joyfully on the delights that would soon be filling their stomachs.

They had never eaten in this particular restaurant before, but Madison and Evie had eaten in many others all over New York and saw themselves as amateur connoisseurs of this kind of cuisine, so it was not surprising that after a few minutes of reflection they were offering suggestions to Gary as to what he should sample off the menu.

The young Aussie, who was still scratching his cheek in disappointment - and only listening with one ear after his moment of disillusion - nodded in agreement to almost all their suggestions while next to him, *the Bishop* who had already made up his mind what he would like to eat, had taken to looking out of the window with a detached, passing interest.

Indeed, he was simply scanning the street idly from left to right when suddenly a bill-board across the way caught his eye.

It was for a weekly magazine and it featured as its headline, an article about pampered pets being offered their own dedicated airline flights.

'You can understand why some people despise the American way of life', he commented dryly, 'when you see some of the self-indulgent and ostentatious decadence they lavish on their pets…when elsewhere in the world there are people; men, women and children…dying of starvation'.

Nobody answered, the girls preferring to ignore him and finish ordering while Gary was still muted after his non-celebrity encounter.

'I mean, do these pets really need the diamond studded collars and clothes?' *the Bishop* insisted, gesturing to the photo on the magazine's front page.

Madison turned to him and seeing the poster too, she tried to brush it off saying that that kind of thing only happened in California and not in New York…but even as she was saying it, *the Bishop* quickly pointed out several mutts being treated with just as much deference in the street in front of them.

She frowned, lost for words.

'I hate to see those poor animals being used as fashion statements and being bred for cosmetic reasons just to fit inside a handbag', *the Bishop* continued; 'those poor animals are no more than mutant hybrids, created by mad-scientists and exploited by irresponsible and bloody-minded, self-obsessed dog breeders who are in complete denial as to the harm they are causing to the animals…just so that they can satisfy their own greed for monetary gain and enhance their standing and their reputation within the closed in-bred world of dog-breeding', *the Bishop* ranted as he unfolded his napkin.

'That is some analogy', Madison remarked as she handed back her menu.

'What do you mean by that?' Evie asked having missed the gist of what was being said while she was ordering.

'Well'; Madison explained, taking on the role of educator much to *the Bishop's* great surprise, 'pedigree dogs are in-bred in order to maintain the purity of the gene pool and what Tob…TB here is saying, is that if you look at the people involved in this practice…well, they do all seem to look pretty similar, don't they?', she concluded.

'It's not only the official breeders', Gary chipped in; 'there are plenty of criminal gangs breeding these animals for profit, pandering to the trend'.

'Did you know that in L.A. they even organise dog marriages and take them to be psycho-analysed…and that they even have their own Twitter accounts and Facebook accounts…and YouTube accounts', Evie added, inadvertently adding fuel to the fire.

'Ridiculous', *the Bishop* scowled.

'….but what I really can't handle', Gary complained pursuing the subject, 'is those people who treat their dogs like surrogate children, flying them first-class, feeding them only the best food, teaching them to dance and worst of all, expecting others to treat them like they do – letting them jump all over them, sniffing and licking them'.

'Yeah, they lick their balls and then they lick your face', he said contentiously, tacitly encouraging the argument.

'Eew', the two women screeched in chorus.

'No, but the worst thing has to be those who let their dogs sleep with them in their beds leaving hairs and god knows what else in their wake', Madison griped adding to the discussion.

'That's so unhygienic, but I think that the worst thing about it all, is that these people leave those animals millions of dollars in their wills; surely that money could be put to better use', Evie quipped, unconsciously revealing her priority in life.

'In England, I know two owners who send their dogs post-cards when they go on holiday', Gary added.

'That's nothing; in LA, they have pigs and pet monkeys that they dress up and treat like children; they even make them wear diapers', Evie declared.

'That's just sad', Madison commented.

'Where are these people's priorities?' *the Bishop* suddenly interrupted..

'Don't get me wrong; I do understand people's affection for…and attachment to…their pets; I'm not completely without a heart, and I would never deliberately harm or hurt an animal but the monetary expense aside, I find the extreme, soppy devotion that some people exhibit towards these creatures…especially those who enter their precious pets into dog-shows…completely ridiculous…pathetic…and bordering on madness in some cases', he concluded, and everybody agreed.

There was a lull after that as everybody paused and took stock of what had been said.

'Listen, all I wanted to say when this discussion started…' *the Bishop* reiterated, '…was that I don't believe that it is right to lavish excess on these creatures when people, human beings around the world are suffering'.

'Yeah, I suppose that when you come to think of it; it is all rather ridiculous', Madison concurred but 'you've made your point', she added, looking at *the Bishop* with an insistent stare, thinking to herself how yet again he had managed to attack her countrymen.

'Hey, let's lighten up', Evie suggested. 'Let's talk music'.

'Did anybody see the Music Awards the other day?' she asked excitedly; 'the Rappers took all the spoils'.

'That my dear, is another perfect example of American decadence', *the Bishop* announced reigniting the argument.

'Rap Culture is the epitome, the greatest example of American decadence', he declared, 'because when Rap Music emerged, those 'artists'…and I use the word lightly…were considered the scum of the earth by many of those in the establishment, because of their association with drugs, the way they glamorised guns and their disrespect for women'.

Madison heaved a heavy sigh while Evie threw her hands in the air.

'…but now', *the Bishop* continued, ignoring their disinterest, 'thanks to their streetwise culture where women are all considered as cheap ho's, guns and drugs are cool and the dollar is almighty, they have risen up through the layers of puritanical hypocrisy inherent in the American system to become icons of society…and more fool the USA and the record company executives who have promoted this cultural trash and made a string of gutter-snipes multi-millionaires', he concluded.

'Wow, that's quite a statement; do you have an opinion like that about everything?' Evie heckled facetiously.

'The short answer is 'yes', Madison interrupted, hoping to change the subject again before *the Bishop* could expand any further.

A brief resume of the reasoning behind the Bishop's comments on Rap Culture

Today's Rap culture grew up in the streets and on the corners of our inner-cities where groups of disinherited young men gather in order to sell drugs.

Bored with hanging around, waiting for clients they began to use their creative talents to organise what they called 'battles' (a form of verbal jousting).

At first, they rapped about what they knew, about their lives… about the street but unfortunately as time went by, those among them who were already gang-members began to influence the content of the songs and the gang-related lyrics which soon crept into the songs led to Rap Music being used and abused for more sinister agendas like boasting about criminal activity or sending messages to other gangs seen as a threat.

This went on for a while but then – *seeing the market possibilities that music could offer them* - the street gangs decided that selling drugs on corners was not enough; they wanted to claim their part of the American dream.

They started by demanding 'respect' in their lyrics – but not respect in the noble sense of the word – the respect that these young men were demanding in their songs was the respect of their peers on the streets based on the un-written rules of the gang-culture that they belonged to; i.e. Respect me, because if you don't, I have a weapon and I'm not afraid to use it.

(Noticeably and quite conveniently, the respect for human-life doesn't seem to come into the equation at that point).

This threatening tone is a constant feature of the Rap culture; it shows -

1) in the way that they speak and in the crude, controversial language that they use (mofo, nigger)
2) in the subtle and not so subtle threats of violence implied in the grammatically threadbare lyrics of their songs – where they regularly glamorise the carrying and the use of guns and knives
3) in their reputations as bad-boys / ex-criminals (drug pushers, dealers etc.)
4) ...and finally in the arrogant way that they dress and behave with their posturing attitudes (even when they dance, their body-language is threatening, inciting violence).

Now, the fight against injustice is laudable in any section of society but how hypocritical is it of these people to be demanding respect for themselves while they talk about young girls and women in the most horrendous, derogatory fashion;

- constantly denigrating and running them down as 2nd class citizens
- referring to them simply as 'pussy'
- ...and reducing them – in their uncultured, misogynous minds – to mere sexual objects of mass consumption (ho's (whores) and bitches)

Then, they invite these same young girls to appear in their music videos and deliberately dress them as scantily as possible (skin-tight fluorescent hot-pants and crop-tops or bikinis) to re-affirm their hypothetical male superiority / dominance over them, humiliating them further by imposing dance routines on them created with no other purpose than to flaunt and exploit their feminine sexuality (grinding hips, undulating mid-sections and constant pelvic thrusting).

The subliminal concept of dominance / subservience is present throughout.

That said, the question needs to be asked; do these young women, these 'Hip-hop honeys' as they are called, not realise that they are being exploited? – Does the miserable pay-check that they pick up in appearance fees (if they are paid at all) compensate them for all that humiliation?

In the 21st century; does the almighty dollar and the opportunity to appear on a TV screen trump even the basic human qualities of dignity and self-respect?

This new 'raunch-culture' is synonymous with sleaze and exploitation, but it has become so ubiquitous in these music videos that the younger generations are being completely de-sensitised to the concept of morality that should surround their sexuality.

In fact, young girls and women these days – thanks also to the superficially inept and vacuous celebrity culture – now see the Playboy bunny logo as cute and sexy – a symbol of their independence, empowerment and sassiness – and no longer as an offensive symbol of sexist oppression – indeed they aspire to it,

......so what hope do we have?

Just some of Rap-culture's role-models that are currently 'inspiring' the younger generation

Chris Brown – convicted of assault on singer **Rihanna**

Clifford Harris aka **TI** – convicted of possession of two machine-guns and silencers – **N.B.**; as he had to wait for a prison space, he did a few more gigs while he was waiting, where he was roundly applauded by the crowd for his conviction

Corey Miller aka **C Murder** – currently serving a life sentence for murdering a 16 year old fan

Curtis Jackson III aka **50 Cent** – a man who is constantly bragging about being shot nine times

Dwayne Carter Junior aka **Lil Wayne** – convicted on drugs charges and gun possession

Earl Simmons aka **DMX** – convicted on drugs and theft charges

Marshall Bruce Mathers III aka **Eminem** – drug and alcohol dependence, assault and weapons charges

Snoop Doggy Dogg – considered the 'coolest dude on the planet', has been convicted several times on drug and fire-arms charges

Trevor Smith aka **Busta Rhymes** – convicted of assault

Then there was **Tupac Shakur and Christopher Wallace** aka **Notoriuos B.I.G.** – two big influences on today's youngsters - who were both assassinated on the street with fire-arms.

...as were...

Patrick Lamark Hawkins aka **Fat Pat**,

Raymond Rogers aka **Freaky Tah** and

Deshaun Dupree Holton aka **PROOF** (a friend of Eminem).

...and finally, no list of influential, celebrity rappers would be complete without the shameless, self-promoting narcissists who are **Sean (Puffy / Diddy) Combs** and **Kanye West** who was also convicted recently for assault.

These are just some of the high-profile people who represent the Rap scene; the problem gets worse and more violent further down the social scale.

One last comment;

These people may drive fast, expensive cars and live in huge 'pimped-out' houses to showcase their flash life-styles, but could somebody please inform them of how ridiculous they look in their outsize basketball jerseys and their baggy pants that somehow they have difficulty pulling up further than their thighs, not to mention the over-sized trainers and the baseball caps which they still haven't figured how to wear (hey guys, the visor goes at the front).

Oh, and then there's the bling (the flashy gold jewellery); has anybody ever explained to these people that wearing a lot of 'bling' is all about inadequacy – the greater the outer show – the more the inner lack of self-worth.

Conclusion;

Rap feeds on cultural, moral and social subversiveness and represents a worrying undercurrent of the dark side of society (pimps, ho's, drugs and guns)

A typical slogan often quoted by those in the Rap movement is;

'Life ain't nuthin' but bitches and money'

Now, if that is the ideology that Rap culture is based on, and if that is the ideology which the younger generation now wants to embrace and aspire to, on top of the spiralling drug culture, then society as we know it will be taking a few more 'hits' in the coming years.

A final thought; 'Music pollutes young minds quicker than any bacteria ever could'.

♝

'Okay, so what else do you want to talk about, politics'? Gary asked innocently.

'Oh, please don't get him started on that again', Madison pleaded.

'Why?' Gary asked again, naively.

'Don't ask; just take my word for it', she insisted plaintively, but unfortunately it was too late, *the Bishop* had taken the bait.

'Well, you have just been through the presidential election process recently and it is too early to comment on the new administration, but I would say that in my opinion, US politics seems to be a very cut-throat business'.

'It seems to be full of shadowy figures intent on manoeuvring their candidate into position by whatever means possible using the most devious methods, conniving, back-stabbing, dirt-raking, mud-slinging and sleaze-trawling – and at the end of the day, if all that work doesn't produce the desired result, then the campaign organisers have teams of faceless individuals prepared to make unsubstantiated claims and insinuations about rival candidates' personal lives in order to destroy their reputations and denigrate / destabilise them in the scramble for the top job'.

'I have a fascination for politics but I have no time for politicians', he declared.

'They are the same, the world over, they lie, they cheat, they make promises that they can't keep – and then they ask you…no, they plead with you, to vote for them again so that they can continue lying, cheating and milking the system for another term'.

The Bishop realised that he was being ignored, so for once, he ceased his rant.

'Whatever happened to truth, honesty and integrity?' Gary asked idealistically; whatever happened to being fair and the idea that the best man with the best policies wins?'

'Oh surely, you are not that naïve', *the Bishop* countered, re-engaging.

'Politics is not about the best guy winning', he snapped a little impatiently; 'it's not about dignity, honour and sincerity; there is no place in politics for such noble human qualities'.

'Today's politics is all about corporations deciding which candidate will do best job for them, take the best care of their interests'.

'It's not democratic; there is no real democratic process; the voters are just pawns manipulated from above by those with the biggest publicity campaign, who in turn are financed by those bigger corporations', *the Bishop* fumed.

'I have to say that you are being very irreverent with your hosts', Evie interrupted; 'After all, we are in New York here'.

'Oh believe me', *the Bishop* sighed with audible irritation, 'as I told Madison before, UK politicians are no better; they have all got their snouts in the trough too, as we say in England; in fact they are currently doing everything they can to pass a law, desperate as they are to prevent the British taxpayers from finding out what they earn and what they claim in expenses - but it's the US that goes around the world handing out lessons on how people should run their affairs when the example they set at home is far from perfect…and *that* makes them hypocrites and an easy target to criticise', he explained logically.

The food arrived at that point, cutting short *the Bishop's* oratory and everyone breathed a sigh of relief as the rest of the evening took on a more convivial tone.

Next day;

The presentation wasn't until noon and so, having spent the night with Gary...*in his room, in order to avoid a repeat of Madison's comments the previous day*...and enjoyed a rather eventful breakfast in bed with him, Evie just about had the time to race down to her room to get showered and changed before they were all due to reconvene again downstairs at eleven.

She did this in record time...and just as she was coming back out of her room spruced up and ready for the day ahead, who should come wandering nonchalantly along the corridor...looking like a lost dog...but Gary, who was clearly anxious to join up with her once again.

He stopped in front of her...and she gave him a discreet little peck on the cheek as she brushed down her dress, looking for the customary compliment that women expect from a man in this situation...but alas, Gary didn't pick up on the subtlety of her body language...as his attention was being drawn away in that instant by a group of uniformed air-hostesses who were making their way down the other side of the plush corridor towards the lifts.

Disappointed...and curious to see what was distracting him, Evie quickly pivoted on one heel and on seeing the group of young women she could not help but roll her eyes in exasperation as she turned again and knocked on Madison's door, expecting to walk straight in.

Strangely though, there was no answer.

She tried again, pushing the door-handle but the door was clearly locked...

...then she looked at Gary and almost simultaneously, they had the same thought; that Madison was probably already downstairs with *the Bishop* checking over some last-minute details before the event.

They waited a few moments and Evie knocked once more, a little louder this time, just to make sure that her friend hadn't simply overslept... or not realised the time, even though she knew viscerally that that scenario was highly unlikely.

Still, there was no answer, so with that Evie decided that the best thing to do would be for them to go down to reception and wait for Madison or *the Bishop* to find them as they had arranged.

'That's sweet with me', Gary agreed on hearing Evie's suggestion.

Evie smirked at his Aussie brogue and as she turned a half-circle and walked off in the direction of the lifts following the air-hostesses, a dubious smile curled in the corners of her mouth and stars twinkled in the pupils of her eyes.

Gary stood for a moment and watched her walking away from him… enjoying the view of her rolling hips…but then just as he was about to catch up with her, Evie suddenly stopped as she reached the end of the corridor, before turning the corner where the lifts were situated.

The young Aussie stopped too, thinking that Evie had probably forgotten something in her room, but to his great surprise, instead of turning around, she simply reached behind her and discreetly lifted up the hem of her short black, crochet-dress…rather coquettishly…to show him that she was not wearing any underwear.

'I did not expect to be staying in town this long', she lied cheekily pursuing her mischievous conduct; the wink in her eye, promising him a fun-filled morning.

Gary was gob-smacked and his jaw almost hit the floor but his embarrassment was pretty short-lived as almost immediately they were joined by several other guests who were also on their way down to reception; their presence forcing the young Aussie to contain his emotions.

One of the other guests pressed the call-button and for an awkward moment the group waited patiently in silence, acknowledging each other only with polite smiles or brief nods of the head.

A few moments later, the light above the lift doors lit up and the doors suddenly parted in front of them.

The men invited the women to step inside – *it was all very formal for some reason* – and they followed on behind, shuffling in carefully beside their respective partners.

The cabin was rather crowded as there were already three people in there from the floors above, but during the brief ride down, among the polite coughing and throat clearing, Evie managed to catch Gary's eye with a couple of smouldering looks, revelling triumphantly - albeit in silence - at his stunned reaction to the surprise that she had just revealed to him.

Gary looked at her then looked away again until moments later, the lift landed at ground level.

The doors opened and Evie was one of the first to move, stepping out confidently into the bustling lobby where Gary joined her, seconds later, his mind scrambled with a myriad of raunchy scenarios.

Unfortunately though, all those naughty cameos would have to be put on hold for a while, as coming out of the lift they walked straight into the waiting arms of Madison and *the Bishop* who promptly turned them around and marched them back into the lift and up to the roof-top restaurant where Madison had organised another impromptu interview.

The Bishop was interviewed first, and while he was enthralling the reporter, and the camera, with his usual charm, Madison stood to the side of him, just out of the camera's angle, fielding a number of other questions about the impending exhibition match via her mobile phone which was ringing incessantly with queries about the event.

Meanwhile, spying an opportunity to be alone for a couple of minutes, Gary and Evie wandered out onto the roof-top terrace while he waited for his turn in the spotlight, and as they stood there side-by-side like a couple of love-struck tourists looking out over the Hudson, the young Aussie's hand slowly slid down, very discreetly over the curves of Evie's derriere.

'I like your…audacity', he whispered softly in her ear, enjoying the thrill of public intimacy.

Evie smiled back at him politely - as if butter wouldn't melt in her mouth - but before she could speak, one of the camera crew interrupted them, calling for Gary to follow her back inside.

The young Aussie was introduced to the reporter and while he was answering the usual set of questions, about himself, his background and the reasons he had chosen to take up the game of chess, Evie noticed *the Bishop* on the other side of the room helping himself to another glass of orange juice…and decided to take advantage of the opportunity to sidle up next to Madison and thank her.

'Thank me; why?' Madison asked with a puzzled look.

'Well', Evie explained naughtily, cupping her hand over her mouth; '…

because Mr Grumpy over there gave Gary some lessons in the finer art of seduction, and ever since he has become a lot more adventurous'.

'He did?' Madison queried.

'He did…and his previous awkwardness has given way to new more confident approach', Evie disclosed contentedly.

Madison looked at her friend a little confused, her head too full of organisational imperatives to be worried about the details of her relationship with Gary.

'Yeah…he even taught him all about going 'down-town'', Evie whispered with a discreet hand gesture.

'Eew; too much information E', Madison remarked, recoiling slightly, taken aback as she was by the idea that *the Bishop* of all people had been giving Gary coaching lessons in the art of bedroom gymnastics.

The interviews were wrapped up and from there, they moved on to the presentation at the exhibition centre, igniting considerable public hysteria in the process, and an hour or so later, once Gary had fulfilled all his commitments, Evie asked Madison if it was okay for her to take Gary off for a couple of hours.

'I could do with a little distraction so I am going to treat him to a tour of Yankee Stadium', she murmured, taking out a new digital camera that she had brought along.

'…in fact, while we are all here, maybe I could get a couple of shots of you guys', she suddenly piped up; 'everybody else is doing it', she confirmed looking around at the prevalence of cameras and mobile phones.

Madison was about to dissuade her, but before she knew it she was wedged in between *the Bishop* and Gary…and Evie was snapping the three of them from all angles.

She then went on to capture *the Bishop* and Gary randomly several more times, before finally putting her camera away and signalling to her new 'partner' that, if he was ready, then they had the green light to leave.

Gary looked at Madison for confirmation that this was the case and the latter…having checked her schedule one last time…quietly dismissed them with a friendly wave.

'Just try to stay out of trouble', she remarked, looking at the pair with a knowing smile.

'Awesome Mad…Madison', Gary replied.

'Where the fun in that?' Evie mocked as she turned and started for the exit.

'See you back at the hotel', Madison called after them.

Evie raised a hand in acknowledgment but she didn't turn back around.

'Congratulations', *the Bishop* announced as he re-joined Madison after yet another photo-op, catching her off guard.

'Don't speak too soon', she warned; 'it's not all over until the Fat Lady sings'.

'No, no; I don't mean all this', *the Bishop* countered, 'I mean that…' he added gesturing with his head to the lifts where Evie and Gary were waiting impatiently for the cabin to arrive.

'That was a fine piece of psychology', he announced.

Madison's brow furrowed momentarily.

'You killed two birds with one stone', *the Bishop* summarised filling in for her hesitation.

'I'm sorry', Madison queried still unsure as to what he was on about.

'We both win', *the Bishop* stated without malice.

'First, you suggest that Gary accompanies me on this trip - which has so far proved to be a great success; the media already loves him and I'm sure that in the not too distant future those that run the game of chess will learn to appreciate him too, thus benefiting the game and all those involved in it'.

'…and then of course', he paused, glancing in the direction of the lift; 'your friend Evie seems to be enjoying herself too'.

Madison nodded in agreement.

'Yeah, I suppose so', she concurred, busying herself by writing another useless note to herself on her file to avoid looking at him.

In reality, she had been hoping for something a little more personal in *the Bishop's* reasoning but evidently it wasn't to be, and although she was getting used to his non-committal manner Madison was nevertheless disappointed that he always seemed to deliberately avoid even the slightest allusion to the fact that they had spent that one glorious night together.

Her mind was in turmoil.

She had so much going on in her head that she didn't know if she was coming or going but while she stood there, wrestling with her dilemma over the past and her desires for the future, her focus was suddenly brought back to the present by the raucous sounds of Evie and Gary joyously belly-laughing at each other as they disappeared together into the lift.

That image annoyed her more than she cared to admit and she was still digesting her frustration when one of the other organisers came up to her with a few more questions about the timing of the event.

He shook hands with *the Bishop* and while he and Madison began cross-checking their schedules, *the Bishop* leaned in and discreetly whispered in her ear, without interrupting her, but with a small note of admiration in his voice and a fleeting but sincere smile on his lips, that while she was tying up the loose ends, he would make his own way back to the hotel.

CHAPTER FIFTEEN

Having finally been left to their own devices, Evie and Gary were delighted to get away from the false sophistication surrounding the exhibition centre.

The match was really being marketed like a corporate event and much as they both wanted it to succeed for Madison's sake, neither really felt comfortable in that kind of environment.

Instead, they jumped into a cab and just a short taxi-ride later, the incongruous couple found themselves standing proudly in front of the Yankee Stadium where, having negotiated the bogus photographers preying on the blissfully unaware tourists, they quickly joined the expectant crowd of people waiting to visit what is known as one of the most iconic and recognisable of sporting grounds the world over.

Gary was stoked…and as they stood in line waiting impatiently for their turn to be called forward to the cashier's booth, he was almost pinching himself to make sure that what his eyes were seeing all around him was indeed reality.

Evie meanwhile stood by his side watching him carefully, sensing his growing enthusiasm, but while she was a keen fan herself, she was a typically smug New Yorker, blasé and unfazed by anything that life could throw at her…or at least that was how it appeared on the outside.

'Why does coming here mean so much to you?' she asked nonchalantly, commenting on Gary's adrenaline-fuelled demeanour, for no other reason really than to fill in time; '…after all, it's just a stadium', she declared dismissively, toying mischievously with his mind.

Gary looked at her in disbelief, falling for her wind-up; 'Don't you understand?, this is the Holy Grail for a sportsman; to play here, to step out onto that hallowed turf in this magnificent stadium is the pinnacle of any player's career…it would be like, like playing in the Grand-Final at The G for an Australian', he announced, drawing a parallel from his own culture.

'The G', Evie queried.

'Yeah, the G', Gary confirmed; 'the Melbourne Cricket Ground, it's our Yankee Stadium; the place where dreams come true'.

Evie smiled and nodded her head briefly in understanding, just as the uniformed security guard unclipped the barrier in front of them and waved them forward.

Gary paid for the tickets and as they made their way inside, he stopped to pick up a souvenir magazine from the young man hawking them next to the cashier's booth for ten dollars.

'That's what I call enterprise', he commented as he caught up with Evie; 'that young guy can't be more than twelve and he's already got the world sussed'.

A little further on they met up with the guide who was going to show them around…and while they waited for the rest of the group to form around them, Evie took out her camera and took a few photos of Gary's beaming self-satisfied smile, until the guide eventually raised his hand, hushing the excited flock and signalling the start of the tour.

The tour lasted just over an hour during which time Evie took endless photographs of Gary, in all sorts of poses, in the locker rooms, in the club-house and next to the field…and when it finally came to an end…though it was still too soon for both Gary and several other die-hard fans in the small group of starry-eyed visitors…the tour-guide purposely led them to a meeting point in front of the stadium's merchandise store and coffee-shop, where he shared one last anecdote with them before inviting those who wished to do so, to go in and browse, while indicating the exit route to those who preferred to opt out of the loaded invitation.

Unsurprisingly, still wrapped up in the magic of the experience Evie and Gary took the first option and joined the majority of the group heading towards the souvenir and merchandising store, where after a brief look around, they decided to stay for a coffee.

Ten minutes later;

Sat at one of the tables in front of two rather large lattes, Evie asked Gary for his considered opinion on the tour.

The young Aussie sat back and paused rubbing his chin in reflection.

'Well…I have to admit that I found the whole thing really fascinating; the new stadium is magnificent', he declared with false enthusiasm; '… but I have to say that while I was very impressed by much of the set-up, I would really have liked to experience the aura and the mystique of the house that Ruth built', he concluded with more than a hint of disgruntled disappointment.

'Oh, you mean the original Yankee stadium next door', Evie sympathised.

'Yeah, now that would have been sweet', Gary lamented.

A pregnant pause followed as Evie's mobile phone rang and Gary turned his attention to his latte…but when she had finished her conversation, the young Aussie decided to restart the conversation by lightening the mood and explaining the 'Tim-Tam suck' to his unsuspecting companion; (the 'Tim-Tam' is a type of cookie).

'The Tim-Tam suck; what the hell is the Tim-Tam suck?' Evie enquired with a hint of dread, wondering anxiously about the connotation and innuendo of such a strange gesture.

'Well', Gary continued, picking up a cookie; 'The Tim-Tam suck is the way we Australians eat Tim-Tams', he explained.

'First, you have to bite off the opposing corners', he demonstrated with great dexterity; '… then, you dip the biscuit into your tea or coffee…and then you suck the tea or the coffee-soaked filling out of the biscuit like it were a straw'.

'Eew; that's gross', Evie scoffed, appalled…and ignoring Gary's triumphant hand-slapping which drew a few disapproving looks from the other customers, she quickly moved on, asking him more about Australia, never having been there herself.

'So, other than the Tim-Tam suck, what else do you Aussies have to show us?' she enquired with a rather ambiguous smirk.

Gary could see that Evie hadn't been impressed with his attempt at caricature-comedy so rather than come out with yet another boorish joke he decided to show off his cultural knowledge by explaining to her all about a little town in South Australia called Coober Pedy.

'Coober Pedy is the most extraordinary place you'll ever see', he confirmed.

'Oh yeah, and why is that?' Evie questioned in typical, unimpressed New York fashion.

'Well', Gary continued; 'Coober Pedy is considered to be the opal capital of the world and here's the incredible part', he insisted building up her expectation.

'It is only a small town but seventy per cent of the population lives underground in converted opal mines', he announced.

'Are you serious?' Evie asked, expecting some kind of punch line to follow.

'Deadly serious', Gary assured her; 'it's amazing, they have taken the excavated mines and turned them into four-bedroom homes, shops and hotels, all underground', he confirmed.

'Wow, is that so; now that is interesting', Evie replied finally showing a hint of admiration.

Gary was pleased with himself; at last he had managed to astound Evie's blasé New York attitude…but then, just as he was congratulating himself on his success he spoiled it all by telling Evie all about the Gaslight music shop in Melbourne where they have an Annual Nude Day, during which patrons strip off and get free CD's and a free buffet served by naked waiters and waitresses while a naked pianist entertains them.

'Eew, now that sounds even more gross', Evie remarked, screwing up her nose.

'Yeah, I suppose you're right', Gary agreed, 'but that's Australia for you', he concluded unapologetically.

Another of the couples from their group brushed by their table at that moment and once Gary had exchanged polite nods with them, he began explaining to Evie how the guy, with whom he had struck up a conversation during the tour, had been saving up for ten years for this trip and how his wife had almost divorced him on three occasions because of his obsession with the Yankees.

Unfortunately though, Evie was only half-listening to his commentary as her mind had suddenly wandered elsewhere.

She was a little disappointed that the visit had not been as memorable for Gary as he had expected and while he was rambling on about that other couple's life history, she was naughtily elaborating a plan in her mind which would top any guided-tour and render their visit unforgettable for a whole other reason.

Discreetly, she took out a pen and a pad and began scribbling a little note to him; then when she had finished writing; she turned the piece of paper over and covering it with her hand, she pushed it slowly across the table.

Gary picked it up and read it studiously.

'I'm horny; I want you', he read, moving just his lips and looking at her with a stunned expression.

'Is this another wind up?' he asked inquisitively.

Evie shook her head, the sparkle in her eyes relaying her response.

Gary couldn't believe what was happening to him; he'd never had so much action in his life.

'Okay, I'll just finish my coffee and we'll be right', he stated boldly, pocketing the little note simultaneously.

'Forget the coffee…' Evie insisted getting up and holding out a hand in encouragement.

Right on cue, Gary did just that, pushing his cup away and getting up in turn to follow her out.

Once outside the coffee-shop, though still within the confines of the stadium, Evie spotted the entrance to the underground car-park and seeing that the guard there was distracted by some other tourists, she pulled Gary behind her and they managed to duck into the concrete structure away from prying eyes.

The car-park was a little deserted and smelled of fresh paint but enjoying the illicit nature of the moment, they quickly found a quiet corner where they could give free reign to their desires...Gary, trying desperately to quench his new friend's surging libido level with his moderate talents, over the bonnet of a gorgeous blue Cadillac that just happened to be parked there, while remembering *the Bishop's* pertinent advice that 'if a woman makes the first move, then there is no need for foreplay'.

Twenty minutes or so later, they re-emerged from the shadows of the car-park's imposing architecture, Gary with a beaming grin on his face... and Evie looking happy, if a little flushed.

Later...

When they got back to the hotel, Evie went straight to her room, telling Gary to go to his...and get showered...and changed...for what she assumed would be another group dinner organised with military precision by her bff.

She then took a long shower herself and having re-applied her make-up, she slipped on a little 50's-style Tea-dress and popped next door to Madison's room, to find out what the plans were for that evening's entertainment.

She was buzzing after her afternoon spent with Gary but much to her dismay she found her friend completely embroiled in contingencies and last-minute organisational details for the exhibition match the next day... and in no mood to socialise.

Nevertheless, despite her busy demeanour Madison did notice the barely-disguised grin on Evie's face as she sat down on the bed opposite her, and knew instinctively that she had a confession to make.

'Have you guys been misbehaving again?' she asked curiously.

Evie blushed and looked away, but then recovering her composure she could not help but gush about the day she had spent with Gary and most importantly their cameo performance on the bonnet of some guy's car in the parking lot at Yankee Stadium.

'Whatever possessed you?' Madison protested, turning back to her files to cover her own embarrassment.

'Oh, it was just one of those spur of the moment things', Evie explained; 'Gary was a little dis....'

'Whoa, spare me the colourful details', Madison interrupted holding up her hand defensively.

'Aw, Maddy, you are such a prude at times', Evie commented, standing up and checking her hair in the mirror.

'Anyhow, what about you and 'TB'; how is that going?' she enquired casually.

Madison paused, flicking her pen repeatedly.

'I don't know', she replied sullenly; 'that time in England, we were like poetry in motion but ever since...well, I just don't know'.

'Maybe he doesn't find me that attractive', she grumbled uncharacteristically.

'Hey girl', Evie countered, 'attraction is all about personality and chemistry; heck, I should know; look at me and Crocodile Dundee'.

Madison smiled stiffly.

'Yes, you've got a point there', she said satirically, 'but relationships need more than just chemistry to work, they need exchange, they need kindness and laughter...and sharing'.

'Well, you two definitely have chemistry; ...believe me; I can sense it', Evie declared trying to boost her friend's sagging morale.

'I know; I can feel it too', Madison agreed; 'the guy's magnetism is irresistible but I just can't get close to him; he doesn't really socialise, he doesn't dance, he doesn't show any affection...never mind cuddling, apart from that one time – so what does define a relationship?'

'I mean, we go through life forging friendships and alliances, but to what end?' she lamented.

'Are we all just using each other to blot out the fact that one day we are all going to die?'

'Oh, cheer up and don't be so pessimistic, hon', Evie chided.

Madison looked at her friend in the mirror; 'there's plenty more fish in the sea, right', she reasoned.

'That's right girl, so get yourself out of that chair and let's go eat', Evie chanted.

'I can't; not tonight; I've got all this stuff to go through...and anyhow

TB has isolated himself in his room for the evening to prepare for tomorrow, so we won't be eating out tonight', Madison confirmed.

'In that case, are you sure I can't tempt you to join us?' Evie insisted.

'No thanks hon, I'll just order something from room-service later', Madison replied picking up her file again.

'By the way; cute dress', she remarked.

'You like it; I'm having a retro-moment', Evie replied…smiling sweetly before she turned to leave.

'I do', Madison replied, smiling graciously and with that Evie opened the door and was gone.

Evie was disappointed to see her friend so down, so once she was back in the corridor she took a moment and decided to try and fix the problem.

She made her way upstairs to *the Bishop's* room, hoping to persuade him to join them for dinner, if nothing else, but when she got there, much to her annoyance, the 'do not disturb' sign was clearly in evidence on the door handle…and try as she might, she just couldn't bring herself to knock, unprepared as she was to deal with *the Bishop's* potential outrage at having his concentration rituals interrupted.

So, admitting defeat and mouthing the words 'I'm sorry Maddy' to herself, she quietly tip-toed away from *the Bishop's* door and down the corridor to Gary's room where the young Aussie was all ready and waiting for another New York experience.

She explained the situation…and two minutes later, the incongruous couple were once again in the lift, making their way back downstairs.

Evie wasn't quite sure where to take Gary. She usually hung out in the Singles bars on 3rd Avenue but tonight, because the onus had fallen on her to provide the entertainment as it were - not that she was complaining - she decided to take her new 'plus one' to the Harley Davidson Café at 1370 Avenue of the Americas.

Of course, Gary was delighted with her choice as he had always wanted to visit one of these branded watering-holes but his excitement soon turned to disappointment once again when on entering the place he did not see a single one of the stereotypical leather-clad biker-types sat at the bar.

Still, they took up residence on adjoining stools and once they had settled in and relaxed into the mood, they began chatting more freely.

Their meals were served and almost immediately Gary raised his glass to Madison and *the Bishop*, thanking them both for giving him the opportunity to meet Evie who did the same.

'You know what I like about you', Gary announced as he prepared to tuck in to his Fat-boy steak.

Evie shrugged, fearing the worst.

'What I like about you Evie Finch is your confidence', he continued without waiting for her input.

'I liked that from the moment you came and joined me on the dance-floor the other night; that took some guts', declared the young Aussie.

Evie looked at him, a little confused…and seeing her puzzled expression Gary explained his propos.

'I mean it took some guts for you to dance with someone like me', he affirmed self-deprecatingly. 'I mean; you saw me dance'.

'What can I say; I'm the kind of girl who likes to take a risk now and again', Evie intimated in reply.

'Oh, I know that', Gary scoffed, turning to face her wide-eyed, making an allusion to their earlier exertions at the baseball stadium.

'…and as I said, that's what I like about you, your self-confidence', he insisted kindly.

Evie enjoyed the compliment and as she thought about what he had said, she suddenly realised that there was probably more depth to this young stranger than she had given him credit for.

'I like a confident woman', Gary continued, 'who is prepared to go out there and take risks, someone who is not afraid of her sexuality…'

Evie stopped chewing and braced herself, wondering where he was going with his thoughts, but Gary saw her reaction and quickly reassured her.

'Nah, all I'm saying is that I'd rather be with someone like you than with someone like….oh, I can't remember her name right now, off the top of my head…but anyway', he continued, '…we have a rather staid TV presenter, back home in Australia who must be all of 35 or 40 years old, and the poor woman always gets so embarrassed and coy whenever she has to read out anything that might contain the slightest sexual reference…'

Evie frowned.

'Even an unintentional metaphor or innuendo', Gary continued; '…and whenever her colleague makes a comment on the subject, she immediately dismisses it with a mandatory 'let's not go there', hiding her blushes behind a convenient sheet of paper and moving on to the next report'.

'How sad is that, do you reckon, to be 40 and still so bashfully naïve?' Gary asked.

Evie didn't comment, defending the sisterhood. *(Women rarely like to criticise other women in front of men)*

'On the other hand', Gary piped up more cheerfully; 'we do have another presenter, Sandra Sully, and she's a right 'corker', so I suppose these things balance out', he judged objectively.

Again, Evie didn't comment, deciding that Gary's awkward, puerile and slightly misogynous remarks were best ignored.

The rest of the meal went off without incident and a while later Gary and Evie were back in the hotel bar having one last drink.

It had been a long and eventful day and as they sat there, enjoying the relaxing surroundings and the comfort of the hotel's amenities Evie suddenly remembered that she owed it all to Madison, a thought which prompted her - without thinking of the advanced hour - to ring her friend in her room and ask her to join them.

Her mobile-phone was out of battery so she got up and walked over to the bar, where in reply to her request, the barman instantly directed her, with the greatest of deference, to a telephone on the wall.

Evie nodded politely to show her gratitude to the young man, and then gliding to the end of the bar, she picked up the receiver and rang Madison's room, waiting for several rings before her friend answered.

'Hi M; we're down in the bar; do you want to come down and join us...?' Evie asked.

'No…I'm good', Madison replied.

'Aw come on Mad; just for a night-cap', Evie insisted…but despite several further attempts to sweet-talk her into coming down, Madison politely refused the temptation, explaining that she had had to work all evening and that because it was so important to her career, she would rather keep a clear head and get a good night's rest before the big day.

Evie understood and rather than insist beyond the point of nuisance, she ended the conversation with a gentle word of encouragement for the success of her friend's event, before returning to her seat, having ordered another round of drinks from the young barman, which she and Gary then quickly polished off, before retiring, each to their own respective rooms for the night.

♗

Next day, the exhibition match was a resounding success and as *the Bishop* was glad-handing just about everybody...showing great diligence and professional conscience...and Gary was being snapped by yet another gaggle of photographers, people were already beginning to disperse when all of a sudden Amanda...dressed immaculately, as usual, with not a hair out of place...appeared in their midst talking to the photographer she had booked to cover the event.

Naturally Madison spotted her from afar...and having dealt with yet another enthused spectator...she immediately made her way over to where her boss was standing, greeting her in her customary polite manner.

'Amanda...I didn't think you would be coming today', she remarked, watching intently for her boss's reaction.

'I wasn't going to...' Amanda explained, her eyes scanning the room inquisitively, 'but I was in the area so I thought that I might as well look in and see how things were going'.

In fact, Amanda had arrived unannounced half-way through the game and had watched the last few moves of the match on a monitor, out of sight.

'...and I have to say', she continued, 'I found the whole experience... unexpectedly gripping'.

Madison was delighted. She knew that a good report from her boss would go a long way to smoothing out any remaining wrinkles to her reputation around the office.

'Now then Madison', Amanda suddenly announced as the photographer who was with her pointed out *the Bishop*; 'I think it's time you introduced me to this Mr Byron character'.

'Of course, right this way...', Madison responded, raising her arm... but before the two women could move, Amanda's photographer-friend and a couple of his professional cohorts asked them if they would mind posing for a photo or two, just the two of them.

Astonishingly, Amanda...*who was not one for self-promotion*...agreed to his request, albeit a little grudgingly, but as she stood next to her boss Madison could not help but notice that the top two buttons of her blouse had come undone.

This was most unlike Amanda...who was normally the consummate professional in these kinds of situations...and so believing it to be a mistake - between photos - Madison discreetly pointed out the wardrobe malfunction to her boss, thinking that she would probably want to correct it before any more were taken and she was introduced to the man of the moment...but inexplicably and quite contrary to her usual nature, Amanda just waved away her junior's concerns, surprising the latter with a smile that let her know that she knew exactly what she was doing.

The photographers finished up...and as Madison dealt with yet another request, this time concerning the dismantling of the podium that had been constructed for the event, Amanda began making her way over to where *the Bishop* was standing...parrying the demands...for answers to their questions from a group of sycophantic media people who were trailing in her wake...with her usual disdain.

Madison watched her boss go, admiring the sharp lines of her perfectly-cut designer jacket, but as she stood there with the technical director, subliminally pondering which collection it was from, the penny suddenly dropped and her boss's intentions became clear; Amanda was obviously working on her own agenda as far as *the Bishop* was concerned.

Swallowing hard, Madison couldn't believe what she was seeing, but while she was undoubtedly upset at her boss's blatantly provocative behaviour, she also knew that she didn't really have any reason or grounds to be jealous of her...because despite having had numerous opportunities to do so, the Bishop had never once mentioned the night that they had spent together, nor made any hint that he would like a repeat performance in all the time he had been back in New York.

Of course she was disappointed, but Madison realised that any show of petulance on her part, any womanly display of territorial demarcation, in these circumstances would probably be seen by those present as highly inappropriate, not to mention catastrophically detrimental to her career prospects, especially with her boss playing the role of the other woman.

It was a perplexing dichotomy…but because of her position she could not reveal her inner turmoil…in this context…to the outside world, and so, masking her deception and maintaining her professional demeanour through gritted teeth, she rushed over to join her boss, catching up with her just as they both reached the spot where *the Bishop* was engrossed in a tactical conversation with the amateur player he had just beaten in the exhibition match.

She almost slipped in her heels as she came to an abrupt halt but Madison immediately turned on the charm, tactfully interrupting the guys' conversation, before turning to her boss and introducing them all to each other.

The two men smiled politely and while all three of them were shaking hands and exchanging social courtesies, Evie suddenly appeared behind Madison, tapping her on the shoulder.

'Do you need Gary to stick around for anything else, hon?' she asked, 'because if not, we're going to head out. Gary wants to go for pancakes', Evie whispered, shaking her head and rolling her eyes in false irritation.

'Pancakes?' Madison repeated, '…really?'

'Aha', Eve confirmed looking a little awkward.

'Is that what were calling it now', Madison whispered, '…is that some kind of metaphor…?'

'Hey, a girl's gotta eat', Evie retorted with an impish smile.

Madison stepped back and after pausing momentarily, she cunningly tried to introduce Gary to Amanda…in the hope that it would distract her attention away from *the Bishop*…but the withering look on her boss's face and her ensuing disregard for the young Australian after only the briefest of glances in his direction, served only to confirm Madison's suspicions that on this occasion, no question, her boss's intentions were more personal than professional as far as *the Bishop* was concerned; she was certainly *not* interested in the future of chess.

A little demoralized, but still maintaining her professional demeanour as another group of media people came over to congratulate her on the organisation of the event, Madison confirmed to Evie that Gary was free to leave…and moments later she waved them both goodbye with a brief 'see you later'.

She then turned back to introduce these new people to Amanda, hoping that their compliments about her wonderful organisation of the event would also register in her boss's memory, but as she did so, she realised that Amanda and *the Bishop* were no longer there.

Momentarily caught off guard, she quickly apologised to the group of well-wishers and began looking around the room; urgently scanning every nook and cranny like a jealous lover, until she finally spotted her quarry in a quiet corner where they were apparently deep in discussion.

Her blood beginning to boil, Madison immediately made her way over to join them but just as she reached them, Amanda was already getting ready to leave having complimented *the Bishop* once again on his talented performance; *as ever, she had another appointment to get to and couldn't stay any longer.*

Relieved, Madison bit her tongue and thanked her boss…with her best passive-aggressive smile…for at least taking the time out of her busy schedule to come down and run her eye over the fruit of her endeavours.

Amanda stopped in her tracks and looked Madison directly in the eyes; her stony smile, as hard as diamonds. 'I wouldn't have missed it for the world', she announced with her usual patronising self-confidence, her gaze slipping back to *the Bishop*, before she headed off.

Little did anyone know but Todd was at the event too, on his own little sabotage mission, still trying to work an angle, still trying to discredit Madison.

In fact, he even caught Madison's eye at one point, to let her know that he was there…but there was no direct contact between them.

That said; he tried everything he could during the event to get close to *the Bishop*, to try to get a comment from him or to engage him in a brief exchange that he could ultimately turn to his advantage, but alas, he was unsuccessful every time.

Nevertheless, still hoping for something he could use to paint Madison in a bad light to their employers, he did manage to get a word with Gary to ask him if there was anything that could have been organised better in his opinion…but sadly, Gary just gave him a glowing report of Madison's organisational skills and her all-round professionalism.

At this rate, I'm just going to have to make something up, Todd thought to himself as he slinked back out of the building.

At that moment, *the Bishop* was assailed by the group that had followed in Madison's slipstream and while he seemed to be enjoying the attention, a few minutes later he managed to get the message through to Madison that whenever she could arrange it, he would be more than ready to go back to the hotel.

Madison took the hint, called the car around and within minutes *the Bishop* was being ushered out of the hectic exhibition room and into the calm haven of an air-conditioned limousine.

'Aren't you joining me?' he asked, breathing a sigh of relief as he settled onto the back seat.

'No'; Madison replied a little curtly, a slight tremor in her voice. 'I've still got things to sort out here'.

The door closed and seconds later the car pulled away.

'Damn', she heard herself say out loud as she stood there on the sidewalk and watched the car disappear into the traffic.

That man had tested her emotional resilience to the limit…and she had had enough of the waiting…and the anticipation…and the frustration which had been whipping her mind into a frenzy for the past couple of months.

Not only that, she was tired of his non-committal attitude towards her and his evasive, if not hollow replies whenever she tried to get close to him.

It was all getting too much for her…and now, now that she felt that she had finally made a connection with him, by proving her worth, proving what she was capable of doing, by successfully organising this event which she had only agreed to be involved with because of him, it would appear that she was now going to have to contend with her boss as a potential love-rival.

'That isn't going to happen'; Madison decided in her own mind, because now that she had fulfilled her professional role, the way was clear for her to confront *the Bishop* on a more personal level in order to find out, one way or the other, if he wanted to pursue a relationship…or a friendship…or whatever it was that they had…together.

Only then would she know where she stood and only then would she be able to move on with her life – and she would do that as soon as she got back to the hotel, she resolved; she would strike while the iron was hot and while the adrenaline was still pumping through her veins.

At that point, she looked up and the skies above her head seemed to clear spontaneously as if nature itself was suddenly in harmony with her thinking.

This metaphorical sign from above…of impending clarity…was an inspiring moment and it instantly galvanised Madison in her determination to resolve her issues with *the Bishop*…while the accompanying breeze on her cheeks provoked a self-satisfied smile on her lips as she closed her eyes and revelled in the intake of a few deep lungfuls of revitalising but chilly New York air.

She stood there for a while longer, pleased with her decision, and after another few moments of secret reflection, Madison composed herself once again, before turning and going back into the exhibition centre to oversee the clear-up…and tie up all the loose ends with her fellow organisers.

Meanwhile, *the Bishop* had made his way back to the hotel and having showered to relax himself after the rigours of the day, he immediately began the long and tedious job of packing his suitcases; a chore which he always loathed but one that he was quite pleased to undertake on this occasion as he was desperate to get back home to the peace and quiet of the Abbey and his solitary existence.

He carefully emptied the drawers, filling the bottom of his suitcase making sure that everything was placed just so, and then satisfied that he had everything, he turned his attention to the wardrobe, opening the doors to their fullest.

The rail inside was full but despite the boring aspect of the task ahead, *the Bishop* was still in quite a good mood.

He had thought about it on the ride back from the exhibition centre and overall he was pleased with the results of his…and Gary's…trip to New York.

He felt that things had gone well; that he had fulfilled his commitment to the game he loved and to his supporters back home, and that by introducing Gary as his potential successor, he had also passed the baton on, as it were, to the next generation.

Yes, he was pleased with himself, but his self-congratulation was suddenly interrupted by a knock on the door, bringing him instantly back to reality.

He stopped what he was doing and without considering his attire, he casually sauntered across the room in his white towelling robe to answer the knock, expecting to find one of the maids or a room-service employee outside his door, delivering yet another bouquet of flowers or maybe a small gift from one of his many admirers.

However, this time he was wrong.

This time, it was Madison who was standing there; she had finished up at the exhibition centre and had come to confront him about what had been said between him and her boss, Amanda…and about his role as Gary's new unofficial mentor.

'Wow; you girls really do tell each other everything, don't you?' he commented dryly.

'Well, that's because whenever I have a question about the incomprehensible behaviour of a member of the opposite sex, I can always rely on Evie for an honest opinion and vice-versa', Madison replied, walking in without being invited.

'Very well then', *the Bishop* declared as he returned to his packing, 'if you must know, your boss was simply asking me if I had been taken care of during this trip; if there was anything that could have been changed or that I would have done differently…and I told her, no'.

'As for Gary; he needed a little manly advice so I gave it to him; it's no big deal', *the Bishop* explained with his usual direct, no-nonsense tone.

Madison looked at him in mock surprise but didn't speak; then she noticed his open suitcase and her heart fell, though she tried hard not to let it show.

The Bishop saw her expression and stopped what he was doing; he had been fighting with his emotions ever since he and Gary had arrived in New York, trying to work out his feelings towards Madison, but now as he was getting ready to leave, and she was standing there in his room, looking a little despondent, giving him one last chance to make a move, all the theoretical formulas and complex mathematical hypothesising that he had been tormenting himself with, seemed to suddenly resolve itself.

He put down the suit that he had just taken from the wardrobe and slowly walked over to where Madison was stood, just inside the doorway.

As he got closer she felt her body tighten in expectation and a shiver of anticipation run up her spine…and even though she would never admit it, she also felt her mid-section tingle with the thought of another moment of illicit pleasure.

'There is one thing that I might have changed', he said softly, without a hint of his usual obnoxious tone.

'Oh, and what's that?' Madison asked a little defensively suppressing her emotion, her eyes looking into his for longer than was strictly necessary.

The tension in the room was almost palpable.

'This'; he replied in a whisper…and with that, against all convention, he took her face in his hands and kissed her gently on the lips.

The spontaneous nature of his approach seemed a little out of character for TB but Madison wasn't complaining after he had made her wait so long before renewing the experience

All at once she wanted time to speed up and go as slow as possible… all at the same time.

The kiss took her by surprise but Madison succumbed gladly and as she closed her eyes to prolong the moment, *the Bishop* instantly pulled her towards him, spontaneously igniting the tacit desire they felt for each.

Madison responded by throwing her arms around his shoulders and returning his kiss with interest making it clear that she was on the same page.

The kiss was long and wet with open mouths and active tongues.

The Bishop then reached around behind her and Madison felt his hands run slowly down her back until they came to rest on her hips. He kissed her again…deeply…and she found herself melting against him, her legs going weak at the knees.

Eventually, they pulled away from each other to draw breath and *the Bishop* promptly dropped his hands onto the curve of her backside, where with a sudden jolt of ardour, he took instant possession of her derriere through the thin material of her skirt.

He looked into her eyes and held her like that for a moment before kissing her again more tenderly, after which he relinquished his hold.

Taken by surprise, Madison announced that she needed a moment and headed for the bathroom but even as she walked across the room she could still feel the heat from his hands where he had grabbed her.

'Hell yeah', she thought to herself as she closed the door behind her, brushing the back of her skirt.

Their first night together had been pretty magical and Madison couldn't wait for round two.

While she was in the bathroom *the Bishop* quietly secured the door against any further interruptions and when Madison came back out a few moments later, he whisked her into bed immediately…where they spent the next couple of hours having glorious, loud, exciting, exhausting and mutually satisfying sex, trying out just about every position that either of them could imagine.

It was the most memorable sex that Madison had ever had - even better than the evening that they had spent at the abbey - and after almost three hours, as the sweat dripped off her chin and onto *the Bishop's* rippling body beneath her, she implored the heavens above to never let it end…ever.

Madison was still feeling all warm and fuzzy inside and didn't want to move from *the Bishop's* snuggling embrace to go and shower…but all of a sudden she caught sight of the time on his watch on the night-stand and realised that she would have to, as Evie was bound to come a-knocking at her door to see what she had decided to wear for their final meal together.

She lifted herself onto her elbow and looked at *the Bishop* for a moment or two before jumping out of bed and leaving him still slumbering, his face glowing with pleasure and satisfaction.

She gathered her clothes together and quietly got dressed again making every effort not to wake him as she did so; and then, once she was ready to leave, she went over to the bed and shook *the Bishop's* arm gently, to remind him, with a half-whisper in his ear, that he would have to get up soon as it was nearly 6 p.m. and they were all supposed to be meeting down in the lobby at 7 p.m.

The Bishop mumbled an incoherence and raised a hand in acknowledgement before turning over and pulling up the covers as Madison slipped on her shoes and rushed downstairs to her room to shower and get changed in a desperate race against time.

It was touch and go, but she had just about managed to take a quick shower and wash her hair when the sound of Evie's familiar knock rapped against her door.

She wrapped a towel around herself and discreetly opened the door to her friend who was rather surprised to see her in such a state, and while she rushed back into the bathroom to dry her hair, Evie sat on the bed and gave her a running commentary on how she and Gary had filled their afternoon visiting the Guggenheim museum and how quite inadvertently, they had almost gotten caught by one of the security guards in 'flagrante delicto'.

Madison squealed in the bathroom; 'You did not; seriously', she cried out.

'Yeah, we did…I mean, we almost got caught…but we didn't', Evie confirmed, swinging her feet like a naughty schoolgirl.

'Why would you do that?' Madison called out, feeling a little embarrassed for her friend.

'Well, Mad', Evie explained; '... having sex in a bed, in the missionary position, might be the ideal context for some…in terms of comfort and security, but for me it lacks the audacity, the ingenuity and the spontaneity of basic sexual expression, of bodice-ripping passion'.

She paused for a second and then added; 'What can I say; I like innovation and an inventive mind'.

'So, anyway; blah…what have you been up to…?' Evie enquired, changing the subject intentionally; 'Did you get the chance to do anything else this afternoon?'

Madison popped her head around the bathroom door; she wanted to tell her friend everything; she wanted to tell her that her afternoon had been so immensely enjoyable that every fibre of her being was screaming at her to reveal her secret, but wisely, suspecting that *the Bishop* would rather she didn't, she bit her tongue, indeed she lied, telling Evie that the wrap had taken far longer than expected and that she had not long gotten back to the hotel.

Evie accepted Madison's explanation without question and then made a snide comment about Amanda along the lines that she hoped she knew what a great person she had working for her.

Madison didn't catch this as she re-emerged from the bathroom and grabbed some clean underwear - but to avoid any further questioning on the matter and to allay any suspicions that her friend might have, she quickly launched into the discussion as to what they were going to wear for their final dinner, pulling out several dresses from her wardrobe which, with Evie's help, she quickly narrowed down to one of three.

Evie then got up and left her friend to make the final call, returning to her room to get herself ready, before coming back thirty minutes or so later looking absolutely stunning in a beautiful peek-a-boo Versace dress which was gathered at the waist before flaring out into a coquettish hemline just above her knees that she had matched with a pair of sling-back ivory stilettos…and as a surprise for Gary, she had accessorised her look with a sexy black suspender belt and stockings.

Madison was still putting the final touches to her make-up when Evie came waltzing back in to her room.

'Damn girl, that dress is hot', Evie exclaimed; 'you're gonna have every guy in the place drooling all over you'.

Indeed, she looked resplendent in her beautiful blue-satin cocktail dress.

'I feel a little...conspicuous', Madison replied, looking into the mirror and sliding her hands through her golden blonde hair.

'Pfff, gimme a break', Evie retorted; 'you look stunning…and if Mr. Grumpy can't see that...'

She didn't finish her comment; just shook her head in feigned despair.

It was almost 7 p.m. and as she refused to be fashionably late, despite what her friend might say 'that it was a lady's prerogative to do just that', Madison quickly checked herself one last time in the mirror, before pushing Evie out the door and cajoling her towards the lift in a desperate attempt to be on time.

The lift doors opened into the lobby just as the clock struck seven and when the two women stepped out of the cabin, and approached the waiting men, they could see that both *the Bishop* and Gary were suitably impressed by their outfits, the expressions on their faces speaking louder than any words could have done.

Indeed, the women had both done themselves proud…and despite the fact that they had concurred beforehand, the dresses they had chosen were not too dissimilar, as…understandably…each of them wanted to leave a memorable psychological impression on their respective men.

That evening, Madison had decided that they would have their final meal together at the hotel's very own gastronomic restaurant, in order to thank the hotel and its staff for their hospitality and the service that they had provided to her and her guests over the duration of their stay.

It was a wonderful gesture and to mark his appreciation the restaurant manager sent over a bottle of champagne for them to savour as an aperitif, which they all thoroughly enjoyed, raising their glasses gladly in a toast of thanks both to him and to Madison, while wishing her every success in the future.

It was a very satisfying moment for Madison who revelled in the attention and the compliments that not only those at her table, but also those from other hotel guests were paying her - to the point where even a rival editor who was there dining with a client of her own raised her glass to her in a discreet show of professional appreciation for what she had done.

They then settled down to eat, and with the tension of the event behind them - which had been an unqualified success, if the number of text-messages Madison had received was anything to go by - the mood at the table soon relaxed as everyone tucked in hungrily to the gastronomic delights set out before them.

Silence followed for a moment but when the conversation started up again, it was quite light-hearted for a change; none of the usual philosophical lecturing or politically-inspired diatribes from *the Bishop*, just a succession of jocular anecdotes, mostly from Gary, about what they had all seen and done in New York over the last few days interspersed with some almost sensual remarks of appreciation for the hotel chef's undeniable culinary talents.

Part of the conversation…

At one point they were discussing confidence and the lack of self-confidence…when *the Bishop* happened to mention TV presenters and Gary immediately picked up on it saying that he and Evie had discussed something similar the day before…

'Yeah, we were only talking about the 'Coy Club' yesterday', Gary imparted.

'The what?' Madison asked prudently.

'The Coy Club', Gary explained, '…you know, all those...middle-aged, forty year old women who lack the self-confidence to discuss normal human behaviour…'

'My question is this', he continued, having taken another swallow of beer. 'Why are these women, these mature, intelligent women still so embarrassed about discussing natural human interaction? I mean, sex is not dirty, is it? It is not immoral; it is all part of the human experience and we wouldn't be here without it…so why the reticence?'

'Well, some wom…' Madison began.

'I just think those shrinking lilies need to chill a little; that's all I'm saying', Gary concluded interrupting Madison before she could finish. 'What do you guys think?' he enquired.

'Well of course it's true, religion and the unwarranted guilt it makes people feel about engaging in normal human activity has a lot to answer for', *the Bishop* agreed.

'It's violets by the way', Evie interposed, raising her glass to her lips.

Gary looked puzzled.

'It's shrinking violets…not shrinking lilies', she clarified.

Gary just shrugged. 'No, but seriously', he continued, laying out an argument for the first time any of them could remember. 'In England the TV news-presenters really are that naïve; they reach forty and still can't say the word 'sex'; they have to mouth it through their blushes and then shuffle their papers noisily before quickly moving on to the next topic; it's embarrassing'

'That's not the reason', *the Bishop* countered; 'It's true that the British people are a lot more uptight than most other nations because of their religious conditioning, but those TV presenters you are talking about have to contend…not only with the political-correctness culture that dominates all of British life these days but also the rules imposed on them by their employers…'

'…and the media regulators', Madison interjected.

'Yes…and the media regulators…' *the Bishop* concurred.

'I still maintain that they are all frigid', Gary insisted. 'Look; I understand that not everyone is as comfortable talking about sex as I am, but if you get to forty and you still can't even say the word 'sex'…a three-letter word…without blushing like a schoolgirl, even after the watershed…I doubt you will have enjoyed your life up to that point in the way you could have; that's all I'm saying'.

'I'll tell you what's worse', Evie announced suddenly, taking the conversation in a slightly different direction; '… political correctness has ruined comedy;, every joke I hear these days is about bodily functions…'

Her comment was met with a chorus of distaste and repulsed expressions.

‘You see what I mean’, she continued; ‘I would much rather talk about sex; talking about sex is interesting…and educational; talking about bodily functions is embarrassing…and gross’.

‘My point exactly; I think we’re on the same page, you and me’, he said.

‘You and I’, Evie corrected him again.

‘Too right’, Gary agreed without realising that Evie was rectifying his grammar.

Evie then took another sip of wine and raised her glass.

‘Man, I haven’t had this much fun since we played strip-dodge-ball in senior grade’.

That comment took everyone by surprise.

‘Oh, come on; don’t tell me you never played…’, she shrugged, looking at Madison while Gary instantly imagined two teams of hot young women in various states of undress, playing an x-rated version of dodge-ball.

Evie stopped talking and began fiddling with the silverware in front of her; ‘Okay…it was just me then…’

(It wasn’t true of course; Evie was just being deliberately mischievous…and provocative…but that didn’t stop her secretly enjoying the shocked expressions on the faces of her table companions…especially that of the Bishop)

Now, throughout the meal…and unbeknownst to the others, Evie had been trying constantly to distract Gary by pressing her leg against his …and despite *the Bishop’s* tacit but unspoken rule, both had been texting the other under the table like a couple of silly teenagers.

And, as they waited for the dessert menu…and *the Bishop* and Madison were engaged in a little small talk about the wine…they exchanged the following;

> Evie’s text; ‘I’m horny; I want you...again…now’.
>
> Gary’s reply; ‘Gimme a few minutes; can’t move; crowd is on its feet’.
>
> Evie; ??????

Gary's reply to that; two emoticons: a 'smiley-face' and a 'banana'... the sight of which immediately had Evie scoffing and chuckling to herself, much to the others bewilderment.

A pleasant atmosphere reigned in the dining room and as the waiter arrived with the dessert-menus and she looked around trying to take it all in...knowing only too well that she probably wouldn't be eating there again in the foreseeable future...Madison noticed that Gary and Evie seemed to be enjoying a much more open liaison as they sat there laughing and joking, than she was enjoying with *the Bishop* – even though what they had, seemed at times, to be bordering on exhibitionism as far as she could make out.

She herself had never been as promiscuous as Evie but rather than dwelling on her friend's questionable moral choices...as she would never begrudge her friend a moment of happiness knowing what she had been through...Madison began wondering what she would have to do herself in order to make that kind of connection with the brooding Englishman that was currently sat opposite her.

She would have loved to have been able to reveal to Evie what she and TB had really spent the afternoon doing - if for no other reason than to assuage her competitive streak vis-à-vis her friend and Gary - but unfortunately as she looked across the table into *the Bishop's* unfaltering blue eyes, she knew that she would be committing emotional suicide if she were even to dare allude to the fact without having cleared it with him first.

It was nevertheless a surreal moment of enlightenment for Madison - as she sat and watched Evie and Gary touching hands again across the table and sharing yet another of his silly jokes - when she suddenly realised that part of what she had with *the Bishop*, part of the make-up of their relationship together - if indeed that's what it was – and probably one of its most important parts in some respects, was the element of secrecy that surrounded it and gave it its intensity.

Madison was disappointed that she couldn't share, but of course, she knew what had happened...and as she caught *the Bishop* staring at her, she smirked back at his blank face with veiled self-satisfaction.

The meal continued towards its natural conclusion without further incident, but the longer it went on, the more painful it became for Madison to sit there and make small talk when all she wanted to do was grab *the Bishop by* his face, trace his full lips with her tongue and kiss him again and again, just as she had done earlier, especially as Evie and Gary were themselves becoming increasingly more tactile.

However, she managed to restrain herself all the way to the end.

They decided to bring the evening and the whole New York experience for the men to an end with one last round of champagne in the roof-top bar.

Madison and *the Bishop* went on ahead and Gary and Evie followed a few minutes later once Evie…who was getting a little tipsy…had been to the ladies-room.

Little did he know but Evie had another surprise for Gary as going up in the lift, she reached into her bag and discreetly removed something from it which she stuffed hastily into the breast pocket of his jacket.

'Just a little something to remind you of your time here', she whispered, putting her index finger in front of her mouth.

The lift doors opened and Madison was standing there waiting for them.

She saw that it was them and with a secret smile she turned away expecting them to follow her lead.

'Just so as you know; that purple pocket-square doesn't match your outfit', she aimed at Gary over her shoulder while glancing knowingly at Evie.

'Ever the fashion critic', Evie retorted glibly, grabbing Gary's arm.

Gary reached up and pushed the silky fabric down further into his pocket…and out of sight.

The little group joined *the Bishop* who was already at the bar and as the men took the drinks to one of the tables, Madison pulled Evie back to inform her of what she had seen.

'What are you doing; you forget I was there with you when you bought that…set of underwear; remember?' she whispered.

Evie shrugged her shoulders and grinned; 'I thought the colour matched his eyes', she remarked playfully before turning on her heels and sashaying her way over to the table, Madison following on behind, lost for words.

They all drank down the champagne and while Evie and Gary did suggest pursuing the evening and going to a club, Madison was the first to decline saying that it had been a long day and that she was drained.

That didn't deter Gary though; he was still pumped and as it was his last night in New York, he easily persuaded Evie to join him for one last hurrah.

The two of them quickly disappeared…and a few moments later, once she had signed the chit for the barman, Madison and *the Bishop* followed suit, retiring to their respective rooms, having shared just a brief but meaningful goodnight kiss on the cheek, before he exited the lift on the 6th floor and she continued on down to her room on the 4th.

Madison had wanted to invite the Bishop to her room…and had thought about it a thousand times during the evening but in reality, the hours had passed…and her libido had finally thrown in the towel. It had been a long and strenuous day, she was out on her feet and all she wanted to do was to get her head down.

As the lift doors closed, she waved *the Bishop* goodnight and quickly made her way to her room, reaching behind her almost immediately she was inside the door, to unzip her dress which she draped carefully over a chair.

Then, only a few minutes later, after a quick bathroom stop, she slipped under the bed-covers and melted into a fitful sleep…as soon as her head hit the pillow almost…the smile on her lips testament to the successful result of her day's work.

The next morning, Madison awoke feeling refreshed but slightly confused.

Where did she stand now; what did that afternoon of passion mean;

was it just cause and effect, or had it simply been an opportunity for them both to release all of the adrenaline and the pent up emotions that had been steadily building ahead of the exhibition match in a cascade of sexual frenzy?

She knew that she was attracted to *the Bishop*, but what were his thoughts on the matter, she wondered?

Madison decided to find out.

She took her usual shower and seeing that it was still rather early, she headed up to *the Bishop's* room, hoping to catch him there - or at the very least intercept him as he made his way down to the breakfast room - in order to get some answers from him before they joined the others.

However, unfortunately for her, when she knocked at his door there was no reply…and as she checked left and right, there was no sign of him either in the corridor.

Disappointed, she rushed down to the breakfast room still hoping to corner him before the others arrived - assuming logically in her own mind that they would probably be down a little later, having been out on the town - but alas, as she walked through the door, Evie and Gary were the first people she saw.

They were already seated and enjoying a hearty meal, though as she approached their table, Madison noticed on closer inspection that Evie was quite obviously suffering the effects of a late night and was just sipping silently on a cup of black coffee.

Madison looked across at the buffet and saw that *the Bishop* was there too; her heart jumped, but as she took her seat and the pretty waitress came over to offer her coffee, she realised intuitively that she had missed the chance to talk to him in private about what had happened between them…and her face fell.

At that point *the Bishop* came over to the table and joined them, but once everybody had greeted everybody else, breakfast was a quiet affair as they all tucked in – except for Evie – and used the tacit silence to reflect on the impending conclusion of the two men's New York escapade.

An hour or so later, the bags were packed, the car was waiting outside... with irrepressible punctuality...and within no time the girls were waving the two men off as they disappeared behind the security screens at JFK airport without Madison ever having gotten the chance to speak to *the Bishop* one-on-one about their tryst, leaving her frustrated and a little sad... though she did her best not to show it.

Inside the airport terminal;

Once they had complied with all the official requirements imposed on them by the US customs personnel, *the Bishop* and Gary made their way to the departure lounge for their flight home, and as they did so *the Bishop* turned to Gary and asked him about Evie.

'Yeah, she really likes the old beef bayonet', the young Aussie commented, reverting back to his innately crude vernacular, 'but we were just bum-buddies really'.

'I see', *the Bishop* replied, looking at his young companion rather circumspect.

'As I see it, any action I can get, is good action', Gary confirmed, trying desperately not to reveal the depth of his feelings for his new friend, Evie.

'...and what about you, champ? I mean you and Madison...anything going on there', Gary enquired casually.

The Bishop smiled stiffly; 'no comment', he replied flatly as they arrived in the lounge joining multitude of eclectic travellers who had already congregated there.

The flight back to England went without a hitch and no sooner had they touched down at Heathrow, Gary's mobile phone began to ring out, much to *the Bishop's* horror, drawing the attention of all those around him. (*The Simpsons' theme tune*)

It was an e-mail that Dave, his flat-mate had left on his message-service informing him that Rory Campbell-Brown had won a tournament while they were away, and that the Scot was now leading the chase, ahead of Gary, for the prize of challenging for the next world title.

'Looks like I've got some work to do', Gary commented as they walked along the travelators towards the passport desks.

'You sure have', *the Bishop* replied, as he shook the young Aussie's hand before they went their separate ways, '...but I'm sure that you are up for the fight, right', he confirmed confidently as he moved to enter the passport channel for UK residents.

'Aaw mate; I was born to fight', Gary whined with an unshakeable confidence of his own, as he threw his travelling companion one last smile before making his way further up the line towards the channel reserved for foreign nationals.

CHAPTER SIXTEEN

After the triumph of the exhibition match...and the follow-up article that she penned in its wake…extolling *the Bishop's* unprecedented mastery of his craft…Madison's life quickly returned to 'normal' and she quietly resumed her role as Gretchen's assistant in the paper's fashion department.

However, a week or so after the event, Gayle (Amanda's secretary) was typing away diligently at her computer…updating a report on one of New York's trendiest new bars…when out of the blue she received a rather cryptic call from Conrad Elliott (the paper's Head of Finance) asking to see Amanda on a matter of some urgency.

Caught somewhat off-guard by the call…as she rarely had any direct contact with the paper's executive level…Gayle hesitated momentarily, before quickly composing herself and informing Mr Elliott that Amanda was out of the office at that particular moment, but that she would be back at her desk within the hour.

'Should I ask her to come up to your office when she gets back?' she enquired courteously, while simultaneously bringing up her boss's afternoon schedule on the screen in front of her.

'No; that won't be necessary…I'll come down…' the executive retorted rather abruptly, ramping up the intrigue.

'Very well Mr Elliott; I will tell Amanda to expect you…at…1.15', Gayle confirmed politely, before the line suddenly went dead.

And so it was, that an hour or so later, at 1.15 precisely, Mr Conrad Elliott, a man who rarely ventured down to the lower floors walked straight out of the elevator and into Amanda's office…with barely a nod of recognition for Gayle who was sat there at her desk…followed close behind by a very smug-looking Todd Klingenschmidt.

Inside Amanda's office;

Conrad and Amanda exchanged greetings in the usual manner…and while Todd closed the door behind him…Conrad walked directly over to one of the chairs placed opposite Amanda's desk and sat down.

'…So Amanda', he began, not waiting for Todd to join him; 'I know you're a very busy woman but I just wanted to see you in order to find out if you knew anything about the allegations that Mr Klingenschmidt here has brought to the attention of the management.'

He gestured towards Todd.

Amanda looked him in the eye, frowned and sat back in her chair. 'And what allegations are those?' she asked, glancing at Todd who was just taking his seat.

The latter cleared his throat and was just about to speak when Conrad raised his hand and insisted on taking the lead.

'Well; it would appear…', the financial executive continued, '…that Mr Klingenschmidt here interviewed that...Bishop guy…after the chess-event that we held a couple of weeks back…and apparently the guy told him that our Miss Chatfield had not been...how can I say this...up to scratch... in her organisation of the event'.

'He did, did he?' Amanda responded, raising her eyebrows.

'Aha', Conrad confirmed, suddenly looking a little uncomfortable.

'And...?' Amanda pursued with her usual calm; 'why are you telling me this?'

'Well', Conrad pursued, '…you were involved in that event too… and we...'

'We..?' Amanda interrupted, tapping her pen against her bottom lip.

'…Management', Conrad clarified; '...were wondering if you had heard anything similar'.

Amanda leaned further back in her chair and looked up at the ceiling as if giving the news some thought.

'I see...', she answered after a moment's reflection; 'Well no, I haven't heard anything like that...but as you quite rightly said in your opening remark, Conrad, I am a very busy woman and I do have a meeting in a few minutes that I simply cannot defer, so if you could just leave that…

rather troubling information…with me...I will look into it and get back to you. Would that be okay…?'

'Of course…I understand; thank you Amanda', Conrad quickly acquiesced, feeling a little awkward, all of a sudden; 'I knew that we could rely on you'.

The two men then got up to leave and as they did so, Gayle just happened to pop her head around the door…

'Miss…Webster is here for you', she announced quietly to her boss, almost in a whisper.

Amanda replied with a curt nod, waited for the two men to make their way out and then quickly instructed her secretary to ring Madison in the fashion department.

'Tell her I want to see her A.S.A.P.' she intoned…quietly but forcefully; '…Oh…and send in Miss Webster', she added with a rolling hand-gesture… almost as an afterthought.

Gayle nodded, invited the waiting Miss Webster into the office and then without another word returned to her desk to call Madison in the fashion department.

The next day;

When Amanda arrived at her office the next morning, Madison was already there waiting, sat on the edge of Gayle's desk, chatting with her about fashion.

Gayle spotted her boss exiting the lift from afar and with almost military precision stood up to greet her with her usual professional courtesy.

'Good morning Amanda', she announced as Madison turned around to do the same.

Amanda looked at them both**…**but barely bothering to acknowledge their welcome she immediately launched into a violent rant about the early-morning commuter traffic…before raising a hand, crooking a finger and indicating to Madison that she should follow her into her office.

'Hold everything…' she called back to Gayle.

In the office;

'Close the door…' Amanda insisted brusquely as she hung-up her coat and made her way around her desk.

Madison closed the door…and having been in the office a few times now, didn't wait to be invited to sit.

'So what's all this about?' she asked curiously; '…Gayle wouldn't tell me anything'.

'Of course she wouldn't…' Amanda responded, showing that her cantankerous character was never far from the surface, '…because what I am about to tell you now is sensitive…and confidential…and Gayle knows better than to gossip about what happens in this office'.

Amanda then sat down, pulled her chair forward and with a stony look on her face, began to explain the situation with Todd and Mr Elliott.

Madison…*who was naturally wary and even a little suspicious given her previous dealings with management*…listened carefully to what Amanda had to say before ultimately springing to her feet, filled with indignation and a smarting sense of injustice.

'Are you kidding me?' she railed flippantly, aghast at her boss's insinuation. 'I did everything I was asked to do…and more…to make sure that that match was a success and everyone knows that around here…everyone'.

'…Igniting considerable public hysteria in the process, might I add' Amanda appended.

'Exactly', Madison blustered, 'and if those people up…'

'Look, Madison', Amanda jumped in; 'I know what you did on that mission…and clearly, a lot of people really enjoyed the article you wrote…but we both know that life isn't always fair…and that…not everybody around here appreciates you and your work'.

Madison was suddenly speechless; surely it couldn't be true that *the Bishop* had filed a complaint against her; could it?

Then Amanda's phone started to ring and its annoyingly repetitive ringtone quickly snapped her out of her reverie.

'Okay Madison; I have to take this', Amanda informed her young colleague, pointing to her phone'...but I have promised Mr. Elliott that I will look into this, so for the moment...go back to what you were doing and I will call you again later...once I have had time to make a few calls'.

She then pressed the screen on her phone and put it to her ear; 'Amanda Brooke speaking...'

Madison could do nothing but shake her head in disgust...and unable to hide her frustration she stormed out of the office, rushing past Gayle and taking a few steps down the corridor...*so that she was out of sight of everyone*...before she stopped again to take a couple of deep breaths.

She was still stunned...and a little confused by what she had just heard...but at the same time she was also strangely heartened...to some extent at least...by the fact that Amanda seemed to have her back on this occasion...even though she knew herself that she had done nothing wrong.

That said, she (Madison) was under no illusion that there were still people in the boardroom who wanted to get rid of her by any means possible...because of her previous history.

Back in Amanda's office;

Amanda was well aware of the management's position towards Madison after the sexual-harassment case that she had brought against them but that afternoon she made a number of calls to people she knew... who had been at the event...in order to find out if there was any truth to what Todd was alleging ...and she even tried calling Todd himself to find out from the horse's mouth so to speak, but he was unavailable and nobody else could offer anything but praise for the way the exhibition match had been organised.

She then called Conrad Elliott to inform him that she had looked into what they had discussed earlier and found nothing and no-one who could corroborate Todd's story, believing that that would put an end to the 'misunderstanding'.

Conrad listened to her report and thanked her for her diligence…and as far as Amanda was concerned, that was that.

She then tried calling Madison in the fashion office to explain what she had done…but it was getting late by then and sadly there was no reply.

Next morning;

Madison and Gretchen were busy in Gretchen's office going through hundreds of wedding-dress photographs, looking for something original that they could use in a bridal-themed feature that they were working on… when all of a sudden a stylish young woman with short blonde hair and a vibrant smile appeared in the door-way.

She knocked politely and…reaching forward…announced; 'Your mail, Mrs Olsen'.

Gretchen stopped what she was doing; put down the photograph she was studying and strolled over to the door.

'Thank-you...'

'…Kimberley', the young intern interjected, '…but Kim is good'.

'Thank-you…Kim', Gretchen remarked with a sympathetic smile as she took hold of the parcel of letters.

'You're welcome', the young girl replied, lingering there a little longer than she needed.

'Cute look' Gretchen quipped, as she began flipping through the pile and handing one particular letter to Madison which had come up from the HR Dept.

'Thanks', the delighted young intern replied again before turning and going on her way.

Meanwhile, Madison looked at the letter that Gretchen had given her…and without a second thought, tore it open.

The letter inside, printed on company paper, explained that 'management' had received a complaint about her and that she should expect to be summoned to a meeting in the next few days to explain herself.

'What the f…udge' she exclaimed with indignation…and without a word to Gretchen, she grabbed her suit-jacket from the chair where it was hanging and raced upstairs to see Amanda…convinced that her boss had somehow betrayed her.

Upstairs;

Madison bolted out of the lift and with only a fleeting glance at Gayle…she rushed into Amanda's office to find her boss…as usual…on the phone;

'…I'm sure I can make myself available for that John…; let me check my schedule and I'll get back to you', Amanda was saying in conclusion to her conversation…before she pressed the red button on her phone and dropped her hands into her lap on seeing Madison's agitated state.

'Madison; are you okay; is there something I can do for you?' Amanda asked, tempering her usual indifference.

Incensed, Madison tossed the letter she had just received onto her boss's desk, her insides churning with pent-up emotion; 'I thought you were going to sort 'this', she blustered with uncontrolled rage; '…but it looks like you've just sold me down the river'.

'This? What is this?' Amanda questioned as she took hold of the letter and started to read, a look of barely-disguised irritation spreading quickly across her face.

'I should have known better', Madison continued, shrieking with righteous anger before Amanda could even finish reading; 'what is it with you people; why do you all have it in for me?'

Amanda put the letter down, joined her hands in front of her on her desk and frowned noticeably.

'Firstly, Madison', she chided, staring calmly back at her junior's impassioned face

'...before you say anything else that you might regret, just remember where you are'.

'...But you once told me that your door was always open' Madison snapped back belligerently putting her hands on the back of the chair in front of Amanda's desk.

'Don't be flip Madison; that's just a metaphor that all management use to...; never mind...' Amanda replied, her nostrils flaring as she sat back in her seat, making no attempt to conceal her displeasure as she tried to assess the situation objectively.

'I don't understand this', she declared, flicking the letter with her right hand; 'I called Mr Elliott yesterday having made a few enquiries...to tell him that nobody I had spoken to could corroborate Todd's claims...and I assumed that that would be the end of it. And in fact Madison...' she added for effect, 'I tried calling you too, just after...but there was no reply'.

Madison grimaced awkwardly ... fighting hard to control her emotions...but knowing only too well that she and Gretchen had gone home early the previous day having decided to make an early start today.

'Look Madison, let me give him another call to see what's going on' Amanda suggested, raising her mobile up and tapping in Mr Elliott's number.

The phone rang twice but unfortunately it was Mr Elliott's secretary who answered only to inform Amanda that Mr Elliott was unavailable.

Amanda thanked the young woman abruptly and then frowning again in frustration she noticed that the letter had come from the HR office.

'Maybe Svetlana didn't get the message', she pondered out loud; 'Let's try her'.

Again the phone rang but again Amanda was thwarted. Svetlana too, was out of her office.

'Look Madison', Amanda argued cogently, hoping that rational judgment would prevail; 'I'm sure this will all be straightened out...as soon as all the players involved are on the same page...but...'.

Madison wasn't listening; she was still bristling with rage and Amanda's comments were doing little or nothing to assuage her obvious frustration... but rather than dig herself a hole even bigger than the one she was already in, she decided to storm out of the office at that point, without another word.

Amanda watched her go and then immediately picked up the phone on her desk and called Gayle in the internal line; 'Its 10; 20 now. Wait an hour or so for her to calm down…and then get her back up here'.

'Yes Amanda; anything else?' Gayle asked politely.

'No that will be all…' Amanda replied; '…but don't take 'NO' for an answer'

'Yes Amanda', Gayle confirmed with her usual perspicacity.

An hour later;

Once again Madison was standing in front of Amanda's desk.

She was still annoyed…but after a rational, level-headed exchange with Gretchen… her fury had abated and she was in a more conciliatory mood.

'Sorry about earlier', she mumbled apologetically as she sat back down; 'I got a little carried away'.

'Look Madison; it's not my job to get involved in this…' Amanda retorted with conviction…and a hint of annoyance '…but as I was saying earlier…before you so rudely stormed out… I'm sure that this will all be straightened out; I can't see it being a problem but if you would like me to, I will come upstairs with you and speak up in your defence'.

'Defence…defence…I don't need any…defence; I have done nothing wrong', Madison ranted again; 'these people just want me out because I exposed them as misogynist dinosaurs. That's why they are doing this… no other reason; you know that…and I know that'.

Amanda grimaced, unable to contradict that statement.

Madison sat back and paused, thinking of what to say next.

'Look Amanda, I don't want to lose this job' she mumbled almost, her voice cracking slightly.

'I understand that…and I'm reliably informed that you won't; not this time at least. Trust me', Amanda stated, trying to find the path of least resistance…and hoping to curtail the discussion.

'Trust is a rare commodity in life…and needs to be earned; especially in this business', Madison countered stubbornly in reply.

'I know; I know that we don't always get along' Amanda responded again, 'but despite what people might think I am not without compassion. Just don't sell yourself short Madison…and don't let yourself be defined by that one event in your life', Amanda offered, still trying to resolve her own internal struggle.

Madison shrugged and leaned forward to pick up the letter.

'Look Madison, if you hear anything else on this matter, if it doesn't get resolved beforehand, I want you to come and tell me…and I will give you my full support…if you want it…when you go in front of management', Amanda concluded.

Madison nodded and forced a smile, before turning to leave.

'Oh…and Madison, just one more thing before you leave…' Amanda remarked, reverting back to type; 'Don't mistake my kindness for weakness'.

Madison took a deep breath and left without further comment.

'Management' wasn't available for a few days thereafter…but eventually, a meeting was convened and at the appointed time, as arranged, Madison joined Amanda in her office before the two women made their way upstairs…together…to confront Todd and his scurrilous accusations.

Outside the conference room, before they went in, Amanda put her hand out and stopped Madison in her tracks.

'Whatever you do…and whatever happens in here, don't over-react and don't let what happened to you that day define your time here', she said with ominous prescience.

Madison nodded politely, then followed her boss into the room and sat down on one of the two chairs that had…quite obviously…been placed there for that reason.

In front of them…on the in-house disciplinary-panel…sat the CEO, Mr Hines, with…to his left Conrad Elliott, and to his right Svetlana Joric, from HR.

Todd was sat off to the side almost like an interested spectator.

Mr Hines thanked them all for coming and then to begin proceedings he made a short introductory speech…with practiced gravitas… in order to comply with the legal protocols put in place for such circumstances… where he explained…for the record, who each of his colleagues were, their roles and the reasons why they were all there.

Then, he turned to Todd and asked him to stand up and repeat his allegations…which he did with almost gleeful disdain…reading from the notes he had made on his phone…and glancing several times in Madison's direction as he did so…with that snide grin of his that she had so come to detest.

Madison glanced back at him too, wanting to slap that smirk right off his face…and in her mind she even imagined herself doing just that… but in reality she just sat there and listened, her arms folded in passive-aggressive frustration.

The panel-members listened quietly and attentively to everything Todd had to say… as did Madison and Amanda…and then after a brief, whispered consultation, Mr Hines asked Madison to stand up in turn and give her version of events.

Inhaling deeply, Madison did just that…ready to give the panel a piece of her mind…but before she could speak, Amanda got up too and stepped forward.

'I got this…' she said, motioning for Madison to keep her counsel.

Slightly confused by this sudden…and very unexpected…development in proceedings Madison glanced at her boss, a little puzzled. The two women shared a look…and in that split second images of the conversation she had had in Amanda's office when this 'allegation' had first been aired, and the others since flashed through Madison's mind.

She held her breath for a moment or two…and then nodding reluctantly she agreed to let Amanda…who all of a sudden had that arrogant, no-nonsense look about her…have the first word.

I can always dovetail in behind…if necessary, Madison thought to herself as she took a step back and the room suddenly hushed.

'Okay people', Amanda announced loudly, glancing at Mr Hines before focussing her attention on Todd, '…we have all listened to Todd here…and what he has said is indeed worthy of sanction…if what he has said…is true…but what if Todd had simply misheard what *the Bishop guy* had said…because of his English accent…or gotten his facts wrong in some way; again because of the guy's unusual vocabulary. Could that be an explanation for this '*misunderstanding*'?'

She paused for a second and then repeated her suggestion asking Todd directly if it was possible that he could have misheard what *the Bishop* had said…or mixed up his facts in some way.

She was trying to introduce an element of doubt into Todd's story…so as to give him the opportunity to retract his allegations…even if he was one of… if not the most obnoxious and perfidious of colleagues.

Her eyes searched his, looking for some kind of apology or regret but Todd stuck to his guns.

'No; no…everything I have said is word for word what *the Bishop* guy told me…and that's the truth', Todd insisted, throwing another grotesquely insincere smirk in Madison's direction as the tension in the room began to grow.

Amanda frowned and clearly dismayed, she took a few steps back and stood directly in front of the panel.

This was the moment; the moment of truth; the moment when her whole career could come crashing down around her ears, Madison thought to herself.

Mr Elliott, clearly feeling guilty, shifted uneasily in his seat while Mr Hines…*not averse to a little journalistic skulduggery himself in his early years*…stared fixedly at the file in front of him while Svetlana…in her temporary-role as company secretary…kept her head down and continued to scribble away diligently, determined to record every detail of the meeting for 'the Minutes'.

Another excruciatingly long pause followed…but then, as she glanced to her left and caught Todd's eye, Amanda found herself shrugging her shoulders wearily. She had opened the door for him to retract his allegations, she had given him the opportunity to modify his claims…

but sadly he had chosen to plough on with his lies…and now she was left with no choice but to reveal the truth.

She rolled her eyes, shook her head and threw her hands in the air.

'Well gentlemen…' she said, '…and ladies', she added, looking at Svetlana and then back at Madison; 'believe me, I take no pleasure in saying this…but I feel that Mr Klingenschmidt here has backed me into a corner'.

She sighed loudly before continuing.

'I spoke to Mr Byron…*the Bishop*…myself during the event and he had had nothing but praise for the work that Miss Chatfield here had accomplished'.

This new information was like a bolt out of the blue and caught everybody in the room by surprise. Nobody was expecting it…and as it began to sink in the panel-members were left looking at each other, completely bemused and bewildered; Svetlana even stopped writing.

'…And if you'd like', Amanda added, pulling out her phone…and pausing again for dramatic effect, 'I can call him right now and we can have him re-iterate his 'grievances' for the panel to hear straight from the horse's mouth…so to speak'.

Silence filled the room…but then all of a sudden the penny dropped, Todd's smirking face blanched and he slowly hung his head as he realised what was happening…that he had been undone…that Amanda, Amanda Brooke, the notorious 'office Rottweiler' who had seen off many an adversary in her time…and adversaries a lot more worthy than him…was putting her reputation on the line against his.

'That won't be necessary Amanda', said Mr Hines, realising the situation.

Throughout all this, Madison just stood there in stunned silence. She couldn't believe that Amanda would fight her corner like this…and even put herself in the firing line, in order to defend her...

'So guys; it looks like it's my word against Todd's...' Amanda continued advocating, driving home her point with her usual unshakeable confidence.

The panellists looked at each other again and shuffling the pages in the file in front of him, Mr Hines then asked Amanda and Madison to leave the room while they (the panel) continued their deliberations.

'We'll let you know our decision in due course', he added, trying to conclude proceedings in the appropriate manner.

'I look forward to it', Amanda concurred, and with that, after another cursory glance at Todd, she tucked away her phone and strolled out of the room with Madison close on her heels.

Still in shock, the latter closed the door behind them and no sooner had she done so, than the arguments and the recriminations broke out between all three of the male participants.

Outside the room;

While Amanda headed straight for the lifts...Madison took a moment to glance back through the glass panel in the conference-room door… where she could just about see Todd…with his back to her, his arms spread wide…clearly arguing his case and protesting his innocence.

'I was just following orders', she could hear him saying, as he gesticulated wildly.

'That's all on you; sucker' she murmured to herself as she turned and followed Amanda to the lift trying desperately hard to hold back the smuggest of smiles.

In the lift down;

'Thank-you for that; it really wasn't the outcome I was expecting…' Madison admitted as she stepped into the cabin and pressed the button to her floor '.

Amanda's only reaction was an aloof smirk.

'…But…well…I…I didn't know that you had that…Bishop guy's… number', Madison added, her mind racing and her thought full of curious inquisitiveness.

'I don't...' Amanda replied; '…but you might want to rectify that'.

(There was a pause after that as the lift stopped one floor down for no reason)

'…Wait; you're not telling me that you are 'interested' in him, are you?' Madison remarked, almost choking on the words, as the doors closed again.

'What can I say…?' Amanda crooned, still basking in her victory; 'I'm sapiosexual; get over it'.

'Sapio…what now…?' Madison blurted out.

'Sapiosexual', Amanda repeated; 'it means that I am sexually attracted to intelligence'.

Madison grimaced.

'Oh, come on Madison; you have to admit that the guy is easy on the eye', Amanda cajoled.

'He's okay, I guess', Madison conceded, not wanting to give anything away.

'Oh, don't be so diplomatic, Madison; we both know the guy exudes charisma, charm…and sensuality', Amanda specified, deliberately teasing her younger colleague.

Madison was suddenly lost for words; her brain was in turmoil; Amanda had just saved her job...not that she had done anything wrong... but now she wanted to 'get to know' *the Bishop…her Bishop…*better…and she wanted her to facilitate it!!

At that moment, the lift stopped again, this time on Amanda's floor and before Madison could say another word, Amanda had stepped out of the cabin…with her usual poise and confident stride…and was already on her way back to her office.

'Thanks again', Madison called after her as she pressed the button for her own floor, still shaking her head in confusion.

Amanda raised a hand as she narrowly avoided a temp who dared to get in her path but deliberately ignored the acknowledgement, not wanting any other staff-members who might be watching to know that she had a compassionate side.

During the confrontation Amanda had been more than a little conflicted in her loyalty...due to her position in the company and her inside knowledge of its workings...but when had Todd started to tell his story which was so clearly a trumped-up attempt to discredit Madison and ruin her professional reputation...which would then be used as an excuse to fire her...she just couldn't stand by and say nothing. It was a decision she knew that would have consequences for her down the line...but, she just couldn't side with 'management' on this occasion from a moral standpoint. Yes Madison could be difficult and yes she had brought unwanted attention to the company... and embarrassed the family of a major-share-holder at the same time...but she didn't deserve to be treated the way she had been in the aftermath of 'the incident'...and realising this, albeit a little late in the day, she had decided to try and do something to redress the situation; especially as she had indeed been at the event, had spoken to the Bishop and had found out exactly how he felt.

The next day, having just dropped off the Fashion-department's rewrites for the Sunday edition with Alex in the editor's office, Madison was already on her way back downstairs when out of the corner of her eye she spotted Todd across the way carrying his office in a box.

He was clearly still smarting from his defeat the previous day...and now his dismissal...and the sour expression on his face did little to mask the hostile thoughts that were going through his head.

Nevertheless, Madison tried to make eye-contact with him...briefly... although she didn't really know why.

Across the divide, it was pretty obvious that Todd saw her too… but using that very moment to reposition something in his box that was 'potentially' going to fall over, he just blanked her completely before turning and heading back in the direction from whence he came.

Perplexed, Madison just stood there for a moment…bemused by Todd's rather strange behaviour…but then in the great scheme of things, it really didn't surprise her…or matter to her…as the guy had shown nothing but contempt for her since the first day they had met.

That said; Madison was very curious by nature…and despite what had happened with Todd, she would have really liked to know why he had always been so vindictive towards her…what she had ever done to him…if anything at all…that would have made him act in the way he had; however, his speedy 'about-turn' and quick disappearing-act was a clear indication that that was never going to happen and that he had no interest in talking to her.

Shrugging her shoulders…and exhaling a brief pffft of disdain, Madison pressed the call-button for the lift…and even though she knew that it was uncharitable of her to gloat over another person's misfortune, she decided that on this occasion, she would make an exception.

What the hell, she thought to herself; I can't feel sorry for somebody whose only goal seemed to be getting me fired.

At that moment, the light above the lift 'pinged' loudly, the doors opened and a stunning young woman with model-like poise, wearing a pretty, full-skirted swing dress and a beautiful, self-satisfied smile stepped confidently out of the cabin and headed directly for the executive offices.

The young woman's dress instantly caught Madison's eye and as she took her place in the cabin…and watched the young woman's pert derriere slowly disappearing behind the lift's closing doors…she made a mental note to buy one for herself just like it.

CHAPTER SEVENTEEN

Back in England;

Meanwhile, one morning back in England, *the Bishop* was sitting quietly in the Abbey's conservatory …enjoying a new book entitled 'Aphrodite's Wrath'…when his house-keeper, Rosa suddenly appeared at the open door.

Knocking politely on the door-frame, she paused for a moment and then walked slowly into the room.

Now it was most unusual for Rosa to do this…*as she never interrupted him when he was reading*…so realising that whatever she had to say must be important…*enough for her to disrupt his morning routine…the Bishop* immediately stopped what he was reading and lowered the book to his lap, raising his eyes slowly as he took in the meaning of the last few words that he had read.

'Rosa…what is it?' he asked quietly, turning to face her.

Rosa just stood there for a moment…in silence…but the expression on her face told him that she had something on her mind…something that she wanted to say.

'Come and sit down…' *the Bishop* beckoned, tapping the arm of the chair placed at right-angles to his.

Rosa thanked him kindly…but politely refused, preferring to stand.

'I have received some news from my family in Portugal', she announced quietly in her soft Madeira accent. 'My parents' fiftieth wedding anniversary is coming up…and as they haven't seen me in a while…they have asked me to go and visit them', she explained, holding out the letter for him to read.

The Bishop listened attentively to his loyal employee - *who had in fact become more of a friend over the years* - and then reassured that it wasn't bad news…he quietly waved away the letter with an understanding 'that won't be necessary', agreeing immediately to her request…almost before she had finished formulating it…and even offering to pay for her flight.

Rosa smiled appreciatively. *The Bishop* had been more than generous to her over the years but this time, she politely declined his offer.

'That won't be necessary either', she affirmed enjoying the exchange of etiquette.

'Very well then', *the Bishop* concurred, '…and when would you be thinking of leaving?' he asked calmly.

'Oh, it won't be for another month or so… but when I do go, I will probably be away for about…four to six weeks…to make it worthwhile', Rosa informed him folding the letter away into her apron.

'I see; very well…take all the time you need; you deserve it', *the Bishop* concluded with a benevolent smile, raising his book once more.

Rosa thanked him for his understanding and then …stopping briefly on her way out to plump up a cushion on the couch, she returned to her chores in the kitchen.

The Bishop watched her leave, still smiling kindly, but as soon as she was out of sight he slowly leaned back in his chair and winced visibly, the shaking pages of his book the only expression of his distress as he tried desperately to control the nervous spasm that was ripping through his body.

A week or so later, back in New York, a handwritten letter was delivered directly to Madison's desk…in the cramped little office she shared with Gretchen…by one of the interns.

At the time, she was very busy…up to her eyes in fact, in runway photographs…and didn't want to be disturbed, but when she saw the postage stamp on the front of the envelope and recognised the handwriting from the note that he had left for her all those months ago in that hotel in England, she immediately stopped what she was doing and marched over to her desk.

She picked up the envelope and raised it to her nose…weirdly…sniffing it for a few moments like a tracker-dog trying to pick up a scent. Then, having looked at it from just about every angle she turned it over and carefully slid her thumb-nail under the seal to open it.

Inside, she found a short note from *the Bishop* written quite formally thanking her…albeit belatedly…for her work during his visit to New York.

Secretly thrilled, Madison felt a strange feeling wash over her…but then as she continued reading, she realised that it was not only a thank-you note, it was also an invitation…a personal invitation…from him to her… to go and spend the summer with him in England.

Well…that's…a surprise, she murmured to herself as she sat down on the corner of her desk to re-read the note…twice more…just to make sure that she had understood its meaning correctly.

Now naturally, Madison was more than a little surprised to receive this correspondence from *the Bishop* as she hadn't heard from him in almost two months; indeed she hadn't heard from him since he and Gary had left New York…and if she was honest with herself she had begun to wonder if she would ever hear from him again, so her surprise was well founded.

However, as she read the note for the third time, memories of the time she had spent with him suddenly filled her head…and as she turned around in response to a co-worker dropping a pile of catalogues outside the office, her eyes were immediately drawn to the photo on her desk that Evie had taken…and had framed for her…of her with Gary and *the Bishop* just before the 'now infamous' exhibition match.

She sighed out loud…and without her realising it, her mind instantly cast itself back…to that wonderful afternoon she had spent with *the Bishop* in his hotel room…and the thought of re-living that experience just one more time, instantly made her heart race.

'Brrring, brrring…brrring, brrring'

The annoying sound of the office phone put a sudden end to Madison's 'romantic' musings…and as she picked up the receiver with her left hand, she slipped the note and its envelope into her handbag with her right before taking the call and carrying on with her day.

Gretchen walked back into the office an hour or so later, having fulfilled her weekly obligation to assist at the HoD (Heads of Department) meeting…to find Madison still sorting through the pile of fashion pics;

'Find anything interesting…?' she inquired nonchalantly as she set down her phone and bag on her desk.

'Only if you think 'Boho' is making a comeback…or mis-matched patterns…or leggings', Madison replied holding up a few hideous examples from a recent fashion-show.

'Eeew', Gretchen squealed, sauntering over to where Madison was working.

'…Or jeans under a skirt…' she scoffed as she picked up another random cliché.

'I know, right? What were they thinking…?' Madison agreed, shaking her head in disbelief.

Gretchen smiled at her young colleague; 'Believe me, that's not the worst thing I've seen since I started doing this job', she commented as she grabbed a pile of photos and busied herself, helping Madison sort through what was left of the mountain of glossy photos.

In fact, the two women spent the next hour or so picking through the photos, discussing this design and that… either praising it for its innovation or ripping it to shreds for its lack of imagination, until, taking advantage of their relative privacy…and the growing rapport she had built up with Gretchen…*who, despite her position as her 'boss' had become more of a friend than a mentor to her since they had started working together*…Madison decided to bring up the letter she had received earlier that morning.

'I think it's a great idea…' Gretchen commented sympathetically when Madison handed her the letter to read, '…If you're interested, that is; after all, you haven't had a real break since you started her'.

Madison pursed her lips, deep in thought, as she tapped the edge of the envelope against the desk-top, but didn't respond.

'Just check your holiday entitlement with the accounts department and book it', Gretchen advised with a pout of her own as she walked over to the other table full of run-way photographs that Madison had sorted earlier; 'Oh…and I'd run it past Amanda too', she added as she picked up the first photo she saw; '… just to keep things official and above board'.

Madison smiled warmly at her new 'boss'. Gretchen was wonderful to work with, and she couldn't do enough to encourage her in her quest to move up the ladder, but she was also one of those people desperate not to annoy 'the Nanny' - *as some people around the office called Amanda* - and suffer her wrath.

She (Madison), on the other hand had no such problems; she wasn't particularly comfortable being in Amanda's presence but since her *contretemps* with Todd, she and Amanda had been on far better terms… and where others wilted and retreated in Amanda's presence, she was one of the few who could stand up to her and look her in the eye.

A while later;

Back at her desk after lunch, Madison picked up the phone and rang the accounts office to confirm her entitlement to holiday-time only to be informed that she didn't have enough time in the bank to take the whole summer off…as she would have liked…but she did have enough to make a trip to England worthwhile.

'Thank you for the information', she responded politely to the rather dour accounts-employee before quickly hanging up the phone and immediately ringing Gayle (Amanda's secretary), to set up a time for her and Amanda to meet so that she could…hopefully…get Amanda's authorisation if not her approval to take the time off.

Gayle answered the phone with her usual efficiency, and after a brief chat about how Madison was getting on in the fashion department, she booked the latter in to see Amanda at 10:30 the following day.

'Thanks Gayle; I'll see you then', Madison remarked confidently…and as she hung up the phone she suddenly realised that that was the first time she had followed protocol and gone through the proper channels in order to get something done.

Huh, she thought to herself with more than a little smugness; I think I'm getting the hang of this office malarkey.

'Madison…Madison; come out here and tell me what you think of this…' Gretchen suddenly called out from the outer office.

'Sure; I'll be right out', Madison replied, standing up and brushing herself down before making her way out into the main office…where she found Gretchen in the corner stood behind the chair of a hunky young technician who…by the evidence spread all over the desk in front of him… was in the middle of installing some kind of newfangled software onto their computer-system.

'What are we looking at here?' Madison asked as she reached them; '… the computer graphics…or…him?' she whispered playfully into Gretchen's ear, nodding discreetly in the direction of the muscle-bound technician.

'..The graphics, of course', Gretchen mouthed quietly in reply, turning her head and elbowing her younger colleague gently in the arm.

'Bring it on is what I say…' Madison quipped with a smile as she turned and headed back to her desk, '…technology is the future'.

Later that evening; Madison's apartment

It had been quite an eventful day at the office and after finishing her rather generic 'meal-for-one', Madison decided to give Evie a call. She hadn't spoken to her friend in a while and she felt that it was about time they met up again for one of their 'catch-up walks' around central Park.

She grabbed her mobile and having checked it first for any new e-mails she quickly brought up Evie's number…and hit the 'call' button.

The phone rang a couple of times but Evie didn't pick up. She was in the middle of a new episode of her favourite TV series and didn't want to be disturbed.

In fact, she was tempted to let the call go to voicemail so as not to interrupt her viewing experience but when she glanced at the screen…and saw that it was Madison calling…she reluctantly hit the pause-button on the TV remote and answered the call.

'Hey stranger', she chirped happily, making herself even more comfortable on her couch than she was before, ready for a good old girlie chin-wag. 'What's new?'

'Oh my god; where do I start', Madison replied, a distinct note of irritation…and frustration in her voice.

'At the beginning, hon', Evie opined, reaching for an apple on the table behind her.

…and with that, Madison began to relate all her recent trials and tribulations at the office.

Now, Evie knew Madison very well. She knew that when Madison needed to get something off her chest, her job as her BFF, was just to sit there and listen, which she did patiently for the next twenty minutes or so…offering her support, her understanding and her advice wherever possible…but as soon as she got the chance to do so…when Madison finally paused for breath after describing the rather strange events with Todd the day after the confrontation…she jumped on the opportunity to change the subject to something a little more up-beat.

'So anyway…how's your social life?' she asked abruptly hoping to steer Madison in a more positive direction.

'Pffft; what social life?' Madison responded, somewhat offhand, 'I don't have a social life at the moment…but…'

She paused.

'But…but what?' Evie jumped in with sudden enthusiasm.

'Well, I did receive a letter today…' Madison announced nonchalantly, a hint of mischief creeping into her voice, '…from England'.

‘Oooh…, tell me more’, Evie prompted quickly, her gossip-radar suddenly on red alert.

‘Well, as you can guess…’ Madison revealed candidly, drawing the detail out somewhat; ‘it’s from ‘you know who’…and he’s invited me over to England’.

‘He has…and are you going to go?’ Evie asked, jumping up, suddenly more interested.

‘I don’t know yet’, Madison replied, not wanting to confirm anything until it was definite.

There followed another long discussion about the implications…and the pros and cons…of such a trip…but eventually…after exhausting every possible scenario and every possible angle over the next hour or so…Evie finished by agreeing with Madison that she should indeed take up *the Bishop’s* offer, if for no other reason than to get closure.

‘You can’t change what is in your heart…’ she remarked philosophically between bites of apple stump, ‘…and until you know where you stand with this guy…you can’t…you won’t move on…so go for it’, she concluded, a note of sympathetic tenderness in her voice.

‘Yeah; you’re right’ Madison concurred, ‘but hey, here’s an idea’, she added after a brief pause; ‘…why don’t you come with? You’ve never been to England... it would be fun, like Boston?’

Evie scoffed noisily. ‘I’d love to Mad…you know I would…but sadly I just don’t have the time…nor the money for such an excursion. No, you go; find your truth and come back and tell me all about it. I’ll be right here, waiting’.

‘Okay…that’s what I’ll do then’, Madison agreed, and with that she wrapped up the call with her usual comment for her friend to ‘stay safe’.

(Fun fact; the girls had spoken for almost two hours and there was not one mention of the walk which was Madison’s initial reason for calling)

Evie’s support notwithstanding, Madison still wasn’t sure about her decision…and for the next week or so she mulled it over in her head…

repeatedly; some days she wanted to go and on others…seeing the work piling up on hers and Gretchen's desks… she didn't, but in the end, having gotten the green light from Amanda; something which had surprised more than she would care to admit, despite her legal entitlement to time-off… she decided that she was prepared to tempt fate, to take a leap of faith and make the trip to England.

Besides, she thought to herself; she needed a break after all the stress of her in-house troubles…and yes it was true, she had never really had any closure on whatever it was that she had shared with *the Bishop*, so this trip would be the ideal opportunity for her to do just that.

However, knowing *the Bishop* and his unpredictable character she also decided that if she was going to do this, she was going to do it on her own terms…and with that in mind she spent the next couple of days looking into flights and finding herself somewhere to live in England for the duration of her stay.

This, she felt would not only respect *the Bishop's* privacy…if and when he needed it…but also provide her with an environment where she could work and stay in touch with Gretchen if she needed to.

After all, she reasoned, she really didn't know what to expect from this invitation or what *the Bishop's* intentions were going to be during her time there.

A few days after that, having confirmed her flights, Madison quickly typed out a brief thank-you…and acceptance letter…in reply to the Bishop's invitation, which she printed off from her computer and addressed to the abbey, together with the details of her arrival time.

Of course, in this kind of situation, she would normally just fire off an e-mail or a text message to confirm all this…but as the Bishop was somewhat of a latent technophobe, that wasn't an option; a fact which irked the modern New-Yorker more than she cared to admit.

And so it was that a few weeks later, Madison was back in London's Heathrow airport, where to her great surprise…when she walked out of the arrivals doors…dressed in her sensible, travel-friendly, chocolate-brown, cashmere-knit jumper dress…it was *the Bishop* himself who was there to meet her.

(She didn't know what she was expecting or who she was expecting be there to meet her, but for some reason she didn't think it would be him.)

However, what really surprised her was seeing him dressed in a white, Cuban-collared shirt and casual sand-coloured trousers rather than one of his usual ultra-chic Italian suits.

This guy really is so…unpredictable, she thought to herself. I never know what to expect next.

♝

The Bishop greeted her with his customary consideration and having exchanged the usual social courtesies…though they did not kiss…he politely led her through the busy terminal to the car park, even offering… rather generously…at one point, to push her baggage-trolley for her …*which she (Madison) respectfully declined.*

At the car, they quickly loaded up and within minutes they were making their way back to the Abbey…*or at least that was where the Bishop assumed they were headed, even though he hadn't really made it clear in his invitation*…but a little while later, as the Aston approached the Abingdon turn-off on the M40 motorway, Madison suddenly pulled a piece of paper out of her purse on which the address of the cottage she had rented was printed.

'I didn't know what arrangements you had made, so I made my own… just in case', she explained calmly, opening the page out fully in order to show him where she needed to go.

'I'll be staying here', she revealed confidently, trying to be light-hearted about it; '…at this cute little cottage known as Tanglin'.

'Have you ever heard of it?' she enquired casually, trying to be as diplomatic as possible; 'it's not too far from your place, I think'.

The Bishop glanced at the sheet of paper with its photo and its summary description of the rental cottage's amenities…and in that split second, his mood changed visibly; he looked straight ahead, his demeanour stiffened and he gripped the steering-wheel a little tighter than was probably necessary.

'Yes, I know the place…more or less', he murmured, looking in the rear-view mirror to avoid looking straight back at his passenger, before flicking the indicator to warn the car behind that he was about to turn off the motorway.

The news had clearly come as a disappointment to *the Bishop*, but realising that he wasn't blameless either in the lack of communication between them, he didn't show his indignation to any great extent, preferring instead to maintain his inscrutable chess-face as he concentrated on the traffic and the road ahead.

Meanwhile Madison took out her mobile phone…and in her best professional manner, she called Mr Douglas - *the estate agent who was dealing with the let* - to inform him where they were, so that he could co-ordinate his arrival at the property with theirs - bringing with him the keys and the lease for her to sign – so that she could take possession of the cottage in a smooth contractual operation.

It was another ten minutes or so before they arrived…but caught up in the excitement of her adventure Madison didn't even pick up on the fact that *the Bishop* had driven straight to the cottage without asking her for any further precision as to the address.

Nevertheless, moments later, they pulled off the road and into the little drive-way that led to the cottage, Madison looking all around and pointing out the little wooden sign as they passed-by, which announced the property's name as 'Tanglin'.

Mr Douglas was already there, pacing to and fro in front of the property. He had come straight over after her call to open up the little cottage…in order to air it out a little…before she arrived, as it had stood vacant for some time.

The Bishop parked up next to the estate-agent's Land Rover and as soon as she saw it, Madison immediately fell in love with the little cottage; something about it just said 'home'.

She got out of the car…and while *the Bishop* and Mr Douglas greeted each other politely with a respectful British nod, the enchanted young New Yorker quickly took a few steps back from the car in order to take in the full perspective of her new residence; including the white-washed walls, the cute leaded-windows, the trellises around the doorway… entwined with an array of pretty lavender flowers…and…the rather singular smell of the thatched roof.

There was not much of a garden with the property and what there was, was overgrown and unkempt; but that aside, everything else looked just like she had always imagined an English cottage would.

'Would you like a guided tour, Miss?' Mr Douglas asked courteously, going through his usual routine as he walked towards his client.

Madison looked at him and smiled in response to his offer…but then taking him by surprise, she held up a halting hand, stopping him in his tracks.

'That's very kind of you…sir…but if you don't mind, I would rather look around on my own first, in order to get a feel for the place', she insisted, showing the confident authoritarianism that she was now cultivating in her new role.

'By all means', the agent agreed, looking over a little bemused at *the Bishop* who simply shrugged and waved her on.

Madison took a deep breath; then stepped forward, walking cautiously through the front door and across the cottage's tiny threshold. Inside, it was like walking into another world; stone walls, wooden floors, antique beams across the ceiling and furnishings from another age - but as she stood there in the middle of the tiny living-room, admiring the quaintness of it all, she suddenly felt a strange energy, in the air around her.

It made her shiver…in the moment …but doing her best to ignore it, she carried on with her visit, walking over to the staircase and slowly making her way upstairs…where the well-worn wooden boards creaked and groaned with every step of her ascent.

She quickly reached the landing area and pausing for a moment to look left and right, she quietly lifted the latch on the door to her left and peeked inside. This just happened to be the smaller of the cottage's two bedrooms but despite its secondary status and its simple decor, the room still had the most beautiful oak-beamed ceiling.

Madison walked on in…and as she caught sight of herself in a mirror hung by design on the far wall to make the room look bigger than it actually was, the blurred vision of what she could only describe as a couple of amorous lovers flashed briefly before her eyes …while the muted sounds of their tempestuous embrace rang disquietingly in the sound-box of her mind.

It was a little unsettling…and most people would have probably turned and hightailed it out of there without a second thought, had they experienced such an event, but Madison had been taught from a young age – *probably in the stories told to her by her grand-father* - that houses in England were often haunted, so dismissing the phenomenon as more of a moment of over-excitement than any folkloric hallucination, mind-trip or 'goings-on', she calmly checked out the other, larger bedroom…before quietly making her way back downstairs, deciding that…despite its strange energy…she would still like to rent the cottage as it was close enough to the abbey – *where she hoped to be spending most of her time anyway* - to be convenient…and yet not too close if she or *the Bishop* needed some space.

'…And you are within easy walking distance to the abbey', Mr Douglas confirmed as she walked out, one hand raised, gesturing to *the Bishop* to come and have a look inside her newly acquired…albeit temporary…home.

He and the Bishop had clearly been conversing while she was inside taking a look around.

The Bishop…not uptight but clearly not in his usual controlled state… glanced briefly at Madison and then at his watch, before politely refusing her invitation…much to her dismay…announcing rather cryptically instead that 'time was of the essence' and that '…Mr Douglas here needed to get on to his next client, as they had just called and were already waiting outside the property that they were hoping to rent out'.

The latter, looking rather puzzled, glanced briefly at *the Bishop* with raised eyebrows...as he had received no such call...but then feeling a little awkward, he simply stepped forward and invited Madison back inside the cottage so that he might show her the layout in greater detail...even though it was only small...as she would need to know where the electric, the gas and the water supply stop-cocks were situated in case of an emergency.

It only took a few minutes and once they had completed the inventory and Madison was satisfied that everything was as it should be, they reappeared, walking over to the Land Rover where, after a brief re-read of the contract, using the car's bonnet as a prop, Madison began signing the rental papers, reminding Mr Douglas as she did so that she had sent a deposit in advance plus payment for the first two weeks of her stay.

The latter smiled at her courteously, confirming readily what she had just referenced before counter-signing his name at the bottom of the lease, and handing her the keys; the deal was done.

He then got into his car and took his leave, surprising Madison...as he pulled away...with a blast from his car's rather powerful horn, which made her jump.

In the meantime, *the Bishop* had opened the boot of his car...and once she had finished watching Mr Douglas's car disappear into the lane at the end of her little driveway, Madison quickly turned around and began walking towards him...a beaming smile on her face and a twinkle in her eye as she swung the keys to the cottage in front of her like the cat that had gotten the cream.

She was clearly excited and expecting him to stay for a while...if for nothing else than to help her to get settled in...but still looking at her with a rather indifferent expression on his face, *the Bishop* immediately dashed those hopes, by informing her quite summarily that he had organised dinner for them at the Abbey later that evening '...for her first night' – and that, '...if it was alright with her...', he would rather get back home to make sure that everything was in place for that.

Madison was stunned...and a little disappointed...that the guy who had invited her over, the guy, for whom she had travelled thousands of miles, would just drop her off and leave...having totally brushed aside her excitement and her enthusiasm for her new abode...and she could quite easily have had a go at him for that...but knowing how much of an enigma the Bishop was, and not wanting her trip to get off on the wrong foot, she managed to restrain herself, bite her lip and accept his reasoning without question.

He then removed her suitcase from the boot of his car...and without another word quietly deposited it by the front door, before marching straight back to the car and getting in behind the wheel.

Madison, still dumbstruck, just stood there and watched, not really believing what she was witnessing...and as the car-door closed...somewhat abruptly...with quite a resounding 'thunk', she could do nothing but look on, totally mystified.

It was a weird, almost surreal moment but the next sound that she heard was that of the Aston's engine...roaring back into life, as *the Bishop* switched on the ignition and gunned the engine a couple of times...before shifting it into gear.

Then, just before releasing the hand-brake, he calmly lowered the driver's-side window and leaned out;

'I'll be back to pick you up again at seven', he informed her, in a rather brusque and peremptory tone.

'Can't wait', Madison threw back at him with more than a hint of sarcasm, her arms now crossed firmly in front of her chest.

And with that, the Aston started rolling forward, following the same path as Mr Douglas's car had, just a few minutes earlier, leaving Madison all alone for the first time in the quiet stillness of her new surroundings.

'Unbelievable!' she mumbled to herself, kicking the ground below her feet in frustration.

Clearly miffed...and a little disconcerted...by *the Bishop's* rather odd behaviour...*but refusing to be aggrieved by his uncharacteristic and quite frankly unwarranted display of churlishness,* Madison just turned back around and stood there, facing her new abode.

She had never seen anything quite like it...and almost bewitched by the little cottage's uniquely original architecture, she remained standing there...for a good minute or two...marvelling at the wonderful tableau... and revelling in all its timeworn splendour, before quietly picking up her carry-on bags and marching inside...coming back out almost immediately to grab her suitcase from the doorstep...before closing the door behind her one more time, ready to...finally...get her vacation under way.

Once inside, Madison calmly set about unpacking all her bags and as she did so she began pondering on why *the Bishop* had been so unwilling to share in her excitement over her new 'residence'...even if it was only temporary.

Had she done something wrong?

Was he upset about the fact that she had rented the cottage – and if so, why?

He hadn't mentioned in his invitation that his hospitality extended to her staying at the abbey, and he would certainly have let her know if she had presumed that that was the case...when it wasn't...so why the long face and the surly attitude?

'Whatever...; that's his problem', she decided boldly as she opened the bedroom window and looked out onto the cottage's diminutive back garden; 'I'm not going to let his weird behaviour spoil my vacation...or put a damper on my otherwise buoyant mood', she resolved candidly.

An hour or so later, having put away all her bits and pieces...in the tiny closet...and the even tinier wooden drawers...*remembering at the last minute to leave out her outfit for the evening ahead, which she laid on the bed,* Madison decided it was time for her to unwind and take a nice, hot bath. It had been a long day and she had been looking forward to this moment ever since she had touched down at Heathrow.

However, her first experience of quaint English living was to be a very brief one, as the little cottage did not have a bath…only a shower, and the trickle of water that came out of the antique shower-head left quite a lot to be desired in comparison with the high-powered pressure jets that she was used to, back in New York.

Nevertheless, she managed as best she could…and within no time at all she was primped and ready…looking very 'New York chic'…in an asymmetric black and white print dress and designer heels.

She had picked out the 'chess-inspired' designer dress so as not to look like she was trying too hard to be provocative.

Her hair and makeup done, she even had time…

> to pack a small overnight-bag…just in case…
>
> to check her mobile phone for any urgent messages…*of which there were none*…and
>
> to finish an article on her lap-top…which she had started to read on the plane…

while she waited…with great anticipation…for *the Bishop* to return.

18:58

It was still warm outside…but by the time the Aston rolled back into the cottage's little drive-way…at two minutes to seven…the light from the sun had started to fade and a gentle evening breeze had started to rustle the leaves on the trees as twilight approached.

Madison was still on her lap-top…but when she heard the tyres crunching on the loose gravel outside…and saw the wash of car headlights chasing shadows across the cottage's tiny rustic windows, she quickly closed it down and made her way to the door, grabbing her overnight-bag from the couch as she went.

She switched off the lights...and stepped outside onto the little porch, feeling an instant early evening chill on her exposed arms as she did so; I should have put a jacket on, she thought to herself as she retrieved the keys to the cottage from a handy little pocket in her overnight bag and locked the front door...turning the key twice just to make sure.

Then, having checked the door-handle twice too...to be doubly certain that she had locked up properly...Madison turned and set off down the little path...keeping her eyes on her feet all the while...*wary that she might just ruin her favourite Louboutins if she was to slip on the somewhat uneven surface*...reaching the car-door, just as *the Bishop* was pushing it open for her.

'Good evening', he announced with a rather sardonic smile, the look his eyes betraying his surreptitious cynicism for her security-conscious New York paranoia as he re-engaged the gear-shift.

'Hi', Madison announced in reply, casually dismissing her host's barely-disguised critique as she settled into the passenger-seat beside him.

'You look stunning tonight', *the Bishop* appended as he released the hand-brake.

'Thank you...' Madison replied, strangely taken aback...but nonetheless delighted...that he would compliment her on her appearance.

The car started moving...and in no time at all...having carefully negotiated the half-mile or so of twisting lanes that separated the two properties...they were back at the abbey, where, once *the Bishop* had parked up in his usual spot, Madison got out with a spritely step, delighted to be back once again at his singularly-unique abode.

She slammed the car-door behind her in typical New York fashion and without waiting for any prompting from her host...who had clearly put his earlier vexation behind him...she immediately made her way directly to the front entrance, her footsteps crunching noisily on the uneven ground.

It was a little strange, but as she stood there at the front door, waiting for *the Bishop* to catch up to her, Madison felt somewhat different this time, more at ease and less uptight; not that she had been intimidated the last time she was there, but as with most things in life, familiarity breeds confidence.

The Bishop joined her a few moments later and having opened the door, he stepped back and invited her inside once again with a gentle helping hand placed delicately in the small of her back.

Madison smiled at him politely…and with a carefully-placed step, she preceded him into the hallway where…just as it had done on her first visit…the strong scent of testosterone filled her nostrils which flared noticeably as she breathed in the intoxicating lure.

She closed her eyes briefly…to enjoy the moment of recognition, but then as she continued walking, she was rather taken aback to see that a table with two place-settings had been set up in the conservatory.

'Wow, I'm impressed', she remarked, trying to manage her expectations; a hint of ambiguity in her voice nevertheless.

Smiling stiffly, *the Bishop* ignored her tone…and without further ado he ushered her inside, pulling out her chair in an exaggerated, over-chivalrous manner.

He then poured them each a glass of crisp white wine before casually excusing himself and disappearing to the kitchen, only to return a minute or so later with two wonderfully presented and beautifully-cooked fresh-salmon dishes.

Madison was a little confused.

This was not the man she thought she knew…and all through the meal that followed, she remained on tenterhooks, waiting for *the real Bishop* to make himself known, expecting him to revert to type at any moment and embarrass her over something she or one of her fellow countrymen might have said or done in recent weeks.

However, it never happened; her fears turned out to be unfounded; the expected outburst never materialised and instead of a dictatorial speech on whatever subject he cared to broach, an air of serenity and calm seemed to reign over the proceedings.

It was almost romantic…and even the conversation was more bi-lateral than it had ever been before, *the Bishop* agreeing to compromise on most of the topics they discussed…which was so unlike the man she had come to know previously.

They finished the meal and Madison's first day in England…for this trip anyway…drew to a close with *the Bishop* proposing a toast…to her, to thank her for all she had done for him in New York; another compliment which surprised her but which she accepted graciously.

He then concluded his flattering remarks with an invitation for her to stay over, explaining rather conveniently that her little cottage would need to be 'aired out and warmed through' properly before she could settle in and be comfortable.

This made Madison smile; she had heard a lot of chat-up lines in her time, and much better ones at that, but as she was determined to make the most of whatever happened during this trip, she accepted his invitation with barely a hint of feminine guilt.

In fact, feeling a little flirtatious, she even decided to take the lead in this curious game of cat and mouse, taking a final sip from her glass and putting it down slowly before getting up from the table … *pausing for only the briefest of moments*…and making her way out to the spiral staircase… which led up to the first floor.

The Bishop, his glass of wine still in hand, watched his guest's movement across the room with interest, his piercing eyes fixed firmly… and very indiscreetly…on the sway of her rather bewitching hips…while the anticipation of what she apparently had in store for him instantly increased the blood flow to every part of his body.

On reaching the bottom of the stairs Madison brazenly checked herself for another brief moment…clearing her throat nosily and throwing her host a discreet glance… *to make sure that he was watching*…before grabbing the mitre-shaped stair-cap and slowly beginning her ascent.

She climbed a few steps…but then, aware that *the Bishop* had yet to move from his seat at the table, she immediately stopped again, took a deep breath and leaned over the hand-rail.

'Should I leave the light on…?' she asked almost in a whisper, her eyes sparkling with enticement and promise.

Madison couldn't in fact believe what she was dong; she had never been promiscuous in her life…and she still wasn't… but since meeting the Bishop she had clearly blossomed both as a person and as a woman.

The Bishop raised his glass, took one last sip of nectar…and smiling back at her, got to his feet, ready to take up the challenge that his guest was so obviously throwing down.

He made his way out of the conservatory…and having turned off the conservatory lights, he advanced at a steady pace to the bottom of the stairs, ready to follow her up.

Madison had waited for him to start his ascent but then as she felt him behind her, feeling more excited than she had in a long while, she accelerated the pace, rushing up to the landing with a nervous snigger.

She was definitely looking forward to spending another night with this enigma of a man…despite the fatigue of her long day…but when *the Bishop* caught up with her on the landing and put a shepherding arm around her, walking her past his door to the guest room at the far end of the corridor, her growing excitement instantly waned.

What the hell was he thinking? She wondered as they came to a halt in front of the guest-room. Was this another one of his games?

Indeed, the confident young woman that she was, the liberated New Yorker who had seen and done it all, felt a little affronted if not insulted and embarrassed by this turn of events; surely he wasn't going to invite her to stay over and then ask her to sleep in the guest room, she thought to herself.

The Bishop slowly pushed open the guest-room door and seeing the puzzled look on Madison's face, as she stood her ground, he quickly reassured her by explaining…*with a strangely self-satisfied smile*…that since her last visit his antique Mongolian swing-bed was in need of some critical structural repairs, and as a consequence, he was using this room as his bedroom until those repairs could be carried out.

'It needs a lot of expert attention and I have yet to find the master craftsman capable of doing the job', he announced calmly, elucidating the mystery much to his guest's relief.

Madison didn't know how to take that comment; as a compliment or a critique, but pleased to have had her self-esteem re-affirmed, she just smiled at him cheekily, draped her arms around his neck and kissed him gently on the lips.

The Bishop responded, seizing her firmly by the waist…and stepping forward into her embrace, he pinned her against the frame of the door with a kiss of his own which became increasingly more passionate as he slowly caressed her top lip with his - and then the bottom one - in anticipation of an imminently deeper exchange.

Madison froze momentarily, unsure what she should do next, but then as his tongue softly parted her own warm, welcoming lips; she relaxed again, her body flooding with feel-good endorphins.

They moved into the bedroom, and without a second thought, Madison allowed her host to guide her gently towards the bed. She was suddenly desperate for his maddening touch …and as she stood there expectantly, *the Bishop* didn't disappoint, reaching nimbly behind her back to grasp the zipper of her dress as her whole body shivered in anticpation.

Their eyes met…and as their minds fused in a single goal, Madison felt her stomach tighten.

The Bishop didn't speak; he didn't have to…but all of a sudden he stopped what he was doing… pausing just long enough to prolong the moment and tease the flames of her desire.

All the while he stared at her…intensely…as if trying to read her thoughts…and then slowly, very slowly, pulled down on the zipper of her dress, milking the moment for maximum theatrical benefit as he revealed her beautiful womanly charms…once again…to his stern yet captivating masculine gaze.

Within no time they had slipped into that timeless rhythm…and for the next few hours liquid noises, rhythmic moaning and a never-ending chorus of soft gasps and contented sighs filled the small bedroom with an orchestra of delight, Madison revelling in the expert attention that her accomplished lover lavished relentlessly on every inch of her willing body.

She had missed him since he had left New York…more than she was ever prepared to admit.

Next morning, Madison was still in bed ensconced under sheets and pillows, doing her best to recover from a combination of jet-lag and an incalculable number of hours of love-making when all of a sudden *the Bishop* appeared at the door with a tray full of steaming hot coffee and warm croissants.

Peering at the clock on the bed-side table, she rubbed her eyes and just about managed to sit up, brushing her hair loosely out of her eyes.

'Good morning', *the Bishop* announced with an air of misplaced formality.

'Yeah, morning…' Madison replied sleepily, tucking the sheet around her.

The Bishop smiled uncharacteristically.

'Hard night?' he asked, in an attempt at humorous sarcasm.

Madison looked at him, unimpressed by his sexist comment - *even though it was said in jest* - but she didn't answer, preferring instead to let her disdainful expression convey her obvious feminine displeasure.

The Bishop saw her reaction and immediately regretted his awkward attempt at humour.

'I'm sorry; that was meant to be fun…'

He didn't finish his sentence but rather than dwell on the embarrassment of the moment he sat on the bed next to her and…by way of apology…

offered her a cup of hot freshly-brewed coffee, the aroma of which had quickly infused the air in the room with roasted splendour.

Madison accepted his contrite peace-offering with good grace…but as she reached out to take it from him, the balance between them was quickly restored when the sheet around her slipped, and she found herself inadvertently exposing herself once again to his gaze.

The Bishop thought nothing of it however…*as they had just spent the most wonderful night of passion together discovering every inch of each other's body*…though he was somewhat amused by Madison's rather flustered reaction to the sheet's disloyal collapse, as she tried desperately to cover herself up again in order to protect her modesty… *like an embarrassed teenager on her first date*…there-by demonstrating all the complexities of being a woman that neither he…with all his intelligence…nor any other man would ever really understand.

Nevertheless, he stood up chivalrously so that his disconcerted guest could pull more of the sheet around herself until…reassured that her modesty was once again intact…she invited him to sit back down.

A moment of awkward unease then punctuated the mood…each of them having been suitably embarrassed by a couple of those awkward instances which always tend to happen at the beginning of a relationship when two people are adjusting to each other…but in order to avoid a prolonged silence ruining their first moment of closeness – the 'night of passion' aside - Madison took it upon herself to make the next move, by remarking favourably on the softness of the silk sheets, admitting that she preferred them to cotton.

'…but tell me this, man of mystery', she enquired curiously…guessing that there was a reason; 'why do you have silk sheets on this bed and cotton…on the other one?'

The Bishop who was chewing on a rather jagged morsel of croissant finished swallowing before offering his reply.

'It's quite simple really', he explained in his typically English tone. 'I too prefer the silk kind…but for practical reasons I have to put Egyptian cotton on the swing-bed to reduce the slip-sliding effect…', and with that he imitated the rocking movement of the bed with a gentle motion of his hand.

'I see', Madison acknowledged, blushing slightly.

They finished breakfast and still looking a little dishevelled Madison got out of bed and walked over to the bathroom completely naked, allowing *the Bishop* yet another chance to stare with impunity at the perfection of her body.

'I'm going to take a shower…' she advised calmly.

'Well, if you want a shower, you'll have to take it in the other bathroom; that one only has a bath', *the Bishop* disclosed politely, as he began tidying up the breakfast tray.

Madison pouted for a second; she would have loved to take a long, relaxing bath but she still wasn't sure if she could impose her presence on him for that long, so erring on the side of caution, she grabbed a robe that was hanging from a peg on the bathroom door…noticing on the wall beside it a framed quote which read; 'Love will find a way through paths where wolves fear to prey', as she tied the belt around her waist. The quote was signed; Lord Byron.

She didn't comment on it…but she did find it rather curious.

'Very well, then', she insisted returning to the bed to give him a peck on the cheek before disappearing out the door.

Moments later, Madison entered the master-bedroom and headed for the shower, noticing as she rounded the bed that *the Bishop* had replaced the photo she had seen on his bedside table on her previous visit with yet another framed quote; this one reading; 'The scars you can't see are the hardest to heal'; Astrid Alauda.

Curious, she bent over to read the quote twice…but then bemused by both its meaning and how it related to *the Bishop*, she just shook her head and continued on her way into the shower which she dragged out for far longer than she would have done normally, in order to compensate for the paucity of the shower she taken the night before in her little cottage.

In fact, it took her at least forty minutes to shower and get dressed again…this time a little more casually than she had the night before…but feeling refreshed…and having collected all her personal belongings…*which she threw somewhat haphazardly into her overnight bag*...she eventually made her way back downstairs where the *Bishop* was waiting patiently to drive her back to the cottage.

The drive only took a couple of minutes and within no time, *the Bishop* was pulling back into the cottage's little driveway, rolling the car to a stop just next to the front-door.

Madison looked at him curiously, wondering what he was going to do next, if he was going to stay...or if he was going to propose some other kind of excursion they might enjoy together later on in the day ...but having left the engine running...*thereby signalling his intention*...he simply reached into his pocket and pulled out a piece of note-paper on which he had scribbled a telephone number.

'This is the number for the Abbey...' he explained very matter-of-fact, '...so whenever you're ready to be picked up again, just give me a call...'

And with that he handed her the piece of paper.

Surprised and a little taken aback by his very dispassionate demeanour... especially after the night of passion that they had just shared...Madison took hold of the piece of paper and reached for the door-release, her head filling with myriad questions she knew she just couldn't ask; at least not yet.

'...Oh and if you do call; just let it ring three times and hang up', *the Bishop* then instructed; 'that way; I'll know that it's you'.

'Are you for real...?' Madison blurted out without thinking.

'I just hate answering the phone to strangers', he explained flippantly as he put the Aston back into gear.

Madison shook her head and without another word, she pulled on the lever and got out of the car, searching for the keys to the cottage in her overnight-bag as she went.

The Bishop waited for a moment to make sure that she got the door open...*knowing that the lock on the little cottage door could be sticky*...and then just before he pulled away, he opened the passenger-side window and called out to remind her that...despite the sun which was slowly beginning to peek through the clouds above, she should still turn the heating on for a few hours to warm the cottage through…in order to get rid of the stale and musty smells.

Madison nodded and thanked him for the advice…and for the lift…pleased in some way to see that he hadn't completely changed from the fascinating paranoid character she had first met.

Now, this rather singular arrangement set the tone of their liaison for the next ten days or so and all things considered, it worked well. Madison would call the abbey and hang up after three rings…*though she felt ridiculous every time she did it*…and then twenty minutes later *the Bishop* would pull up outside, like her own personal chauffeur, greeting her with all his usual courtesy.

He would then take her to lunch…or to dinner…during which they would discuss an eclectic range of topics including both British and American politics…and then, depending on the hour…he would either drive them back to the abbey where they would spend the rest of the day in each other's company…Madison, sometimes staying over…and sometimes not…

…or…if she preferred to be taken straight back to the cottage…to her own little piece of England's green and pleasant land…he would do that too…without a word of contention or disappointment.

This became the pattern of things…and when *the Bishop* wasn't available…for whatever reason…Madison would just hang around the cottage…or sit in its tiny garden…and work on her computer…keeping in touch with her office and her friends via 'Skype' or her mobile phone.

It was a strange arrangement in many ways… each of them keeping to their respective homes

…despite *the Bishop's* initial reluctance…but there was one particular detail…among all the eccentricity of the situation…that Madison found more puzzling than all the rest…and that was the fact that *the Bishop* never once stayed over at the cottage…*indeed he never even set foot in the place.*

This intrigued her more than she was prepared to admit…but despite their growing familiarity she could never find the right moment to bring it up…or to ask him about it.

And besides, when she did think about it… she realised that it was probably much easier…and a lot more convenient for her to go to the Abbey whenever she and *the Bishop* wanted to be together…as there was more space there…and more comfort…and the Abbey's fridge was always stacked full of food…thanks to a regular delivery service…which certainly wasn't the case in her little homestead.

One morning however Madison was in for yet another surprise.

It was a beautiful sunny day and rather than call *the Bishop* to come and pick her up, she decided after a light breakfast…a very light breakfast consisting of just an energy bar and a mouthful of mineral water…to walk over to the abbey…at her own leisurely pace... and arrive there unannounced.

It was only about half a mile from the cottage to the abbey and by following the lanes that she had seen *the Bishop* use when she had been in the car with him, Madison calculated that she could be probably make the trip easily enough in twenty minutes or so.

It would be almost like an adventure for her, she thought to herself, as in New York nobody ever walked anywhere if they could possibly avoid it.

The sun was bright but the air was still cool and crisp when Madison stepped out of the cottage that morning, a happy, pleased-to-be-alive smile on her face.

She locked the door behind her and set off down the little driveway at a leisurely pace …only to realise when she reached the gate that…despite her designer sun-glasses…she still had to squint against the strong sunlight when checking the road both left and right…for any oncoming traffic… before stepping into the narrow lane which led ultimately to the abbey.

The lane was deserted, but almost immediately…as her shiny blond hair began to blow gently about her face…Madison was hit by the fragrant smell of freshly-cut grass which filled the air all around her, the natural scent seemingly hemmed in and held prisoner by the roughly cut hedges that bordered the lane either side.

She stopped in her tracks and took a couple of deep breaths; then looking up…above her head…she was beguiled by the filtered strands of sunlight beaming through the billowing clouds…while to the left and right of her…in the overhanging leaves of the trees that bordered the lane… she could hear the mischievous, free-spirited breeze gently rustling those otherwise static miracles of nature.

It was a wonderful moment; a moment of communion with nature… and pushing her sunglasses back into place on the bridge of her nose… while enjoying the feeling of the sun's rays on her face…Madison decided there and then that she would make a habit of repeating this amazing experience as often as she could.

It took her a little longer than she had expected, but thirty minutes later, Madison was knocking on the door of the abbey after the most invigorating stroll of her life.

There was however no answer to her first knock, so she knocked again, and this time *the Bishop* came to the door, a look of frustrated surprise on his face.

'You didn't call', he remarked rather bluntly with a frown.

'No, I didn't; is that a problem?' Madison asked, a little out of breath… and somewhat surprised to see him still dressed in a towelling robe, another towel draped over his arm.

'No, I suppose not, but I would rather know that you are coming', *the Bishop* declared flippantly trying not to get irritated.

'How come you're not dressed already; that is so unlike you?' Madison commented making her way to the kitchen, desperate for something to drink.

'I was just about to go and relax in the spa', he informed her in measured tones, following her into the kitchen.

'Spa…you have a spa…where?' she exclaimed as she poured herself a glass of juice, looking at him, completely bemused.

The Bishop didn't answer.

'You're winding me up, right?' she continued, raising the glass to her mouth and swallowing a large gulp of orange juice.

Being the investigative journalist that she was...Madison had made it her business to visit every room in the abbey...or so she thought...but she had never seen anything that vaguely resembled a spa.

The Bishop turned on his heels and walked off in front of her; 'Come along; I'll show you', he responded as he opened the back door and disappeared into the garden.

Intrigued but still convinced that he was toying with her - *even though that was not really his style* - Madison finished her juice and followed him out.

Outside, *the Bishop* walked on ahead...but Madison quickly caught up, scuttling along behind him as they made their way down the path and through the tightly planted rose gardens.

It was another one of those surreal moments that Madison was slowly getting used to when in *the Bishop's* company and as she walked behind him, being careful not to trip on the uneven flagstones, she could not help but sneeze as her city-living, olfactory senses were once again inundated, this time with the heavily perfumed bouquet that wafted up from the flowers all around them.

Indeed, she was just about to comment on the overpowering nature of the scent when *the Bishop* suddenly stopped in front of her and turned sharp-left, making his way over to a little thatched structure, situated away from the main garden and half-hidden by a thicket of purple and white hydrangeas.

Madison stopped in her tracks too, surprised that he had veered off when he had...but she quickly caught up again, just as *the Bishop* came to a halt in front of the little cabin where, taking a key out of the pocket of his towelling robe, he calmly unlocked the padlock that evidently held the door secure.

'There', he announced almost triumphantly as he pushed the door wide open with a sweeping gesture of his hand.

'Would you like to take a look inside?' he enquired, savouring the moment over his guest's doubting mind, a self-satisfied grin on his face.

Madison was still convinced that he was winding her up for some reason, but as she boldly accepted his invitation to step forward and peer through the doorway, her jaw almost dropped to the floor when her eyes caught sight of the view.

Inside the little cabin *the Bishop* had installed what she could only describe as an all-singing, all-dancing, state of the art Jacuzzi unit…and as she caught her breath again, Madison could do nothing more than stand back in disbelieving admiration.

'Well, Mr Byron, you never cease to amaze me', she commented, turning back to *the Bishop* who was stood there with the smuggest of smiles on his face.

Of course, Madison had indeed noticed this little cabin several times before, but she had always assumed that it was just one of those sheds used to store gardening tools and the likes which held little or no interest to a city girl like herself.

How wrong could she have been?

'Never judge a book by its cover', *the Bishop* announced as he walked inside leaving his guest still completely bemused at the door.

The air inside the cabin was warm and humid and while Madison continued to look on, still filled with frustrated disbelief, *the Bishop* simply went about his business, programming the integrated music unit on the spa's console and checking the settings for the water's temperature.

Then, once he was satisfied that everything was just right, he turned to look at Madison again, staring at her for a few seconds before removing his robe.

She took that as a signal that she should look away or at least avert her eyes which she did respectfully, but while she did shield her face with one hand, she nevertheless took a sneak peek at him through her fingers while he wasn't looking, curious as always not to miss a trick.

She had expected to see him completely naked, after the way that he had looked at her, but she was pleased – and reassured in some way – to see that he had in fact maintained his usual decorum in her presence, though she had to admit that the slightly pretentious pair of cotton monogrammed shorts that he was wearing had seen better days.

The Bishop hung his robe on the hanger which had obviously been placed there for exactly that purpose and having removed his plastic footwear, he proceeded to lower himself into the steaming, bubbling mass of water as Madison continued to look on incredulously.

'Would you care to join me?' he asked courteously. '...it's wonderful for relaxing and de-stressing tired, weary muscles'.

'No thanks, I'm not really dressed for it', Madison argued, gesturing to her attire; a beautiful summer print dress from Dolce & Gabbana.

'In fact, I don't even have a swimsuit with me', she remarked, '... because when I packed for England, the idea of bringing a swimsuit never crossed my mind', she added with a hint of irony.

'Hey, who's watching?' *the Bishop* asked cheekily.

Madison rolled her eyes and looked up at the sky; there was no way she was getting into the hot-tub, stripped down to her underwear.

'Maybe next time', she concluded.

'Look, I came over to surprise you but I think that I would rather go back to the cottage and catch up with some more paperwork while you are enjoying your spa', she confessed, feeling a little awkward.

'That's fine by me', *the Bishop* agreed, nodding his head.

'...Oh, and I'm sorry for not calling ahead', she declared apologetically.

'Think nothing of it; I'll see you later', *the Bishop* confirmed.

'...for dinner', he added, after a brief pause; 'I've got some work to do myself later on'.

'Sure', Madison concurred as she turned to leave.

She closed the door behind her, still in a state of shock really, but then just as she began to walk away, she was jolted back to reality by the sound of a loud thud and water spilling down, splashing onto the floor.

Quickly, she back-tracked and re-entered the little cabin, only to find *the Bishop* standing upright in the middle of the Jacuzzi, drenched from head to foot, water dripping from his now straggly black hair and the man himself looking rather churlish.

'It's okay; I just lost my footing. It's no big deal', he reassured her, trying to hide his embarrassment as he wiped his brow.

Madison accepted his explanation without question…and reassured that the moment of panic was over, she turned to leave again, knowing that he would prefer that she left him alone to recover his composure in his own good time.

She waved goodbye once again over her shoulder and returned to the cottage without further incident, enjoying the walk back just as much as she had the walk there, even stopping off about half-way to watch a flock of sheep grazing in a field…and contemplate on her life…before continuing on her way.

Back at the cottage, Madison was again gasping for something to drink, so she immediately put on the kettle and while it was boiling she collapsed onto the small Chesterfield couch, kicked off her shoes and began to check her e-mails on her laptop.

She wanted to call Evie for a chat as they hadn't spoken in a while, but as she glanced at her phone, she realised that the time difference meant that her friend would probably still be in bed.

Consequently, lost for something else to occupy her…*as she had tabled on spending the day at the abbey…*Madison decided that rather than just hang around the cottage all day, she would go into the nearest town and have a look around.

She knew from her time at university that Oxford was well known for its culture…and its architecture…and presumed that while she was there, she would also be able to look for a swimsuit for the next time that *the Bishop* invited her into the spa - as despite her reticence earlier, she quite fancied the idea.

And so it was that half an hour later, having changed out of her dress and into a practical little blouse, her favourite pair of jeans and some comfy shoes, the taxi she had ordered on her new phone-app was dropping her off in Queen Street in the centre of Oxford.

She paid the fare and stepping out of the cab Madison was immediately overcome by the beauty and the historic nature of the famous old town; everywhere she looked was spectacular...and while she was no expert in architecture she could not help but be impressed by the cathedral, the museum and the array of other buildings that lined the narrow streets.

Enjoying the sights and the warm afternoon sun Madison ambled around the city-centre for quite some time, window-shopping here and there for over an hour before finally finding a boutique that specialised in lingerie and swimsuits.

She went inside and having had a good look around, she picked out almost a dozen items to try on – including a number of bikinis, *which, if they fitted her well enough, she would keep for her next beach holiday* - and several other one-piece swimsuits which she thought would be more suitable for the spa, were she to be given a second chance to take advantage of it.

The assistant indicated a cubicle to her and for the next forty minutes or so she tried on every one of the articles, at least three times before finally settling on two modest, one-piece swimsuits and three different bikinis.

'Would you like them wrapped, Madam?' the young assistant asked politely as Madison put her chosen outfits on the counter.

'No..., just put them in one of those carriers; that'll be fine', Madison replied, enjoying the typically British service, as she handed over her card.

The card-transaction completed, Madison smiled politely at the young assistant and left the shop delighted with her purchases; the grin on her face proof that the retail therapy had had its usual uplifting effect on her mood.

Turning left out of the shop, she continued her way down the High Street…where there was still a multitude of shops for her to check out… and as her mind began to wander and wonder how *the Bishop* would react to seeing her new swimsuits, Madison found herself coming to a halt once again, only a few doors further down, in front of yet another boutique which this time specialised in perfume.

Once more, she could not resist going inside to take a look…and still on a high with those romantic thoughts of what *the Bishop* might say about her swimsuits running through her mind, she bought herself a new bottle of Fendi perfume to replace the bottle that he had bought for her previously, calculating that if he had bought it for her, then he must like it himself.

The next stop was the Market…which was to be another incredible experience…but on the way there, as she passed by one of the many little side-streets, another strange little shop caught her eye.

It wasn't a fashion shop; in fact she would not normally have paid any attention to it as the window-front was simply piled high with baby-linen, coloured towels and assorted bed-sheets, but on several of the items displayed, Madison noticed those same monogrammed initials that she had spied on *the Bishop's* shorts earlier…and in the corner of the window a small notice which read 'Any initial, any style; ask inside'.

She pondered on whether she should go inside and investigate further; she even considered maybe buying him a new pair of shorts, to replace the old ones - if they still sold them that is - but then after playing tug of war in her mind for a while…of should she, shouldn't she…Madison suddenly realised that in fact she didn't actually know the *Bishop*'s waist-size, so to go ahead and buy a pair would probably be pointless.

Besides, she thought to herself, it was better that she erred on the side of caution as far as *the Bishop* was concerned, because although they were getting closer by the day, it would probably be a little presumptuous on her part to buy him something so intimate at this stage of their bourgeoning relationship despite the fact that they now knew each other intimately.

How strange is that?, she mused to herself, because while *the Bishop* had offered her a set of lingerie after only two or three meetings…which men of all ages have a tendency to do without even a second thought…the other way around seemed a little awkward for some reason.

Madison got back from Oxford just before six o'clock and after a quick shower, she called *the Bishop* to let him know that she was ready to be picked up, smiling to herself smugly as she waited for the phone to ring three times before she hung up…as was their rule, and remembering only too well the look on his face earlier in the day when she hadn't followed the procedure.

She slipped into her chic plum-coloured body-con dress, then quickly packed herself a little overnight bag…in case she stayed over…and as she wasn't sure if she might need them, she threw in her new swimsuits too, just to be on the safe side.

A few minutes later, as had become their routine, *the Bishop* pulled up in front of the cottage and only ten minutes or so after that, they were back at the abbey, sitting at the breakfast-bar in the kitchen enjoying another one of his speciality pasta dishes.

He had opened a bottle of wine and as they sat there and discussed their respective day's occupations, in between mouthfuls of delicious tagliatelle, just like a pseudo-married couple, the mood in the room was one of relaxed reciprocated enjoyment.

'I have to say that I am amazed by your culinary expertise', she remarked as she popped another forkful into her mouth; 'I would never have pegged you for a chef'.

The Bishop smiled. 'I'm sure that there are a lot of things you don't know about me', he responded.

Madison smiled, then finished off her first glass of wine…and as *the Bishop* poured her another, he asked her if she was going to put on a fashion show for him later.

She blushed slightly at his suggestion; her conservative upbringing showing through once again in her self-consciousness.

'I don't think so, wise guy', she teased, trying to recompose herself by distractedly running her fingers through her hair.

The Bishop shrugged his shoulders in disappointment; then smiled again.

'Oh, alright, you can have a look… but I'm not modelling them for you', Madison relented, screwing her face up facetiously; the look in her eyes contrasting strongly with the words coming out of her mouth.

The Bishop scoffed playfully as he cleared his plate. 'Did you know that in the game of seduction, the smile is the number one weapon?' he asked calmly.

Madison smirked back at him but didn't answer, realising suddenly, in a moment of pure mind-blowing clarity, that being in the company of this man meant her having to be constantly on her toes, constantly ready with a wise-crack or some creative thought to counter him, because once again he had outmanoeuvred her...and this time, all it had taken was a smile.

They finished eating and while *the Bishop* cleared up, Madison excused herself momentarily in order to pop to the loo, and fetch her swimsuits so that she could show him, as promised.

When she came back, they moved into the conservatory and while *the Bishop* sat at the piano, lazily tinkering with the keys, Madison opened up her bag and showed him what she had bought, having to refuse twice more - point blank - his suggestion that she should model the swimsuits for him.

The evening continued and just as they had been doing almost every evening since the day she had arrived, they discussed a number of different topics, rarely agreeing but always finding out more about each other through the positions that they defended.

The banter between them was like a game of cat and mouse and this particular evening, with the effects of the wine slowly rounding the edges of their respective characters, the flirty innuendo being exchanged around the design of her different swimsuits, slowly turned into frivolous, pre-bedtime foreplay as each of them tried to outdo the other.

However, Madison was soon bored with that game, and in an effort to encourage open debate and break off from the reductive objectification of women that *the Bishop* had begun to pontificate about once again... in response to her throw-away comment about beauty pageants and their obvious propensity to attract those with voyeuristic tendencies...she suddenly jumped up and challenged him to a game of snooker.

The Bishop stopped talking instantly and looked at her, rather amused, never having seen or heard her ever mention the word sport before...but as her suggestion challenged his competitive spirit, he agreed without a moment's hesitation to show her how the game was played, standing up in turn and leading the way across the hall to his study.

In the study;

The Bishop set up the game and handing her a cue, he invited Madison to break.

'Break?' she questioned, tossing her head defiantly.

'Start the game', he clarified, in his usual polite...but emotionally detached...manner.

Madison nodded and walking around the table she took up the stance she had seen so many guys take in the pool-halls of her youth.

'Am I good?' she asked, feeling a little gauche as she looked over her shoulder for his assistance.

The Bishop smiled politely, unable to hide a playful smirk. 'Not bad... but you need to plant your feet like so, bend at the waist and...'

He moved behind her and leaning over her...he gently guided her action, pulling the cue back and driving it forward again...without actually striking the ball.

He repeated the action twice more and then, feeling a little awkward they both stood up.

The Bishop then showed her the correct position one more time...on his own...before handing her back the cue.

Madison took up the stance again, and then after quite a long, drawn-out pause she pulled the cue back and smashed the white ball...known as the cue-ball...into the pack of colours scattering them randomly all over the baize-covered table.

The Bishop then took his turn, potting a red and then a blue ball before missing a long shot on the next red which brought the white ball back up the table to rest right against the top cushion.

Madison stood there defiantly, biting the corner of her lip as she weighed up her next move.

Then she took up the stance again and this time *the Bishop* averted his eyes slightly not wanting to be caught staring at her prostrate and slightly vulnerable position for a second time.

This time she did manage to 'pot' a red ball, but having missed the pink, which was an easier shot, she couldn't help but frown and let forth a pout of consternation.

The Bishop fluffed his next shot too, and in fact his shots rarely found the pocket thereafter, the cue-ball often ending up almost in the middle of the table which meant that Madison had to stretch her body across the table for almost every shot she took, much to her host's delight.

Indeed, one time, as she was stretched out and ready to shoot, he bent down and quietly whispered in her ear how much he was really enjoying watching her play.

Instinctively, Madison rolled her eyes at him, in mock indignation but said nothing as she sent the white ball ricocheting around the table and into the pocket right beside her.

'Damn', she blurted out. 'You put me off'.

'Tactics', *the Bishop* explained quietly, 'the key to winning any game... good tactics'.

Madison smiled, realising that it was a deliberate ploy and then prodded him firmly in the chest.

'I'm taking that shot again...tactics or no tactics', she insisted, and with that she retrieved the white ball and took up her determined stance once again.

The next couple of hours were spent playing game after game...and indeed as time went on, *the Bishop* was quite surprised at how quickly Madison picked up the rules...and how competitive she was once she began to get the hang of it.

'That's what Gary said when we went karting', she revealed elatedly.

'And what would that be?' *the Bishop* questioned making her repeat herself.

'Well, that I am quite competitive when I get the hang of it', she repeated as she potted another ball.

'I didn't know that you had gone…karting with Gary', *the Bishop* commented a little amused.

'You see, I'm full of surprises too', she smiled.

CHAPTER EIGHTEEN

(Part one)

The next morning, after another night of passion and transcendent bliss, the *Bishop* was busy rustling up breakfast when Madison quietly sauntered into the kitchen, wearing his dressing-gown.

Yawning and rubbing her eyes she plonked herself down on a stool at the breakfast-bar…looking on with quiet appreciation as he cracked eggs, grated cheese, diced vegetables and whipped up the perfect frittata in next to no time.

(**Frittata**; an Italian dish similar to a Spanish omelette)

'What's in that exactly?' she asked, screwing up her nose comically.

'Eggs, smoked salmon…some herbs and a dash of cream', *the Bishop* replied succinctly.

Madison frowned.

'You, young lady, have trust issues'; *the Bishop* remarked…a hint of paternal judgement creeping into his tone; '…especially where food…and women are concerned'.

'I do not...I have no such thing', Madison retorted, slowly raising a glass of orange-juice to her mouth.

'Oh yes, you do', *the Bishop* countered; 'I noticed it the first time you were here…when you asked about my cleaner and the photograph on my bed-side table', he continued, picking up a spatula and sliding it around the edge of the pan.

'That was just curiosity…I don't trust men more', Madison riposted again, an image of her assault in the office flashing through her mind.

'Very well then; if you don't have trust issues let's try this…' *the Bishop* suggested, walking behind her and slowly pulling the silk belt from the loops either side of 'her' robe.

Madison's hands immediately came up to protect her modesty which again provoked a rather wry smile on *the Bishop's* face as he ran the belt through his fingers…*to straighten out the creases*…before pulling it taut and tying it neatly around her eyes.

In that moment, Madison felt very vulnerable...but in spite of her innate wariness about any situation where she wasn't in complete control, she felt she knew *the Bishop* well enough now for him not to take any undue advantage of her.

'What are you going to do?' she asked inquisitively.

'I'm going to test your capacity to trust me', *the Bishop* whispered in her ear before sitting down on the seat beside her and making himself comfortable.

As he sat there, *the Bishop* studied Madison's features for a moment... and then watching her closely; he raised his right hand and ran a finger along her lower lip...very slowly and very deliberately.

Madison froze, making her host smile yet again.

'What are you doing?' she repeated.

'Don't you trust me?' he murmured.

Madison frowned behind her blindfold.

'Of course I do', she stated, wanting to get this over with as quickly as possible.

The Bishop then deftly transferred the omelette onto a plate, picked up a fork and began to feed her.

Ten minutes later;

'Well; did you enjoy that...?' he asked as he wiped her mouth with a cloth; '...trusting me'.

'I did...I was kinda weird...but...yeah...and that was delicious', Madison replied, quickly pulling off the 'blindfold and pointing in the direction of the pan'.

'Let that be a lesson to you', *the Bishop* remarked as he stood up and served himself his own plate of frittata.

‘You like teaching me a lesson...don’t you?’ Madison commented, a twinkle in her eye.

The Bishop didn’t respond; he just smiled that infuriatingly sexy smile as he calmly chopped up a piece of frittata with his fork, before devouring it.

A while later, *the Bishop* was relaxing in the bath, when Madison walked into the bathroom wearing just a sky-blue blouse over her delicate pearl grey underwear to ask if he had any plans for the day?

He looked at her with recognisable approbation, stroked his chin and then…observing the morning sun blazing through the window… suggested that they take advantage of the good weather and go for a drive, maybe stop off somewhere for a traditional pub lunch.

‘Fine by me; is there a dress-code for that kind of jaunt’, Madison asked. ‘I know you British are all about etiquette’, she added flippantly.

The Bishop smiled and waved for her to come closer.

‘Let me tell you…’ he began…and with that…as she leaned forward, he quickly pulled her into the bath on top of him, sending the splashing water in every direction.

‘What the ffff…?’ Madison screamed, trying to recover her balance.

‘That’s for being facetious’, the Bishop remarked before kissing her gently on the forehead.

‘You see; that’s why I have trust issues with men’, Madison shrieked as she scrambled back out of the tub and reached for a towel, thankful that her hair hadn’t gotten wet.

The Bishop just smiled and chuckled quietly to himself as she scurried away.

‘Oh and by the way’, he shouted after her as she rushed out; ‘I’m sure that whatever you choose to wear will be perfect’.

An hour or so later, as they made their way out of the Abbey, Madison asked if they could swing by the cottage before they hit the road so that she could change. ‘I need to change this…’ she explained, gesturing to her water-stained blouse.

The Bishop grimaced but could hardly complain as it was his fault that her blouse was all creased.

As a consequence, they drove over to the cottage; the *Bishop* choosing to wait outside by the car…as was his habit…while Madison hurried inside to get changed.

♗

She re-emerged ten minutes later, in a completely different outfit…having swapped her skirt and blouse combo she had been wearing for a smart short-sleeved tunic dress…and as she reached the car, she decided that it was her turn to tease…

'Can I drive...?' she asked playfully, running her fingers along the car's sleek paintwork; 'I have never driven in England…apart from that time I went karting and I don't think that really qualifies…'

The Bishop looked at her, hesitated and shook his head.

'You're not insured', he mumbled, opening the car-door and getting behind the wheel.

'I was only asking', Madison shrugged, secretly pleased to have put *the Bishop* on the spot for once.

♗

They drove out into the country and twenty minutes or so later they came upon a pub where a number of people were sitting outside at tables chatting freely and laughing overtly as if they had not a care in the world.

'This place looks cool', Madison commented, indicating her approval and expecting *the Bishop* to slow down and pull into the car-park.

However, he did no such thing and instead, his eyes fixed on the road, he carried straight on to the next pub which was a little more out of the way.

This time, reassuringly, he did slow down…and having indicated his intentions to the car behind, he carefully pulled off the road and into the car-park, manoeuvring the Aston in the largest of the spaces available.

Madison waited patiently for him to switch off the ignition…and maybe explain why they hadn't stopped at the previous establishment…

but as no explanation was forthcoming she simply shook her head, rolled her eyes in frustration…and got out of the car.

The Bishop, seemingly unaware of his passenger's perplexity, did the same and without a word being spoken, other than Madison's undirected 'this is cute' comment, they both ambled…separately…towards the pub's well-worn doorway.

Once inside, while *the Bishop* went to organise a table for them, Madison made a bee-line for the ladies-room…aided by a helpful female employee, who…having noticed her 'searching' demeanour…and caught her eye…indicated where the rest-rooms were situated with a discreet gesture of the hand.

Madison smiled back at her in reply and as she turned to the right and entered the narrow corridor she was somewhat amused to see the two rather-quaint ceramic door-plaques that indicated the different conveniences; foxes on the one…hounds on the other.

How fitting, she thought; seeing women as foxes…and men as hounds.

For the next two hours or so they enjoyed a traditional ploughman's lunch of cheese, pickle, boiled eggs, ham and bread…while discussing a number of topics…before driving back to the abbey where they spent the rest of the afternoon enjoying the abnormally good weather and relaxing in the Abbey's huge private garden.

The next day, the *Bishop* decided to repeat his morning spa and this time, as Madison had stayed over again, he insisted that she join him.

She wasn't really in the mood for such early-morning activity but brushing aside her excuses; he pulled out a couple of towels for her and went on ahead telling her to catch up with him when she had changed into her swimsuit.

'I don't have it with me…' she began to say, trying to remember where she had put the bag after the other night.

'You'll find them in a drawer in the master bedroom', *the Bishop* declared; 'you forgot to pick them up the other day, so I put them away until you needed them', he added from the corridor.

'I see; which one should I wear?' Madison asked, raising her voice to make sure he heard.

'Surprise me', he shouted back as he made his way downstairs.

Madison got out of bed and dressed in his robe…which she had more or less adopted as her own…she went into the master-bedroom to find her swimsuits…still yawning and stretching.

She looked out of the window and after one particularly enjoyable and relaxing limb-extension, she began opening a couple of the drawers looking for her costumes.

They weren't in the top drawer, nor were they in the second, but quite by accident in that second drawer, she did come across a small cigar box in precious wood, hidden amongst her host's monogrammed handkerchiefs.

Her eyes instantly narrowed and her eyebrows arched. She knew that he didn't smoke, so why would he have a cigar-box stashed away in one of his drawers. She was intrigued…her journalistic instincts were suddenly roused…and without thinking of the consequences of her actions, she immediately tried to open it.

The box was locked.

She picked it up, placed it against her ear and shook it.

The box was full…but full of what; what could he possibly keep in there? She wondered curiously.

Once again, the journalist in her was tempted to try to open it, but then overcome with guilt and images of his reaction, were he to find her snooping around in his personal belongings, she decided to put the box back in its place making sure that everything was just as she had found it.

She closed the second drawer and opened the third, where sure enough, sitting there neatly on the top of it, she found the instantly recognisable logoed-bag containing her swimsuits.

She quickly pulled them out, laying them all haphazardly on the bed, and having rejected the bikinis out of hand…after a speedy comparison of the other two in the full-length mirror, she opted for the more modest of the one-piece models, deciding that the morning and the occasion didn't really lend itself to the more seductively-cut articles.

Two minutes later, she was changed - and after barely showing the brush to her hair, she was rushing down the stairs with a huge fluffy towel wrapped tightly around her, ready to join her host in the Jacuzzi.

It was a most enjoyable experience.

Madison really got a lot of pleasure out of that first-time in the spa - even though her mind was a little distracted by what she had discovered – and from that day forth, over the next couple of weeks, it became somewhat of a routine, whenever she stayed over, for the two of them to start the day with an hour or so in the Jacuzzi, before returning to the house to enjoy a hearty breakfast in the kitchen.

They would then move to the conservatory, often still dressed in their robes and while Madison relaxed languidly on one of the couches, *the Bishop* would sit at the piano and play for her.

It was a very calming interlude to begin the day with, and even though Madison wasn't particularly musically-minded, she easily understood the benefits that *the Bishop* seemed to draw from the experience; it honed his concentration and allowed him time for reflection, deep reflection on all those subjects which seemed so important to him.

Knowing this, she never interfered or interrupted him during this time, but on the odd occasion, when the mood suited, she did get up and join him on the piano-stool, just to show him her appreciation of his talent, often amazed as she sat there by the speed and precision of his fingers as they danced across the keyboard to produce any number of her favourite tunes – though she stopped short of lionising him – his inflated ego had no need of the extra compliment.

Then, in the afternoon, when she decided not to go back to the cottage, they would spend their time relaxing in the garden, where the Bishop would bury himself in a newspaper or a book…when he wasn't dispensing a lecture or explaining another part of his particular brand of philosophy to her that is…while Madison would sit quietly reading a magazine or tapping away on her lap-top.

It was a peaceful and pleasant existence…almost idyllic in fact…with only the faint sounds of the country disturbing their silence as they whiled away their time – until the evening when after eating, they would often challenge each other to another game of snooker.

It was a surreal existence and Madison began to wonder quite where it was all leading; she and TB seemed to be living in a bubble, just the two of them, in a world where nothing else mattered, and yet despite the fact that her infatuation and her fascination for him was growing steadily stronger by the day, they never ever discussed the growing dynamic of their relationship or its evolution into something more permanent…

THE CONVERSATIONS

This idyllic existence was typical of the way that Madison and *the Bishop* spent their days during her stay. In fact, they spent many an hour relaxing in the garden…weather permitting… enjoying endless discussions on all manner of subjects, *the Bishop* taking it upon himself to broaden his guest's outlook on just about everything, lecturing her on all those areas of life that he himself found fascinating.

For her part, Madison quite enjoyed the intellectual repartee, sitting for hours mesmerised by *the Bishop's* cultured English accent…and the calm authority in his voice. She was always amazed…and sometimes confounded…by his turn of phrase, but his voice was always so clear and concise that even when she felt that she was drowning in a sea of words, she still found the experience fascinating.

And she learned so much; *the Bishop* not only widening her intellectual horizons but also teaching her some new life-skills, like how to use chopsticks during one of their more romantic evening meals.

At one point he even tried giving her a few lessons in chess…but sadly, that proved to be a lesson too far for her volatile impatience.

It was nevertheless a great vacation, and in his company Madison felt that she was both maturing as a person…becoming more rounded and more poised…and more importantly she was learning about subtlety, compromise and negotiation which were all areas of her character which she knew needed improvement.

These are a few random snippets from the conversations they had as they whiled away their time, lounging in the garden, relaxing in the Jacuzzi or just hanging around the abbey.

Discussion on Politics; (1) Tony Blair

M - 'Look at this headline', Madison announced pointing to the front page of her magazine; '...somebody has poured red paint all over the hands of Tony Blair's statue in Madame Tussaud's'.

TB - '...No more than he deserves...' *the Bishop* responded flatly without raising his eyes from his book. *(He was reading 'The Deconstruction of Society' by Trufeemu)*

M - 'Oh, you are such a cynic...' she countered.

TB - 'Well, the man does have blood on his hands...metaphorically speaking', *the Bishop* mumbled; 'he took this country to war on a dodgy dossier and a web of lies…and quite a few innocent lives were lost'.

M - 'Maybe, but it seems to me that these people are just jealous, Madison confirmed after a brief pause. 'It says here that the guy is a millionaire several times over...' she added, reading directly from the article.

TB - 'Yes, but at what cost...?' *the Bishop* continued, lifting his head slowly from his page and glancing across at her; 'He lost his dignity, his integrity and his reputation over that decision...'

M - 'You think...? She gasped. 'Wow, how does he sleep at night...?'

TB - 'He probably doesn't; he probably just sits there at the kitchen table of Brand Blair HQ with his rosary clasped tightly to his chest - saying a never-ending series of Hail Marys while his wife sits opposite him busily surfing the internet for new properties to buy.'

M - 'My god...humour...' Madison remarked. 'I never thought I would see the day...'

TB - 'Not humour, sarcasm...' *the Bishop* corrected her.

Madison shrugged her shoulders and flipped over to the next page of her magazine, knowing that she didn't have a good enough grasp of the events in British political life to continue the argument. However the Bishop wouldn't let it go so easily.

TB - 'You know, that man felt so guilty about taking this country to war on the back of his dodgy dossier...that once it was all over he converted to Catholicism just so that he could go to the confessional and ask for forgiveness'; he lectured, following up his comments with more uncharacteristic witticism.

M - 'Do you think God listened? Madison enquired irreverently.

TB - 'He didn't have to...Blair was looking in a mirror at the time', *the Bishop* quipped curtly.

(Madison smiled discreetly)

There was a pause in the conversation at that point before the Bishop added...

TB - '...You know...it's a real shame, because Tony Blair could quite easily have gone down in history as a decent PM. It's just unfortunate that like so many politicians before him, he caught the fever…the power fever…the sabre-rattling war-mongering fever passed on to him by your president George W Bush...'

The Bishop looked straight at Madison at this point;

'... and once that blew up in his face and he realised that his time in office was about to end, he spent whatever time he had left desperately milking his position for all it was worth, creating a network of powerful and influential friends that would subsequently finance his post-mandate lifestyle.'

M - 'He did?' Madison exclaimed.

TB - 'Of course, and lucrative offers came flying in from all around the world...and as you so rightly pointed out...having caught the political bug for greedy self-enrichment, he now has a portfolio worth millions...'

He paused and then added...
'...but at the risk of repeating myself...at what cost?'
Madison smirked but didn't answer.

TB - 'You wouldn't know this'...*the Bishop* mumbled in conclusion, 'but no PM has ever made as much money or accumulated as much wealth as Tony Blair has, since leaving No.10.'

'It's sad, but his legacy - *which he tried so desperately hard to create and nurture during his time in office* - will forever be tainted by his lack of morality...and <u>that</u> headline' – he nodded in the direction of her magazine – 'is the proof that the people of this country will never let him forget it...'

Discussion on Politics; (2a) Politicians

The Bishop, reading an article in the newspaper;

TB - 'I really abhor the way we are skewing humanity in order to indulge the selfish demands of all these minority groups who are using the ridiculous European Human Rights Act and the current wave of political correctness to bully spineless politicians into consenting to their demands, even when it is *contra-nature*...'

M - 'What do you mean?' Madison asked.

TB - 'Well for example, if somebody went up to a politician and said 'I want you to paint all the trees pink, the politician would tell that person to go away and get some help...'

M - 'I guess...' Madison responded with a shrug.

TB - 'However, if that person then said to the politician; I represent two million voters and there is an election coming up, the politician would immediately ask the guy to sit down…and while his secretary served him a glass of his finest malt…he (the politician) would be straight on the phone to the local DIY store to ask what shades of pink they had...'

Madison smiled silently and stifled a chortle.

'Because you see...politicians are not really interested in the future or the environment, they are not interested in the morality or the ethics of such a concept; all they are interested in is their own personal seat on the political gravy train…and if painting the trees pink pacifies the 'movement for pink trees committee' and gets them two million extra votes, thereby allowing them to keep that seat...then, hey...we get pink trees; politicians will sell their souls for votes'.

Madison looked skywards as the Bishop continued.

'It's like Gordon Brown, another of our ex PMs', he affirmed; '…here we had a 56yr old Scottish Presbyterian pretending to listen to the Arctic Monkeys, just so that he could tap into the youth vote...it's so cynical'.

M - 'The Arctic who?' Madison quizzed.

TB - 'Exactly', *the Bishop* blustered.

M - 'I think the liberals tried a stunt like that in the States a while back promising to legalise marijuana for medicinal purposes...but it didn't work...', Madison remarked.

TB - 'It didn't work for Gordon Brown either...' *the Bishop* confirmed.

M - 'Ah, poor Gordon Brown; didn't I read on the internet that he is considered the worst British PM ever – is that true?' Madison asked.

TB - 'Well, I believe that I mentioned this in passing once before but let's see...' *the Bishop* crooned, folding his arms. 'Gordon Brown was a career politician who had a dream; a very honourable dream; he wanted to be PM and he spent his whole life working towards that goal; ...somehow, he saw it as his destiny.'

M - '...and he succeeded, right...?' Madison interjected.

TB - 'Yes, yes he did; he got to the top...but unfortunately, while he wanted the job, the People of this country didn't want him...and when they were given the opportunity to tell him so, during the election, they let him know, in no uncertain terms.'

M - 'It was that bad?' Madison frowned.

TB - 'Yes, it was that bad', *the Bishop* confirmed; '...because despite it being his own personal ambition he should never have been handed the job; the man just wasn't up to the task, he didn't have the right profile or the necessary statesman-like qualities.'

M - 'What are you saying', Madison queried; 'He bullied his way into the job?'

TB - 'More or less', *the Bishop* replied; '..., and if only his spineless colleagues in the Labour Party had stood up to him during the sham leadership election and not been such a bunch of cowardly wimps, the country could have avoided his bumbling premiership altogether'.

M - 'You're very harsh', Madison remarked.

TB - 'Harsh but fair... and besides, in politics there is no room for sentiment', *the Bishop* confirmed again.

(Pause)

'…and by the way...that should never be allowed to happen again....' he added after the fact.

M - 'What should never be allowed to happen again?' Madison responded, a puzzled expression on her face.

TB - '…that somebody should be allowed to take up office at No.10 and lead this country without an official mandate from the voters', *the Bishop* explained. '...that kind of thing just shouldn't happen in a democracy.

A few days later...

Discussion on Politics; (2b) Politicians

M – (Lifting her head from a crossword puzzle) 'What is your definition of the word subversion?'

TB – (rubbing his chin) 'Well, let's see, subversion means to undermine the authority or the power of something or someone.'

M – 'Give me an example.'

TB – 'Well, I suppose there is no better example of subversion than Gordon Brown, the man we were talking about the other day. He personifies what the word subversion means in the way he plotted against Tony Blair in order to take his place.'

M – 'You really don't like that guy, do you?'

TB – (raising his tone slightly) 'I don't like anybody who is sly, devious and conniving...'

M – 'That pretty much rules out anyone in politics...'

TB - (with a shrug of the shoulders) 'Yes, it does, doesn't it...sadly?'

M – 'Do you want to elaborate?'

TB – 'I'd rather not, not on an empty stomach; it would take too long.'

Another time...

Discussion on Politics; (3) Politicians

TB – (laying back in reflection) 'If only we could have a politician in this country who actually listened to what the British people want'.

M – 'What do you mean by that?'

TB – 'Well; if we had a politician who actually listened to the voters of this country;

- We wouldn't have signed up for Europe where we are slowly but surely relinquishing our sovereignty over our borders, our justice system and to be honest, our independence.
- We wouldn't have gone to war in Iraq and Afghanistan.
- We wouldn't have let private enterprise exploit our elderly for financial gain

...and more pertinently, we would never have given up our passports.

M - 'Your passports'

TB – (reminiscing) 'Yes; our passports...they were black and sturdy and actually meant something...that you were British and proud of it.'

M – 'You're kidding me, right; you're living in the past?'

TB – 'Maybe so; but it was a much better time.... a time when the Great British passport was accepted and respected the world over.'

...and on another day...

Discussion on Politics; (4) Politicians

M – 'Who was Robin Cook?'

TB – 'Robin Cook?'

M – (Looking up from her laptop) 'Yes, Robin Cook; they are holding some kind of memorial service in his honour next week.'

TB – 'Aah, Robin Cook...Well, Robin Cook was a rather unique individual.'

M – 'How come?'

TB – 'He was the only non-eunuch in the Blair Cabinet.'

M – 'You mean, the only one with, ahem...balls.'

TB – 'Yes; he was the only one with any back-bone or moral fibre; the only one who would stand up to Blair; the only one in a bunch of spineless wimps and yes-men.'

M – 'Oh...'

TB – 'Yes; Robin Cook served as Secretary of State for Foreign and Commonwealth Affairs (Foreign Secretary) until he resigned in protest in 2003.'

M – '...and why did he do that...?'

TB – 'He wouldn't go along with Blair's lies on the Iraq War.'

M – 'So, he quit...very noble...'

TB – 'Yes, and you know what...when he died in 2005, Blair was so bitter and resentful that he didn't even break off from his holiday to attend the funeral.'

Madison frowned

TB – 'Yes; the man was part of Blair's cabinet for several years but because he wouldn't go along with the lies, Blair snubbed his funeral; that's how much of a statesman Blair is...'

M – 'You should be careful; Tony Blair is a powerful man'.

TB – 'I know; I've read the stories, but I'm of the belief that the truth should never be wrong. You wouldn't know this, being American, but by the time he left office Tony Blair was so hated by the British people that he had to travel the 250 yards from his office in Downing Street to Westminster in a bullet-proof limousine surrounded by four armoured Range-rovers?'

M – 'Who'd be a politician...right?'

The Bishop just nodded and grimaced visibly.

And yet another time...as they lounged in the garden

Discussion on Politics; (5) Labour Party

M – 'What do you think about the Labour Party leadership race?'

TB – 'Well, I am no expert on the matter but as far as I can see, because of Blair's clear-out, there is no obvious choice, no outstanding candidate; Diane Abbott, Ed Miliband and Andy Burnham are all too light-weight, politically-speaking, so I would guess that it will be a two-horse race between Ed Balls and David Miliband, with Miliband winning on the strength of his experience as foreign secretary...especially as Ed Balls is just a clone of Gordon Brown'.

M – 'A clone of Gordon Brown?'

TB – 'Yes, a clone of Gordon Brown; somebody who suffers from the same sense of deluded entitlement as he did; someone who believes that he has some kind of divine right, that it is his destiny to be the leader of this country whether the British public want him there or not...and don't even get me started on his wife...'

M - (Sarcastically, remembering their previous discussion) 'At least they are having an election, not like when your friend Gordon Brown got in unopposed.'

TB - (scowling) 'Can you believe that? That man was running this country without being elected to do so; he had no mandate from the people, no legitimacy, no credibility, he wasn't even elected to lead his own party; they just couldn't find anyone to oppose him so he was installed by default. And you know what...when he got into No.10 his two closest advisers were Alastair Campbell and Peter Mandelson, neither of whom were elected either, so we had a trio of people running the country, none of whom had been elected by the people to do so. I've said it before and I'll say it again; that kind of thing should never be allowed to happen again.'

M – 'you have said that before...but why didn't anybody stand against Gordon Brown?'

TB – '...Because, obsessed with his own legacy, Tony Blair had already gotten rid of the old-guard, of anybody he considered might be a threat to him or might steal his lime-light during his time in office; he just wanted wimps and yes-men in his cabinet and when he stepped down as the incumbent Gordon Brown was the only one left with any experience; nobody else had any real experience of government which is why the Labour Party now lacks leadership. They have nobody left with any experience, any gravitas or any statesman-like qualities.'

M – 'Wow; you really don't like politicians, do you?'

TB – 'I don't like Tony Blair and Gordon Brown because, between them, through narcissistic self-belief and bumbling incompetence they completely wrecked this country during their thirteen years in office'.

Discussion on Politics; (6) More discussion on elections

TB – 'Politicians lie to get elected.'

M – 'They lie?'

TB – 'Sorry; I'll re-phrase that. In order to get elected, politicians make the trusting, gullible electorate promises...that they know they will not keep.'

M – 'They would probably say that they just bend the rules a little... enhance the detail.'

TB – 'Typical rhetoric; but don't be so naive; it's simple; if they told the truth they wouldn't get elected...they have to sell the idea that they could make a difference, and you have to say that when all is said and done they are just human beings looking to keep their jobs...and with that in mind, they will say or do anything to keep their seats on the gravy train.'

M – 'So basically they lie; I get it.'

TB – 'Some pretend to be well-meaning and idealist but basically, yeah, they lie.'

M – 'So what's your point?'

TB – 'My point is this; they lie to get in there...but when they do get in, by default or however, rather than be grateful and humble, rather than represent their constituents...i.e. the people who put them there...they spend all their time looking after Number One or toeing the party-line (*under the threat of the whips, the enforcers*) whether it's in the interest of their constituents or not; that is why they are perceived by the public as greedy, self-serving frauds... and there have been too many scandalous examples over the years for anyone to deny that that is the case...herein lies the disconnect between the political classes and the British public.'

M – 'Wow; I've said this before but I'll say it again, you really don't like politicians do you?'

TB – 'I don't like anyone who takes advantage of others – whether it be physically or intellectually – in order to benefit themselves... and politicians just happen to be top of that list.'

Discussion on Politics; (7) Politicians

One morning Madison glanced over and noticed the headline on TB's morning newspaper;

M – 'Who is Ed Balls?'

TB – 'I think I've mentioned him before; Ed Balls is a man who wants to run this country.'

M – 'I see; well he'll have to change his name.'

TB – 'Why is that?'

M – 'Because…who's going to vote for a guy called Balls?'

TB – 'Now, now; as much as I disagree with the man's politics, that's unfair.'

M – 'Look, we've had a couple of politicians in the US with dodgy names; like Krystal Ball, Frank Shmuck, Young Boozer or Wankard Pooser, for example...'

TB - 'Wankyard Pooser?' *the Bishop* queried.

M - 'Yep, good ole Wankyard Pooser', Madison confirmed reading from her phone. '…but that said, even us untutored Americans who may not have your sophisticated British background would never vote for a President Balls or a President Richard Head...you know; Dick Head. Don't get me wrong; we might have come close with Dick Swett and Ben Bushyhead, but...Dick-Head, sorry Balls; it's just not going to happen...' she concluded.

TB – 'You have a point; a person's name is important, no matter how good he or she is in his or her field…even though it shouldn't actually have any bearing…'

M – 'Yes, and talking of fields, the British tabloid press with their love of word-play and innuendo would have a field day with it...I mean, look, even his wife doesn't want to be known as Mrs Balls. She insists on calling herself Yvette Cooper', Madison asserted, pointing to the front page of the newspaper.

Discussion on the EU (European Union)

TB – 'All three of the major political parties promised the British voters a referendum in their manifestos before the last election but they have been dishonestly dodging the question ever since. That is what is so frustrating about politicians; the lies and the hypocrisy. Cameron, the current PM says that a debate on the EU would be a distraction. A distraction! How can he possibly describe an issue that is so huge that it affects the fundamental way in which we govern ourselves as a country and the way we spend our own money as a 'distraction'? Surely, denying us the right to decide, denying us the chance to vote on issues that directly affect our very lives is scandalous...and undemocratic.'

M – 'I agree.'

TB – 'The political elite all know that an overwhelming majority of the people in this country want a referendum on the EU but they are determined not to give it to us; same thing with capital punishment. It's just another example of how the ruling class over-rides the democratic feelings of the people. Is it any wonder that the people feel disenfranchised?'

M – 'Yeah.'

TB – 'One of the great tragedies of modern Britain is that our leaders are not honest with us and then they wonder why there is a fracture between them and us.'

'Our mainstream politicians have done all they can to ignore the British public on this issue, wilfully refusing to accept the glaringly obvious sentiment of the people.'

'The truth is that the political classes are horrified by the prospect of a referendum as they fear that they would not receive the response that they want. That is where the fracture between the people and the ruling elite is so clearly evident.'

'If they were to give the public a choice on issues such as the death penalty or our participation in Europe then they would not receive the response that they want so they don't give us, the voting public that chance.'

M – 'That's democracy.'

TB – 'That's not democracy; that's self-serving arrogance.'

M – 'Why do you say that?'

TB – 'Because if it was real democracy, politicians would be elected and they would use their position to defend the ideas of those who put them there.'

M – 'Well; isn't that the case?'

TB – 'No, it isn't; once they get into power politicians stop listening to their constituents and start listening to their party while they feather their own nests; their priorities go like this; party, career...and then if they have any time left after filling in their expenses claims...their constituents.'

M – 'So, they are only human.'

TB – 'True, but by simply following the party line they keep making decisions and taking the country in directions that, given the chance the British public would choose not to go; Tony Blair for example, took us to war against everybody's will, while successive governments have buried us in European legislation, handing over our sovereignty little by little without ever consulting us; it is that arrogance that we abhor, that they the politicians believe that they always know best when quite clearly in many cases, they don't; they are constantly undermining our heritage and our way of life while at the same time being careful to prevent the voters from ever being able to voice their opinion; its un-democratic.'

'Ultimately, even if the politicians believe that the voters are wrong, it is their duty - as the people's elected representatives - to act as their voice, not to put forward their own personal opinions or agenda.'

(Pause)

TB – 'Of course, Europe is in the same position as us, only on a greater scale; it is another example of the ruling classes doing one thing while the population wants another.'

M – 'What do you mean by that?'

TB – 'Well, the people of Europe are being held hostage by the political classes who have a vision of the future with Europe as a united federal state…and to this end the politicians are forging ahead with a constant stream of creeping legislation which is slowly unifying every element of peoples' lives whether the people of these individual countries want it or not.'

M – 'You reckon?'

TB – 'Yes; given the choice, none of these countries would have given up their proud history, their heritage, the diversity of their culture, their money or their intellectual independence…but the grey suits in Brussels who believe that they connect with each other on a higher plane than the rest of us are systematically eradicating and painting over hundreds of years of history and cultural diversity with great swathes of homogenous beige paint in the name of Europe, while at the same time sucking the joy of human existence out of the many for the benefit of the few – i.e. themselves on their own personal MEP gravy train.'

'Now these people with the self-appointed superiority complex should be the most intelligent among us – how else would they be able to conceive of such a vast if somewhat costly and ultimately futile project – but unfortunately they are not as their arrogance and superior grey-matter does not stand up to any scrutiny.'

'Indeed. their incompetence, their inability to manage a budget and their failure to eradicate the inherent corruption within their ranks demonstrates, that they are not fit for purpose, and their accounts which they have failed to get signed off for eighteen straight years do no more than confirm this.'

M – 'I guess they are much like the bankers. Those guys were supposed to be the best in their field too, and look what they did to the world's economy.'

TB – 'I rest my case.'

(Pause)

TB – 'BTW; Tony Blair once said of democracy; 'The British people get to choose once every five years, in the meantime I make all the decisions'; that is not democracy...its autocracy.'

M – 'Now you're just being belligerent.'

TB – (smile)

One time they even discussed Climate Change;

TB – 'I wonder what the next dogma will be; what the politicians and the grey suits will come up with next in order to control the masses and make them pay more taxes; it will probably have something to do with outer-space.'

M – 'Outer-space?'

TB – 'Yes; something like...if you don't pay your taxes on time, the little green men will come knocking in the middle of the night and you will never be heard of again.'

M – 'Wow, that's ridiculous...and scary.'

TB – 'That's why it would work; that's why religion works; the fear of hell and the promise of heaven...and its why the climate change lobby works too; fear, fear that our world might come to an end if we don't pay more taxes to multi-national corporations so that they can save us from oblivion, while incidentally helping themselves and their shareholders to a life of luxury; it's simple mathematics; control the people's fear and you control them.'

M – (Bewildered look)

TB – '...look Madison; as a species, we humans are afraid of the unknown so we would rather pay our taxes and be sure to wake up the next morning in our own beds than to suffer the consequences of the unknown.'

M – 'Even if the unknown is absurd.'

TB – 'Yes, even if the unknown is absurd; would you be willing to take the chance?'

Madison repeated her look of bemusement.

TB – 'You see; people believe in all kinds of absurd concepts, heaven and hell as I said before, reincarnation, eternal life for those who are religious, eternal youth for you women, vampires, ghosts, UFO's, extra-terrestrials, voodoo, astrology, psychics, horoscopes, magic, luck etc.; the list is endless but the common denominator in all these phenomena is the unknown and therein lies the key; our fear; control that, tap into that part of the human psyche and....as any of those who make a living out of such phenomena would attest....you are onto a winner.'

M – 'I see', Madison agreed, letting slide his barely-disguised slant against female vanity tucked in discreetly amongst the other supernatural phenomena.

Discussion on fashion;

Madison was once again sat reading a magazine when *the Bishop* approached with two fruit-juice cocktails;

TB – (Pointing at the magazine) 'Did you know that there has been an 80% rise in young girls, girls as young as nine, being hospitalised with anorexia in the past ten years; all of them influenced by those ridiculous images of unreal, un-natural and completely air-brushed stereotyped models.'

Madison glanced in his direction and shrugged but didn't respond as she accepted the drink.

TB – 'Someone should do something to stop those fashion fascists from selling false hope to those girls; they are wrecking their young lives.'

M – 'You're right; it is wrong, but I have to say that…while the bookers and the magazines are the driving force, it is the casting directors who are the worst offenders for insisting on ethereal, stick insects as models. In fact, in 2008, when asked why Chanel did not use normal-sized women on its catwalks and in its advertising campaigns Karl Lagerfeld replied 'no one wants to see curvy women.'

TB – 'Well I disagree, and so…might I suggest…would a great many other red-blooded men because in a recent survey that I saw, 78% of men said that they preferred curvaceous women while only 7% favoured the skinnier models that the pseudo-oracles of fashion insist upon.'

Madison didn't reply but took a sip from her glass

TB – 'Fashion should be about celebrating women; their sexy curves and their fuller silhouettes... not pandering to these self-styled industry gurus…most of whom wouldn't have the first idea about how to appreciate a woman.'

Madison still didn't respond.

TB – (insisting) 'The bony, androgynous look might be what those self-centred fashion designers with their monumental out-of-control vanity want to see on the cat-walk but it is not what real men want; not on the cat-walk...and definitely not in the bedroom. Nobody finds a lollypop-head attractive; this ridiculous and harmful size zero fascism should be stopped.'

M – 'I'm sensing that you don't like the fashion industry.'

TB – 'Not true; I adore women's fashion; I find it fascinating but what I don't like is...those who work in the business, the fashion executives with their grating air of assumed privilege and the haughty way that they treat 'the little people' (with air-quotes)

'Do you know; high fashion or 'couture' as they so pompously describe it doesn't really exist for women per se; it exists solely to flatter and satisfy the bloated egos of the painfully insecure, emotionally fragile self-important prima-donnas that are the fashion designers.'

M – 'You exaggerate slightly.'

TB – 'Maybe…but...'

Reference *– due to the pressures put on her by the fashion industry Colombian super-model Lina Marulanda tragically jumped to her death on April 22*[nd] *2010 – while Luisel and Eliana Ramos, two Uruguayan sisters died trying to lose enough weight to further their modelling careers...and Ana Carolina Reston, another aspiring Brazilian model also died of starvation through anorexia.*

Discussion on Fashion...and money

One evening as they were getting ready to go out;

TB – 'Did you know that women in the UK spend more than a £1 billion a year on clothes that they will never wear...?'

...and another billion on cosmetics alone; all to satisfy the vain 'because you're worth it' generation; in fact, overall the hair and beauty industry here in the UK generates a massive £5.25 billion a year.'

Madison refrained from taking the bait and finished applying her lipstick.

TB – 'Yes indeed; you ladies have the choice of thousands of different colours and shades of lipstick...and meanwhile the children of Africa are dying of starvation.'

M – 'But men want us to look good, don't they?'

TB – 'No! Men want sex; if the package is nicely wrapped it's a bonus, but it's not essential.'

Madison looked in the mirror and grimaced comically.

TB – 'It's true; men don't put pressure on women, women put pressure on themselves - on each other - to look good, because despite what you women might say you are all constantly competing with each other to be the prettiest, the slimmest or the sexiest etc.'

'Men, on the other hand, really don't care; they like all sorts of body-types – variety is the spice of life as far as they are concerned. It's insidious magazines like those that you read…and the so-called, self-styled fashion experts that go with it who impose those unattainable beauty standards on women, just so that they can sell their wares...'

M – 'Excuse me; I read those magazines as part of my job.'

TB – 'I'm sorry but the fashion industry is just a billion-dollar con, foisted on insecure women by clever global conglomerates who prey on their vanity and their insecurities…

…and I have to say that I find it shocking to see the sums of money that are spent on the frivolity of being feminine in the western world today; from the initial research, all the way through to the often mendacious ad campaigns which market these products to gullible women all over the world...'

M – 'Maybe, we could say the same about...sports; look at all the money that goes into that; guys back home in the NBA, and the NFL all have multi-million dollar contracts; ...isn't <u>that</u> frivolous; do they really need all that money...?'

TB – 'Don't get me started on sportsmen; we have people in this country earning three hundred thousand pounds a week for kicking a piece of plastic around a field...'

M – 'I know, I know...meanwhile others starve...' (She chipped in facetiously)

TB – 'Yes; ...and then of course we have the bankers with their multi-million pound bonuses....'

M – 'Stop; I get it; life isn't fair, but you're starting to ramble.'

(Pause)

M – 'So what is worse in your opinion; vanity or greed...?'

The Bishop didn't answer…

Discussion on Religion;

Lying back in her transat, Madison suddenly held up the front page of her magazine which featured the Pope;

M – 'What do you think?' she asked bluntly, knowing that she was probably poking the bear.

TB – looking non-plussed - 'I'd rather not discuss religion with you... because when it comes to spirituality and the god-concept, every person, every individual has to make up their own mind, go on their own voyage of enlightenment, to experience their own cognitive awakening.'

M – 'Yeah, I get that', she agreed.

TB – '...Just know this', he added after a brief pause...unable to resist the red-flag that she was dangling in front of his eyes; 'The earliest record of humanity on this planet goes back 75000 years...while the earliest record of religion only goes back 5000 years.'

M – 'So, what are you saying...?'

TB – 'Well, what I am saying is this; for 70000 years mankind lived happily on this planet without the bane of religion; then 5000 years ago somebody had the bright idea to invent the concept...'

M – 'Who was it...?' She asked, curious, expecting him to have the answer.

TB – 'It doesn't matter who it was', he retorted dismissively. 'Different faiths have different versions of the story but what matters is the fact that religion was invented by mankind...and therefore - by definition – there is no divine or supernatural component to it'

M – (Apathetic shrug)

TB – (leaning over) - 'However, if you need to believe in some imaginary supreme being from somewhere out there in the universe; I totally understand...that's fine by me...a lot of people do...and it's your choice to make...but just be clear about one thing; Religion and the god concept is a human construct invented by mankind for no other reason than...as a control mechanism, a way of influencing the gullible masses. . .of offering them false hope; it wasn't 'revealed' to us by the universe...but as I just said; if that is what gets you through the day, who am I to say otherwise...?'

M – 'I never said I was religious...'

TB – 'True; but let's not discuss it any further...I'll just get annoyed...'

(A call coming through on Madison's mobile-phone interrupted the conversation)

TB – (mumbling to himself as he returned to his reading) 'It is just such a waste...that the fate of humanity on this planet will one day be decided by the followers of one apocryphal supernatural deity... rising up and going into battle with the followers of another apocryphal supernatural deity...until there is simply no-one left...; Why can't people see that...why can't humanity see that...?'

He turned back towards Madison...

TB – 'You know; Albert Einstein is credited with saying that insanity is doing the same thing over and over again and expecting different results. Well I would like to offer an alternative definition of that word...'

M – 'You would...and what might that be...?'

TB – 'Insanity for me is this...the believers of one apocryphal deity...'

M – 'Hold on...apocryphal...?'

TB – '...it means fictional or imaginary...'

TB – 'So, as I was saying; insanity for me is this...the believers of one apocryphal deity...fired up with evangelical zeal going to war with the believers of another apocryphal deity...and the result of this battle of imaginary supernatural entities being the very real destruction and obliteration of mankind.'

M – 'THAT IS INSANITY'! She exclaimed.

TB - 'It is indeed and I'm telling you Madison', he said; 'We, human beings do not need to believe in some mystical supernatural power - of whatever persuasion – for us to live decent, honest and fulfilling lives; all we need...is to believe in ourselves, to have the right principles, the right moral values...and a set of unquestionable human and social ethics. We don't need all this medieval hokum.'

Madison stared at him, incredulous.

TB - 'I'm telling you. . .because of the sheer stupidity and ignorance of the human race, Armageddon is a real possibility in the not-too-distant future...and when that day comes, and those that survive stand knee-deep in the ashes of civilisation, mankind will have nobody else to blame for his oblivion other than himself.'

A brief exchange on men and women;

TB - 'Look at this survey', he said, pointing to his newspaper. 'Over the last forty years women have slowly…but surely…frozen men out of their lives...to the point where men can no longer be bothered with relationships and prefer to just watch pornography instead'.

He paused for her response but Madison didn't take the bait.

'Looks like the feminists are slowly getting their wish; a world without men', he concluded.

Knowing that she could not win the argument, Madison didn't even bother to comment, she just shrugged her shoulders and carried on reading her magazine.

…and finally, a couple of prickly exchanges on the USA… and its guns…

TB – (looking up from his latest read; America's Book of Secrets) 'Did you know that since the 1970's the USA has produced 1400 known serial killers…and that the FBI believes that there are up to 50 serial killers active around the USA at any one time?'

M – (Blank expression) 'Really?'

TB – 'Yes, and according to the Brady Campaign to Prevent Gun Violence, the USA averages 20 mass shootings a year; in fact, a conservative estimate sets the figure at 30.000 deaths a year from gun-related wounds; murders, suicides and self-defence situations including the police...'

M – 'Wow, when you lay it out like that, it's frightening.'

(Pause)

M – 'Let's see', she said, picking up her phone and tapping the screen...; 'we've had...

Sandy Hook School (*in 2012, 26 victims*)
...the movie theatre in Aurora, Colorado (in *2012; 13 victims*)

and then there was...

(she paused)

Fort Hood, Texas *(in 2009; 13 victims)*...
Virginia Tech *(in 2007; 32 victims*),

and of course...

Columbine, *(in April 1999; 13 victims*)

TB – 'You see; you are constantly killing people.'

M - (Sounding a little facetious); 'We're Americans; it's our God-given right to carry guns.'

TB - (perplexed); 'God gave you that right; to kill innocent women and children, in schools and cinemas?'

M – 'Well, not him exactly, but the American constitution; written over 200 years ago.'

TB – 'That's all very well...but don't you think it's time you people updated that dusty charter?'

M – 'No, it's written in stone.'

TB – 'You mean it's written in blood; the blood of innocents.'

(Pause)

TB – (starting to lecture) 'Look, I understand that the second amendment of the American Constitution's Bill of Rights allows every American citizen to bear arms…but I'm pretty sure that when they wrote that, the founding fathers of America meant that every citizen has the right to pick up or carry a weapon in order to defend themselves and protect their families from attack. They could never have envisioned the issues of the 21st century where people are roaming the streets with high-powered, military-grade, automatic weapons, slaughtering dozens of innocent people in random killing sprees.'

M – (*Knowing that there was no defence to the cold-blooded murder of innocents*) 'Let it go; it is what it is.'

TB – (insisting) 'You know, it's a shame, because America has so much to offer the world…but it will never move into the 21st century until the current generation of paranoid, gun-toting ignoramuses has passed into history.'

M – 'Hey, you can't call my fellow citizens ignoramuses.'

TB – 'I can't? What should I call them then…because it seems to me that the great majority of the American people is lacking in the cognitive maturity to realise that allowing everyone and anyone to possess a gun is a bad idea.'

M – 'Hey, you can't say that either.'

TB – 'What? All I am saying is that America is a great country…but its mentality has not evolved one iota since the 18th century…and its citizens' desperation to hold onto their guns at all costs - *as if the*

Wild-West was still there to be conquered - shows their complete lack of progressive thinking or modernisation.'

His words were intense and achingly passionate…but acutely embarrassed by his attack on her countrymen Madison felt obligated to defend them.

M – 'Look, this is an unwinnable argument; America loves its guns and the American people – or at least its politicians – are prepared to accept that…as part of the ruling that allows every citizen to carry a weapon…there will be…from time to time…an outrage such as Colombine, Aurora or Sandy Hook.'

TB – '…and you are happy with that…?'

M – 'No! Of course I'm not happy with that, but what can I do…?'

TB – 'What can you do…? Something…anything; get a leader with some courage and a backbone who is not in the pockets of the National Rifle Association for a start.'

(Pause)

TB – (mumbling) 'The political cowardice of American politicians is a monumental disgrace.'

At this point Madison just shook her head and shrugged her shoulders; there was clearly no point in continuing the discussion.

Follow up conversation, the next day…

TB – 'I was just thinking about our conversation yesterday…and you know what; there is something bothering me…'

M – 'There is?' (Nothing unusual in that Madison thought to herself)

TB – 'Yes indeed. You remember telling me that you believe that the American constitution…and the 2nd Amendment is written in stone…and therefore cannot be changed.'

M – 'I do…but I didn't mean anything by it.'

TB – 'I see; I just wanted to make sure that you understood what an amendment is…'

M - 'Of course I understand what an amendment is; don't be so patronising…'

TB – 'Well what if I told you that there have been 33 amendments made to the American constitution down the years, notably concerning slaves, the gay community...and votes for women.'

M – 'I would be surprised…'

TB – 'Yes, even the Pledge of Allegiance that all American children learn to recite in school…written initially in 1892…was changed in 1954 to include the words 'under God'.'

M – 'Really?'

TB – 'Yes, really…so you see America can embrace change if it wants to…and yet you…as a people…cannot see that…in the 21st century…the problem of gun-control needs to be addressed…'

(Pause)

TB - 'It's just common sense really…but sadly common sense has no place in the USA where money equals power, irrespective of morality…especially in the gun lobby...so there will be no change there; Americans will simply carry on killing each other every day...because that's what they like to do and they are just not prepared to evolve that frontier mentality.'

M – 'Aha…', she replied…hoping that her disinterested response would put an end to the conversation.

TB - '…But you know what really irks me; it's not the 2nd Amendment arguments per se; it's the way that the NRA uses the 2nd Amendment to maintain a wild-west, frontier mentality amongst American citizens…because without it their product has no market. They don't really care about defending the 2nd Amendment; that's just a convenient cover story. All the NRA really cares about is business…big business. The sale of weapons and ammunition is a multi-billion dollar business. That is what they are defending. They don't care who gets killed. Killings are just free publicity for them to promote their products and their warped ideology that says everyone should carry a gun; it's the ultimate marketing and advertising campaign.'

M – (getting frustrated) 'Look, what you have to understand is that in the US, we have been governed by generation after generation of power-hungry…but ultimately toothless politicians incapable of enacting any worthwhile legislation because they are in thrall to big business and the paymasters who fund their political campaigns…and sadly…that is not going to change anytime soon.'

TB – 'Aah, a reaction at last.'

M – (Playing the devil's advocate) 'What can I say; we're Americans; we are brought up on a diet of mass murder and political gerrymandering; we love shooting our guns and killing people. We'll kill anyone; from presidents to little children...and everyone in between; we just love killing; it's our thing…and the NRA tells us it is our right to do so; well not directly but they defend our right to do so with such vigour that they are almost condoning it, justifying it if you will.'

TB – (ironically) 'A round of applause for the Land of the Free.'

M – (more conciliatory) 'Okay, I'm getting carried away – but just look at Hollywood; if you don't kill 50 or 60 people in an action movie, the film bombs.'

TB – 'That's true; Hollywood can hardly play holier than thou with the gun problem when it uses guns to make itself billions.'

M – (Drained) 'Look, can we get off this subject.'

TB – 'Very well, but can I just make one final point…?'

M – 'Okay…go on.'

TB – 'You Americans all defend the 2nd amendment as if your lives depended on it…but not a single one of you is complaining about your 4th Amendment rights being trampled on.'

M – 'Our what…rights?'

TB – 'Exactly! You are all so busy defending your rights to carry guns; meanwhile the NSA is using drones to monitor and pry on every one of you as you go about your daily lives…which is a blatant abuse of the 4th amendment…and nobody gives a damn.'

M – 'What are you saying?'

TB – 'I'm saying that the 4th amendment…which is there to protect your citizens' right to privacy is being trampled on by the NSA, which is collecting each and every one of your text messages, your e-mails, your phone-calls and your internet searches and nobody is bothered.'

(Pause)

TB – 'Your government is taking away your freedom as an individual, one piece of information at a time and nobody seems to care.

However, if anyone even dares to suggest taking away your guns, you all go completely crazy.'

M – (Looking skyward) 'That's not right...'

A few days later...

TB – 'You know what I don't understand; the fact that you cannot drink alcohol or have sex in the USA until you are 21 years old...but that it was okay to give a nine year old...a nine year old girl lessons in how to use an Uzi sub-machine gun'. *(Sadly the young girl couldn't control it and accidentally killed the instructor; Arizona 2014)*

M – (Irritated) 'What do you want me to say...because we've already had this conversation and I've already told you that Americans love their guns and they like killing people; whether it be in Hollywood in blockbuster action movies or in all those detective series that fill our TV screens 24/7'.

TB – '...or on your streets', he interjected.

M – '...or on our streets', she repeated, feeling a little uncomfortable.

TB – '...or in your schools', *the Bishop* insisted.

This time Madison didn't reply.

TB – '...and let's not forget all the wars', he added annoyingly.

M – 'I was being sarcastic', Madison retorted, exasperated by his unrelenting agenda.

TB – 'That's as may be' he added, '...but the sad thing is...it's all true. On average, 87 people are shot in the USA every day'.

M – 'Shot...but not necessarily killed', she snapped trying once again to defend her country.

TB – 'No, shot...and killed; 87 every day', *the Bishop* insisted.

M – 'Every day? That is a lot of people.'

TB – 'I couldn't agree more.'

M – 'Okay', she consented; 'you've made your point...now let it go.'

The Bishop tilted his head and stared in her direction for a moment before returning to his newspaper.

For information;

More than 1.5 million Americans were killed by guns between 1968 and 2014 which is more than in all the American wars combined (1.4 million)... and four US presidents have been assassinated with guns (Lincoln, Garfield, McKinley and of course, JF Kennedy). More recently unsuccessful assassination attempts were carried out against Ronald Reagan and Gerald Ford, twice, by two different women...all with guns.

These are some of the most notorious mass-shootings in American history;

2017 - First Baptist Church, Sutherland Springs, Texas - 26 dead / 20 injured
2017 - Mandalay Bay Hotel, Las Vegas - 58 dead / 489 injured
2016 - Pulse Orlando Night-club, Orlando, Florida - 49 dead / 50 injured

2015 -	Inland Regional Centre, San Bernardino	- 14 dead / 22 injured
2013 -	Washington Navy Yard, Washington DC	- 12 dead
2012 -	Sandy Hook School, Newtown, Conn.	- 26 dead
2012 -	Aurora, Colorado	- 12 dead / 58 injured
2009 -	Fort Hood, Texas	- 13 dead / 30 injured
2009 -	American Civic Assn, Binghamton, NY	- 13 dead / 04 injured
2007 -	Virginia Tech, Blacksburg, Virginia	- 32 dead / 17 injured
1999 -	Columbine High School, Littleton, Colorado	- 13 dead / 24 injured
1991 -	Luby's cafeteria, Killeen, Texas	- 23 dead
1986 -	Edmond Post Office, Edmond, Oklahoma	- 14 dead
1984 -	McDonald's restaurant, San Ysidro, California	- 21 dead / 19 injured
1966 -	University of Texas tower in Austin, Texas	- 14 dead / 31 injured

These are the incidents that have claimed most lives in one single event...but sadly shootings take place all over America every day; in fact, over 12000 Americans are killed by guns every year ...the figure rising to 33000 if suicides are included...and inevitably this kind of event will continue to happen...over and over...again and again...until the American people choose to update their constitution and join the rest of the developed world in the 21st century.

Author's comment;

On April 28th 1996, a young man (Martin Bryant) walked into a popular tourist-site in Port Arthur, Tasmania and massacred 35 people, injuring dozens more. Within weeks the Australian Government had drawn up the National Firearms Agreement which banned automatic and semi-automatic weapons. A buy-back scheme funded by the government was also put in place and this helped to rid the country of thousands more guns.

There has not been a single multiple-killing in Australia since that law was introduced.

So you see America; it can be done...but you have to want it...and sadly... you just don't want it enough...so innocent children will just continue to be slaughtered in their schools...and defenceless citizens all around your country will just keep on being murdered every day...in their homes and on the streets of your towns and cities...because that...people of America... that is the society you choose to live in.

In the UK, there has only been one mass-shooting in recent times; 16 children and their teacher were killed in their school in Dunblane, Scotland in 1996. This led to strict new gun laws and nothing like it has ever happened since.

Irony;

New US President Donald Trump recently gave a speech in front of the NRA…informing them that he would never take away their 2nd amendment rights; i.e. their right to bear arms; the irony; everybody who attended that meeting was asked to check their guns at the door for security reasons.

Final discussion on the USA;

TB – (back-handing his newspaper) – 'You know, the US brings all this ire on itself.'

M – (No reaction)

TB – (insisting) – 'Do you know why the world doesn't like you... doesn't trust you...and by you, I mean America...because you're hypocrites, you're two-faced. You go around the world rattling your sabres and banging your drums, acting as the world's policeman and its moral arbiter while at the same time repeatedly disrespecting sovereign states by spying on them... friends and foes alike.'

M – 'I resent that characterisation; we wouldn't do that.'

TB – 'Well, how do you explain the recent revelations that your spy agencies were listening to the German chancellor's phone...and that, even more recently, they admitted to listening in on the last three French presidents?'

M – 'What...?'

TB – 'That's why people don't trust you, and what's more, you conduct covert operations in allied countries without informing the relevant authorities; it's no wonder you have a dubious reputation.'

M – 'Look, we intervene where we feel it is necessary', she argued trying to defend her country. . .again.

TB – 'No you don't; you interfere where you feel it would be beneficial to you. You violate sovereignty and then expect to be absolved systematically because of the sanctions you would impose if the violated country complained; you're bullies'.

M – (Pout)

TB – 'And here's another double standard; the US has the greatest stockpile of nuclear weapons in the world, but it won't 'allow' Iran to have nuclear weapons. Now, of course I understand the politics of the argument – especially after what the former leader Mahmood Ahmajenidad said about Israel, but on a purely equitable level, why should the US dictate what another sovereign state should or should not have, when they themselves have the biggest stockpile of 'said weapons'; it's double standards yet again; one rule for you and one rule for everyone else.'

M – (Shrug and look of resignation)

TB – 'Look; you Americans are not bad people; you believe that you are doing the right thing...every time; but more often than not your 'super-power' status and your paranoia about your place in the world supplants your fundamental desire to help out; your interventions are often gauche or premature – usually accompanied by threats of the military kind; *you do like your guns* - and as a consequence you come across as overbearing, bullying and dogmatic. It's either do as we say...or we'll bomb you out of existence...'

Madison sat up ready to offer a rebuttal but thankfully, her phone rang at that very moment, cutting the conversation short.

Discussion on humanity;

TB having just read a report on the latest terrorist atrocity;

TB - 'How stupid is the human race?' He asked out loud.

M - 'What now?' Madison queried.

TB - 'I said; how stupid is the human race?' he repeated, pointing to the article in his paper. 'I mean, we have received the most wonderful gift; the gift of life...and what do we do with it; we spend all our time devising ways of killing off as many of our fellow human beings as possible, in the most destructive and efficient ways possible.'

M - 'Not guns again…?' she said.

TB - 'No, not guns again', *the Bishop* replied with a hint of indignation.

'My question is this; are we human beings really that intelligent when all we can do with that intelligence is try to find the best ways of destroying ourselves?'

Madison just frowned, knowing that she was in for another lecture.

TB - 'Don't you find it sad…?' he quizzed, leaning over, '… that we... human beings...are capable of such creativity and such ingenuity yet we choose to use those talents mainly to invent weapons of mass destruction?'

M - 'I do', Madison agreed concisely.

TB - 'And how much sadder is it that the war-mongering governments who run our countries...with their short-sighted self-interest... base all their policies on military supremacy, on who can kill the most people and cause the most devastation...thereby engineering and even precipitating the eventual extinction of the whole human race.'

M - 'It's terrible, but there are good people out there; there have been people who want peace; like JFK…Martin Luther King Junior… Ghandi', Madison argued timidly.

TB - 'Yes, that's true', *the Bishop* agreed, '… and what happened to all those people you just mentioned?'

Madison shrugged and grimaced knowing what was coming.

TB - '…They were all assassinated…with guns'

Madison frowned again, deciding to keep her counsel.

TB - 'Of course, world peace should always be everybody's ultimate goal…' *the Bishop* continued, pursuing his ramble, '…but passivity and non-violence have their limits and do not work in the real world. Yes, they are laudable concepts but human beings are natural born killers programmed to use lethal force on each other whenever necessary…and if you do not defend yourself and your ideas, then those who do not agree with those ideas will simply cut you down. You might not realise this Madison but our blood-lust as human beings knows no bounds; look at our history.'

M - 'But surely there are some good people around today', Madison replied, trying to be positive.

TB - 'I'm sure there are…and it is fantastic to have dignified, stoic, peace-loving, morally-upstanding people as part of our communities…but unfortunately those wonderfully warm qualities are not enough to resolve the more divergent or divisive issues of humanity. We need people with other qualities; people who are firm, steadfast, decisive, confident, bold, courageous, fearless and brave…to stand up and lead us to a better future… but sadly those people are few and far between. In fact, I cannot name one leader currently in office whose goal is world peace.'

'One thing is sure though. Passivity, as practiced by Ghandi, is not an option. We simply cannot sit back and allow ourselves to be massacred ad infinitum by those with no morality…the criminals, the terrorists and the corrupt politicians…all in the name of peace; there has to be a point where we say STOP.'

M - 'Wow; are you going to start a revolution?' Madison scoffed.

TB - 'Of course not…', *the Bishop* huffed, '…but my conclusion is that mankind has failed to evolve; it is still fundamentally flawed, innately cruel and inherently barbaric…and if mutually-assured destruction is our goal; if that is our destiny...if that is all we can do with this wonderful gift that is life…then do we really deserve to survive?'

Madison often played the 'devil's advocate' during these learned exchanges…and while she did - at times - try to offer a counter-argument to the Bishop's steadfast and unequivocal points of view…more often than not… she just let him have the last word.

CHAPTER NINETEEN

(Part Two)

However, although they never ventured far from the Abbey during those idyllic few weeks, it wasn't all insular living, sedentary activities and private discussions…because the Bishop knew full well that Madison was a city-girl… and as a compromise to the sedate life that he was more-or-less imposing on her, he often invited her out to sample the culinary delights of some of the most renowned restaurants in the area.

These were the times that Madison looked forward to…and enjoyed…the most - and the Manoir aux Quat'Saisons at Great Milton quickly became her favourite dining experience, after he had taken her there for the first time – as a surprise – to celebrate her birthday.

That morning, Madison had woken up in the cottage…having agreed with TB that she would spend that particular day on her own catching up on some work that Gretchen had e-mailed over to her…when all of a sudden, just as she was getting herself settled, her phone rang and he came on the line to inform her that he was on his way over to pick her up as he wanted to take her into Oxford to buy her a present for her birthday.

The call came really out of the blue and Madison was more than a little taken aback by the unexpected content…as she had never even mentioned the fact…to him…that it was her birthday, but then as she ended the call with a secretly joyous prod on the screen, she quickly realised that she had long stopped marvelling at how *the Bishop* always seemed to find these things out.

Clearly, she was delighted by his thoughtfulness and even though it was short notice…and meant her stopping what she had started…which she really hated doing as a rule…Madison quickly readied herself and within minutes she could hear the sound of the stones out in her driveway being crunched under the Aston's tyres as it glided elegantly to a halt outside her door.

As usual, *the Bishop* didn't get out of the car; he never did when he came over…or indeed when he dropped her off, and instead it was Madison who rushed out to join him, thanking him enthusiastically for his consideration through the open window of the car with a brief peck on the cheek.

The Bishop smiled stiffly…as he hated PDA's…but once Madison had gotten into the car and closed the door, he released the brakes, the Aston purred and they were quickly on their way into the centre of Oxford… deciding between them as they drove, that a pair of shoes would be the ideal gift for her birthday treat.

He parked the car, and for the next couple of hours he showed the greatest patience and indulgence that any man has ever shown as Madison…who for once was in her element…dragged him around what seemed like hundreds of exclusive city-centre boutiques trying on every shoe she could find until finally settling on a pair of wonderfully-crafted Manolo's.

Detail;

at one point…just to tease him, Madison stopped at a lipstick counter and picked up the brightest, richest red lipstick she could find. Then, with a coquettish smile, she asked the Bishop what he thought. Somewhat predictably, he just frowned and shook his head much to the sales-assistant's chagrin …but it was a surprise moment of levity which, despite the Bishop's adverse reaction, had the desired effect, lightening the mood and reducing the boredom threshold as they continued on to the next boutique.

That was followed by a quick, revitalising snack before they strolled back to the car and drove back to the cottage where *the Bishop* politely dropped Madison off again, informing her before he left that he would be picking her up again at seven thirty to take her to dinner.

She thanked him for her present…for his patience…and for the few hours that they had spent in Oxford. She even invited him in…to be polite…knowing instinctively that he would probably refuse…but as she turned and made her way towards the cottage's front-door, carrying her new shoes in her left hand and waving briefly to him with her right, her mind immediately began racing as to what else this strange enigmatic man might have reserved for her that evening…because knowing him as she now did, she knew that it would almost certainly be a special treat.

Madison was not to be disappointed.

The Bishop picked her up as arranged and without telling her their destination, he whisked her off to the afore-mentioned, world-renowned Quat'Saisons restaurant, taking her breath away as they pulled up outside the exclusive address, nestled discreetly in the picturesque Oxfordshire countryside.

Once inside, the pretty hostess and the immaculately-dressed head waiter showed them to a table and as they took their seats *the Bishop* immediately ordered a bottle of champagne, asking for it by name, which really impressed his American guest.

'Champagne; am I missing out on the sub-plot here?' she asked cheekily, returning his flirtatious eye contact with a wide-eyed grin of her own.

The Bishop smiled again, complimenting her on her choice of dress.

(She looked fabulous in her favourite vintage black dress, black stockings and birthday heels.)

'Why Mr Byron; are you going to try to seduce me over dinner?' Madison insisted playfully, milking the moment.

He didn't reply but instead looked deeply into her eyes for a long moment…and for the first time Madison saw a depth of tenderness there she would never have imagined possible.

'You know what they say about champagne?' Madison continued cheerily, opening the menu which almost masked her face.

'…it makes girls want to dance and drop their pants'; she announced coquettishly, lowering her voice and the menu in order to check out her companion's reaction.

The Bishop looked over at her, studying her sparkling eyes and enquiring face framed perfectly by her silky blond hair, but just as he was about to respond to her audacious comment, the sommelier appeared next to him clutching a silver ice-bucket; his presence interrupting TB's momentum and spoiling the moment.

They ordered 'a la carte' and over the next two hours, *the Bishop* maintained the romantic theme of the evening by recounting several risqué anecdotes from his vast repertoire, mentioning by-the-by that Casanova recommended eating oysters as an aphrodisiac, while respectfully omitting to mention what the celebrated lover did with lemons, in order to avoid offending Madison's feminine sensibilities.

'He used to recommend chocolate to people too, because it excites and stimulates the brain', *the Bishop* explained, disclosing the fact that he enjoyed a square of chocolate himself from time to time for its morale boosting qualities.

The conversation lapsed at that point while they took a moment to digest what had been said and enjoyed another succulent morsel from their respective dishes…but as Madison looked up again to admire the superbly decorated surroundings and the carefully manicured grounds just visible through the glass conservatory (l'Orangerie), she suddenly spied *the Bishop* looking at two other women across the way.

'You know, despite your obvious differences, you and Gary do have some things in common' she commented in mild indignation at having the spotlight temporarily taken away from her.

'We do?' *the Bishop* enquired, focussing his attention back on the birthday girl, his eyebrows angling quizzically.

'Yes', Madison confirmed teasingly as she swallowed another gulp of champagne, deliberately drawing out her explanation.

'I saw Gary one time, looking at two women just like you did then …with that same predatory look in his eye.'

The Bishop smiled; 'You did …then you are a very observant young lady', he acquiesced.

'...however on this occasion my dear, you are wrong', he pursued, covering his tracks without explanation as he wiped his mouth.

'Oh please, everybody knows that the definitive male fantasy is to watch two women getting it on', Madison affirmed, a little irritated by his blatant masculine denial.

The Bishop smiled again but rather than accepting the stereotypical idea that Madison was putting forward, he turned the tables on the assured young New Yorker by suggesting that in fact, it was what every woman secretly dreamed of doing, but...in reality...could never bring herself to try.

Madison had no answer to that, knowing full-well that she herself had been witness to some strange goings-on in the VIP rooms in the clubs in New York...which pretty much confirmed *the Bishop's* suspicions...and while the man himself sat back and revelled in her confusion and the fact that he had cleverly managed to take her out of her comfort zone once again, she could only shrug her shoulders in frustrated capitulation.

The rest of the meal went off without incident and having thanked their celebrity-host personally for the quality of the restaurant experience that he and his personnel had provided, *the Bishop* and Madison were soon driving back to the Abbey, looking forward to finishing off her birthday celebrations in a more intimate setting.

Thirty minutes or so later, they arrived back at the abbey, where all fired up by the adrenaline and the sheer emotion of the day's events, they tumbled onto the bed entwined in a kiss, their embrace bathed in the moon's spotlight that was nature's paparazzi.

Madison pulled away to catch her breath and while *the Bishop* loosened his tie to make himself more comfortable, she took the opportunity to thank him once again for her birthday treats.

'It has been a most memorable day, and one of the best birthdays that I have ever had', she acknowledged enthusiastically, leaning back over to give him another peck on the cheek, the smile on her face speaking a thousand words.

The Bishop accepted her expression of gratitude with a wry smile but then as she prepared to get back up off of the bed to get undressed as she normally would have done, he suddenly took hold of her waist and pulled her back down onto the bed beside him.

'Hey', she cried out in surprise as she lost her balance and fell back heavily onto the bed.

'What are you doing?' she asked impishly as he climbed on top of her, pinning her to the mattress under his strong masculine body.

The Bishop didn't reply but just looked into her eyes…almost lost in a trance…and without speaking a word, slowly lowered his lips back onto hers.

He kissed her once …and then a second time…and then nudging her lips apart, he kissed her more deeply, caressing her top lip softly with his own before biting gently on her succulent lower lip to solicit a response.

Madison was in heaven and even though she knew that it was quite out of character for *the Bishop* to be doing this - when she felt his tongue slowly entering her mouth she could not help but respond with a fevered kiss of her own.

The kiss led to caressing and much, much more and in the passionate clinch that ensued, which saw them tearing at each other's clothes like a couple of horny teenagers as they rolled around frantically on the huge, king-sized double-bed, Madison's dress got caught between them and was torn from her body like a chiffon rag, buttons flying around like shrapnel.

This did not stop them however; *the Bishop* was like a man possessed and after only a momentary hesitation, used to disentangle and discard the remains of her shredded garment, he overpowered Madison again like a marauding Viking, returning home to claim his trophy after months if not years of bloody conquest.

Madison had never seen him like this before, impulsive, spontaneous and domineering but as he finished stripping her of her clothes, she was quietly thrilled to discover this other side of him, to see that the mask did slip from time to time and that under the controlled exterior that he presented to the world, there was a man beneath who reacted to nature's impulses just like any other.

In fact her birthday had ended up being one of the most romantic… and sexually fulfilling…evenings of her life.

Next morning, relishing not having to get up for any particular reason, they stayed in bed for a few hours longer than they would normally do, dozing and cuddling each other to their hearts content, but as the clock struck ten Madison finally decided to get up and make some breakfast, leaving *the Bishop* to loll around in bed.

She threw on his robe – which she was slowly appropriating – and within twenty minutes she was back, carrying a tray full of coffee, tea, fruit juice and toast which she set down carefully on the bed.

TB thanked her politely for her diligence and immediately took hold of a glass of fruit juice which he downed in one, before grabbing a slice of toast and collapsing back onto his pillow, one hand placed stylishly behind his head.

Meanwhile Madison went over to the window and opened the curtains, stretching herself out fully as she enjoyed a well-deserved morning yawn.

'Well, whadda you know; the sun is shining', she quipped sarcastically.

The Bishop turned to face her.

'It is the middle of summer', he retorted, almost choking on a crumb of toast.

'...as if that means anything, here in England', Madison insisted, smirking from ear to ear as she sat back down on the bed and poured herself a cup of coffee.

TB looked at her and with a twinkle in his eye; he brushed the mattress beside him, inviting her to come closer.

Madison smiled and waved her fore-finger at him reprovingly.

'I'm eating', she declared, picking up a piece of toast and biting into it with gusto.

'Aie....' *the Bishop* winced playfully.

Madison rolled her eyes, but having made her point he left her alone to drink her coffee and finish her toast...without further interruption.

She offered him a cup of tea before tidying the tray away - which he gladly accepted - and once she had placed the tray over on the dresser Madison happily climbed onto the bed again and snuggled up beside him.

It was a wonderful moment and as she lay there next to him, her head resting comfortably on his chest, *the Bishop* began to stroke her hair and repeatedly run his fingers through it, remarking on how much longer it had grown since they had first met.

Madison could see where this was going but before *the Bishop* could jump-start his virility…again, she decided that she should to go home to the cottage to check on her e-mails as she hadn't completed the work that Gretchen had sent her…nor heard from Evie for a while…and she was looking forward to having a nice long chat with her friend as a belated birthday celebration.

The Bishop was disappointed but ignoring his pleas for her to stay, Madison cleverly slipped out of his grasp and made her way into the shower.

He watched her go and then to occupy his mind differently, he picked up one of the books that he was reading from the pile on his bed-side table…only to be jolted out of his concentration a few minutes later by the sound of Madison's screeching voice as she looked in horror at what was left of her favourite dress.

'Oh my God; look what you've done', she complained as she held up the dress.

'…what I've done', *the Bishop* countered, looking up from his page; '… we were both there….' he added.

'Yeah, but I didn't realise….oh, never mind…' Madison conceded, the look on her face clouding over into a frown.

'…but what am I going to wear to get home?' she asked out loud, holding the dress up to the light to see if there was any way of repairing the damage.

The Bishop shrugged his shoulders a little dismissively and quietly returned to his book.

Madison was riled but looking around the room for inspiration, her eyes fell on the formal white shirt that <u>he</u> had been wearing the previous evening flung haphazardly on a chair.

'This will do; do you mind?' she asked, holding the shirt up for his approval.

'You want to wear my shirt instead of your dress?' he queried, lowering his book once again, an inquisitive look on his face.

'Yeah, with this belt; it'll be fine', Madison declared, re-discovering her devil-may-care, New-York swagger as she stripped the leather band from his discarded trousers.

'If you're going to wear one of my shirts, at least take a clean one', he suggested graciously, pointing limply towards his dresser.

'No, this one will do', Madison insisted with growing confidence as she buttoned up the shirt and slipped her shoes back on.

It was a rather incongruous outfit but as she buckled the belt around her waist and checked herself out in the mirror, Madison realised that it would have to do until she got back to the cottage as she didn't really have any alternative; there was no way that she could put her dress back on.

'...and I'm keeping this so that you have a reason to come over and visit me some time', she advised as she kissed him goodbye, alluding to the fact that he had yet to visit her in the cottage.

The Bishop smiled at her and nodded his head politely.

'Would you like me to drive you home now?' he asked; 'you might get arrested dressed like that...' he added, gesturing towards her get-up.

'Nah; I'll be fine', Madison asserted; 'I've yet to come across anyone walking through that lane'.

TB shrugged acquiescently...and with that, Madison stood up and gave him one last wave before making her way downstairs, dropping what remained of her dress in the bin as she went.

Outside, the sun was shining and before she set off Madison stood in the Abbey's driveway for a minute or so, inhaling huge lungfuls of fresh country air which was heavy with the taste of summer, cut grass and gorged fruits.

She brushed her hair from her eyes and adjusted her sunglasses. Then, taking her courage in both hands, she started off on her walk back to the cottage, as quickly as she could, winding her way through the narrow lanes, her long blond hair blowing freely in the breeze and her right hand hovering close by her side, poised ready to intervene in case of emergency... in order to protect her modesty...should any stray gusts of wind decide to blow up and try to embarrass her.

...and sure enough, she had only gotten a few hundred yards down the road when the wind did pick up - for no apparent reason - catching her out as it blew her make-shift outfit rather indiscreetly up around her waist.

Thank god I'd left that bag of swimsuits in the drawer, she thought to herself, as she fought to preserve her dignity, her eyes scanning the surrounding countryside for the slightest sign of life. (*She had discreetly slipped on a swimsuit under the shirt before leaving*).

The wind died down again almost as quickly as it had sprung up and as nobody had been around to witness her flustered reaction...as far as she was aware...Madison saw the funny side of the situation and began laughing at herself as she continued on her way, reliving the moment in her mind and wondering what Evie's reaction would be when she told her.

She carried on walking and as she did so, enjoying the protection of the trees on each side of her, which were green and full of life, Madison began to analyse her situation, coming rapidly to the conclusion that in fact she should have taken up TB's offer to give her a lift back to the cottage, as after all, he was the one who had ruined her dress.

Her mind flashed his picture in front of her eyes and as she looked down at the shoes that he had bought her, her thoughts immediately filled with images of their meal at the Quat'Saisons the night before and their subsequent passion-filled finale which had resulted in her current state of undress.

It had definitely been the best birthday that she had ever had; better than anything she could have ever planned herself...and it was, or at least it had been part of her job to organise things like that, in a manner of speaking.

Whoever would have thought that *the Bishop*, the irrepressible master tactician, the man who controlled everything, would be capable of such urgency, she mused to herself as she re-lived his libidinous onslaught, shivering in silence as the images flashed through her mind.

It had come as a real shock to her but Madison had to admit as she walked out of the shaded cover of the trees and back into the bright sunlight, that *the Bishop* throwing off his usual reserve like that had kinda added a new dimension to their liaison.

Of course, like most women Madison tended to err on the side of romance when it came to relationships and intimacy but despite her preference for the clichéd encounter, she also found that a quick vigorous thrusting once and awhile could also do the trick, and in fact she had quite enjoyed being ravished by *the Bishop's* alter-ego.

Indeed, she already knew what an accomplished lover he was, having luxuriated in his talents on more than one occasion, but now, he had added spontaneity to his register as well; the guy was a genuine schizoid enigma, she decided, throwing her hands up in the air.

I wonder if I should mention it or question him about it, she asked herself, before revising her thought, presupposing with growing maturity that he probably wouldn't appreciate her trying to analyse him.

The sun had gotten warmer and a little further along in a neighbouring field two men were working on a tractor. They were already sweating profusely with the heat and both had removed their shirts which were draped haphazardly over the tractor's mirror-supports.

Madison hurried past, not wanting to draw their attention but as she did so one of the men happened to look her way…and without thinking she raised a hand to acknowledge them.

She carried on a little further, savouring the warmth of the summer sun on her face and as she rounded the next bend she realised that she was within sight of the cottage.

A sense of relief suddenly washed over her on seeing the proximity of her refuge…and with her confidence returning, she deliberately slowed her pace down to a leisurely stroll in order to enjoy the remaining hundred metres or so of her rather eventful walk.

Back at the cottage Madison opened her laptop and set it on the small coffee-table facing the couch. Then she logged onto Skype and waited for Evie to respond…while she looked over the work that Gretchen had sent her and started to make some notes.

It was Sunday so Evie would probably be having a lie in, but eventually after a while she did answer the Skype request and this is a snippet of the conversation that took place;

E – *(Still dressed in her night-shirt with a big-smiley-face on the front as she had just woken up)* 'How's things?'

M – 'Fine; the cottage is a little dilapidated; what with the dry rot, the wet rot and the ancient electrics, but it's very cute and at least it has WIFI.

E – 'Life saver…

M – 'Yeah'

E - 'Well; don't leave me hanging; how are things with you-know-who?'

M – (*Trying not to give too much away*) 'Oh, he's…just as you would remember him; all preachy and OCD.'

E – (*Cutting to the chase*) 'And…was he as good as you remember?'

M – (*Instantly forgetting her attempted reserve*) 'You know, E; most men have no idea how to please a woman...but they refuse to accept their shortcomings. This guy', she added '...has no such shortcomings. He is so...masterful, like a lion.'

E - 'Masterful?' Evie queried.

M - 'Okay…maybe masterful is a bit strong. Let's just say he takes control. Sex with him is almost like an out-of-body experience. The guy's a force of nature.'

E - 'Yeah, that figures', Evie acknowledged.

M – (*Trying to avoid any more discussion about TB*) 'But that's enough about me; what are you up to?'

E - 'Watching TV.'

M - 'What are you watching?'

E - 'Re-runs of Craig Ferguson's 'Late, Late, Show'.'

M - 'Oh, I miss Craig Ferguson…and Geoff; …who's the guest?'

E - 'Carrie Keagan…again!'

M – 'Yeah, she made quite a few appearances on that show'…

(Pause)

E - 'Oh, I almost forgot…I went to a tantric work-shop last weekend; you know, to work on my mojo.'

M – (*Scoffing*) 'Yeah, right; like you need to work on that…'

E - 'You'd be surprised, Mad; it was all about getting in touch with your 'inner goddess...about connecting with your...you know.'

M - 'Eeew, that sounds gross…but did you meet anybody interesting while you were there?'

E - 'No, nobody I would want to get horizontal with…apart from the instructor…you?'

M - 'You mean apart from…'

E - 'Yeah…apart from…'

M - 'No.'

E – 'Silly me…'

The exchange continued a while longer covering the more mundane subjects of human existence…but as both women had things to be getting on with, they brought it to an end with the promise to speak again soon…

It was a day or two later, while they were lounging about again in the garden; him with a book on advanced theoretical strategy…and her with the latest fashion magazines, that Madison decided that it was about time that she broached the subject of the mysterious cigar box hidden away in his dresser.

Of course, it was none of her business really but having bitten her tongue for long enough - as far as she saw it - her inherent curiosity was desperate to be satisfied and now that they were more or less 'dating', she felt that her position had shifted enough to allow her the possibility and the liberty of asking him about it, without it appearing like she was prying.

She cleared her throat nervously before speaking.

'Oh by the way', she remarked casually, looking up nonchalantly from her page; 'while I was looking for my swimsuits the other day…up in the bedroom, I noticed that there was a cigar-box in one of the drawers; …did you used to smoke?', she enquired calmly after a brief pause, trying to appear almost disinterested and wary that it did not to appear as if she had been snooping.

She was pretty sure that he didn't smoke but she knew that she had to tread carefully and approach the subject with caution if she was going to get the response she was after.

The Bishop didn't react; in fact he deliberately ignored her probing and when she repeated her question, with a little more insistence, thinking that maybe he had not heard her question, he simply blanked her coldly, obviously irritated at the thought that she had been going through his drawers.

Madison sensed the tension beginning to build in his demeanour as he sat there, but thinking on her feet, she quickly managed to diffuse the situation by explaining why she had had to look in the drawers – *so that she could find her swimsuits* - and satisfied with her reasoning her host began to relax again, conceding chivalrously that it was his fault, that he should have told her exactly where he had put the swimsuits before leaving her to get changed.

The moment passed but while Madison had vindicated herself for her actions she was no nearer to finding out about the cigar-box and its contents as *the Bishop* offered no further information, preferring instead to return quietly to his book.

For the next week or so, Madison forgot all about the cigar-box but one afternoon while idly looking around his bedroom, she came across a weird-looking figurine carved in wood that was sat discreetly at the back of his dresser behind his collection of grooming products.

The sculpture was that of a cheery-faced, friar with chubby little hands rubbing his rather rotund stomach.

She picked it up out of curiosity more than anything else…as it really did look so out of place among his more stylish curios…and as she lifted it, it clunked.

Surprised and intrigued, Madison twisted the little figurine at the waist and as it came apart in her hands, she was amazed to discover that it concealed a small key.

Of course, the journalist and the fledgling investigative reporter in her immediately put two and two together, but as *the Bishop* was downstairs and liable to walk in on her at any time, she knew that, that was not the moment to put her theory to the test.

She waited a few more days until one afternoon she could resist no longer.

TB was in the conservatory playing the piano, as he did for an hour or so on a daily basis, and as he was engrossed in perfecting a new tune, Madison got up and told him that she was going to the Lucy (WC).

He nodded his head by way of understanding and without another word Madison coolly made her way out of the conservatory.

However, instead of heading for the downstairs facilities like she would normally do, feeling very guilty, her heart pounding a thousand to the dozen in her chest, she crept up the staircase as stealthily as she could and stole into the master-bedroom.

Once there, being as quiet and discreet as possible she removed the key from the little wooden figurine, opened the drawer with a rush of guilt-ridden excitement and inserted it into the keyhole in the box.

Lo and behold; it opened.

Almost frozen with the fear of being discovered she slowly raised the lid and as she did so, a waft of perfume escaped from the box filling her nostrils with its scent.

In a panic almost, she closed the box again and looked around guiltily before opening it again.

Inside, she found a bundle of letters, all addressed to a certain Jane, and all full of warm, passionate scribbling which seemed so unlike the man that she had gotten to know.

She picked out the first letter and looking warily in the direction of the door, she began to unfold it, careful not to rip it or damage it in any way.

She hesitated momentarily, unsure of her motives, but unable to resist the temptation, her eyes were gradually drawn to the page and she began to read;

My Dearest Jane,

I think of you often, with fondness, despite what happened between us, because I still care.....much more than I should, given the circumstances.

I fell in love with you and I cannot regret that, nor can I lie about it...or deny that it ever happened – and while I do sometimes wonder if I am ever going to exorcise you from my thoughts, I cannot pretend that what we had never existed – it was too real.

Of course, only you and I will ever know what really happened between us during those heady days...but I want you to know that ever since that time, despite the tribulations of life's challenge and the distance that now separates us, I have never stopped loving you...

Madison caught herself gasping as she read some of the words and her hands started to shake between the emotion she was reading on the page… and the growing fear she felt of being discovered.

The feelings being expressed in the letter were so truthful, so heartfelt… so full of romantic torment that…at one point…she had to stop reading, deliberately censoring herself from reading on, as she felt more and more ashamed that she was reading his private thoughts without his permission… and suddenly overcome with guilt, she hurriedly put the letter back into the box, closed the lid and locked it again, returning the box to its rightful place in the drawer, before she could be found out.

Then, having replaced the key where she had found it, she rushed back downstairs, cannily stopping off in the kitchen on her way back to the conservatory to pour them each a glass of fruit juice.

Later however, over dinner, still desperate to know more…more about him, more about his past, Madison mentioned the funny little sculpture on his dresser, hoping that it would plant a seed in his mind and develop into a conversation, but unfortunately *the Bishop* simply brushed it off, announcing rather brusquely that the little monk with his beaming grin and his big fat belly had been a gift, given to him from a friend - *who is no longer a friend* - as a sarcastic statement on his surly character.

Madison let it pass on that occasion, knowing that to insist would only cause tension, but from that day forth, whenever the opportunity presented itself and she knew that she couldn't get caught, it became a guilty pleasure of hers to sneak upstairs and read one or more of his private letters, each time falling more and more in love with the author and his romantic prose.

She knew that, by doing this, she was putting her relationship with *the Bishop…if indeed that was what it was…*in jeopardy, because if he ever caught her, she would die of shame and embarrassment…and yet, despite the inner conflict between her morality and his right to personal privacy Madison just couldn't deny her inherent feminine inquisitiveness or her journalistic instinct to find out more about this man and his past.

CHAPTER TWENTY

Madison was coming to the end of her stay in England, when over breakfast one morning, *the Bishop* announced, somewhat unexpectedly that he had to go into London for a few days…and that if she was interested; she was welcome to join him.

'You bet I want to come', she replied in the next breath without thought or hesitation, trying hard, but failing miserably to disguise her response with any kind of restraint.

'Hey; it's just a trip into London', *the Bishop* quipped as he got up, walked around the table and brushed a stray hair out of her eyes – a gesture of affection that had become surprisingly more frequent as the weeks were going by.

'Yeah, but a change of scenery will do us good', Madison mumbled in a more moderate tone, trying desperately to reign in her enthusiasm.

'Besides, while we are in London I could look for some more heels', she reasoned frivolously.

'What is it with you women and heels...and why do you seem to think that towering heels that you can't even walk in without potentially breaking your ankles is a good look', *the Bishop* questioned.

'You don't like women in heels', Madison queried inquisitively.

'I didn't say that; I don't like them in ridiculously high heels…; my rule of thumb…'

'Hold up! You have a rule of thumb...for women's heels'; she interrupted with a withering look.

'My rule of thumb is this...' *the Bishop* continued, ignoring the interruption.

'…a two inch heel improves a woman's posture and gives the appearance of narrower ankles',

'…a three inch heel enhances a woman's silhouette by making her backside stick out slightly as the body equals out the centre of gravity',

'...but anything four inches and above...well…as you Americans would say…that is hooker territory, not to mention a health hazard', he concluded.

'Yeah; as much as I hate to admit it, I think you might be right', Madison concurred grudgingly with a nod of the head.

'The current trend for sky-scraper heels is ridiculous, but we women are slaves to fashion even if it is to the detriment of our own health; you know, I have a friend who has to take two pre-emptive pain-killer tablets every morning just to deal with the pain of walking around all day in her heels'.

'That is just preposterous', *the Bishop* remarked, while lifting up the coffee decanter and waving it in her direction.

'So; more coffee?' he asked good-naturedly.

'No, I'm good', Madison replied, placing her hand over her cup to signal that she had already had her fix of caffeine, her mind already kicking into gear.

The Bishop poured himself another cup and while he was over getting some fresh milk from the fridge Madison's thought process immediately began to wander, making a mental list of everything she was going to do in London.

The Abbey was a beautiful place, a wonderful haven from the outside world and while she was enjoying spending time there…*and at her pretty rented cottage whose peaceful tranquillity was only ever disturbed by the chorus of birds in the morning or the sound of an occasional passing car*…the young New-Yorker that she was, was nevertheless beginning to miss the buzz of the big city.

Oh, how she missed Manhattan, she mused to herself longingly, but at least she now had London to look forward to…

…and so it was that, after lunch the next day, having each thrown… no…placed a suitcase into the back of the Aston, *the Bishop* drove them into London where, with a seamless and effortless transition, they checked smoothly into the Hempel Hotel.

The Hempel is a beautifully appointed boutique hotel situated in the centre of London; it is set back slightly from the main thoroughfare, but it is close enough to Hyde Park for its guests to enjoy spectacular views of it from the upper floors.

They were shown to their room…*which thanks to the Bishop's quasi-celebrity status, just happened to be one the more exclusive of the hotel's many suites*…and a few hours later, once they had had time to settle in and freshen up, *the Bishop* called down to the concierge's desk and asked him to book a table for them at one of his favourite restaurants.

The taxi was ordered and an hour or so later they were sitting in one of Mayfair's finest restaurants, ready to indulge themselves in some of the most exquisite culinary delights.

The mood was relaxed, the conversation was light-hearted and on several occasions during the course of the evening, much to her surprise Madison found herself bursting out spontaneously in fits of laughter in response to some of *the Bishop's* uncharacteristic wit and innuendo.

'You know; you will never cease to amaze me', she commented as she recovered her composure after yet another particularly humorous anecdote.

'…Oh really?' *the Bishop* quizzed, waiting for her to qualify her statement.

'Yeah, because when we first met', she explained, '…you were very distant, remote even…and very unforthcoming'.

'I was?' *the Bishop* cajoled, raising an eyebrow.

'Yeah, in fact I thought you were….' Madison hesitated, still feeling a little reticent about criticising him to his face, despite their ongoing idyll.

'Yes…?' he prompted.

'Well I thought you were a little…obnoxious and self-obsessed', Madison commented.

'…but now that I have come to know you and appreciate your rather unique personality…' she pursued, without waiting for him to comment; '…let's just say that …as I said before, that you never cease to amaze me', she declared after a brief pause, not wanting to dig herself into too big a hole.

The Bishop sat motionless, studying her and pondering his reply.

He was being his usual non-committal self and he had no intention of changing that stance, but somehow, for some reason, the mood and the frivolous nature of their exchanges was tempting him, inciting him even… to say more than his cautious nature would otherwise divulge – because even though they had never really discussed it, their relationship had now gone way beyond the teacher and pupil concept of its origins.

However before he could say anything Madison unexpectedly broke into another nervous giggle.

'…And now you are making me laugh; is there no end to your talents?' she asked, reaching for a glass of water.

'Apparently not', *the Bishop* replied flattered and amused at Madison's endearing behaviour.

'You know, I have always liked a man with confidence who can make me laugh like that', she confessed regaining her composure…again.

'Is that so?' *the Bishop* replied confidently; as he leaned forward, feeling the tension of anticipation begin to build.

'Well, what I like about you is…' he paused, wondering how far he should go in his flattery.

'…your accent', he announced awkwardly, unable at the last moment to reveal his true thoughts.

'…it's alluring …soft and seductive', he added quickly, regaining his focus and his intensity, accompanying his words with a gesture of the hand…*a l'italienne.*

'It is?' Madison queried, a little surprised at his hesitation and clearly disappointed at his rather weak praise.

'Yes it is', *the Bishop* confirmed, looking across the table at her stunned expression.

He wanted to say more; he was desperate to tell her how he was feeling but before he could find the words, the waiter came over, interrupting the conversation and when it resumed, he conveniently avoided returning the delicate subject of 'them', preferring instead to turn his attention to his itinerary for the following day.

'I hope you don't mind but I have an early appointment tomorrow morning with a couple of the senior members from the ECA', he informed her.

'We are going to discuss the new season and maybe change the calendar around a bit, …but after that, maybe we could meet up and I could show you around', he suggested rather considerately.

'That's fine by me', Madison agreed without discussion, '…but don't worry, I'm sure that I can find something to occupy me in this big city of yours…while you are in your meeting', she assured him, with her incorrigible New-York chutzpah, her eyes suddenly sparkling at the thought of being let loose on the hundreds of fashionable boutiques that abound in the English capital.

Next morning, *the Bishop* got up early for his meeting...but before he left, he took the time to carefully whisper into Madison's ear...as she continued to blissfully slumber in the immensity of the huge king-sized bed...that he would rendezvous with her at Speaker's Corner at noon.

The latter heard his words through the pillowy clouds that were enveloping her mind but as she slowly emerged from the depths of her sub-conscious, stretching herself out like the proverbial cat that had gotten the cream, Madison could do nothing else but offer him a sleepy smile.

The Bishop repeated the message.

'I get it ...twelve noon', she confirmed in a whispered breath, not even opening her eyes; preferring instead to simply raise a hand to his cheek to show that she had understood.

TB instantly took hold of her hand, kissed it softly and tucked it back in under the quilt before getting up and turning to leave.

Madison woke up again, forty minutes later and after another wonderfully invigorating shower she wandered into the living area in her robe, still drying her hair, to find a note on the table next to the breakfast tray, re-iterating what *the Bishop* had already told her, along with an improvised street plan giving her directions.

She picked it up and read it out aloud;

'Speaker's Corner at noon;
... and wear something sexy!'
TB

Wear something sexy; who does he think he is? Madison said to herself in indignation under her breath; her irritation at *the Bishop's* sexist demand all too obvious.

The Bishop had been giving her advice on the way she dressed…and the way he thought she should dress…from the very first time that they had met, so it was no surprise to her that he had done this, but his suggestion that she wear something sexy for a meeting in the park, left Madison a little perplexed.

She folded the note in two and placed it back down on the table, before taking a sip from one of the glasses of orange-juice on the breakfast tray and returning to the bedroom, where, not wanting to disappoint *the Bishop* despite her latent feminist indignation, she found herself rummaging through all the clothes that she had brought with her in order to find her secret weapon; the one grey dress - which buttoned-up in the front - that she knew could either be dressed up for the evening or left unadorned for an afternoon stroll in the park, which is what she guessed *the Bishop* had in mind…though why he should want her to look sexy while doing that, completely escaped her.

She pulled the dress out and laid it on the bed before grabbing a fresh set of underwear and returning to the bathroom to attend to the rest of her morning rituals.

It took a while for her to do her hair and make-up, but within half an hour or so Madison appeared again in the bathroom doorway, ready to apply the finishing touches to her persona.

She grabbed the dress from the bed and made her way over to the full-length mirror on the far side of the room, holding the dress up against herself before she put it on, just to check that it would meet with *the Bishop's* approval.

It was a pretty dress that she had worn on several occasions previously, but unfortunately on this occasion she was a little disappointed with it… because while it still looked good, it did look a little plain, and she knew that *the Bishop* wouldn't be impressed by 'plain'.

She pondered accessorising it, with maybe a belt or a brooch but as her mind wandered off in several directions, the dress slipped out of her hand and she suddenly realised that she was committing a cardinal sin in her dress-sense as far as *the Bishop* was concerned; *her bra did not match her underwear.*

Almost immediately she saw him in her mind's eye pontificating across a table at her.

'...women need to realise that men, real men, men who adore women in all their feminine complexity and glory prefer to see them in matching underwear...never mind what the fashion industry might say...'

Madison chuckled to herself; a lot of good that advice is doing for me, she thought to herself as she turned almost one hundred and eighty degrees to see her reflection from the back.

'Owch', she groaned in derision, almost curling up with embarrassment at the sight of her mismatching under-garments.

Then, facing the mirror again, she placed the dress back in front of her.

It was in no way a sexy dress, but as she didn't really have an alternative with her, she decided that it would have to do.

But then as she looked in the mirror again she suddenly had a brilliant idea.

She would leave the sexiness to *the Bishop's* imagination by wearing her most daring lingerie-ensemble under her 'plain' grey dress, thereby allowing her to surreptitiously call his bluff whenever she might choose... *and counter his argument if ever he dared question or criticise her choice of outfit*...knowing full-well that a discreet whisper in his ear at the right moment to inform him of what she was wearing under her rather prim cotton dress would almost certainly give her the upper hand in any... discussion.

It was almost 9 a.m. by the time she made her way out of the hotel ready to launch her one-woman blitz on London's fashion boutiques, but for the next three hours or so, Madison was determined to make the most of it.

London looked so vivid, so alive that morning...and as she turned left out of the hotel, finding herself almost immediately in the middle of Oxford Street, she slowly made her way towards Regent Street, consciously taking note of all the new trends…and original ideas being thrust at her… both in the shop-window displays and on the street around her.

Madison was like a kid in a candy-shop and she stopped frequently on her walk to wander inside one or other of the more fashionable big-name stores along the way…in order to check out their new fashion-ranges… justifying her keen interest of all things 'fashion' under the banner of competitive comparison, knowing that she could always use any ideas that she might glean from these visits in discussions with Gretchen when she got back.

The morning just flew by, and not surprisingly, by the time she reached Carnaby Street, a cursory glance at her phone told her that it was already eleven twenty.

'Goddamit', she mumbled under her breath, 'if there was only some way that I could contact TB to put back the rendezvous for an hour…. or two'.

There wasn't; she couldn't (*TB didn't carry a mobile phone*); so instead she began looking around for a taxi to get her back to Hyde Park because there was no way that she was going to battle her way back up Oxford Street on foot. It would have been like trying to wade against a fast-flowing current…but as she scanned the street for that elusive black-cab, her eyes suddenly caught sight of a quirky little boutique across the road from where she was standing, which was displaying in its window a range of the most original modern print dresses that she had ever seen, full of eye-catching colour and amazing geometric designs.

Ever the opportunist, Madison couldn't resist taking a closer look despite the fact that she was already tight for time and without a second thought, she quickly crossed over the road, gave the window-display a fleeting glance and stepped inside the little boutique.

The assistant at the counter welcomed her politely with the customary offer of help but pressed for time Madison brushed it away with a smile and an 'I'm good' before rushing over to the rail on the far side of the boutique where the dresses that had caught her eye in the window had been set out.

She riffled through them, picked out a couple in her size and with a glance up at the sign which indicated their whereabouts, she immediately headed for the fitting rooms, noticing as she went – on a huge antique clock on the wall - that it was already eleven-twenty-three.

The pretty assistant whose job it was to oversee the fitting-rooms indicated a cubicle to her and within minutes Madison had slipped off her own dress and tried on the two new ones, checking them out from every angle as she twisted and turned in front of the mirror provided.

She liked them both but as was often the case, she was a little disappointed to see that while the dresses were beautifully-made and stunning to look at, they looked so much better on the tiny mannequins in the window than they did on her size twelve frame.

This really frustrated her and throwing her hands in the air, she could not help but vent that frustration by screaming at her reflection which immediately brought the assistant running to see what was wrong.

'Can I help you with anything, madam?' the young woman enquired politely.

Madison pulled back the curtain and while she stood there still berating the fact that the dresses were not quite sitting right on her, the young assistant immediately began to fuss around her, promising earnestly that with only the slightest of alterations the dresses would fit her perfectly.

...but it was no use; Madison had heard it all before; she knew the routine and the techniques that these people use to make a sale and she wouldn't be swayed by the young assistant's obviously-rehearsed sales pitch.

'No, this is not going to do it for me', Madison concluded as she unzipped the dress, much to the assistant's dismay.

'Well...maybe you could try one of our other models', the young woman suggested, used to pandering to the whims of her clientele and anxious too, to make a sale.

'No, I'm sorry, I would love to, but I just don't have the time', Madison commented, glancing again at the clock on the wall.

'...maybe next time', she added, handing back the two dresses with a disconsolate shrug of the shoulders.

'Yes...next time', the assistant repeated with a patronising smile as she turned on her heels and walked off to resume her other duties.

Madison got herself dressed again...rushing so as not to be late...but then as she made her way back out of the shop, she could not help but notice several of the other creative new designs and styles being displayed on the walls and on the racks around the shop.

Her heart sank instantly in frustration and she began to rue the fact that she couldn't stay in the shop a while longer, to try on a few more of the fabulous creations, just as the young assistant had suggested, because despite the latter's rather surly attitude, she was probably right; there was such a diverse choice available that she was certain to find - eventually - something that would suit her among all the wonderful and crazy new asymmetric designs.

Alas, for Madison, she just didn't have the time to do that and another quick look at the imposing clock on the wall told her that she now had less than half an hour to get back to Hyde Park for her rendezvous with *the Bishop*.

♗

It was tight, but Madison made it back to Speaker's Corner, just in time to hear Big Ben striking the twelve chimes of noon in the distance.

She looked up at the cold English sky and could see the dark clouds forming above her head.

The Bishop was late; she was on time but he was late.

Shaking her head, she walked over to the benches which had been installed there for just such an occasion and passed by a group of youths... all tapping frantically on the screens of their mobile phones like an army of witless zombies; a sight which made her feel a little sad.

To think that their whole world had been reduced to a 3-inch rectangle, she thought to herself.

She approached the next bench and a pensioner quickly stood up and offered her a seat.

'Thank-you', she mouthed discreetly as the old-timer doffed his cap and walked away with a gentle wave of the hand.

Madison sat down expecting to see *the Bishop* arrive at any moment - as punctuality had always been his forte - but as she checked her phone a few minutes later, she was more than surprised to note that he was already almost fifteen minutes late.

He had never made her wait before and as she sat there a little perplexed, wondering if she was at the right spot - *getting a little frustrated that she could have spent more time in her favourite new boutique* - her thoughts began to wander and she began to speculate about the lives of all the people who were rushing by in front of her, going about their everyday chores, their everyday lives.

A young man caught her eye momentarily and as she followed his progress for a few yards, she began thinking about her own life, her own situation and about *the Bishop*...because although they were from completely different back-grounds, the haphazard mechanics of life had thrown them together and ever since that time, despite their obvious disparities and disagreements they had somehow gravitated towards each other to a point where she now felt that she had almost inadvertently become his sounding-board if not his touch-stone.

It was a strange feeling and yet for some reason his opinion had come to matter to her too; more than she probably realised.

Of course, she still had a few niggling reservations about *the Bishop*... due to his typically-male emotional hang-ups but while she knew that she was still loathe to admit it openly, she also knew in her own mind that with every passing day she was falling for this enigma of a man, and had been doing so almost since the first time they had met - despite his sometimes erratic and irrational behaviour like today's incongruous request for her to dress up 'sexily' for this rather trivial meeting in the park.

'Just another one of his idiosyncrasies', she thought to herself as she brushed her dress absent-mindedly...though she was convinced, knowing the man as she did, that there was an ulterior motive hidden somewhere in his cryptic manoeuvrings.

Being reminded about her dress and what she was secretly wearing beneath it, Madison's mind continued to wander deeper into her sub-conscious and as time began to tick by, the romantic thoughts that it prompted together with the threatening black clouds above suddenly inspired her to imagine a secret fantasy scenario where she was walking along the deserted streets of London, late one night when;

Suddenly a flash storm breaks out.

She runs for cover, sees a red telephone box and quickly makes her way over to it – her clothes getting drenched all the while by the rain.

Splashing through the puddles she reaches the phone-box at the same time as another person; a swarthy stranger who was also looking for shelter

After a moment's hesitation they both get inside out of the rain.

A flash of thunder and lightning rips through the sky above them, frightening her and instinctively she grabs hold of the man.

Her hair is dripping wet; he inhales her scent

They embrace tightly as the rain lashes against the glass panes of their haven…

Real droplets of rain falling on her cheeks suddenly brought Madison back to reality and just as she was deciding where she could go to take shelter, lo and behold, **s**he spotted *the Bishop* in the distance, arriving in the nick of time to usher her into the sanctuary of a nearby department store, offering her a cursory but tactful apology for his tardiness as they went.

Surprisingly, Madison accepted his explanation without taking offence, her mind still preoccupied with processing the events of her previous thoughts but once they got inside the store, she didn't waste any time in suggesting that he could have at least called her, on her mobile, to let her know that he was going to be late.

The Bishop agreed guiltily with a nod of the head and as they stood there in an awkward silence just inside the store's heavy main-doors …outside in the street…much to Madison's amusement, the wind suddenly picked up and began playing havoc with the women's skirts as they scuttled along in the rain desperately trying to hold them in place.

Two or three more people joined them in the crowded store-entrance and as they did so, parking themselves off to one side, the heavens opened again outside and the rain re-doubled its intensity bouncing off the pavement like a storm of ball-bearings.

The shower was very heavy but no sooner had it started, than it stopped and all those who had gathered around for shelter were soon filtering back out of the store and onto the rain-soaked street to carry on with their lives.

Madison and *the Bishop* held back until the last, but eventually they made their way out too, glancing up at the sky as they did so, to make sure that the worst was over.

Once outside, *the Bishop* put his hand in the small of Madison's back and with a gentle prod, he guided her to the left down Park Lane… stopping briefly, for just a moment or two, *to listen to a young guy playing a stripped-back version of Gerry Rafferty's 'Baker Street' on his sax*…before they continued on towards Mayfair and Hyde Park Corner.

'Let's take a stroll down here', he suggested, much to Madison's surprise.

'Why, where are we going?' she asked curiously, still believing that he must have an ulterior motive or some kind of destination in mind; why else would he have asked her to dress 'sexy'!

She looked into his eyes searching for a response but though they were sparkling, they were giving nothing away.

'You'll see when we get there', he insisted, teasing her.

The rain-shower had washed the streets clean and the volume of people had largely diminished…but nevertheless as they turned right onto Knightsbridge, Madison was slowly becoming irritable, her mood beginning to sag; after all, she had been walking around all morning, had waited patiently for him in the park for longer than she had ever waited for anybody, and as they turned yet another corner she still didn't know where they were headed or why *the Bishop* had insisted on her dress-code.

The frustration was building, her patience was getting thin and just as she was about to let him know it, he suddenly took her by the hand and guided her into the hallowed halls of Harrods.

This was a real shock to her system; not because they had entered Harrods, she had been in there before; but what really surprised her, destabilised her and left her mind reeling with disbelief was the fact that *the Bishop* had taken her by the hand.

He had never been one for public displays of affection and had always made sure that the relevant social protocol was respected whenever they were in company, but here he was, in the most iconic of places, grabbing her hand and holding on to it tightly as they made their way through the different aisles into the heart of the store.

Madison was a little overcome at first but once she had gotten used to it she couldn't stop smiling, squeezing his hand back two or three times to reassure herself that it was real and to let him know that she was okay with it.

The Bishop led her directly to one of the jewellery counters and as they approached, the assistant saw them coming and…recognising him instantly…immediately stooped down and took out a small square-shaped box from under the counter.

On seeing this, Madison suddenly checked her step and as they came to a halt, her heart lurched at the unexpected and presumptuous nature of his gift.

Of course, her first thought, as she saw the assistant placing the little box gently on the glass display case in front of her was that it was a ring - and almost instantly a million considerations flashed through her mind;

…was this really what she wanted?
…where would they live?
…her job, what would she do with her job?

…all the things that a woman thinks about in a situation such as this…

…but then all of a sudden her heart fell because she wasn't sure… they had never even discussed being an item yet…never mind anything more…permanent.

Now I know why he wanted me to make an effort, Madison thought to herself, as she felt herself blush as red as the silk scarlet thong that she was wearing under her now 'wholly-unsuitable-for the-occasion' summer dress, but she managed to recompose herself, brush a stray hair out of her eyes and do the same with her rain-spattered dress.

The Bishop politely introduced her to the assistant and the latter immediately handed over the precious little box accompanied by her most professional smile.

Madison cleared her throat nervously and still looking a little stunned, she accepted the box, looked at the assistant and then paused before turning to look at TB.

It was an almost imperceptible pause but with his usual razor-sharp behavioural analysis *the Bishop* had no trouble picking up on it and immediately began wondering if he was doing the right thing in buying her this kind of gift.

Time seemed to stand still as Madison took a couple of deep breaths... but then she spoke.

'I can't accept this', she said, her voice betraying her emotion.

'I know that it is disingenuous of me to refuse', she continued, treading a fine line between being honest and being tactful, 'but I just can't accept it...not until we discuss...'

The Bishop interrupted her before she could finish.

'Nonsense', he trumpeted.

'You haven't even seen what's in it yet...and besides, you might just like it', he insisted, casually dismissing her caginess.

'Look, I don't want to sound ungrateful', Madison argued, 'but...'

'Just open the damned box', *the Bishop* persisted, his probing eyes trying to understand her reticence to accept his gift.

Madison smiled at him and then at the assistant, and then slowly, very slowly, her heart pounding at fifty to the dozen, she pulled open the top of the little case.

Her immediate reaction was one of disappointment when she saw what was in the little box...but that was soon replaced by an overwhelming feeling of relief and delight as the contents were revealed...relief because she really wasn't ready for marriage; not that *the Bishop* had even asked her...and delight because instead of the ring she had been expecting in her own mind – the little box contained a solid-gold pendant that *the Bishop* had ordered for her in the shape of what else but a bishop chess-piece, suspended from a pretty gold chain that was both simple and elegant in design.

Madison stared at it for a few seconds and then as her emotions began to settle down again, she puckered up, ignoring *the Bishop's* usual rule of no PDA's and gave him a gentle peck on the cheek together with some heart-felt words of thanks.

'Happy Christmas', he announced quietly in his usual imperturbable manner, shattering into a thousand pieces with just those two little words, all the romantic illusions that had been running amok in Madison's head for the last five minutes.

'…but it's not Christmas for another five months', Madison countered, still a little flattened by the realisation that his surprise was no more than an early present.

'I know that, but it soon will be', *the Bishop* explained; '…and as I won't be there then to give this to you, I thought it would be a better idea to give it to you now so that I could see your reaction.'

'Well, I'm flattered that you would do that and as you can see I'm delighted by the extent of your generosity', Madison confirmed, kissing him again and handing the box back to the assistant to be gift-wrapped.

'Good; now that that's done, how about some lunch…I'm famished', *the Bishop* announced bringing a conclusion to the proceedings.

They made their way out of Harrods and moved on to a little Persian restaurant called Hafez, situated just around the corner from the hotel where they were staying…and although it was getting a little late for a lunch reservation they managed to persuade the manager to give them a little table in the corner where they sat for over an hour enjoying some of the most original exotic cuisine.

It was a delicious interlude in the day's events and while *the Bishop* revelled in explaining the history of Persian culture to Madison as they ate, her mind seemed to wander off in several emotionally-charged directions; although when a particular detail, usually relating to fashion did ignite her interest, she immediately focussed again and questioned him about it in great detail, marvelling at the range and the depth of his eclectic knowledge.

Nonetheless, although he was holding court as usual, *the Bishop* did make sure that the culture lesson that he was dispensing was interspersed with a variety of current topics too, so that Madison could add her views to the conversation, offering some balance to their otherwise lopsided exchanges.

They also swapped some rather flirtatious banter too, over dessert, but then all of a sudden, without warning, as the waiter cleared away their plates, Madison's mood changed; she went all quiet and her focus seemed to narrow.

'What's wrong; have I said something to upset you?' *the Bishop* asked, quizzing her while mentally reviewing his last comments for any critical content.

'No', Madison answered feebly, feeling somewhat embarrassed for bringing it up and letting him see her confusion.

'So what is it?' *the Bishop* repeated, his look of concern turning to a frown.

'Oh, it's nothing really', Madison explained; 'it's just that, for a moment there, back in Harrods I stupidly thought that…that it was a ring in the box and that…; it just got me thinking…' she mumbled, not really wanting to reveal any more of her feelings but unable to stop herself.

'Young lady; you should know me better than that', *the Bishop* countered instantly, short-circuiting her thought process and not wanting to reveal the depth of his emotions either.

'Yeah, of course', Madison conceded in a rare moment of self-deprecation; 'whatever was I thinking?'

The Bishop smiled; the look of relief all too apparent in his eyes and with that Madison took hold of her glass of Persian tea and proposed a toast.

'To independence…' she announced raising the glass and chinking it curtly against his.

'To independence….' *the Bishop* agreed as he took another sip of his delicious doogh cocktail *(a drink made from yoghurt, water and dried mint)*, his mind working overtime as it tried to decipher the content and the meaning of her unspoken words.

Madison slumped back in her chair and looked out of the window.

She was obviously disappointed inside…*her body language spoke volumes*…but she couldn't really explain why; after all, she didn't want to get married either; not right now anyway, in fact it had never even crossed her mind but the dogmatic manner in which *the Bishop* had so coldly brushed aside, even the possibility of them consolidating their relationship - timescale or no timescale - left her with a feeling of deep disenchantment.

The Bishop saw this; he saw her fighting with her moral dilemma – and he sympathised with it more than she would ever know - but rather than let it spoil what had been a wonderful moment up until then, he tried to revive the conversation by suggesting that while they were in London they should take in the Tate Gallery, the National Gallery or even the V&A Museum.

Madison sniggered at this…*remembering Evie's anecdote about the museum in New York*…and it brought her back down to earth.

'Is that your idea of a good time in London?' she asked playfully; '…a trip to a museum?'

The Bishop shrugged his shoulders; 'it was just a suggestion…' he explained, brushing his fingers through his hair and scratching the back of his head.

'…maybe another time', Madison quipped sarcastically.

However, as she finished her tea and his words began to slowly filter through the confusion of her jumbled thoughts…to her forefront of her consciousness Madison suddenly realised that something had changed; that the man sitting across from her was no longer the man she had first come to know…because that man had categorically refused to do the sight-seeing tours both in Boston and in New York when she had offered to organise them for him, and yet here he was spontaneously offering to be her cultural guide in London.

Was that a subtle sign of change and hope for the future, she wondered, or was he just humouring her, trying anything he could to shake her out of her current frame of mind?

After all, the man was a master at psychological manipulation and had proved it to her already time and time again.

'Why don't we take a trip on the London Eye?' Madison proposed frivolously trying to put the ball back in *the Bishop's* court.

The Bishop looked out of the window, up at the sky.

'…maybe another time', he suggested, mimicking her previous reply; '…the weather looks rather unsettled'.

'Yeah right…the weather in London looks unsettled', Madison repeated with a wry smile.

'Okay, we'll go tomorrow…' *the Bishop* agreed, smiling at her glib remark; '…weather permitting'.

Back at the hotel, in the privacy of their room, Madison carefully removed her new necklace from its case...and walking over to the vanity mirror, she held it up against herself to gauge how high or how low she should wear the chain.

'What do you think; like this or...like this?' she asked, looking at *the Bishop's* reflection in the mirror for an opinion, her hands holding the chain high against her neck and then a little lower on her chest.

'It's not a choker', he commented critically, 'so the lower option would probably be best', he confirmed.

Madison huffed...and continued striking poses, holding her hair up in several more formal postures, before letting it drop back down again and then draping it loosely around her shoulders.

She was actually quite taken with her pendant but as she inspected it a little more closely in her hand, she suddenly turned to *the Bishop* and said;

'Hey, I'm curious; why did you ask me to 'dress sexy' in that note that you left this morning...I mean, we didn't really do anything during the day that warranted me being 'dressed sexy'.

'I don't really know...' *the Bishop* replied flatly, not wanting it to sound like he was indulging himself in another bout of psychological manipulation.

'...but I bet it made you feel pretty and sexy all day long; didn't it', he argued, as he came up behind her and kissed her softly on the neck, his hands placing themselves almost naturally on the swell of her hips.

She didn't admit to it of course, but it <u>was</u> true, Madison thought to herself; she was feeling a bit 'hot and bothered' – *as all women seem to when they put on their best lingerie* - but nevertheless she was still a little disappointed that *the Bishop's mise-en-scene* hadn't pre-empted something a little more...extraordinary than an early Christmas present.

Still standing behind her, *the Bishop* began taking off his tie, his thoughts obviously on spending an hour or so relaxing before dinner, but as he did so, much to *his* disappointment this time, Madison slipped away from his grasp and made her way into the ensuite bathroom; she really was feeling a little 'hot and bothered' in more ways than one after her morning shopping trip, the rain shower and the emotional episodes in both Harrods and the restaurant, all of which had taken their toll on her stress-levels and she needed a moment to herself, to chill.

She closed the bathroom door…and glancing briefly in the mirror at her slightly dishevelled appearance - *which she had worsened with all her posing* – she decided that the best thing for her to do, in order to cool herself off physically and calm her down emotionally, would be for her to take a nice long, relaxing bath.

Reaching down, she turned on the taps and as soon as he heard the water running from the other room, realising what she was about to do, *the Bishop* immediately put his own plan into action.

He crept towards the main door and being as discreet as possible, he checked that the lock was engaged before calmly returning to the bedroom, where again, being as quiet as possible he got undressed and slipped silently under the covers of the huge double-bed to wait patiently for Madison to reappear.

Ten minutes later, having run her bath and fussed about with all her essential oils and essences Madison nonchalantly wandered back out of the bathroom to get herself undressed, going straight over to her suitcase to sort out a few things for the evening.

She didn't even notice the bump in the bed until she raised her head to ask what they would be doing that evening.

'You have got to be kidding me', she blurted out as she turned around to see *the Bishop* lying in the bed, his hands enlaced behind his head and a large, smug smile plastered across his face.

Madison was more than surprised. Thus far in their relationship *the Bishop* had never really been one for spontaneity – *although there was that one time in New York* – but to see him lying there stretched out in the bed, apparently waiting for her to join him, suddenly left her lost for words – for once - the look on her face summing up her complete disbelief.

'Would you care to join me, Miss Chatfield', *the Bishop* asked mischievously with an impish twinkle in his eye, his right hand holding the quilt open as a welcoming invitation.

Suddenly the mood in the room changed and the air crackled with sexual tension.

'Why Mr Byron; now I know why you wanted me to feel sexy…and horny', Madison whispered softly, as she ambled towards the bed rolling her hips seductively.

She stopped a few feet from the bed.

The Bishop looked so handsome and so inviting as he lay there, that all she wanted to do was to strip off all her clothes and dive in beside him… but as he had upset her and made her wait around earlier in the day, she decided that a little pay-back was in order and that she would make him wait a while before eventually surrendering to his irresistible manly charm.

'You are such a bad man', she teased, '…but on this occasion I think I will pass on your invitation', she declared, indicating that her bath was ready and waiting to soothe away the stress of her day.

The Bishop was disappointed but as he mumbled something under his breath about knowing of another way to take away her stress, Madison began undoing the buttons of her dress, beginning deliberately with those immediately in line with her chest.

The sight of her cleavage immediately got *the Bishop* interested, but he was still unsure whether it was for him or whether she was just getting undressed in order to go and take her bath.

He raised himself up onto his elbow and as his interest grew further, Madison got a little more into the mood, watching him closely as she moved her hands down further, swaying her hips gently and pulling up on the dress's fabric so as to bring the buttons up to her fingers, rather than bending down to reach them; a deliberate move which treated her spectator of a lover to several deliciously tantalising glimpses of her legs and thighs as the dress slowly revealed the treasures it hid beneath, turning the whole scene into a saucy striptease.

The sexual tension in the room cranked up another notch and as she opened the last few buttons, Madison suddenly felt a frisson which made her shiver with delight.

She shrugged the dress from her shoulders and with the adrenaline now pumping, drawn like a magnet, she slowly sauntered closer to the bed with just a hint of sway in her hips.

The moment was both very erotic and highly romantic and *the Bishop's* eyes could not mask his feelings as he gazed on the wonderful curves of Madison's body as she stood before him in nothing but her racy red underwear.

Madison leaned forward on the mattress and as she did so, rather than kiss her, which she was expecting, *the Bishop* cleverly slipped an agile finger between the embroidered cups of her dainty front-fastening bra and with one quick movement of his thumb, snapped it open and flicked it clear of her beautiful feminine attributes which tumbled immodestly into view in all their glory, sending the level of his testosterone into overdrive.

His eyes glinted as he beheld their sight and the lurid thoughts that accompanied that look left him cognitively impaired momentarily as he stored away the memory.

'My, my Mr Byron, you are a scoundrel', Madison declared playfully, her eyes filled with sexiness and mirth.

'A wonderful scoundrel', she repeated in a whisper as she raised a leg to kneel on the bed in order to kiss him on the cheek; the drawl in her voice reminiscent of that of Scarlet O'Hara's in Gone with the Wind.

She kissed him a second time and then stood up again, pausing momentarily to remove the bra which she tossed in his direction with mischievous abandon.

The Bishop reached out and caught it in mid-air before throwing it to the foot of the bed with equal disregard.

It was another very erotic moment and Madison shivered again as she watched her lover's eyes as they drifted casually down her body to her… now, soon to be exposed…hips.

She brought her hands to her waist and deliberately maintaining eye-contact with him to enjoy his reaction; she hooked her thumbs into the waistband of her tiny briefs and slowly slid them down her thighs and past her knees, much to *the Bishop's* obvious delight.

She then wiggled her hips again and a moment later her tiny red underwear dropped quietly around her ankles.

Their eyes met again and as *the Bishop* raised the quilt again, ready for her to slip in beside him, Madison took a step back, gracefully removed one leg from her discarded undergarment and kicked it off theatrically with the other in the direction of his head.

Sadly, her aim wasn't that good and the little red garment landed squarely on one of the reading lamps above the bed…but *the Bishop* completely ignored this fact, preferring to focus his attention instead on each and every curve of Madison's beautiful, supple body as she stood there in front of him like a naked Venus.

Madison herself scoffed and chuckled at her vain attempt at a grand finale but then feeling a little over-exposed she suddenly turned sideways on and raised her arm slightly to shield her nudity from his piercing gaze.

The Bishop, meanwhile could not stop applauding her performance and in recognition of his appreciation - and to prolong her tease - Madison began to dance for him again as an encore, undulating her body and rotating her hips enticingly – *a la Beyoncé* - her hands clasped together modestly in front of her.

She was getting more and more caught up in the mood and having seized the initiative Madison was enjoying her own game of 'tease and denial' - delighted to have gotten her own back on him after what he had contrived to do to her earlier in the day.

The man himself looked on patiently for as long as the pressure in his veins would allow him to, while Madison continued to tease and taunt him with her dancing…but finally he could take no more and patted the mattress beside him almost begging her to join him.

Madison smiled and thrust her arms in the air; she had won and she knew it as she walked casually towards the head of the bed, pulled the covers back and slipped in beside him.

The Bishop took her in his arms and they kissed.

…she never did get to take her bath….

The next morning however, after a night full of fun and frolic, filled with endless hours of creative love-making *the Bishop* had a couple of real surprises in store for Madison as they sat at the table replenishing their energy levels, not having had dinner the night before.

They had asked for a late-breakfast to be served in their room - as they had not wanted to leave the special little bubble that they had created for themselves - and as they sat there enjoying what was probably enough food for four served up on two huge silver breakfast trays, *the Bishop* quietly announced…between sips of steaming black coffee…that to end their stay in London, he was going to take her to the Annual American Embassy Summer Ball; a lavish costume gala organised for all the expatriate Americans who live in London, where they meet up with each other and those that are just in town for a couple of days or weeks.

Flabbergasted, Madison didn't reply immediately…but after a brief moment of reflection, her first remark was that…among the clothes that she had brought with her, she didn't have anything to wear that would be suitable for such a lavish occasion.

The Bishop shook his head.

'Don't worry about that', he said, reassuring her immediately.

'I'm sure that whatever you choose to wear will be perfect', he insisted, leaning over to kiss her gently on the cheek.

'…in fact, you could even wear that', he commented, nodding his head in the direction of the quilt in which Madison had wrapped herself in order to eat breakfast.

'…though it might need a belt', he added diligently with his subtle eye for detail, noticing the gap starting to appear around her waist as the heavy protective layer that she was using to cover her nakedness tried inexorably to slide off of her, despite her best efforts to keep it in place.

'I don't think so', Madison complained, covering herself up again bullishly.

'I can hardly go to the Embassy Ball looking like a swaddling baby', she added flippantly as she finished another slice of juicy melon.

The Bishop glanced at her with the beginning of a smile.

'I'm sure you won't let me down, whatever you wear', he confirmed, and with that he disappeared into the bathroom to get showered, leaving her to ponder her dilemma over the remains of her breakfast tray.

The Bishop re-appeared twenty minutes or so later, dressed in his usual Italian design and looking over at Madison who was still sitting at the table, he informed her, rather brusquely, that he was popping out to take care of some very important business that he hadn't been able to attend to the day before - and that he would be away for a couple of hours.

Madison, who was still in shock after the bombshell that he had just dropped on her, barely registered what he was saying as he walked up to her and kissed her goodbye...but before he left, she did manage to get an undertaking from him, that as soon as he got back from wherever he was going, they would sit down and discuss the details of what would be expected of her during the evening's proceedings.

With *the Bishop* gone, Madison finished her third cup of coffee and standing up a little awkwardly, she slowly dragged her weary body to the bathroom - leaving the heavy quilt in her wake half-way across the room.

She was hoping that the regenerative properties of warm soothing water would somehow clear her head and refresh her mind so that she could work out how she was going to get through this high-society event... *without having had the time to do the necessary planning*...and a quick look in the mirror at her tousled blond hair in complete and utter disarray, told her that she had one mighty job on her hands if she was going to be the Belle of the Ball later that evening.

Stepping into the shower, she turned on the tap and the cold water almost took her breath away as it hit her skin before warming slowly up to the correct temperature.

That woke her up a little and as she reached for the shampoo, she began to think about *the Bishop* and how he had dropped this invitation on her out of the blue.

What an enigma this guy really is, she thought to herself as she stood under the warm stream of revitalising wetness, washing out all the knots from her hair.

He is just so full of surprises, she mused; after all, he spent most if not all of his time criticising her fellow countrymen and yet, just like that, out of the blue, he manages to conjure up two tickets to what must surely be, a rather exclusive event; the American Embassy Ball.

It was a real conundrum and Madison really had no idea how to resolve it – *indeed she doubted that she ever would* - but the truth was that she probably didn't want to know because it was part of his charm; part of the mystery of what made him the most interesting person that she had ever met.

She turned off the water, having come to the conclusion that it was no use her trying to understand how *the Bishop* worked…and satisfied with that result, she brushed the last few droplets of water from her body as her mind switched almost immediately to a more pressing and urgent matter; that of what the heck she was going to wear to this damned Ball.

Stepping out the shower she reached for one of the smaller towels provided by the hotel…which she wrapped tightly around her head… before grabbing one of the larger ones to dry off the rest of her body.

Having done that, she then donned one of the hotel's luxurious towelling robes and with a determined stride marched straight into the bedroom on a mission to find a miracle outfit in amongst her 'weekend in London' wardrobe, that would be suitable for her to wear for this 'once in a life-time' American Embassy Ball.

Opening the wardrobe, she began riffling through the clothes that she had hung there and then, without missing a beat she picked up her suitcase and emptied the entire contents of what was left in it, onto the bed, hoping desperately for a moment of creative inspiration.

Then, after a brief glance at the clock on the bedside table, she began mixing and matching potential outfits with the corresponding shoes, coming up, rather surprisingly, with a number of different options…but after a good hour of trying almost every combination…none of which she really felt made the grade…her self-control slowly began to fray.

Frustrated, Madison threw her hands in the air, because having followed the female bible to the letter…when packing – i.e., bringing something for every occasion - she really thought that she had every angle covered. How was she to know that *the Bishop* was going to take her by surprise and serve her up with such an unexpected curve-ball; never in a million years could she have predicted or foreseen them going to a formal ball while they were in London.

Nevertheless, she had to do something…and in a moment of angst-driven clarity she suddenly remembered the shop that she had visited the day before.

That was it, she thought; she would rush over there, pick up one of those modern designer dresses and all her problems would be solved.

Glancing again at the digital clock next to the bed she tried to calculate whether or not she would have the time to make the trip and get back before *the Bishop* returned, but after a few minutes of 'should she, shouldn't she' reflection, she finally decided to err on the side of caution – which was quite unusual for her – and somehow make do with the clothes she had.

As a result, she chose three of her more formal dresses and having cleared away all the other stuff, she laid them out on the bed – each one with its matching accessories, so that when he got back *the Bishop* could give her his expert opinion on them…as he would know better than she did, just what the women in England wore at these kinds of events…even though the women in question would be Americans living in England which might mean them wearing something completely different again from what they would choose to wear back home.

It was a nightmare, but having made the decision – whether she felt the dresses would be suitable or not – Madison returned to the bathroom, slamming the door behind her rather petulantly - showing more than a hint of her feisty character.

In the bathroom she tried putting her hair in a few different hairstyles… but as time went by and she found herself getting more and more stressed, she decided that she needed to do something to relax her.

She thought back to what *the Bishop* had told her on her first visit to England and wandering back out of the bathroom, she sat on the edge of the bed, picked up the phone and tapped in the number nine, for reception.

'Hello; is that reception', she asked casually.

'Yes Madam, how may I be of service?' a jaunty male voice responded.

'I'd like a massage…do you have somebody who does that here?' Madison enquired a little more cautiously.

'We do Madam; do you have a preference?' the receptionist asked, very matter-of-fact.

'A preference…?' Madison repeated, a little confused.

'Gender Madam; do you have a preference for the gender of…?'

'Female…definitely female' she interrupted before the man could finish.

'And do you have a time in mind, Madam?' the employee prompted conscientiously.

'As soon as poss…' Madison indicated, slightly amused by the conversation.

'Very well Madam; I'll get right on it…and ring you back in about ten minutes with a time for your appointment', the receptionist confirmed.

'Thank you', Madison agreed in the usual polite manner, before putting down the phone.

'The English are weird', she mumbled to herself as she got up, re-tying her robe.

True to his word, the receptionist rang back ten minutes later and forty five minutes later; a smiling young Asian woman came knocking on the door, carrying her table in one hand and a small suitcase containing her lotions and potions in the other.

The Bishop arrived back just as the young woman was leaving, an hour or so later.

He walked into the room but Madison wasn't there; she had already locked herself in the bathroom again to work on her hair and make-up for the evening's event…and on hearing the hair dryer whining away behind the bathroom door, TB decided, rather astutely, that it would probably be best that he not interrupt her at that particular moment.

Instead, he took off his jacket, poured himself a drink of water and took a seat in one of the comfortable chairs which looked out onto the Park, to wait for his 'princess' to emerge; they were…after all…going to the Ball.

It had been a hectic few hours for him too and as he relaxed and unwound from the tensions of the day, he took advantage of the moment of solace to close his eyes and gather his thoughts.

Unfortunately though, that moment of silence was very short-lived as almost immediately a howling scream of frustration came rumbling from the bathroom shattering the quiet mood.

The Bishop smiled and chuckled to himself, imagining the war zone behind the bathroom door, and that image got him thinking about Madison, about how he had grown to like her, to like spending time with her and how being with her had mellowed him and made him a lot more spontaneous again.

'Oh, I see you're back', Madison exclaimed rather ironically as she appeared in the room behind him, still dressed in her robe, the expression on her face betraying a mix of emotions.

'I am', *the Bishop* replied calmly, bridging his hands in front of him and looking at his watch.

'We have to be at the welcoming reception for seven; do you think you will be ready by then?' he teased.

'Of course I will', Madison retorted, picking up a cushion and throwing it in his general direction in response to his flippant remark.

'…but first I have to decide what to wear, and as you have sprung this Ball on me, very last minute', she contended, walking over to where he was sat, '…and I don't really have a cocktail dress with me suitable for the occasion, you are going to have to tell me what you think I could wear among the clothes that I do have with me.'

'I would be delighted to...' *the Bishop* agreed, trying to appease her latent aggression.

Madison then turned on her heels and disappeared back into the bedroom - and for the next hour or so she improvised a little fashion show for *the Bishop*, trying on each the three outfits she had originally put together plus any number of other combinations that he suggested might do the trick.

It went on for ages and as time went by...and Madison's mood began to mellow...they both seemed to enjoy the whole dress-up session using it rather subtly and sometimes not so subtly as the backdrop for some rather barefaced flirting if not thinly-veiled foreplay in the lead up to the Ball.

Finally though, having tried on every possible combination of shoes and dresses, the consensus was that she would go with the blue-silk dress that she had brought along as a stand-by for just such an occasion, as although it was not technically a ball-gown, it was the fanciest thing that she had in her travelling closet.

The Bishop then got up to stretch his legs and while he prepared to get himself ready, Madison returned to the bathroom still wearing the blue dress, in order to touch up her make-up - *which had gotten a little smudged with all the changing* - and arrange her outfit as best she could...still a little down-hearted, all the same, that she didn't – in her opinion - really have a dress worthy of the event.

A few moments later, Madison had just begun dabbing the mascara in the corner of her eyes when all of a sudden she heard *the Bishop* calling her back into the living-area, pretexting that he had something to show her.

'I've seen it before', she shouted out naughtily in reply, allowing herself a little snigger in the mirror at her own remark.

'Come on; I want you to see this', *the Bishop* insisted.

Madison stormed out of the bathroom; 'what...is so important that you have to show me right now', she complained, huffing at the interruption, her mascara still a little smudged around her eyes.

The Bishop was standing in the middle of the room, a smile across his face from ear to ear.

'This is for you', he commented awkwardly, producing a large, shiny box from behind his back.

Madison's jaw dropped; she was speechless and for once she really didn't know what to say.

He held the box out and she took it carefully from his grasp, laying it gently on the table beside her.

She wanted to say something, something funny or something appreciative of his generosity, but she couldn't think of either; all she could do was hold her breath in anticipation of what she was about to discover.

'Go on, open it', *the Bishop* encouraged, desperate to see her reaction too.

Madison removed the top of the box and carefully opened the delicate tissue-paper surrounding the contents to reveal the most beautiful black evening gown she had ever seen.

'It's to replace the one that I ripped on your birthday', he explained with humility.

Madison was stunned but she smiled broadly.

She took a step back and then without thinking flung herself into *the Bishop's* arms, kissing him chaotically, all her previous frustrations and glumness banished without trace, as if by magic.

'Thank you, thank you,' she screeched with a vigour and excitement in her voice that he had not heard in a while.

'Thank you so very much', she repeated again as she took the dress out of the box and held it against herself.

'It's beautiful, so beautiful', she screamed as she rushed over to the full-length mirror to check it out.

'I have never had anybody do something like this for me before', she remarked breathlessly, and with that she fell silent, lost in the mirror's reflection.

The Bishop came up behind her and brimming with uncharacteristic emotion Madison immediately turned around and hugged him again warmly, kissing him again too, before rushing back into the bedroom and removing the blue dress - which suddenly became the 'old dress' - discarding it almost with disdain as she threw it on the bed with abandon.

She couldn't wait to try on her new dress and stepping into it, Madison savoured every moment as the super-soft silk fabric slipped gracefully up over her scented body.

Her mind was in a whirl but looking in the mirror she managed to hook the halter-strap around her neck and reach behind her to carefully fasten the strategically-placed single clasp which held it all together in the small of her back.

All of a sudden she felt gloriously sexy and wondering how she looked from behind, she quickly turned around and looked again in the mirror.

Meanwhile, *the Bishop* took over the bathroom and when he re-appeared again, a half hour or so later, dressed only in his towel, he could not believe what was there to greet him.

Madison stood in the doorway looking sophisticated and…beguiling; a picture of feminine beauty.

She had literally transformed herself again while he was showering; her long blonde hair now wrapped in a tight bun and her make-up as flawless as ever…but with her new dress she looked absolutely stunning as she twirled around for him, delighting him with the sway of the soft chiffon skirt as it… and he…followed her movements back into the bedroom.

'What do you think, handsome?' she asked, turning again and flicking her skirt seductively for his benefit as she reached the other side of the room.

Madison was hoping that she looked as sexy as she felt and her new dress which plunged daringly low before falling away in a multitude of tight pleats definitely fit the bill…while her Grace Kelly hairstyle and her new pendant complemented both the dress and her neckline perfectly.

'What do I think?' *the Bishop* answered, repeating her question.

'Well, if you want an honest answer', he commented, 'I can't wait to see that dress in a ball around your ankles.'

Madison smiled, tut-tutted and then waved a finger at him…teasingly.

'Hands off', she announced playfully, doing one more twirl just to taunt him, her dress sparkling brilliantly as it caught the light.

'Okay then, let me get dressed and we'll be on our way', *the Bishop* declared calmly unhooking a tuxedo from the rail in the wardrobe.

Madison nodded; 'Sure...but don't make me wait too long', she pouted as she walked out of the room, rolling her hips one last time for his delectation.

Out in the living-area Madison tried to recompose herself, suddenly aware that she was acting a little crazy.

She took a couple of deep breaths and brushed her dress down again frivolously, realising immediately that the feel-good endorphins that were swimming around in her brain were quite clearly preventing her from acting like her normal self...and that there was absolutely nothing she could do about it.

She turned on the radio and tried to distract herself momentarily by flipping through an old magazine that she had left lying around earlier... but her mind just couldn't concentrate and she quickly abandoned that idea, preferring instead to go over to the window and peer out pensively at the slowly darkening sky and the randomly twinkling lights of London.

The Bishop appeared ten minutes or so later, looking very stylish as he walked towards her, jacket in hand - and as she turned around to face him, sensing his presence, Madison immediately complimented him on the fact, much to his delight.

She then reached for her handbag, expecting him to confirm that they were at last ready to leave, but surprisingly, rather than putting on his jacket, he went over to the table and draped it on one of the chairs before turning towards her again and astounding her with the strangest of requests.

He called her forward and taking her in his arms he reached around and carefully unhooked the halter neck of her dress.

'No; I told you, not now', Madison murmured softly, taken a little by surprise, her hands crossing instinctively in front of her chest to preserve her modesty.

...but *the Bishop* wasn't listening, and with an agile flick of the wrist he managed to unclasp the skirt of the dress too...

A second later, the whole dress simply slid away from Madison's body, fluttering lightly to the floor around her feet...leaving her wearing nothing but her lacy black boy-shorts and heels.

'Hey, what are you doing?' she argued, trying desperately to control her tone, her arms still crossed against her chest.

Again *the Bishop* didn't answer, but looking at her with a pinch of mischief in his eyes, he simply brushed a stray blond hair out of her eyes and began to nibble ever so gently on the soft delicate tissue of her ear-lobe.

Madison wanted to push him away in embarrassment but the feel of his tongue on her skin rendered her all of a quiver, and despite the weird context, *the Bishop* slowly moved his head lower and began to nuzzle and kiss the smooth skin of her neck...drinking in her fragrance while behind her his free hand rubbed gently up and down her back.

It was a very tender moment - the context aside - and despite her desire not to tarry or spoil her make-up, Madison found it strangely enjoyable.

However, she was more than a little embarrassed to be standing there in just her underwear, not to mention being a little upset that her beautiful new dress was in a puddle around her feet, so as soon as it was possible, she pulled away and held him at arm's length.

'Stop...we have to get going', she chided, bringing them both back to reality.

...but again *the Bishop* didn't stop.

Instead, much to her utter astonishment, he took her by the waist, lifted her out of her dress and holding her very close, he began to improvise a slow-dance with her, to the sound of a song on the radio – which quite serendipitously happened to be the haunting saxophone solo from George Michael's 'Careless Whisper'.

Madison closed her eyes and tried to sway to the sound of the music. She couldn't believe it; this man, who had systematically refused to dance with her on so many previous occasions, was dancing with her now, in a hotel suite, while she was wearing nothing but her underwear and her three-inch heels.

She was stunned…and as she tried to rationalise his action and make up her mind if the moment was romantically risqué, kinky or just plain weird, the song came to an end and *the Bishop* leaned in and whispered in her ear;

'This is how I will be imagining you, when we dance again, later on tonight in front of all your countrymen', he explained a little bewilderingly.

Madison pulled away from him, her eye-brows raised, still in shock.

'What the…?' she began to say but *the Bishop* interrupted her.

'Come on, where is your sense of theatre?' he remarked as he reached down and picked up her dress, helping her to pull it back into place.

Madison inhaled deeply and bit her tongue so as not to spoil the evening.

She then brushed herself down and checked herself one last time in the mirror, rewarding herself with a cheeky self-congratulatory wink.

'By the way', *the Bishop* commented with mock consternation as they headed for the door; 'I was led to believe that when women dressed formally, for this kind of occasion, they avoided wearing any underwear at all…because underwear creates lines under clothes which take away from the elegance of the gown'.

'Isn't that the case?' he questioned mischievously.

'Only in your dreams', Madison replied, grabbing her handbag and picking up the skirt of her dress so as not to tread on it.

The Bishop just smiled, opened the door and with a courteous gesture of the hand, he invited his 'princess' to precede him down the corridor without saying another word.

At the fund-raising ball, which was being held at the Royal Lancaster Hotel, not far from where they were staying, *the Bishop* did his best to introduce Madison to as many of his British-based American connections as possible, as they wandered through the hotel's lavish surroundings… mingling effortlessly with the eclectic muddle of well-heeled Anglo-American guests.

It was a wonderfully stylish event and while people were obviously there to enjoy themselves, a lot of those present were also using the evening to network and further their own careers in one way or another; a fact reflected in the conversations taking place.

The main-foyer was crowded full of people of all nationalities and persuasions…but *the Bishop* – who hated crowds at the best of times – quickly led Madison into the inner sanctum of the ball-room… acknowledging smiles and nods from various people as they went…

… and as they passed by yet another group of beautiful people, stood in a huddle, one of the women among them who was dressed in a stunning Vera Wang gown – *Madison picked up on it immediately* - looked over and mouthed a hello at him.

The Bishop checked his step and politely did the same back to her, vaguely aware that they knew each other from somewhere, but unable to place exactly where.

This annoyed Madison slightly and with a look of consternation she quickly hurried her man along, somewhat surprised by her sudden attack of jealousy, even though she easily stood the comparison with her imagined rival's play for his affection.

A few metres further along, they came across another cluster of people, stood around laughing and enjoying a joke - and beyond them, standing on his own, *the Bishop* spied Clifton Walters, a small, portly and unassuming little man who was a long-standing acquaintance of his.

He led Madison over to him.

'Madison, this is my good friend Clifton', *the Bishop* announced warmly, indicating his friend, who looked a little out of place, standing there on his own.

'Clifton, this is Madison Chatfield; she's a journalist from New York', he explained politely, grabbing his friend's attention.

Madison was happy for the distraction and walked up to *the Bishop's* friend confidently, holding out her hand politely, expecting him to shake it.

However, instead of complying with the customary social etiquette Clifton took her somewhat aback by dodging her hand and planting a well-mannered peck on her left cheek.

'Very pleased to meet you', he remarked in complimentary fashion, '… and might I say that you look absolutely stunning tonight Miss Chatfield', he added, looking at Madison and then at TB for his endorsement.

The Bishop nodded; 'Yes, she does look wonderful in that dress, doesn't she?' he commented piously, flashing one of his inscrutable, enigmatic smiles in her direction.

Madison frowned facetiously and rolling her eyes widely she threw an evocative smirk at her man, knowing exactly what he was thinking, before turning back to Clifton and thanking him for his compliment.

'...Champagne?' Clifton enquired, stopping one of the passing waiters who was circulating with a tray full of complimentary drinks.

'Sure; why not?' Madison agreed, taking the glass from Clifton's outstretched hand.

'Not for me ...not just yet, anyway', *the Bishop* declined, raising an apologetic hand.

'I have something to take care of first, so if it's okay with you', he said turning to Madison; 'I will leave you in the very capable hands of Clifton here, just for a few minutes, while I fulfil my obligations, and after that, I will be all yours for the rest of the evening', he whispered into her ear, the tone in his voice betraying the ambiguity of his thoughts.

'That is alright with you, isn't it Clifton?' *the Bishop* confirmed, brushing his friend's arm amicably.

'Oh sure, that's fine by me', Clifton agreed, wiggling his eyebrows and smiling at Madison paternally.

Madison returned the smile but she wasn't very impressed; indeed she was a little disappointed that *the Bishop* would choose to abandon her in the company of somebody she didn't even know at a party where she was no more than his plus-one.

However, as he walked away and she noticed a couple of other women following him with their eyes, she did nevertheless feel very proud that she was the one that he would be taking home later.

The Bishop disappeared into the crowd and a few awkward minutes went by, while Madison watched and waited for him to re-emerge from the scrum of people that had engulfed him on the other side of the room.

His friend Clifton stood uneasily by her side, not knowing what to say to this beautiful young woman...but as time went by, and *the Bishop* didn't re-appear, Madison decided that it would probably be better that she initiate a polite conversation with him rather than stand there, in a state of complete inertia.

After all, *the Bishop* had introduced the guy as a 'good friend', so maybe, by talking to him, she could find out more about how he knew him, where they had met, and if possible - *without being too indiscreet and treading very lightly so as to avoid another lapse in her journalistic standards* - about the women that TB had dated, hoping specifically that the name 'Jane' would inadvertently crop up in the conversation.

Clifton was delighted by her initiative and with a sigh of relief he smiled at her approvingly…even though he was a little hesitant at first about divulging the details of his friendship with *the Bishop*, knowing the sort of private person that his friend was.

A pregnant pause followed while he grabbed two more glasses of champagne for them and reflected on the implications of what he might say, but then concluding rather self-indulgently that *the Bishop* must have been aware of what might happen when introducing them to each other, Clifton's tongue soon loosened.

He was flattered by Madison's interest in him and his friend - and believing that she was acting in her capacity as a journalist, not having been made aware that she and *the Bishop* were in fact *romantically involved* – he began responding to her careful prodding and clever journalistic interrogation without reserve or restraint, even embellishing his replies at times with the usual, less than subtle coating of male bravado, hoping both to impress the young American journalist and enhance his friend's reputation in her eyes at the same time.

'Yes, *the Bishop* has enjoyed a steady string of conquests over the years'; he disclosed indiscreetly, his eyes scanning Madison from head to toe.

'In fact, he once told me that he always enjoyed playing on a new chess-board', he pursued, punctuating his questionable remark with air-quotes.

Madison frowned and looked puzzled as Clifton leaned towards her, swaying slightly;

'…the game is always the same…but the thrill comes from playing on a different board each time…is what he says', Clifton joked inelegantly, trying to be humorous through the use of a lame chess-based analogy as he polished off another flute of champagne;

'...but having said that', he affirmed, qualifying his previous statement, before Madison could express her distaste at his sexist metaphor, '*the Bishop* himself has always been very choosy and extremely discreet on the subject of women.'

'...Really?' Madison remarked with barely-concealed contempt, as all of a sudden the pangs of jealousy began pulling at her heart-strings once again.

'...unlike you, it seems', she thought to herself, trying desperately to suppress the demon within.

♗

Madison decided shortly after that, that she had heard enough...and excusing herself rather abruptly from Clifton's company, she turned on her heels and walked off in search of her elusive companion.

'Clifton would you excuse me?' she said as she began to weave her way...in as straight a line as she could...through the thick crowd, leaving the latter bereft of company and in a state of complete bemusement.

♗

She spied *the Bishop* across the room in amongst a throng of people and quickly made her way over.

As she drew nearer, he looked up and saw her coming, bringing a warm smile to his lips.

'Hey, you promised me a dance; remember', she whispered in his ear, having finally caught up with him.

The Bishop stopped in mid-sentence and broke off from the conversation that Madison had so rudely interrupted. He turned to look at her and with a tactful excuse to those gathered around him...*about why a gentleman should never keep a lady waiting*...he quietly followed her onto the dance-floor where, with an unexpected and unscripted display of public unity they prepared to dance their first ever dance together.

♗

It was quite a formal dance and Madison had to pinch herself… *metaphorically speaking…*when *the Bishop* took hold of her…with a gentle firmness…and began leading her around the dance-floor, with the grace and agility of a professional dancer.

In fact, she was quite taken aback…but also very impressed…not only because of her latent scepticism about his ability to dance…but because *the Bishop* carried himself with such masculine poise and elegance as he piloted them around the floor that his technique was almost flawless…and the way that he kept his eyes fixed firmly on hers all the way through… *thereby maintaining the focus on their mutual connection…*had her senses working overtime.

They danced a second dance after that…and even a third – *during which the Bishop discreetly leaned into Madison's ear and reminded her of his quip in their hotel room* - but pretty soon thereafter, once he was certain that he had shown his face to all the right people, *the Bishop* quietly took her aside and suggested that they call it a night.

Madison was not one to leave a party in full swing…but on this occasion she was quite happy to leave all the razzmatazz and sparkle behind, because for once in her life, she just wanted to be with her man and was in no mood to share.

So, without further ado, she carefully linked her arm through his and they slowly made their way out through the crowd, waving polite goodbyes to anybody who noticed them going by.

They got back to their hotel within no time and just inside the door to their room…while *the Bishop* was locking the door behind them… Madison stopped again, to admire herself…and her dress…in the full-length mirror.

The Bishop, following close on her heels stopped right behind her, and together they shared in her obvious delight at what was being reflected back at them.

Their eyes met in the mirror and as *the Bishop* placed his hands on the smooth skin of her shoulders Madison could feel his warm breath in her hair.

It was a very romantic moment and as she turned around to face him, filled with anticipation, the idea of what was about to happen both thrilled…and mystified her…all at the same time.

What was he going to do next? She wondered.

The Bishop remained motionless for a few seconds…time seemed to stand still…but then as he stepped forward, closing the gap between them to almost nothing…Madison suddenly put a hand up to his chest, blocking his advance.

This gesture immediately stopped *the Bishop* in his tracks and he quickly pulled his head back, a look of mild confusion on his face …but then…as their eyes locked…he slowly reached out a hand…and gently brushed away a couple of strands of hair that had strayed across Madison's face.

This was another tender moment and as Madison slowly relaxed into the mood…*taking control somewhat*...she raised both of her hands and calmly ran them down *the Bishop's* chest, her fingers slowly undoing the buttons on his dress-shirt as she went.

She managed to open the first three buttons…but before she could get any further, *the Bishop* took her by the hips and… rather brusquely… swivelled her back around to face the full-length mirror, creating a very sensual tableau of her watching herself…and him…as he began placing warm, gentle kisses on that most sensitive part of her neck.

Madison watched for a few moments…but then slowly closed her eyes as she felt *the Bishop's* hot breath cascading enthrallingly down into the cleavage of her dress, provoking a shiver and a tingling sensation within her that reached deep into her core.

'You looked stunning tonight', he whispered in her ear, his lips almost touching her cheek as the words fell smoothly from his mouth.

'I did…didn't I?' Madison responded confidently.

The Bishop smiled to himself and then slowly raised both of his hand.

Their eyes met again in the mirror…and again Madison wondered what he was thinking.

'I have wanted to do this all night', *the Bishop* whispered again in her ear…and with that, he unclasped the halter-neck of her dress…for the second time that evening…their eyes remaining locked in the mirror's reflection during the whole process.

Madison's heart began to beat, to pound like it had never done before… but as she spun back around, her arms crossed modestly against her chest, she'd never felt more alive.

'I get the feeling that you like doing that; don't you?' she murmured, summoning up her most seductive voice.

The Bishop just smiled…in silence…and then slowly stepped forward again, backing Madison up against the mirror and pinning her there, his arms resting either side of her head forming a trap from which she was not meant to escape.

He waited thus for a moment…and then satisfied that they were both on the same page he reached behind her head and pulled the pin out of her luxuriant blond hair which fell instantly down around her shoulders, like a golden mane.

All of a sudden, the air between them crackled with sexual tension and Madison felt powerless to resist.

They stared at each other for a long moment…as if trying to read each other's minds through their eyes…but then as the adrenaline kicked in Madison quickly raised her hands up to the Bishop's head and buried her fingers in his hair pulling his face towards her.

Their mouths locked…and almost instantly sparks began to fly.

A succession of torrid kisses followed and as Madison relaxed into his embrace, their respective senses shifted into over-drive.

The Bishop's hands dropped slowly down to her waist and while they kissed…in one fluid movement…her beautiful dress slipped effortlessly to the floor…once again.

A little embarrassed, Madison pushed *the Bishop* away, trying to gain a little control of the situation but after a brief pause to catch his breath he came right back at her, his mouth assaulting her neck like a vampire going in for the kill.

The passion of those kisses and the many that followed was so breath-taking and frantic that they didn't make it past the entrance to their suite…and as *the Bishop* tore off his jacket and then his shirt, Madison was suddenly reminded of two memorable scenes from the films *Disclosure* and *Basic Instinct*…where the intensity of the Michael Douglas character's frustration – in both films - turned him into an animal-like predator ready to ravish his prey in his haste for sexual release.

It was a rather incongruous situation to be in…and she certainly didn't recognise *the Bishop* in the overpowering, dominant male in front of her… but lost in his touch Madison was in no way put off by his sudden sexual euphoria and she responded in kind to her lover's assault with a passionate gusto of her own, fuelled not only by the day's events but also by her closet jealousy which had unwittingly been brought to light by Clifton's unfortunate comments.

Suddenly though, she broke the kiss and pushed *the Bishop* away again, breathing heavily, her face flushed with excitement and embarrassment at the fact that she was standing there, almost completely naked.

Undeterred, *the Bishop* pulled her close again and without the need for any more words, their enraptured bodies quickly gave vent to all the raging carnal desires that had built up within them throughout the day and during the evening's cleverly orchestrated foreplay.

There was no romance to it, *per se*, just pure, unadulterated, raw sex… and each new thrust was met with a thrilled moan which echoed eerily around the room.

It was 'hotel sex' at its best; loud and urgent, full of unrestrained moans, uncontrolled gasps and lots of lascivious grunting.

'Oh god, yes, that's good', Madison cried out as she rode her personal wave of ecstasy all the way to its natural conclusion, just as her paramour was exploding in simultaneous release.

It was a wonderful moment and one that neither of them would forget for a very long time, but once all the pressure of sensual overload had been released…and they had regained control of their senses…*the Bishop* carefully lifted Madison up and carried her over to the comfort of the big double bed where they could pursue their nocturnal register into the small hours.

Madison shivered briefly as *the Bishop* laid her on the cool satin of the bedspread but…while he finished getting undressed…she quickly removed her shoes and crept under the covers ready to continue their rapture.

The rest of the night was magical…and entwined as nature had intended…they continued to make love slowly and very tenderly until both were exhausted.

'God, I enjoy you', Madison whispered as she climaxed for the umpteenth time a few hours later, pleasure still rippling through her sweat-soaked body.

'Ditto', *the Bishop* replied economically, as he rolled off of her onto his back, completely spent, his body glazed in a similar film of ecstasy-induced lustre.

A few minutes went by thereafter, while each of them took time to catch their breath; the *Bishop* lay there inhaling deeply trying to re-oxygenate his lungs, his chest rising and falling rapidly with the effort, while Madison remained perfectly still, her eyes fixed on the ceiling as she waited patiently for her own emotions to subside and her cognitive senses to return.

It had been another extraordinary day full of unimaginable surprises to add to the many that she had already experienced since first meeting *the Bishop…what with the new dress, the weird dance in her underwear, the Ball and then the unexpected ravishing she had undergone in the hall-way…* and she was absolutely drained.

Indeed it took her quite some time to recover…but when her breathing did finally calm down and her energy levels slowly began to return, Madison eventually managed to haul herself up onto her elbow; a feat of strength in her weakened, bed-worn condition.

She glanced at the clock hoping to see the time but unable to focus on the LCD display she turned her attention back to her lover who was still lying there exhausted by her side.

She smiled at him - though as his eyes were closed, he couldn't possibly have seen it - and as she did so, her mind flooded almost immediately with a cascade of pleasant memories and sound-bites from all their time together, some very amusing, others less so.

She reached out a faltering hand and as her memory continued to replay some of their more dubious escapades through the rose-tinted lens of her mind, Madison started to toy gently with a lock of *the Bishop's* dark wavy hair, wrapping it idly, time and time again, around her finger.

She couldn't believe how happy she was, and as she contemplated him lying there next to her, fatigued and seemingly oblivious to the world, it suddenly dawned on her just exactly what this man had come to mean to her, not only because he had been instrumental in getting her career back on track but also as a person; he had taught her so much.

He was by far the most intelligent person that she had ever met, but not only that, he was resolute and principled - qualities she had always sought out in the men that she dated – and even though, at times, when in one of his more belligerent moods he would criticise the USA no end, she knew that any viewpoint that he put forward would have been researched and reasoned to a point where it would be indisputable in its logic and its veracity.

The man had a self-awareness about him which he wielded with an edgy flair, constantly pushing the boundaries but never allowing his supreme confidence to turn to arrogance; a commendable quality, Madison thought to herself, especially when she compared and contrasted it with the extremely disagreeable and cringe-worthy nature of his long-term adversary 'Copperfield', for instance.

However, *the Bishop* was more than just that too; he also had a sensitive side; a vulnerable side that not many people had ever been witness to, because while he presented this cold façade to the world, in private, when he was in the mood, he was quite capable of contrasting those seemingly inflexible qualities with a kindness and a gentleness of spirit that any woman would be delighted to encounter in the person she gives her heart to.

...and indeed, he had proved that to her on several occasions already, with some rather grand, romantic gestures and gentlemanly considerations, most of which she would never have expected from him...if she hadn't gotten to know him intimately...although it had to be said that some of his more recent behaviour did seem more than a little out of character.

Nevertheless, it was a win / win situation for her, Madison thought to herself as she continued playing with his hair, because not only was *the*

Bishop the perfect partner, but being with him had also smoothed some of the rough edges from her own character.

She already saw herself as a strong-willed, intelligent and independent young woman but he had taught her patience and a little humility; he had taught her to think on her feet, to improvise when necessary and had given her a much more balanced perspective on life, honing her sense of purpose and encouraging her to pursue her goals with the same determination that he did his…and whether she liked it or not, he had also introduced her to emotions…and even, heaven forbid, to love, something that a string of pretenders back in the Big Apple had never been able to achieve.

These thoughts waltzed randomly through her consciousness for quite some time and then…suddenly caught up in a spontaneous wave of post-coital admiration for her prostrate lover…she broke out of her reverie, propelled by the desire to lean over and whisper into his somnolent ear, those three little words that have tolled the death-knell of so many relationships down the ages. She even began to formulate them on the tip of her tongue as she slowly leaned towards him, but then at the very last moment, she hesitated – deciding very wisely that to do so, to say those three little words and to reveal her innermost feelings to him, would only serve to complicate what was - despite the evidence to the contrary - a finely balanced situation, which could not easily be resolved because of their respective circumstances.

However, as she lay back down, Madison did wonder - as she brushed a strand of her own hair out of her eyes - if it really changed anything or not, to admit one's feelings verbally as they are still there, they still exist whether they are expressed or not?

A cold chill suddenly crept over her cooling skin…and in response Madison quickly reached down the bed and grabbed what she could of the sheet…which had been cast aside earlier in a moment of unbridled passion.

Meanwhile, *the Bishop* still hadn't moved, so trying hard not to disturb him she pulled the sheet up over them both and carefully re-adjusted her position, snuggling into his warm body, her head resting softly on his chest.

This did cause him to stir…but even though his slumber was slowly deepening, his arm immediately rose up and enveloped her, his hand coming to rest gently and reassuringly in the small of her back.

Madison felt secure and comforted in the fact that even in his somnolent state *the Bishop* had responded to her touch…and recognising his gesture of masculine protection she squeezed him gently in return and kissed his chest lightly before quietly drifting off to sleep in his arms.

They lay like that for a while, until an hour or so later, when realising that his mouth was dry *the Bishop* decided to get up to get himself a drink of water.

Madison was still tucked into him, her right arm draped lightly across his chest but with a little delicate manoeuvring he managed to extricate himself from the bed without waking her.

He made his way over to the mini-bar and quietly helped himself to a bottle of mineral water which - because of its chilled state - made him shiver momentarily.

His senses roused by the cold shock to his system, he decided to use the bathroom and returning to the bed a few minutes later, dressed in one of the hotel's robes, he could not help but admire his sleeping companion.

She looked so sexy, lying there naked in the bed covered only by the sheerest of sheets but as he stood there contemplating Madison's natural beauty the expression on his face - which should have been one of complete satisfaction and contentment - betrayed a worrying mix of emotions; admiration for sure…but also a hint of melancholy.

In that moment, Madison felt him standing over her and though still in a dream she raised herself onto her elbow to ask what he was doing, the movement causing the sheet that was covering her to fall away and reveal her nakedness once more.

'What's wrong?' she asked sleepily as she tucked the sheet back around her.

'Nothing…just a little thirsty', *the Bishop* replied flatly, offering her a drink.

'No thanks', she replied with a tired shake of the head, curling back up in a ball with her back to him.

The Bishop shrugged his shoulders and gently sat on the side of the bed.

Then…having placed the bottle of water carefully between his feet…he dropped his head into the palms of his hands and…with all his might…tried to control and contain the juddering nervous spasms that had suddenly taken over his body, straining his every sinew.

CHAPTER TWENTY-ONE

Next morning, it was Madison who was up first while not surprisingly *the Bishop*, who had obviously over-extended himself the night before, preferred to tarry in bed, and having retrieved her dress from the hallway… and grabbed the essentials for her morning routine…she went straight into the bathroom to run herself a nice hot bath.

Fuck; what a night! She thought to herself as she eased her aching body down into the tub full of steaming hot water topped off with a just a soft airy layer of fragrant foam.

She lay her head back against the rim of the bath and as she started to relax, playing with the foam and languorously splashing the water between her fingers…her mind started to wander, flashing back a few weeks to the morning she had playfully splashed *the Bishop*…soaking both his shirt and pants…in retaliation for the time he had pulled her into the bath a few days before that;

'That's for dragging me in the other day', she had called after him as he scuttled away'.

The funny memory instantly made Madison scoff and snigger but at the same time it also made her realise what a gentleman *the Bishop* was… as just a few minutes after she had soaked him, he had come right back, carrying a towel…and proceeded to help her out of the tub, embracing and kissing her tenderly, without a second thought for his wet clothes.

That thought made her smile and filled her with optimism for the future as she slowly lowered herself further into the water, submerging herself completely until her blonde hair spread out like jellyfish-tentacles on the water's surface.

Seconds later, a sudden knock on the door interrupted Madison's languorous immersion; it was room-service delivering their breakfast tray just as they had requested.

'Just a minute', she called out, before hastily jumping out of the bath, wrapping a towel around her head and throwing on a robe, tying it at her waist as she made her way to the door.

'Good morning madam', the young hotel-employee announced as she slowly opened the door. 'Room Service', he confirmed with a smile.

'Yeah…of course…thanks', Madison replied languidly.

The young man entered the room…and while he went over and placed the loaded tray on the table using the greatest of care Madison quietly ambled over to the panoramic windows to open the blinds and let in a little natural light. Then, thanking him politely for his service, she followed him back to the door, locked it carefully behind him and returned to the bathroom, to finish her daily pampering routine…pinching a tiny chocolate muffin off of the tray as she went.

Back in the bathroom, Madison emptied the bath and quickly jumped into the shower to wash the bath-water out of her hair.

She re-emerged fifteen minutes or so later with her hair still wrapped tightly in a towelling turban…having replaced the wet robe that she had grabbed earlier with a set of turquoise underwear…and applied enough make-up to make her look presentable for that time of the morning.

Then, peeking into the bedroom on her way through to see if *the Bishop* was still asleep – which he was – she carried on into the living-area where she sat down to eat, deciding quite deliberately that she wasn't going to wait for her lover to wake up and join her as she was more than a little hungry after yet another night of nocturnal gymnastics.

The breakfast tray was a sight to behold and as she sat down and prepared to tuck in, Madison's eyes sparkled with delight in anticipation of what she was about to devour.

She rubbed her hands together and even licked her lips hungrily as the various aromas of freshly-baked French pastries; freshly-pressed fruit juice and freshly-brewed coffee rose up in unison from the tray to titillate her olfactory senses.

Grabbing the coffee-pot, she poured herself a cup of coffee and while that was cooling she picked up a glass of fruit juice, sat back and enjoyed the view looking out over London's roof-tops.

'I could certainly get used to this'; she thought to herself as she picked up a croissant and tore it mercilessly in two.

A quarter of an hour went by and Madison was just finishing her second croissant when *the Bishop* finally appeared in the frame of the bedroom door, wrapped in the bed-sheet.

He had finally been roused by the unmistakeable and irresistible aroma of freshly-brewed coffee which had slowly filtered through into the bedroom from the living-area.

'Pour me a cup, would you?' he asked in a rather subdued manner, as walked towards her, gathering the sheet awkwardly around his waist.

'Sure hon', Madison replied sympathetically, only too happy to oblige.

The Bishop didn't say anything else for a minute as he stood there a little unsteadily, but he did notice immediately how scrumptious Madison looked sitting at the table eating her croissant wearing nothing but a touch of make-up and a matching set of turquoise underwear.

'Wow, you look stunning again this morning', he managed to express, rewarding her domestic brinkmanship with a contrived but nevertheless flattering comment.

'Well, you ripped my dress off again last night, so I have nothing else to wear', Madison joked playfully, feeling kind of pleased with her lover's look of appreciation.

'Hey…for the record, I didn't rip your dress off this time, *the Bishop* retorted as he raised the cup of coffee to his lips, keen to point out the fact;

'…and if I'm not mistaken you have a whole suitcase full of clothes over there', he added indicating her suitcase;

'…though I have to say that turquoise really suits your skin-colour', he added, the expression on his face suggesting that his mind was not completely engaged in what he was saying.

Madison smiled at him again, the look in her eyes full of a thousand questions that she would like to ask…and have answered…but knowing instinctively that this wasn't the right moment.

The Bishop tasted the coffee and his face contorted immediately into a horrendous scowl.

'This coffee is cold', he complained, putting the cup down and walking straight over to the phone, picking up the handset and ringing down to reception.

'Hello; yes, good morning; this is room twenty; could we have another pot of coffee…fresh coffee please', he asked politely.

'Certainly sir', came the reply without hesitation; 'I'll have it sent it right up'.

The Bishop thanked his respondent, hung up…and walked right back across the room, sitting down at right-angles to Madison who had…in the meantime…started on a yoghurt.

'Look…Madison', he declared, a little hesitantly, 'I must apologise if my impetuous nature upset you, last night; I don't know what came over me', he explained, raking a hand through his hair.

'Hey, don't knock it'; Madison replied reassuringly as she plunged her spoon back into the yoghurt.

'I kinda like the new impetuous, spontaneous you', she assured him, ruffling his hair in turn; astounded that he should use the word impetuous where he was concerned.

The Bishop smiled, got up from the table again and…much to her surprise…went right back over to the phone and made the exact same call to the hotel's reception, using almost the exact same words.

'Hello; yes, good morning; this is room twenty; could we have another pot of coffee…fresh coffee', he repeated.

Madison was somewhat stunned by this rather strange behaviour and uncharacteristic impatience; *the Bishop* had never shown any kind of weakness or vulnerability before and patience had always been his greatest virtue because of his profession.

'Hey, give them a break', she scolded as she got up herself;

'I'm sure they'll be right up', she pouted, as she waltzed back into the bathroom shaking her hair loose from the towel; 'there is no need for you to keep on at them'.

This time, it was *the Bishop's* turn to look confused;

'...keep on at them? All I want is some fresh coffee', he mumbled to himself.

Shrugging his shoulders *the Bishop* sat down again, picked up a glass of freshly-squeezed pineapple juice and before long there was another knock on the door.

He got up again...re-arranged his sheet to make sure that he was decent...and then without further ado, duly answered the door.

Standing there was the same young man as before with a fresh pot of coffee.

'Coffee sir', the young man announced chirpily.

The Bishop held out his free hand, took the pot and thanked the young man with his usual polite manner before closing the door firmly behind him and returning to finish his breakfast.

They checked out of the hotel a few hours later but before travelling back to Abingdon, reluctant for their brief stay in London to come to an end, *the Bishop* suggested that they go for lunch first.

'Great idea', Madison agreed without a moment's hesitation, because as much as she enjoyed life back at the Abbey, London was fast becoming her city of choice to spend time in.

Acknowledging her response with a wry smile *the Bishop* returned to the concierge's desk to make arrangements for their luggage to be stored temporarily while they were at lunch...and then without further ado, they made their way out of the hotel turning left in the direction of Oxford Street, Madison linking her arm possessively inside *the Bishop's* to pull him closer as they went.

They soon arrived at Edgware Road and as they hurried across, harried by the impatient oncoming traffic, Madison suddenly realised that her life had never been better.

Everything was going so smoothly. London was amazing, life at the abbey was more than pleasant...most of the time...and her relationship with *the Bishop* was really blossoming; they were great in bed together... sharing a natural chemistry in that department...and while the balance of their relationship wasn't quite fifty-fifty, she did feel that they had made a connection outside the bedroom too, on a more intellectual level, with each of them having made allowances...and learned to accommodate the other's idiosyncrasies.

Compromises; it's all about compromises, she thought to herself as they reached the other side of the road and she steadied herself again, looking around at the bustling hub of people and cars; that's the secret.

Yes, everything was going along perfectly, but then, all of a sudden, without warning, *the Bishop* veered off to his right, yanking Madison with him...rather unceremoniously...and ripping her instantly out of her reverie.

'Hey, where are we going?' she asked rhetorically, not expecting a reply...but *the Bishop* did reply, jerking his head succinctly in the direction of a couple of restaurants on the opposite pavement from where they were standing.

'Over there', he announced confidently.

Madison squeezed his arm and followed his lead as they crossed the road again and stopped in front of a little Italian bistro, allowing a couple of ambling tourists to pass in front of them before they approached the establishment.

They checked out the menu on the outside wall and then with Madison's approval, *the Bishop* led the way inside where they were immediately shown to a little table by the window.

Once again, the moment was somehow romantic – probably because of the typically warm ambience in the Mediterranean-styled restaurant - and as they settled down for a light pasta lunch, still caught up in her own private little feel-good bubble Madison rather uncharacteristically allowed her aspirations to get ahead of her.

She didn't mean to, but having decided that her life could hardly get any better...because she was already in such a good place...she unwittingly let her guard down...and by doing so, made the most fatal of mistakes.

She had never really thought about it before, but having spent the last few weeks in *the Bishop's* company she was finally ready, for the first time, to take a relationship that she was involved in, to the next level.

What that meant, Madison wasn't quite sure, but what she did know was that she wanted to know more about the enigma that was *the Bishop*... about what made him tick, and as he had very kindly introduced her to a number of his friends and acquaintances during the American Embassy Ball, she decided to use that as an excuse to be a little more inquisitive, casually mentioning in passing that Clifton had spoken to her about his previous girl-friend.

'Janet was it...or Jean?' she suggested nonchalantly, trying to play a little reverse psychology.

The Bishop, who was a master of reverse psychology himself immediately put his glass down...very deliberately...and looked across the table at her with his usual self-control, managing to keep any signs of mistrust or paranoid suspicion from appearing anywhere on his face.

He knew for a fact that Clifton had never met Jane, and that he himself would never have mentioned her to him in a million years...so how, he wondered, did Madison know about her?

'Oh, and what exactly did he have to say?' *the Bishop* asked politely in a very controlled and focussed tone, keeping his cards close to his chest as he tried to confirm his suspicions.

Madison fell into the trap; her usually-reliable intuition failing to warn her, as her treacherous tongue loosened and she revealed another intimate detail from one of the letters she had read.

It wasn't a startling revelation but, as soon as she said it, she felt something flip in the pit of her stomach and she knew that she had messed up.

Across the table, *the Bishop* sucked in the air through his nostrils and held his breath; his poker-faced expression changing instantly from mildly annoyed to an icy stare as the realisation that Madison had been prying… and spying on him…suddenly hit home.

'Do you remember our first ever conversation?' he asked churlishly, his voice now indicating considerable disapproval.

Madison frowned but did not answer; preferring instead to push the pasta that she had just been served around the plate in an effort to gain time as she desperately searched her mind for a solution to her predicament.

'Do you remember me telling you how I always avoid the paparazzi because people like that cannot be trusted', he insisted with ominous calm, after an uncomfortable and slightly embarrassing pregnant pause, his eyes narrowing and his jaw tightening.

He didn't raise his voice but there was no mistaking the authority in his tone.

Madison sat back and swallowed deeply as the realisation of what she had done slowly seeped into her consciousness, and in that instant she could feel the blood rushing to her brain.

He knew her secret; she had been found out…but despite her shock and embarrassment she managed to keep her emotions under control while her mind raced back to that day in the Crown in Amersham when he had first given her a chance.

She remembered his comments – almost word for word - on how he despised exploitative paparazzi photographers who intruded on his private life and how he avoided them like the plague.

'If there is one thing, one thing that I abhor, it is people who invade my privacy', *the Bishop* commented, his voice still calm and controlled but now a little more forceful.

Madison blushed scarlet and grimaced at his knowing look, trying desperately to think outside the box and conjure up a believable explanation as to how she might know these things, realising that denial was not an option.

She had never felt pathetic before in her life…but in that moment she felt the shame of the world invading her every pore.

Indeed, she could quite easily have curled up and died right there in the restaurant given half the chance, but she knew that he was waiting for her to respond…and rather than wait for him to drag it out of her, she decided to cut to the chase by apologising profusely for her betrayal of his trust, expressing her remorse as best she could.

'I'm sorry', she blurted out, the synapses in her brain working overtime; 'It was a total impulse-call'.

'I found the key in that little friar-sculpture on your dresser and I just couldn't help myself', she began to explain in a voice that would normally have softened the hardest of hearts…but *the Bishop* cut her short, shushing with a raised hand in front of his face, to show her that he didn't want to listen and was not interested in her explanation.

She was slowly dying inside but despite her embarrassment Madison tried to redeem herself once again with a chastened smile, hoping beyond hope that it would deflect *the Bishop's* incipient anger and maybe win back a little of her self-respect.

It didn't work; *the Bishop* simply ignored her and calmly raised his glass to take another sip of wine, his eyes filling slowly with cold anger.

A heavy, lasting silence ensued but not wanting the situation to fester for too long Madison leaned forward and tried again to explain herself.

She opened her mouth; the words were there but unfortunately, because of the emotional guilt she was feeling, her voice seemed to choke in her throat.

'Sorry is nice to hear; it shows that you were taught manners', *the Bishop* suddenly remarked '…but unfortunately it doesn't change anything', he informed her, in a slow and deliberate tone.

Madison cleared her throat and apologised again, desperately trying to keep her whole world from falling apart…but seeing that her humble attitude wasn't getting a result, she suddenly reverted back to her natural, brash New York character, her hands clenching in fists of frustration.

'You're so fucking sanctimonious; how dare you judge me, like this?' she squealed with indignant rage, visibly shaken by the emotions now coursing through her body.

'…and how could I possibly have been so stupid as to think that maybe, just maybe, for one second, for just one tiny second, you might actually have cared about me, enough to put your stupid paranoia aside for a moment?' she rasped tersely while pushing away her plate.

The Bishop remained impassive as the waiter and two other customers turned to see what was going on.

'You know what; I'm leaving', Madison announced curtly, shoving back her chair and standing up.

Then in a sudden show of unprovoked aggression…reacting on the impulse of somebody who had just been caught red-handed…she leaned right across the table and lashed out with her right hand, catching *the Bishop* directly on his left cheek with a loud open-handed slap.

This time, several more customers turned their way and in the confusion of the moment Madison quickly turned and rushed out into the street, hailing the first cab she saw as the tears…that she had managed to hold back up until then…began to pearl in the corners of her eyes.

She quickly jumped into the cab, grateful for her dark sunglasses, and no sooner had she made herself comfortable on the back seat…waiting for the driver to engage a gear…than the tears began to flow.

In her distraught state, Madison didn't really know where to go, so in a moment of panic, unable to think straight, she gave the cabbie the only address she knew in London…and that was…Gary's.

The cabbie nodded his acknowledgement of the address and having enquired politely about her emotional welfare, to which she replied with just the briefest of nods, he pulled away from the kerb.

The situation could not have been any more harrowing but
then in the most cruel, serendipitous and poignant reminder
of her betrayal, Madison suddenly realised that
the song playing on the taxi's radio was
'Honesty' sung by New York's very own piano-man Billy Joel

(She asked the cabbie to switch channels)

Madison sat there alone on the back seat, in a state of complete emotional distress. She could almost feel her heart breaking in her chest… and as warm tears continued to trickle down her face she started to think about the sad…but oh so true…analogy that *the Bishop* had made between her and his hated nemesis, the paparazzi.

She had never meant to hurt his feelings; on the contrary, she just wanted to get to know him better, more intimately, but because of her rather indiscreet and overly inquisitive mind, she had let herself down and she knew it.

…but how he could possibly compare her with those insincere, opportunist creeps, she still heard herself protesting in her mind.

Slivers of thought began slicing through her sub-conscious like random shards of an unsolvable puzzle but then, as she broke it down and analysed the facts, she soon realised that while those persistent photographers did indeed try to steal his intimacy away in their long-range lenses at any opportunity, she had actually gone into his home, into his bedroom and stolen it from behind a secured lock.

The Bishop had welcomed her into his life - which he didn't do very often - and she had betrayed his trust…so who was really the worst offender, she wondered, deliberately bowing her head in shame to avoid crossing the driver's reflection in the rear-view mirror.

Meanwhile *the Bishop* had left the restaurant…and to collect his thoughts he had taken a walk which took him past the spot where they had previously stopped to watch the busker playing his saxophone…but this time everything was quiet; nobody was there.

He carried on, back to the hotel…still a little disquieted by what had happened…and having picked up their suitcases and retrieved his car from the hotel's underground car-park, he drove home.

During the drive, still fuming from Madison's revelations, he cast his mind back to the first time that Madison had stayed over at the abbey… and vaguely remembered that…when he had performed his ritualistic kiss on his 'special note', before transferring it from the shirt he had been wearing to the clean one he was about to put on...he could smell Madison's perfume on it. He hadn't thought anything of it at the time just dismissing the idea as a lingering memory of her recent presence in his bedroom... but now...after what his inquisitive guest had confessed, he wasn't so sure.

On the other side of town;

When he opened the door to his flat, Gary was more than a little surprised to see Madison staring back at him...but even though he hadn't seen her since New York he welcomed her straight away as if it had only been the day before.

'Hey Maddy', he exclaimed, forgetting conveniently that she didn't like to be called by that particular diminutive.

Madison just stood there on the doorstep looking completely disconsolate, her make-up obviously smudged and her hair blowing all around her face...but she was nevertheless happy to see a friendly face and her spirits were instantly lifted on seeing Gary...if only for a moment.

'Come on in', the young Aussie beckoned, without waiting for her to say a word, explaining simultaneously as he closed the door behind her, that he and his flat-mate Dave were just chilling and about to sit and watch a DVD.

Madison nodded in acknowledgement and having been there before, made her way straight through into the living-room where Dave...still wearing his tartan pyjamas bottoms and a 'Keep calm and get the beer in' tee-shirt...immediately got up to greet her too, offering her the comfortable chair that he was sitting in...and a beer; both of which she accepted with gratitude.

Then, while he disappeared into the kitchen Gary quickly busied himself clearing away the empty bottles...and a couple of take-away cartons...that had been sitting on the coffee-table in front of them before plumping up the cushions on his chair and sitting back down, just as Dave reappeared with three beers in one hand and an empty glass in the other.

In the kitchen Dave had grabbed three cold beers and picked up an empty glass too for their guest, assuming rather chivalrously that Madison would not want to drink directly from the bottle as he and Gary were doing.

'Sweet...', Gary declared as his flat-mate shuffled over to where Madison was sitting and reached over her shoulder with the empty glass...expecting her to take it.

'Thanks Dave...but if you don't mind, I'll just take the bottle like you guys', she announced quietly as she turned, reached up and took hold of one of the beers.

(This was not Madison making a statement for feminism; she just didn't trust the cleanliness of the glass)

'Okay...fine by me', Dave shrugged as he handed the second beer to Gary before putting the glass down on the table behind him and pulling up an extra chair...from the dining table...which he positioned diplomatically off to one side, thereby allowing Madison and Gary to talk if indeed that was where this was going.

However, for the next twenty seconds or so, a strange, awkward silence seemed to descend on the room as all three of them just sat there sipping quietly on their beers, the two guys looking at each other with puzzled expressions, Dave, feeling more than a little uncomfortable as he tried to find out...using discreet hand signals...if he should stay or make himself scarce...and Gary just shrugging back at him in bewilderment.

They could both see that Madison was upset; that much was obvious, but neither of them was going to push her for an explanation, realising instinctively that she would probably tell them...or at least that she would tell Gary...whatever her problem was, when she was good and ready.

They waited...and waited...until eventually, Gary broke the silence... *in an attempt to jump-start the conversation*...with a rather weird quote from his childhood.

‘My father used to say; “There’s a difference between scratching your arse and ripping it to pieces”, he suddenly announced out of the blue, before taking another long swallow of beer.

‘Huh; what’s that supposed to mean?’ Madison mumbled, still sitting there looking glum and pensive.

‘It means…’ Dave interjected, as he turned to remove a Rubik’s cube that had been stuffed behind him, into the corner of his chair, ‘that whatever’s happened; you don’t need to beat yourself up about it’.

Madison just nodded in reflection and took another swig of beer too.

Meanwhile Gary finished his beer…and then lost for any more words of wisdom …*but still looking for something else to take her mind off of what it was that was bothering her*…he turned to Madison and suggested that maybe she should choose the film that they were about to watch.

He leaned forward and grabbing the two DVD’s that were lying on the table, he casually handed them to her, offering her the choice of either the quirky Australian film Muriel’s Wedding - *full of Abba music* - starring Toni Collette…or his favourite baseball film, For Love of the Game with Kevin Costner and Kelly Preston.

Madison took them from him and frowned; she didn’t know either of the films, nor was she particularly interested, but in her current state of mind she certainly wasn’t in the mood for a *rom-com*…and so with no other option available, all she could do…with the greatest of indifference… was point to the baseball film.

This was however, quite obviously the choice that Dave and Gary had been hoping for…and they immediately jumped up as one, shouting out their mutual accord and performing a rather theatrical high-five with each other before Gary grabbed the film and installed it in the player, much to Madison’s unspoken irritation.

The film started…and at first, Madison didn’t really pay any attention to it…or its storyline, wrapped up as she was in her own personal drama, but as the tension of the film began to build…with Gary giving a non-stop running commentary on the events as they occurred, from his sprawled position on the chair next to her…she slowly became a little more interested, realising that it was not just a film about baseball but also a romantic tale about unspoken love.

Two hours seventeen minutes later the credits went up and as he turned to ask her, her thoughts on the film, Gary was more than a little taken aback to see that Madison was sat there dabbing her eyes with a tissue.

Without thinking, he immediately sat up and tried to comfort her, telling her that he understood how she felt…which was a strange admission for a man to make, especially a man like Gary…and as she wiped her eyes with the back of her hand, Madison wondered instinctively if there was a hidden message in her saviour's comforting words.

Gary saw her dubious expression and immediately reassured her, explaining that he knew that it was a bit of a chick flick but that the last line of the film always brought a tear to his eye too. *(Last line of the film – I love you Jane, believe it)*

Madison smiled stiffly, though her demeanour suggested disbelief…

However, what Gary didn't know, and what Madison still wasn't ready to reveal to him, was that the real reason she was crying was…not because of the film's sad denouement but because she had just had an almighty row with the Bishop over her reading all of his private love-letters…which were also addressed to a certain woman named Jane…and that she felt so guilty, so jealous and so absolutely ashamed of herself because of it that she just couldn't bring herself to talk about it.

'What?' Gary retorted with a shrug; '…can't men be sensitive too?' he asked, looking over at Dave for some masculine support.

Dave didn't answer…but just got up and was about to offer Madison another beer when his mobile phone suddenly sprang into life on the table behind him.

He picked it up and having checked to see who was calling, he disappeared into his room using a few hand signals to excuse himself and explain his movements.

Meanwhile Gary turned off the TV and removed the DVD, still

waiting for Madison to explain how and why she had turned up on their doorstep.

However, she was still unforthcoming…so, lost for another way of broaching the subject…diplomatically…he just crouched down in front of her, looked into her eyes and asked simply if there was anything he could say…or do…to help; his straightforward manner, a refreshing change from the complex mind-games that were *the Bishop's* trademark.

In reply, Madison just screwed up her face, shook her head disconsolately and waved her hand dismissively.

'Don't worry about me; I'll be fine', she then mumbled unconvincingly, brushing aside Gary's awkward attempts at sensitivity…*because although the young Aussie had always been good to her…and had already helped her out of several sticky situations in the short time that they had known each other… she felt that, on this occasion - while she didn't want to hurt his feelings - he was not the right person for her to confide in.*

At that moment, Dave walked back in and picked up his guitar which was leaning up against one of the chairs. He sat down and started strumming.

'Do you play?' Madison asked politely, trying to shift the focus away from her.

'Yeah, a little bit', Dave confirmed, continuing to strum.

'Play something then', Madison encouraged…humouring the guy as he clearly wanted her to ask.

'Well, as we're going to a Jim Jefferies gig tonight in Logan Hall, why not something from Down Under', Dave announced, looking at Gary for his approval.

'Yeah…go for it Bud', Gary agreed as he got back to his feet.

'Okay then; this is a little song you might know...or not...written by one of Australia's best-ever song-writers' Dave explained…and with that, he launched into a stirring rendition of Peter Allen's timeless tune 'I still call Australia home'.

As she listened, Madison's eyes filled with tears once again…prompted by the emotion in the song…and as she wiped the corner of her eye, Gary immediately went to move closer again, to try and give her a hug.

'No, Gary, I'm good…I'm good…thanks', she declared quickly, waving away his concerns yet again, '…but I would like you to call me a cab', she added as she brushed some imaginary crumbs from her skirt. 'It's time I headed back'.

'Sure thing Mad', Gary responded, taking out his phone.

The taxi arrived ten minutes later and when it was time to say goodbye, Madison quietly turned to Gary and gave him a great big hug...and a little kiss on the cheek...before thanking him...and Dave...for both their hospitality...and the beer.

'No worries Mad; you know you're always welcome here', Gary assured her as he escorted her back to the front door...where she gave him another huge hug...before turning away and making her way down to the taxi which was waiting patiently by the kerb...motor running.

She slipped into the back-seat...and with just the briefest of waves, she was gone...without ever having furnished any kind of explanation as to how...or why she had turned up there in the first place.

It was a long ride home to the cottage...and as she fought to contain the tears Madison replayed the events of the restaurant in her mind, over and over again, the images streaming through her thoughts like a speeded-up disaster movie. The look on *the Bishop's* face...as she admitted her mistake...kept hammering its way to the front of her consciousness and eventually...as they left the bright-lights of London behind...she could no longer hold back the tears which leaked unhindered and continually from the corners of her bloodshot eyes.

Madison arrived back at Tanglin an hour or so later and as she stepped through the front door, still dabbing at her eyes, her attention was immediately drawn to the red light blinking furiously on the slightly-dated answer-phone sat on a small table in the corner.

Who could it be? She wondered curiously ...surely it wasn't *the Bishop* apologising!

She edged over to the phone and having stared at it for several very long moments she reached out very tentatively and pressed the 'play-messages' button.

There followed a moment of silence filled with panic and anguished apprehension...but then just as she was about to throw her arms up in despair, Evie's dulcet tones filled the tiny room asking repeatedly and insistently where she was.

Madison quickly checked her watch, with the cross-Atlantic time difference in mind and having taken a few minutes to get herself sorted, she sat down and called her friend, to explain how she and *the Bishop* had been away in London, that it had all been rather rushed and that consequently she had forgotten to take her charger with her, leaving her mobile phone uncharacteristically without back-up power.

Evie was both delighted and relieved to hear from her friend…and reassured that she was okay she immediately teased her, that it was so unlike her to be forgetful like that.

'It must be love', she mocked playfully exaggerating the last syllable.

Madison didn't respond to her friend's unwittingly poignant quip - preferring instead to turn the tables on her and ask if there were any new developments in her own life - but after a few minutes of listening to the same old inane comments that Evie usually came up with, she finally broke down, as the blanket of despair that had been hovering over her, finally settled on her shoulders and she began to explain rather dejectedly all about the argument with *the Bishop* and the reasons behind it.

It took a good twenty minutes for her to recount the whole story and when she finally finished and sat back on her chair Madison suddenly realised – *on analysing the situation simultaneously in her mind* - that she had lost *the Bishop's* trust for the most selfish of reasons – because even though she was naturally curious…like most women…her journalistic instincts to always dig a little deeper than was necessary, had ultimately pushed her beyond the acceptable boundaries of social etiquette and it was that, that had probably ruined her relationship.

'What have I done?' she lamented dolefully to her friend as the tears began to well up in her eyes once again, despite her having resolved not to let it happen.

'Aw hon, don't beat yourself up about it', Evie rallied, sensing her friend's sorrow and trying to be supportive.

'Why, why do we do it?', Madison continued, sniffling into the phone; 'why can't we just leave things alone; why do we always have to go rooting through their personal stuff as soon as they have their backs turned – checking their pockets, their mobile-phones, their e-mails…?'

'Listen hon… as women, it's just what we do …it's in our genes to be suspicious', Evie tried to explain…rather ineptly.

'No…no it's not', Madison countered rather forcefully regaining her composure; 'it's because we are insecure and we don't dare trust men to be honest with us; that's the problem and now I've gone and messed it all up', she raged disconsolately.

'Listen hon,', Evie repeated, trying to sympathise, 'if he loves you, he'll come around…they always do, it's a no-brainer', she encouraged, though in her own mind she couldn't believe she was saying that about *the Bishop*, a man who she really hadn't connected with, either in Boston or in New York.

'Yeah, I suppose you're right', Madison replied, thanking her friend for those heartening words of comfort.

'Of course, I'm right'; Evie responded again… insistently…still trying desperately to boost her friend's morale from the other side of the Atlantic.

'Look Mad', she continued; 'You can't put the toothpaste back in the tube...but the point is that there is a line…and while I love you more than I love myself; you did kinda cross that line…big-time. Geez, you must have known that you were playing with fire…you know…given who you were dealing with', Evie tried to reason.

'Aha', Madison huffed…and as she changed her sitting position on the rather uncomfortable antique chair that she was sitting on, the conversation suddenly lapsed into an exchange of hypothetical ways and means, options and strategies as to how she should handle redressing the situation, Evie suggesting some more light-hearted and even humorous scenarios while she herself…who was all together more conservative in her thinking…put forward some more subtle and conventional ideas.

Eventually though, after a good hour of friendly chitchat the conversation had to end when Evie had to hang up in response to somebody knocking rather insistently at her door.

For her part, Madison would have liked it to continue; chatting to Evie again had been surprisingly comforting as they hadn't spoken much of late...but as the phone went dead and she sat there...the hand-set still glued to her ear...she suddenly felt very alone; her head was in turmoil and as the tears of solitude bubbled to the surface once again it seemed that the self-confidence which had always been her saving grace had inexplicably deserted her.

For the first time in her life...or at least for the first time she could remember in a very long time, she felt isolated and out of her depth...not in control, and she really didn't like it.

She slumped back in the chair, feeling forlorn and frustrated...and as she closed her eyes and took a deep breath, her father's face suddenly appeared in front of her eyes and Madison instantly remembered that day when she had flunked one of her exams in high-school.

Her father had sat her down and told her; 'You can disappoint me; you can even disappoint your mother...though I wouldn't recommend it...but never, ever disappoint yourself.'

Madison <u>had</u> let herself down and she knew it.

CHAPTER TWENTY-TWO

Having decided that a cooling-off period was probably the best plan among the plethora of suggestions that she and Evie had discussed, Madison waited a couple of days thereafter, before trying to get in touch with *the Bishop*...in the hope of making things right with him.

She had made a mistake; she knew that...and now she just wanted to make it right, to apologise and put the whole sorry episode behind them.

Those few days dragged by very slowly...but while Madison did spend more time than she should have, analysing the reasons for her actions... and mulling over the consequences, she also managed to keep herself busy doing other things too...such as ringing the hotel in London to find out how she could retrieve her suitcase...and catching up on all the work she had left unfinished because of their trip to London.

For information; having checked his log the hotel concierge politely informed her that Mr Byron had picked up all their belongings before leaving.

By the third day she was very frustrated not to have heard from him and unable to settle to anything else that morning...until she had some kind of resolution, she decided that if he wasn't going to ring her, then she would ring him.

She picked up her phone and called his number, both comforted and terrified at the same time by the instantly recognisable ringing tone emitted by the Abbey's very old-fashioned telephone system.

The phone rang time and time again but *the Bishop* didn't answer, and when the answering-machine did eventually pick up the call, she decided to simply hang up.

A little downhearted, she wandered into the cottage's tiny kitchen to make herself a drink and as she stood there sipping from her oversized mug she looked out through the lead window…*the design of which strangely resembled the bars of a prison*…and saw a flock of birds rise up out of the neighbouring field and head towards the Abbey; how I wish I could be coming with you, she whispered to herself sorrowfully.

Then, lost for something else to occupy her mind…or at least to distract her…Madison started wandering around the cottage without purpose… randomly opening cupboards and drawers, that she had previously ignored…and in one of those drawers she came across an old newspaper that had been left there by a previous tenant. She picked it up and even though it was crispy and yellow in places…next to the main title in the right-hand corner, she could just about make out the 'quote of the day' which read;

'The tongue like a sharp knife…kills without drawing blood' – Buddha.

Madison stared at the paper for quite some time, soaking in the words one by one as the tears of guilt and despair began once again to prick her eyes. The words were so true and so pertinent to her current situation that they dealt yet another devastating blow to her already fragile heart.

She tried ringing the Abbey twice more later on in the day but each time she was met with the answering-machine's cold, business-like invitation to leave a message, which she did at the third time of asking, leaving a brief but contrite apology and asking him to please return her call. She even left a couple of messages on his mobile-phone…even though she knew that he only kept it for emergencies and took the battery out when he wasn't using it.

As it was, none of her calls were dignified with a reply; in fact her mobile phone lay silently on the kitchen table all day long like a tiny oblong coffin abandoned to its fate.

Another day went past, and then another.

What was his game? She wondered. Was he trying to punish her or break her resistance…or simply stretch her patience to the limit; what was his end-game? She pondered as she lay there in bed on that fifth night.

Finally, the next day, the sixth since it had all happened, Madison decided that she couldn't wait any longer; her holiday was coming to an end and she needed to clear the air before leaving to go back to the States

She got up that morning and having conjured up all the inner-strength she could muster; she charged over to the Abbey.

It was a trip that she had made on numerous occasions over the summer and as she made her way once again through the leafy lanes, her mind focussed on exactly what she wanted to say to him, a thousand and one more questions went racing through her mind creating doubt in her pre-rehearsed argument.

She reached the Abbey in record time and without hesitation, glancing over to see that his car was indeed parked there in its usual place, she strode up to the front door with great purpose and determination.

Once there, she composed herself, brushed down her dress which had ridden up slightly during the walk and rang the bell.

It took a minute or so, but eventually the door was eased open by a beautiful, professional-looking, young woman in a stunning violet-coloured business suit, followed by the unmistakeable aromas of hot toast and freshly-brewed coffee.

'Hi, I'm Olivia', the pretty brunette announced with a pleasant smile as Madison recoiled in shock on the door-step; 'I was just about to leave'.

Stunned into silence Madison looked like she had just been hit in the face with a glass full of ice-cold water…and her pent up frustration… which was already at breaking point because of the strained situation…was suddenly cranked up another notch with the sight of this strange woman opening *His* door.

Time seemed to stand still there in that moment but then as the irrational penny of feminine presumption dropped, she saw red and the inevitable pangs of jealousy began to tighten almost immediately in her chest.

'Are you alright', Olivia asked, noticing Madison's rather shocked expression.

Madison didn't respond and…ignoring the young woman's kindly concern…she threw her hair back disdainfully, stepped forward and stormed past her into the hallway, the look of contempt in her eyes enough to warn off any potential rival.

Olivia took a step back…and as Madison walked on in she followed her with her eyes from her position in the door-way, wondering if she should alert *the Bishop* of this other woman's sudden presence in his home.

However, the rhetorical question was quickly answered when the latter paused in front of the full-length mirror to catch her breath and smooth down her dress, making it obvious that she was quite comfortable and familiar with the layout of the house.

Olivia therefore concluded that – knowing *the Bishop* as she did - it would probably be best if she just left, which she did with a shrug, closing the door firmly behind her.

Meanwhile, having composed herself in front of the mirror Madison strode confidently up to the door of *the Bishop's* office…paused again to take another deep breath…and without bothering to knock, forgetting all the normal civilities, she rushed straight in like a bull in a china shop, ready to demand an immediate explanation as to who this 'Olivia person' was…and why he hadn't returned any of her calls.

♗

Once inside the hallowed sanctuary of his office which she had come to know so well over recent weeks, Madison came to a rather abrupt halt right in front of his desk; the look on her face expressing both bewilderment and confusion as she stood there, hands on hips, shaping up for a showdown.

She looked rather menacing but in reality, her surface anger notwithstanding, she was really quite full of remorse and regret, fearing that after her revelations and their subsequent disagreement in London that he might not actually want to see her again.

'…So who is she; who is this…Olivia person?' She demanded, clenching her fists in frustration as she stood there in front of him, waiting impatiently for him to react…and sensing most definitely that her presence wasn't particularly welcome.

♗

The Bishop, sat quietly behind his desk, didn't react immediately to her aggressive stance, and only when he had finished the paragraph of the book that he was reading did he look up, draw a deep breath and lean back self-assuredly in his heavy leather chair…steepling his fingers in reflection.

'It never ceases to amaze me…' he began grabbing the edge of the desk, '…just how much jealousy, resentment and injustice there is in this world; jealousy is such a destructive emotion'.

Madison could see in his eyes that he clearly resented her intrusion; she knew full well that he hated anybody arriving at his house unannounced, but this time, despite his latent irritation he calmly asked her to take seat – which she promptly refused, throwing her arms in the air in a classic show of petulance.

He waited a while longer for her to cool down and once he was satisfied that she was ready to listen, he calmly went about answering each of her questions one by one, pulling off a masterful display of self-control and unruffled masculine charm…the secret of which he alone knew the key.

'Olivia is my house-keeper'; he lied, his voice cold and unemotional as he said it.

'She is?' Madison scoffed incredulously, biting the inside of her cheek and brushing her hair back nervously.

'Wow; she's kinda hot…for …for a house-keeper', she commented after a brief pause, trying to lighten the mood.

It didn't work.

'I think she would prefer the term glamorous', *the Bishop* lectured, a little annoyed by Madison's somewhat derogatory American terminology; 'it doesn't sound so vulgar'.

'Yeah, you're right, that does sound better'. Madison agreed, feeling nevertheless that the strength of his rebuke was unwarranted.

'…and for your information, she isn't working today, she was just dropping something off for me', *the Bishop* added while marking his page and closing his book.

Madison wasn't entirely convinced by his explanation but as she stood there a seed of uncertainty suddenly clouded her previously self-assured mind…and her aggressive stance slowly softened as *the Bishop* got up from his desk and joined her in front of it.

He stood facing her, and though neither of them spoke for a moment, when he reached out his hand and brushed it lightly against her hair, Madison's reassurance level quickly soared.

'I have told you before, Madison; you have trust issues', he said; '…especially where women are concerned'.

'I don't…I don't have a problem with other women…just…' Madison began to respond…but before she could finish her thought, *the Bishop* placed his fore-finger against her lips and stopped her in her tracks.

This gesture instantly triggered her memory and in that moment she was instantly transported back in her mind to when she had done exactly the same thing to him all those months ago, just before their first ever kiss.

The recollection warmed her soul and almost as a reflex reaction to it she closed her eyes in expectant anticipation. Had he forgiven her? She wondered with renewed optimism.

She waited a few moments for that blissful contact to be resumed - remembering just how much she enjoyed his kisses - but then when nothing happened, she carefully opened one eye and then the other to find that *the Bishop* had discreetly stepped away from her and was resting nonchalantly against the edge of his desk, his arms folded across himself in a typically defensive manner.

'…So, tell me', he asked, speaking slowly and pausing momentarily to add weight to his question; 'why are you making such a big deal out of something so insignificant as Olivia opening the door to you?'

Madison frowned, disappointed that he wasn't going to kiss her after all…and frustrated by the realisation that her pardon wasn't going to be granted that easily.

'…Well; let me see now', she began, collecting her thoughts.

'I was under the impression that we kinda had something going on here…between us', she then declared regaining her composure; '…and seeing Olivia at the door…well, let's just say I jumped to the wrong conclusion', she added, unintentionally revealing more of her innermost thoughts than she probably should have.

'Indeed…and is that how you see it?' *the Bishop* queried, rubbing his chin; 'Is that how you see me?' he insisted, the tone of his voice one of controlled irritation; 'Am I just another one of those perfidious men that can't be trusted; one of those men that women ignorantly judge and criticise…all because they choose not to disclose the details of their private life to anybody that asks?'

Madison blinked, was going to respond but then thought better of it.

'Is that how you see me?' *the Bishop* continued in an even and commanding tone that belied his growing internal conflict.

'…Because I try to protect myself and my privacy; is that why you went snooping around my house looking for the proof that would confirm the label you wanted to attach to me?' he asked without breaking eye-contact and raising his voice a little further just to show his indignation.

The tension in the room was suddenly thick with consequence.

'I'm sorry; I know I screwed up', Madison blurted out, trying to atone for what she had done and retrieve the situation which was once again slowly spiralling away from her; 'I didn't mean…'

'Sorry is all well and good', *the Bishop* interrupted, speaking to her again in a very controlled and focussed manner, '…but this is not about Olivia; it is about you', he added insistently, wrong-footing her completely.

Madison frowned again and realising what was surely coming her way, she braced herself for the inevitable onslaught - feeling that any control she might have had when she first walked into the room was slipping slowly but inexorably through her fingers; it was time for her to eat a very large slice of humble pie.

'You had become an important part of my life', *the Bishop* announced quietly; 'I had come to trust you…but for whatever reason, you betrayed that trust…and while it might be a cliché, I suppose what I'm trying to say is that just because we had a past together, it doesn't necessarily follow that we have a future', he declared with a look of resignation in his eyes.

Madison swallowed deeply, crushed to hear him speak of their relationship in the past tense…and though she held her head high trying not to let her feelings show, her heart immediately dropped through the floor.

'Look, people make mistakes'; she argued desperately, taking a step forward; 'it doesn't necessarily make them bad people…it just makes them human', she declared…

'…and in my defence I am a journalist…and maybe on this occasion I overstepped the line' she explained cautiously, knowing that she was on rocky ground.

'There is no maybe about it', *the Bishop* retorted quickly, pulling the metaphorical rug of conciliation out from under her; 'that is exactly what you did…you overstepped the line…and in my house, you might be surprised to discover, I didn't consider you a journalist, I considered you a guest…'

'…and guests don't go snooping around; I get it', Madison agreed, finishing his phrase for him while choking back the emotion.

The Bishop nodded; he could see the moisture of tears gathering on Madison's eye-lashes and ever the gentleman, despite the context, he reached forward to offer her a tissue from the box on his desk.

Madison thanked him, dabbed her eyes gently and then began to crumble contritely in front of him as her inner strength disintegrated under the weight of her shame.

It was a first for her; she had never allowed this to happen before… in front of someone…but *the Bishop* - the master tactician - had managed to pierce her hard, protective shell and expose her most basic human emotions.

Desperation suddenly took hold of her and as she wiped her eyes again, she apologised once more, hoping that this time he would accept it and end this rather strange stand-off.

It was a sad picture but bizarrely Madison's plight didn't seem to move *the Bishop* and he just stood there impassively watching her for a moment, apparently intrigued by the confused array of emotions on her face.

Time stood still for a moment and then suddenly without warning *the*

Bishop's whole demeanour seemed to change; his legendary patience and renowned self-control unexpectedly replaced by an impenetrable curtain of red-mist.

'Stop crying', he barked abruptly.

'You have already lost my trust; are you now prepared to lose my respect?' He insisted harshly, his chastening tone quite unbecoming of the man she thought she knew.

Madison was shocked by this sudden mood swing but she quickly averted her eyes, knowing that what he said was true.

She was crest-fallen by his rebuke and her heart began smarting from the rejection in his voice.

Her emotions began to escalate out of control and despite her feelings of guilt and shame; she made one final impassioned plea for forgiveness.

'Don't you care about me?' She asked through her tear-stained eyes, bracing herself again for the hammer blow of his reply which would surely send all her hopes and dreams crashing through the floor to oblivion.

'Yes I care about you…much more than I should', *the Bishop* confirmed after a brief pause.

'Then please don't do this, Tobias'; she beseeched him with one last entreaty - *suddenly conscious in her mind that that was the first time she had called him by his first name*, as he got up, turned his back on her and walked over to the window, unable to assuage his own internal conflict any longer.

'I said I'm sorry; what more do you want?' she insisted, hoping that her plea would somehow change the outcome of the argument.

'It's too little too late…', *the Bishop* lamented, twisting the metaphorical knife in her back as he turned to face her once again; '…the bond of trust has been broken'.

Madison caught his eye as he brushed his hair back, but strangely in that split-second she didn't recognise him; he had always been opinionated, ever since she had first gotten to know him; indeed she had witnessed it a thousand times already, but for him to be so callously cold-hearted and uncaring like this was so truly out of character with the man she thought she knew; …had what she had done really been that bad?, she wondered to herself.

The Bishop looked into her eyes as he sat back down in his chair…and seeing the hurt and the confusion in her face, he immediately tempered his tone, but he would not entertain any further discussion on the subject of their relationship and Madison knew as she stood there, that it would be fruitless to try to force the issue, even though she had so much more to say and a host of unanswered questions still waiting for a reply.

The mood in the room was intense like the moment before a gunfight but they had reached a stale-mate and this was a fight Madison knew she couldn't win, so she wisely boxed the remaining questions in her mind, and putting on a brave face to hide the hurt that she was so obviously feeling inside, she backed away slowly, turned and rushed out of the house, petulantly slamming the hallway door on her way through, with such force that it shattered one of the ornamental stained-glass panels, sending several shards crashing to the floor in a tinkling of rhythmic chimes.

Outside, her eyes filled again with tears and as she turned into the lane and began the long trudge back to the cottage – *the Bishop's* cold, harsh words still fresh in her mind - Madison suddenly disintegrated; her shoulders dropped, her head fell forward and when her hair conveniently covered her face, obscuring her features from any prying eyes she let the flood-gates open.

It took her almost an hour to make her way back to the cottage and just as she was about to turn into her driveway, having sobbed her heart out most of the way, the rain-clouds that had been steadily gathering above her head suddenly burst their seams, forcing her to run the last few metres to her door.

She rushed inside and having kicked off her wet shoes, she made her way straight upstairs, where without even bothering to get undressed or close the curtains, she crawled under the covers of her bed, buried her face in the pillows and cried herself back to sleep, drowning herself in another river of her own shiny tears.

The next morning, Madison was still wallowing in the quiet of unconscious sleep, when all of a sudden she was woken up by the sound of somebody knocking loudly on her door, downstairs.

She raised her head slowly from the tear-stained pillow and with her puffy, blood-shot eyes she caught a glimpse of the unforgiving, grey sky above through the rain-soaked panes of her bedroom windows.

Then, exhaling a deep sigh of despondency, she looked at the clock on her bed-side table; it was almost 8:00 a.m.; she had slept for nearly eighteen hours.

Her head felt heavy - like she had been drunk and had a hangover - but as she slowly emerged from the depths of her emotional stupor, the knocking downstairs was repeated a little more insistently, the noise reverberating through the thick stone walls of the tiny cottage.

Madison sat up slowly and through the opaque haze of her muddled mind she began wondering who could possibly be hammering on her door at that time of the morning.

A third knock, although less persistent, finally pushed her to react… and prising herself reluctantly out of bed, she forced herself to leave the sanctuary of her little bedroom, to find out who it was.

It was cold and she shivered as she hurried down the stairs in the forlorn hope that it might be him at the door…completely forgetting in the moment that she had gotten up in the middle of the night to use the loo and had changed out of her clothes and into the white shirt that she had borrowed and worn home from the abbey after her birthday treat.

She reached the door becoming steadily more cognisant, and her heart immediately jumped in expectation at the sight of what she assumed was the outline of *the Bishop's* silhouette behind the frosted glass.

However, when she flung the door open - almost taking it off its hinges - ready to welcome him with open arms, her hopes came crashing down once again.

Standing there on her door-step, dripping wet in his fluorescent jacket was the postman; he was new to the job and had a package in his hand for another address somewhere in the area which he had been looking for, but couldn't find.

'Hello there', he chirped merrily, despite his sodden appearance; 'you wouldn't happen to know where Rossway is, would you?' he asked hopefully.

Madison's face dropped on seeing him but she managed a stiff smile as she shook her head in disappointment.

'No I don't, I'm sorry; …I can't help you', she replied, closing the door a little due to the draught which was suddenly making her aware of her scant attire.

'Never mind', the postie retorted with a warm smile, putting the package back in his bag and gesturing his thanks to her with a friendly wave; 'I'm sorry to have troubled you', he declared before turning and continuing on his way.

Without another word, Madison quickly closed the door and slowly traipsed her way back upstairs, a mournful look on her disconsolate face.

She got back into bed and as she pulled the covers back over her weary limbs, the rain outside seemed to double in intensity, in a rather accurate reflection of her sombre mood.

Madison still had another week or so to go before she was due to leave, but later that day having come to the conclusion - after many hours of horizontal reflection - that there was no longer any point in her prolonging her stay, she decided to ring her travel agent to see if she could organise an earlier flight back to New York.

The guy who answered her enquiry was most helpful…*even though her request was a little awkward to deal with because of the short notice…* and within the hour he had rung her back with the offer of a flight to JFK leaving two days later.

Without a moment's hesitation Madison duly accepted his offer, even though there was a hefty admin charge, confirming the reservation immediately with her credit card number.

Then, with a heavy-heart, she rang the Abbey one last time - knowing full well that *the Bishop* wouldn't pick up - and left a last message for him on the answering-machine, informing him of her departure and of the fact that she would be arranging for the taxi taking her to the airport to stop by the abbey on his way through in order to pick up the suitcase that she had so frivolously abandoned in the hotel in London; could he please have it ready.

It was a poignant call but once it was done, Madison recomposed herself and spent the rest of the afternoon tying up all the loose ends; organising the taxi to the airport and sorting through the restitution details of her rental contract with Mr Douglas.

The evening was spent sorting out her clothes ready to pack and reminiscing warmly and almost nostalgically on what she and *the Bishop* had done on the days when she had been wearing those particular outfits.

The next day was rather quiet, though it still rained on and off outside, and Madison spent most of it on her laptop, catching up with a host of unanswered e-mails, updating and tidying a couple of files and getting up to speed with what was going on back in the office, determined not to let her personal crisis interfere with or impact on her professional bearing.

The day after that was the day of her departure and as planned the taxi arrived on time, having stopped off to pick up her suitcase from the Abbey beforehand.

It rolled up to her door and as it came to a halt in the little forecourt, Madison came out and greeted the driver with a wave as she made her way over to him.

She waited for him to get out and as he moved around the car to open the boot, she followed him and asked, as nonchalantly as possible, if there had been any problem with picking up her other suitcase from the abbey... hoping secretly that the man might have a message for her from *the Bishop*.

The cabbie just looked at her and shook his head; 'No love, no problem'.

'So there was no message from the guy at the abbey', Madison repeated insistently, desperate for a sign of reconciliation.

'No, no message', the cabbie confirmed, holding up his hands apologetically; '...though...it was a young lady who handed me the case...and not a...a gentleman', he added apathetically as he made room for her suitcases.

Madison's face froze momentarily but then with a look of resignation and a shrug of the shoulders, she turned away and made her way back into the cottage, indicating the two suitcases that she had gotten ready by the front door with a curt, almost indignant flick of the hand as she went.

The cabbie took note and while he was busy loading the suitcases into the boot of the car alongside the one he had picked up at the abbey, Madison took one more look around the cottage to make sure that she hadn't forgotten anything.

Five minutes passed and just as the cabbie was starting to get impatient; she re-appeared, stepping outside and putting her computer case on the floor next to her while she closed the door and locked it for the very last time, trying the handle twice to make sure that it was secure.

Then, having done that, she slipped the keys into an envelope alongside the covering letter that she had prepared for Mr Douglas and very carefully posted it back through the letterbox for him to find when he came on his next visit, as arranged over the phone.

She paused momentarily, took a deep breath and picking up her computer-case, made her way over to the cab without another look back.

She got into the car, the cabbie did likewise and without further ceremony they drove off, bringing what had been the most exciting period of her life to a premature and sadly, desperately unhappy end.

'At least it's stopped raining', the cabbie commented blandly as he turned left onto the open road.

Madison looked at his reflection in the rear-view mirror but didn't reply.

On the plane home, thanks to some clever seat manipulation by one of the flight-attendants, Madison managed to get a seat on her own and... *once the plane had settled into its cruising altitude and all the passengers had finally calmed down*...she quietly rested her head against the window-surround where her thoughts began to drift and she started to reflect on what she had left behind.

She thought about London and its wonderful choice of shops, she thought about the Abbey, about her cute little cottage…and about Gary who had selflessly come to her rescue on more than one occasion over the past few months.

That last memory made her smile; she liked the young Aussie, he was one of the good guys and one of the few people she had met who had always been straight with her - even more so than she probably had been with him, but as much as she liked him, Gary just couldn't stand the comparison with *the irrepressible Bishop* whose enigmatic face suddenly replaced the young Aussie's in her mind's eye as if by magic.

'Chicken or fish?' the flight-attendant repeated politely, interrupting her daydream and dragging her back to reality.

'Chicken, please', Madison answered decisively, correcting her posture.

The young woman smiled and handed her the meal-tray which Madison took from her graciously, setting it down carefully on the mini drop-down table in front of her.

She looked at the tray's rather meagre and un-appetising contents, and as the flight-attendant continued on her way with her droning 'chicken or fish' proposition, the sound of children squabbling suddenly drew her attention.

A family of four were sitting across from her in the middle aisle and the two young children sandwiched between their parents were arguing over who would get the square of chocolate from their mother's tray.

Madison tried to ignore it at first but as the quarrel continued and the parents seemed unable to quell their unruly offspring, she decided, rather spontaneously, that the best solution would be for her to take the square of chocolate from her own tray and hand it to the harassed-looking mother so that she could even things out and settle the dispute.

The mother thanked her…as did the father with a grateful smile, and with that everybody returned to their food, Madison feeling rather pleased and somewhat surprised by her selfless show of consideration; she didn't really like children.

A few minutes later, the flight-attendant came around again with tea and coffee, and a further twenty minutes or so after that, once the trays had all been collected again, everything settled down again as the passengers returned to their preferred distractions.

Madison relaxed again too and as she settled into her seat again, her thoughts immediately returned to *the Bishop*.

Her mind began to wander into dangerous territory, opening a door that it should really have left closed and all of a sudden she found herself reliving the ill-fated argument in London and its follow-up at the abbey.

The recollection of that and the streaming images of so many other things that she and *the Bishop* had done together, steadily created a wave of emotion in her head and without her realising it, those emotions were transformed into hot, wet tears which began to leak again from the corners of her eyes onto the cold skin of her cheeks.

If only she had stopped and thought it through before she had gone snooping around his house, she thought to herself…but unfortunately her journalistic instincts had led her astray, forcing her to abandon her moral principles…and regrettably that one mistake had scuppered her chances of a lasting relationship with the most fascinating man she could ever have hoped to meet.

She wiped away a tear and as she looked back on the whole episode, she had to agree…with the benefit of hindsight…that what she had done was totally irrational; to jeopardise her relationship with *the Bishop* in the way she did was unforgiveable and sure enough he had not forgiven her.

Of course, she knew that with time, the hurt would pass, that even the shame would eventually disappear, but she also knew that the guilt, the guilt that she was feeling right now, like a stab to the heart, would last forever… like a permanent scar on her emotional landscape; it had been a valuable if somewhat painful lesson and she swore to herself in that moment that she would never let it happen again, she would never cross that line again in any possible future relationship.

After all that soul-searching Madison took a deep breath and recomposing herself, she decided that it was time for her to stop looking back…and look ahead.

She had enjoyed her trip to England - for the most part - but now she was really looking forward to getting back to New York, to reality, or at least what she called reality; her apartment, her job and her friends…and that perspective instantly brought the smile back to her face, lifting her spirits and making her feel much more confident about the future.

CHAPTER TWENTY-THREE

Madison had been back at work for a couple of months after her summer escapade in England and had begun…slowly but surely…to cement her place in the fashion department alongside Gretchen when one day…while she was happily working away at her computer…another of her colleagues popped her head around the office door to inform her that she had just read online that that 'Bishop guy', that she (Madison) had written about all those months ago, had just announced that he was going to retire at the end of the year…and that the tournament he would be participating in just before Christmas would be his last.

The news came as rather a shock to her…but while she paused momentarily in what she was doing and looked up, Madison didn't react with any great emotion to her colleague's excited comment preferring instead to ignore it almost, as she returned to tapping on the keys of her computer, albeit a little harder than previously.

'…Oh, and the meeting is about to start', her young colleague then added breezily, popping her head back around the door before rushing off, obviously delighted to be the proud bearer of some breaking news, however insignificant that news might be.

Madison waited a minute or two, then got up, sorted out the files on her desk relevant to the meeting that was about to take place and made her way down the hall to the glass-walled conference room where Amanda was already waiting, ready to chair her weekly brain-storming session…with her, Gretchen and several other members of the magazine's creative team.

She reached the door…followed closely by Gretchen…and as they walked into the room the air suddenly came alive with excited whispers… *thanks to the extraordinary powers of the gossip grapevine.*

Amanda, who was sat at the head of the table, looked up slowly from the file laid out in front of her and greeted them both with a tight smile… and a very-deliberate finger-tap on her bare wrist.

'Sorry everyone', Gretchen offered, looking a little flustered as she made her way around the oval-shaped table.

The usual assortment of mumbles and social indulgences reserved for such occasions quickly rolled around the room but as Madison followed in her 'boss's' footsteps she couldn't help but notice the expressions on the faces of all those present.

Clearly the story of *the Bishop's* retirement was already on everybody's lips.

Madison had never spoken about her relationship with the Bishop within the confines of the office – either to confirm or deny it - but somehow it seemed to be common knowledge that something had gone on…and like all rumours, if they are repeated enough, people will eventually begin to believe them, whether they be based on fact or pure invention…so, despite her silence it was inevitable that the rumour-mill would connect her to the news about his retirement in some way.

They reached the head of the table…and with another brief apology to Amanda…Gretchen quickly took her seat, followed swiftly by Madison who nonchalantly pulled out her chair and sat down next to her 'boss' in her usual spot.

The other team-members then settled into their seats too and… after a very awkward pause…the subject of *the Bishop's* retirement was immediately tabled by one of the newer interns, desperate to stand out and ingratiate herself with her superiors.

'As I'm sure that you are all aware', she blurted out from the far end of the table, glancing at Amanda for a sign of her tacit consent; 'Tobias Byron, the British chess champion…that Madison interviewed last year…has just announced his retirement, and as our first item for discussion…even though it's not on the agenda…I would like to propose that we do a tribute article on the guy in the weekend magazine leading up to Christmas to celebrate his career'.

She then paused for effect, to take a breath and look for the support of her colleagues.

'After all, he has become a celebrity…' she insisted.

'A minor celebrity', Madison interjected with a hint of acrimony in her voice.

'Okay, a minor celebrity', the young intern repeated, '…thanks to this magazine…so it seems only logical that we do something', she concluded, waiting nervously for her peers' reactions.

Others immediately began to voice their opinions and the idea went anarchically around the table before Amanda raised a hand to resume control of the proceedings, secretly enjoying the moment.

She sat forward, rested her arms on the table in front of her and deliberately prolonging the moment for maximum effect, she turned and looked directly at Madison.

Everybody waited with bated breath to hear what she was about to say.

'What do you think Madison?'; Amanda enquired, not wanting to put too fine a point on it…but putting her young colleague on the spot nevertheless, '…you introduced this guy to us, and now that he's jacking it all in, maybe it would be a good idea for you to do a kind of wrap-up assignment, to tie up the loose-ends so to speak', she reasoned, mirroring her thoughts with a circular gesture of the hand to illustrate the full-circle nature of the idea.

'…After all, he has become a *minor* celebrity thanks to your coverage of his previous exploits', she confirmed, insisting on the 'minor' just as Madison had done, picking up on her younger colleague's unspoken disenchantment.

The silence in the room was palpable while Madison thought about her response but then as several of her colleagues started shifting uncomfortably in their seats the buzz of chattering voices slowly built again.

Gretchen turned to her assistant waiting for her reply too…but sensing the latter's hesitation or at least her reluctance to answer, she decided to short-circuit Amanda's rather blatant and insensitive grilling of her protégée by drawing the focus away from her, jumping on the opportunity of a lull in the conversation to call for everybody's attention.

'Listen up, everyone…' she announced hesitantly, standing up; '… before we get on with whatever else we are going to discuss, I've got something that I would like to share with you all.'

The buzz around the table quietened again, momentarily.

'Everybody…I'm pregnant', she declared gleefully throwing her arms out in celebration…and with that the whole room erupted in unison… congratulatory comments and clapping hands filling the air once again, this time with joyful energy.

Even Amanda joined in tactfully, but as she was on a tight schedule, she quickly brought the meeting back to order, thanking the new intern for her suggestion and repeating her offer to Madison, informing her that she had first refusal on that particular assignment if tempted.

Madison smiled politely in response to Amanda's renewed offer and then leaning on the files on the desk in front of her she looked around at all her colleagues' expectant faces, took a deep breath and announced confidently;

'Look; thank you Amanda for your vote of confidence', she began… gesturing appreciatively towards her boss, 'I'm flattered; I really am that you would consider me again for this new mission …but on this occasion I really think that I should sit this one out…because…under the current circumstances…and especially after Gretchen's wonderful news…I think I need to concentrate on my new role in the fashion department…rather than take more time off to go and do another feature', she explained, sensing the possibility of another promotion thanks to Gretchen's timely revelation.

'…I don't know… maybe you could give one of these 'newbies' here, her…or his…chance', she suddenly suggested out of left field, gesturing with an open palm around the table.

Amanda frowned, looking pensive for a moment, her eyes scanning around the table at the array of hopeful faces looking back at her.

'No…no, no, no; this is not an assignment for a newbie to cut her… or his teeth on', she declared objectively; 'this is the Christmas issue; it's time-sensitive and needs someone with experience'.

Hearing these words all the hopeful faces dropped and a murmur of grumbling disappointment circled the table.

'However, you know what'; Amanda suddenly announced, after a brief moment of reflection, 'I find that Bishop guy quite intriguing myself, so maybe…maybe I will just go ahead and do it myself', she reasoned, 'After all, I'm overdue a holiday and two weeks in London would be just what the doctor ordered', she added, her mouth twitching in an involuntary smile as she thought it over.

'…After all…people…don't you just love that cultured English accent', she gushed with deliberate ambiguity, aiming a discreet wink in Madison's direction.

The latter shook her head slowly, thought about it for a moment and then just smiled inwardly. She knew that just like her, Amanda would never shy away from a challenge…but she also knew that like many women of her ilk, Amanda was permanently dissatisfied with life due to her perennial hankering for the unattainable…and with that in mind she (Madison) decided, somewhat surprisingly, that Amanda would be the ideal person…and a worthy adversary…for *the Bishop* in the war of words that would inevitably oppose them, if and when they ever met and clashed.

'Now', Amanda said, focussing everybody's attention again and continuing the meeting, '…about next week's cover photo; 'I think we should go with….'

A few days later, Madison was sat in her office again, when Amanda appeared in the doorway.

'Is it alright if I come in?' she enquired with uncharacteristic courtesy.

'Sure'. Madison nodded, surprised by her boss's unexpected visit.

Amanda sauntered in and sat down without being asked.

Madison stopped what she was doing, sat back in her chair and prepared to listen.

'I met with Gretchen earlier today and I have just come from the boardroom', Amanda announced…getting straight to the point without any unnecessary preamble; '…and as Gretchen is going to be otherwise engaged for the next few months, it has been agreed that you be put in temporary charge of her diary while she is away; are you okay with that?' Amanda questioned coldly.

'Does it come with benefits?' Madison retorted immediately, with the same lack of emotion, expecting her insolence to be rebuffed.

'…Benefits, maybe, conditions definitely', Amanda declared without reprimand; '…three month trial and if all goes well, a revenue-linked bonus after six', she rattled off, scrutinising Madison's unruffled reaction.

'Very well, that all sounds good to me', Madison agreed, trying not to reveal any emotion at hearing that the dream she had chased after for so long was finally taking shape.

'HR will be in touch with you about the paperwork', Amanda confirmed as she got up; '...Oh and by the way', she added with a hint of provocation, almost as an afterthought as she walked out, 'I have decided to go ahead and do the interview with that bishop guy in London'.

'Great news' Madison commented a little sarcastically, trying not to let her displeasure show through in her voice as she watched her boss leave.

However, as soon as Amanda was out of sight, she could not help but glance at the framed photograph of her with *the Bishop* and Gary...*which had now been relegated to the far corner of the office between two piles of fabric samples*...realising as she did so that she had no right to be jealous of Amanda going over to London to interview him.

After all, she had been given first refusal on the assignment...*and had turned it down*...and more importantly...she and *the Bishop* were no longer an item anyway...if indeed they ever really were.

It was just that the mention of his name still pulled at her heartstrings - and as she got up and walked over to the photo, picking it up to wipe away a smudge that had caught her eye, she also realised in retrospect that if Amanda was now prepared to entrust her with the responsibility of running Gretchen's diary while she was away having her baby, it was due in no small part to the fact that he had come into her life.

He had taken the person she was and had subtly moulded her into the person she had become.

Oh, it wasn't the classic story of the ugly duckling morphing into a beautiful swan, nor was it Eliza Doolittle blossoming under Henry Higgins' guidance in 'My Fair Lady' but, in his own way *the Bishop* had helped to fashion her future by teaching her some basic lessons on life, along with some patience, some humility and some manners; in fact, even the length of the skirt that she was now wearing, was down to his influence, she acknowledged, looking down at her hem-line.

Madison put the photograph back in its place and as she regained her chair, it suddenly dawned on her that Amanda must have picked up on those subtle changes too and...having recognised that new maturity...now felt more comfortable in delegating more responsibility her way, knowing that despite the subtle changes she was still as driven and motivated and determined as ever.

She turned and looked again at *the Bishop's* face, staring back at her from the photo and brushing her hair away from her face, she mouthed a grateful 'thank-you' in his direction.

Three weeks later Amanda disappeared off to London to watch the Bishop in his final tournament having negotiated the rights to an exclusive interview with the master himself - to be conducted a couple of days before the tournament started…and thanks to her professional guile and her years of experience she managed to conduct a more in-depth interview with him than Madison could ever have hoped to do, the Bishop rising to the challenge once again to offer her the benefit of his rather outspoken opinions on a number of subjects.

She met him at the headquarters of the ECA in London and when she walked into the small room that they had reserved for the interview… wearing a pinstriped trouser-suit from Yves Saint Laurent…*the Bishop* was already there waiting for her, looking suave but clearly on edge as he sat there toying with his favourite fountain-pen.

Amanda looked around the room feeling a little claustrophobic - *as coming from the States she was used to a more spacious environment in which to work* - but nevertheless, when *the Bishop* stood up and greeted her with his usual gentlemanly propriety, recognising her instantly from their brief introduction in New York, she was quickly put at her ease.

'Nice to see you again', he declared warmly, extending a welcoming hand.

'Likewise', Amanda replied, offering her own hand in return…and reacting favourably to his invitation for her to take a seat across from him.

A brief pause followed while Amanda settled into her chair and pulled out her digital voice-recorder ready to start the interview, but then, almost before she could set it up, just as he had done previously with Madison, *the Bishop* began to talk, taking the unsuspecting Amanda completely by surprise and swamping her almost immediately with his vast knowledge of American culture in general…and its politics in particular.

He asked her about the recent elections, congratulating her as an American citizen for the resounding message of hope that she and her countrymen had sent out across the world…and for a split-second Amanda gloried in the praise as if the compliment was directed at her personally.

'Yes, that is the best piece of news that the world has had for a while', *the Bishop* went on; 'I just hope that the new president, President Obama and the rest of the political community is aware of how much the core of their country needs help'.

Amanda's expression suddenly changed. 'Help?' she quizzed, meeting his gaze.

'Yes, help', *the Bishop* insisted. 'America is a country bursting with suppressed emotions, emotions which have been ignored and glossed over with a paper-thin crust of political and religious hypocrisy for far too long…and this new hope, this new beginning that President Obama is promising with his 'Yes we can' slogan, could mean that there is a real potential for that powder-keg to explode', he preached.

This outburst, which had nothing to do with why she was there, left Amanda feeling a little bemused and while she acknowledged *the Bishop's* concerns about her country's fragile state, humouring him with an indulgent smile, she was not really interested in getting into a political discussion with him.

'So, what's in the future?', she asked politely, cleverly steering him away from the subject and back onto neutral ground.

'…The future?' *the Bishop* repeated.

'Yeah, the future…now that you're retiring from tournaments', Amanda clarified, locking eyes with him for the first time.

'I shall probably spend my time reading', *the Bishop* replied simply.

Amanda nodded and shrugged without comment.

'…I am fascinated by high-profile cover-ups, like those of JFK, Robert Kennedy, Marilyn Monroe and Martin Luther King', *the Bishop* admitted, refocusing the conversation back on America.

'I see', Amanda noted, without further comment.

This remark brought up the subject of censorship, which, because of her many years in publishing, Amanda thought she would be able to trump him on – but once again, unfortunately for her, *the Bishop* knew a lot more about the MPAA than she did, and for the next ten minutes he drilled that advantage home.

MPAA;

Motion Picture Association of America.

Amongst its many roles, the **MPAA** is the US censor which regulates censorship and hands out movie ratings. It is an organisation cloaked in secrecy made up of a small number of faceless, nameless individuals… including representatives of the clergy…who make decisions of morality and decency for the majority.

They are moral dictators who decide what the masses can and cannot watch, based on their own political, military or religious judgements.

It is another example of a small body of people (between 10 and 12 people make up the panel at any one time with an average age of between 45 and 50) having the power to decide what you and I, who represent the millions of potential viewers, are allowed to watch, as if we were incapable of deciding for ourselves, refusing certificates on films that they consider unsuitable for whatever reason while handicapping others with R ratings so that they cannot be properly marketed.

Their decision is final and unquestionable – and the film-makers are given no chance to defend their work or discuss its content.

Appeals are allowed however…to give the impression of arbitration or a veneer of legality to the process…but in reality they are systematically refused.

'So, once again hypocrisy rules', he declared; '...while socially-created problems such as violence and murder get PG ratings from these people (*the body-count in a typical action movie can easily reach 80 individuals*), anything pertaining to human sexuality, anything inherent in our nature... that these people disagree with for whatever reason, gets an R+ rating' (18 in the UK)...and therefore a reduced audience'.

'Surely this is sending the wrong message to the public?' he pontificated.

'Guns and murder is okay; human sexuality is not...and we see the result of this hypocrisy on the streets of America every day', he concluded, bringing his rant on censorship to a close.

Amanda sat back in frustration, waiting for the storm to pass, just as Madison had done before her.

It was unlike her to be so passive but just like her younger colleague, she too, was left speechless by *the Bishop's* intelligent, indisputable argument...and unable to come up with a reasonable defence for her country's undeniably questionable institutions.

'Of course, there is a way around this anachronistic institution', *the Bishop* added as an aside, '...for those film-makers intent on getting their work out there without these people meddling in it; ...the internet', he announced smugly, a hint of mischief in his voice.

'My, you really seem to have a grievance against these people', Amanda suggested calmly, trying to maintain her professional façade, even though her patience was running thin.

The Bishop looked at her and frowned; 'No, not a grievance, not a personal grievance at least; I just hate hypocrites and anybody who tries to tell me what I should think - and the MPAA is just another one of those cases of 'the-few-choosing-for-the-many' which as I see it, is not a democracy', he reasoned logically.

'I see your point', Amanda conceded, trying to get back to the questions she felt her readers would be more interested in...but unfortunately, as ever, *the Bishop* wouldn't let it go;

'Are these people really that naive?' he continued, developing his thought.

This time it was Amanda's turn to frown and wonder what was coming next.

'...I mean, do they really believe that by beeping out the words *drugs* and *pills* from that Rockstar video by Nickelback for example…that the kids watching it at home won't understand what the song is all about - that it is about the 'sex and drugs and rock 'n' roll lifestyle of celebrities?'

'…Come on America; the girls are in bikinis throughout the video and the men barely disguise the fact that they have all dabbled in drugs', he affirmed, pausing just long enough to throw his hands in the air.

'What a crazy country; you can carry a gun around, but whatever you do, don't use bad language', he muttered.

Amanda grimaced again with frustration but more so at the fact that this rather incongruous Englishman should have even heard of a 'rock-music video'.

'…I just find it so sad that these blinkered people with their outdated values are still trying to exist in a world rapidly passing them by', he concluded, once again, shaking his head almost disconsolately.

The Bishop's sanctimonious rant was getting out of control as far as Amanda was concerned, side-tracking her from her real mission and looking for a way of breaking his flow, she spied a jug of water sitting on a side-table behind him.

'Is that water over there; could I have a glass?' she asked politely, gesturing towards the carafe.

'Why of course; by all means', *the Bishop* confirmed, getting up and pouring each of them a glass, while Amanda checked the settings on her voice-recorder.

'Sorry, no ice', he apologised as he handed the glass to her; 'this is England'.

Amanda smiled at his quip and the tension that had built up in her mind abated slightly.

The Bishop sat back down and after a brief pause, during which each of the enjoyed the refreshing qualities of the most basic of pleasures, he carried on with his rant, going off at a tangent that left Amanda more than a little perplexed.

'Take the biggest subject of the last ten years', he proclaimed, raising an arm in a gesture of irritation; 'climate change and global warming'.

Amanda slumped back in her chair, wondering what she had to do to get her interview back on track.

'Climate change has been going on since the beginning of time, since the big-bang', *the Bishop* announced, 'and will probably continue long after we are gone…that is if we don't manage to blow the planet up first', he added as an aside.

'…Are we humans - and when I say humans I mean politicians - so arrogant, so pretentious or so presumptuous that we think we can control nature and the universe?'

'…Of course we can't, but there are those amongst us, like Al Gore and all his merry men who have whipped up such a hysteria around the idea that we can – *creating wonderfully new and lucrative careers for themselves in the mean-time, might I add* – …and in doing so, they have opened the door for any number of exploitative and financially incompetent governments around the world to jump on the bandwagon and impose as many extra taxes as they can on their long-suffering citizens as long as they label them 'green''.

'…Don't get me wrong', *the Bishop* pursued; 'I am totally against wasting anything, especially energy; anything we can do to improve the way we use the resources available to us is good, but let's get a grip here'.

'…Our planet has been changing and evolving for 400 million years and it will continue to evolve and change, whether mankind likes it or not'.

'…Who the hell do we think we are, that we believe we can change the evolution of this planet and by extension, the whole universe simply by imposing more taxes on people and forcing them to change the voltage in their light bulbs, pretexting that it is a man-made problem'.

Amanda started fidgeting in her seat which was a bad sign.

'…We are insignificant in the universe', *the Bishop* exclaimed, ignoring her patent disinterest, 'but those who are fanatical about this cause should really look at the bigger picture and prioritise their attacks against the world's biggest polluters first; i.e. the USA, China and India – because, it is all very well, us in the UK *going green*, or even the whole of Europe *going green*, it will not make an iota of difference if the rest of the world isn't doing the same'.

Amanda wanted to interrupt at this point but again she didn't get the chance, taking his hand signal as a sign that he wanted to finish his thought.

'…Now', he said, '…going back to Al Gore, one of those making a pile of cash from this issue'.

'…Studies have shown that his scare-mongering film, An Inconvenient Truth, contains at least nine glaring, scientifically proved errors which completely discredit the film; even a US judge called it 'distinctly alarmist'.

'…the man is a total hypocrite, flying around the world in private jets and preaching to others about cutting their carbon emissions'.

'…Did you know', he asked, staring directly at his indifferent audience, 'did you know that this 'defender of the environment', this 'prophet of profit', served up an endangered species of fish for his daughter's wedding reception?…that's how much he cares about saving the planet; that's how much he cares about protecting the environment'.

'…He is just using the Climate Change and Global Warming bandwagon to feather his retirement years, and very successfully too;…he has, after all, become the first carbon billionaire', *the Bishop* confirmed.

Amanda raised an eyebrow and cleared her throat. 'I'm sorry; you're losing me slightly; …what's the connection here exactly', she asked flippantly.

'The connection is that once again, it is the few – and in this case the conceited, hypocritical, conniving few – who are dictating to the many – and I would also like to add at this point, that since the Nobel Prize committee became politically correct and contrived to attribute the peace prize to this man for his misleading film, they have gone right down in my estimations too….although they did already have form in that regard; by handing the same prize to Henry Kissinger during the Vietnam War, which I suppose set a precedence in poor integrity', *the Bishop* snarled.

Amanda jumped in again, not to be denied.

'Obama's just got it', she chimed in without thinking, hoping that the image of the as-yet-untarnished new president would somehow offer her country a little respite from the mauling it was taking from *the Bishop's* unending verbal onslaught.

However, even as the words left her mouth, she regretted it immediately, realising too late that she should have bitten her tongue.

A deafening silence instantly engulfed the room.

'That figures', *the Bishop* pounced sarcastically, with surprisingly measured hostility considering his propos; 'the USA is currently fighting two wars in Iraq and Afghanistan and its president gets the Peace Prize…'.

He shrugged his shoulders and gulped down the rest of his water while Amanda did the same, kicking herself for slipping up like that.

'…And do you know who Al Gore was in competition with for that prize; who he beat with his misleading error-ridden slide-show', *the Bishop* piped up again after another brief pause for reflection; 'Irena Sendler; Irena Sendler', he insisted; 'a woman that nobody knows but a woman who single-handedly saved 2500 children from the Nazis; that's who', he exclaimed in frustration.

'Okay, point taken', Amanda acknowledged; annoyed with herself for being rattled and destabilised by *the Bishop's* overpowering dialogue.

'…But tell me sir', she hit back facetiously, a rare blush of embarrassment on her cheeks;

'…As you seem to know all the answers; what would you do about the problem?', she insisted, a little flustered, not used to playing second fiddle in a two way conversation…and this time, it was *the Bishop* who sat back, pensively.

'Look, Ms Brooke…Global Warming or Climate Change is a reality; nobody disputes that, but I repeat, it is something that our planet has been doing cyclically for millions of years. It is not man-made and the carbon-management business which has now sprouted up and swept the world is no more than political and corporate greed gone mad; they have tapped into the psyche of normal people, into their natural, inherent fears of the unknown, and are exploiting it to the max, supporting it with phoney scientific evidence that they are manipulating to make it fit the cause'.

'I know, as you do I'm sure that immoral people capitalising on the innocence and naiveté of others to attain their own goals is a story as old as mankind itself, but rather than watch Al Gore's misleading film, I would suggest that people watch Dr Iain Stewart's programme; Earth; The Power of the Planet…or Tony Robinson's film 'Catastrophe'…or read Ian Plimer's book; 'Heaven & Earth; global warming; the missing science'.

'These programmes show the reality of how our planet has evolved and will continue to evolve without the exploitative, apocalyptic imagery currently being flashed across our screens daily by the scare-mongering powers that be'.

'That's what I would recommend as a way of getting a better understanding as to the evolution of our planet', *the Bishop* affirmed in conclusion.

Amanda was left dumbstruck; she was still really frustrated that she hadn't yet been able to ask the questions she wanted, but at the same time, she could not help but be lost in admiration for *the Bishop's* intelligence, his knowledge and his passion for the things in which he believed, despite his tendency to overcook it.

'I once heard that fear, fear of the future, fear of the unknown, is just man's attempt to justify his own ignorance', she countered, out of the blue.

'Good comment', *the Bishop* applauded, looking directly into her eyes.

'Environmentalists often use the *fear of the unknown* concept to sensationalise their actions and gain some free publicity; then they follow it up with some misinformation to scare and alarm the public; it's just how they operate', he explained looking away pensively.

'The *Great Global-Warning Swindle* was another programme made for Channel Four here in the UK which showed just how the carbon problem had been created and perpetuated by politicians, despite scientific evidence to the contrary, because basically the industry that's grown up around it now keeps hundreds of thousands of people in jobs...and the politicians would rather that than have thousands more unemployed'.

'Their theories, in this programme, based on fact going back many, many years showed that it is actually the sun and the clouds which create cyclical change over the centuries and that the human input to the problem is minimal, ...but of course, their conclusions are ignored because they do not tie in with the official line'.

Amanda just nodded, trying to keep up.

'...But as I said before; who do we think we are that we can cover ourselves with that much self-importance, to the point where we believe that that by our actions alone...and more taxes...we can change the cyclical occurrences in the wider universe?'

'Global warming happens naturally and will continue to happen naturally on a cyclical basis over thousands and millions of years'.

'The politicians of today are simply scare-mongering to maintain control of the masses and using the issue to exploit them'.

'Again, I know that I might be repeating myself, and I assure you that I am not against doing whatever we can to avoid polluting the atmosphere of our planet, but I refuse to accept the psychosis and hysteria put in place by the world's political powers to frighten the masses into paying more taxes for useless environmental measures'.

'Here in England, the former prime minister introduced a stealth tax on air-travel; it was a blatant stunt which did absolutely nothing to help the environmentalists cause...but it did a wonderful job of bringing in more revenue for the incompetent and cash-strapped New Labour government which is basically political fraud.'

Amanda yawned discreetly; she had been a patient audience but time was going on and she had heard enough of his ranting.

The Bishop saw this and recognising that he had gone on for a lot longer than he should have, he apologised unequivocally.

'I'm sorry if I've bored you' he said; 'I'm just fed up of politicians and ex-politicians milking peoples' fears and brow-beating them with error-riddled propaganda so that they can exist and pick up another pay-cheque towards their cosy retirement plan'.

'Evolution is an imperfect and often violent process...but it is inevitable...and doubling the cost of flying or forcing people to change their light bulbs isn't going to alter that', he concluded with finality.

For information;

The Bishop's arguments on Climate-change have been borrowed from 'A Citizen's Blueprint' by Emgee.

Amanda acknowledged his apology and to lighten the mood, catching him completely off-guard, she asked him subtly if he had ever thought of getting married.

The Bishop looked up and paused for a moment before continuing;

'Well, I believe that marriage is a wonderful tradition', he declared; '...but after a while men start to stray when they get disappointed by their wives lack of desire for sexual adventure', he added bluntly, adding a tone to the conversation that was not there previously.

Amanda's eyes bulged, stunned by his response...and despite her confident New York demeanour, she was a little unsettled by its content which she saw as rather inappropriate and sexist. However, before she could voice her disapproval, clasping his hands together tightly in front of him, *the Bishop* qualified his statement.

'Ms Brooke, we are all walking contradictions', he explained, '...and I believe that you are given a choice in life; on the one hand, you can choose hours of fantastic, unbridled sex with as many different partners as you can find...or...on the other...you can choose shared values and common goals...companionship and friendship with one special person, but you can't have both'.

'So, you don't think that it's a commitment issue then?' Amanda prodded, regaining her composure.

The Bishop smiled enigmatically.

'Look', he insisted; '...men are notoriously commitment phobic; it's not really in our genes to be monogamous ...but even those who do want to conform to the social stereotype are now thinking long and hard before doing so...'

'...and why do you think that is?' Amanda queried, finally becoming interested.

'Simple mathematics really', *the Bishop* replied, shrugging his shoulders.

'Men these days are reluctant to commit to long-term relationships because of the divorce laws and the settlement packages being handed out to their ex-wives by the courts, which force them to hand over huge chunks of their hard-earned capital when the relationships turn sour'.

Amanda nodded; 'Yeah'.

'Here in England', *the Bishop* continued 'we have had a series of high profile cases where ex-wives have walked away from their marriages with extraordinary amounts of money and property, and unfortunately a lot of men are no longer prepared to take that risk', he reasoned logically, pausing momentarily.

'It's selfish, I know…from the woman's point of view…but don't you just hate gold-diggers', he complained rather misogynistically.

'Yeah, I understand that', Amanda agreed. 'In the US, we tend to think of gold-diggers as hookers, only smarter'.

'That's one way of putting it', *the Bishop* sniggered, pleased to have found a fellow sceptic and delighted with himself to have once again managed to avoid answering her original question directly.

They both relaxed after that and Amanda was able to conduct a more conventional interview with *the Bishop* from there on in, discussing his life, his career and how the game of chess had flourished since his first meeting with Madison, who he mentioned frequently during the next hour or so of intensely personal conversation…either to compliment her, to flatter her or to shower her with praise.

Finally though, a knock on the door brought the conversation to an end when the Association's secretary popped her head around the door to announce that *the Bishop* had another appointment to attend.

'I'm sorry to interrupt', she declared; 'but the committee is waiting for you Mr Byron in the conference room'.

'Thank you', *the Bishop* acknowledged with an appreciative wave, and with that he stood up and walked around the table to thank Amanda for coming, apologising again for his angry tirades and reminding her politely that they would be meeting up again later anyhow, if she had any further questions to ask.

He then escorted her out of the office, and as they walked down the corridor towards the entrance-hall, being the consummate professional that she was, Amanda quickly resumed the conversation in her mind, just in case anything immediately came to mind.

However, nothing did and as she shook his hand at the front door, the seasoned media executive concluded that while it had been exhausting and frustrating at times, the **tête-à-tête** with *the Bishop* had been the most fascinating and enlightening experience she had had in a very long while… and that the material she had gathered would most definitely make for a very intriguing article.

That evening, as part of their agreement, Amanda was invited, along with the rest of the chess fraternity, to a banquet organised by the ECA to celebrate *the Bishop's* stellar career.

It was a rather staid, typically-British, black-tie affair, but during the evening Amanda was introduced to many of *the Bishop's* contemporaries… and each of them in turn showed their respect and admiration for the retiring champion, by providing her with a pertinent comment…or an amusing anecdote about him…which she jotted down with her usual perspicacity, knowing that she would be able to sprinkle them throughout her up-coming article, just as Madison had done before her.

CHAPTER TWENTY-FOUR

Ten days later, back in New York;

The elevator emitted its familiar 'ping'…announcing its arrival…and when the doors opened, and the two people waiting for it, parted to let her through, Amanda emerged onto the office-floor with her usual sure-footed strut…and her inimitable self-confident manner.

Her hair was pulled back in a ponytail…*which was unusual but not uncommon*…and her eyes were hidden behind dark sunglasses…because of the jet-lag…but what was most-startling about her…was…her outfit.

Amanda always, but always, wore a pristine, dark-coloured business suit…often with matching trousers…but here she was dressed in a scarlet-red couture-dress accessorised with a classic Chanel jacket, a colourful Hermes scarf…and heels a little higher than usual, looking absolutely stunning.

People all around looked at her with amazement as she strolled past, their eyes widening in shock and their jaws dropping in disbelief as they followed her 'almost regal' progression down the corridor towards her office.

In fact, many of those in the immediate vicinity found themselves doing a double-take…*because it was so out of character for Amanda to dress this way*…although predictably not one of them dared to comment or even catch her eye as the woman, known by most as 'the nanny', sauntered past oblivious.

Even Gayle… who had worked for Amanda for longer than she cared to remember…was suddenly taken aback when she saw this person coming towards her…not realising until almost the very last moment…that it was indeed her boss.

'Oh…, good…good morning Amanda…' she stammered, suddenly finding herself scrambling to remain cool, calm and collected as she grabbed Amanda's diary…*and all the notes and messages that she had accumulated during her absence*…before following her boss into the office…and closing the door behind them.

Meanwhile, down in the Fashion department, the morning meeting was already under way.

Gretchen was still there supervising and overseeing everything… but for the most part it was Madison who set the agenda…and led the discussion…although she was careful to take on board any ideas and suggestions that her colleagues around the table might come up with…in an effort to include them…and to start gaining their trust.

The meeting took just over an hour to complete…and when it came to a close…and everybody else started wandering back to their workstations…Madison stayed behind with Gretchen for just a little while longer, *in order to go through a quick debrief of what had been said…and decided*…before gathering up all her bits and pieces and making her way upstairs.

(She knew that Amanda was due back that morning and had arranged with Gayle to see her straight after the morning meeting at 11:30)

Ten minutes later;

Her shoulders back and her chin up, Madison strolled confidently into Amanda's office, Gayle waving her in from across the corridor where she was stood by the photocopy-machine.

Amanda was sat there behind her desk, deep in thought, her elbows planted firmly on the desk and her hands clasped together under her chin.

'So…how was London?' Madison asked inquisitively, getting straight to the point as she sat down.

Amanda reached idly for a glossy magazine that just happened to be lying there on her desk and stared at the cover photo for a moment or two, using the time to formulate her response.

'London was great', she replied, very business-like.

'And the…the Bishop', Madison asked haltingly, not wanting to be too obvious.

Amanda leaned back in her chair and took a deep breath, making Madison wait again for her response.

'The…He was very civil…and very gentlemanly', she remarked with unexpected courtesy.

Madison nodded politely, her stomach tightening.

'You know Madison…I can see now why you liked….why you enjoyed…that guy's company. He just exudes charm…and charisma…' Amanda then observed, sitting forward again in her chair.

Madison just sat there…her arms crossed…but sensing a hidden meaning to her boss's characterisation of *the Bishop*, her blood pressure started to rise.

'…In fact, I would have to say Madison…' Amanda continued, as if she was deliberately trying to provoke her young colleague, '…that meeting him…one on one…was one of the most exhilarating experiences I have had in a long while…and it left me drenched in sexual energy'.

'Eew', Madison replied with a grimace, doing her best not to take the bait…; 'Anyhow, I have the provisional-template here for next week's issue…' she announced quickly, changing the subject as she flipped through her folder and produced the 'said file'.

'Thank-you Madison; just leave it there', Amanda responded, gesturing to the corner of her desk.

The sound of Gayle's voice on the intercom suddenly interrupted this awkward exchange.

'Amanda…Quinton Booth from Marketing is here to see you', she announced.

'Who?' Amanda queried, sounding more than a little disinterested.

'The new guy', Gayle explained succinctly.

'Fine; show him in, we're done here', Amanda instructed.

Moments later, the door opened and a rather tall man with a strong, muscular build entered the office and strolled right up to the desk.

Amanda didn't get up…but with just a tired gesture of the hand she quickly introduced the 'new guy';

'Madison, this is Quinton Booth…Todd's replacement in Marketing; Quinton this is Madison Chatfield from our Fashion department'.

A little bemused, *her mind still assimilating what Amanda had said about the Bishop*, Madison slowly got up from her chair and shook the guy's hand; 'Welcome to the team', she said with a friendly smile before turning back to Amanda to signal that she needed to get on.

'Of course Madison…I'll have a look at that template when I get a minute', Amanda announced assertively as her younger colleague headed for the door.

'Nice to meet you too…Madison', the new guy commented as he watched her leave.

Madison reached the door, half-turned and smiled again stiffly…but she didn't respond.

'I hope he's better than the last guy', she whispered to Gayle as she made her way past, still having a little difficulty keeping her emotions in check after what Amanda had said to her about *the Bishop*.

Gayle…ever the professional…just looked up, smiled diplomatically and then carried on typing.

Madison carried on walking and was just about to press the call-button on the elevator when the doors opened and two middle-aged men came rushing out;

'Happy wife; happy life' the one was saying the other. 'Great formula', the second man replied with a snort as they brushed past Madison and headed off down the corridor.

She watched them go and then, as she stepped inside the cabin Madison allowed herself a brief, self-satisfied smile. Maybe the feminist message is finally getting through, she thought to herself, her spirits suddenly lifted by that moment of positivity.

Later that same day, Madison was making her way down to the Admin office on the ground floor when who should be in the elevator but Amanda, on her way out to a meeting downtown.

The two women exchanged a cursory smile and having checked that the button for the ground floor was lit-up, Madison immediately took advantage of the fact that it was just the two of them, alone in the cabin, to compliment her boss on her new look.

'I didn't say anything earlier…because the new guy was there…but I like the new image', she murmured with a discreet hand gesture.

Amanda didn't reply but her rather hard stare did fade slightly as the doors suddenly re-opened to allow another young woman with stylishly-short blonde hair to join them on the ride down.

'Thanks', the young woman mumbled to nobody in particular as she turned around to face the doors and began rummaging in her bag for her phone.

The doors closed again and moments later all three women stepped out of the elevator on the ground floor, the young blonde-woman hurrying away in one direction just as a weird young man…*carrying a beat-up folder and wearing a pair of ill-fitting jeans slung low around his thighs…* approached Amanda and Madison from another…to ask them if they could direct him to the HR office.

Slightly taken aback, the two women looked at each other…and seeing Amanda's horrified expression Madison quickly took it upon herself to ask the young man if he had an appointment…*which he did…*before immediately redirecting him to the reception-desk across the lobby, informing him that somebody over there would be able to take care of him.

'Appreciate it', the young man acknowledged with a grateful smile as he turned and walked away.

'I see you've learned the security protocol', Amanda remarked before turning away…and then turning back again…having seen the waistband of the young man's underpants as he sauntered away from them across the lobby;

'Heads up Madison; if that guy can't even figure out how to pull his pants all the way up, I think he might find working here too much of a challenge.'

Madison just stood there, shrugged and rolled her eyes, before turning herself and making her way through the security doors to the Admin office.

The rest of that week went by pretty quickly with Madison managing to keep the Fashion department on an even keel…for the most part… thanks to Gretchen's steadying hand.

However, Amanda's comments about *the Bishop* had played on her mind more than she would care to admit…during her rare moments of down-time…or when she was alone in the office…and as the weekend approached she decided that she needed to talk to somebody about it; that and all the other pointless feminine jealousies and frustrations that had built up in her head.

Of course, Evie was her go-to person in these kinds of situations…and as they hadn't had a chance to meet up since her return from England, Madison decided that this would be the ideal opportunity for them to get together.

Unfortunately, it wasn't convenient for her to call Evie right in that moment…what with all the people coming and going in the office…but a while later, she did manage to take a minute, to bring up Evie's number on her phone's contact list and call it.

Evie's phone rang reassuringly…but for once it went straight to voice-mail…*which surprised Madison somewhat as Evie always picked up her calls*…but then as she noticed the time on the top of the phone's little screen Madison suddenly realised that Evie was probably busy in her job too…and as a consequence she rang off and just keyed in a text message instead, asking Evie to call her when she had a moment.

That call came through thirty minutes later …bringing an instant smile to Madison's face when she saw Evie's name written large on her phone's little screen…and filled with the warmth that only a genuine friendship can ever provide she promptly picked up the phone.

The two women briefly exchanged the usual heartfelt cordialities that their friendship epitomized…but then…not wanting the call to get too involved, *because she still had a thousand things to do*, Madison quickly suggested that they go for lunch…or for one of their long walks in Central Park on the weekend.

'Yeah; of course…why not?' Evie responded immediately without thinking…

…but then there was a pause on the line as she hesitated…

'Ohhh, sorry; sorry Maddy, I just remembered, I'm busy this weekend…I've got a thing…'

'You've got a thing…?' Madison repeated with a frown.

'Yeah, sorry Mad…but…I could meet you for a drink tomorrow evening (Friday)…if that works for you', Evie offered, sensing her friend's disappointment.

'That would be great; where should we…?' Madison was about to ask before Evie interrupted her again.

'Sorry Mad, my boss is coming; let's say 'The Deuces…at 6:30'.

'Fine; I'll see you there 'E'…6:30 at the De…' Madison barely had time to confirm before the phone went dead.

The following evening;

Madison walked into 'The Deuces'…a typical Manhattan bar full of clean-cut smiles and trendy clothes…at precisely 6:30 to find Evie already sat there waiting for her.

'Wow; you're early', she exclaimed, her surprised tone tinged with more than a hint of irony.

'I am, but don't be flip, girl', Evie replied, getting up off her stool and giving her friend a big hug.

'…And looking good', Madison commented, throwing her friend a warm and sincere compliment.

'You know me Mad.' Evie retorted, clicking her fingers and performing an impromptu dance-move, '…classy but sassy'.

It was true; Evie looked stunning in her monochrome dress…the black and white checks of which ironically resembled a chess-board…while in comparison, Madison looked quite demure and boring, still dressed as she was in her charcoal-grey, cropped-trouser work-clothes

'Oh my god…' Madison suddenly shrieked looking down at herself, 'I just realised that I'm turning into my boss'.

'Yeah, if she was twenty years younger…and hot', Evie scoffed as she turned to the barman and ordered two mimosas (champagne and orange juice) while Madison settled herself down on the stool next to her…the image of Amanda's stylish new look suddenly flashing annoyingly in front of her mind's eye.

The drinks were served and then, having taken their first sip, the two friends quickly caught up with each other's lives, Madison quickly updating Evie on *the Bishop…which was quite brief as there was nothing to tell…*before she moved on to Amanda, telling her all about Amanda's trip to London…and her comments about *the Bishop* after their meeting while she was there.

'Can you believe what she said to me…?' Madison asked…almost rhetorically…and barely concealing her indignant rage.

Evie didn't answer but just waited for the inevitable follow-up.

'…That meeting him had left her...and I quote; 'drenched in sexual energy'', Madison spat out, throwing up imaginary air quotes around those last two words.

'Eew', Evie did reply this time, looking incredulous as she took another sip from her glass, '...but I can see what she means...' she added mischievously; '...That guy has a kind of raw, animal sex-appeal that you can almost smell'.

'Woah...hello...!' Madison remonstrated, rolling her eyes and fighting to maintain her composure.

'I'm just saying...' Evie teased with a saucy grin, being deliberately provocative in order to gauge her friend's reaction; '...if I were you, I'd watch that bitch; next thing you know her panties will be draped over you-know-who's bed-post'.

'Amanda? No...I don't think so; she's not that kind...' Madison pooh-poohed, her eyes suddenly narrowing with uncertainty as her voice trailed off.

'Anyway...' Evie remarked nonchalantly, raising a hand to gently rub her neck, '...why do you care; the guy's history; right?'

'Right', Madison agreed, taking another sip from her drink; '...but you know...girl code'.

'Girl code?' Evie questioned.

'Girl code', Madison repeated, '...that unwritten rule which states that no woman should ever go after another woman's man...' she clarified as if it was some kind of feminist mantra.

'That's bullshit' Evie spluttered; 'there's no such thing. This is the 21st century Mad; women go after each others' men...and their friends' exes all the time.'

'We just can't help ourselves', she continued, '...we are sexual beings filled with passion and desire...and when it comes to men...we are not the angels of integrity that we like to tell each other we are...'

'Wow; where did that come from; who are you and what have you done with my friend?', Madison suddenly questioned, a look of complete bewilderment on her face.

'You see Mad...', Evie explained, having taken another sip of her delicious cocktail, '...it's all down to feminism; the feminists came along and told women that they could go out and do whatever they wanted...that they no longer had to wait around for a man, that it was okay for them to take the lead...to take control and to enjoy their sexuality...so that's just what women are doing.'

'Yeah, but that doesn't mean you get carte-blanche to go out and grab any man that takes your fancy…' Madison retorted with more than a degree of tension in her voice.

'Interpret it as you like, Maddy girl, but this is our time…and I for one am going to enjoy every moment of it…as I'm sure your boss is', Evie replied, raising her glass with another of her impish grins.

'Thanks for that reassuring pep-talk', Madison exclaimed a little sarcastically, before taking an extra-large swallow from her own glass.

'Maaad…you need to lighten up girl and get back in the game', Evie suddenly urged, tapping her friend on the forearm.

'But E, I'm not like you', Madison quickly responded, feeling a little confused.

'Like me?' Evie questioned, raising her eyebrows

'An exhibitionist', Madison clarified, lowering her tone.

Evie scoffed. 'I'm not an exhibitionist', she countered again almost choking on her cocktail, 'I'm just somebody who likes to enjoy those moments when spontaneity and lust overcome discretion and precaution.'

Madison could only shrug, lost for a follow-up comment. 'So anyway; what's wrong with your neck…?' she asked trying to steer the conversation away from *the Bishop* or any more potential, inter-personal, feminine controversy; '…Long day?' she added as a prompt.

'Heavy night' Evie joked, looking at her friend and trying to suppress a titter…before she exploded in a burst of uncontrolled laughter.

This time Madison just shook her head and rolled her eyes.

'What can I say Mad', Evie exclaimed, shrugging her shoulders and throwing up her arms like an Italian; '…the best things in life are free!'

Just at that moment, the guy who was sat next to them…and *who had been listening idly to their conversation…*suddenly got up to go to the men's room and unfortunately knocked Evie's elbow on the way past spilling what remained of her drink.

'Zookers', Evie cried out, as she looked down to see if her dress had taken a hit.

'Zookers?' Madison repeated questioningly, grabbing the serviette from under her glass and handing it to her friend.

'Yeah…Zookers', Evie explained as she took the serviette and brushed off her dress; 'I'm trying to get it trending instead of '*for fuck's sake*'…; it sounds a little less vulgar'.

Again Madison just shook her head.

'I'm very sorry…are you okay?', the guy asked, turning around and holding up his hands apologetically, before addressing the barman and asking him to serve the two women two more of the same, on him.

'…That is, unless you ladies consider me buying you another drink as sexual harassment in this brave new world', he remarked, looking directly at Evie.

'Actually, I heard just yesterday that they were going to upgrade it to a hate-crime…but on this occasion we'll let it slide', Evie riposted with her usual quick-witted repartee.

The guy just smiled…apologised again…and then carried on to the men's room while Evie and Madison settled back down and returned to their conversation.

However, while they continued chatting Evie started checking her phone at regular intervals.

'Do you have somewhere else to be?' Madison asked inquisitively, after about the third or fourth look.

'I do actually…' Evie explained, '…We're having a 'girls' night out'; …it's Michelle's birthday'.

'Aha, so that's why you're all 'glammed-up', Madison interjected, suddenly feeling a little awkward.

'Yeah', Evie confessed, looking down and brushing her dress again, '…but, you know Mad, you rang me last minute…and I wanted to be here for you…just in case it was something urgent.'

'You should have said E; this could have waited…we could have rescheduled…' Madison argued, suddenly starting to feel a little uncomfortable.

'I know…' Evie agreed, '…but…'

'Look', Madison remarked, resting her hand on her friend's arm; 'If you need to head out 'E'…it's no big deal…really…go for it', she encouraged.

'Are you sure?' Evie responded…

'…You know, you're welcome to join us…' she added, suddenly feeling her own rush of guilt over the eagerness in her voice.

'No…no…I'll pass this time…' Madison countered with an understanding grin, '…but you go ahead; enjoy'.

'Okay then…as long as you're sure', Evie confirmed, before checking her phone once again…and finishing her drink.

'I'll be in touch', she announced as she slipped on her rather distinctive bubble-gum-pink jacket and gave Madison another huge hug before heading out…pausing just briefly at the door to turn and wave her friend goodbye.

Madison waved back with a smile…and then…feeling suddenly alone…she just sat there at the bar…playing with the rim of her glass and staring out the window, a look of despondent abandonment settling slowly into the tired features of her overworked face.

A while later, as Madison was quietly making her way home…alone; Evie was walking into Frank's bar to be met with a barrage of hollers… 'Evie; where the hell have you been?'

Diane, Kelly and Kim had clearly been sat there for quite some time, and had already started the celebrations without her…or indeed the 'guest of honour'.

'We were just about to send out a search party for you', Kim shouted out.

'Yeah; we thought you might have gotten yourself lost…' Kelly threw in.

'…Or side-tracked by some hunk', Kim added, jokingly.

'Is Michelle with you?' Diane asked, pushing away her empty glass.

'Yeah, is Michelle with you?' Kelly repeated, 'After all, it is <u>her</u> fricking birthday'.

'No', Evie replied, making her way over to the table; 'she's not…'

The three women looked at each other a little confused…but Evie had barely reached the table and removed her coat when Michelle did appear…

right behind her…doing just the same with her coat as a chorus of 'happy birthday' shouts rang around the table filling the air in the immediate vicinity with a cacophony of sound.

'Oh my god Michelle, you look like Lana', Kim suddenly blurted out, spraying Diane…who was sat opposite her…with 'champagne bubbles'.

'Lana…?' Michelle queried, looking puzzled as she folded her coat.

'Lana…Lana Kane! Surely you've heard of...; oh, never mind', Kim groaned, brushing aside Michelle's obvious bewilderment…and ignorance of her pop-culture reference.

'Yeah, it's true; that mini sweater-dress with its thigh-skimming hemline is enough to send any red-blooded man's pulse racing skywards', Diane quipped, while still wiping her face.

…and with that the three women…Diane, Kelly and Kim…all raised their glasses and clinked them to a chorus of 'Danger Zone!'

Evie just smirked at her friends' teasing and quickly ordered two more glasses of champagne…for herself and Michelle…before they took their seats too…and within no time all five women were toasting Michelle's birthday once again.

♝

The last person in their group, Octavia, arrived just a few minutes later.

'Who do you think you are…Lana Kane?' she said on seeing Michelle.

'Told you', the other women all cheered as one.

Michelle just grimaced and…feeling slightly put-upon for a 'birthday-girl'…she quickly took another drink of champagne…gulping down a little too much in her haste…which made her cough and splutter as a consequence…much to the amusement of the rest of the group.

'Now look what you've made me do', she blurted out as she tried desperately to regain her composure.

♝

Octavia pulled up a chair and while she and the others started catching up on the latest gossip, Michelle discreetly wiped down the table in front of her before grabbing her phone, opening Google and searching for images of this 'Lana Kane' person, whoever she might be'.

More drinks were brought to the table and within no time, the whole group was laughing out loud again as they all sat there…enjoying the teasing, the sharing and the camaraderie that only a close-knit peer-group can offer.

Then, all of a sudden, in the middle of all the joviality and high-jinks going on at the table Evie's phone began to ring.

She let it ring for a while and then putting down her glass, she idly checked the caller-ID, thinking that it could be Madison.

However, on this occasion it wasn't; in fact, the screen read simply 'unknown caller' which intrigued Evie somewhat as most of the people she knew were indexed in her contact-list.

'Looks like I'm going to have to take this; it might be important', she announced to the table…not having a clue who was on the other end of the line but unable to stymie her curiosity.

Her statement prompted a chorus of remarks from all around the table, *some filled with risqué innuendo…others suggesting simply that she should ignore it*…but Evie being Evie, she wouldn't be swayed and cutting short any discussion, she quickly got up from her seat, took a few steps away from the table…to isolate herself from the crowd…and then put the phone up to her ear.

A weird voice came on the line….

'Gary…is that you?' she asked.

A few weeks later;

Amanda's article was published on the weekend just before Christmas and naturally it was given all the preferential treatment that her position in the paper afforded her; a glossy centre-spread combined with a brilliant photo display…both of the Bishop himself and some of the people who knew him… and anybody who read it, lauded it as a great success.

Everybody found it tougher, more pertinent and much more journalistically competent in the way it portrayed the Bishop, which contrasted quite unashamedly with the original picture that Madison had painted of him as a dour, humourless recluse – and the very nature of that contrast intrigued readers to the point that sales figures for the paper went through the roof that weekend.

On the Monday morning Amanda's article was on everybody's lips and as always rumours had started to fly around the building...*on the gossip grape-vine*...about how 'the Nanny' (Amanda) had somehow succeeded in finding out so much more intimate detail about *the Bishop* than her younger counterpart had done previously.

Of course, like the rest of the staff, Madison heard these rumours too...and as Gretchen had now gone off to fulfil her maternal duty...*after a small but very enjoyable baby-shower that she (Madison) had organised*... she decided, as acting head of fashion, that she would pop up to Amanda's office once again...after the morning meeting...to congratulate her on her article, in the vain hope that maybe her boss would let something slip on those rumours...or indeed dismiss them completely...which seemed the more likely option in her view.

She was also curious to find out whether or not *the Bishop* had mentioned her at all during the interview as she had not heard from him since her return...especially as Evie's comments in the bar...although wildly speculative...had unsettled her more than she cared to admit.

The morning meeting lasted just over an hour, during which time Madison's thoughts wandered constantly...but once it was over, she immediately headed upstairs only to be confronted outside the conference room by a couple of young interns who were bubbling over with excitement at the gossip going around the building.

'Hey Madison...' one of them asked; 'What's with all these stories about 'the Nanny' hooking up with that bishop guy?'

Madison just shook her head and continued walking, 'Don't take any notice girls; it's just office gossip', she replied confidently without turning around, thereby avoiding any attempt the two young women might make to engage her in a more prolonged and embarrassing discussion.

The two young interns followed on behind for a moment…but then stopped at the water-cooler, still giggling and hypothesising while Madison continued on until she came to a halt in front of the elevators, where she took a moment or two to compose herself before pushing the call button.

A few deep breaths helped calm her nerves but then, before she knew it, one of the elevator doors opened and a UPS delivery-guy came bowling out of the cabin, a package in one hand and his electronic delivery monitor in the other.

'Hi there', he mumbled; 'Mr Dupree's office?' he asked hurriedly.

'That way', Madison indicated, pointing off to her right.

'Thank-you Miss', the guy replied before rushing off without further ado.

Madison watched him go, then stepped into the lift and pressed the button which would take her up to the executive level; it only took a few seconds and as the doors pinged and swept aside like the doors to the bridge on the USS Enterprise, her mind which had already begun to wander and wonder again after the intern's question, suddenly regained its professional focus.

She walked out…smiling pleasantly at two or three people who were milling around in the hallway-area…and made her way directly to Amanda's office, checking briefly with Gayle that she was free…and given the green light…continuing on in.

However, as she approached the actual door itself Madison was suddenly stopped in her tracks; hit by an invisible force.

The door was ajar and inside, she could hear *His* voice.

He was here; *the Bishop* was here, her mind screamed at her...in Amanda's office.

Madison's heart jumped with conflicting emotions and equal amounts of excitement and panic as she shuffled closer to the door, not wanting to give away her presence…but hoping secretly to overhear something that she might enjoy…an indiscretion or a compliment.

Leaning forward, she listened at the door for a few moments, just to make absolutely certain that she wasn't hallucinating, but knowing *the Bishop's* voice like she did; there was no way that she could mistake it.

Meanwhile, behind her, two other people were approaching Gayle's desk…*probably Amanda's next appointment*...so, forced into action Madison quickly composed herself once again, cleared her throat and knocked on the door, walking straight into the office with her usual nonchalance, even though she felt her heart thumping so loud that she thought that Gayle might hear it from where she was sat…at her desk.

However, the office was empty…even though *the Bishop's* voice continued to fill the empty space.

Madison took a deep breath and held it momentarily to settle her nerves.

It was a little weird but staring at Amanda's desk, she suddenly realised that the voice she had recognised so instantaneously was in fact being relayed by a small digital recorder.

Her shoulders fell and as she took another deep breath - which could have doubled as a sigh - Amanda appeared from her private bathroom, obviously very pleased with herself.

'Oh, I was just checking on something he said', her boss explained casually, noticing immediately that Madison's attention was fixed on the little gadget.

'John from legal wanted to…never mind; what brings you up here', Amanda asked coldly, walking back to her chair.

Madison shook her head to bring herself back to her senses.

'Oh I…um', Madison stuttered, sitting down without being asked.

Amanda sat down too, pulling herself forward behind her desk and breathing in deeply, before reaching out and stopping the little machine.

'Handy little thing this', she quipped, before storing it away in the top drawer of her desk.

'So…; what brings you to my office', she repeated with prescience.

'Well…as acting head-of-fashion…' Madison announced, her mind still a little confused…and somewhat disappointed, '…I just wanted to congratulate you on your article…'

'You did? Thank you', Amanda replied, enjoying the compliment. 'I had forgotten just how much fun it could be; it's been such a long time since I did a piece like that', she declared extravagantly, obviously basking in all the attention and the plaudits that were being thrown her way since the article had been published.

Madison frowned. 'Amanda, I hope you don't mind me asking this …but…did he…umm…did he…mention me at all during your discussions', she enquired.

Amanda paused deliberately, to keep Madison waiting for her reply… and as luck would have it, the phone on her desk began to ring too, prolonging the wait even further.

'Well?' Madison prompted, once her boss had hung up; '…Did he?'

'No, as a matter of fact, as I recall, your name never came up', Amanda lied, simultaneously writing down the new appointment in her diary so as not to look Madison in the eye.

'Never', Madison queried in consternation; 'not even once?'

'No', Amanda confirmed; '…but I have to say that I did find the guy fascinating, if a little unpredictable at times…just as you had mentioned previously', she stated, cruelly exploiting Madison's show of weakness; 'As I said in the article, the guy has a natural presence, an authority about him that…'

She was disappointed but seeing the look of self-satisfaction on her boss's face and hearing the way she was showering her former lover with praise - which really wasn't her style - Madison immediately jumped to the erroneous conclusion that something must have gone on between them.

'Are you saying that he made a pa…?' She began to ask, cutting off her boss in full flow.

Amanda interrupted her in turn with a very authoritative tut, tut, tut, and dismissed Madison's question with her staple response that she didn't discuss personal issues with her subordinates.

'…and besides, even if he did, it is none of your business'; she confirmed crushing Madison's show of thinly-veiled jealousy.

Madison was suddenly speechless and feeling reprimanded for the first time in a long while, she quietly apologised and smiled; a smile so tight that her features barely moved.

She had seen how Amanda had looked at the Bishop when she had come to visit the exhibition match that they had organised, and as far as she was concerned, her boss's lack of denial...and her new softer, feminine style...was as good as an admission of guilt.

'Okay then, back to work,' Amanda declared guiltily, looking at her watch.

Madison took this as her cue to leave, got up with a nod of the head and then left without another word, feeling somehow betrayed...by both her boss and her ex-lover.

But why, she wondered as she made her way back to the lift; why were her emotions so conflicted; after all, she was no longer with him...she had no intention of ever seeing him again...so why the show of jealousy?

She could only put it down to that very succinct feminine logic which suggested in her own mind that Amanda had somehow committed the ultimate sisterhood betrayal...and that...*despite what Evie had said about 'girl-code' in the bar*...it had sparked her emotional confusion, even though she and *the Bishop* were no longer an item, if indeed they ever were.

♝

Christmas came and went that year and for the next few months Madison was inundated with work due to Gretchen's absence...and didn't have much time to herself for socialising.

Even her regular chats with Evie dried up as she began spending more and more time at the office doing longer and longer hours in order to keep on top of all the work that was being pushed her way.

This was good for her in some respect as once again it proved her commitment and dedication to her 'bosses upstairs'...but it also kept her from indulging her demons and thinking about what might have been... with the maddening enigma that was *the Bishop*.

Then one day, in mid-March, while taking a short-cut through Macy's, her head full of the new season's fashions, Madison unexpectedly bumped into Evie who was there checking out the perfume section.

It had been a while since they had seen each other but their warm embrace left no doubt that this was two life-long friends, pleased to be renewing their bond, no matter the circumstances.

Evie was clearly in one of her excited moods but once they had exchanged the usual social pleasantries, her first concern was for Madison whom she had tried to call on several occasions over the Christmas period without ever getting a response.

'Where have you been; I've been trying to get in touch with you?' She scolded.

'Did I say something…or do something to flip you off?' she enquired anxiously, her natural paranoia coming to the fore.

'No, of course not 'E'' Madison replied, resting her hand on her friend's arm.

'So why haven't you been returning my calls?' Evie insisted heavily; 'that's not like you; is something wrong?'

Madison frowned; 'I'm sorry; it's a poor excuse I know, but I have just been so busy since stepping in to replace Gretchen that I haven't had time to think'.

Evie gave her another hug.

'So, what's up with you?' Madison asked, pulling away from the embrace and smartly diverting the attention back to her friend; 'you seem…happy…is there something I should know?'

Evie grinned and took another step back, having difficulty disguising the stars in her eyes.

'Look…Vivian Westwood', she announced, opening her powder-blue coat to show off her new bold-patterned statement dress.

'I picked up in London' she confirmed, mentally rememorizing the fun she and Gary had had in the changing rooms when doing so.

'You were in London?' Madison repeated, not sure that she had heard right.

'Yes, that's what I was trying to tell you about, but you weren't answering my calls', Evie confirmed in a tone of false reprimand; 'I went over to see Gary'.

'Really…? Gary?' Madison quizzed; 'how is he?'

'Gary…? Oh, he's fine but I was sorry to hear about your guy's illness', she sympathised, assuming wrongly that Madison already knew.

'Whose illness, what illness?' Madison questioned trying to digest the information calmly, even though the words had hit her like rifle shots; 'You mean…?'

'Yeah…him'; Evie confirmed.

'Oh my god; I haven't heard from him since last summer…but it never occurred to me that he could be…ill', Madison confessed feeling a little guilty, all of a sudden.

'Oh, I'm not exactly sure what's wrong with him…nor the prognosis', Evie continued, surprised by her friend's revelation…'…but Gary did say something about him trying to surprise you with a visit at New Year… probably to tell you all about it himself', she explained; '…unfortunately, he was stopped at the airport by the immigration services and refused entry'.

'Are you serious?' Madison exclaimed ruefully, a sinking feeling suddenly gripping her in the pit of her stomach.

'Yeah, apparently', Evie confirmed, lowering her tone; '…since 9/11, Homeland Security has stepped up airport security; …they are all paranoid over there about terrorists getting into the country'.

'In fact, when I came back through myself last week, some guy I was talking to, told me that they were using those new powers to stop anyone with an opinion from entering the country…and after your boss's article about your guy being so outspoken and all, I suppose they deemed he was a threat and put him on the list of *persona non grata*', Evie surmised distractedly; her gaze suddenly drawn to a rather handsome-looking passer-by.

Madison shook her head and rolled her eyes, deeply shocked by the news of the *Bishop's* illness…and especially by that of his aborted visit to see her…but rather than show her frustration in front of Evie - and then have her friend bombard her with a thousand questions, none of which she wanted to answer – she decided not to let her emotions transpire.

Evie focussed again and looking into Madison's eyes she suggested they go for a coffee.

'Sorry 'E', I'm pushed for time today', Madison replied, '...but we should get lunch...at Carlo's...some time soon.'

'Yeah...I suppose that could work too', Evie responded, shrugging her shoulders in disappointment.

'Okay hon, I have to get going now', Madison announced,' ...but give me a call to sort out that lunch...'

'No...; you call me Mad', Evie replied a little despondently, '; you're the one with the busy schedule.'

'Yeah, that would probably be best', Madison agreed...and with that Evie quickly turned around and disappeared into the crowd with a flustered wave.

Meanwhile, still a little baffled by what she had learned, Madison stood motionless for a few seconds in the middle of Macy's, her face turning paper-white as the blood and the colour drained away from her cheeks.

It only lasted a moment but for that split-second she felt faint, her insides suddenly awash with emotion.

She rushed outside and it was only when the cold New York air hit her face that she realised how thoughtless and unsupportive she had been with Evie.

The news about *the Bishop's* illness had completely thrown her and she had totally forgotten to compliment her friend on her dress or show any interest in her visit to see Gary in London.

She would have to call her later and apologise.

A wailing police-car siren suddenly brought Madison back to her senses...with a jolt...but then, as she hurried back to the office, visions of her time together with *the Bishop*...and of him being turned away at JFK suddenly clouded her mind.

Her emotions were in turmoil but then as she entered her office building...*where the receptionists were ready and waiting to pounce on any hint of weakness they might discern to add to the office gossip*...she managed to push all those negative thoughts aside in a desperate attempt to recover her professional demeanour.

She rushed upstairs...and back in her office, she immediately tried calling the abbey.

The phone on the other end rang almost instantly...and when the rather distinctive tone...*which she could see in her mind's eye ringing forlornly in the abbey's polished hallway*...began resounding in her ear, Madison's heart almost jumped into her mouth.

The phone rang and rang, but despite her insistence, nobody answered...not even the answering-machine...and so with a heavy heart... but no other option available to her...Madison simply hung up with a deep disconsolate sigh, before turning to her computer, typing in her password and carrying on with her life.

In the following weeks, despite her heavy work-load and her imagined if unconfirmed belief that he had betrayed her with Amanda, Madison did try...on a number of other occasions...to get in touch with *the Bishop* in order to enquire about his health...but each time her call was unsuccessful and eventually, lost in the clutter of her mind, it slipped back on her agenda of things to do.

CHAPTER TWENTY-FIVE

Almost five months later

Gretchen had decided that maternity and looking after her new-born son easily trumped a stressful career in fashion and as a result, thanks to her dedication and devotion to hard work Madison was in line to replace her permanently on the fashion department roster as Fashion News Editor

It was a Tuesday morning and upstairs, in one of the executive suites a group of high-ranking managers and shareholders were discussing the possibility of Madison's promotion.

Mr Vance Morgan, one of the major shareholders (who just happened to be the father of the young executive who had propositioned Madison) was speaking…and he was in a typically bombastic mood;

'Listen to me', he was saying with the confidence of a man who was used to people taking notice of what he said; '...the current role of women...in society at large...and in the work-place in particular...is a complete fabrication; an artificial construct created by men to appease people like you...', he pointed at Amanda, '…and the feminist movement…and it has become the bane of our lives...not only here at the paper but everywhere we turn'.

He paused to take breath; '...but let me just say this'; he added slamming the palms of his hands on the table; '...there is no doubt in my mind that before too long the natural order of things will be restored... and women will once again return to their fundamental role of childbirth and childcare – which is – after all – what their bodies are destined to do.'

The room fell silent until Mr Morgan suddenly piped up again; 'Aw, come on people; it's simple biology, for heaven's sake; it might not be in my life-time but one day the men of this country will come to realise the error of their ways ...and they will regain control of this madness...hopefully before it is too late.'

'Now hold on a minute Vance; I can't just let you say that...' Amanda suddenly countered; jumping to her feet, feeling compelled to respond and stand up for her gender. 'I'm sorry but that kind of sexist attitude is no longer acceptable in the modern world. Equality is not some kind of experiment dreamed up by men; it is a right that women have been denied for far too long…and it is time that men like you...'

A knock on the door interrupted her flow, cutting the discussion short.

It was Mr Morgan's PA who was stood there pointing to his watch.

Mr Morgan acknowledged the signal and…inhaling deeply through his nostrils…he immediately suggested they go around the table and take a vote on the proposal in front of them.

'Very well then…' Bruce Hines (CEO) announced; 'All those in favour of the proposal please raise your right ha...'

'You're all fools', Mr Morgan suddenly declared, interrupting the vote and slamming his closed fists down on the desk once again in disapproval.

'You know what Vance; you need to stop being so fucking vindictive and mean-spirited', Amanda argued across the table at him. 'This young woman has already proved that she can do the job…and she deserves to be given a chance…'

'…especially after what you…and all your associates…have put her through', she added as she looked around the table, showing little concern for the fragile masculine egos that stared back at her.

'Is there no-one else you could put forward for the position?' Conrad Elliott (Head of Finance) suddenly chipped in, trying to offer the paper's major shareholder a little moral support; '…Someone a little less… controversial.'

'No, there isn't', Amanda insisted; 'this young woman has already proved that she can do the job…so why would you…why would we, go looking for anyone else?'

'We could always out-source', Milton Harvey (lawyer) interjected casually.

Amanda sighed loudly. She was a master of office guerrilla-warfare and was clearly not going to back down.

'Why would we do that when we already have a perfectly suitable candidate here in the building, who knows the job and all it entails?'

‘But that bitch ruined my son’s career…’ Vance Morgan mumbled as he got up, ‘…and you people want me to agree to giving her a promotion.’

‘I vote against…’, and with that…he stormed out of the room adding one of those dismissive hand-gestures to his posturing gait that left nobody in any doubt of how he felt.

There was an uneasy silence around the table after that…which lasted a good thirty seconds or so…but eventually Bruce Hines took charge again and calmly repeated the question.

‘All those in favour of the proposal please raise your hand...and all those against...’

It took a minute or so…while a number of conditions were proposed and clarified…but after a couple of hesitations, the vote was carried… with a small majority …and the decision to offer Madison the position as Fashion Editor was confirmed…on a trial basis…on the condition that Amanda would oversee her work until all doubts, misgivings and reservations had been put to bed.

Later that day;

That afternoon Madison received a call from Gayle informing her that Amanda wanted to see her, indicating a time after lunch the following day when Amanda would be free.

‘Fine by me’, Madison agreed without a moment’s hesitation.

(This was no big deal for Madison as she had grown accustomed to Amanda’s controlling if somewhat annoying oversight of her work)

The next day; 2PM

Madison headed for the lift and as the doors opened she caught some of the conversation that the two guys in the cabin were having;

'Apparently, there is a strict, 'no banging the interns' policy here', the one guy was saying.

'Really; I didn't know…that', the second guy was replying as he caught sight of Madison.

'That's right guys; so be warned; keep it in your pants if you know what's good for you…or face the consequences' she remarked as she joined the two men in the cabin and pressed the button for the executive floor, allowing herself a secret smile.

Moments later, when the cabin jolted to a halt and the doors opened, Madison stepped forward first before turning around to face the two young men; 'Remember guys; no impropriety will be tolerated in these offices'.

The two young men both nodded, the one blushing a deep shade of red as they exited the cabin and scuttled away.

Madison took a deep breath…and then feeling more than a little pleased with herself, she calmly strolled up to Gayle's desk…and refusing to follow protocol…as usual…she just waltzed straight past into Amanda's office, clearing her throat as she entered…with discreet, 'Ahem', before sitting down.

Amanda was on the phone;

'…Suave like Jon Hamm? Oh please; Cary Grant was Don Draper when John Hamm was still in diapers. No, find another angle and get back to me' she insisted to the person on the other end of the line, before brusquely hanging up.

'Madison; good; you're here', she then remarked, as she looked up; 'I have something to tell you.'

Madison immediately sat bolt upright.

'You do?' she said, trying to keep her poise and composure.

‘Yes…’ Amanda confirmed, cracking her knuckles and pausing for dramatic effect.

‘Look Madison; here’s the thing. Through a combination of luck… circumstance…and dare I say, hard work…you have managed to get yourself noticed around here…which has brought us to this point…’

And with that Amanda announced the news.

Madison sat back in her chair…pretending to look calm and collected… but inside she was giving herself the biggest of high-fives, having just been told that she had finally obtained the reward that she had been working so hard to achieve.

‘There are however, two more things you should know before you go’, Amanda announced making direct eye-contact with her young colleague.

‘Aha’, Madison responded, her mind already in meltdown.

‘Firstly…’, Amanda counselled,; ‘…professional alliances can be solid like a rock or ephemeral and fragile like a snowflake melting in the sun; you need to realise that and be aware!’

‘And secondly’, Madison asked as she started to get up.

‘Secondly…’ Amanda warned, as she picked up a random file from her desk; ‘just remember, Madison; no-one LIKES the people who make the tough calls, but they DO respect them’.

‘Thanks Amanda; I’ll be sure to keep that in mind’, Madison confirmed…as she turned and made her way out…offering Gayle a discreet thumbs up as she walked past.

There was no fanfare, no big announcement of her promotion but the very next day Madison set to work on resolving that most negative and disruptive aspects of office life – *which is office-gossip* - by trying to create a more harmonious working environment in which everyone felt happy and valued for their contribution to the team effort.

She felt that a good working environment was essential to her future success…but it was not only for that reason. She wanted to make it one of her priorities because having experienced the humiliation of being snubbed and cold-shouldered herself after the *infamous incident*...as well as being gossip fodder for longer than she could remember...she was adamant that there would be no catty, back-biting...and no simmering bitterness or tension in the new office environment that she was going to create.

Madison knew exactly how the office worked after years of waiting for her moment to shine, and while it had toughened her up...and helped to make her the person she had become, it had also made her desperately unhappy on the odd occasion...and now that she was in a position to do something about it, she was determined not to allow that kind of situation to develop or fester ever again in her newly-reorganised department.

She had changed and she believed rather unselfishly that everyone had the potential to do just as she had done; and that everybody deserved a second chance in life, no matter how much they had made her life hell in the past.

Consequently, buoyed by her new sense of responsibility and encouraged by the general acceptance of her appointment, her first action was to call each of those under her charge into her office for an informal chat, to clear the air and to deal with any outstanding issues and criticisms.

It was a stroke of genius on her part...and during these conversations which took place one after the other on the first few days after her appointment, every single one of her staff, even her most ardent detractors had been impressed by her confidence, her poise and the surprising new maturity that she displayed while setting out her vision for the future.

Her humbling experience in England had obviously taught her a painful...but a very useful...life-lesson and because of her change of attitude, it appeared that Madison was somehow more in tune with those around her; an attitude which clearly agreed with her team who were all delighted with their new boss, and one that contrasted noticeably with that of Amanda whose withering looks and old-school methods still haunted their expressions and struck fear into their hearts.

There were still of course, some people in the building who were rather surprised by her appointment - especially those in the boardroom who had consistently blocked her attempts to climb the ladder over the years - *citing her involvement in the messy sexual harassment lawsuit which had threatened to ruin the paper's reputation several years earlier, as their reason for doing so* - but their reticence and resentment notwithstanding most of Madison's other colleagues agreed that she deserved her promotion because of all the hard work and effort that she had put in, even though, there were still the inevitable two or three who were a little suspicious and possibly jealous of her success.

About a week later Madison was in her office...busily tapping away at her computer...totally absorbed in what she was doing...when all of a sudden she sensed a presence.

Looking up slowly she instantly recognised the new guy, Quinton Booth standing there in the doorway, leaning against the door-frame and watching her with an obvious interest.

'You know who you remind me of...?' he remarked without so much as a 'Hello'; '...the tennis player...Chris Evert.'

Madison paused to reflect for a moment.

'Is that a line you use?' she asked, sitting back in her chair.

'No!' Quinton countered; 'It's true...you have that same aura about you.'

'I do? Well in that case...I'll take it as a compliment; thank you', Madison answered politely trying not to antagonise the new guy before really getting to know him.

This time it was Quinton who paused.

'Anyhow; I just thought I would come by and congratulate you on your promotion', he announced, flashing a mouthful of white teeth.

'Oh yeah; thanks', Madison replied again, finding his lack of self-awareness a little disconcerting.

'...And I was wondering...if maybe I could invite you out for a drink... or dinner...to celebrate', he continued suddenly...out of nowhere.

'That's very kind of you...but I don't think that would be a good idea', Madison responded as she picked up a pile of papers and started flicking through them to indicate that she had a lot of work to do.

'Okay...maybe next time', Quinton responded taking the hint before turning to leave, 'but seriously...congrats on the promo...' he added before disappearing back to wherever.

Madison watched him go and then just scoffed, shook her head and returned to her work. She had no time for dating and especially for dating someone in the office. Besides, she thought to herself, he would never compare with *the Bishop.*

A few days later;

Madison was once again sat at her desk answering e-mails and multi-tasking in her usual manner, when out of the blue Gretchen appeared in the doorway;

'Hey, Madison; I've come to pick up my stuff', she announced excitedly.

'Oh my God, Gretchen…how are you?' Madison responded, getting up and giving her 'old boss' a hug.

'Things are great' Gretchen replied, taking a seat.

'And you…you're in charge here now?'

'Thanks to you', Madison smiled, arms outstretched.

'Oh please', Gretchen countered; '…You were always going to take over here; it was just a question of time'.

'Thanks for the vote of confidence, Gretch' Madison replied gratefully, sitting back down.

'Oh…and by the way, before I forget…which I seem to be doing a lot since little Rafa came along…' Gretchen remarked; '…Do you know where my copy of 'Fashion Down the Ages' is? My mom gave it to me when I first started here, so I wouldn't hear the last of it if I forget to take it home.'

'Erm…, I think it's '…Through the Ages'…and yeah…it's over there…with a couple of other things you left behind', Madison signalled, motioning across the room.

'Silly me; that's baby-brain for you', Gretchen scoffed, throwing one hand up in the air.

'Oh…and this is yours too Gretch', Madison then remarked, sorting through a pile of files and other things that were sitting on her desk.

She handed Gretchen a second book entitled, 'A history of fashion.'

'Oh my god; I'd completely forgotten all about that one', Gretchen exclaimed, taking the book, before thanking Madison again and then launching into an excited narrative about her new life as a mother with the usual clichéd photos on her phone to prove it.

Madison listened for a while with polite fascination. She was happy for her former 'boss'…and her new life…but her gushing about motherhood and all that it entailed was clearly going straight over her head and thankfully…after about ten minutes or so…a call came in which she indicated she would have to take.

'Oh yes, of course', Gretchen acknowledged as she got up, gathered her bits and pieces together and prepared to leave.

'We must get lunch sometime' she whispered as she stuffed her belongings into her extra-large tote-bag, not wanting to interrupt Madison's call.

'Great idea…call me' Madison replied, blocking the phone's microphone with her hand as Gretchen turned and walked away.

♗

Moments later, Madison had just gotten back to work when Quinton walked in again.

'I came to apologise', he announced as he wandered into her office.

Madison frowned, clearly not happy with the constant interruptions.

Gretchen had just left and while she had been pleased to see her ex-boss, their chat had seriously screwed up her schedule…so she was not in the best of moods.

'Last time, when I came to congratulate you...I did so, empty-handed…' Quinton announced, '…but this time I have come prepared', he declared, holding forth a coffee-tray and a small box of doughnuts.'

'Seriously?' Madison remarked forcing a rueful half-smile.

'I know it's a cliché, but hey; it is what it is', Quinton stated almost apologetically.

'Oh…and by the way…' he followed up as he placed the coffee and doughnuts on the corner of Madison's desk; 'I was wondering…if you had reconsidered my offer for drinks or…dinner?'

Madison looked her new colleague straight in the eye.

'I have…and I'm still not interested', she replied dispassionately.

Quinton grimaced as if he had received a thump to the stomach.

'…Okay then, maybe next time', he announced, not giving Madison a chance to reply before he turned and continued on his way.

'Strike two', he whispered to himself as he headed down the corridor.

A few weeks later;

It had only been almost two months since Madison had taken on her new role but she had quickly become the archetype of the successful, professional woman with her new open-door policy and her modern style of leadership.

Indeed, her laid-back approach had so dramatically changed the mood around the office that a new sense of camaraderie had been established; one which had never existed previously; everybody was suddenly more friendly towards each other, joking among themselves, when appropriate, and even going out to lunch together which had never happened before.

Madison was delighted with the result and in an effort to assert herself further, she decided to instigate a few subtle changes to the fashion pages of the magazine which were now more or less her responsibility; changes which she called her 'reality policies'.

Her ideas were a little *avant-garde* and met with some resistance at first…but thanks to some clever…and very persuasive…argument she eventually won her case and was able to impose age limits on the models when she felt it necessary, and insist whenever possible, that the models used in her fashion shoots be of a more natural shape and size, rather than the un-natural, unhealthy-looking stick-like figures sent down the cat-walks by self-absorbed stylists and divas of the fashion industry.

She also pioneered the idea of placing a small paintbrush symbol at the foot of each page, to indicate whether or not a particular photograph had been air-brushed or not, as the case might be.

Things were going very well for Madison and anybody who had dealings with her; found her very fair and considerate; though, they soon found out if they put her to the test, that she could be just as decisive and single-minded as any of her corporate contemporaries.

Compliments rained on her from all quarters and even the bosses who had previously been fairly hesitant about offering her the role, had changed their opinion of her, thanks to the attention that her edgy style had brought to the magazine's profile and the increased sales that had ensued.

Indeed, the only person that she hadn't managed to win over since moving up was her immediate boss Amanda, but that was probably more to do with the latent animosity that existed between them, than any professional divergence or artistic discord, because unfortunately, no matter how hard she tried Madison could never see past her suspicions that her boss had somehow dashed any chance she might have had of patching up her relationship with the only man who had ever captivated her.

She remained convinced that Amanda was hiding something from her about her trip to London - *the details of which she steadfastly refused to divulge, if indeed there was anything to divulge* - and because of that suspicion and the possibility that the article that her boss had written might well have been the reason why *the Bishop* had been prevented from entering the country to come and see her, Madison couldn't bring herself to treat her with any warmth or camaraderie.

This created a little tension around the office whenever Amanda made an appearance but despite the uneasy truce both women remained very professional at all times, disguising their apparent contempt for each other behind the typical feminist guise of a condescending glare or a hypocritical smile whenever they didn't see eye to eye – *just as the feminist bible would dictate*...and the regular antagonism aside, their working-relationship had blossomed, getting noticed both in house and in media circles all around New York.

It was an alliance built on a tacit understanding and an unspoken professional respect, but there were still times when the two would clash, usually for the most insignificant of reasons and on those occasions, when the electricity between them arced, the sparks did fly…though generally, after turning the air blue for a good twenty minutes or so, they would usually settle on a compromise or agree to disagree when neither was willing to let the other get the upper hand.

This tension was never more evident than the day Madison had organised a recruitment drive for new interns.

As time was going by Amanda was allowing Madison greater and greater rein, but because of the conditions imposed on her…during the infamous management meeting…she still insisted on over-seeing certain details of office-life in order to make sure that Madison was adhering strictly to any new company policy.

It was a Tuesday morning and Amanda just happened to wander into the fashion department where she was confronted…metaphorically speaking…by a long line of candidates waiting patiently for their turn to be interviewed.

She smiled politely at the first couple of hopefuls and then…without further ado…made her way directly to Madison's office where, without bothering with any of the usual social protocols, she simply popped her head around the door and announced rather curtly;

'No rips…and no holey jeans'.

'Sorry… what was that…Amanda?' Madison asked, as she looked up from the pile of CV's that she was perusing…unsure that she had heard correctly…the expression on her face one of surprise and confusion.

'No rips and no holey jeans' Amanda repeated on seeing Madison's puzzled reaction. 'They can think it's cool; they can think it's edgy. They can even think it's fashionable…but they are not getting a job here' she insisted, in a way that wasn't to be questioned.

'What…what are you saying?' Madison asked again, curious for a more detailed explanation.

'I'm saying…', Amanda explained, standing half in and half out of the office now, the door held tight against her so that she could not be overheard'… that anybody who's been hoodwinked into buying jeans with rips, tears or holes in them is not a suitable candidate.'

'…But…what if they come back for the second interview…with you…in a smart suit…looking a million dollar?' Madison answered back swiftly, putting down the CV that she had just checked out.

'It doesn't matter' Amanda countered with one of her stern looks; '…they've already bought the jeans and that tells me all I need to know.'

'Wow…okay', Madison replied, a little taken aback by her boss's sudden show of unbending dogmatism.

'Good; as long as we're on the same page', Amanda confirmed as she started to pull the door closed…only to push it open again and pop her head back around.

'Just one more thing Madison…' she hastened to add with a fixed stare; '…no visible tattoos…and absolutely no weird piercings….'

'Sure thing…got it; no visible tattoos and no weird piercings', Madison repeated, sitting back in her chair and looking completely bemused as she watched her boss disappear off to her next appointment.

Now who does that remind me of? She thought to herself, as she sat forward again and picked up the next candidate's CV, knowing full-well that she would have to abide by Amanda's stipulations if she wanted to stay on the right side of her.

Paris;

September arrived and as part of her new remit, Madison was sent to Paris to cover the autumn fashion shows for the following summer's collections.

It all sounds very glamorous, working with the fashion houses, turning up at the runway shows and enjoying the creative spectacle from a privileged front-row seat, but actually Madison found the whole routine of running from one venue to the next rather tedious…and boringly repetitive.

However, one day towards the end of her trip, as she was making her way through the busy reception area of her conference hotel…dressed immaculately as always in a new Chanel twin-set…her attention was suddenly drawn to the lobby bar where, by sheer fortuitous consequence, she thought she spotted Gary sat on one of the stools.

The man she saw had his back to her…and even though she thought she recognised his shirt, she still wasn't sure that it was him at first - *even though the guy's fashion sense more or less confirmed it* - but to make certain that it was him, she circled around quietly and stood behind the guy, like a cat ready to pounce, waiting patiently for the right moment to surprise him.

The barman saw her arriving and moved to greet her but she quickly waved him away, putting a finger to her lips discreetly in response to his inquisitive air.

Then, all of a sudden, a phone started ringing and Madison instantly recognised the drum beat and sax riff; it was the same riff she had heard at his flat in London.

(Who can it be now? by Australian band Men at Work)

So, having confirmed that it was indeed Gary, she leaned in and whispered coquettishly in his ear;

'Okay, wise guy, what do you like to do?' she asked huskily, disguising her voice as best she could, with what could only be described as a poor attempt at a French accent.

'Well, beautiful', Gary answered cockily, playing along without turning around, flattered somewhat by the unexpected feminine inquisition; 'If you must know; I like to play chess and screw'.

'Okay zen, let's play chess…' Madison responded cheekily, trying to keep a straight face; '…where eez ze chessboard?'

Gary stiffened and straightened up, suddenly recognising her voice…

and while Madison took a step back to enjoy his reaction, he swivelled around on his stool to face her.

'Geez, I'm sorry, Maddy' he blurted out apologetically in his Aussie twang; 'I didn't know it was you…you know I didn't mean it like that…I was just quoting a line from Mel Brooks' film Blazing Saddles', he mumbled contritely, the words tumbling out of his mouth indiscriminately; '…but… as you know, I do actually play chess', he hastened to add, trying to soften his momentary embarrassment.

'Yeah, yeah…but you need to work on your pick-up lines', Madison cautioned, smiling at him and slapping the young Aussie's arm playfully.

Pleased to see her again, Gary slipped off his stool and after a brief moment of hesitation they greeted each other warmly with a hug.

'What are you doing here in Paris?' Madison asked curiously with a fixed stare, once they had separated once more and exchanged the usual common courtesies.

'Aww well Mad…Madison', Gary began to explain, correcting himself automatically; '…we are in the middle of a walkabout tour of Europe', he informed her, '…taking in Paris, Amsterdam, Berlin, Geneva and err… Brussels'.

'…Brussels indeed?' Madison remarked, raising a curious eyebrow, '…a place where all the washed-up politicians go to die in the hope of perpetuating their…

…money-grabbing lifestyles for a few more years at the tax-payers expenses', Gary joined in, echoing her imitation of their mutual acquaintance.

A complicit look finished breaking the ice and with that they both sniggered happily, enjoying the moment at *the Bishop's* expense.

'Yeah; they're calling it the European Challenge Circuit…it's been arranged as part of a series of events to promote the game around Europe', Gary explained further.

Madison nodded her head in understanding.

'…and…they're also using it to decide who is going to get the No.1 ranking position to replace Toby…you know, as the official contender to go on and face the world champion in the World Series next year', Gary added with renewed assurance.

'I see', Madison acknowledged, pursing her lips and smiling.

Gary's lip curled too into an insouciant smile; he was in high spirits having just won his match.

'Look Maddy…I was just about to have another celebratory drink; would you care to join me for a swifty?' he enquired politely, in his own inimitable style.

'…My shout…for old time's sake', he insisted with a smirk, jerking his head in the direction of the bar.

'I'm sorry Gary; I can't', Madison replied frankly. 'I'm on my way to a show…but tell me…talking of *the Bishop*, how is he doing these days?' she asked solicitously, expecting the young Aussie to update her on the chess-master's health.

'Oh, I don't really know much about that', Gary answered, shrugging his shoulders unenthusiastically; '…you know the guy…he's keeping it all very hush-hush.'

Madison frowned thoughtfully…and looked away, barely able to hide her disappointment.

'He's just that sort of guy', Gary insisted; '…he doesn't like fuss, never has, never will.'

'Yeah, I guess you're right', Madison agreed reluctantly.

'…So, Maddy, are you staying here…in this hotel?' Gary asked inquisitively, trying to change the subject.

'Aha', Madison replied rather absent-mindedly, throwing a cursory glance at the clock behind the bar.

'…So…do you fancy a quick grind later, for old time's sake?' Gary suddenly proposed out of nowhere, as much in hope as in expectation.

'What…?' Madison exclaimed abruptly, her mind still processing the young Aussie's lack of updated news on *the Bishop's* health.

'…Do you fancy an egg-sandwich…upstairs…later?' He insisted, jerking his head and directing his eyes towards the lifts.

Madison's expression remained blank and somewhat perplexed as she tried to keep a lid on her emotions.

'…I thought…you know, maybe we could spend the evening getting sticky again', Gary repeated again cheekily, lowering his tone.

The penny suddenly dropped in Madison's overworked brain.

'Eew…keep dreaming Gary', she scoffed churlishly as she suddenly came to her senses, not wanting to put too fine a point on the memory of the disaster that had been their brief and oh-so-forgettable coupling back in London.

Gary saw her repulsed reaction and before she could remonstrate further, he apologised again…contritely.

'I'm sorry Mad…pull your head in…I didn't mean to upset you or anything'; he joked, trying to smooth over his outrageously inappropriate suggestion with a little humour; 'but you know me…for me, women are like muffins…when you've tried one, you'll do anything to get another bite', he declared theatrically, raising his arms in self-embarrassment.

'Behave yourself Gary', Madison reprimanded scornfully, her eyes flashing while a hint of annoyance crept into her voice.

'…and I've told you before, the name is Madison', she insisted, correcting him prissily.

'Aaw, don't kick off Mad; you know I'm only playing with you', Gary whined sluggishly.

Madison sighed with audible irritation and rolled her eyes in mock despair.

'Anyhow; aren't you seeing Evie?' she asked curiously, crossing her arms in front of her as the memory of her friend's trip to London suddenly popped into her head.

'Well, yeah', Gary admitted with another lazy shrug of his broad shoulders, 'but in Australia we have a saying which goes like this; …never take sand to the beach.'

Madison shook her head; '…you Australians are incorrigible', she remarked, a little taken aback by what she saw as a rather disrespectful comment on Gary's part as far as Evie was concerned even though she had lost touch with her friend of late due to her workload - and as she reached into her handbag to grab her mobile phone which had fortuitously chosen that particular moment to come alive, she suddenly realised that a metaphorical chasm had opened up between her and Gary since their time in London, all those months ago.

Previously, she had found his puerile sense of humour somewhat endearing if not amusing…and he had definitely been her rock at times during her time in England…but as she checked the caller ID on her phone and decided to let it go to voice-mail, she recognised with a pinch of sadness and a little regret that his type of humour no longer had a place in her new world of cosmopolitan sophistication; the young Aussie hadn't changed one iota, which was good in a way, he was still the same old Gary, but she, she had changed… and as her thoughts drifted back to *the Bishop*, Madison knew that an integral part of that change was down to His influence.

'No…but seriously…' Gary continued, interrupting her nostalgic musing; 'Evie did come over to London a few months back. I even got a tattoo while she was there…' he announced, pulling up his sleeve to reveal his 'ink'. (*a chess-piece, a bishop, with the word 'inspiration' underlining it*).

'Evie suggested a mitre but you know what Toby's like about religion', he proclaimed.

'I do indeed', Madison concurred.

'So, let me get this straight; you and Evie…' she pursued, accompanying her question with a hand gesture.

Gary interrupted; 'Look Mad, Evie's great but she's in New York and I'm…well, I'm over here…' he explained with guilty masculine logic.

'…She still calls me though, now and again…for phone sex', he concluded, putting another nail in his reputation as far as the sophisticated New-Yorker was concerned.

Madison didn't respond to this latest crudity and noticing the blank expression on her face, Gary quickly deduced that her mind was elsewhere, probably still thinking about *the Bishop*.

'You know Mad, Toby once told me that the secret to keeping a partner happy is twofold', he blurted out without warning, trying to regain Madison's attention.

'I'm sorry; what was that?' she muttered distractedly.

'Toby…*the Bishop*…once told me…that the secret to keeping a partner happy was twofold', Gary repeated, pausing to wait for her reaction before delivering the punch-line.

None was forthcoming…

'…Keep making them laugh and keep making them cum', he joked contentedly, enjoying the saucy albeit distasteful nature of his vicarious pearl of wisdom.

'That was rich…coming from him', Madison retorted dryly, a knowing smirk slowly spreading across her face.

'…the laughing part I mean', she added, qualifying her statement with a hint of irreverence.

This time it was Gary's turn to look away and chortle.

'I couldn't possibly comment', he managed, before turning back to the bar and handing his glass to the barman for a refill.

'…Are you sure I can't twist your arm?' he enquired, looking back at Madison who was once again checking text messages on her phone.

'No, I'm sorry Gary, I really should be going now', she replied, shaking her head.

A second mobile phone suddenly burst into life in her handbag and as she motioned to Gary that she would have to take it…as it was from her boss back in New York; Madison signalled to the barman - who had just brought the young Aussie another beer - that in spite of everything she had just said, a glass of refreshing mineral water probably wouldn't go amiss.

He duly complied…and once she had finished her call, Madison licked her parched lips thirstily before picking up the glass from the bar and swallowing half its contents in one single gulp.

Gary looked on, impressed, a silly smirk on his face.

'Nice ring-tone…what's that tune?' he asked inquisitively.

'You wouldn't know it Gary; its Alicia Keys and Jay Z; Empire State of Mind…' Madison smirked disdainfully.

'Nah, I suppose I wouldn't', Gary agreed nonchalantly.

'You really haven't changed, have you Gary?' Madison commented, shrugging her shoulders and putting the glass back on the bar having quenched her thirst.

'Whadda you mean…Mad?' the young Aussie enquired, the froth from his beer comically lining his top lip.

'Well…how can I put this delicately?' she chided, slowly looking him up and down over the top of her designer sunglasses.

'…You're still wearing the same lame clothes…and have been for years, probably. You need to change it up a bit, get yourself a smart suit….and a new hat', she added, gesturing in abhorrence at his lucky green and gold beanie.

Gary raised his eyebrows and shrugged his shoulders, before taking another swallow of beer; he wasn't interested in changing; his clothes were a part of who he was and nobody would ever change that.

'Aaw look, Mad; that's just not me….all those sharp suits and stuff', he argued loosely, brushing away her annoying criticism.

'Yeah, I suppose you're right', Madison conceded, looking at the clock again; 'it doesn't suit everyone…but you could make an effort to look a little smarter', she concluded, reaching out and pulling off his cherished beanie.

Gary gasped theatrically, and feeling a little hesitant, a little defensive all of a sudden, he grabbed his treasured possession back off of her, taking Madison very much by surprise.

'Sorry Mad, but that's my lucky hat', he explained, slapping the worn out piece of head-gear against his thigh before replacing it on his head.

'Really?', she exclaimed; 'well; all I can say is that while you keep wearing that yellow hat on your head and matching it with red shirts, then you're never going to get a regular girlfriend…', Madison advised disapprovingly.

Gary shrugged his shoulders again, wondering if he should tell Madison his news but then, uncharacteristically taking umbrage with her rather haughty and judgemental manner, he decided not to and instead - despite his joy at seeing her again – he started looking around for an excuse to escape from her rather unwelcome and patronising sartorial examination.

He reached for his beer again and as he did so, providence was on his side, as two of his fellow players came into the bar just at that moment, causing a bit of a commotion amongst the more staid Parisian clientele, by announcing their arrival with a series of raucous victory chants.

Indeed, everybody in the bar turned to look at them as they made their way over to a table in the lounge area, and in the confusion that followed their entrance even Madison was distracted from her critique, allowing Gary some much appreciated respite and the time he needed to gather his thoughts.

The two men sat down and although they were still hyped up on adrenaline, they both recognised Gary through the crowded bar and acknowledged him with a nod of the head and a victorious clenched fist; a sign that one of them at least had made it through to the next round of the competition…and…thankful for the reprieve that they had presented him with, albeit unwittingly, Gary gladly responded to their salute with one of his own, raising his glass in the air and toasting their success loudly.

At the same time, through the glass panel separating the bar from the lobby, Gary caught sight of a young woman sitting quietly on her own, reading a fashion magazine and almost immediately he perked up again, his calculating mind deciding in a flash to use her presence, as an excuse to get away from what he saw as Madison's intensely critical scrutiny which, despite their history together, was making him feel a little uncomfortable.

Madison sensed the sudden change in Gary's demeanour and discreetly following his line of sight, she soon spotted the leggy model too, out of the corner of her eye.

'Do you know her?' she asked facetiously, her eyes smiling playfully.

'No, never met her', Gary replied spontaneously, regaining his usual composure, '…but as we say Down Under; a stranger is simply someone you haven't had sex with yet.'

Madison cringed; appalled once again by Gary's continued - albeit deliberate - attempts at machismo and all she could do was look up at the ceiling and shake her head in disgust.

'Look Mad', Gary announced with sudden urgency, shifting his position slightly so as to keep his prospective target in his line of sight; 'it was nice seeing you again, but…well, I can't stand here chipping all day like this…you do understand, right?'

'Yeah; I can see that', Madison conceded mischievously, glancing sideways at the unsuspecting young model, the smile in her eyes now curling slowly along her lips as she studied Gary's watchful gaze across the lobby.

'Thanks Mad…Madison, you're a star', Gary announced, before downing the rest of his beer and signing his bill, making sure that her drink was charged to his room too; '…maybe we could catch up more, later', he suggested, his mind already elsewhere.

‘Sure; why not’, Madison agreed unconvincingly…and with that Gary began walking out.

He took a few steps and then stopped. Madison thought perhaps that he had forgotten something, but just as she was about to look around at the bar to check, he turned around and gesturing proudly towards his impressive physique, he shouted back smugly;

‘Hey Mad…you don’t need to dress like a rock star to get laid, you know.’

Madison smirked, sniggered and waved him on his way.

Then, having taken a final sip of water, and nodded politely in the direction of the barman, she turned on her heels and made her own way out too, passing right in front of where Gary and his new acquaintance were now sat chatting.

She smiled silently at them as she went by but they didn’t react, too caught up as they were in their exchange.

Outside, she got into a taxi and as it pulled away, leaving Gary, she assumed, to pursue his eternal quest, Madison realised that her brief meeting with the young Aussie had not-unsurprisingly brought to mind a flurry of memories of her time with *the Bishop*, memories which were slowly but surely being erased, one after the other, by time and the mountain of work that had come her way since…and all of a sudden the realisation of that loss started to make her feel…nostalgically miserable.

♗

The fashion shows and all that they entailed took up most of her day but after bumping into Gary in the foyer-bar earlier, Madison could not get *the Bishop* out of her head and several times, during the presentation of some of the smaller labels, she found her thoughts wandering back to the abbey and reliving some of the happy moments she had spent there.

It was most distracting but she couldn’t deny her concern for *the Bishop’s* well-being and when she got back to her room later that evening, worn out by her day’s work and loaded down with yet another armful of catalogues, it suddenly struck her, as she threw off the trappings off her success, ready to jump into her daily bath of perfumed bliss, that despite the way that it had ended with *the Bishop*, she owed a lot of the success she had since achieved, to the subtle, subliminal advice that he had dispensed to her over the time that they had spent together.

I really should do something to express my gratitude to him…and show him that I still care, she thought to herself as she wandered into the bathroom to run her bath… and as she turned and gazed at her tired eyes in the mirror, a moment of inspiration suddenly lit up her face;

I know; I'll pay him a surprise visit on my way home from Paris. Oh, he'll hate it; somebody…anybody turning up at the abbey without prior arrangements; he always did…

…but as she slipped into the warm embrace of her luxurious bath a few minutes later, Madison could not help but smile to herself mischievously.

CHAPTER TWENTY-SIX

It wasn't easy to change her flights last minute, but with a little feminine charm and persuasion Madison somehow managed it…and two days later, having completed her mission in Paris, she was on her way to London.

The plane was late taking off that morning but it landed safely and on time at Heathrow, despite the British weather, and having assured herself via the transfer desk that her suitcases would be taken care of and reassigned directly to her evening flight home to New York, Madison made her way out of Terminal 3 full of confidence.

It felt strange being in England again and as she got into one of the many waiting taxis and gave the cab-driver her instructions to Abingdon, her mind was suddenly and uncharacteristically overcome with self-doubt.

What was she doing here? She thought to herself.

The Bishop had been on her mind constantly…*because of his illness…* since her unexpected encounter with Gary two days previously but now that she was here, and on her way to the Abbey, what was she going to say to him?

Over a year had passed since their 'difference of opinion' and neither had made an effort in that time to heal the rift that had torn them apart… *unless his aborted but as yet still unconfirmed visit to NY could be taken into account…*but as the black-cab pulled away from the kerb and she slowly settled back into its comfortable leather bench-seat, Madison began to relax again and the positive attitude which had now become her trademark, gradually returned.

The taxi-cab made its way through the tunnel at the airport's exit and as they hit the roundabout which followed, Madison began absent-mindedly wiping away the condensation that had formed on the window beside her.

She had always enjoyed the journey from Heathrow to Abingdon…

especially the last part when they left the motorway and continued along the narrow English roads which meander endlessly through the countryside - *taking in a succession of villages and farming communities…all of which contributed to the olfactory experience of the trip…*as coming from Manhattan with its bright lights and its oppressive skyscrapers, lined up like menacing sentinels along every major artery, she always felt as if she was somehow going back to nature, if not back in time when travelling this route…and as the taxi continued on towards its destination, she began looking forward to seeing some of the more familiar milestones which she knew appeared at regular intervals along the way …prompting her mind, inevitably, to wander once more.

These landmarks were all such trivial things, probably of no importance to anybody else than to her own subjective memory-bank - *much like a personal diary where thoughts, impressions and observations are re-grouped for future reference with no meaning for anybody other than the author* - but somehow, as they raced along, lost in the busy flow of late-morning traffic, Madison took comfort from seeing these objects again on this road that she had gotten to know so well; the solitary tree that stood forlornly in a fallow field, the seemingly abandoned barn with its rusting corrugated-iron structure…and as they neared Oxford, quite surprisingly, the blue sign at Junction 7 of the motorway which indicated unerringly that her journey was nearing its end.

Strangely, it felt like she was going home.

Then, all of a sudden, the traffic on the motorway heading west began to build-up and as the line of cars slowed, almost to a standstill at one point, the cabbie up front tried to strike up a conversation with his American fare.

He was only trying to be friendly; to pass the time, but Madison was in no mood for small-talk…lost as she was in her memories…and after several unsuccessful attempts he gave up, preferring instead to turn on the radio.

Another twenty minutes or so went by but eventually, the signposts for Abingdon began to appear on the side of the road and with a sigh of relief the cabbie glanced into his rear-view mirror ready with another frivolous comment for his passenger on the time it had taken them to get there.

He looked once, and then again, but observing that his sleep-deprived passenger had been lulled into an awkward slumber by the rhythmic, rocking motion of the car, her head lolling uncomfortably on the head-rest, he held his tongue and fixed his attention back on the road, ploughing on for another fifteen minutes or so in almost complete silence with only the radio on his dashboard to keep him company.

They passed through another couple of villages, around a series of twisting bends and then, just as they were negotiating their way through the last of the narrow lanes which led inexorably to the Abbey, the cab hit an unexpected bump in the road and the sharp jolt woke Madison up with a start.

The cabbie quickly checked his mirror, hoping that the shock hadn't disturbed his slumbering passenger - *acutely aware that in these times of political correctness he should not be seen to be staring at her for too long* - but seeing her stir, he immediately apologised for waking her by raising his left hand.

Madison was momentarily disorientated but she quickly gathered herself together and acknowledged the cabbie's apology with a sign of her own, before immediately checking out where they were with another glance out of the window.

Outside, the late-autumn sun was beginning to shine and its strong reflection in the side-window made it difficult for her to see; however, blinking discreetly and looking over her shoulder, out of the rear window, Madison instantly recognised the tiny post-office-come-grocery store that she had used once or twice during her stay, as it disappeared in the distance.

This made her heart jump…and as the reality of the situation and the imminence of her arrival suddenly hit her, an uncharacteristic nervousness began to take hold in her stomach.

The cab carried on around the last few bends and moments later, the Abbey's driveway appeared on the right hand side of the road between two rather scruffy-looking hedges.

It was an awkward driveway to get into, the angle being rather obtuse, but the cabbie negotiated it perfectly and without a second thought he drove on in, straight into the courtyard, bringing the cab to a complete stop about ten yards from the main entrance.

'Here we are, love', he announced with a jaded sense of accomplishment, once they were stationary; 'that'll be one sixty, please'.

Madison frowned warily, surprised at the cost, but then opening her purse, she handed over the cash without comment before slowly opening the door and carefully getting out; the butterflies that had taken hold in her stomach moments earlier suddenly gorging themselves on the adrenaline that was now pumping through her body.

The journey had taken longer than expected…and as she stood there in the courtyard Madison was desperate to stretch out her stiff limbs… *after the awkwardness of her sleeping position*; however, she was reluctant to do so in front of the cab-driver's curious gaze and rather than embarrass herself - even though there was nobody else around - she waited for him to turn the cab around and disappear out of sight, before treating herself to a very satisfying, fully-extended, finger-popping yawn and stretch in order to shake off her residual slumber and refocus her befuddled mind.

Then, pausing deliberately for a few more precious seconds to enjoy the moment, she breathed in two or three more lungfuls of air, noticing immediately…with some nostalgia…how its sweet-smelling scent contrasted so distinctly with the electrically charged, neon-scented atmosphere that she was used to in New York.

It felt strange being there at the Abbey again after all this time and as she made her way over to the front door, her stomach still full of angst and her head just as full with apprehension, her mind began racing again with thoughts of what she was going to say when He opened the door.

She couldn't imagine what he was going to say either, but as she stood there at his door, Madison knew that whatever happened when the door opened, she would have the satisfaction of being the one who had made the effort at least to reconcile with him; she will have offered him the olive branch, come all this way to show him her concern for his welfare…and if he couldn't or didn't want to accept that for whatever reason…then that would just have to be his problem.

She cleared her throat nervously one last time and after a few more deep breaths, she pressed the door-bell, brushing away a stray hair from the sleeve of her jacket as she did so.

The sound of the antiquated door-bell immediately resounded in her ears as it reverberated around the solid walls of the medieval masonry and while she waited patiently for him to answer…for anybody to answer… Madison took a step back and tried to relax, jiggling her shoulders to loosen the tension.

She waited a couple of minutes but unfortunately nobody came.

Madison was a little disheartened by this, her patience not being her biggest quality…but undeterred; she tried the bell again, pressing it more insistently the second time around. She even gave the brass knocker a yank …but despite her persistence there was still no answer.

Suddenly the apprehension and the trepidation that she had been feeling were replaced by disillusion and frustration…and the butterflies of excitement that had been fluttering with wild abandon in her stomach began to slowly die off in the growing pool of her disappointment.

She had come all this way to surprise him…for nothing.

Madison took a couple of steps back into the courtyard and looking around despondently for any sign of life, she took out her mobile phone, deciding that the only option she had left was to give his house-phone a call.

Maybe he was asleep or worse, confined to bed by his illness, she thought to herself… but then as she scrolled-down her contact list, she also remembered his tendency to screen his calls and immediately thought better of that idea too.

Her head dropped and she sighed out loud in frustration…but then out of the corner of her eye she noticed that the Aston was parked in its usual place in front of the garage.

This gave her morale a much-needed boost…but then as she looked closer, she was more than a little surprised to see that the car was covered in dust…and in dire need of a good valet-service...as like many men *the Bishop* had always prided himself in keeping his car in pristine condition.

That can't be good, she thought to herself…but the car's mere presence there…in its usual spot…gave her renewed hope that he must be at home, somewhere.

Madison looked up to the sky for inspiration and seeing the sun glaring back at her she was immediately reminded of all the times that they had spent in the garden.

It was a long shot as they were almost into October…but she had come all this way and was determined not to leave without having explored all her options.

And so, without further ado, she made her way around to the side of the house; just like she had done on so many previous occasions and as she reached the corner she called out *the Bishop's* name…several times, to let him know that she was there.

'Tobias; are you here…Tobias…?'

There was still no answer and indeed the only sound that could be heard as she advanced a little unsteadily along the narrow path which bordered the house was that of the fallen leaves that she was crunching underfoot.

It felt a little strange, to be re-entering his world like this…via the garden gate…and as she pushed it open, Madison found herself suddenly overcome by a sense of guilt, like a burglar or a thief might feel when trespassing on somebody else's private property.

Isn't it weird how being at someone's house when they are not there makes you feel spooky, she thought to herself, even when you know the person and you have been invited there a thousand times before.

At the back of the house, she called out again; 'Hello…Tobias, are you there…it's me…Madison'.

Still nobody replied.

Disappointed that she had come all this way, made all this effort and not been rewarded for it, Madison sighed out loud again in growing frustration.

However, after a furtive glance through the kitchen window to check for signs of life, she decided to off-set her disappointment by taking a stroll down into the garden, for old time's sake, curious as she was to see how things had changed, if at all, since the last time she had been there.

She stepped onto the paving-stones which led through the depleted rose gardens...*whose bushes were now no more than a series of twigs and thorns*...mindful not to scuff her rather expensive heels and followed them through till they opened out onto the un-tended grassy area which then led further on into the orchard beyond.

The garden was just how she remembered it and despite its stark autumn coat, Madison stood there for several minutes enjoying the memories of the time she had spent there.

She closed her eyes and in an instant her mind began to recall all those delicious smells of summer that had been indelibly stamped in her memory ever since; the fragrant flowers, the luscious fruits and the unmistakeable bouquet of freshly-mown grass.

Of course, those thoughts also included *the Bishop* and once again, as she inhaled deeply to recapture the memories that she had subliminally released, she began wondering where he could possibly be; he wasn't answering the door but his car was there in its usual spot, so surely he couldn't be far; she reasoned...her disappointment beginning to show.

She stamped her foot in frustration and as she did so, it suddenly dawned on her why she had come; she wanted validation, she wanted the man who had shaped her career...and possibly her life...to see the results of his endeavours.

However, she hadn't come under any false pretences either...because despite their estrangement...she really was genuinely concerned about *the Bishop's* health and would have loved to see him again...to make sure that he was okay...especially after the way that they had parted...even if, in her heart, what she really wanted more than anything else, was to show him what she had become since.

She wasn't looking for his seal of approval as such; it was more like she wanted him to acknowledge her success...while recognising his part in it.

Unfortunately though, it seemed like that wasn't going to happen; she wasn't going to get that satisfaction...and disenchanted...and frustrated in her quest, Madison resolved to leave.

She turned on her heels and just as she was about to storm off, she noticed something moving in the second of the two cabin-like structures situated on the far side of the garden near the entrance to the orchard. She was unsure of what she had seen at first, but her curiosity had been spiked and screwing up her eyes as she advanced further into the garden to get a better look, Madison quickly realised that what she had seen was a person, and probably *the Bishop*, since, as far as she knew, he still lived alone.

Suddenly her whole mood changed, and buoyed by the fact that he was indeed at home after all, she began ambling towards the gazebo, quickly regaining her poise and confidence, swinging her large Gucci briefcase and looking every bit the stylish fashion executive that she had become, in her smart but demure purple roll-neck and elegant grey suit.

'I debated about whether I should come'; she called out nonchalantly from afar, to fore-warn him of her imminent arrival…

'I wasn't sure that you would want to see me', she added speculatively as she approached, passing a hand through her carefully-managed shoulder-length hair as she did so…convinced in her own mind that the person she was addressing was *the Bishop*.

She stopped about ten metres from the open-fronted wooden structure, waiting expectantly for a response to her calls, but once again, much to her dismay, none came…and indeed it was only when she repeated her call with a bit more insistence that the person inside - who was stretched out in what looked like some kind of hammock - managed to drag his eyes away from the book he was reading and smile at her belatedly on recognising her voice.

'No, don't be silly…you are very welcome', he said quietly, in his usual controlled tone, waving her forward from behind his blanket.

Madison advanced cautiously; she couldn't see him clearly from where she stood, but as she got up close and was able to confirm that it was indeed *the Bishop* who was lying there, she was stopped instantly in her tracks by what she saw.

The confident smile on her lips vanished immediately and despite her perfect make-up, her complexion suddenly turned a ghostly shade of white as the blood drained from her cheeks; she looked like she had been hit in the face with a glass-full of cold water and as she stood there facing him the only words she could summon were;

'Oooh mmmy Goood.'

Of course, she knew that he had been ill, but the person Madison saw in front of her was not *the Bishop* she had come to know and love; his hair was greying at the temples, his skin was pale, he had a five o'clock shadow around his chin…and once the welcoming smile had abated, he looked gaunt and prematurely old.

Indeed, his overall appearance was haggard, dishevelled and unkempt; even the mischievous glint that had always epitomised him was absent from his once-sparkling eyes.

This was all so incongruous for a man who had always taken so much pride in his appearance and been renowned and respected by so many for his impeccable grooming and dress-sense.

Rooted to the spot, Madison was visibly shaken to see how much his health had deteriorated and as she stood there paralysed trying desperately not to let it show, a host of emotions, conflicting emotions began racing through her mind.

The Bishop didn't say anything for a moment or two; he just lay there quietly observing her reaction, taking in the shock and the concern that had suddenly registered in her eyes.

'I know…I know…that the person you see in front of you is just a pale imitation of what he once was', he admitted honestly, after the pause, trying to pre-empt her inevitable questions with a self-critical analysis, '…but what can I say; he confessed bluntly, the irony in his tone clearly evident; 'I'm just not the man I used to be'.

Madison was devastated, but not because of his condition; she could deal with that; it was because that statement was the first time that she had ever heard anything resembling an admission of weakness come out of *the Bishop's* mouth; it was the first tear, the first rip in the fabric of the illusion that he had spent his life creating around his persona…and hearing it pained Madison more than she could ever have imagined it would.

She didn't know what to do with herself; she tried to move but she couldn't and as the tears began to well up in her eyes she just stood there meeting his gaze, ashen-faced and open-mouthed; the shock of seeing him like this having knocked the wind right out of her sails.

'Take a seat', *the Bishop* said, gesturing for her to sit down beside him…and as she did so and made herself comfortable in the appointed chair Madison managed to get her emotions under control again, just as another woman, an older woman, one who she had never seen before, appeared in the distance at the end of the garden, coming from the house, carrying a meal-tray.

The woman approached them slowly and once she had set the tray down on the small table next to him, *the Bishop* turned to Madison and – *ever the perfect host, despite his condition* – he took care of the introductions.

'Madison, this is Rosa', he announced formally, raising a hand towards the rather matronly-looking older woman; 'she's my house-keeper; she looks after me.'

'That I do, Mr Byron…and have done for years…ever since his parents died', Rosa added with deference, turning to look at Madison.

'…and Rosa, this is Madison; she is a journal…;' *the Bishop* bit his tongue; 'she is an old friend of mine from New York.'

'Pleased to meet you', Rosa announced courteously with a smile.

'Pleased to meet you too', Madison reciprocated with a friendly smile of her own, trying hard to disguise her confusion at the fact that *the Bishop* had told her previously that Olivia – *the young brunette that she had met at the door that time* - was his house-keeper…though the frown on her face as Rosa turned away again quite clearly betrayed her bemusement.

'Would you like a cup of tea, dear?' the house-keeper asked politely, returning to her duties.

'I would, thank-you…Rosa…white, no sugar', Madison responded pleasantly; 'that taxi ride seemed to take forever to get here and my throat is as dry as a bone.'

Rosa smiled again…silently…and busied herself with the tea while *the*

Bishop marked his page and Madison tried to make herself comfortable, still completely baffled by all these new developments.

'What are you reading?' She asked casually, catching *the Bishop's* eye and changing the subject.

'Oh…I'm…I'm reading 'New Labour; the politics of greed, incompetence and self-interest'…by Doonby, *the Bishop* mumbled slowly, his tone laced with irony.

'Not again', Madison lamented, a distinct note of exasperation in her voice. 'Look Tobias…' she said as she pulled her chair closer, '…I never mentioned it before…and please don't get all bent out of shape by what I'm about to say…but politics has never been a passion of mine; I am passionate about a lot of things…but politics has never been one of them.'

The Bishop looked at her with wistful eyes. 'I know that…and I understand that it's not everybody's cup of tea…no pun intended…' he whispered almost…gesturing towards the teapot that Rosa was holding, '…what with all the lies, the corruption and the self-interest...'

During the short pause that followed, the investigative journalist inside Madison's head began to wonder what was going on; she was already having difficulty processing the self-evident extent of *the Bishop's* health problems, but on top of that, another altogether more intriguing question now needed an answer, regarding the duplicitous nature of the housekeeper's position…because if Rosa had been his house-keeper for all these years, then who was Olivia?

The question went around and around in her head; indeed it was starting to burn the tip of her tongue…but even though her journalistic instincts had been roused Madison knew that she couldn't, she shouldn't mention it, not while the older woman was still standing there between them; a show of restraint which was excruciatingly frustrating for the New York fashion executive who had gotten more and more used to speaking her mind in recent months thanks to her new standing.

However, on this occasion she decided to bite her tongue and maintain a dignified silence until once again she was alone with *the Bishop*, thereby avoiding any embarrassment for all concerned.

'Here you are, dear', Rosa announced graciously, handing her a steaming cup of Earl-Grey.

'Thank you Rosa', Madison offered in response, reaching out a hand and shuffling forward again in her seat.

The old house-keeper nodded her head benevolently and having served *the Bishop* his cup too, she stepped back and watched on curiously as their guest raised the cup to her lips and took a large sip.

'God, I needed that', Madison exclaimed appreciatively as *the Bishop* leaned towards her, precariously holding a plate from the tray.

'Would you like a muffin?' he asked courteously.

Madison shook her head politely, alluding to her figure, but she could not help but smile fleetingly at the sight of the toasted tea-cakes, remembering back to the joke that Gary had cracked on that same subject in the hotel in Paris only a few days earlier.

At that point Rosa disappeared back to the house and while *the Bishop* got himself organised, tea in hand, in his rather awkward-looking contraption, Madison let her eyes roam around the garden; her gaze rather inevitably and unavoidably coming to rest on the other wooden cabin across the way which she knew from experience housed his private hot-tub.

Indeed, they had spent many a happy time in that little cabin during her stay at the abbey…and the sight of it instantly triggered two of her most vivid memories of that time in the secret movie-theatre of her mind, each of which had taken place behind that rather inconspicuous-looking door; one which still made her blush to this day whenever she thought about it… and the other, which had always made her smile too, up until now, being the time that *the Bishop* had lost his footing and almost drowned in front of her on her very first visit.

The cabin had been their little hideaway of sorts during her stay - hidden away as it usually was behind an all-encompassing floral disguise, but as she contemplated it now, in its current state, exposed and stripped of its colourful camouflage, it suddenly struck her that it looked much like its owner at present, sad and neglected.

Her thoughts and memories of that summer began to stack up as her eyes continued to scan the rest of the garden, bringing a whole host of emotions to mind, but her musing was suddenly cut short by the heavy thud of *the Bishop's* book as it tumbled from his lap onto the floor bringing her back to the present with a jolt.

The noise caught Madison off-guard in the moment but after a shake of the head to clear her mind…and a reproving roll of her eyes; she reached down and picked the book up for him.

'Wow; that's quite a…heavy book', she commented dryly as she handed it back to him, trying to lighten what was slowly becoming a rather tense and uncomfortable situation.

The Bishop didn't respond to her comment but simply thanked her quietly with a raised hand as she laid the book next to him.

'That reminds me…' she announced, reaching into her Gucci briefcase and handing him a book she had come across at the airport 'I picked this up for you.'

The book was entitled 'Lovers and other strangers'; a compilation of Jack Vettriano's work.

Again, *the Bishop* looked up at her…and with a great fondness in his eyes he thanked her with a cracked smile.

He seemed a little subdued which worried Madison somewhat, as amongst other things she had been looking forward to discussing their romantic entanglement and the reasons which had led to it falling apart after their summer tryst…but as she looked at him, slouched listlessly in his hammock, his eyes half-closed as he savoured the aroma of his favourite tea, she quickly realised that if she was expecting an afternoon of light-hearted repartee, she was probably going to be disappointed.

Of course, the demise of their affair wasn't her only concern either, she had plenty of other questions to ask too, about his health, about his retirement plans…and not least about his house-keeper situation, but not wanting to aggravate his condition in any way possible she determined that she would not bring any of it up until he took the lead.

Again, this wasn't easy for Madison, to remain quiet and restrained, but as she sat back in her chair, nursing her cup of tea, her mind quickly filled the void in the conversation with a series of flashbacks to some of their other, more memorable conversations.

She pictured them in Boston, in New York and in London and as the minutes went by, she began dissecting the images, analysing them one by one…finding it intriguing and enlightening even to re-visit the arguments with the benefit of hindsight, though she had to admit that while *the Bishop* had often frustrated her with his unwavering logic during these exchanges, she had always enjoyed the cut and thrust of his intellectual argument and the incisiveness of his wordplay, even when he was playing the devil's advocate just to annoy her.

This brought a smile to face…but then, as she looked over at him, her face fell again as she was brought back once again to the present.

Another minute or so went by without a word being spoken…and then Alicia Keys suddenly burst into song again from the depths of her briefcase, breaking the silence and forcing Madison into a reaction.

She quickly put her cup down on the little table that separated them and looking at *the Bishop*, invoking his indulgence, she pulled out her mobile phone, checked the message and decided to ignore it before returning the phone to whence it came as quickly and as discreetly as possible.

'So, what brings a successful, high-powered, fashion executive from New York back to the relative peace and tranquillity of rural England?' *the Bishop* suddenly enquired, staring deliberately out into space to avoid eye-contact.

Madison cleared her throat and sat up straighter; this was the invitation she had been waiting for.

'Well, firstly, I wanted to find out how you were doing, obviously… and then I wanted to thank you for intervening on my behalf', she began.

'I don't know what you mean', *the Bishop* countered, shrugging his shoulders and feigning an expression of blithe indifference as he swallowed a bite of his muffin and washed it down with a large slurp of tea.

'Come on Tobias; don't sell yourself short; I might live across the pond but we both know that there are people out there, people you know, people from your inner-circle who have been making calls and opening doors for me over the last year or so…', Madison persevered.

The weakened master turned his head and looked at his *protégée* with a pair of emotionless eyes.

'Listen', she continued earnestly, sitting further forward '…I'm pretty sure that my career has gone forward in leaps and bounds because of those interventions…and I just wanted you to know that I appreciate what you have done for me…no-one else could do what you have done for me and I want you to know that I will be eternally grateful to you for that', she declared almost in one breath.

'I see', *the Bishop* concurred, quietly flattered by the sincerity in her voice.

He smiled at her wanly.

'Look Tobias', Madison insisted, taking hold of his hand and enjoying reconnecting with him through the skin on skin contact, 'You were the one who told me on our first meeting that…every experience that we go through in life is a building block to understanding who we are; a test to find out our strengths and our weaknesses…and that our goal, in order to succeed…is to extract the positives from those experiences and use them to further ourselves – to our best advantage…'

'…while also being aware of the negatives and working to reduce them', *the Bishop* joined in, finishing the last line of his mantra for her.

'Well, that advice has stuck with me…' Madison confirmed proudly; 'I now know what I want out of life and I am confident that I can achieve it…'

'Oh, I might not have shown it at the time, but in recent months I have put your advice to the test and thanks to you I am well on the way to succeeding beyond my wildest dreams', she gushed.

'You know; since last year, I have been presented with a multitude of opportunities…inundated with offers of work…it has been extraordinary and I have to say that while I always knew I could do it, I'm pretty sure that a lot of it is down to meeting you', she insisted, showering him again with more appreciation.

The Bishop inhaled slowly and then exhaled loudly; 'I appreciate your candour and your exuberance but it was nothing really', he commented with cool, emotional detachment.

'Yes it was…I'm serious', Madison insisted again pointedly, '…you smoothed out the edges of my sometimes…uncompromising character… and taught me all about respect, humility and diplomacy…'

'Hey, my self-esteem is now booming and my self-confidence is at an all-time high because of you…not that I was really lacking in that department', she tempered humorously, trying to get him to crack a real smile.

There was a natural lull in the conversation after that as each of them finished their tea and reflected on what had just been said, Madison sitting back in her chair and *the Bishop* carefully tucking himself back under his blanket, even though the sun was now shining…but the moment was short-lived as Madison suddenly realised that she had been selfishly hogging the conversation, monopolising the exchange, gushing about herself…and hadn't given him the chance to answer her first question about his health.

Disappointed with herself for her lack of good manners, she immediately tried to correct it by asking him again about his health… but *the Bishop* just waved her enquiry away, dismissing any further discussion about it out of hand…and Madison knew by his reaction that it would be fruitless for her to try to force the issue - even though she sensed that he wasn't telling the whole truth about it - as like all men, *the Bishop* deliberately avoided discussing any issues that might threaten his masculinity.

Instead, they began to reminisce about the old times, reliving some of their more adventurous if not scandalous escapades and while they were on the subject and emotions were running high, Madison decided to strike while the iron was hot and ask why – even though they had been lovers – he had never really allowed her get close to him.

'You do know that you stole my heart…right?' she murmured poignantly, thinking back fondly.

'I did?' *the Bishop* mumbled solemnly, pausing to enjoy the comfort of her words for a moment.

'If only you could have cut me a little slack, applied a modicum of rationality to your rather parochial stance…who knows what might have happened?' she complained with a hint of petulance.

'…but you crushed any chance we might have had with your stupid rules and your inability to commit', she suddenly protested, finding it difficult to remain objective and non-judgemental, her voice rising slightly and her frustration resurfacing spontaneously.

'I know all that…but I just couldn't let it happen', *the Bishop* answered after a brief pause, his voice softening in a way that touched Madison deep inside.

'Why?' she asked with growing zeal, tossing her hair flamboyantly, 'Why wouldn't you let me in?'

Another moment of silence followed; it was an inauspicious moment and *the Bishop's* voice, sounding like broken glass, was barely audible as he began to explain why.

He kept it as vague and ambiguous as possible – deliberately glossing over most of the real reasons why he had not wanted to get embroiled in a full-on relationship - and hadn't done for quite some time, citing his lifestyle and the usual male commitment issues for not wanting to get involved, none of which rang true in Madison's ears, but at the end of a rather drawn-out and frankly dubious soliloquy he looked over at her and concluded his somewhat lacklustre rhetoric with one of his favourite quotes, imparting a sincerity into it that had been lacking in most of what he had just expressed;

'The best and most beautiful things in life can't be touched or seen; they are felt in the heart', he declared rather cryptically.

'What does that mean?' Madison responded with mounting dismay; 'I mean, what are you trying to tell me here Tobias? Are you saying that it was doomed from the outset and that whatever we might have had together, regardless of what I did to sabotage it…was never going to work out… no matter what? Is that what you are saying? She countered with growing anger; her rebuke taking the prostrate champion somewhat by surprise.

‘Please; calm down’, *the Bishop* beseeched her, looking off into the distance again and raising his hand defensively.

‘All I am saying is that…as we navigate our way through life we are constantly faced with decisions which will take us on one path or another…I chose the path of solitude and as Lord Byron once wrote; It is in solitude where we are least alone.’

Madison shook her head in frustration and disbelief; the emotion of the moment was getting to her but determined not to let it show she turned away and focussed her attention for a moment or two on the solid white-washed walls of his home, drawing strength from their stoic resilience.

The tension in the little wooden shelter was palpable, but before it got out of hand, before she said something she knew that she would later regret, Madison got up and excused herself, pretexting that she needed to go to the bathroom.

The Bishop nodded politely. ‘You know the way.’

‘Yeah, I do, don’t I’, she quipped sarcastically with a mixture of regret and anger in her voice as she stepped back out onto the grass and turned towards the house.

The Bishop watched her go and once she was a safe distance away, he picked up his book again, hoping to finish the chapter he had started, before she came back.

Madison took her time walking back to the house, using the time to compose herself and reflect on what *the Bishop* had just said, and as she passed by the infamous cabin that housed the hot-tub she noticed that the door was slightly ajar.

She stopped in her tracks and then without thinking, she glanced back to see if *the Bishop* was watching her; he wasn’t…so deviating off her path slightly, she walked over to close it, surprised to see it so, as he had always been so meticulous in padlocking it.

Memories flooded her brain and curious to see if anything had changed, she slowly opened the door a little further and sneaked a peek inside for old time's sake.

What greeted her was demoralising…and her heart sank when she saw the tub, dry as a bone, the side-panels dismantled and all its internal wiring and tubes exposed; obviously in need of some expert intervention.

Deflated, she quickly closed the door again and without further ado she carried on into the house, knocking on the back-door politely to warn Rosa…*who was in the kitchen busily preparing the ingredients for dinner…* of her imminent arrival.

Madison walked in and on her way through she poked her head around the kitchen door, hoping to get an answer to the one question that she had never been able to ask her host.

'Rosa', she enquired, unburdened by the usual British need for social protocol, 'I hope you don't mind me asking this, especially as this is the first time that we've actually met, but if you have been working for T… Mr Byron for so long, perhaps you could answer a question for me; you know…woman to woman.'

Rosa didn't react immediately; she just kept on peeling the vegetables for the evening meal, but then after a few more scrapes, she looked up, questioningly.

Madison advanced cautiously into the kitchen.

'I know that this might seem a little forward of me', she announced brazenly, 'but I am intrigued and a little curious', she admitted, trying to present her case with tact.

'…and I have always been captivated by the grainy photograph that Mr Byron keeps on his bed-side table; would you by any chance know who that person is ….was? She asked tentatively.

Rosa stopped what she was doing and looked out into the garden to check that her employer was still there in his hammock.

Then wiping her hands, she turned slowly towards Madison and replied quietly…with studied politeness.

'That my dear is a very private matter…and between you and me, I really shouldn't be telling you this', she whispered, '…so you'll have to promise me that this will never reach his ears.'

'Of course', Madison agreed without reflection, nodding cautiously.

'Well, young lady, we've never met', Rosa reiterated, but I've heard so much about you over the time that I feel as if I do know you.'

A little puzzled, Madison nodded again in heightened expectation.

'Okay then; as long as this stays between us…' the old house-keeper suddenly explained, '…that photo represents ten, no eleven years of unrequited love.'

'It does?' Madison questioned, pricked with emotion…her puzzled look conveying her lack of real understanding.

'Yes, my dear', Rosa continued; '…that woman used to live in the cottage down the road.'

'You mean Tanglin?' Madison exclaimed incredulously.

'Yes, that's the one', Rosa confirmed nodding her head, surprised that Madison knew the actual name of the cottage so spontaneously.

'Was her name Jane by any chance?' Madison asked expectantly.

Rosa paused and took a deep breath.

'Yes, I do believe it was', she confirmed with unflinching candour.

So that's why he never came to visit me in the cottage, Madison reasoned to herself quietly.

'Remember…this stays between you and me', Rosa repeated, confirming their pact with a simple hand gesture.

'Sure; you have my word', Madison agreed before turning on her heels and making her way to the bathroom, using the time to digest this new development.

Then, a few minutes later, while washing her hands, Madison suddenly remembered *the Bishop's* quote in the restaurant all those months ago in New York and it all made sense.

(*Reminder of what TB said in New York*; 'As my name-sake Lord Byron once said; 'Sometimes it is easier to die for the woman you love, than to actually live with her'.')

Meanwhile the doorbell rang, dragging Rosa away from her culinary occupations.

It was Olivia…and in what seemed like a routine that had developed into a habitual occurrence the old house-keeper casually opened the door to let her in, greeting her with her usual courtesy.

'He's out in the garden', she announced quietly with muted deference as the young woman stepped inside.

Olivia nodded and returned Rosa's greeting, smiling politely as she followed her back through the hallway and into the kitchen.

'Has there been any change?' she asked as Rosa returned to her culinary duties.

'No, still the same', the old house-keeper offered reverently, shaking her head; the sorrow in her voice suddenly audible.

Olivia frowned fleetingly and nodded in understanding before turning and continuing on her way, out through the back door and into the garden.

At that moment Madison came back into the kitchen…and flaring a new perfume in the air she just caught sight of the back of Olivia's head as the smartly dressed brunette was making her way through the thorny rose gardens and into the main garden.

She noticed that the young woman was carrying what looked like a doctor's bag and despite her new resolution not to pry into *the Bishop's* private affairs ever again without a prior invitation she felt compelled to ask Rosa who she was;

'I've seen that woman here before', she commented, looking in Rosa's direction, while keeping one eye on Olivia; 'Who is she?' she enquired, a hint of latent jealousy betraying her attempt at nonchalance as she approached the window and sneaked another peek.

Rosa took a deep breath, Olivia's arrival having obviously affected her in some way, and looking despondently back at her inquisitor, her eyes filled with unspoken emotion.

'I think you should ask Mr Byron to answer that one', she replied turning away to check her oven and alter the setting, 'but if I were you, I would give them a few minutes before going back out there', she advised with considered aplomb.

Madison backed off immediately, sensing intuitively that there was a reason for the old house-keeper's pre-emptive tip-off.

'Oh, right', she acknowledged, plunging her hand into her handbag to check the whereabouts of her mobile phone; 'I have a few calls to make… so that's fine by me', she concurred, trying to maintain a neutral expression on her face while the curiosity alarm in her head went off the scale.

Rosa smiled stiffly, appreciating Madison's courteous and considered response…and making her way over to the other side of the kitchen she started to weigh out some flour on the heavy, well-worn antique scales.

'What are you making?' Madison enquired, joining her and trying to make polite conversation in the vain hope that the old house-keeper might open up to her and reveal a little more about the identity of the mysterious brunette.

'Lemon meringue pie', Rosa replied flatly; 'it's his favourite.'

'I see'; Madison conceded, lost for a more pertinent response.

Rosa wiped her brow with the back of her hand. She was feeling a little uncomfortable with Madison's presence in her kitchen as like most women, she was very territorial; this was her domain and she wasn't used to having people around while she went about her business.

Madison understood this and sensed her unease but while she didn't want to make a nuisance of herself her journalistic persistence told her that if she hung around a little longer Rosa might just let something else slip about Olivia, if for no other reason than to get rid of her.

She checked her watch…and while she was no longer thirsty, having enjoyed her cup of tea in the garden she decided that it would be as good an excuse as any to loiter, so she asked Rosa politely if it would be okay for her to grab a glass of orange-juice from the fridge while she was there.

The old house-keeper smiled generously and wiping the flour from her hands on a cloth she had handy, she opened the cupboard above her head and to her right.

'Here you go' she responded, reaching up and taking out a glass which she set down carefully on the work-top beside her. 'I believe you know where the fridge is', she commented, a hint of comedic irony in her eyes despite the tense mood.

'I do; thank you Rosa', Madison declared, picking up the glass and sashaying her way over to the fridge where, to her amusement, she found the orange-juice stored in its usual place, as it always had been, on the middle shelf.

♗

It felt a little strange for Madison, being in *his* kitchen again after all this time and while she was pouring herself a glass of juice, her mind suddenly wandered back again to that day when *the Bishop* had made them both a full English breakfast after their early-morning adventure in the hot-tub.

Time stood still for a moment and in that split second as she stood there musing, hidden by the fridge door, the memory of him chasing her back into the house that morning, with them dressed in only their towels, instantly brought a smile to her lips and a hue to her cheeks.

The flashback was quite vivid and in it Madison saw herself perched on one of the breakfast-bar stools sipping a glass of the same juice she was now holding, watching attentively as *the Bishop* stood manfully by the stove, in just his towel, his skin glistening and his hair slicked back from the spa water, looking a picture of health and vitality.

It was a delicious moment and as she closed her eyes to capture the mental image for future reference, Madison was suddenly transported back in her mind to that wonderful summer morning.

Out of nowhere, the aroma of freshly-brewed coffee suddenly filled her nostrils and as the rest of her senses tuned-in to her reflection she could even hear the bacon sizzling and the eggs being cracked into the pan as *the Bishop* went about producing his culinary masterpiece for them to share.

He looked magnificent as he stood there, full of life, spatula in hand… but then as the image began to fade again, almost as quickly as it had come into focus, the smile on Madison's lips disappeared just as quickly as the contrasting reality of *the Bishop's* current plight took centre stage once again in her thoughts.

She sighed in dismay at the cruel irony but there was no time for her to linger on the memory of her lost romance as the sound of a blender bursting into life quickly snapped her back into the here and now, startling her and filling the whole kitchen with what must surely have been an illegal number of ear-splitting decibels.

'Sorry…sorry if I made you jump', Rosa cried out, as best she could over the nerve-shredding din.

Madison closed the fridge door sharply, ready to vent her displeasure at being taken so deliberately by surprise but then remembering that it would probably be better for her to have Rosa as an ally rather than a foe, she bit her lip, feigned another bogus smile and raised her free hand limply in a gesture of surrender.

'I'm outta here', she shouted, grabbing her handbag and subliminally making the connection between her cookery flash-back and the six empty egg-shells now sitting on the counter.

Rosa just nodded in reply, too busy to stop what she was doing…while, desperate to get away from the deafening noise of the blender, Madison quickly retreated into the hallway and continued on, past *the Bishop's* office and through into the glass-doored reception area, looking for some peace and quiet where she could make her calls.

She set her glass down on the conveniently-placed table just inside the door but the noise from the kitchen was still too loud for her to hear and carry on a professional conversation, so rather than fight the odds Madison decided to take her business outside instead; that way at least she would be able to enjoy the sun's warm rays on her face while making her calls in a more conducive setting.

She opened the door and slipped outside, being careful to leave it ajar so that she could get back in, and once she was out of the shadow of the house, she reached into her handbag and pulled out her mobile phone.

There were three missed calls and several text messages for her to deal with and as she brought up the first of them Madison smiled to herself and shook her head, enjoying the fact that these people, who at the beginning of her career would not have given her the time of day, were now ringing her to consult her, obtain her approval or get her opinion on any number of issues, some of which had nothing to do with the world of fashion.

She dealt with each of the calls very succinctly one after the other and having answered each of them she then proceeded to make a few new calls of her own; to her office, to a fellow journalist with whom she had agreed to have lunch in a few days time and finally to the taxi-company she had booked to take her back to the airport later that afternoon, to re-confirm that that was still the case.

Twenty minutes or so later, having finished that last call Madison strolled nonchalantly back inside, picking up her glass of juice as she went and finishing it just as she reached the kitchen again.

She deposited her empty glass on the breakfast bar - with a whispered thank-you to Rosa – and as she did so, she just happened to notice a DVD case that was lying there on the counter.

'Gran Hotel; what's this about', she asked Rosa, picking up the DVD case.

'Ah, that my dear…' said Rosa turning her head; '…is the story of Alicia and Julio…a pair of star-crossed lovers embroiled in impossible love.'

'I see', Madison acknowledged, nodding her head.

'Alicia is the married daughter of a wealthy hotel owner and Julio... Julio is just a waiter in the hotel…albeit a very handsome one', Rosa explained, walking over and taking the DVD back out of Madison's hands.

Madison smiled. 'My, my; the age old 'Lady Chatterley' dilemma', she commented as she started for the door, on her way back out into the garden…where - sat in the seat that she had vacated earlier – she found Olivia and *the Bishop* engrossed in deep conversation.

'I hope I'm not interrupting anything' she called out as she approached.

'No, of course not', *the Bishop* replied, waving her forward; 'come and join us.'

Madison did just that, stepping warily into *the Bishop's* rather incongruous little bolt-hole, her mind working overtime as she wondered rather vainly if they had been discussing her and what kind of reception she was about to receive if they had.

Inside the wooden shelter it was a little cramped due to *the Bishop's* rather over-sized hammock arrangement and as Olivia was occupying the only available chair, Madison was forced to just stand there, feeling a little awkward.

'Oh, I'm sorry…let me get you a chair from the orchard', *the Bishop* offered apologetically, throwing off his blanket in a gesture of belated gallantry.

'Don't worry about me Tobias' I'll be fine here', Madison announced amiably, raising a hand to stop him as she took up a position against one of the cross-beams which held the structure together, having first checked it for dirt and any lurking insects.

The Bishop nodded his head quietly and with a strained smile, he settled back down, making himself comfortable again under his heavy blanket.

There was a pause while he did this and as she waited somewhat impatiently - *her arms crossed defensively in front of her* - to finally learn the truth about Olivia's identity…and how she fitted into *the Bishop's* world, Madison's brain – probably still high on the oxytocin from her kitchen daydream - began messing with her emotions, feeding her random feelings of jealousy and betrayal.

She had long since moved on from her summer idyll with *the Bishop*, but nevertheless, to see Olivia sat there, so obviously at ease in his company, she couldn't help but feel slightly jealous of the young brunette.

Something inside, if no more than her competitive spirit was all of a sudden reignited and the presence of a potential rival, who might quite rightly be diverting *the Bishop's* attention away from her - if, as she suspected, they were closer than he had let on - was having an adverse effect on her, making her suddenly very uncomfortable.

Of course, she had no idea what she was about to hear and whatever it was, it shouldn't have bothered her anyway, because of the fact that she had moved on, but for some reason it still did...and the reason for that she decided, was probably because, during their time together, she had often felt - be it through her feminine intuition or through her journalistic *naus* - that *the Bishop* had been keeping something back from her.

She had never been able to put her finger on it, but as those suspicions suddenly resurfaced – and Olivia's presence seemed to confirm them - she began feeling somewhat aggrieved that he had criticised her previously for her human failings - which had ultimately led to them breaking up – and yet here he was about to admit to a far greater crime in her eyes, the ultimate betrayal for any woman; that he had been cheating on her with another.

The Bishop looked at Madison, gauging her mood and then at Olivia.

It was a strange moment of calm and once again time seemed to stand still as the anticipation of what was to come crescendoed.

The Bishop knew that the game was up at that point; that the time had gone when he could get away with being economical with the truth...and realising that there was no escaping from the situation, there was no more holding back, he proceeded to formally introduce the women to each other.

'Olivia, this is Madison; she is an old friend of mine from New York… and Madison, this is Olivia…she is a doctor…and when you met that time…it was because Olivia had promised to look in on me while Rosa was away in Portugal', he announced, pausing for effect.

'No; in fact she is more than that', he continued, reaching out a grateful hand in Olivia's direction; 'she is my…my personal physician… and she has been treating me for some time.'

'Treating you…treating you for what', Madison enquired abruptly, almost before he had the time to finish his declaration, her eyes switching alternately between Olivia and their ailing host; her thoughts of jealousy instantly dismissed.

The Bishop grimaced; he really hated talking about himself.

'Well Maddy', he continued, abridging her name mischievously just to tease her; 'I have been diagnosed with an incurable disease…which is the real reason why I never let you get too close', he explained, speaking calmly and evenly, but avoiding any hint of self-pity.

'…and as I'm sure you will have noticed on the odd occasion, my behaviour can be a little erratic…well, those mild schizophrenic episodes are also symptoms of the disease', he confirmed getting a bit fidgety and uncomfortable at being the case-study.

'So all those times that you were being obnoxious and gross, you were doing it deliberately to prevent me from getting close to you…to protect me' Madison jumped in again, a little taken aback by the revelation and torn between her feelings of anger and compassion.

The Bishop closed his eyes and frowned, breathing in heavily, but he didn't respond.

Olivia chose that moment to get up and leave.

'Well; I have to go…' she announced calmly, '…as despite what Tobias here says, I do have other people to see; I just popped in to give you these', she declared, handing him a new box of pills.

'It was nice meeting you…again', she remarked, turning to Madison.

'You too…' Madison responded, still a little shocked by what she had just heard.

'Olivia, on your way out, could you ask Rosa to bring me a fresh glass of water for these', *the Bishop* requested, raising his box of pills.

'I'll go and get it for you', Madison offered, and with that the two women walked away together.

They took a few steps and once they were out of *the Bishop's* earshot, Madison seized the opportunity to ask the young doctor to explain his illness further and to suggest a prognosis.

Olivia did so, very eloquently, as they continued walking towards the house, explaining that Huntington's disease – which is what *the Bishop* was suffering from – is an incurable degenerative genetic disorder.

'But he's going to be okay…isn't he?' Madison murmured as if not understanding the concept of 'incurable'.

'The symptoms are many', Olivia continued confidently, '…and while it is a slow process…over time…they gradually begin to adversely affect the person's cognitive abilities, their personality, their physical capacity and their all-round behaviour – to a point where eventually they overwhelm the person's rational judgement, their patience, their comprehension and their dexterity.'

'Basically', Olivia resumed; 'Mr Byron's brain cells are slowly wasting away…which will eventually lead to him losing his ability to walk, talk, think…and reason.'

'It starts with confusion and clumsiness, loss of co-ordination, spilling things, dropping things etc and develops terminally; it's all very sad', she lamented.

Madison shook her head in horrified disbelief but even as she endeavoured to hide her emotions…and battled to maintain her composure, a series of images flashed through her mind…of *the Bishop* losing his balance in the spa and spilling drinks. At the time it had never occurred to her that he might be ill but as the full horror of what was happening to him started to sink in she began to understand; isolated phrases…and solitary words…were suddenly brought into focus, given meaning where no meaning had existed previously…and while he had only raised his voice to her once or twice during their time together, she definitely remembered him being excessively obnoxious and critical on more than one occasion.

They reached the house and walked straight through together, Olivia waving politely at Rosa as they passed by the kitchen.

Madison opened the front door and watched in a daze almost as Olivia walked to her car and stored her doctor's bag in the boot before getting behind the wheel.

The two women exchanged another polite wave and as Olivia drove off Madison slowly closed the door again before turning and exchanging sad looks with Rosa who was stood in the kitchen doorway, a fresh glass of water in hand.

'So…now you know', the old house-keeper said softly, her voice tinged with sadness.

Madison nodded but rendered speechless, she didn't comment.

She simply took the glass of water and returned to *the Bishop's* side in the garden with a heavy heart.

Once there, having taken up her seat…and waited for him to swallow his pills, Madison tried to direct the conversation away from the pathos of the moment, suggesting that they play one of those silly games that people play when they are lost for a topic of conversation.

'If you had been given the chance to be anything, anything at all; what would you have liked to have been…' she asked curiously, as the tears began pearling in her eyes.

'Is that a rhetorical question?' *the Bishop* enquired flatly.

'No, I'm serious; if you could be anything, anything at all, what would it be?' she repeated, choking slightly on the emotion.

The Bishop thought about it for a moment and then taking inspiration from the expression on her face, he replied rather poetically that he would have liked to have been one of her tears.

'Oh and why would that be?' She asked, her eyes already brimming.

The Bishop looked up directly at the sky and after taking a deep breath to focus his concentration, he quoted 'The Tear'.

'I would have liked to have been one of your tears because…a tear is born in the eye…lives on the cheek…and dies on the lips', he announced rather prosaically.

Madison stared at him and almost immediately big wet tears began rolling down her cheeks.

'I'm so sorry Tobias; is there really nothing that can be done?' she sighed.

He reached out and took her fingers in his. His hand was soft and gentle but his grip was still firm.

'I'm afraid not my dear; death is an incurable disease', he disclosed rather morbidly, a note of finality in his voice, 'but that said…' he continued, '…I cannot…and will not complain; I've lived a fabulous, rewarding…and enviable lifestyle.'

'Doesn't it scare you…are you not afraid…how are you not afraid?' Madison blurted out, the emotional ache in her voice choking her words.

The Bishop turned again and looked into her eyes; 'People fear what they don't understand; I know what awaits…' he murmured. 'You see, Madison; when you die; when you shuffle off this mortal coil, you're just dead, expired, deceased, no more; that's all there is to it. All these existential concepts about an afterlife, about purgatory, angels and demons, heaven and hell are just ways for us as human beings to deal with our mortality and the fear of death that religion and society have bred into us over our lifetime.'

'But…but people want to believe in these things; they want to believe that there is a heaven and a hell', Madison countered, wiping her cheek.

'Of course they do…', *the Bishop* concurred with his usual quiet intensity; '…that's what human beings have been conditioned to believe; that's the narrative that religion has sold to humanity for centuries…and who I am to question that…but the reality of our existence is that we are just mortal souls with a finite life-cycle. When you die, you are just a corpse, a heap of biological matter that, having served its purpose, slowly breaks down again until it is just a pile of dust, which by the way, is the only thing religion gets right.'

Madison pouted.

'The only existential afterlife you might enjoy…the only way you might 'live-on'…posthumously…so to speak…', *the Bishop* continued, '… is in the hearts and minds of those you have left behind, in the thoughts and memories or your shared existence; other than that…you just slip into the 'next room', never to be seen or heard from again…'

'I'm not so sure', Madison argued pulling back her hand; 'I think that there might be something else…out there in the universe.'

'That's very sweet Maddy…' *the Bishop* replied, this time with a wince, '…but we have sent probes and satellites to the far reaches of the galaxy… and guess what…there have been no reported sightings of any pearly gates…or signposts to the Promised Land or to Nirvana or Paradise; what does that tell you…?', he continued, his tone laced with more than a hint of irony.

Madison shrugged as she looked at him in wistful contemplation.

'It tells you that these concepts are all in the mind, in the minds of scared human beings who cannot believe that they, with all their flaws and failings could possibly be the best that the universe has to offer. There must be more…right…? We, as human beings cannot be the summit of creation; the definitive experiment…; there has to be something else out there better than us…surely…? I mean look at us, we are not worthy, we have no honour; we kill each other, we buy and sell each other on a daily basis…we…'

'I get it; we're animals…' Madison interrupted, not wanting another lecture on the short-comings of humanity.

'No, no, not animals', *the Bishop* corrected her; 'we are afraid; afraid that we are the best the universe has to offer…and by the way…picking up on what you said just now; have you noticed that nobody actually ever goes to hell; whenever someone dies people always say that they have gone 'up to heaven' and that they are 'looking down on them', nobody is ever looking up from the 'fires of hell'…are they…huh?'

The overriding mood in the little shelter was one of sadness but the pregnant pause and the reflective mood that followed allowed each of them the time to recompose themselves…and after that, despite *the Bishop's* quiet, almost sullen demeanour, the rest of the afternoon was filled with lots of flowing intelligent conversation, reminiscent of their summer idyll.

They discussed a whole range of topics and not unsurprisingly *the Bishop* spent quite some time discussing his succession and who he thought would be the best pretender to his crown.

That debate went on for quite a while but in due course, bored with listening to all the possible permutations, some of which *the Bishop* inadvertently repeated, Madison's attention began to wander and she decided that it was time to change the subject to something she was more interested in.

She waited for a natural pause in the conversation and while *the Bishop* was catching his breath one time; she jumped in with a question of her own, interrupting him before he could continue his monologue.

'So; is it true that you came to New York…and got thrown out?' she teased, offering him the bait to develop the narrative.

She had been dying to hear the story of his aborted visit to New York, ever since Evie had inadvertently mentioned it to her in the middle of Macy's.

The Bishop sighed at her suggestion…and initially he was a little reluctant to talk about his experience; he never liked discussing weakness or embarrassing situations, especially where he was concerned…but eventually he relented and told her the whole story, recounting it with all the eloquence, drama and pathos that the situation imposed…while of course exaggerating his own role of wronged-innocent and inevitably decrying the frustrating intransigence of the American Authorities.

It was an amazing story which Madison found quite captivating but when he had finished she could not help but feel a little despondent at the realisation that somehow the hand of destiny had prevented her from enjoying that lost opportunity.

Nevertheless, she was quietly flattered by his story...and while *the Bishop* continued to pontificate and berate those who had refused him entry to the USA, albeit a little less vigorously than he had previously because of his failing health, her focus seemed to drift off...to ponder a more personal issue which had been driving her to distraction ever since her very first visit to the Abbey.

Casting her mind back to that evening when she had first noticed the photograph of a woman in his bedroom…and then forward to the day when she had come across those infamous letters in his drawer, she re-lived those moments in her head, as she had done on many occasions over the past year.

Neither of those rather delicate matters had ever really been adequately explained to her, but she knew that because of her rather tenuous position after the incident with the letters, and several other more minor indiscretions, none of which she was proud to be the perpetrator of, she had never been in a position to ask the one question that had been haunting her, tormenting her ever since;

Who was this Jane person...and why did she mean so much to him?

She was still desperate to find out, to elucidate the mystery of the woman behind the letters…and indeed on more than one occasion during the afternoon, she had been tempted to broach the subject...but each time she had managed to bite her tongue, well aware from previous experience that she would be on shaky ground with *the Bishop* if she did so.

It was however torturing her not to know - despite it no longer serving any purpose, because who Jane was and what she meant to *the Bishop* was really none of her business any more - but her ego wouldn't be ignored, especially after the cryptic discussion she had had with Rosa earlier - which had done no more than pour hot oil on the braise of her simmering curiosity.

Madison sat there in frustration, desperately looking around for something else to focus her attention on, something that would take her mind off of her obsession and release her from the self-inflicted pressure she had put herself under...and then suddenly, without warning, it happened... she had an epiphany.

She looked over at *the Bishop*, swaying gently in his hammock, enjoying the peace and calm of his now sedentary existence and out of nowhere she suddenly realised that, actually it didn't matter anymore, that she had been right to let this one slide because there was no longer any point in opening that particular can of worms...even though her information-hungry, journalistic demons were still secretly howling away inside her head, demanding appeasement.

The pressure disappeared almost instantly like a weight being lifted off of her shoulders and she quietly enjoyed the irony of the moment at the realisation that the tact he had counselled her in, on so many occasions, was finally bearing its fruit.

Besides, she thought to herself, if this was going to be the last time that she and *the Bishop* met, she didn't want his final memory of her to be one of confrontation.

She sat back in her chair and as she tilted her head and looked up... prompted by the unmistakeable whup-whup noise of its rotors...Madison noticed a rescue helicopter in the sky up above them...circling around and around like a hungry vulture biding its time, waiting for its time to strike.

Thankfully, it wasn't headed their way...not right then at least...but as she wiped her eyes and glanced once more at *the Bishop* in his hammock, the irony of that analogy wasn't lost on her either.

Another hour or so flew by, and in what seemed like no time at all, Rosa appeared again at the far end of the garden, waving her hands at them in a come-hither fashion - and doing a rather poor imitation of a steering-wheel – to let Madison know that her taxi had arrived.

Madison saw her out of the corner of her eye and acknowledging the old house-keeper's signal with a raised hand of her own, she looked at her watch and sighed tiredly as she realised that it was already time for her to leave; she was on the evening flight back to New York and with her busy schedule she knew that - while she would have loved to have stayed a while longer - she just couldn't afford to miss it.

She looked over again at *the Bishop*, trying to maintain her composure, but as she gathered herself together and got up to leave, bending over him carefully to kiss him goodbye, the sadness was still clearly evident in her eyes.

Emotion coursing through her veins, she kissed him tenderly on the cheek not wanting to believe that she might be seeing him for the last time, and as she hesitated to move away from his side, another untimely tear pearled in the corner of her eye.

The Bishop saw this and without saying a word, he slowly raised a hand to brush it away.

'Just remember', he said quietly as she slowly straightened herself up, '...you're swimming with sharks now...so in the immortal words of Michael Corleone (from the Godfather); always keep your friends close and your enemies closer.'

Madison nodded her head and smiling stoically through the melancholy of the moment she grabbed his outstretched hand and squeezed it as tightly as she could, the impending sense of loss suddenly surging once again through every nerve and sinew of her being.

Time stood still for a moment, but then realising her situation Madison distracted herself with another glance at her watch.

'I have to go', she whispered, though the sound barely passed her lips.

The Bishop recognised her predicament and sliding his hand back under the blanket he responded with a simple smile and an understanding nod.

It was a poignant moment and as she turned away, ready to make her way back to the house, Madison felt emotionally drained…and a little unsteady on her feet.

She had hoped that this visit would be a cathartic experience; one which would provide her with some answers and maybe some closure even on the time that she and *the Bishop* had spent together, but unfortunately, because of circumstances which were way beyond her control, it had instead been quite the opposite.

She set off for the house, her mind in somewhat of a whirl, trying to analyse and dissect the meaning of his parting words, but after only a few steps, she stopped in her tracks and turned back almost in slow-motion to look at the wooden shelter one last time, hoping possibly for a final wave from her ailing mentor.

Unfortunately though, her view was obscured by one of the wooden balustrades and as *the Bishop* had already picked up his book again, she couldn't see him.

At that point, her fixed smile faded instantly and her shoulders slumped as she turned once again and continued the walk back to the house, taking a series of deep breaths, one after the other, in order to regain her composure.

Rosa was there waiting at the back door, ready to escort her through to the front the house - which she did in silence - and having signalled to the taxi that she needed just one more minute, Madison turned to the wise old house-keeper and handed her, her business card.

'If there is anything I can do, anything at all; please...call me', she declared, the words trailing off a little as she choked once again on the emotion.

Rosa courteously accepted the card and smiling politely, she nodded in an understanding manner.

Madison returned her smile as best she could and as she stepped out into the forecourt where the cherry-red taxi was waiting patiently for its fare, she stopped once again and took a moment to look around and admire the Abbey's impressive yet homely exterior.

So many memories, she thought to herself and as she walked on towards the taxi, with a heavy heart after what had been a rather emotionally-charged afternoon, snap-shots of her time together with *the Bishop* began flashing through her mind once again.

She knew how grateful she was to have met the man, and even if he had been a little belligerent at times, which she now understood was possibly a symptom of his illness, he had been a wonderful companion and had taught her so much about life, about self-belief and about thinking outside the box; she had even learned a little bit about patience and strategy from watching him and the others play chess.

Indeed, he had given her all that and so much more - opening doors for her professionally and introducing her to some very influential people - but her one regret, the one thing that still rankled with her as she got into the taxi and closed the door behind her - other than the fact that there was nothing she could do to help him fight his illness - was that she had never gotten to meet the one person whose ghostly presence had had so much influence on her time at the Abbey.

Jane was obviously *the Bishop's* one true love, she thought to herself as she made herself comfortable; after all, he kept all the rhapsodic letters she had ever written to him in a drawer…her photo took pride of place next to his bed…and more frustratingly…as far as she was concerned… he kept her memory etched indelibly on his heart...and sadly there was just no competing with that kind of devotion, she concluded, as the taxi pulled away.

Nevertheless, I would still have liked to have met the woman, Madison mused to herself as she brushed a stray hair away from her face…because she must have been one hellofa woman to enchant a man like *the Bishop* to that extent.

The cab came to an abrupt halt at the gate to let some oncoming traffic go past and as she looked back at the abbey, sighing despondently Madison realised that she would probably never get that chance...

CHAPTER TWENTY-SEVEN

Another few months slipped quietly by;

It had been a rather difficult start…but Madison had slowly blossomed in her new role, earning not only her team's respect but that of her peers…and her bosses too…and as a consequence…with a little help from Amanda…she even managed to get the necessary authorisation to completely redesign and revamp the fashion department.

Naturally, Madison had always had big plans and big ideas…and having been given the go-ahead to implement them she wasted no time in transforming the whole department into one big user-friendly environment; her goal being not only to facilitate more interaction between colleagues but also to create a more positive vibe generally around the office.

It was an ingenious idea…and everyone was delighted with their new open-plan workspace…but Madison's plans didn't stop there…because not only did the new lay-out make the workplace more convivial for everyone, it also freed-up quite a bit of floor-space which she had every intention of using…to increase the team's capacity…when the time was right.

That said, the new open-plan lay-out wasn't Madison's main goal in all this; no, her main goal in all this was to create a new glass-fronted corner office for herself; one which would not only overlook the world-renowned 'Avenue of the Americas' but also give her the status that she felt she now deserved.

(She had never liked the cramped and windowless little office that Gretchen had used; she felt it lacked any cachet and pizzazz)

So…this is what she did…and as part of her plans, she also had all the latest technology installed in the new office too, including a bank of TVs along one wall…which were tuned to multiple channels which constantly updated the news…and kept her regularly informed of any new developments or recent events in the world of fashion and celebrity.

Life was good; Madison was finally moving up. She had a new office; her reputation was growing, her open-door policy had proved to be very successful, and even the little changes she had made as part of her 'reality policies' were having their effect on hearts and minds.

Then one day, while she was busy looking through a bunch of new fashion photos, Nicole…*one of the three new interns that Amanda had approved…*appeared in the doorway to her office looking a little confused.

(Nicole was typically French…and so strikingly beautiful that she could easily pass for a model. She was very stylish…if a little provocative...in the way she wore her crisp white blouses, tight-fitting pencil-skirts and killer heels…but her sexy look aside she had a good attitude and a decent work ethic.)

'Madisssonn', she said in her strong French accent; 'Can I ask you about 'ze…nanny.'

Madison stopped what she was doing, turned her head and found herself looking directly into Nicole's liquid brown eyes.

'…She's always so glamorous...so why 'ze nanny', Nicole questioned curiously.

Lowering the photo she had been studying, Madison thought about the question for a moment…and was sorely tempted to caricature her boss in a way that would back up her 'ice-queen' reputation…but being the person she had now become, mature and responsible, she managed to resist...just.

'All I can say Nicole…is that Amanda is…'a trailblazer', Madison replied succinctly, avoiding the 'nanny' reference altogether.

'Uuumm; I don't know about…how you say…trailblazer…' Nicole retorted with her charming French candour;

'…but when I see her…she always makes me feel a certain…'froideur'', she added, while wrapping her arms tightly around herself and feigning a shiver.

'Look Nicole…', Madison began to preach; '…if I were you, I wouldn't go making any impertinent…or disrespectful assumptions about the people who work here; you just need to do your job…and if you do that, then Ama…Ms Brooke won't be a problem for you.'

As luck would have it, Quinton…who had become a regular visitor to Madison's new office… just happened to arrive at that very moment…strolling in with his usual self-confidence and overbearing demeanour… forcing the young French intern to quickly sidestep out of the way…like a redundant air-hostess.

'What was all that about?' he asked as Nicole turned and flounced away muttering in French under breath; 'Oh, la, laa...quel con!'

'…Nothing that concerns you', Madison answered back; 'She just wanted to know about Amanda.'

'Aaah, your friend Amanda', Quinton quipped nonchalantly; patting his jacket as if to check that he had his phone with him before taking up a casual stance against her desk.

'…Hardly my friend', Madison countered, returning to her photo-selection.

'…Oh; that's not what I heard', Quinton teased, moving from the desk to the table where Madison was trying to work.

'I'm sorry; what did you hear?' she enquired casually, forgetting…in the moment…all about her own rules on office hear-say.

'…Oh nothing…' Quinton tormented as he flashed his winning smile at her; 'I wouldn't want to get a reputation as a gossip', he whispered, leaning in closer.

'Probably for the best…' Madison argued as she picked out a couple of her favourite photos and set them aside.

An awkward pause followed while each of them decided on what they should say next.

'Okay, I'll tell you…', Quinton suddenly conceded…*after what seemed like an interminable silence*…clearly hoping that by telling Madison what he had heard, he would somehow endear himself to her and have a better shot at asking her out;

'…but this has to stay between us…' he insisted.

Madison just shrugged her shoulders, a barely perceptible smile flickering across her lips.

'Well…', Quinton announced, having first checked that nobody else was in ear-shot; 'I heard that Amanda fought very hard for you to get this job…and that without her backing you would not only…not have this job…but you would not have any job at all, at least not in this building.'

'Whaaat…; that's bullshit', Madison scoffed, without deviating from what she was doing, 'You really shouldn't believe everything you hear Mr Booth', she added while brushing a stray hair off of one of the photos.

'Yeah…you're probably right', Quinton quickly concurred while flashing his winning smile again, '…but anyway…' he resumed as he checked his phone which had just rung in his pocket; '…have you reconsidered my latest offer?'

'I have...' Madison replied firmly, her mind suddenly reliving the day that Amanda had defended her against Todd's false accusations, '…and the answer is still no. So if there's nothing else, I need to get on', she insisted as she picked up the photographs that she had picked out and made her way back over to her desk.

Quinton shook his head…a little dismayed…but he made no attempt to leave.

Madison looked up again…to see what more he wanted. 'Do I need to call security?' she asked coldly.

'No...I'm good', Quinton replied slowly, realising that his ploy to wriggle into Madison's affections had come up short once again.

Madison watched him leave…and as he disappeared into the distance, stopping briefly to exchange a word of wisdom with Nicole, she started wondering how Quinton could have possibly known the things he had just spoken about…who it was that could possibly have told him…and how in

God's name he thought that embarrassing her like that would ever make her reconsider his request for a dinner-date…which was never going to happen no matter how many times he asked.

A few days later, Madison had arranged to go for lunch with Evie at Carlo's Italian diner, one of their favourite haunts.

They had been keeping in touch with each other via text…but because of their busy lives / work schedules…they hadn't seen each other in person in months;. in fact they hadn't seen each other in person since that brief encounter in Macy's back in March when Evie had informed Madison of the Bishop's illness…so this was going to be their first chance for a real catch up since then.

Detail; As it was a week-day both women were wearing their work clothes; Evie was wearing a 'ying & yang' print top and a beautiful…but surprisingly demure…silk handkerchief skirt – while Madison was once again in her charcoal grey, cropped-trouser business-suit.

'How are you doing E?' Madison asked as Evie joined her at the table.

'Living the dream hon…living the dream,' Evie replied, her whole demeanour radiating elation as she sat down and caught the waiter's eye.

'I'm starving', she announced, barely allowing the waiter to pull out his pad, before she ordered her usual; a grilled chicken sandwich and a small salad.

'I can see that', Madison remarked as she opted for a small Caesar-salad.

'Sooo…tell me more about your trip to London', Madison prompted… as the waiter disappeared…hoping to get a handle on the situation, as Evie was so clearly on a high.

'Well…' Evie began without any of her usual preamble. 'He rang me a couple of times…we got talking…and it just kinda developed from there... organically' she announced, before pausing to take a sip of water.

'...And then, before I knew it, I was on the plane to England', she continued, getting a little over-excited.

'Wow', Madison exclaimed with a hint of ambivalence, before taking her own sip of water.

'I did try to call you...' Evie interposed; 'but...'

'Yeah...I know; sorry about that' Madison interrupted; '...and <u>this is Gary</u> we're talking about...right?' she confirmed, trying to strike the right balance between pleased and concerned.

'Aha...it's crazy; right...who would've thought?' Evie confessed, beginning to see the humour and the irony in the situation.

'Oh, I know he's a bit rough around the edges...' she conceded...

'And a bit young...' Madison interjected, screwing up her face.

'And a bit young...' Evie acknowledged; '...and...not my usual type...' she added before Madison could do so, 'but he's got a real heart of gold.'

Madison sat back and frowned, still unsure about all this...but while she could not question the fact that Gary had a heart of gold, as he had already demonstrated it to her on several occasions...she still felt that she should voice her concerns.

'Look E, I don't want to 'harsh your mellow' here...' she remarked while simultaneously straightening her cutlery, '...but I met Gary a couple of weeks ago in Paris ...and he didn't seem so...he didn't seem... as excited...as engaged as you seem to be.'

'Yeah...but he's a guy; guys don't like to show their emotions, do they?' Evie countered clearly engrossed in her new pursuit of happiness.

Madison just smiled and shrugged. She still wasn't convinced but she decided to let it slide as she hadn't seen Evie this enthusiastic about a relationship in a long while.

'Okay then; as long as you're happy; that's all that matters' she agreed.

'So anyway, enough about me...what about you Mad...anybody on the horizon?' Evie suddenly enquired, changing the subject just as their meals were being served.

'No...not really...' Madison disclosed, once the waiter had moved away, '...I'm on a bit of a romantic hiatus...although we have just taken on a new guy; Quinton...'

'Quinton?' Evie repeated as she tucked into her grilled chicken sandwich.

'Yes Quinton…' Madison confirmed, '…but I just don't have the time for all that…and besides… after what happened I have made it a rule that I am never going to date anybody from the office…ever again.'

'Yeah…I can understand that…' Evie acknowledged as she took another bite of her sandwich; '…but Mad, you still need to get your freak on from time to time.'

'Yeah, I suppose I do…I just have to find the right guy…' Madison reasoned before taking another swig of water.

At that point, having practically devoured her sandwich, Evie wiped her hands and pulled out her phone in order to show her friend all the photos she had taken outside the different landmarks she had visited in London.

'Check this out', she said as she handed over her phone.

Madison put down her fork…took hold of the phone…and started flicking through the photos on the tiny screen making a pertinent or a funny comment on just about every one before stopping to focus on two particular outfits that caught her professional eye.

The first was a stunning red and white silk polka-dot jumpsuit and the second was a black bodysuit that Evie had matched perfectly with a full white dirndl skirt which had just a flash of coloured detail splashed on the side.

'Wow; that jumpsuit is…zinging…' Madison remarked pointing to the photo of Evie in Hyde Park, '…and that bodysuit and skirt ensemble; that's the ultimate colour-block combination', she added flicking to the next frame.

'I couldn't have put it better myself', Evie agreed making short work of her small salad.

The two friends chatted for another fifteen minutes or so but as she had to get back to work; Evie was soon readying herself to leave.

'I know it's been a bit rushed Mad…' she explained, '…but I can't be late back to the office; my boss will go kazoo.' *(She accompanied her comment with a crazy swizzle gesture)*

'That's fine E, I understand', Madison declared amicably; '…I'm just glad we've managed to reconnect…and hey…let's not leave it so long next time…'

'Agreed...' Evie replied as she got up and gave her friend another big hug; '...Oh and by the way...' she whispered into Madison's ear, '...thanks for lunch...and thanks again for introducing me to Gary...'

Madison was a little taken aback by the sentiment in those last words but she barely had time to register them before Evie turned and made her way out, raising her right hand to her ear as she went...in that universally-recognised phone gesture that let her friend know that she would be in touch.

At that very same moment, the waiter who had served them stopped by to ask Madison if there was anything else she needed.

'No...no thank-you', she replied a little absent-mindedly, her brain still coming to terms with what she and Evie had been discussing.

'...but I will take the check...' she suddenly prompted, just as the guy was turning to walk away.

'The check? Coming right up', the young man confirmed, before continuing on his way.

Still a little bemused, Madison sat back, took out her phone and started to scroll through her messages while she waited for the waiter to return... but she barely had time to look at an e-mail or two before he was back again...check in hand.

She smiled at him politely, quickly handing over her card...and while the young man dealt with the transaction, she graciously engaged in a little small-talk with him, about the establishment...its décor...and its food.

'Maybe we'll see you again then', the young man remarked as he returned her card and handed her, her receipt, unaware that she and Evie were regular customers.

'Maybe you will...' Madison replied as she put away her purse.

Meanwhile, at the table behind Madison's, another customer was trying to catch the young man's attention and so…while he moved on to deal with her, Madison quietly got up and made her way out, deciding to take a short-cut back to her office, through the walkways of the busy plaza in order to save time.

It only took her a couple of minutes to get back to her office-building and as she strolled through the main doors into the lobby…*being mindful not to step on the wet floor that someone had clearly just wiped*…Madison's eyes were instantly drawn to two young men who were in the middle of assembling some kind of publicity stand over by the reception desk.

Clearly, they were having a little difficulty with the logistics of putting the stand together

…*which pained Madison somewhat*…but it wasn't the sight of these two young executives berating each other for their ineptitude or their lack of ingenuity that prompted her to stop and linger; it was the unmistakeable sound of Nicole's voice.

She couldn't quite see her young intern across the busy lobby…*as she was hidden behind the stand that the two young men were erecting*…but Madison had already gotten used to her Gallic tone and recognised it immediately.

Nicole had been sent down to collect some document or other…and as she stood there at reception waiting for one of the receptionists to hand it to her, she had caught the eye of one…if not both of the bungling young execs…with her stunning figure and her engaging smile…and was clearly enjoying some kind of flirty exchange with one or other of them.

Frowning, she stood there motionless for another moment or so… *not wanting, in her head, to get the reputation of company killjoy*…but then, on hearing Nicole's voice split the air for a second time, with a laugh that drew more than its fair share of curious stares, Madison suddenly felt that it was incumbent on her…given the position she now held…to go and have a quiet word with her young intern…about her professional conduct.

She started making her way over to the reception desk…but unbeknownst to her, her presence in the lobby hadn't gone unnoticed… and as she moved forward, one of the young men picked her up in his peripheral vision and quickly signalled to his colleague to stop chatting and get on with what they were doing.

Madison caught this out of the corner of her own eye and smiled to herself discreetly; *her reputation was clearly starting to build around the building*…but then as she advanced a little further toward the reception desk…hoping to get a quiet word with Nicole…a thousand scenarios began whirling around in her head about the potential ramifications of this kind of innocent, but nevertheless flirty interaction between her intern and the two young execs…notably images of her own unsettling experience with Morgan.

The memory of that event caught her a little off-guard…and distracted by its disturbing nature, she suddenly found herself walking straight into Quinton who had just emerged from one of the elevators followed closely by the Head of HR, Svetlana.

'Quinton', Madison gasped, throwing out a hand to steady herself; '…I'm sorry I didn't see you there'.

'It's all good Maddy', Quinton replied, almost dismissively, raising a hand himself as he stepped around her and carried on strolling towards the exit.

Flustered momentarily, Madison brushed herself off before turning and looking at Svetlana. The two women exchanged an awkward smile but as neither offered any comment, Svetlana just hurried off to catch up with Quinton who was already waiting for her by the main-doors, clearly feeling more than a little uncomfortable with the optics.

Madison watched Svetlana go…with a wry smile…and then, glancing impassively at the two young executives as she passed them by, she continued on towards the reception desk…just as a third man arrived behind her to join up with his two colleagues.

‘She’s very playful; I quite fancy her’, said the first of the young men who had been setting up the stand.

‘Hands off, I saw her first’, the second guy retorted.

‘No, no; I’ve already called ‘dibs’, said the new guy, playfully digging the second guy in the ribs.

‘Hey…you can’t call ‘dibs’ on the new interns; it’s against…’ the first guy quickly countered.

‘It’s against what…?’ the new guy asked, cutting in before his colleague could finish his sentence.

‘It’s against the new company policy’, the second guy explained, using imaginary air-quotes.

‘Tell that to my todge’, the new guy argued, gesturing crudely to his groin.

Madison, who was still in earshot at this point, heard what the guys were saying and immediately stopped in her tracks.

She took a deep breath and then spinning around, her face suddenly contorted in disgust, she quickly confronted the three young men.

‘For crying out loud; don’t you guys ever learn?’ she blasted, catching all three men by surprise; ‘Women are not pieces of meat to be haggled over.’

Stunned…and stung…by this sudden and unexpected condemnation of their male bravado…and somewhat embarrassed too by a couple of the outraged looks from passers-by…the three young men instantly fell silent and just looked at each other with genuine bemusement.

Madison glared at all three them for a moment or two…but she didn’t wait around for a response, preferring instead to just pivot on her heels once again and keep on walking…as she was still hoping to catch Nicole before the young intern headed back upstairs.

However, Nicole was nowhere to be seen; *on seeing the events unfold she had already made herself scarce* …and so, after a quick look left and right, Madison just turned around again and headed over to the lift, announcing quite loudly over her shoulder as she went;

‘Remember the rules guys…; no inappropriate behaviour will be tolerated in this building.’

Moments later, Madison reached the lifts; feeling rather pleased with herself and pressed the call button with a flourish, checking robotically which way the directional indicators were pointing in order to see which of the cabins was on its way down.

The left-hand cabin was still ascending but the right-hand cabin was on its way down.

She took a step to the right and seconds later the lift emitted its familiar melodious 'ping' followed by the even more recognisable whoosh that announced the opening of its doors.

Madison paused for a moment to let anybody who might be inside, out, and then stepped forward…expecting the cabin to be empty…only to be greeted by the biggest surprise…if not the greatest shock…of her life.

Inside the cabin, she found Amanda…and she was in there with a man!

'Oh…Madison…' Amanda stammered while discreetly wiping her lips and recovering her composure; 'This is Mauro…Mauro Hernandez… from Argentina.'

Madison just smiled politely and took a step back, without saying a word.

('Mauro from Argentina' was dressed in a smart Italian-silk suit…which instantly reminded Madison of the Bishop…and had a charming smile which shone through the most striking hazelnut-brown eyes.)

'Hello Madison, it's nice to meet you', Mauro remarked in a deep baritone voice while extending his right hand.

'Enchanté', Madison replied amicably…*working with Nicole had taught her some new French words*…as Amanda quickly took him by the arm and ushered him aside in order to expedite their goodbyes.

Madison looked on as they spoke for a moment or two…and then with one last beguiling grin, Mauro turned and walked away, Amanda standing her ground awkwardly as she waited and watched him leave.

'Going up?' Madison enquired a little tongue in cheek.

Amanda turned and stepped back into the cabin without a word.

'So…Mauro…from Argentina…' Madison commented a little irreverently not deigning to look at her boss; 'He seems nice.'

'Ahaa', Amanda confirmed through tight lips as the cabin began to ascend.

Later in the day, Madison was sat at her desk chatting with Lily from the Research Department about this fascinating new designer who was coming to town, when out of the corner of her eye she just happened to notice Nicole, hovering outside her office, waiting to use the photo-copy machine.

This gave Madison an idea and as Lily prepared to leave, just a few minutes later, she asked her if she would ask Nicole to pop in and see her. '…before she disappears again.'

'Sure thing…' Lily replied very matter-of-fact; '…but do let me know what you think about that guy', she added, motioning to the portfolio she had left behind, 'I need to see if he's available for a 'sit-down' while he's in New York.'

'I will do that,' Madison answered, glancing at the file while brushing a stray hair behind her ear.

Madison knew that she was probably going to regret what she was about to do…because she had gone to a great deal of trouble to make sure that everybody felt comfortable in her department…but she had been in a similar position herself…and she felt that…as Nicole's boss, it was incumbent on her to say something about what had happened earlier, believing that the embarrassment she would no doubt experience in the moment would be a small price to pay for the peace of mind she would get from airing her misgivings about Nicole's 'somewhat-unprofessional' behaviour, however innocent it might or might not have been.

'You want to see me…boss', Nicole murmured as she stood in the door-way, waiting expectantly.

'Oh, hi Nicole', Madison began, beckoning her forward; 'Yes, come on in.'

Nicole took another step forward, a little unsure as to why she had been summoned.

‘Look Nicole’, Madison continued, setting aside the file that Lily had just deposited on her desk; ‘I…I saw you in the lobby earlier with Mr Henderson and Mr Gibbs…’

Nicole bit her lip and smiled coyly. ‘Yeah…nice guys…’ she observed.

‘I’m sure they are’, Madison concurred as she pulled her chair forward and took up a more commanding position, ‘...but I feel you should know… as a new girl here…that all the guys in these offices have a ‘work-hard, play-hard’ ethos.’

Nicole raised her eyebrows quizzically, a little confused by the idiom.

‘What I’m trying to say Nicole…’ Madison pursued, not wanting to shy away from the question ‘…is that you must realise that the guys in this office, in this building have no discernible moral compass.’

Nicole still looked confused, as again Madison paused, trying to choose her words carefully; ‘Look…I know it’s a cliché…and don’t feel as if you have to talk to me about this if you don’t want to…but I feel that it would be remiss of me if I didn’t warn you that...’

She paused again…

‘Look…all I’m trying to say Nicole…is that if you want my advice; just stay clear of office relationships...; there are plenty of other places to meet me(n)...people.’ she added almost as an after-thought.

Nicole frowned, and then finally nodded her understanding before adding…*after a brief pause*; ‘But Madissson, I’m just trying to fit in.’

‘…And I understand that…’ Madison concurred, ‘…but flirting with your colleagues is not the way to succeed. Hard work is…if you want realise your potential…’

‘Maybe for you…but look what I have to work with…’ Nicole suddenly interrupted, gesturing to her figure and wiggling her hips, before shrugging her shoulders and pirouetting 180 degrees.

‘Oh, la, laa...quel Conne’ she mumbled under her breath as she walked away, rolling her eyes petulantly.

Madison watched her young intern walk back over to the photo-copy machine to collect the copies she had made, and all she (Madison) could do was just shake her head in despair.

Oh, the wisdom of hindsight, she thought to herself as her phone began to ring, quickly refocusing her mind on the job she was actually being paid to do.

A week or so later Evie called…as promised…to propose that they meet in the park on the weekend…as they hadn't done so in a while.

'Sorry E; I have plans Saturday', Madison replied; 'my parents are coming into town.'

'Well that sucks…' Evie mumbled, running her fingers through her newly-styled hair.

'I could do coffee though…', Madison quickly suggested, sensing the disappointment in Evie's reaction on the other end of the phone; '…as long as I'm back home by two.'

'Okay; coffee it is then' Evie agreed, perking up a little; 'Usual place… at twelve?'

'Twelve is fine by me', Madison concurred; 'I'll see you there.'

'See you there', Evie repeated before hanging up.

On that Saturday morning the two friends arrived pretty much at the same time.

It was a pleasant day…by New York standards…and as a consequence Madison was wearing a smart, powder-blue trouser-suit over a pristine white-silk blouse while Evie…in her own inimitable style…was looking very cute in a pair of red denim jeans that she had matched with an eye-catching Bardot top, while her hair was shaped into a stylish new pixie-cut that made her look years younger than she actually was.

'Wow; you look amazing; I almost didn't recognise you', Madison cried out as the two women met and hugged.

'You approve?' Evie asked excitedly.

'I do; very much so', Madison replied, reaching out to brush a few stray hairs back into place.

'Can I get that in writing?' Evie quipped, brushing her friend's hand away.

Madison just shook her head and rolled her eyes.

'Okay M…' Evie quickly announced as she headed inside; 'Go and grab a table; coffee's on me today'.

Madison shrugged and then quickly looked around…spying a couple who were just about to vacate one of the wrought-iron tables that had been placed outside the establishment for their patrons use.

She glanced to her left and then to her right…in case somebody else had had the same idea as her…and then quickly made her way over to the table before anybody else could claim it. After all, this was New York and in New York there is no standing on ceremony.

Inside the coffee-shop, where the air was filled with the aromatic scent of roasted coffee-beans, Evie suddenly found herself stuck in line behind a guy who just couldn't make up his mind what to order.

'Can I get…a double…double decaf…with just a soupcon of almond milk and hint of sweetener?' he finally announced to the barista.

'Coming right up', the barista replied as he turned away to fill the order.

Meanwhile, Evie tapped the guy on the shoulder; 'You know what you need to get; …a life', she remarked cheekily as she prepared to put in her order.

Moments later, Evie too had been served, and a few minutes after that the two friends were sat outside exchanging small-talk while they sipped carefully on their delicious cappuccinos.

Scrutinising her hair Madison complimented Evie once again on her new look and then, as a couple of tourists at the next table got up to leave, she repeated her apology for not being able to make their walk in the park, as her parents were flying in.

'That's okay Mad.', Evie replied while stirring the foam around in her cup; 'You don't get to see them very often so I can hardly complain that you're blowing me off to go and spend some time with them.'

'Yeah…' Madison acknowledged without further elaboration.

The two women then went on to talk about what was happening in their respective jobs…and within no time Madison was telling Evie all about her new interns and about one of them in particular. (Nicole)

As usual, Evie listened keenly to all her friend's office tribulations but then, after they had been chatting for a while, she suddenly went all quiet and started to get upset.

'You know Mad; if you're not happy with your new intern…if you think she's too headstrong or too flirtatious…you should have let me apply for the job,' she suddenly announced out of left-field, her voice tense with emotion.

Madison baulked with surprise, taken aback by the idea that her friend harboured her own thoughts and dreams of career in the fashion business; 'But E…' she replied; '…You already have a job'.

'My job…my job? I would pack that in, in a heartbeat…if only I could', Evie blurted out as she swirled the coffee around in the bottom of her cup, her mouth beginning to droop a little.

'You know what…E…you look really cute when you pout', Madison remarked trying to lighten the sudden mood of despondency.

Evie looked directly at her friend and grimaced; 'Oh I don't know…' she continued, ignoring Madison's attempt a humour. 'It's just that I've been talking to my colleagues and chatting to a couple of other paralegals… in other firms…and they're all afraid that their companies are going to downsize in the near future…which is going to leave them…me…out of a job…and working with you could have been the ideal opportunity for me to jump before I'm pushed.'

Madison sat forward, realising that it was her turn to listen…even though she knew that Evie would never have qualified for the position of intern…because of her age.

'Oh, I know that I wasn't as academically precocious as you…', Evie persisted as Madison covered her hand with her own, '…but that would have been the perfect opening for me…and you didn't even consider me', she lamented as she pulled her hand away, before revealing;

'Don't take this the wrong way M…but you do realise that me and my gospel girls helped to get you where you are today. It was us that helped to get your article trending on social media…which ultimately got you that next assignment covering that chess-challenge here in New York', she explained succinctly.

On hearing this, Madison stopped drinking and immediately cast her mind back to that evening at Frank's bar...and to Evie's gospel girlfriends who she had so rudely abandoned without so much as a goodbye...

She then thought back to a phone conversation that she and Evie had had a few weeks earlier when she had ranted over the phone to her friend about needing more help, not knowing that Evie would have jumped at the chance to apply for such a role...and for once she found herself tongue tied, not knowing what to say.

'I just thought that... You know what; just forget it; forget I said anything; idle thoughts' Evie suddenly announced, her body-language suggesting anything but a desire to forget.

'No, not forget it; were you seriously interested?' Madison countered, beginning to feel a little guilty.

'Yeah, I was...or at least I would have been', Evie nodded as she sat back disconsolately, the look in her eyes still one of great disappointment.

'Oh, now I feel like a bitch' Madison declared, sensing her friend's disillusion, even though she knew that Evie would never have fulfilled the necessary criteria for consideration.

Evie waved away her friend's self-critique. 'Whatever', she mumbled; 'It's too late now.'

Madison stared directly at her friend for a moment or two, and then putting down her cup, she sat back in her chair too, taking the time to process the emotional fall-out of what had just been revealed to her.

Not another word was spoken thereafter...for a good minute or so... but then by-the-bye a couple of cute guys just happened to stroll past their table on their way into the coffee-shop, which drew not only Evie's attention but that of several other young...and a few not-so-young...female admirers...sat at the surrounding tables too.

This momentary distraction was just what Madison needed and glancing at her phone...*to check the time*...she immediately announced that she needed to get back, using the convenient excuse that her father was a stickler for punctuality.

Evie looked back and just smiled ruefully as she watched Madison quickly finish her coffee.

She then did the same…and after another minute of banal small-talk, mostly about how they should really make a date for their next walk in the park…the two women stood up, Evie giving Madison a brief and somewhat half-hearted hug before she rushed away leaving her friend to stand there, feeling somewhat abandoned and looking more than a little bemused.

CHAPTER TWENTY-EIGHT

Meanwhile, back across the pond, Gary had won his way through to the final elimination round of the European Chess tour; a match which would ultimately decide who would then go forward to face the reigning champion in the next World Series.

His game had matured considerably since he had first rubbed shoulders with the Bishop - and it seemed inevitable…after his brilliant displays in the qualifying tournaments…that he would go on to fulfill his natural potential and achieve his stated goal of becoming the first Australian to compete for the World Championship.

Indeed, he felt the hand of destiny on his shoulder whenever he thought about it…but Gary also knew that he still had one more person to beat before he could fulfill that dream.

…and how fitting it was, that that person, the person who stood in his way, the person who he would have to beat in the best-of-three contest in order to take his place in the World Series would be none other than the man who had always boasted that the title would be his one day; Rory Campbell-Brown.

London;

On the day of the competition, as Gary walked into the plush London venue where the elimination match was being held…accompanied by his brother Joey, his friend Murray and Murray's sister Roz who had all made the trip over from Australia to support him, there was a real buzz of excitement in the air.

A decent-sized crowd had already gathered in the reception area… including his flatmate Dave…*all ready and waiting to welcome him and offer him their support*…and as he made his way over to the official desk – followed closely by his posse - Gary consciously slowed the pace of his progression in order to enjoy the moment and soak up the electric atmosphere that was clearly beginning to build up around him, reacting calmly and deliberately to each of his well-wishers encouraging comments with a confident smile or a purposeful nod as he made his way through them like a boxer making his way to the ring.

Then, having signed all the official paperwork…*as required by the organisers*… he and his entourage headed straight for the refreshment lounge…carried on a wave of growing expectation and back-slapping… where to their great surprise they found Rory holding court, gloating unashamedly and telling anyone who was prepared to listen, about how many people he had beaten over the years in order to get to where he was today…and more poignantly…how little chance Gary…or as he called him…'the little 'roaster'…had of beating him…as if the result of the match was already a foregone conclusion.

The Aussie clan, spying Rory across the room, stopped abruptly just inside the door…like a small band of warriors surveying the lie of the land before an assault…and then, unfazed by Rory's rather disrespectful antics, Gary walked straight over and stood quietly behind his opponent, listening intently to the latter's nakedly self-serving rhetoric for a minute or so before finally interrupting him in mid-sentence with a discreet tap on the shoulder.

'Hey Rory…' Gary announced politely, feigning ignorance as to what had just been going on; 'I just thought I'd come over and say hello… introduce the friends and family…'

Rory's whole body suddenly stiffened…like a board…as he felt Gary's presence beside him and his ears registered that unmistakeable Australian accent.

'Oh, hi Bruce,' he replied with false regard, his face freezing into a self-righteous smile. 'I didn't see you there.'

'Yeah, I got a feeling you hadn't', Gary riposted frostily, his voice filled with measured menace.

Rory quietly cleared his throat, embarrassed at being put on the spot like that.

'Anyhow...' Gary continued assertively; 'This Rory, is my brother Joey...my friend Murray and his sister Roz...'

'...Guys; this here is Rory Campbell-Brown; known affectionately by his friends in the chess community as...the 'Scottish wind-bag', Gary indicated with a weirdly exaggerated hand-gesture.

Joey stepped forward...followed closely by Murray; both of them looking rather serious as they held out their hands to shake with Rory... *using the firmest of manly grips*...but Roz hadn't really heard what was being said over the noise of the crowd and looked a little confused.

'Is that because you play the bag-pipes', she queried, as she reached forward in turn to shake Rory's hand, not quite getting the sarcasm of the moment.

'People don't really call me that...' Rory began to bluster...but before he could finish Gary quickly interrupted again, dropping a heavy hand on Rory's shoulder and fixing him with a strangely impervious stare;

'Oh...and...by the way...Rory me old mate', Gary quietly whispered into Rory's ear; '... Just so that you know; my name is Gary...and not Bruce.'

'I knew that...of course I knew that' Rory stammered, pulling back and feeling more than a little uncomfortable all of a sudden; 'It was just a wee bit of friendly banter.'

'Well, it stops today, yeah', Gary pressed, the tone of his voice as cold as steel.

'Very well', Rory agreed with a scowl, before turning to the guy stood the other side of him and quickly inventing an excuse to disappear...which he did almost immediately, wandering off towards the exit, sneering and muttering some undecipherable and no doubt disparaging remarks under his breath as he went.

Gary and his posse watched Rory leave, all four of them managing to keep a straight face until the door had closed behind him...

...but then as soon as it had done so, they all burst out in a chorus of raucous laughter.

'You really psyched him out there, bro...' Joey roared, grinning widely and slapping his younger brother fraternally on the back.

‘Yeah, I learned from the master’, Gary replied, elbowing his big brother playfully in the ribs.

Just then, the barman came over and while Gary ordered in a round of drinks, his friends found themselves a nice, quiet table where they could enjoy a couple of beers before the much-anticipated match got under way.

‘We’re all laughing here…’ Murray announced as Gary reached the table and started handing out the beers, ‘…but crikey, that guy sounded pretty cocky…didn’t he?’

‘Yeah, sounds a little too cocky for my liking…’ Roz chipped in boldly, taking a sip of warm beer and grimacing hideously.

‘Nah, don’t worry about him’, Gary reassured them all as he sat down; ‘Rory has always had a propensity for making outrageous statements like that.’

‘Too right…and little bro here is going to take him down…right bro?’ Joey interrupted, slapping Gary on the back again and proposing a toast.

‘To Gary…the future king of chess’, he prompted, raising his glass and bouncing it off of Murray’s.

‘To Gary’, the others all repeated with similarly raised glasses, sealing their faith in Gary’s belief that he could pull it off.

‘Okay boys’, Gary declared confidently, having emptied half of his glass in one slurp, ‘…another couple of these bad-boys and I reckon we’ll be good to go…what do you say?’

‘Sweet’, Joey boomed, swallowing the remaining contents of his glass and showing it to the barman with a nod and an accompanying hand-gesture so that he might start pouring the next round.

‘…But in the mean-time’, Gary persisted, leaning forward towards his friend Murray; ‘I want to hear all the news from back home…so go on, big fella, let’s hear it’, he encouraged; ‘…start spilling your guts.’

‘Right…’ said Murray a little surprised…

‘Well, firstly…’, and while he started to fill Gary in, on what had been happening back home with the rellies…Joey chipping in a detail or two whenever he felt it necessary…Roz got up and walked over to the bar to change her order from a warm beer to a cold one, in a bottle.

An hour or so later, just as they were enjoying their third 'bevvy', one of the blue-blazered officials strolled purposefully into the bar…and made his way directly over to their table.

He stopped right behind Gary's chair and placing both hands on the back of the wooden frame, he leaned down casually… without waiting for a natural break in the conversation…and whispered quietly into Gary's ear that it was time to go.

Gary nodded studiously, thanked the rather staid-looking official for his courtesy and then stood up, stretching out his impressive frame flamboyantly.

'Okay fellas…' he announced confidently as his friends instinctively finished their glasses and followed his lead by standing up, '…it's Showtime.'

He then turned and followed the 'blue-blazer'…and as they fell in behind him, Joey and Murray suddenly broke out in song to the chorus of Shannon Noll's rousing anthem 'Shine';

'This is the time…,
This is the day that we've been waiting for,
When all the world will stop to watch you shine
…this is the time…'

The 'blue-blazer' led the way out of the bar and as they entered the competition room, through two huge swing-doors, Murray leaned in to Gary and whispered a word of encouragement in his young friend's ear.

'Just keep your eyes on the prize, kiddo', he said, slapping Gary on the back again, before breaking off to go and take his seat.

'No worries', Gary replied in his usual relaxed manner, as he dutifully followed the blue-blazer preceding him to the podium at the front of the room.

Roz, Murray and Joey were similarly shown to their seats in the front row and as they prepared to sit down, each of them showed their support for Gary - with either a hand signal or a holler.

Of course this kind of unruly behaviour was very much frowned upon in the rather sedate world of tournament chess…and within seconds one of the pedantic 'blue-blazered' officials had stepped in to restore order, much to the amusement of Joey & Co., who welcomed the former's stern looks and calming hand-gestures with some rather typical and colourful antipodean vernacular about a man…a long pole…and a lake.

It was all a little comical because of the rather incongruous setting, and those who witnessed it could not help but crack a smile…but after that brief moment of light relief, the Aussie clan happily settled down again while the blue-blazers who had moved to intervene, quietly shuffled back to their sentry posts, hands clasped loosely behind their backs.

The rest of the crowd finished filing in and once the doors were closed, signalling that the contest was about to begin, the MC took to the podium to make his welcome speech…which included the usual requests for silence during play in order to respect the players' concentration…as well as the inevitable reminder for people to make sure that their mobile phones were switched off.

Then, without further ado, he introduced the players, both of whom were greeted with spontaneous applause - *and a couple of whoops from the Aussie camp when it was Gary's turn* – but once that excess energy had been liberated and the lights in the room had been dimmed slightly…*to focus attention on the podium*…a religious silence seemed to descend on the audience…despite the sense of excitement…and the bubbling undercurrent of anticipation…that was clearly inhabiting all those present.

♗

Up on the podium, the tension was just as palpable and as Rory got the match under way, using the white pieces…*as tradition required*…the crowd instinctively took a collective breath and held it as Gary prepared to engage his first piece in reply.

This was almost like a show of solidarity from the crowd as Gary was considered the under-dog in the contest…and if the British love anything, they love an under-dog. What is more, many of the 'die-hard' aficionados in the crowd had been unimpressed by Rory's somewhat questionable behaviour over the years and were loath to offer him their support.

The opening gambits were pretty cagey as each player tried to out-smart and out-manoeuvre the other, but within no time – due mainly to Rory's tendency to be over-confident and hence a little complacent - Gary took charge of the contest, dismantling his opponent in clinical fashion to win the first game with relative ease, much to the crowd's delight.

The second game however, was a longer, more drawn out affair which held everybody in transfixed fascination for quite some time, Rory having re-assessed the situation and adjusted his tactics accordingly…and indeed he won it narrowly despite a valiant rear-guard action by Gary which prolonged the game for considerably longer than it should ever have lasted - *making a stalemate seem the most logical outcome at one point* – but just when everything was pointing to a draw and a little unrest could be heard in the audience, Gary finally found himself cornered and had to concede.

♗

That heroic resistance meant that the second game had taken almost three hours to complete, and so, with the scores tied at one a-piece, the lights went up and the MC stepped back onto the podium to announce that there would be a short recess to allow everybody to get up, stretch their legs and refresh themselves as they saw fit, before coming back for the deciding rubber.

Mumbling voices instantly broke out all around the room as people decided what they were going to do, and then seconds later a synchronised rush for the doors occurred by people eager to get either to the bar, the toilets or the designated smoking area.

Of course Gary's clan was no exception to all this, but unfortunately being in the front row they had to wait a minute or two for the bulk of the crowd to funnel out, before they could make their way back to the bar…and by the time they got there it was already overflowing with people having heated discussions in every corner.

♗

It took them quite a while to fight their way to the front of the queue… but when they did eventually reach the bar…and got their hands on some cold beers…the three Australians decided unanimously, after a brief discussion, that rather than return to their seats in the front row of the audience, they would stay where they were for the concluding match-up and follow it on the flat-screens which had been installed in the bar specifically for that purpose.

'Besides', Joey insisted, 'this is where we feel most at home…right guys?'

'Yeah…and we can vent our emotions more freely here, without the worry of disrupting the game', Roz chipped in.

Murray simply nodded in agreement.

'We have to let Gary know though', Roz announced, looking around the bar.

'Go and tell that guy over there, in the blue blazer', she said to Joey, pushing him in the direction of one of the officials; 'he can relay the message to Gary for us', she reasoned out loud.

Joey did just that and as he turned to walk back to where Roz and Murray were standing, the sound of a bell rang out, announcing the resumption of the contest.

Once again, in response to the Pavlovian signal, people started to rush their drinks and hurry themselves up as the team of blue blazers suddenly reappeared in the doorway, ready to herd them all back across the hallway into the arena.

♗

The match started again a few minutes later and Gary seemed to be the popular choice among those who had chosen to stay in the bar to watch it on the two large screens.

However, as the game progressed, one customer – who was sat on a stool just behind where Gary's clan were standing…*and who was completely unaware as to their identity* - happened to shout out a word of encouragement for Rory which at the same time ridiculed his young opponent.

Joey, Gary's big brother, looked over his shoulder and glared at the man.

'Hey mate, bite your tongue; that's my little brother up there'; he announced proudly; '…the new Billy Slater of World Chess.'

'The new who?' asked the bemused Englishman, a little stunned by the strength of Joey's rebuke.

Joey turned to Murray and raising their glasses together, they repeated his shout in unison…and with a lot more gusto.

'Billy the Kid, 'See You Later' Slater, the best rugby league player in the whole damned world', they chanted in heavy Aussie brogue, high-fiving each other loudly above their heads, before launching into their own rendition of…'come on Aussie, come on ….come on', which prompted an immediate torrent of shushing from the bar's other patrons.

'Hey, cut it out, you two' Roz chortled as Joey just missed stamping on her foot and spilling her beer; 'Honestly…you guys are such girls sometimes', she added in jest, playfully elbowing her brother in the ribs.

Murray regained his balance and as he turned his attention back to the screen, the camera zoomed in on Rory's furrowed brow and tortured grimace.

'You should have stuck to being an accountant if you can't take the pressure', he shouted at the TV disparagingly; 'I hear the Scots are good at that', he added turning to Rory's one declared supporter.

'Not all of them', the Englishman retorted, suddenly disinterested.

The game carried on for another hour or so after that…and despite some very astute counter-play by Gary, the consensus in the audience seemed to be that Rory was well on his way to winning the contest.

Indeed, up on the podium the smug-looking veteran seemed to be toying with…if not taunting…his young challenger, often leaning back on his chair and folding his arms across his chest in self-assured fashion, while the sneaky, self-satisfied smirks parading across his face clearly betrayed his rather presumptuous frame of mind.

Meanwhile Gary's crouched position hardly ever changed; his focus and his concentration remaining solely on the game.

Another thirty minutes passed and the crowd began to get restless again, fidgeting noisily in their seats as the players considered each move they were about to make from every possible angle before ultimately confirming their decision and stopping the clock.

The tension was at its zenith…and had been for some time…and then suddenly, out of nowhere, using a variation on the most famous finishing move of all time; *The Paris Opera... which ironically relies on the support of the bishop to succeed...*Gary unexpectedly called checkmate.

For a split-second, there was hesitation and confusion in the room, as people were unsure who had actually called the checkmate...especially as Rory seemed to be in such an unassailable and commanding position... but when the result was confirmed by those at the front getting to their feet to applaud, everybody else rose as one to join in; a reaction which was naturally mirrored in the bar by Gary's clan...with Joey, not unsurprisingly leading the celebrations.

Rory however could not believe what had happened; he couldn't believe that he had been beaten; he couldn't believe that the dream he had worked so hard for, over so many years, had been within his grasp and that he had let it slip at the last moment.

He was stunned...speechless, and as he pushed himself away from the table and got to his feet, his mouth still agape in disbelief, he could not help but shoot a disgruntled glare around the room at all those who were now applauding his defeat.

Gary stood up too...and in typical Aussie-fashion, forgetting all about protocol and the stuffy committee rules, he threw both hands in the air and shouted out at the top of his voice...in the broadest of Aussie-brogue, 'You Beauty!!!'...savouring his triumph for all of two seconds, before suddenly remembering where he was and reaching forward to shake his opponent's hand - as was the custom after every contest.

As he did this, the crowd rushed forward, eager to congratulate Gary and join in his celebrations, while Rory was quickly swept aside, pushed into the background and left to make his own way back to the bar, without so much as a 'good game'.

The podium was subsequently over-run with people but among the furore, the MC suddenly returned and made his way over to Gary's side.

'Ladies and gentlemen', he announced loudly into his microphone while raising Gary's right arm like a boxing-match referee; 'I give you our winner...Gary Bridgewater from Sydney, Australia.'

Another round of applause and victory shouts rang out around the room to celebrate Gary's triumph...*forcing the MC to pause for a few seconds...*but then when the clapping had ceased and the noise in the room had returned to a more reasonable level, he turned to Gary anew and confirmed in an exponentially louder voice, that his reward for his victory, was that he had won the right to challenge the reigning world champion at the next World Series ...'

'So, let's hear it for Gary, people', he shouted into his microphone... and with that another huge wave of applause erupted around the room.

Back in New York;

After Quinton's revelations, Madison suddenly had a new-found respect for her boss...and with Mauro's rather surprising arrival on the scene... *which seemed to have softened Amanda more than she would ever care to admit*...all the old animosities between them were slowly being forgotten.

Neither subject was ever discussed in an open forum...but having finally managed to put aside their differences, their rivalry...*and any lingering resentment there might have been between them after Amanda's trip to London...mainly from Madison*...the professional relationship between the two women began to thrive.

Amanda was still the boss, of course, but both she and Madison had finally realised that the time for them to act like warring amazons... caught in an armed stand-off...was over. They needed to work together for the good of the paper...and with that in mind they had reached a compromise...lines of responsibility had been drawn...and at long last everybody knew where they stood...*although both women made it perfectly clear that they would still reserve the right to defend their corner whenever they felt it necessary; such was the indomitable character of these two strong, single-minded, career-focussed professionals.*

As the weeks went by, this new understanding led to the two women becoming very close allies and forging a unique working relationship... much to everybody's surprise but to nobody's regret, as the edgy articles they produced for the magazine...and the progressive visions they championed for the wider fashion industry...suddenly became essential reading for women all over New York, leading to a noticeable upswing in sales and market share which put a smile on the faces of everybody involved at the paper, employees, executives and shareholders alike.

It was now late February; winter had loosened its grip and the spring Fashion season was in full swing; New York having set the ball rolling with some rather fabulous new collections…and as part of her remit…as the new head of fashion…Madison was once again in London…for London Fashion week – before she moved on to Milan and then Paris to run her professional eye over their spring-fashion shows too.

She hadn't seen or spoken to *the Bishop* since her rather-depressing last visit…and while they had naturally drifted apart since then, as each of them got on with their respective lives – *especially as all thoughts of romance had long since been consigned to the past after their dispute and his subsequent health problems* - Madison still felt somewhat beholden to the ailing master for what he had done for her…and frequently found herself - *often when she was alone* - reminiscing about that wonderful summer she had spent with him…and wondering just how he was coping with his illness.

These thoughts were even more prevalent in her mind while she was in London, and because of that Madison felt that it was incumbent on her, her duty almost, to get in touch with him while she was there to let him know that she hadn't forgotten the role he had played in her life.

She knew that it wouldn't be easy to organise…but nevertheless, having arranged to skip a couple of the smaller mid-week presentations, she managed to free up a couple of hours in her busy schedule to go and pay her mentor another surprise visit.

That Wednesday was a rather cold February day despite the crisp early-morning sun, but as the black-cab wound its way carefully through the last couple of narrow lanes leading to her destination, Madison was feeling rather optimistic.

Indeed, she was feeing glad to be alive and as she looked out of the window she empathised completely with the thousands of spring flowers she could see dotted all over the fields and along the grassy verges at the roadside which were enjoying their first taste of life.

The shows in London were going well; Amanda had just been on the phone to inform her that their most recent article had been lauded in the New York press and she was certain that when she got to the Abbey she would find *the Bishop* on the road to recovery too; that somehow the doctors would have revised their gloomy prognosis and given him a new lease on life.

Yes, Madison was feeling very upbeat as the taxi arrived at the Abbey's gates, but then, as the cabbie turned into the forecourt, her mood suddenly changed and inexplicably...out of nowhere...a strange sense of foreboding seemed to take hold of her...right in the pit of her stomach; a feeling which surprised somewhat...as these days, in the cold, hard world of journalism in which she now evolved, her emotions were rarely solicited.

The taxi rolled to a halt a couple of metres from the abbey's front door and as she straightened out her trendy, new, high-necked sweater dress, buttoned up her beautifully-tailored plum-coloured winter coat and donned her matching cloche hat, Madison dismissed the sinking feeling in her stomach as merely a sign that her dietary regime needed revising.

She paid her fare and having confirmed with the cabbie that she needed to be picked up again an hour later - *so as to be back in London that evening for another show* - Madison stepped out onto the familiar forecourt and walked slowly over to the abbey's imposing front door...being careful where she stepped, *as in some places the morning sun hadn't quite finished burning off the frost from the night before*, her mind still a little troubled by the churning sensations in her abdomen.

Behind her, the taxi slowly turned around before making its way back out onto the road...and as she stood there waiting patiently for a response to her firm knock, Madison suddenly realised that the alien sensation in her stomach had been joined by an equally-unwelcome lump in her throat.

A minute or so went by and just as she was about to berate herself again for not ringing ahead to warn him that she was coming - *which was so unlike her in her meticulously time-managed world* - Madison heard the bolt slide back and the heavy door slowly begin to open.

Rosa appeared in the doorway, still wiping her hands on a kitchen cloth and as their eyes met, Madison immediately noticed in Rosa's harassed expression that something was wrong; she could feel it intuitively in her bones.

It took the old house-keeper a moment or two to recognise Madison - as she had stylishly pinned her hair up under her hat - but after a brief hesitation, she quietly stepped aside and respectfully invited her in.

'I'm sorry for dropping in on you like this...unannounced as it were; I hope I'm not disturbing you', Madison uttered as she stepped over the threshold and walked quietly into the vestibule, unconsciously taking a deep breath as she did so, to clear her throat and regain her composure.

Rosa didn't respond but with her customary deference she smiled stiffly and waited patiently for her guest to walk past before closing the door behind her.

Madison stopped in the foyer waiting politely for Rosa to join her but as she stood there looking around at the décor that she remembered so well from the time she had spent there, she suddenly felt somehow out of place; the mood in the house felt strangely sombre; the light in the hallway was more subdued than she remembered and the strong masculine atmosphere that so typified *the Bishop's* presence…and which had grabbed her attention so-intensely on her previous visits there…also seemed noticeably absent.

Rosa caught up with her…and lost for an introductory declaration of any significance or merit Madison immediately fell back on her b-game and commented on the delicious culinary smells that were wafting out from the kitchen.

'Roast chicken…his favourite', Rosa explained succinctly, her tired features softening slightly into a more natural smile.

Madison nodded in agreement; 'So…how is our patient…any new developments', she asked hopefully, unbuttoning her coat and skimming over the usual exchange of social conventions; the appetising kitchen smells starting to make her sensitive stomach rumble.

Rosa shook her head regretfully and almost instantly the fleeting smile brought on by Madison's appreciation of her culinary talents quickly disappeared to be replaced by a look of utter dejection; 'No, I'm sorry to…'

As she spoke, as if by design, the sound of piano-music suddenly interrupted her flow and recognising the melody instantly, Madison promptly gravitated towards the conservatory door, where she stopped to listen a little more before carefully pushing the door open, *just enough to peek inside*, clearly expecting to see *the Bishop* sat there at the piano in his usual pose, waiting to welcome her back.

Sadly though, instead of experiencing that joyous moment of reunion, her eyes were greeted by a sight which took her breath away and shook her to her core.

Somebody…somebody that she didn't recognise and had obviously never seen before was sat at *the Bishop's* piano playing 'their' tune - Beethoven's 'Fur Elize'- and that somebody, to her even greater surprise was confined to a wheelchair, propped up by a number of tired-looking cushions.

Who <u>is</u> that? Madison whispered to herself, the shock slowly manifesting itself on her puzzled face.

Her view of the unknown pianist was slightly obscured by the angle of the door-frame …but once the initial shock had worn off, Madison quickly realised on closer inspection that the shabby-looking person hunched so awkwardly over the keyboard was no other than *the Bishop* himself…and despite her New York constitution which usually protected her from any unexpected emotional mood-swings, her eyes immediately clouded over.

Up to that point she hadn't really taken the seriousness of *the Bishop's* dwindling health on board, but seeing him like that – so diminished and in such an obvious state of decline – left Madison feeling uncharacteristically distraught. The knot in her stomach returned with a vengeance and without warning her whole body was suddenly a quiver of random emotions (sadness, despair, regret and helplessness).

The poor man looked miserable and forsaken, sat alone in his chair… but what really upset Madison as she stood watching him impassively for a minute or two, was that he looked so dishevelled; his clothes were scruffy and tired, his hair was a mess and what she could see of his expressionless face was grey and sad.

There was no sign of the once proud man she had grown to respect and love and as she turned and looked…almost accusingly…at Rosa, who was stood just a few steps behind her, still clasping her cloth, she tried desperately to mask her despair at this realisation.

The old house-keeper saw Madison's questioning expression and taking a deep breath she sighed quietly and shook her head before looking away, the wistful expression on her face betraying both her understanding of the situation and the genuine melancholy in her soul.

Madison's morale began to sink further, but then, just as she was about to enter the room and announce her presence to her ailing mentor, the piano burst into life again.

Had he spotted her, she wondered, as she paused again to listen to their tune, still hidden discreetly behind the door.

It was strangely uplifting despite the pathos of the moment and Madison's heart unexpectedly missed a beat as the memories came flooding back to her, of them sitting together for hours in that same room while he played his repertoire of music to her…

…but then when he hit a succession of wrong keys, jarring her back to reality, it suddenly dawned on her that he was no longer the smooth, well-oiled machine that she remembered and indeed, as she shifted her position to catch a better view of his frail-looking silhouette, Madison could almost see the gears grinding in *the Bishop's* head as he toiled to remember the notes.

Her face fell again as this new realisation hit home and while *the Bishop* tried desperately to recover his mastery of the keys, her gaze wandered modestly away from the piano in an effort to distract herself from the vision in front of her and stem the rising tide of her emotions.

Unfortunately though, as she scanned what she could of the room, her eyes came to rest on the piano-stool which she had once shared with the man himself; it was just a piano-stool but again the memories came flooding back to her of the time when she had sat with him, side by side, and listened to him play.

Alas, the stool had been pushed out of the way now and into a corner in order to make room for the wheel-chair…and on seeing it there, abandoned, out of place and unwanted, Madison's stomach flipped on itself and her bottom lip started quivering.

She couldn't hold it back any longer and as she raised her eyes again and stared off into the distance, her strong, business facade crumbled and the first of many tears began rolling down her cheek as the emotion finally overwhelmed her.

She shuffled back from the door, pivoting slowly on her heels…and looking despairingly at Rosa who was still stood there disconsolately wringing her hands, Madison revealed her dilemma.

'I can't go in there; I don't want to remember him like this', she cried quietly, her emotions now in turmoil and her distress all too apparent.

'That's alright, my dear…I understand', Rosa conceded sensitively; 'He probably wouldn't remember you anyway.'

'W…wouldn't remember me; what do you mean; wouldn't remember me?' Madison quizzed through her tear-stained eyes; her puzzled look conveying her lack of understanding.

'Well', Rosa began to explain; 'Time…and the illness of course have bleached away Mr Byron's memories of the past and…and some days, sometimes, he doesn't even recognise me', she lamented sadly.

'…but…but he remembers enough to play; he's playing our tune right now', Madison countered defiantly, doggedly defending her former lover as best she could, her mind refusing to accept the reality of the situation.

'I'm afraid that that's not really memory dear, its habit…reflex… or…muscle-memory is how Olivia explained it to me', Rosa declared sorrowfully.

'Apparently, with this illness, the brain decays…but for whatever reason, that muscle-memory remains…and as you know, he's played that tune so many times over the years…' she mumbled, her voice trailing off deliberately. *(She didn't have the heart to tell Madison that that tune was actually the first one that his beloved piano-teacher Jane had ever taught him)*

Madison was deeply grieved by these new revelations and as she tried to regain her composure – unused as she was to making such a spectacle of herself - she instinctively grabbed hold of the pendant around her neck.

She had stopped wearing it after their initial quarrel, but since her previous visit she never took it off - and as she closed her eyes and squeezed it with all her might, *the Bishop* appeared as if by magic through the prism of a nostalgic haze in her mind's eye, just as he had been before, sat majestically at his piano serenading her with his outrageous musical talent.

'Are you okay Miss?' Rosa enquired empathetically, fearing that Madison looked a little unsteady.

'Yes, I'm fine', Madison replied; the old housekeeper's words refocusing her thoughts, '...but is there no hope at all, not even a nugget?' she enquired sadly, slowly succumbing to the melancholy of the moment.

I'm afraid not', Rosa replied ruefully, reaffirming the doctor's prognosis; 'It's just a question of time.'

Madison frowned and began rummaging through her handbag looking for a Kleenex to wipe her eyes and as she did so, she came across the slab of chocolate that she had picked up in the airport duty-free shop.

'Rosa, Tob...., Mr Byron once told me that he enjoyed a square of this chocolate from time to time; could you please give it to him for me', she requested, handing over the somewhat trivial little gift.

'Of course', Rosa agreed politely, 'it will be my pleasure.'

Madison thanked her...and with an understanding nod from the old house-keeper...she quietly turned and made her way back out, sad and despondent that a man who had so often drowned her in a sea of words, a man who had been blessed with such a brilliant and passionate mind should falter and vegetate in the way he had; it was a great loss and for her it seemed like such a waste.

Outside once again, her chest still heaving with emotion, Madison immediately took out her phone and called the taxi service to inform them of her change of plans.

The dispatch operator on the other end of the line notified her politely that there would be a ten to fifteen minute wait because of her rural location but once that had been made clear to her Madison thanked the woman and hung up.

She looked up to the sky to check the weather, and while she waited for her cab to arrive - still a little bewildered by what she had just witnessed inside - Madison couldn't help but wonder if there was anything she could have done to change *the Bishop's* destiny.

There wasn't, she concluded, very matter of fact, but while her thoughts were focussed on him she did suddenly realise why *the Bishop's* demeanour had changed out of all recognition, since they had first met; he had been cramming in the memories before it was too late.

♗

It was quiet and peaceful in the forecourt…which contrasted dramatically with the surreal atmosphere inside the abbey and while she waited, to pass the time Madison ambled over to where the Aston was still parked waiting faithfully, like a loyal pet for its master to decide when he would come and take advantage of its powerful V12 engine.

The car also brought back memories for Madison - *of her time with the Bishop* - and as she began to reminisce on a few of them, the sound of bells chiming in the distant village drew her attention to a group of twittering of birds in a nearby tree.

This took her a little by surprise but as she lowered her gaze once again to the flowers in the adjoining field which were bursting with life and vitality, just like the birds up in the trees, she couldn't help but compare it all to her own flagging morale and that of *the Bishop's* desperate plight as his life slowly ebbed away.

The circle of life, she mumbled to herself, the circle of life.

The irony was not lost on her and as the taxi she was waiting for appeared at the gate and pulled up alongside her, it brought another lump to her throat.

'London?' the cabbie called out as the car came to a halt.

'Yeah; the Landmark Hotel, opposite Marylebone station', Madison responded with difficulty as she opened the door and jumped inside.

The cabbie nodded silently…and as he engaged first gear, Madison could do nothing but look back mournfully as she bid the abbey goodbye, for probably the last time.

♗

EPILOGUE

Eight months later Madison was in the conference room, stood in front of a white-board, discussing female empowerment...and body-shaming...with her team;

'...When a woman stands in front of a mirror...' she was saying, channelling one of *the Bishop's* first rants...

'...naked or otherwise...

...she doesn't see a beautiful female form

...she sees a mish-mash of problems that need addressing;

...her thighs...her stomach...her boobs...her upper arms...and most commonly, her butt.

Women do this all through their lives; measuring themselves against other women and finding themselves wanting...'

She paused at this point for reflection...before continuing...

'...and before you say anything; this has nothing whatsoever to do with men or how men view us...

...because the reality is; we women are our own worst enemies.'

'The perfect images we see...on billboards...and in glossy magazines just like ours...have created a false normal, an improbable standard against which women...young and old...but especially the young...are constantly measuring themselves...and inevitably falling short...

So people, what are we going to do about...?'

Just at that moment, one of the secretaries from the editor's office appeared in the corridor outside...looking more than a little awkward as she stood there trying to get Madison's attention through the glass partition-wall using a number of discreet...but clearly discernible... hand-gestures.

Madison didn't see her at first...caught up as she was in her own thought-process...but after several of the team started to point the young woman out she did eventually clock her in her peripheral vision and stop what she was saying...mid-thought...before making her way over to the door...voicing a brief apology for the interruption to her team as she went.

She eased the door open...just enough to stick her head out...slightly irritated by the interruption, but before she could exercise her authority and ask why the young woman was interrupting her meeting, the latter took the initiative and jumped in first.

'Have you heard?' she whispered, looking slightly pained.

'Heard what?' Madison queried, a little abruptly.

'That guy...that guy that you and Amanda did the articles on; he's dead.'

'He's what?' Madison cried out, her eyes springing open in shock as she tried to take the information on board.

'He's dead', the young secretary repeated, her sullen expression adding extra gravitas to the news. '...We just got a call from England.'

'Oh my god...' Madison gasped, as she raced out of the conference-room and rushed back to her office, almost knocking the bewildered young secretary over as she went.

The young woman watched Madison go and then quickly popped her head around the conference-room door to inform the rest of her team what had happened.

Back in her office, Madison quickly grabbed the remote-control off her desk…and standing there… still in disbelief…she immediately started working her way through the different internet feeds and news-channels that she had at her disposal on her wall of TVs; her eyes scanning every screen and every headline…with ever-increasing urgency…as she sought to confirm or at least find an update on the awful news that the young secretary had just brought to her attention.

She stood there for some time, getting more and more anxious… her eyes glued to the bank of screens…and had just begun to read the tag-lines from one of the European channels…when behind her the digital phone on her desk began to buzz, startling her with its strangely abrupt tone.

Madison glanced back over her shoulder…to check the caller ID screen…hoping with all her heart that she could just ignore the call or let it go to voicemail…given the news she had just received…but then when she saw the international code 44 prefacing the number on the tiny LCD screen…*which she recognised instantly as the code for England*…she knew that she had no choice but to answer it.

Taking a deep breath…and with a look of utter dread and foreboding on her face, she picked up the hand-set and pressed the flashing connection button on the phone's base-unit, steeling herself for what she knew was probably going to be the most difficult call she had ever had to take.

'Hello; hello…is that Madison?' the caller enquired quietly.

'It is…' Madison replied, starting to choke up as she recognised Rosa's voice.

'I'm sorry dear; I tried calling your mobile-phone a couple of times but there was no reply' the old housekeeper announced.

Madison immediately retrieved her mobile-phone from her handbag…

and as she moved around the desk to sit down, she saw the missed calls staring back at her on the little screen.

(She had introduced a rule that all phones be switched off during meetings)

'Anyway...' Rosa announced quietly...and very succinctly; 'I just wanted to tell you...Madison...that Mr Byron left us today.'

'Oh my god...No...I'm so sorry to hear that', Madison murmured, not knowing what else to say as she looked at her computer screen and started to Google *the Bishop's* name.

And with that...the line went dead, as overcome with emotion; Rosa had simply hung up.

♗

Madison was devastated...

Of course she had been expecting the call...one day...but now that that day had actually come, it still came as a shock...and as she hung up the phone, she suddenly found herself reaching instinctively for the pendant that still hung dutifully around her neck, just as she had done at the Abbey on her last visit.

She started biting her bottom lip in an effort to stem the emotion... and was still doing so...when the results of her Google-search flashed-up on the screen in front of her...confirming the sad news; the first headline stating quite simply; British chess master dies.

Madison clicked on the file and for several very long moments, she just stared at the page...transfixed.

She still couldn't believe it; she felt sick...and trying to compose herself she turned away from the screen, only for her eyes to land once again on the photo that Evie had had framed for her...of her and Gary with *the Bishop,* looking vibrant...and full of life during that now-infamous New York 'Chess Challenge'.

The memory of that day immediately stirred her emotions...deep inside...and as she twisted the pendant in frustration...her grip tightened by the pain of her loss...the body of the little chess-piece suddenly unscrewed and came off in her hand.

'Oooohh fuuuuuck', she exclaimed, as she almost dropped the little charm onto the floor, but then as she caught it in her fingers and examined it a little more closely, she suddenly noticed a tiny little scroll of paper that had been pushed inside the charm's hollow core.

Curious…as always…even though her emotions were slowly beginning to register the news…she carefully extracted the little piece of paper with her nails…and slowly unfurled it on the desk in front of her, taking great care not to tear it.

It was really small…but inscribed on the tiny scroll, in His very own hand-writing, were just three numbers; 1, 4 and 3.

What is this? What does '143' mean? Madison wondered as she contemplated her find.

Is it some kind of code?

♗

Time seemed to stand still for a moment but then, as her emotions started to overwhelm her, Madison suddenly felt a solitary tear pearl in the corner of her right eye and pause for a split second on her lower eyelid before gravity dragged it inexorably down over the unblemished skin of her cheek.

This prompted her to reach across her desk for a Kleenex…to prevent her makeup from smudging…and as she did so, her attention was drawn… almost instinctively…back to the bank of television screens on the wall opposite her desk.

Madison noticed that one of the screens was flickering randomly… and made a mental note to inform the technical department…but she also noted in passing that, on several of the other screens some celebrity or other…who had clearly just stepped off a plane after a long flight… was being surrounded and jostled by a whole host of journalists and TV cameramen… as they tried to make their way through the airport.

This was nothing new to Madison; she had seen her fair share of media scrums during her first years as a journalist…but just as she was about to dismiss what was happening on her screens as just another well-orchestrated PR stunt and get back to organising some kind of respectful gesture to mark *the Bishop's* passing…she suddenly recognised the voice of the celebrity in question as he began responding to the journalists' excited clamouring and goodwill messages.

In the moment, she couldn't quite place it, but then she caught sight of the guy's unmistakeable features as they were flashed onto the screen and her jaw almost dropped to the floor at the realisation that the person being interviewed was none other than her old friend…Gary.

Madison couldn't believe it…and jumping to her feet she quickly grabbed the remote again and turned up the volume, just in time to hear the reporter congratulate the young Australian on his victory.

Gary Bridgewater, the young Australian who had been so instrumental in her success…if only indirectly…had just been crowned world chess champion and the local TV channel…together with the usual horde rogue paparazzi… who always seem to hang out in major terminal buildings these days in the hope of bagging themselves that exclusive, money-earning shot…was there at the airport in Sydney, to cover his triumphant return home; just as he had predicted they would in their conversation all those months ago; a fact confirmed by the rolling news strap-line across the bottom of the screens.

Stunned once again, Madison moved back around to the front of her desk…her arms folded loosely across her chest…and as she watched Gary's smiling face on all the different screens…she saw it little more than poetic justice that the young Aussie had realised his dream and become world champion.

After all; she had seen how much he wanted it…and knew how much he deserved it…but for him to actually achieve it…was nevertheless something special.

It was a surreal moment and it had stopped Madison in her tracks… but what she saw next was going to leave her even more dumbfounded.

Accompanying Gary…as he made his way through the airport… followed by the horde of cameras…her arm linked tightly in his…was… her best friend…and his new wife (*if the flashy ring on her third finger was anything to go by*) Evie, looking absolutely stunning in her new black and white, polka-dot couture dress.

Madison was understandably gob-smacked; she and Evie hadn't spoken in a while...because of her busy schedule...but even so, she had no idea that her 'bff' and Gary had been seeing each other on any regular basis, never mind become 'an item.'

Arriving at the airport's main entrance, the happy couple stopped once more to allow the photographers one final chance to blitz them with flashes and Evie played to the cameras for all she was worth...puckering up frequently...like a blow-fish...in reply to every request made of her by the insatiable paparazzi...her whole demeanour just radiating the elation of a person blissfully happy with their life.

Stood next to her, Gary looked as proud as a peacock...but while Madison felt that Evie's look was delightfully *coquette*, she was far from impressed with Gary's new style...and couldn't help but groan out loud at the sight of his white zoot suit, his red shirt and his slightly over-sized Panama hat.

She was nevertheless very pleased for them both and as she leaned back against her desk to take it all in and enjoy the spectacle, her raw emotions were suddenly overlaid with a mixture of pride, happiness and a little jealousy at this undeniable picture of consummate marital bliss.

She knew that what Evie wanted more than anything else in this world was a lasting relationship and if the images on the screens were as real as they appeared, she seemed to have finally gotten her wish granted too.

But then, as she kept watching and noticed Gary's hand brush gently across the front of his new bride's dress...*probably in order to swat away some kind of insect*...Madison was suddenly struck by something even more unexpected.

'Oh my god' she cried out in amazement and disbelief, '...is that a baby-bump?'

She tilted her head slightly...and as she smiled affectionately at the screen, the tear that had now run down her cheek caught unavoidably in the corner of her mouth and its salty taste immediately reminded her of *the Bishop* and his last quote to her, making a second tear appear almost instantaneously in between the lashes of her right eye.

Madison looked around forlornly at the telephone, as if that last call somehow represented the end of something…in some way, but before her mind could drag her back once again to the memories and the regrets of the past, Amanda suddenly came waltzing into the office and handed her the mock-up presentation for the following week's fashion pages.

'…These designs are all too similar; we need something new, something different, something more original for next month', she blustered, hoping that Madison would have an immediate solution.

Madison scratched her head…and while still witnessing her friend's new happiness live on TV…she couldn't help but think back over her own life…and wonder what might have been.

She was now the envy of many of her friends…and colleagues…and yet there was still something lacking, something missing in her life; Jeez; even Amanda now had 'Mauro'.

'How about a feature on polka-dots', she suggested with one eye still on the screen.

'Polka-dots', Amanda repeated, 'Yeah, we haven't done that in a while…but you'll have to find an angle; something edgy, something new; have you got anything here I can look at?'

'No, not right this minute…' Madison affirmed as the mobile phone on her desk sprang to life, demanding attention; '…but trust me, I know just the person who can help us with that.'

The internship was never going to be an option for Evie but a consultancy role would suit her down to the ground, Madison thought to herself.

'Okay; that sounds like a plan' Amanda agreed.

Just then, Nicole knocked on the door, to remind her of her lunch appointment…and as Madison went to answer the mobile phone, the phone on her desk lit up again like a Christmas tree.

Amanda, seeing that her colleague was busy just turned and left, stopping only to confirm their meeting for later that day before she disappeared down the corridor.

Madison acknowledged that…and Nicole's reminder; then, having checked her mobile phone she sat back down in her designer chair and prepared to answer the calls which were lining-up on her desk phone.

However, before she picked up the handset, she took a deep breath and looked slowly around her office, suddenly realising at that precise moment, that finally she was living the dream that she had always wanted.

Her feminist sisters would be proud of her, she thought to herself; she had money, she had status, she had the corner office…she had everything the feminist movement told her she could have…and yet as her gaze landed back on the flat-screens which were still full of images of Gary and Evie's smiling faces, she also realised deep-down that despite her success, despite all her effort and all the hard work she had put into making a career for herself, there was still one thing missing, and that one thing was all that any woman really wants in her life; somebody to love.

THE END

LEXICON OF AUSSIE SLANG PHRASES IN CHRONOLOGICAL ORDER

Okker – uncultivated, boorish Aussie male
Strife – trouble
Blow the froth off a few coldies – have a few beers
That's sweet with me – that's fine by me
No worries – no problem
Fizzing – excited
Giving the ferret a run – chasing women
Footy – rugby league football
Down the track – later on (in life)
Ticked off - annoyed
Siphon the python – urinate
Unload – criticise
Bumpers / sweet potatoes – boobs
Budgie-smugglers – underpants
Bed-swerver – unfaithful spouse
Chubby-chaser – a man who likes plump women
As dry as a dingo's donger - dry
To bail out - to leave
Sanger - sandwich
Holy Dooley - OMG
In the G.O.D.'s - good old days
Bowl of rice - cup of tea
Sticky beak syndrome – nosey person

Kirribilli House	- the official Sydney residence of the Australian PM
FIGJAM (**f**uck, **I**'m **g**ood, **j**ust **a**sk **me**)	– a person with a high opinion of himself
Stonkered	– defeated, beaten
Driving like Jehu	- means driving fast and recklessly - Jehu was the king of Israel in 9 BC known for his furious chariot driving
Okay, who opened their lunch?	- Who farted?
You'd better knock it on the head	- leave the girl alone
Aussie dentistry	- a kick in the teeth
Spanner weather	– cold
Grunt	- sex appeal
Sizzler	- hot woman
To put the bite on	- chat up insistently / come on strong
Woah; take a hike, mate	– stop it!
Aah mate, you're all foam and no beer	– you are full of hot-air, my friend
Five-finger discount	– shoplifting
Spitting chips	– angry
Woolloomooloo uppercut	– kick in the groin
Swifty	– quick drink
Love-gloves	– condoms
Lock it in Eddie	– reference to a game-show in Australia
Snap a yam	- take a dump
Bummed out	– down, depressed
Banged like a dunny door in a gale	– enjoyed sex
Map of Tasmania	– pubic hair
Stoked	– so excited
Beef bayonet	– male appendage

Swifty	– quick drink
Pull your head in	- calm down
Chipping	- chatting
My shout	- I'm paying
Rellies	- relatives
Billy Slater	- Melbourne Storm, Queensland and Australian Rugby League player

Disclaimer

Throughout this story…I have name-checked
a number of people and places…using
information in the public domain…
and when doing so I have always tried to be positive and truthful.
However, if any of these references are considered
unacceptable by those mentioned
then I will happily have them removed from future editions

Note from the author

This story has been written as a potential screenplay
which is why I have concentrated mainly on the dialogue, the characters
…and the issues I want to hi-light through those characters…
rather than any flowing narrative or literary prose.

Lightning Source UK Ltd.
Milton Keynes UK
UKHW041949230919
350302UK00003B/258/P

9 781452 073743